Women in Families

Women in Families

A FRAMEWORK FOR FAMILY THERAPY

Edited by

Monica McGoldrick
Carol M. Anderson
Froma Walsh

W.W.NORTON & COMPANY, INC. • NEW YORK • LONDON

First published as a Norton paperback 1991

Printed in the United States of America.

Library of Congress Cataloging-in-Publication Data

Women in families.

   "A Norton professional book."
   Includes index.
   1. Family psychotherapy. 2. Women–Psychology.
3. Women–Social conditions. 4. Women–Mental health.
I. McGoldrick, Monica. II. Anderson, Carol M.,
1939–   . III. Walsh, Froma.
RC488.5W654 1989   616.89'156   88-25248

ISBN 0-393-30776-X

W.W. Norton & Company, Inc., 500 Fifth Avenue, New York, N.Y. 10110
W.W. Norton & Company Ltd, 10 Coptic Street, London WC1A 1PU

2   3   4   5   6   7   8   9   0

This book is dedicated to women
whose love and inspiration have shaped our lives:

Helen Cahalane McGoldrick
Margaret R. Phiffer Bush
Mary Gertrude Cahalane
Mildred McGoldrick Cook
Elizabeth Cahalane Haney
Joan Cahalane Weaver
Marie Baden Mottram
Anna Anderson
Anita Jurchisen
Myrl Seledic
Joanne Wesley
Mary Jo Weisberg
Frimid Lang
Claire Marie Whitney

Foreword

EVERY REVOLUTION HAS its firebrands and martyrs, its trailblazers and historians, but only *successful* revolutions are blessed with leaders creative enough to grasp and shape new ideas and, at the same time, help us to implement them at every level of the system: in our personal and professional lives, in our clinical practice and in our teaching. Monica McGoldrick, Carol Anderson, and Froma Walsh are such leaders.

In 1977, the four of us who soon called ourselves the Women's Project in Family Therapy (Peggy Papp, Olga Silverstein, Marianne Walters, and I) held our first meeting on the subject of "Women as Family Therapists." In 1978, expecting a small group to attend our second meeting, we were astounded to find an audience of over 400. At about the same time in 1978, Rachel Hare-Mustin introduced feminist ideas to a much larger family therapy audience through her seminal article in *Family Process.* She followed with additional articles in the next few years, and we in the Women's Project, feeling a bit as though we had a tiger by the tail, took a series of workshops on women in families and family therapy to cities across the United States and to London. Articles on the subject of women appeared in family therapy journals or books sporadically—from Judy Libow and her colleagues in California, from Michele Bograd in Boston, Harriet Lerner in Topeka, Kerrie James and Deborah McIntyre in Australia, Jo-Ann Krestan and Claudia Bepko in New Jersey. But none of us knew each other, nor did we have a structure through which to communicate. Feeling isolated, vulnerable, severely criticized and unsupported, we each mushed on alone or in our own small groups, until Monica McGoldrick, Carol Anderson and Froma Walsh, also acting alone and unsupported, brought us and dozens of like-minded women together at the first Stonehenge Conference in 1984. The results of that joyous meeting and the establishment of permanent networks of support and exchange among women family therapists have already made a permanent contribution to the field in the form of the many thoughtful articles, books and presentations that have flowed into the field since 1984.

The second Stonehenge Meeting, in 1986, also produced by the uncompensated efforts of the three editors of this book, was somewhat less euphoric but perhaps more "real," as inevitable tensions emerged between women of different professional experience, different degrees of interest in political activism, and different ideas of the best way to deal with gender issues in family therapy. One concrete result has been the founding of a feminist journal where we can explore these differences. The three organizers of the second Stonehenge Meeting may have felt buffeted by its conflicts; however, it can be argued that it was, in fact, an even greater triumph of female dedication to the principle of collaboration-in-spite-of-conflict than the earlier "honeymoon" conference. Let the history of our field record and appreciate the enormous effort expended by these three women in creating our very productive and collaborative network of women family therapists.

Now the field stands at another crossroads and, once again, Monica McGoldrick, Carol Anderson, and Froma Walsh are here to help us find our way. The question is this: Will discussion of "gender issues" continue to receive token acceptance, be co-opted by every program chair as a "trendy" issue for "debate," and remain absolutely academic and peripheral to mainstream family therapy as actually taught and practiced, or will we now move on to see that these basic ideas are included in every reputable family therapy training program here and abroad? Women in our field have spent over ten years introducing and refining these ideas. The family therapy field has resisted, first overtly, and now, more dangerously, with lip service and indifference. It is now time for serious professionals to insist on the implementation of teaching and practice that recognizes that the family and all of society is organized according to gender.

This book tells us both *how* to bring gender issues into our teaching and practice, and *what* ideas must be included. The editors have gathered an outstanding group of contributors. If this book is not required reading in your training program, it may be a deficient training program, and you should insist on its inclusion. If these ideas are not yet reflected in your clinical practice, then read on, and do whatever it takes to absorb and integrate the complex ramifications of the simple fact that women and men have different and unequal experiences in society, in family life, and in family therapy.

Betty Carter

Acknowledgments

WE ARE GRATEFUL to many people for their support and help with the preparation of this book. We thank the women of Stonehenge for their creativity, support, and encouragement. Jeannine Stone, Adriane Powell, Theresa Vogel, and Sandra Price gave generously and cheerfully of their time and effort to bring the book to fruition. Gary Lamson, Director of the CMHC of UMDNJ, and Thomas Detre, Senior Vice President for Health Services, University of Pittsburgh, provided ongoing support. We also thank Henry Murphree, M.D., Chairman of the Department of Psychiatry UMDNJ-CMHC, David Kupfer, Chairman of the Department of Psychiatry, and George Huber, Administrator, of the Western Psychiatric Institute and Clinic of the University of Pittsburgh Medical School, Mary Scanlon, Library Director, UMDNJ-Robert Wood Johnson Library of the Health Sciences, Betty Carter, Joyce Richardson, Neale McGoldrick, Helen McGoldrick, Karen Welch, John Rolland, Katherine Goldberg, Emily and Kate Erstling for their support in the development of this book. Susan Barrows has been a generous and supportive editor—always as good as her word and very enthusiastic about the book from the first conversation so many years ago. We are very grateful to have been able to work with her and the other staff at Norton.

Monica McGoldrick
Carol M. Anderson
Froma Walsh

Contents

Contributors

James Alexander, Ph.D.
Professor of Psychology
Psychology Department
University of Utah
Salt Lake City, Utah

Carol M. Anderson,
    M.S.W., Ph.D.
Professor
Psychiatry Department
University of Pittsburgh
    Medical School
Western Psychiatric Institute
Pittsburgh, Pennsylvania

Judith Meyers Avis, Ph.D.
Associate Professor
College of Family and
    Consumer Studies
University of Guelph
Guelph, Ontario, Canada

Claudia Bepko, M.S.W.
Private Practice
Fair Haven, New Jersey

Evan Imber-Black, Ph.D.
Director of Family and
    Group Studies Division,
    Department of Psychiatry
Albert Einstein College of Medicine
Bronx, New York

Lois Braverman, M.S.W.
Director, Des Moines Family
    Therapy Institute
Des Moines, Iowa

Pauline Boss, Ph.D.
Professor of Sociology
University of Minnesota
St. Paul, Minnesota

Sita Chaney, Ph.D.
Trainer/Therapist
NASHUA Brookside Hospital
Nashua, New Hampshire

Virginia Goldner, Ph.D.
Faculty, Ackerman Institute
  for Family Therapy
New York, New York

Rachel T. Hare-Mustin, Ph.D.
Professor of Counseling and
  Human Relations
Villanova University
Villanova, Pennsylvania

Sharon Hicks, M.S.W.
Western Psychiatric Institute
University of Pittsburgh
Pittsburgh, Pennsylvania

Paulette Moore Hines, Ph.D.
Project Director
Office of Prevention Services
UMDNJ-CMHC
Piscataway, New Jersey

Diane P. Holder, M.S.W.
Western Psychiatric Institute
University of Pittsburgh
Pittsburgh, Pennsylvania

Joan Laird, M.S.W., Ph.D.
Smith College School
  for Social Work
Northampton, Massachusetts

Evelyn Lee, Ed.D.
Assistant Clinical Professor
Department of Psychiatry
University of California
San Francisco, California

Rosemary Masters, M.S.W.
Center for Anorexia & Bulemia
New York, New York

Monica McGoldrick,
  M.S.W., M.A.
Director of Family Training &
  Associate Professor
Psychiatry Department & CMHC
UMDNJ-Robert Wood Johnson
  Medical School
Piscataway, New Jersey

Lorie A. Miller, M.B.A.
Consultant, Cole Surveys
Boston, Massachusetts

Alice Newberry, M.A.
Graduate Student
Psychology Department
University of Utah
Salt Lake City, Utah

Nydia Garcia-Preto, M.S.W.
Director of Adolescent
  Day Hospital
UMDNJ-Community Mental
  Health Center
Piscataway, New Jersey

Sallyann Roth, M.S.W.
Family Institute of Cambridge
Watertown, Massachusetts

Michele Scheinkman, M.S.W.
Staff of the Student
  Mental Health Center
University of Chicago and on the
  Faculty of the Family Institute
  of Chicago
Chicago, Illinois

Ronald Taffel, Ph.D.
Director of Family & Couples
   Treatment Services at the Institute
   for Contemporary
   Psychotherapy
New York, New York

Morris Taggart, Ph.D.
Psychologist & Family Therapist
Houston, Texas

Barrie Thorne, Ph.D.
Department of Sociology
University of Southern California
University Park
Los Angeles, California

Froma Walsh, M.S.W., Ph.D.
   Associate Professor
School of Social Service
   Administration
University of Chicago
Chicago, Illinois

Janet Warburton, Ph.D.
University of Utah
Salt Lake City, Utah

Dorothy Wheeler, Ph.D.
Director of Family
   Intervention Team
Affiliate of North Shore
   Childrens Hospital
Lowell, Massachusetts

SECTION I

Women in Families: Theory and Therapy

1

Women in Families and in Family Therapy

MONICA McGOLDRICK

CAROL M. ANDERSON   FROMA WALSH

THE EVOLUTION OF THIS BOOK AND THE STONEHENGE CONFERENCE

THE HEART OF THIS BOOK lies in some very specific concerns about women's lives, yet its ultimate purpose is the greater good of both sexes. We expect that healthier relationships between men and women will result from an examination of our assumptions about women and the roles they play in the family and work systems within which we all live.

We began focusing specifically on the ideas in this book when we arranged a meeting of 50 women at the cutting edge of family therapy training, theory, and research, which took place at Stonehenge in Connecticut in 1984. The aim of the colloquium was to share and build on our mutual efforts to understand the issues of women in families and in family therapy.

The initial reactions to the idea of the Stonehenge conference were many and surprisingly negative. One leading woman said there was no need for it, adding, "There are no women out there I would be interested in meeting." Another rejected the invitation out of hand, saying she had never concerned herself with gender, since it was a trivial level of difference holding no interest for her. One woman said she had no "legitimate excuse" to go off for three days "with just women," particularly since she had been away from her husband too much already. Others wondered what it would be like to meet "with only women" for three days, and a few were concerned that their male colleagues would be upset with them for attending. In other words, few women were unambivalent about the idea of a conference of and about women. Several joked that 20 years ago the idea of a meeting without men would never have occurred to them and, if it had, would have been immediately dismissed as too boring to consider. Even we as the initiators wondered at times about the possible negative effects of such a meeting. Would it unite us or divide us? Would it alienate those who could not attend? Would it do more harm than good?

Men who heard about the meeting also reacted strongly. Several expressed fears that we women were trying to mobilize a takeover of the field to oust the male leaders. A few tried to get themselves invited or to at least be allowed to send a representative. The meeting was compared to a coven of witches. Women who were interested in attending were called radicals, men haters, and—the worst of all possible insults—"nonsystemic thinkers." Something about this topic stimulated emotional reactions and fantasies far beyond our expectations. As the emotional climate intensified, so did our commitment to the meeting and our curiosity about the causes of such extreme responses from otherwise rational people. It became clear that some very powerful issues were being raised, some very important unspoken rules were being challenged.

Stimulating turmoil had not been our intent. In developing the plan for Stonehenge, we saw the need for a network, for more visible women mentors and role models, and for hearing the many wonderful voices of women in the field, who were so often overshadowed by the men in their lives. Although some men and, surprisingly, some women reacted negatively to the Stonehenge meeting, once the conference occurred almost everyone found it to be an experience that brought together thoughtful, articulate women family therapists to talk about their lives, their ideas, and their experiences in the field. What we found remarkable about the meeting and the many connections it helped to foster among women in the field was the energy, intelligence, and power that were there to be mobilized. We had all struggled with gender issues at various levels all our lives, but we were only beginning to articulate the issues as they confronted the field of family therapy. It had been, for most of us, as Betty Friedan described it, "the problem with no name."

As we talked together, we learned that we all experienced problems with the unequal division of power and labor in our own families, in the families we see in treatment, and in our professional relationships. We found that we contributed to these problems by our own attitudes and behaviors—lacking confidence to assert ourselves and feeling guilty when we did not take total responsibility for our homes and children or did not protect and defer to men.

PERSONAL CONNECTIONS: THE IMPORTANCE OF A SISTERHOOD

We three co-editors have been friends for 20 years, even though for most of that time we have lived in different geographic regions and made time together primarily at professional meetings. Like the women in Hennig and Jardim's (1977) study of successful women in management, not one of us had a brother. Perhaps this accounts for the fact that some of our parents' dreams and expectations, which might otherwise have been concentrated on sons, went instead to us, their daughters. Unlike the women in Hennig's sample, however, only one of us was an oldest and an only child (Froma); one was the middle of three sisters (Monica), and one the youngest of four sisters (Carol). Perhaps our different and complementary sibling positions facilitated our collaboration as friends over the years. As we thought about our ties to each other and their meaning for us in both our personal and our professional lives, we came to appreciate the importance of women's relationships to one another through the life cycle, as well as the importance of not letting those ties weaken in the competitive struggles that have so often separated professional women from each other. Having all experienced in our own families the importance of deep bonds with other women, we know well the importance of our biological sisters (see McGoldrick, Chapter 13). But we also know the importance of our sisterhoods through friendship, colleagueship, and mentoring. We need each other; further, we appreciate the need to validate not only our intellectual bonds but also our emotional and spiritual bonds. As we articulate and respect our differences and varied perspectives, we hope to contribute to a fuller appreciation of women's experiences.

We each began our development as family therapists in the late 1960s, when Virginia Satir was the only major female voice among primarily male virtuosi. Although she was one of the earliest and most influential pioneers in the family field, she was often derided by both men and women for her emphasis on feelings (a "feminine" concern) at a time when her male colleagues were presenting revolutionary models that downplayed emotions and emphasized "masculine" priorities—i.e., rational planning, instrumental problem-solving, hierarchy, neutrality, and power. Her "experiential" mentality was almost embarrassing, as was the fact that she was "touchy-feely" rather than distant and conceptual in her orientation and her practice. Nevertheless, Satir stood her ground for many years, becoming the only woman who regularly had a place among the "stars" of family therapy. During that same time, Lynn Hoffman, who has played such a key role in the development of our theories, was never in the limelight; only recently has she received recognition for her pivotal role in shaping and articulating the ideas credited to so many of her male collaborators.

THE DEVELOPMENT OF A NEW CONSCIOUSNESS AND A NEW NETWORK

Since the late 1970s a shift has occurred, in part due to changing times and in part due to the efforts of a number of women in the field. Rachel Hare-Mustin's landmark article in *Family Process* in 1978 called attention to the traditional one-down position of women in families. The Women's Project in Family Therapy, developed by Betty Carter, Peggy Papp, Olga Silverstein, and Marianne Walters, began to conduct workshops addressing roles and relationships of women in families. Further papers from Hare-Mustin (1979, 1980, 1983, 1987; Hare-Mustin & Marecek, 1986), and from such writers as Michele Bograd (1982, 1984, 1986, in press), Lois Braverman (1986a, 1986b), Kerry James (1984) and Debra McIntyre (James & McIntyre, 1983), Jo-Ann Krestan and Claudia Bepko (1980, in press), Harriet Lerner (1983, 1985a, 1987), Judy Libow (1985; Libow, Raskin, & Caust, 1982), Sally Ann Roth (1985), Morris Taggart (1985), Virginia Goldner (1985a, 1986b, 1988), Judith Myers Avis (1985a, 1985b, 1986, in press), and Dorothy Wheeler (1985; Wheeler, Avis, Miller, & Chaney, 1985), stimulated a reevaluation of gender in family therapy theory and practice. We have included some of these major articles, revised and updated, in this volume: Goldner (1988) is Chapter 3; Hare-Mustin (1987) is Chapter 4; Roth (1985) is Chapter 15; and Wheeler et al. (1985) is Chapter 8.

Women have also become more active in the politics of the field and have assumed major leadership positions in national organizations. Florence Kaslow served as editor of the *Journal of Marital and Family Therapy*. Since 1984, two women have been presidents of the American Family Therapy Association — Kitty LaPerriere and Carol Anderson. Clearly, the doors to powerful leadership positions are opening to women, and they are willing to pay the price of leadership and the price for raising controversial issues.

In addition, recently we have seen the publication of several books articulating new perspectives on women's relationships: *The Dance of Anger* (1985b) and *The Dance of Intimacy* (1989) by Harriet Goldhor Lerner; *Feminist Family Therapy* (1988) by Thelma Jean Goodrich, Cheryl Rampage, Barbara Ellman, and Kris Halstead; *The Invisible Web: Gender Patterns in Family Relationships* (1988) by Marianne Walters, Betty Carter, Peggy Papp, and Olga Silverstein; *The Responsibility Trap* (1985) by Claudia Bepko and Jo-Ann Krestan; *The Family Interpreted* (1988), Debra Luepnitz's feminist critique of the theories in our field; Marianne Ault-Riche's edited volume, *Women and Family Therapy* (1986); and the journal issue edited by Lois Braverman, *A Guide to Feminist Family Therapy* (1988). Under the editorship of Lois Braverman, a new journal, *Feminist Family Therapy*, has been launched; moreover, the number of presentations at major forums in the field on the subject of women, as well as articles in the leading journals, grows each year.

You've Come a Long Way, Baby—Or Is the Route Circular?

Despite all this activity, "women's issues" as an appropriate topic of concern continue to be dismissed or regarded with suspicion, criticism, and fear by many in the field. The assumptions appear to be several, including: Any attention focused on the concerns and needs of women is a "special issue" and not really scientific or important; if women attend to or assert their needs, men, children, and families will suffer; women who focus attention on their relationships with other women must be angry at men. For instance, a close male friend of one of the editors, when he heard we were working on this book, said, "Oh, are you still involved in that fad?" Another warned one of us not to abandon science for "popular passion" and cautioned that such an endeavor could "tarnish" her reputation. And another very thoughtful colleague said that he felt forced to conclude that feminist ideas were bad for families, because they led to their breakup and to the neglect of children.

This last reflects the cynicism evident, for example, in Arnold Bloom's best-selling *The Closing of the American Mind* (1987):

> The feminist response that justice requires equal sharing of all domestic responsibility by men and women is not a solution, but only a compromise, an attenuation of men's dedication to their careers and of women's to family, with arguably an enrichment in diversity of both parties but just as arguably a fragmentation of their lives. The question of who goes with whom in the case of jobs in different cities is unresolved and is, whatever may be said about it, a festering sore, a source of suspicion and resentment and the potential for war. Moreover, this compromise does not decide anything about the care of children. Are both parents going to care more about their careers than about the children? Previously children at least had the unqualified dedication of one person, the woman, for whom their care was the most important thing in life. Is half the attention of two the same as the whole attention of one? Is this not a formula for neglecting children? Under such arrangements the family is not a unity, and marriage is an unattractive struggle that is easy to get out of, especially for men. (p. 128)

Bloom seems to believe a most absurd idea—that we have already reached a point of gender equality: "The female career . . . is now precisely the same as the male career. There are now two equal careers in almost every household composed of educated persons under thirty-five" (p. 127). The existence of two careers does not mean the existence of gender equality. Bloom further asserts that it is pointless for women to seek equal rights because men will not and cannot change:

> Men tend to undergo this re-education somewhat sullenly but studiously, in order to avoid the opproprium of the sexist label and to keep peace with their wives and girlfriends. And it is indeed possible to soften men. But to make them "care" is another thing, and the project must inevitably fail. It must fail because in an age of individualism, persons of either sex cannot be forced to be public-spirited, particularly by those who are becoming less so. (p. 129)

Bloom would have us think that, because men are not inclined to change, women should give up the project or else their children will suffer. We are neither as cynical about the potential of men to be caring nor as optimistic about the extent of the change that has already occurred. Certainly more women have careers and more women are successful. However, even though today's young married women are setting higher goals in education and employment, their marital relationships are likely to revert to more conventional patterns as soon as children are born (see McGoldrick, 1988, Chapter 11, and Walsh, Chapter 14). Throughout the life cycle both men and women are bombarded by influences from the larger social system that reinforce gender inequities. In our educational system the teachers are primarily female, but men run the schools and are the administrators who determine what and how teachers teach. The health care system is female at the level of actual caregiving, but male-dominated at the level of decision-making; men control the economics of care, as well as hospitals, clinics, and insurance (see Imber-Black, Chapter 7). The media send messages from the cosmetics industry and numerous other advertisers that women are valuable primarily for their looks, their youth, and their caretaking ability, while men are valuable for their intelligence, wit, power, and assertiveness. Cartoons and toys for children continue to reinforce the stereotypes of the "macho" male hero and his cute, adoring female companion. In short, it is clear that we have made hardly a dent in the gender inequities built into the basic structure of our society.

WHERE WE'VE BEEN IN THE FAMILY THERAPY FIELD

In one sense the family therapy field has always worked toward balancing the equation between men and women by emphasizing so-called "female" values of relationship and family. Specifically, we have encouraged men to develop the hidden and devalued side of themselves by attending to their family connections, their emotions, and their relationships with their wives, their parents, and their children. Our efforts to involve men more in family relationships have made important contributions to the lives of all family members. However, these moves have not rebalanced traditional family patterns so that the needs, goals, and dreams of women are more fully addressed; nor have we substantially changed men's primary commitment to a world dominated by competition and power relationships to the neglect of human connectedness.

The family therapy field has been very late in coming to the awareness that gender plays a differential role in families. For the first 20 years the field operated in a gender-blind fashion, as if family members were simply interchangeable units of a system (see Goldner, Chapter 3). Gender was one of those "content" areas regarded as less significant than the "process" of interaction in a system. Family therapists have given token acknowledgment to the context in which families exist, yet have focused only on the interaction of family members, as if they were interchangeable parts with equal control over the outcome of family interactions (Taggart, 1985). As Goldner (1985a) has stated, despite documentation from sociologists and demographers about the differences for men and women in family participation:

> The category of gender remains essentially invisible in the conceptualizations of family therapists. This blind spot seems extraordinary when one considers the embattled condition of the contemporary family and the extent to which the battle lines have been drawn around conflicting ideologies about how gender relations should be structured. (p. 33)

Goldner goes on to point out that changes in the traditional family have not necessarily helped women toward greater equality. In fact, she points out, these changes have "too often meant a new kind of freedom for men and a new kind of trap for women" (p. 41).

Because of the way women and men have been socialized, and because our increased awareness of problems with gender strikes at the interior of the family, at everyone's closest relationships, these issues have been even more threatening and difficult to recognize than ideas about differences in class or ethnicity. As James (1984) states,

> Patriarchal structures are transmitted through the acquisition of culture, language and gender identity and the family is the site of this transmission. . . . To the extent that there is a disjunction between the ideology and a woman's experience, she will tend to blame herself, lose herself and shape herself to fit the picture. This ideology creates women's silence—to speak out against it risks incurring labels and sanctions that mark her as deviant. . . . Women's worth is very much dependent on their roles as wives and mothers. Their value is tied to and derived from their relationships with men. (pp. 244, 247)

In the past few years we have come a long way toward removing the blinders which kept us oblivious to the power politics of families, determined by and reinforcing of the power politics of the larger culture, which define women as less valuable members of the culture in virtually every respect. Throughout the life cycle, women's roles, apart from their functions as wives and mothers, have been negated (see Hicks & Anderson, Chapter 16; Braverman, Chapter 12; McGoldrick, Chapter 11; and Walsh, Chapter 14). Even within their roles as wives and mothers, women have been left at a serious disadvantage by our family therapy models and our male-determined definitions of dysfunction (Taggart, Chapter 6; Anderson, Chapter 19; and Walsh & Scheinkman, Chapter 2). Within the organization of family therapy training, women's perspectives have, until very recently, been ignored (Wheeler, Avis, Miller, & Chaney, Chapter 8; Warburton, Alexander, & Newberry, Chapter 9). In other words, our history has tended to ignore women's voices and experiences. It has become increasingly apparent that we need to "restory" the history of the family therapy field, the families we see for therapy, and the families in which we live (Laird, Chapter 21).

Since the field has been defined primarily by men, our definitions regarding the family and family therapy have been determined by male language, which objectifies human relationships and puts distance between us and our clients. "Enmeshment" has been regarded as bad; "differentiation" as good. Emotion has been regarded as bad; thinking as good. We use "joining techniques" and we help families "detriangle." We worry about being "epistemologically correct" and talk of "co-constructed realities," "strategic interventions," and "systemic dysfunction." In other words, in some ways our language differs little from the very depersonalized analytic notions of "object relations" and "narcissistic introjects." We seem to have almost a pathological fear of direct, personal language and of expressions of caring or tenderness. Unless carefully muted, emotional realities are somehow dangerous or embarrassing. We talk of love only in clinical terms such as "bonding" or "attachment," and we drug ourselves and our patients or others to avoid facing those aspects of life that don't fit in our neat categories (see Bepko, Chapter 20).

But since the late 1970s an increasing number of women and a small number of men have forced our attention to the underlying assumptions about gender on which the family therapy field, like the culture which created it, is based. Those concerned about the inequalities women face inside and outside of their families are raising many serious questions for the family therapy field. Unless we are committed to the task of rebalancing and redefining families, we unwittingly promote family patterns in which women are devalued, blamed, and made to feel guilty for patterns and lives they have little freedom to change.

Despite the impressive body of scholarship and research on women's issues in our culture over the past 20 years, and specifically the more recent acknowledgment in our field of these issues, women's concerns have not yet been integrated into family therapy training and practice. We have not incorporated what we know about gender issues, even those that would not seem controversial. Family therapists still tend to hold women primarily responsible for what goes wrong in families (Caplan & Hall-McCorquodale, 1985; see Goldner, 1985). Leading therapists still talk about maintaining "therapeutic neutrality," an absolute impossibility in a clinical situation (Boscolo, Cecchin, Hoffman, & Penn, 1987; see also Walsh & Scheinkman, Chapter 2). Books on marital therapy fail to discuss the different implications for men and women of questioning their commitment to their marital relationships (see Walsh & Scheinkman, Chapter 2). Most of the literature and discussion regarding facilitating change in family therapy still occurs without reference to the unequal division of power between men and women in families and in larger social systems, or to most women's lack of freedom to alter their life circumstances without severe penalties (for example, Kerr & Bowen, 1988). And books in our field still appear using the masculine pronoun to refer to all people (for example, Kerr & Bowen, 1988), in spite of the nonsexist publishing guidelines which have long been established by many publishers and by the APA (1983). Even therapists who are overtly aiming to help a symptomatic wife become more functional may unthinkingly form a coalition with the husband, putting him in charge (Fishman, 1988; see Walsh & Scheinkman, Chapter 2).

The recognition and advancement of women professionals in our field still lag behind those of men, and in many cases behind their actual contributions. Men control the major accrediting organization in the field, the American Association of Marriage and Family Therapy, while the most influential journals have disproportionately low numbers of women on their editorial review boards and almost no representation on their boards of directors.

In spite of the change in the number of women in the workplace, and the number of writings that are drawing attention to inequities for women in our society, women remain overburdened within their families, and all the more so when they also work outside the home, as most wives and mothers do today. Beyond the confines of the family, women confront serious obstacles to advancement in the workplace and in other meaningful pursuits. Wife abuse and intimidation occur with astounding frequency; moreover, women have fewer options than men when the family dissolves or does not meet their needs, since women who divorce generally end up with less money, less earning potential, and less likelihood of finding a new partner.

Our culture must come to value women, even those who do not marry or form nuclear families. Too often such women become invisible; they are seen as "not yet complete" because they have not united with a male who will help them fulfill themselves as wife and mother (see Hicks & Anderson, Chapter 16). As family therapists we must recognize the strengths and contributions of women on their own, rather than consider them as tragic figures because they have lost the male who centered their lives, providing their financial security and even their very identity. We must expand our respect for women and our awareness of their options and priorities, so that women without men can be seen as whole beings with their own identities. Statistically all women can expect to be alone for a substantial portion of their adult lives; this should not make them less legitimate, valued, or respected.

Although the family therapy field has tended to ignore the larger context, it is increasingly obvious that family relationships cannot be separated from the wider culture that defines the types of relationships which are possible in families and who is available to participate in those relationships. Brief family therapies have tended to promote the myth that the problems are small and can be solved by small interventions. We think that problems may indeed be big and will take generations to resolve. While brief interventions can at times be very helpful to families, we do not want to promote the idea that the problems families encounter because of their basic structural imbalances should be swept under the rug, that the status quo should be preserved by encouraging minimal changes or by the clever reframing statement of a smart therapist.

In our view attention to the unequal positions of women and men in our society is necessary for all family therapists. A therapist who is not aware of the gender inequities embedded in our culture and conscious of the need to change this imbalance is contributing to the problems of families and couples attempting to survive in a new and complicated world. A therapist who fails to respond to a families' presentation of their problems with a framework that takes into account the inequities of the culture, and who attempts to maintain a so-called "neutrality" vis-à-vis the family, is necessarily doing sexist family therapy.

The implications of this perspective are many and complex. There is no formula for gender-sensitive family therapy. We have heard colleagues at family therapy conferences, frustrated with the presentations of feminist family therapists, complain: "Why don't they get practical? What should we do differently?" This question reflects a lack of understanding of the magnitude of the problem. We are not going to be able to come up with quick "technical" or "strategic" solutions, cookbook fashion, which will make this problem evaporate. This is going to take us all working together for many years — or probably more accurately, many generations.

We hope that this book will provide a beginning contribution to the development of a new way of understanding families and family therapy, one which takes into account the biological and social differences of men and women. Feminist scholars have rightly criticized our field for its inattention to gender-based roles, assumptions, and interactional rules in families and to the sociocultural and historical context in which families are embedded. If the field is genuinely to respond to this critique and to the very real dilemmas facing families today, we must examine and expand our theory and practice to confront the unequal distribution of power between men and women in the larger culture and challenge the severely constricting role expectations and impossible binds that have been placed on women.

If the field cannot move to integrate current and developing information about gender and its impact, if it regards such criticism as simply representing extremist notions that concern only a few radical women, then none of us, male or female, will develop our abilities to the fullest. Family therapy should not be used as an agent of social control or as a way of perpetuating the existing inequities for women in families and in society. To ensure that it does not, we must address the problem. We must move to assume a truly systemic perspective, one which takes into account all system levels, from the microbiologic to the sociopolitical structure of society. Only then can we expect change in the patterns which have for so long limited and denigrated women's possibilities, positions, and options.

This book builds on our awareness of systems, and of the problems women experience in the systems that matter most in an attempt to rebalance thinking and practice in the family therapy field by including and valuing the female voice and experience. We know this work is still in its formative stages. The problems are not completely defined, and solutions are out of the question. We look forward to being able to follow up this work, perhaps from a new vantage point, as our field and our culture move toward redefining relationships within and beyond the family in ways that are more satisfactory for us all.

REFERENCES

American Psychological Association (1983). *Publication manual, third edition* (pp. 43–49). Washington, DC: author.

Ault-Riche, M. (Ed.) (1986). *Women and family therapy*. Rockville, MD: Aspen Systems.

Avis, J. M. (1985a). The politics of functional family therapy: A feminist critique. *Journal of Marital and Family Therapy, 11*, 127–138.

Avis, J. M. (1985b). Through a different lens: A reply to Alexander, Warburton Waldron and Mas. *Journal of Marital and Family Therapy, 11*, 145–148.

Avis, J. M. (1986). Feminist issues in family therapy. In F. Piercy & D. Sprenkle (Eds.), *Family therapy sourcebook*. New York: Guilford.

Avis, J. M. (in press). Deeping awareness: A private study guide to feminism and family therapy. *Journal of Psychotherapy and the Family, 3*(4).

Bepko, C. (1985). Mary & John: Power, power, who's got the power? *The Family Therapy Networker, 9*, 47–49.

Bepko, C., & Krestan, J. (1985). *The responsibility trap*. New York: Free Press.

Bepko, C. (in press). Female legacies: Intergenerational themes and their treatment for women in alcoholic families. *Journal of Psychotherapy and the Family, 3*(4).

Bloom, A. (1987). *The Closing of the American Mind*. New York: Simon & Shuster Inc.

Bograd, M. (1982). Battered women, cultural myths and clinical interventions: A feminist analysis. *Women and Therapy, 1*, 69–77.

Bograd, M. (1984). Family systems approaches to wife battering: A feminist critique. *American Journal of Orthopsychiatry, 54*, 558–568.

Bograd, M. (1986). Holding the line: Confronting the abusive partner. *Family Therapy Networker, 10*, 44–47.

Bograd, M. (in press a). Scapegoating mothers in family therapy: Re-exploring enmeshment. In M. Mirkin, (Ed.), *Social and political contexts of family therapy*. New York: Gardner Press.

Bograd, M. (in press b). Gender, power and the family: Challenges of feminism to family systems theory. In L. Walker and M. Douglas (Eds.), *Feminist psychotherapies: Integration of therapeutic and feminist systems*. Norwood, NJ: Ablex Press.

Bograd, M. (in press c). A feminist examination of family therapy: What is woman's place? In D. Howard, ed., *Women and Family Therapy*.

Boscolo, L., Cecchin, G., Hoffman, L., & Penn, P. (1987). *Milan Systemic Family Therapy: Conversations in Theory and Practice*. New York: Basic Books.

Braverman, L. (1986a). Beyond families: Strategic family therapy and the female client. *Family Therapy, 13*(2), 143–152.

Braverman, L. (1986a). Reframing the female client's profile. *Affilia: Journal of Women and Social Work, 2*, 30–40.

Braverman, L. (Ed.). (1988). *A guide to feminist family therapy*. New York: Haworth.

Caplan, P. J., & Hall-McCorquodale, I. (1985). Mother-blaming in major clinical journals. *American Journal of Orthopsychiatry, 55*(3), 345–353.

Carter, B., Papp, P., Silverstein, O., & Walters, M. (in press). *Rethinking Family Relationships*. New York: Guilford.

Fishman, C. (1988). *Treating troubled adolescents: A family therapy approach*. New York: Basic Books.

Goldner, V. (1985a). Feminism and family therapy. *Family Process, 24*, 31–47.

Goldner, V. (1985b). Warning: Family therapy may be dangerous to your health. *The Family Therapy Networker, 9*, 19–23.

Goldner, V. (1988). Generation and gender: Normative and covert hierarchies. *Family Process, 27*(1), 17–32.

Goodrich, T. J., Rampage, C., Ellman, B., & Halstead, K. (1988). *Feminist family therapy: A casebook*. New York: Norton.

Hare-Mustin, R. T. (1978). A feminist approach to family therapy. *Family Process, 17*, 181–194.

Hare-Mustin, R. T. (1979). Family therapy and sex role stereotypes. *The Counseling Psychologist, 8*, 31–32.

Hare-Mustin, R. T. (1980). Family therapy may be dangerous for your health. *Professional Psychology, 11*, 935–938.

Hare-Mustin, R. T. (1983). An appraisal of the relationship between women and psychotherapy: 80 years after the case of Dora. *American Psychologist, 38*, 594–601.

Hare-Mustin, R. T., & Marecek, J. (1986). Autonomy and gender: Some questions for therapists. *Psychotherapy, 23*, 205–212.

Hare-Mustin, R. T. (1987). The problem of gender in family therapy theory. *Family Process, 26*(1), 15–34.

Hennig, M., & Jardim, A. (1977). *The managerial woman*. Garden City, NY: Anchor/Doubleday.

James, K. (1984). Breaking the chains of gender. *Australian Journal of Family Therapy, 5*, 241–248.

James, K., & McIntyre, D. (1983). The reproduction of families: The social role of family therapy? *Journal of Marital and Family Therapy, 9*, 119-129.

Kerr, M., & Bowen, M. (1988). *Family evaluation: An approach based on Bowen theory.* New York: Norton.

Krestan, J., & Bepko, C. (1980). The problem of fusion in the lesbian relationship. *Family Process, 19*(3), 277-289.

Krestan, J. (in press). Lesbian daughter and lesbian mothers: The crisis of disclosure from a family systems perspective. *Journal of Psychotherapy and the Family, (3)*2.

Lerner, H. G. (1983). Female dependency in context: Some theoretical and technical considerations. *American Journal of Orthopsychiatry, 53*(4), 697-705.

Lerner, H. G. (1985a). Diana and Lillie: Can a feminist still like Murray Bowen? *The Family Therapy Networker, 9*, 36-39.

Lerner, H. G. (1985b). *The dance of anger: A women's guide to changing the patterns of intimate relationships.* New York: Harper & Row.

Lerner, H. G. (1987). Work and success inhibitions in women: Family systems level interventions in psychodynamic treatment. *Bulletin of the Menninger Clinic,* July.

Lerner, H. G. (1989). *The dance of intimacy.* New York: Harper & Row.

Libow, J. A. (1985). Gender and sex role issues as family secrets. *Journal of Strategic and Systemic Therapies, 4*, 32-41.

Libow, J. A., Raskin, P. A., & Caust, B. L. (1982). Feminist and family systems therapy: Are they irreconcilable? *The American Journal of Family Therapy, 10*, 3-12.

Luepnitz, D. (1988). *The family interpreted.* New York: Basic Books.

McGoldrick, M. (1988). The young couple: The joining of families in marriage. In B. Carter & M. McGoldrick (Eds.), *The Changing Family Life Cycle,* 2nd Ed. New York: Gardner Press.

Roth, S. (1985). Psychotherapy with lesbian couples: Individual issues, female socialization and the social context. *Journal of Marital and Family Therapy, 11*(3), 273-286.

Taggart, M. (1985). The feminist critique in epistemological perspective: Questions of context in family therapy. *Journal of Marital and Family Therapy, 11*, 113-126.

Walters, M., Carter, B., Papp, P., & Silverstein, O. (1988). *The invisible web: Gender patterns in family relationships.* New York: Guilford.

Wheeler, D. (1985). Fear of feminism in family therapy. *Family Therapy Networker, 9*(6), 53-55.

Wheeler, D., Avis, J., Miller, L., & Chaney, S. (1985). Rethinking family therapy training and supervision: A feminist model. *Journal of Psychotherapy and the Family, 1*, 53-71.

2
(Fe)male: The Hidden Gender Dimension in Models of Family Therapy

FROMA WALSH   MICHELE SCHEINKMAN

At a time when long-standing assumptions about families are being challenged throughout American society, gender has become one of the most controversial issues in the field of family therapy. Tremendous social changes over the past two decades have generated an upheaval in beliefs and practices concerning what it means to be male or female and what gender-linked rules govern interactions and expectations within the family and in the social world in which gender and family norms are embedded.

This chapter will examine the place of gender in family therapy theory and practice as it has been explicitly addressed, or merely implicit, in the literature relevant to the development of major approaches to family therapy. It presents an overview of the most influential approaches for comparison and contrast. We will consider the following questions in relation to each model:

1. *Family processes:* What are the assumptions about the role of gender in family functioning and in problem development and maintenance?
2. *Therapeutic change processes:* How is gender considered in the therapeutic objectives, intervention strategies and techniques, and in the therapist's use of self?

In contrast to some family therapists who maintain that feminist positions are incompatible with systems theory and practice, we argue that to ignore gender is, in fact, nonsystemic. Rather than suggesting that we abandon systems therapies, here we attempt to advance theory and practice by suggesting ways to incorporate an awareness of gender in the various models of family therapy. Gender, until recently a hidden dimension in family therapy theory and practice (Goldner, 1985), must become a visible and vital component in all models of family functioning and all approaches to change if our field is to develop.

Our review of family therapy models begins with the brief, problem-solving approaches, and in particular the strategic/systemic and structural models of family therapy. Next, we consider intergenerational growth-oriented approaches, and in particular the Bowen family systems model.

STRATEGIC/SYSTEMIC APPROACHES

Strategic/systemic approaches to family therapy have been most strongly represented by the interactional view and brief therapy model developed at the Mental Research Institute in Palo Alto, the problem-solving approach of Haley and Madanes, and the Milan systemic model.

Interactional View/Brief Therapy Model

The interactional view was launched by the Bateson group investigation of double-bind communication in the etiology of schizophrenia (Bateson, Jackson, Haley, & Weakland, 1956). On rereading the early papers we were struck by an apparent blind spot in conceptualization. Despite the paradigmatic shift from linear to circular causality, and from individual and dyadic units of analysis to the family as a system, there persisted a tendency in case examples to focus narrowly on mothers' pathogenic communication to their schizophrenic offspring. *Parent* was equated with *mother* and the influence was linear: Mother's behavior produced certain responses in her offspring. Only much later was this tendency corrected (Sluzki & Ransom, 1976).

Don Jackson and his M.R.I. colleagues established a language and conceptual foundation for the interactional paradigm. In two seminal papers, Jackson (1977a, 1977b) introduced the concepts of "the family as a rule-governed, homeostatic system" and "the marital quid pro quo." He also addressed explicitly the question of gender. In his description of "family rules" he contrasted this new concept to sociologist Talcott Parsons' widely accepted sex-role theory of marriage and family. Jackson's critique underscored the primacy of transactional phenomena, asserting that individual vocabulary was inappropriate to describe interaction. He introduced the novel idea of rules rather than roles as determinants of human behavior. However, in his fervor to refute the sex-role model and establish the interactional paradigm, Jackson threw out the baby with the bath water. Jackson not only discarded sex-role theory as epistemologically ill-suited for the study of human interaction, but also, in focusing exclusively on communicational process, took an extreme position in which he negated the relevance of gender as a dimension in family theory. As one of the forefathers of the interactional view, Jackson's dismissal of gender differences initiated a taboo so strong that it is only now, 20 years later, being challenged.

Jackson (1977a) defined the concept of family rules as implicit or explicit norms which organize family interaction and function to maintain a stable system by prescribing and limiting members' behavior. He contrasted rules to roles and criticized sex-role theory on the following grounds:

1. The sex-role construct is an individual concept, while the concept of *rules* refers directly to the redundancies we can observe *between* individuals.
2. Sex-role theory was proposed as a normative theory in which it was not possible to separate the role concept from cultural preconceptions about "proper" sex roles. In this view men's and women's behavior was classified and measured against stereotypic ideals of masculinity and femininity, with no allowance made for the *relationship* which underlay and maintained this arrangement or for the possibility of a variety of ways of working out rules for a relationship.
3. Sex-role concepts are based on a priori categories rather than on observed phenomena. In Jackson's view, more important is the circularity in the evolution and maintenance of the differences.

Based on his concept of rules, Jackson (1977b) suggested a theory of marriage which emphasized the interactional and collaborative aspects of the marital relationship rather than individual gender-based roles. The marital quid pro quo refers to the rules about the exchanges between two partners: Each partner, as in a bargaining relationship, must receive something for what he/she gives; these exchanges consequently define the different rights and duties of the spouses. (See Walsh, Chapter 14 for a reappraisal of this theory.)

Considering that Jackson's ideas were developed during the early 1960s — a time when prevailing theories were monadic, normative, and a priori — his pioneering work elucidated a language for understanding interactional phenomena. In his critique of role theory he anticipated the recent feminist criticisms of Parsons' functionalist model of the family (Hare-Mustin, Chapter 4; Boss & Thorne, Chapter 5). Moreover, he offered a conceptual tool that advanced the field from the stereotypic and prescriptive theories in which normality was viewed as adaptation to a patriarchal model of the family.

Jackson's interactional view is consistent with feminism in that the concept of rules implies that relationships are not destined by our biology, but can instead be defined potentially in a variety of functional ways. Nevertheless, by focusing exclusively on the interior of the family, he decontextualized human interaction, as if interactional processes could be understood in a vacuum. He narrowly equated "system" with "family" rather than recognizing the reciprocal interplay between individual, family, and other social systems. His theory of the marital quid pro quo implied that each spouse enters the relationship as an equal partner and as a "blank slate," i.e., with freedom to define *any* rules. Actually, each spouse is already "rule-governed" by larger systems, especially by the family of origin and culture, which co-influence socialization processes in human development.

Jackson's cybernetic model accounts for neither the social and economic context in which the family is embedded nor power differentials between family members (James & McIntyre, 1983). The most problematic aspect of Jackson's work however, is his contention that "sex roles" are not based on biological givens but are actually the end result of the bargaining between two people trying to define rules of collaboration. He failed to see that roles and rules are reciprocally constructed. Moreover, since men and women are social beings constrained by their history, culture and social condition, they enter relationships with different kinds of knowledge and experience and different degrees of power. He asserted that most of the dilemmas in marriages are not due to sexual differences but instead result from difficulties in working out rules for collaboration. He concluded, " . . . *it is possible that one could outline marriage as a totally nonsexual affair, nearly excluding all sexual differences, or at least minimizing the causal role usually assigned such differences*" (1977b, p. 23).

Jackson came close to addressing today's gender issues in his assumption that our behavior cannot and should not be reduced to or explained in terms of biological differences. Yet, in order to avoid the pitfall of the theories of his time, which viewed sex differences in a causal and deterministic way, he dismissed gender altogether. In doing so he unwittingly established a false dichotomy between the interactional point of view and the inclusion of gender as a self-evident concept in family theory.

In subsequent work at the M.R.I., therapists in the Brief Therapy project (Watzlawick, Weakland, & Fisch, 1974; Fisch, Weakland, & Segal, 1982) developed a strategic model for working with individuals, couples and families. Based on an integration of systemic/communicational ideas (Watzlawick, Beavin Bavelas, & Jackson, 1967), and on the work of Milton Erickson, the brief therapy team evolved a problem-solving model focused on how problems come to be and how to resolve them:

> "Problems begin from some ordinary life difficulty, of which there is never any shortage. This difficulty may stem from an unusual or fortuitous event. More often, though, the beginning is likely to be a common difficulty associated with one of the transitions regularly experienced in the course of life—marriage, the birth of a child, going to school, and so on. . . . But for a difficulty to turn into a problem, only two conditions need to be fulfilled: (1) the difficulty is mishandled, and (2) when the difficulty is not resolved, more of the same 'solution' is applied. Then the original difficulty will be escalated, by a vicious-circle process, into a problem whose eventual size and nature may have little apparent similarity to the original difficulty." (Fisch et al., 1982, p. 14)

The authors contend that individuals do what they do because of their beliefs and values (their "position") about what they think is the best way to approach a situation. The model was not proposed as a comprehensive theory about human nature or the family. Instead, it was intended as a map of interactional patterns that maintain or intensify problems and of interventions to intercept these dysfunctional processes.

Like Jackson, the brief therapy team is wary of normative theories. As a result, they attempt to maintain neutrality by offering a minimalist model limited to initiating changes that will get the individual or family "unstuck." They believe that each individual or family must define what is normal and healthy for itself and that it is not the function of therapy to direct how people live their lives. Although this is laudable as a theoretical principle, in being so parsimonious the brief therapy model is too incomplete a map for so large a territory. While the model is extremely helpful in focusing the therapist on the interactional sequences that maintain a problem, its exclusive attention to changing attempted solutions omits all else, including the context of the attempted solutions or the alternative "appropriate" solutions.

The M.R.I. therapists consider the patient's beliefs and values as essential in maintaining erroneous solutions, but they deal with the patient's position neither in terms of gender patterns nor in relation to social context. This omission is critical to the plight of women, especially in terms of the planned direction of therapy. The model posits that if the dysfunctional pattern is interrupted, alternative solutions will emerge. However, it is unclear how such solutions are generated and maintained. Even if only in indirect, paradoxical, or subtle ways, it seems unavoidable that, as long as we are in the business of being therapists, we will rely implicitly or explicitly on some notion of individual, family, and gender functioning. Our questions, our reframes, and our definitions of therapeutic goals are all value-laden. Even when working within a symptom-focused model, the omission of gender-based patterns can be limiting to the therapist in understanding the problems of women and the solutions available to them. Although a value-free model of therapy might be ideal, in actuality neutrality seems utopian and a poor fit with the complexity of the psychotherapeutic process.

Recent work by the brief therapy team (Fisch et al., 1982) reflects increasing attention to the individual. Recognition of the importance of the patient's "position," involving the operation of beliefs, values and attitudes in the maintenance of attempted solutions, can be a point of entry for integration of gender as a dimension in the model.

The M.R.I. brief therapy model has been developed exclusively by men and, in fact, team members have claimed that the model appeals more to male than to female therapists. This can be understood if we take into account recent work describing how, typically, men and women follow different paths in the process of acquiring knowledge (Belenky, Clinchy, Goldberger, & Tarule, 1986). The M.R.I. model was from the beginning advanced with rational, abstract, impersonal language and metaphors. Also, the model's instrumental nature and narrow focus, as well as its emphasis on behavior and cognition, omit important aspects of women's "connected" ways of learning and knowing, which utilize contextual understanding, intuition, and self-knowledge. In this vein it is important to mention Virginia Satir, who was the first director of training at the M.R.I. Although Satir's therapy approach was strongly influenced by the early M.R.I. development in mapping communication principles, her direction was diametrically opposed to the model that evolved out of the Brief Therapy Project. While the brief therapy model was presented in a logical and pragmatic style, with a narrow focus and emphasis on behavior, cognition, and problem-solving, Satir refused to be confined to the "black box" and instead tried to broaden the interactional view by integrating individual psychology and the importance of social systems (Satir, 1972). In sharp contrast to the brief therapists' cognitive style, Satir valued the intuitive and experiential modes of change and centered her approach on feelings and growth.

Problem-Solving Approach

The strategic model advanced by Jay Haley (1973, 1976) integrated the cybernetic/communicational orientation from his early work at the M.R.I. with assumptions derived from his observations of Milton Erickson and structural ideas formulated in collaboration with Salvador Minuchin. Like the M.R.I. group, Haley's major concern has been with developing a model of therapeutic change rather than a theory of the family. However, as he shifted focus from communication to family structure, he added two key tenets about the family to the M.R.I.'s parsimonious model.

First, Haley stressed the importance of viewing the family and problem formation within a life cycle perspective (Haley, 1973). He stated that "families undergo a developmental process over time, and human distress and psychiatric symptoms appear when this process is disrupted" (p. 41). Secondly, he conceptualized the family as hierarchically organized (Haley, 1976). In doing so, Haley recognized that power differentials do exist among family members. However, continuing the taboo on gender, he paid exclusive attention to power differences across generations and did not address gender as a basic demarcation of family organization. In his writings, Haley made references to gender differences and the plight of women, but he looked at gender only as a secondary, extrafamilial social variable and ignored the power differential between men and women *within* the family. As a result of this omission, Haley's writings present a contradictory view of women's predicament. (See Goldner, Chapter 3, for a fuller discussion.)

On one hand, Haley presented a view of the life cycle which is culturally relativistic and contextual. He stated that the goal of therapy is "to free the person from the limitations and restrictions of a social network in difficulty" and that "a symptom cannot be cured without producing a basic change in the person's social situation, which frees him to grow and develop" (p. 44). It is in this light that Haley showed a sensitivity to women's dilemmas, considering their problems as deriving from an oppressive social situation. For example, in arguing against a view of therapy that would foster "adjusting" a person to his situation, he says: "Many wives, for example, discontented with the narrow pattern of suburban life, have been stabilized for years by intensive analysis. Instead of encouraging them to take action that would lead to a richer and more complex life, the therapy prevents that change by imposing the idea that the problem is within their psyche rather than in their situation" (p. 43).

On the other hand, as Haley described of the stages of the life cycle more specifically, at several points he portrayed women's dilemmas with mixed sensibilities. Not only was his account tinted with a male bias, but he also did not address the dilemmas of gender *within* the family. For example, when describing the stage of childbirth and caring for young children he described how a special problem arises for women:

> Having babies is something they [women] looked forward to as a form of self-fulfillment. Yet caring for small babies can be a source of personal frustration. . . . The wife who finds herself confined largely to conversation with children can also feel denigrated with the label of "only" housewife and mother. A longing for more participation in the adult world for which she was prepared can lead her to

feeling discontented and envious of her husband's activities. The marriage can begin to erode as the wife demands more child-rearing help from her husband and more adult activities, while he feels that he is being burdened by wife and children and hampered in his work. Sometimes a mother will attempt to exaggerate the importance of child rearing by encouraging a child to have an emotional problem, which she can then devote her attention to. The task of the therapist is to help the problem of the child by helping the mother disengage herself from him and find a more fulfilling life of her own. (1973, p. 55)

Haley began this formulation sensitive to the woman's experience as one of pleasure and frustration. However, to our surprise, he left the man and the couple's interaction out of the "problem" situation. He ended by placing sole responsibility for change on the woman, while the husband was portrayed as incidental and as simply reacting to his wife's problem—a rather linear view. Haley seemed to have recognized the oppressed nature of the woman's position on a societal level without recognizing it also as an interactional and hierarchical problem within the family.

Haley's mixed views are also found in his discussion of the stage of middle marriage: "One of the inevitable human dilemmas is the fact that when a man reaches his middle years and has gained in status and position, he becomes more attractive to young females, while his wife, who is more dependent upon physical appearance, is feeling less attractive to males" (p. 58). By portraying this crisis as an "inevitable human dilemma" Haley did not recognize the sociocultural basis of the problem. He missed the point that the stress in these middle years can be the life cycle culmination of a patriarchal asymmetrical arrangement in which the wife, having taken an auxiliary role all along, is now faced with social powerlessness, while the husband may be collecting the benefits of the asymmetrical arrangement.

Haley (1976) postulated the necessity for clinicians to recognize that families are hierarchically organized. He introduced the idea of inequality of power among family members but then limited his attention to inequality of power across generations, stating that the most elementary hierarchy involves the generation line, i.e., between grandparents and parents, parents and children. He then posited that symptoms usually reflect a violation in the family's hierarchical arrangement, in which a member from one generation forms a coalition across the generational boundary. An organization is viewed as malfunctioning when a coalition across generations occurs repeatedly and the parents are not relating as peers in the executive capacity. By limiting his view of the husband and wife as equal peers in an executive team, Haley addressed hierarchical problems between the husband and wife not in a fundamental way but only as incidental to generation (Goldner,

Chapter 3). What he failed to recognize is that cross-generation coalitions are often secondary to the inherent power inequalities between the men and women within families, the pattern that prevails in our society.

The best response to the problems in Haley's theory is Goldner's proposition that we transform our theory of the family to include gender at "ground zero" as a basic category of family structure. In other words, gender and generation should be understood as the *two* fundamental organizing principles of family life.

Cloe Madanes, a collaborator with Haley and a leading strategic therapist in her own right, deserves comment. While not explicitly addressing gender issues, Madanes (1984) has shown sensitivity to the unbearable situation of low-income single mothers. She has criticized traditional mental health services for their tendency to make things worse by admonishing overburdened single parents for neglecting their children and, in effect, blaming the victim. We agree with her assessment that efforts directed at increasing the mother's executive functioning by giving her more responsibilities generally fail and only make the mother feel all the more incompetent while neglecting her very real needs.

The Milan Approach

The Milan approach, developed by Mara Selvini Palazzoli, Luigi Boscolo, Gianfranco Cecchin, and Guiliana Prata, was influenced initially by the work of the M.R.I. team. They adopted a strategic mode and elaborated their own methods of positive connotation and prescription of rituals. Rediscovering Bateson, the group edged away from the strategic approach, developing a new mode of interviewing that emphasized circular questioning, the formulation of systemic hypotheses, and the maintenance of neutrality (Selvini Palazzoli, Boscolo, Cecchin, & Prata, 1980).

As Boscolo and Cecchin moved toward a non-instrumental/"esthetic" view of therapy, they increasingly adopted a position of neutrality and gave up the notion of directing and maneuvering people towards change. They have repeatedly distinguished therapy from education and have expressed a strong bias against "instructive interaction." Cecchin has stated:

> As family therapists, we cannot invent a family. What we do best is bringing [sic] forth of patterns through interacting with a family. We cannot think of ourselves as teachers instructing families in better scripts for being families. Yet, because we do not know what specific script will be successful for a specific family, we are left to interact in a way that will perhaps perturb the system such as it finds its own new (or rewritten) script. (1987, p. 408)

The purpose of circular questioning, thus, is simply to generate new systems of meaning and to challenge the premises the family has had about their present situation, their relationships, and their problem. Like the M.R.I. group, they see change in behavior as closely intertwined with change in the basic premises individuals have about their problems. They utilize rituals as interventions to effect behavior directly. However, a distinctive aspect of their work has been their increasing attention to the meaning system—i.e., the premises, values, myths—as their primary focus (Boscolo, Cecchin, Hoffman, & Papp, 1987).

The Milan approach is a method of practice rather than a theory about the family. They refer to families only in abstract and cybernetic terms; in doing so they do not address gender explicitly as a dimension of family functioning. They acknowledge that families can have premises regarding gender, but they seem to accept those premises rather than question them. In a discussion of their ideas and practice (Boscolo et al., 1987), Peggy Penn asked how premises are learned. Boscolo replied, "From their present relationships, from their history, and also from the general culture. You can have very powerful religious premises which are handed down by the culture in which a family lives. Or you can have premises regarding gender: what a woman is supposed to do, what a man is supposed to do' (p. 149). Cecchin then shifted the discussion away from gender, but Lynn Hoffman returned to the topic to raise the question of neutrality in cases of physical and sexual abuse:

> Hoffman: " . . . It is hard to see a therapist take such a hands-off stance with behavior that is not only morally repugnant but defined as criminal. Could you state in more detail what you mean by 'neutrality'?"
>
> Boscolo: "Neutrality is the result, over time, of the interaction between the therapist and the family. If you ask the family 'What does the therapist think you should do?' or 'Whose side is the therapist on?' and if the family cannot answer these questions, the therapist has achieved neutrality. They might say he's 'tough' or 'warm,' but if they cannot state his position about what they should do, then he has achieved neutrality." (p. 149)

As a (non)reply to Hoffman's question, Boscolo's apparent indifference to issues of abuse is rather alarming. Reminiscent of psychoanalysis, the achievement of neutrality seemingly overrides all other concerns, implying that the therapist should strive not to let a family think that he or she has any position on what they should do about abuse. However, revealing no position can communicate indifference or even support of the abuse. The ethical implications of such neutrality demand more serious consideration.

Although there is brief mention that gender-based premises may be part of the problem, this point is not specifically elaborated. It is left to the particular sensibilities of the therapist to determine whether or how to focus circular questions on gender-based premises and myths. We see this as an important direction to pursue for clinicians working with the Milan approach. Rigid, normative assumptions about wives' and husbands' roles, rights, or obligations can and must be questioned if other possibilities are to be imagined. For example, one might ask family members their views on how it was decided that mother, who like father has a full-time job, is to be in charge of all household duties. Noticing and questioning differences between male and female experiences and perceptions can facilitate the appreciation of other positions and perspectives. What is called for is more explicit attention to gender in the circular questions that are asked, in systemic hypotheses that are posited, and in the stance of neutrality. Evan Imber-Black's utilization of rituals and attention to larger social systems (Chapters 17 and 22) are valuable models in addressing gender within a systemic approach to intervention.

Structural Model

The structural model of family therapy emphasizes the importance of family organization for the functioning of the family unit and the well-being of its members. Minuchin (1974) proposed a conceptual schema of family functioning to guide therapy. He viewed the family structure as an open social system in transformation, operating within a particular cultural context. Accordingly, the family progresses through successive stages of development, each transition requiring restructuring. The family must also adapt to changed environmental circumstances in ways that allow members to maintain continuity and to further their psychosocial growth. Individual dysfunction is viewed as symptomatic of a family's difficulty in restructuring in response to a developmental or environmental challenge. At this theoretical level, the structural model is quite congenial with feminist values in its attention to context and in the normalizing of problems as adaptational dilemmas.

Family structure is defined as the invisible set of functional demands that organizes family interaction. Transactional patterns defining relationships and regulating behavior are thought to be maintained by two constraints: (1) universal rules governing family organization, especially the power hierarchy; and (2) mutual expectations in particular families—explicit or implicit contracts that persist out of habit, mutual accommodation, and functional effectiveness. Each system maintains itself according to preferred patterns, resisting change beyond a certain accustomed range. This conceptualization is similar to Jackson's constructs of family rules and marital quid pro quo. To this, Minuchin added the rules that govern family organization, especially the power hierarchy. However, like Haley, Minuchin did not apply these principles to gender. Yet one can readily consider their specific application to gender-based transactional patterns that define relationships and regulate behavior. Gender patterns are likewise constrained by societal rules governing the power hierarchy, as well as by mutual expectations, or contracts, in particular families.

The structural model offers the conceptual framework and the vocabulary for addressing organizational patterns, boundaries, and subsystems. But it has yet to apply the framework to the dimension of gender—either to the gender-based arrangements in the construction of marital/parental subsystems (Scheinkman, 1988), or to the gendered coalitions across generations and among sisters or brothers. In the collaboration of Haley and Minuchin, it's curious that the generational distinction is a major focus of attention without notice taken of the distinction between genders. Husbands and wives have been conceptualized as a marital or parental unit, with the most salient distinguishing feature between them ignored, perhaps to avoid falling back into an individualistic view in noting sex differences. In fact, structural family therapy diagrams, until recently, made no gender distinctions: There was one symbol for parent and for child, as if individuals were interchangeable and unisex. That ignores the fact that there are fundamental distinctions between wives and husbands, or sons and daughters, just as there are distinctions between children and parents in families. Gender is a structural relationship variable, not simply an individual characteristic (Goldner, Chapter 3).

Minuchin has been keenly aware of the impact of socioeconomic and cultural environment on family and individual functioning. Nevertheless, in practice, when it comes to the position of women in the family, the frame of observation and intervention has tended to focus on the interior of the family. The diagram constructed for planning the phases of intervention is typically restricted to the nuclear family unit or household structure, with the occasional addition of a few key extended family members. Since the model posits the interconnection of family and its sociocultural context, structural family therapists could readily include the linkage of each family with other systems operating significantly in their lives, especially their work systems. Evan Imber-Black (1986, Chapter 17) makes such connections an integral part of her systemic assessment and treatment approach.

For instance, structural family therapy frequently focuses on restructuring dysfunctional triangles with an overinvolved mother and child and a peripheral father. Minuchin (Simon, 1984) has stated:

In this circumstance I tend to use the father to separate the mother from the children. It is an intervention I find useful because it expands the father's function, shrinks the woman's concentration on the maternal, and creates new possibilities for her to function as a more complex, adult woman, and it introduces perturbation in the parental field. (p. 67)

In response to feminist critics, Minuchin acknowledged that this is a skewed way of entering the system that supports male cultural stereotypes. Yet he asserts that this operation "doesn't represent either a coalition of males or a political statement" (p. 67). However, the failure to notice the culturally based hierarchical imbalance within the marital/parental subsystem leaves the husband's relatively greater power and authority and the woman's subordinate position unaddressed in the therapy. Nor does it consider how a woman, socialized primarily for a maternal role, can spontaneously develop meaningful alternatives in a society in which her options are limited. The social pressures and constraints on a husband's position are also not dealt with adequately. For instance, a sense of powerlessness and failure in meeting standards for job success and financial provision to his family may contribute to a father's unavailability and frustration, which may be expressed in neglect or abuse of his wife or children.

As the model was developed to meet the challenges confronting multiproblem inner-city families, structural family therapists have been more sensitive than others to the plight of low-income single parents. With single mothers, the structural therapist actively promotes the authority and competence of the mother, while also normalizing and addressing her unmet needs for adult support and companionship. The therapist is cautious not to "fill in" as the missing father. However, the therapist does need to avoid suggesting to the mother that she—or the family—is incomplete without a husband, or that what she needs is a new man to rescue her, as in the classic case, "Family with a Little Fire," in which the therapist, Braulio Montalvo, ends the therapy by using the metaphor of "setting mother on fire" to attract a new man (Minuchin, 1974, and videotape, Philadelphia Child Guidance Clinic).

The particular style of the therapist and misapplication of the model have at times been problematic. For instance, the forceful manner of a powerful male therapist may be confused as a requisite of the model and viewed as a necessary therapeutic stance for the approach to be effective. Therapists need to be sensitive to the therapy experience of a wife or mother who has been in a subordinate position to the men in her work and family life. Despite her apparent compliance, she is likely to feel intimidated or patronized by an overpowering male therapist. In practice, therapists can promote structural changes by using themselves in a variety of ways that are respectful to all family members.

Structural family therapists need to become more aware of the impact of metacommunication in the therapy context that reinforces gender stereotypes and dysfunction. Fishman (1988) describes his efforts to promote a sense of competence in a 19-year-old girl in a family session at her hospital discharge:

DR. FISHMAN   Congratulations — do you want her at home? Do you want your lovely grown-up daughter to be at home?

MOTHER   She can't leave. She can't do important things.

INGRID   She's right.

DR. FISHMAN   I don't understand. You know a foreign language but you can't boil an egg — you can't cook at all? (p. 214)

Whether intended or not, the therapist conveys the message that domestic activities are the competencies that matter for a young woman.

In another family case, Fishman identifies a skewed marital pattern — in which the husband was always up and the wife was always down and feeling devalued — as maintaining the wife's severe anorectic symptoms and child-like functioning. While he defines the therapeutic objective as correcting this structural imbalance in order to promote more competent functioning by the wife, his interventions actually reinforce her one-down position. At a meta-level, the structure of the therapy is isomorphic to the dysfunctional skewed pattern. The therapist repeatedly interrupts and challenges the wife, allies with the husband's position, and talks to the husband about her; at no time (in the transcripts presented, pp. 261–275) does he interrupt the husband, acknowledge or support the wife's position, or talk to her about her husband.

As the wife attempts to describe her experience of her marriage and her distress, the therapist (like the husband) at no point shows sensitivity to her feelings or validates her position. For example:

HERB   Anybody that has gone through all this crap would have left you long ago (he laughs).

DOROTHY   But maybe there's nothing there anymore. Maybe you're going to stay, but maybe there won't be anything left of *us* anymore. Of course you will stay. It's too convenient to leave. Who else is going to be as good a cook? And who else is going to iron all those shirts real nice, and make sure the collars are starched? You come home at 7:00, you go to sleep at 9:00. But I never tell you anything about it. You say, "Do you mind if I close my eyes?" No, I don't mind if you close your eyes. At

one time I told you I was going to drink too much because then at least
I would go to sleep. I couldn't even do that. Because that was doing
something. I can only deprive myself.

DR. FISHMAN   I see Herb as very committed to this relationship.

DOROTHY   He really is.

DR. FISHMAN   Don't speak for him—because it's not fair. He needs to speak
for himself. (To Herb:) I see you as very committed to Dorothy. But
somehow Dorothy doesn't hear it. So what can you do to help? Do you
feel committed to her?"

HERB   Yes, very much so. I think she knows that. We wouldn't be here
if . . .

DR. FISHMAN   Herb, she doesn't know that. Because she just said she
doesn't. Tell her (p. 263).

Although the therapist defines the structural imbalance as a fixed complementary pattern—Dorothy being sick and Herb responding, he notes only
her contribution, implying that she is to blame for the problem:

DR. FISHMAN   Now you are putting yourself down. You are inviting your
husband to disrespect you.

DOROTHY   Why do I do that?

DR. FISHMAN   I don't know why. After you are better you can find out why
(p. 267).

An even greater skew is promoted by the value-laden objectives the therapist injects for the distant husband's more active involvement. In his case
commentary, Fishman observes that the husband's focus on his wife's disorder has kept him from fulfilling "his parental function, which is to pluck the
adolescents away from her" (p. 256). Fishman puts the husband in charge of
the family, advising him to become the "captain of the ship." Fishman
comments:

I engage Herb directly, trying to increase his participation by using an image of
leadership that has been painfully missing. One would think that Dorothy wants
this, but instead she activates to interfere and to try to arrest the participation. I
resist the intrusion and pull him out (p. 258). . . . To end the session I intensify
the message to the father that he must take control and challenge the mother to
change (p. 260).

As clinicians address structural imbalances in families, they need to become more aware of the gender implications of the positions they take and
the objectives they set for therapy.

MULTIGENERATIONAL APPROACHES

Psychodynamic/Intergenerational Approaches

A number of family therapists, such as Framo (1970), Meissner (1978), and the Pauls (Paul & Paul, 1987), have attempted to bridge psychodynamic, object relations, and family systems views of family functioning and approaches to intervention. Gender has not been addressed explicitly in these fomulations; however, a number of implications are embedded in both theory and practice.

Although intergenerational family therapy models attend to relationship systems, some basic premises in the psychodynamic model have persisted in ways that negatively regard and influence women in families. Traditional assumptions about the locus and source of problems, as well as views of normality and health, are worth noting in order to place our critique of family systems therapies in sociohistorical context.

First, the psychoanalytic model places the locus of problems within the individual, personalizing human distress as individual psychopathology. Women, who have been the predominant consumers of psychotherapy, have disproportionately been pathologized and blamed for their problems by the assumption that their complaints are a symptom of their own inadequacy. Insufficient attention has been given to the context of their distress.

Second, the source of problems was located in the distant past, in the earliest relationship between patient and mother. The mother, as primary caretaker, was held ultimately responsible for all problems in life evidenced by offspring. Thus, pathology identified within clients, both male and female, was viewed as caused by "bad mothering" or maternal character deficiencies. There was a failure to view women and mothers contextually, to expand the frame of inquiry and intervention beyond the mother-child dyad, and to consider reciprocal influences within the broader network of relationships.

Third, the psychoanalytic tradition, wedded to the medical model, was concerned with the diagnosis of psychopathology. Treatment was aimed at reduction of conflicts and deficits. Women as consumers and as mothers tended, therefore, to be overpathologized. Strengths and resources tended to be unnoticed or misconstrued as pathogenic. Treatment was regarded as successful if a (woman) patient came to accept her own limitations and came to terms with (i.e., accepted) her mother's deficiencies.

Fourth, diagnosis and treatment goals were strongly, yet subtly, influenced by gender role expectations consonant with cultural ideals. Although the stance of the therapist was to maintain a value-free neutrality, implicit assumptions and beliefs about proper roles and attributes for males and females operated in unacknowledged and powerful ways. Normative female characteristics (how women *should* be), such as emotional expressiveness, passivity, and dependency, were labeled as pathology, as in the overused diagnosis of hysterical personality. Yet, standards of health fit male models, and a woman adopting those standards was criticized for being unfeminine. Moreover, a double standard operated when the same behaviors in men and women were labeled and connoted as health for men but pathology for women. A strong man in relation to his wife was praised for being dominant (as men should be), whereas a woman stronger than her husband was condemned for being "domineering" or "castrating."

Intergenerational family therapy approaches, like other systemic therapies, have assumed a gender-free position, examining relationship dynamics and transactional processes *as if* spouses were interchangeable genderless units and *as if* they have equal influence on one another and on the system as a whole. Gender differences in socialization require closer scrutiny as they relate to marital and family dynamics (Feldman, 1984). For instance, men and women have quite different experiences and problems around loss issues, with men constrained in the expression of grief and women expected to carry the socioemotional and physical caretaking tasks for the entire family. At the same time, because women are more central in families and are responsible for maintaining extended family connections and traditions, there is a tendency in practice to focus disproportionately on wives and mothers and on the maternal line in families of origin. Our experience as family therapy trainers suggests that fathers tend to offer less information about themselves and to claim that their own family experience was simply "normal" or unnoteworthy. Therapists are less likely to press husbands for more information, and husbands tend to be less forthcoming with their feelings and concerns, so that family assessment and intervention can become skewed toward problems in the wife's family of origin. Moreover, in family-of-origin inquiry, relationships with mothers loom large because of mothers' centrality in families and fathers' shadowy presence. As a consequence, women and their relationships in families remain the predominant focus of therapy. Therapists need more actively to encourage husbands to express their feelings and address their family of origin issues.

Intergenerational approaches have corrected the traditional narrow, linear causal focus on early mother-child dyadic relationships, instead attending to ongoing, circular transactional processes in the family as a system. Yet, when family history is gathered, there persists a tendency to focus more on past relationships and ignore current stresses affecting the family. Moreover, as the source of current relationship problems is located within each spouse's family of origin, problems become pathologized within a particular family in unresolved past relationship conflicts and losses. The historical and ongoing influences of other social systems, particularly economic and cultural imperatives, are outside the frame, hidden from view. Thus, the impact of poverty, work discrimination, or inadequate day care options for a single parent is likely to receive scant attention, and very real culturally determined problems may be interpreted as symptoms of unfinished work with her family of origin. Intergenerational therapists need to attend as fully to social context as to intrafamilial context.

The emphasis on psychopathology has persisted. Despite a systems orientation, intergenerational therapists risk retaining an "individualistic" perspective when they simply shift focus from looking within the individual person to looking within the individual family. In spite of a basic premise of circular causality, family therapists unwittingly revert to a reductionistic, lineal explanation of behaviors when they ignore extrafamilial influences and regard symptoms necessarily as evidence of underlying pathology in the marriage or of unresolved conflicts from the family of origin.

Intergenerational approaches are growth-oriented, with therapy aimed at comparatively vague goals that are often utopian ideals of healthy functioning (Walsh, 1982). Although therapists attempt to maintain a neutral stance in order to avoid imposing their own values, the unclarity of goals leaves a good deal of room for the influence of culturally based and idiosyncratic notions about healthy families. Therapists need to examine their own beliefs and values about gender and the models they have had in their lives.

Bowen Model

The Bowen family system model, in common with psychodynamic approaches, is growth-oriented, with a therapeutic mandate for exploration and change beyond symptom reduction. Both emphasize the gathering of information about family-of-origin relationship patterns and unresolved conflicts or losses, with the objective of changing one's perspectives and current relationships with key family members. These methods and goals are consistent with feminist values, especially when they assist both male and female clients to gain an evolutionary and contextual perspective on women's experience. Harriet Goldhor Lerner has observed,

> Through both Bowen work and feminism, a woman's sense of isolation about her so-called pathology is replaced by an empathic understanding of the continuity of women's struggles through the generations and the ways in which she is both similar to and different from those who came before her. (1986, p. 37)

Yet, in locating the source of individual or marital problems, Bowen (1978) placed particular emphasis on the importance of the maternal line in the transmission of pathogenic multigenerational influences. As Luepnitz (in press) has noted, a consistent theme in Bowen's work is the contention that mothers "overinvest" in their children because they could not separate from their own mothers, who in turn were unable to separate from their mothers. He has therefore focused disproportionately on the maternal line in family-of-origin inquiry and change. Although Bowen has asserted the importance of the father's role, there is scant mention of fathers in the clinical material in his major volumes (Bowen, 1978; Kerr & Bowen, 1988). This bias has been corrected by feminist therapists working with a Bowen orientation, notably Elizabeth Carter and Monica McGoldrick (1976; 1988) and Harriet Goldhor Lerner (1986). The development and application of the genogram (McGoldrick & Gerson, 1985), introduced by Bowen, have been of particular value in enlarging the lens from the narrow focus on mothers to the broader network of relationships.

While psychodynamic approaches promote the sharing of feelings among members in sessions, which is closer to what we regard as "feminine" in our culture, the Bowen approach is closer to the "masculine" model. The therapist assumes the role of coach, takes a highly cognitive stance, and encourages the control of one's emotional reactivity in contact with family members outside sessions. Unlike the psychodynamic and experiential approaches, there is little value placed on direct communication of pentup emotions, especially long-standing and previously unexpressed feelings of disappointment or anger. Rather, communicating with family members is a very planful, thoughtful enterprise in which feelings are well modulated. This can be a highly effective way to work. At the same time, we need to be careful not to communicate to clients and their families that strong feelings must be kept under control or that they are necessarily reactive and dangerous.

Bowen has presented mixed messages regarding the healthy balance of intellectual and emotional functioning and between differentiation and to-getherness (Luepnitz, 1988). While he has repeatedly emphasized the importance of balance, there is little elaboration on these attributes in his work, other than his Scale of Differentiation of Self (1978). Under healthy functioning are the following attributes: "autonomous," "being-for-self," "intellectual," and "goal-directed." The poorly differentiated person is described as: valuing "relatedness," "seeking love and approval," and "being-for-others." From this scale, it appears that a "feminine" relationship orientation is devalued and pathologized, while male norms for autonomy and achievement are the criteria for health, with little balance evident on the scale.

However, it is not a relationship orientation, but rather a fused, reactive emotional position, that is regarded as dysfunctional by Bowen. Those low on the scale of differentiation of self are dominated by their emotions, which override planful, intellectual modes of thought. Their overdependence on others in relationships impedes their ability to pursue independent interests and achievements.

Because the Bowen method focuses on differentiation of self, some critics have misunderstood Bowen to be concerned only with achieving separateness and autonomous functioning. To the contrary, differentiation is promoted in order to achieve the goal of a deeper and richer relationship, which is not possible when members are either too closely fused or reactively distanced, or cut off. The central objective in Bowen therapy is the differentiation of self *in relation to others*. It involves being separate and connected.

Nevertheless, in the Bowen method therapists don't directly promote togetherness. Bowen has assumed that, if clinicians encourage differentiation from families of origin, clients will be able to engage more fully in their current relationships. In other words, togetherness will take care of itself. However, we cannot take that for granted when efforts have been directed toward separateness. Clients, men in particular, because of their socialization experience, are likely to need assistance in developing more intimate relationships.

There are many commonalities between the Bowen coaching method and women's assertiveness training, especially in efforts toward differentiation of self, as in assuming more responsibility for changing oneself in relationships. Taking an "I" position — without attacking, defending, or withdrawing — is close to the notion of asserting one's own position in transactions with others. Gender differences in the typical reactive stance of men and women should be noticed by clinicians: Attacking and defending are more likely to be male responses in an uncomfortable interaction, while women tend to back down and defer to the positions of others. Moreover, men are reinforced positively for expressing their own ideas and opinions strongly; women doing the same tend to be viewed as "bitchy" and "too aggressive."

While Bowen can be criticized for tilting the balance of intellect and emotions a bit too much in favor of the cognitive control of emotions, it should be kept in mind that Bowen has valued the importance of maintaining connectedness and repairing cutoff relationships in families. Working with the Bowen model, clinicians need to strive for a balance that neither pathologizes emotions and closeness nor overvalues an autonomous self at the expense of connectedness, as we have done in our culture. Clinicians need to be careful not to confuse the concept of differentiation with pseudo-autonomy, which is seen when extreme self-reliance and emotional or geographic distance that must be maintained from one's family in order to feel separate. Rather, a healthy differentiation involves the ongoing maintenance of self *in relation to* one's family.

In application of the Bowen model, we have to keep in mind that when we are coaching women to change themselves in relation to others, they are most likely starting from a one-down position vis-à-vis their husbands. It is much harder to change oneself in relation to another when that other holds considerable power over your life. That must be taken into account in setting goals and planning effective intervention strategies. Too often, a woman who attempts to change herself in relation to her partner finds the task impossible from a one-down position, in part because the nature and conditions of the hierarchy have not been fully considered. She may then direct all her energies toward her children or career development, either shutting down in the marriage or experiencing increasing disparity between herself outside the home and inside the marriage. She is then likely to see leaving the relationship as the only viable alternative. A woman may have to take the first steps in changing a marital relationship, but eventually the husband must make reciprocal changes for the marriage to work. Unless he takes an active part in changing himself in relation to her as well, we replicate society's charge to women — that they must bear sole responsibility for change in the family.

Furthermore, the construct "self-in-relation-to-other" must be considered in the broader context. Both husband and wife will likely have to change their respective positions in relation to their work systems if a rebalance in their marital relationship is a goal of therapy. Here, too, it is a formidable task for men as well as women to alter their positions in work systems that hold such power over their lives in terms of economic security, job advancement, time allocation, and expectations for success. Clinicians can be helpful by applying Bowen techniques for change in relation to work systems. For instance, the genogram and coaching method can be used to assess clients' own work systems, noting triangles involving competing demands of work and family, and to alter their position in that system in relation to family life. A clinician might coach an overburdened single mother with the aim of strengthening her job position or joining effectively with coworkers to achieve day care benefits in a firm in which she feels exploited and powerless. One might also coach a father who is constrained by job performance expectations from active participation in parenting to restructure an inflexible work schedule.

In sum, we see many advantages in the Bowen method of therapy in addressing gender issues. We urge that information gathering, genogram construction and coaching techniques be directed to work systems and other contextual influences, in addition to the usual focus on multigenerational patterns. Clinicians need to help men and women in families to achieve a fuller valuing and balance of intellectual with emotional functioning and of differentiation with relatedness.

DISCUSSION AND RECOMMENDATIONS

By and large, the major models of family therapy have not by design promulgated sexist beliefs or practices. However, the architects of our models of family functioning and family intervention have been blind to gender as a fundamental organizing principle in human systems and have not taken into account the differential in power and status between men and women in the larger social systems in which families are embedded (Hare-Mustin, 1978; Goldner, 1985; Taggart, 1985). As a consequence, with the exception of recent feminist critiques, gender has remained a hidden dimension in models of the family and change. The limited focus on current, intrafamilial process to the neglect of historical and socio-political contexts contributed to the gender blindness. The emphasis on circular causality and the maintenance of neutrality fostered a reluctance to confront gender issues in clinical practice.

The cybernetic perspective brought to our attention the circularity of influences in ongoing interactions. However, as family therapists began to reify this model and to regard as important only the transactional sequences and loops between individuals within families, relationships were depersonalized and de-contextualized. In employing the cybernetic metaphor, we began to think of the family as if it were actually a machine (James & McIntyre, 1983), and like machines, genderless. What we failed to see were the gendered patterns both within and beyond that frame, regularities in the interactions between males and females in families and throughout our culture. Since it was very much a "man's world" at the time of the development of systems models, women were "other," defined (by men) by their positions as wife and mother, and their experience was rendered invisible. As Bateson (1979) noted, the ways in which we punctuate human experience determine what we see and how we define that experience. If we are to apply the cybernetic model to families, we need to incorporate gender as a basic element in human systems.

Also, in the early development of the field of family therapy, we were pushing away from the influence of the psychoanalytic tradition. Any attention to "content" issues or history was considered linear, deterministic, and irrelevant to change. However, we must not lose sight of the very process *and* content issues that distress family members. If we are not attending to gender as a distinguishing feature in families, we may fail to notice a woman's subordinate position or to hear her pain. To understand her experience, we must expand our attention to the historical and socio-political contexts of gendered relationships.

Family therapy pioneers mainly developed theories about change and steered away from formulations about the family that could unwittingly be taken as prescriptive. This cautious attitude derived from the constructivist view that all notions about "normality" are merely subjective and that therapists should not meddle with a family's value orientation. Yet, shared beliefs and assumptions about gender are core variables in all families and their contribution to problem development, maintenance, and change must be more carefully examined.

In order to address gender issues, models of change need to be accompanied by models of family functioning, relative to varying economic and cultural contexts and fitting particular developmental tasks and environmental demands (Walsh, in press). We must also be more cognizant that patterns that are functional at one system level may not be functional at another. Traditional roles, rules, and interactional patterns that may have enabled men to fit with societal standards for success have nevertheless been dysfunctional for the family. Families have been organized to support that success, to the detriment of overburdened and undervalued contributions of wives and mothers and to the limited participation of husbands in family life. Now that most women are active members of the workforce and men are seeking greater involvement in parenting, traditional assumptions are being called into question by families we treat, either explicitly or through symptoms of distress. We must neither assume nor tacitly reinforce gender status quo.

Family therapy training should assume greater responsibility for helping therapists to gain more explicit awareness of the values and beliefs about gender that are embedded in practice models and in our own cultural and family experiences. The provision of supervised experience interviewing non-clinical families can also be important in broadening the perspective of clinicians (Walsh, 1987). Our intervention approaches must be more responsive to the diversity of family forms and the unprecedented dilemmas confronting women and men in contemporary families.

The most curious feature in the development of the field was the negation of power as a valid or useful construct. There persists an attitude that it is not "systemic" or consistent with circular causality to talk about power in families. Haley and Minuchin did attend to the power differential in the hierarchy between generations as a universal feature in family systems and focused intervention on structural rebalancing as a chief objective of family therapy. However, the hierarchical imbalance between husband and wife has yet to be addressed in practice models. Given the differential of power and status between men and women in the society that frames all family interaction, it is a fallacy to assume that a power balance is maintained in family systems, with each member having equal influence. The insistence on therapeutic neutrality has left some difficult questions unaddressed. Fundamentally, is it possible to intervene and influence a system and yet remain neutral? Is it ethical even to attempt neutrality when systemic patterns maintain abuse?

We have to construct power on our interactional map if we are to chart the family's territory. We must pay attention to the overt and covert rules that regulate the expression and balance of power between males and females in society and in families (Walsh, Chapter 14). We need to examine what blocks us, as family therapists, from addressing this issue. Discussions about power have tended to focus on hierarchical relations between males of one generation and males of the next, perhaps because that is where the culturally defined action has been. If power is equated with success and success is defined in male terms, then the extrafamilial male arena would be the significant arena of focus and the power differential between men and women would not be, following Bateson's reasoning, "a difference that makes a difference" to men.

Our society is changing and new generations of family therapists are bringing a greater awareness of gender to family therapy theory and practice. It was not possible here to review all models and developments. Noteworthy contributions to the analysis of gender issues in Behavioral approaches to marriage and family therapy have been made by Jacobson, (1981; 1983); Gurman and Klein (1984), and Margolin, Talovic, Fernandez, & Onorato (1983). Avis (1985) and Warburton and colleagues (Chapter 9) have examined gender in the Functional Family Therapy model and the differential experiences and impact of male and female therapists with male and female family members. The formidable challenge of integrating gender awareness in the conceptual frameworks, training, and practice of family therapy still lies ahead.

REFERENCES

Ault-Riche, M. (1986). A feminist critique of five schools of family therapy. In M. Ault-Riche, (Ed.). *Women and family therapy*. Rockville, MD: Aspen Publications.

Avis, J. (1985). The politics of functional family therapy: A feminist critique. *Journal of Marital and Family Therapy, 11*, 127–138.

Bateson, G. (1979). *Mind and nature: A necessary unity*. New York: E. P. Dutton.

Bateson, G., Jackson, D. D., Haley, J., & Weakland, J. H. (1956). Toward a theory of schizophrenia. *Behavioral Science, 1*, 251–264.

Belenky, M. F., Clinchy, B. M., Goldberger, N. R., & Tarule, J. M. (1986). *Women's ways of knowing: The development of self, voice, and mind*. New York: Basic Books.

Boscolo, L., Cecchin, G., Hoffman, L., & Penn, P. (1987). *Milan systemic family therapy*. New York: Basic Books.

Bowen, M. (1978). *Family therapy in clinical practice*. New York: Jason Aronson.

Carter, B., & McGoldrick, M. (Eds.). (1980). *The family life cycle. A framework for family therapy*. New York: Gardner Press.

Carter, B., & McGoldrick, M. (Eds.). (1988). *The changing family life cycle*. New York: Gardner Press.

Carter, E., & McGoldrick Orfanidis, M. (1976). The therapist's own family. In P. Guerin (Eds.), *Family therapy: Theory and practice*. New York: Gardner Press.

Caust, B. L., Libow, J. A., & Raskin, P. A. (1981). Challenges and promises of training women as family systems therapists. *Family Process, 20*, 439–447.

Cecchin, G. (1987). Hypothetizing, circularity, and neutrality revisited: An invitation to curiosity. *Family Process, 27*, 405–413.

Feldman, L. B. (1982). Sex roles and family dynamics. In F. Walsh (Ed.), *Normal family processes*. New York: Guilford Press.

Fisch, R., Weakland, J. H., & Segal, L. (1982). *The tactics of change: Doing therapy briefly*. San Francisco: Jossey-Bass.

Fishman, C. (1988). *Treating troubled adolescents: A family therapy approach*. New York: Basic Books.

Framo, J. (1970). Symptoms from a family transactional viewpoint. In N. Ackerman (Ed.). *Family therapy in transition*. Boston: Little Brown.

Goldner, V. (1985). Feminism and family therapy. *Family Process, 24*, 31–47.

Gurman, A., & Klein, M. (1984). Marriage and the family: An unconscious male bias in behavioral treatment? In E. Bleckman, (Ed.). *Behavioral modification with women*. New York: Guilford Press.

Haley, J. (1973). *Uncommon therapy: The psychiatric techniques of Milton H. Erickson*. New York: W. W. Norton.

Haley, J. (1976). *Problem-solving therapy*. New York: Harper & Row.

Hare-Mustin, R. T. (1978). A feminist approach to family therapy. *Family Process, 17*, 181–194.

Imber-Black, E. (1986). Women, families, and larger systems. In M. Ault-Riche, (Ed.), *Women and family therapy*. Rockville, MD: Aspen.

Jackson, D. D. (1977a). The study of the family. In P. Watzlawick & J. Weakland (Eds.), *The interactional view*. New York: W. W. Norton.

Jackson, D. D. (1977b). Family rules: Marital quid pro quo. In P. Watzlawick & J. Weakland (Eds.), *The interactional view*. New York: W. W. Norton.

Jacobson, N. (1983). Beyond empiricism: The politics of marital therapy. *American Journal of Family Therapy, 11*, 11–24.

Jacobson, N. (1981). Behavioral marital therapy. In A. Gurman & D. Kniskern (Eds.), *Handbook of family therapy*. New York: Brunner/Mazel.

James, K., & McIntyre, D. (1983). The reproduction of families: The social role of family therapy. *Journal of Marital & Family Therapy, 9*, 119–129.

Kerr, M., & Bowen, M. (1988). *Family evaluation: An approach based on Bowen theory*. New York: W. W. Norton.

Lerner, H. G. (1986). Diana and Lilie: Can a feminist still like Murray Bowen? *Family Therapy Networker, 9*(6), 36–39.

Lerner, H. E. (1988). Is family systems theory really systemic? A feminist communication. *Journal of Psychotherapy and the Family, 3*, 47–63.

Lerner, H. E. (1985). *The dance of anger*. New York: Harper & Row.

Luepnitz, D. (1988). *The family interpreted: Feminist theory in clinical practice*. New York: Basic Books.

McGoldrick, M., & Gerson, R. (1985). *Genograms in family assessment*. New York: W. W. Norton.

Madanes, C. (1984). *Behind the one way mirror: Advances in the practice of strategic therapy*. San Francisco: Jossey-Bass.

Margolin, G., Talovic, E., Fernandez, V., & Onorato, R. (1983). Sex role considerations and behavioral marital therapy: Equal does not mean identical. *Journal of Marital & Family Therapy, 9*, 131–45.

Meissner, W. W. (1978). The conceptualization of marital and family dynamics from a psychoanalytic perspective. In T. Paolino & B. McCrady, (Eds.), *Marriage and marital therapy*. New York: Brunner/Mazel.

Minuchin, S. (videotape). "Family with a little fire." Philadelphia Child Guidance Clinic. 34th Street and Civic Center Blvd., Philadelphia, PA.

Montalvo, B. (1974). *Families and family therapy*. Cambridge, MA: Harvard University Press.
Paul, N., & Paul, B. (1987). *A marital puzzle: Transgenerational analysis in marriage*. (Rev. ed.) New York: Gardner Press.
Satir, V. (1972). *Peoplemaking*. Palo Alto: Science & Behavior Books.
Scheinkman, M. (1988). An interactional view of graduate student marriage. *Family Process, 27*, 351-368.
Selvini Palazzoli, M., Boscolo, L., Cecchin, G., & Prata, G. (1980). Hypothetizing-circularity-neutrality: Three guidelines for the conductor of the session. *Family Process, 19*, 3-12.
Selvini Palazzoli, M. (1983). Emergence of a comprehensive systems approach. *Journal of Family Therapy, 5*, 165-177.
Simon, R. (1984). Stranger in a strange land: An interview with Salvador Minuchin. *The Family Therapy Networker, 8*, 20-68.
Sluzki, C., & Ransom, D. (Eds.). (1976). *Double-bind: The foundation of the communicational approach to the family*. New York: Grune & Stratton.
Taggart, M. (1985). The feminist critique in epistemological perspective: Questions of context in family therapy. *Journal of Marital and Family Therapy, 11*, 113-126.
Walsh, F. (1982). Conceptualizations of normal family functioning. In F. Walsh, (Ed.). *Normal family processes*. New York: Guilford Press.
Walsh, F. (1987). The clinical utility of normal family research. *Psychotherapy, 24*, 496-502.
Walsh, F. (In press). *Treating severely dysfunctional families*. New York: Guilford Press.
Walters, M., Carter, E., Papp, P., & Silverstein, O. (1988). *Redefining the family*. New York: Guilford Press.
Watzlawick, P., Beavin Bavelas, J. H., & Jackson, D. D. (1967). *Pragmatics of human communication*. New York: W. W. Norton.
Watzlawick, P., Weakland, J., & Fisch, R. (1974). *Change: Principles of problem formation and problem resolution*. New York: W. W. Norton.

3
Generation and Gender: Normative and Covert Hierarchies

VIRGINIA GOLDNER

THE PRIMARY PURPOSE of this chapter is to rescue the topic of gender from the category of the "special case" or "special issue," and to locate it where it belongs, at the center of family theory. By considering gender a central theoretical category and opposing its marginalization, I am following an established tenet of feminist scholarship. This is to insist on a constructivist view of knowledge that takes nothing for granted and asks the same question of every idea: Does it make room for both male and female experience or does it make man the measure of woman?

Establishing the truth value of ideas by evaluating them against this standard is a habit of mind with a social history. Indeed, it is arguably the single most significant accomplishment of the original, humbly conceived, consciousness-raising groups of the 1960s. As women met together to compare notes on their lives, they began to realize that they had been deprived of their subjectivity by a culture that expected them to be sexual objects for men and facilitating environments for everybody. The more they talked and laid claim to themselves, the more of themselves they found had been left out of the world. And this led to a striking insight: Gender dichotomies were not only restrictive, but also constitutive. In other words, not only did the gendering of social spheres constrain personal freedom, but gender categories also determined what it was possible to know.

Revised from *Family Process*, 1988, *27*, pp. 17–31.

Coming to this discovery was historic. It meant that the feminist project that had brought women together had to be reconceived. It was no longer a matter of demanding equal access to a man's world, but of asking what the world would be like if women had equal power in creating it. This meant that gender could no longer be conceptualized as simply a barrier to be transcended, because it was itself a metaphysical category, a central organizing principle of knowledge and culture.

This paradigm shift in our view of the problem has led academic feminists to theorize about the gendering not only of social spheres but also of the act of knowing itself. There is now a burgeoning literature elaborating the premise that thinking is gendered and that different modes of thought produce different kinds of knowledge (Belenky, Clinchy, Goldberger, & Tarule, 1986; Gilligan 1982; Keller, 1985; Ruddick, 1982). Having staked out this claim for cognitive variation, feminist investigators have been led, inevitably, to challenge the hegemony of traditional (masculine) forms of intellectual inquiry and even to question the fundamental assumptions underlying traditional canons of knowledge.

This conceptual revolution has made its mark in philosophy, literature, anthropology, history, and psychoanalysis. In family therapy, feminist criticism is at an earlier stage. We have done extensive and important work in documenting the androcentric biases of clinical theory and practice, but we have only just begun to tackle the intimidating project of the conceptual transformation of our discipline as a whole (see Taggert, Chapter 6). It is time.

Family therapy, as a field, has finally taken notice of feminism and has taken it seriously. The noisy feminist presence of the past few years has been virtually impossible to ignore, and, in any case, family therapists by political temperament do not like to be on the "wrong side" of a socially progressive issue. Indeed, reactivity to feminism has now become so intense that political responses, which typically take a decade to unfold, seem to have been condensed into a scant few years.

Looking back at this very recent history, it appears that, after a long period of polite silence, family therapists suddenly developed an intense curiosity about what feminists were saying. This was followed by hurried attempts to incorporate feminist concerns into the field, which was ambivalently received by feminists who liked the attention to their agenda but feared that the price of admission would be cooptation.

Not surprisingly, as the dialogue developed, reactivity intensified, generating increasing polarization and even political backlash. More recently, there seems to be evidence that feminist ideas are being assimilated into the mainstream, but the professional climate remains "edgy" and intermittently adversarial. A systems consultant describing the process would probably observe that a short, intense period of uncertainty, ambiguity, and unstable coalitions quickly congealed into a predictable, symmetrical spiral between discrete factions.

If we are to move beyond this rebuttal, retort, and rejoinder mode of transaction, feminists will need, once again, to elevate the level of discourse about gender. This will involve demonstrating that our primary goal is not the moral reform of errant colleagues but the transformation of our theory of families — and family therapy will only gain in the process. Such a transformation requires situating gender at "ground zero."

<h2 style="text-align:center">GENDER AND GENERATION</h2>

Put in formal terms, this means conceptualizing gender as an irreducible category of clinical observation and theorizing, as fundamental to the family therapy paradigm as the concept of "generation." Indeed, the position to be advanced here is that gender and generation are best understood as the two fundamental, organizing principles of family life.

There is nothing revolutionary or even particularly feminist about such a view. Indeed, all classic theories of family and kinship in anthropology and sociology begin with two universals: age and sex (Collier, Rosaldo, & Yanagisako, 1982; Dimen-Schein, 1977; Lévi-Strauss, 1969). In anthropological terms, age and sex, as the only self-evident biological givens, are taken to constitute the two universal principles of kinship organization. Because the distinctive feature of human society is the transformation of nature into culture, these immutable givens — age and sex — become transformed into the complex cultural phenomena of "generation" and "gender."

In the classic sociological analysis of the modern family, the functionalist Parsons (1954) also regards age and sex as the underlying axes of family relations. His way of casting the subject matter has been much criticized by feminists, but that is a separate matter.* For our purposes, the important point is that in academic conceptualizations of kinship and culture age and sex are taken to be co-equal principles of organization. Indeed, it is around the structuring and interpretation of these two social categories that primitive societies and modern families organize themselves. Think, for example, of Bateson's discussion of the Iatmul in *Naven*. Even though his formal subject was social instability (how conflicts and divisions in a group are handled), his argument hinged on an analysis of the balance of power between the men and women of the tribe at different stages of the life cycle.

In contrast to this suddenly self-evident point of departure, family thera-

*See Boss & Thorne, Chapter 5.

py theory seems oddly lopsided. Insofar as we have a theory of the family at all, as distinct from a theory of communication or of structural "good form," it is a theory that relies on a single cultural concept: the idea of the family life cycle and the presumption of the necessity for a hierarchy of the generations. What is fascinating about this view is what it leaves out.

I thought it would be interesting to trace back the history of ideas in family therapy in order to find out how gender, as a co-equal concept, was ignored or erased as a universal principle of family organization, leaving only generation. Rereading Haley's classic chapters on the family life cycle in *Uncommon Therapy* and on hierarchy in *Problem-Solving Therapy* seemed a good place to start because his presentation of these two ideas has been so central to the development of family therapy theory. Moreover, given that both these books are products of their era as well as of their author, I thought they might serve as time capsules back to the recent past, revealing what could be seen and named, and what could not. In this regard, I was intrigued to note how gender appeared and then was made to disappear in Haley's characterization of family life.

In *Uncommon Therapy*, for example, when introducing the historic formulation that "families undergo a developmental process over time, and human distress and psychiatric symptoms appear when this process is disrupted," Haley particularizes his meaning of family development by adding the phrase, "the dilemmas that arise when men and women mate and rear children" (p. 41). Here we have what could have been the beginning of a dual description of family dilemmas, read out in terms of both gender and generation. However, Haley's attention to gender unravels as the discussion proceeds. "Men and women" soon become "human beings" who are then made synonymous with "men," as in: "Men have in common with other creatures the developmental process of courtship, mating, nest building . . . " (p. 44).

Examples of the variety of "mating practices" of the "human species" follow:

> A man can copulate with any woman who passes, the more anonymous the better. Men can also have clandestine affairs. . . . Human beings have also tried out the arrangement of multiple husbands or wives characteristic of some species. Most commonly, men select a single mate for life and remain with her constantly; at least this is the myth of monogamy in middle-class America. . . . (p. 45)

This paragraph is telling in a number of ways. Not only are women made to disappear by use of a universalizing male pronoun, but, when they do appear, they are not represented as sexual subjects who can claim men for anonymous sex, have clandestine affairs, or choose lifelong monogamy.

They surface only as *objects* of male desire, not as subjects in their own right.

In other words, what Haley seems to mean by asserting that the "human species, with its complex capabilities, can follow any of the mating habits of other animals" (p. 44), is that human males have the freedom to "exchange women" for purposes of sex in as many ways as other male animals. Stated this way, Haley has unwittingly observed what anthropologists, beginning with Lévi-Strauss (1969), have had to explain: that men have "certain rights [to] female[s] . . . and that women do not have the same rights [to] males" (Rubin, 1978, p. 177).

By losing hold of gender as an irreducible, orthogonal axis of family organization, Haley buries women in his prose and then intermittently brings them back to life, as in this feminist swipe at psychoanalysis:

> Many wives . . . discontented with the narrow pattern of suburban life, have been stabilized for years by intensive analysis. Instead of encouraging them to take action that would lead to a richer and more complex life, the therapy prevents that change by imposing the idea that the problem is within their psyche rather than in their situation. (1973, p. 43)

A similar incongruity between Haley's protofeminism and his patriarchal presumptions is to be found in his discussion of hierarchy in *Problem-Solving Therapy*, published three years later in 1976. When making the point that every "therapist must think through his [sic] ethical position" (p. 102),* Haley writes:

> Although one must accept the *existence* of hierarchy, that does not mean one needs to . . . accept the status quo either in terms of the economic structure of society or [in terms of] a particular [family] hierarchy. Everywhere there are hierarchical arrangements that are unjust. One economic class suppresses another. Women are kept in a subordinate position in both family and work groups merely because they are female. People are placed in subordinate positions because of race or religion. Children are oppressed by their parents, in the sense of being restricted and exploited in extreme ways. (pp. 101–102)

Here, gender inequality, located inside as well as outside the family, appears along with race, class, religious and even age oppression as "wrongs that need righting" (p. 102). In other words, gender, like race and class, is

---

*Haley does make a formal, footnoted disclaimer in *Problem-Solving Therapy* (p. 2) about his use of "he" when referring to therapists who can be of either sex. Apparently, he became aware of the "pronoun problem" after the publication of *Uncommon Therapy*, in which he uncritically used "men" as a synonym for "human beings."

construed by Haley as a secondary, mediating variable that structures social existence, often in oppressive ways.

But having already distinguished gender from these other mediations by observing that gender (like age) orders *intra*familial as well as extrafamilial hierarchies, Haley drops the subject. Two paragraphs later, gender has already been obliterated as a distinctive social category by use of the generic "people," and generation now emerges as the "most elementary" family hierarchy.

> When we look at the family in terms of hierarchy, the organization includes people of different generations, of different incomes, and of different degrees of intelligence and skills. . . . The most elementary hierarchy involves the generation line [because] at the most simple level it is parents who nurture and discipline children. . . . (1976, pp. 102–103)

Privileging generational relations by presuming there is anything simple and universal about parents caring for children is anthropologically naive and factually inaccurate. Malinowski made this claim in 1913, and revisionist critics ever since have been documenting his errors. Indeed, if there is anything universal about the social organization of childcare it is, as the anthropologist Rosaldo (1980) concludes, that "women almost everywhere have daily responsibilities to feed and care for children . . . while men's . . . obligations tend to be less regular and more bound up with extrafamilial sorts of ties" (p. 394). Similar conclusions were reached by another anthropologist, Fox, who writes that "whether or not a mate becomes attached to the mother on some more or less permanent basis is a variable matter" (1967, p. 39).

In other words, one can never "simply" (to borrow Haley's word) talk about parenthood. There are only mothers and fathers producing progeny, after which fathering seems to be a highly variable social occupation. Thus, it appears that the division of labor by sex, with women bearing primary responsibility for childcare, may be even more "basic" to the structure of kinship than the hierarchical organization of family members by age.

Determining which is more primary, "gender" or "generation," is not as important as establishing that *both* are essential to any description of family relations. Even Freud took this premise as a given, situating the conditions of civilization on the resolution of a universal family drama organized around the erotization of generational relationships—the Oedipus complex. Thus, for Freud, Parsons, and Lévi-Strauss, the politics of age and sex hierarchies constituted the central force field of family life and culture. In the context of this broadly based, intellectual tradition, the mysterious omission of the category of gender from the first premises of family therapy becomes stranger and stranger.

THE DENIAL OF GENDER

Returning to Haley's disarmingly simple paragraphs about hierarchy and injustice, written in 1976, one is tempted to speculate about the meaning of his ability to see and simultaneously *not* to see women as occupying a central and problematic position in family hierarchies. Over ten years later, it is easier to recognize how difficult it is to navigate the ethics of hierarchy for the conduct of clinical work. Musing on the psychohistory of this problem, one might conjecture that by denying the centrality of gender for family relations, Haley (speaking for the field) could avoid confronting the issue of gender inequality in family life.

This strategy was almost certainly not intentional, yet it was accomplished painlessly and elegantly by what, with hindsight, could be called a theoretical sleight of hand. By privileging the category of generation, and trivializing the category of gender, Haley could dispense with the vexing question of sexual inequality in marriage thus: Spouses, by virtue of being at the same generational level, are, by definition, equals. In other words, merely by being age peers, and therefore having generational parity, husbands and wives were presumed to occupy the same level of the domestic power hierarchy.

Haley's cautiously abstract definition of "generation" in *Problem-Solving Therapy* illustrates the elision through which gender becomes incidental to generation: "By *generation* is meant a different order in the power hierarchy, such as parent and child or manager and employee" (p. 109).

THE RATIONALIZATION OF GENDER INEQUALITY

There is an argument to be made that Haley's graceful detour around the reality of gender inequality protected family therapists from ethical dilemmas that we, as a field, were unprepared to face. By speaking only in terms of the universality of generational hierarchies, Haley neutralized the issue of power. There is, of course, something inherently plausible about the notion that older people should be in charge of younger ones. Because it does not grossly violate our democratic ideals to think in terms of age hierarchies, the authoritarian parent who goes too far can easily be seen as merely "doing too much of a good thing." (This is often the way the diplomatic family therapist would frame the issue.)

On the other hand, it is not so easy to rationalize the persistence of gender hierarchies, given our egalitarian values. In fact, the history of the obfuscation of the gender issue in our field seems to suggest that we simply cannot tolerate the idea that arrangements of inequality between men and women may be structurally essential to family relations. In fact, the truth of family life in our time might be described as consisting of two social hierarchies — one acceptable, indeed normative, "generation," and one unacceptable, and therefore covert, "gender."

Unfortunately, much as we might like to think otherwise, the social fact of gender inequality, of man's dominion over woman, has probably always and everywhere been the norm. Although there have been many attempts to read into the anthropological and historical record a matriarchal or sexually egalitarian past, most contemporary scholars lean toward the view that human cultural and social forms have probably always been male dominated. Moreover, there appears to be a universal connection between women's primary responsibility for the care and feeding of children, spouses, and other kin, and their secondary status in both domestic and public domains (Rosaldo, 1980).

What distinguishes our time and place from others is that women's subordination to men has become morally unacceptable. Nonetheless, it persists. This contradiction between our democratic values and our social practice is not easy to rationalize. Appeals to the historical precedent of women's inherent inferiority or to the fictional claim of separate but equal spheres of influence have long since lost their legitimacy. In their place, contemporary strategies for tolerating patriarchy seem to depend on viewing the situation in such a way as to minimize or at least contain the scope of the injustice.

These devices run the gamut from Haley's rhetorical magic, in which the whole problem is made to disappear in one turn of phrase, to Parsons' rationalizations for a sexual double standard written 20 years earlier. Parsons has been an easy target for feminists because his defense of patriarchy is so transparent. Reconstructing his awkward and ambivalent attempts to justify what is unjustifiable will provide an interesting counterpoint to the strategy of simple denial that has characterized the family therapy field.

What Haley could assert as a conceptual given — that spouses, by virtue of being at the same generational level, were equals — Parsons had to "prove." His argument, rooted in a theory of the historical evolution of the modern family, posited that with the development of industrialization, husbands lost much of the legal and material basis of their authority over their wives, so that marriages could now become arrangements of equals, that is, the "companionate marriage." Thus, for Parsons, equality between husbands and wives was not axiomatic, but rather a sociopolitical accomplishment, an achievement of bourgeois democracy at a certain point in its history.

Yet there was too much evidence against this celebratory view of American history, even for such a celebrant as Parsons. Reading his work carefully, as the sociologist Beechey (1978) has done, reveals that he was neither comfortable nor intellectually satisfied with his characterization of gender equality in marriage.

For example, in one essay, "An Analytical Approach to the Theory of Social Stratification," originally published in 1940, Parsons states that in American society members of kinship groups are "treated as 'equals' regardless of the fact that by definition they must differ in sex and age . . . [T]he only differentiation tolerated is that involved in the socially approved differences of the sex and age status" (1954, p. 77). The justification of his claim that marriage is a relationship of "equals" and does not involve structural domination and subordination seems to be based on the inference that, because the wife's social status is established on the basis of her husband's occupational position, the two become equal in marriage even if they were not equals at birth. Thus, inequality between men and women disappears because the woman, by becoming a wife, "acquires" her husband's social position.

Interestingly, in a 1954 revision of the paper, Parsons abandoned this line of argument and actually conceded that some degree of gender inequality was *necessary* for the preservation of the family unit! He rationalized this conclusion with his special brand of functionalism:

> It follows that the preservation of a functioning family system even of our type is incompatible with complete equality of opportunity. . . . [This] is attributable to its conflict with the functional exigencies of personality and cultural stabilization and socialization. (1954, p. 422)

Yet, when stripped of functionalist rationalizations, Parsons' observations were stark and prescient. In his paper "Age and Sex in the Social Structure," for example, Parsons asserted without equivocation or apology that the male world of work, from which women were excluded, was the primary site of power and prestige in America. He went on to speculate that, if women were to compete with men in that public arena, the structure of family life would have to go through a profound transformation:

> [The wife/mother] is excluded from the struggle for power and prestige in the occupational sphere. . . . It is of course possible for [her] to follow the masculine patterns and seek a career . . . in direct competition with men of her own class [but] this could only be [accomplished by] profound alterations in the structure of the family. (1964, pp. 258–259)

These conclusions, which were theoretical hypotheses for Parsons, are now empirically based givens in the sociological research literature on marriage and divorce. But even before the "evidence" was in, Parsons clearly had stated his belief that the maintenance of the nuclear family under capitalism depended upon sexual inequality in the form of role complementarity and the prescription of separate, gendered spheres. This is far more explicit and compromising than Haley's (1976) cool, contradictory assertion that families, by definition, are headed by two co-equal executives, Mom and Dad, although he simultaneously asserts: "Women are kept in a subordinate position in both family and work groups merely because they are female" (p. 102).

This oddly inconsistent position has gone without challenge in our field because the ideas occupying each of those clauses have been kept apart from each other. Contradictions that Parsons had to confront could remain inconsequential in family therapy as long as gender remained a marginal category. In fact, with the exception of Haley's remarks, I could not find a single reference to gender, let alone gender inequality, in any of the classic family texts.* Insofar as feminist concerns entered our field at all, they were kept outside the family. This was accomplished by a reworking of the doctrine of separate spheres.

THE FAMILY VERSUS SOCIETY

In our updated version, public and private domains are no longer taken to be equal, but they are still kept artificially separate. In other words, family therapists do not deny the fact that women are politically and economically one-down; they simply hold onto their conviction that, in the privacy of their own homes, men and women are equals.

This naive and uncritical dichotomization of public and private spheres is especially incongruous in a field that historically congratulated itself on its rigorous commitment to an ecological paradigm. To presume that social hierarchies topple at the domestic portal violates the principle of ecological embeddedness on which our theory depends. How family therapists have kept these two worlds apart for so long and with so little strain is the real subject of this essay.

The resilience of this kind of wishful thinking is a measure of its multiple origins and causes, some of which have already been suggested. An additional factor is the sociohistorical context in which our ideas have been formed.

The illusion of marital equality in a male-dominated society *requires* the illusory division of the world into public and private domains. This bifurcation of social existence can be likened to a kind of cognitive "deep structure" that limits the scope of even the most rigorous, ecosocial paradigm. As

---

*From this perspective, Haley's inconsistencies, however politically problematic, represent an attempt to address a problem that no one else thought to name. See Braverman (1986, p. 149) for other examples of Haley's prescient attention to matters of sexual politics.

participants in a competitive, capitalist culture, it may be that we simply cannot conceive of the family except in symbolic opposition to a harsher public arena.

This juxtaposition of public and private contains a host of elaborated antinomies that cannot easily be brushed aside, even for a more accurate, formal paradigm. When we think of the family, and then think of the world that surrounds it, we tend to think in terms of contrasts like these: love versus work, cooperation versus competition, timeless versus temporary, noncontingent versus instrumental, feeling and morality versus law and contract, altruistic versus acquisitive, collective versus individualistic, equality versus hierarchy, and so on (Collier et al., 1982).

Although family therapists do not sentimentalize these distinctions in the manner of 19th-century popular culture, our training, which was designed to counteract the reification of the individual, does encourage us to think of families as "havens in a heartless world" (Lasch, 1977). This is clearly incompatible with Parsons' admission that gender inequality is structured into domestic life because our theories *presume* an ultimate consensus of interests among family members who are conceived as "parts of a whole."

No matter how academically abstract our descriptions of a family system, there is always an underlying idealization of the family as constituting some kind of poetic, transcendent unity. This vision of ultimate interdependency is covertly ideological because its power comes from an implied comparison with the outside world, a place where individuals are set against each other in the marketplace of daily life. Our holistic conception of human relations, therefore, is compelling not only because of its formal, explanatory power, but also because it evokes a metaphorical critique of capitalist individualism.

Minuchin and Fishman (1981) probably take this imagery the farthest because their preferred metaphor of the family "organism" moves beyond an implicit nostalgia for a pre-industrial past and evokes a timeless analogy to natural, biological systems. "The family as a whole seems almost like a colony animal—that entity composed of different life forms, each part doing its own thing, but the whole forming a multibodied organism which is itself a life form" (p. 12).

This image of the family as body politic, with parts and wholes intricately balanced, cannot be easily reconciled with a view that has husbands and wives engaged in a contest for power because of their irreconcilably conflicting interests.

THE FAMILY VERSUS THE STATE

Minuchin the clinician has no illusions about the "goodness" of families, and has never minimized their terrible, destructive power. Similarly, Minuchin the theoretician is quite clear about what he intends to convey by the organism metaphor, and what he does not. He puts it best in his book co-authored with Fishman:

> [T]hose who attempt to come to grips with man's [sic] interdependence often resort to mystical or holistic philosophies connecting man with the universe. It is less painful to conceive of man as part of a universal intelligence than as part of the family network, a living organism closer to our experience. We can embrace man the cosmic hero, but we would prefer to turn a blind eye to his fight with his wife over who should have locked the front door. (1981, p. 12)

However, for Minuchin the rhetorician (1984) the "family organism" begins to take on an ideological function. Indeed, the organism metaphor seems to fuel his sense of mission since he maintains the political posture that to be for the family *is* to be for the individual. This militant holism is not only an implicit critique of the culture of capitalism, but also an explicit political attack on the modern Welfare State, whose activities he perceives as intrusions into realms of privacy that threaten self-determination, especially for the poor. Thus, by protecting the "family organism," we are protecting our sense of personal integrity and individuality.

This view of the family-as-victim of the public sector has been most systematically developed by Lasch. In *Haven in a Heartless World*, the first of a series of books on this theme, Lasch argued that the modern liberal approach to the family was ultimately an excuse for middle-class professionals to tell private citizens how to live. He attempted to show how the modern welfare state had displaced the family, writing of the "forces that . . . invade the private realm" (p. xvii) and the "assertion of social control over activities once left to individuals and their families" (p. xiv). He even has a section entitled "The Proletarianization of Parenthood" (pp. 12–21), in which he analyzes the means whereby the state has usurped parental prerogatives.

The politics of this account informed the rhetoric and professional agenda of both Haley and Minuchin during the expansion of family therapy in the 1970s. They saw the family as being dismembered, invaded, and regulated by professional experts with their own agendas — bureaucratic, psychoanalytic, medical. Stating it crisply in *Problem-Solving Therapy*, Haley wrote, "Despite its humanitarian nature, the clinical field is also an important arm of social control in society" (p. 196). Protecting the family against intrusive violations by the social welfare and mental health industries became part of the political culture of family therapy, and remains a central focus of Minuchin's current work.

What is important about the history of these ideas is that it highlights how our thinking about families was shaped by this battle with the bureaucrats and the "experts" they relied on. Set against the specter of an enormously powerful, unwittingly destructive, social control apparatus, we conjured up

an image of "family" as a beleaguered, but still hearty, "natural" unit. "The
family," Minuchin and Fishman wrote in 1981, "is the natural context for
both growth and healing. . . . The family is a natural group which over time
has evolved patterns of interacting" (p. 11).

This emphasis on Nature is the key, because it is related to the privileging
of generational relationships and the marginalizing of gender conflicts in
our theory of family systems. Looking back, once again, to Haley's formal
exposition of the family life cycle framework in *Uncommon Therapy*, it is
clear that situating the family in Nature was crucial to his universalizing of
the generational construct.

The intellectual conceit organizing his discussion relies on a semi-whimsi-
cal, semi-serious play of analogies between the social practices of human
beings and those of other "beasts." Haley writes:

> The systematic study of the human family . . . has coincided with the study of
> the social systems of other animals. . . . [H]uman beings as well as the other
> beasts of the field and the birds of the air have been observed in their natural
> environment. . . . Men [sic] have in common with other creatures the develop-
> mental process of courtship, mating, nest building, child rearing and the dislodg-
> ing of offspring into a life of their own, but because of the more complex social
> organization of human beings, the problems that arise during the family life cycle
> are unique to the species. (1973, p. 44)

The power and wit of exploiting this analogy become clear in the next
page with a breathtaking one-liner: "A crucial difference between men and
all other animals is that man is the only animal with in-laws"!

By borrowing metaphors from ethology instead of confronting the dilemmas of cultural anthropology, Haley could keep it simple, generating an
image of "the family" that suited the demands of theory and the political
agenda of the field in general. By suggesting, for example, that symptoms
could be understood as "comments" that conveyed distress about the predictable difficulties of generational development throughout the life cycle,
Haley exploited a developmental metaphor to score a political point. This is
because his assertion contained the implication, made more or less explicit,
that families, *if they were not interfered with*, could evolve home-grown
solutions to many of these developmental crises.

This idea eventually came to incorporate Minuchin's image of family-as-
organism and Bateson's "mind and nature" metaphors. In its current usage,
"family development" is analogically tied to representations of evolution so
that the argument now reads something like this: Were it not for developmental snags and external meddlers, families would "naturally" grow and
develop, and in the process emerge as more complex forms of life.

Much has been accomplished (and obscured) by this evolutionary analogy. By turning families into organisms, a naturalistic, developmental frame could be used to normalize psychological problems. This has been useful in protecting individuals and the sphere of private life from the truly destructive impact of medical and psychiatric interventionism. Moreover, the generational emphasis, with its associated imagery of the timeless universality of cycles of birth and death, has been empowering to parents needlessly intimidated by professional advice-givers. In this regard, we might remember that the standard clinical maneuver of "putting the parents in charge" is less a comment to unruly children than a challenge to interfering professionals.

Thus, by proselytizing about the integrity of the family unit and emphasizing the "natural order" of the generations, family therapists were actually waging a political battle on behalf of parents against the State (and competing with other segments of the mental health establishment for those parents' allegiance).

From "Nature" to "Power"

Unfortunately, this semi-explicit political agenda obscured as many realities as it revealed. As I have argued elsewhere (1985a,b, 1987), the ideal of restoring parental authority often got translated in clinical practice into the attempt to restore *patriarchal* authority by implicitly blaming mothers for fathers' weaknesses. Moreover, by "normalizing" generational hierarchies, conflicts between husbands and wives were depoliticized. The struggle for power between the sexes was relevant only insofar as it compromised parental functioning. Gender conflicts had to be made incidental to generational difficulties because they could not be camouflaged as normal aspects of the natural developmental flow.

In short, to confront gender inequality on its own terms would have meant an end to the idealization of family relationships. "The Family" could no longer stand outside of hierarchical society, just a bit closer to nature and to our pre-industrial past. Instead of the presumption of an ultimate "consensus of interests," we would have to consider that families are also entities divided against themselves, and that they are structured around an inherent "conflict of interests" between males and females — each sex belonging to a distinct social group, but one having more power than the other.

To entertain such a view would undermine, in the most profound sense, the political and philosophical commitments of the family therapy field. It would mean questioning the conceptual transcendence of "The Family" as our unit of description, and with it the epistemological, if not moral, idealization of the family as some kind of "ultimate unity." It would undermine the radical constructivist credo that power is an illusion, or, as Bateson put it, a "myth . . . that always corrupts because it proposes always a false . . . epistemology" (Sluzki & Ransom, 1976, p. 106). It would require instead a reading of family relationships at two levels of description: one elucidating the paradoxes of circularity, the other confronting the realities of domination. Both punctuations are necessary to capture the essentials of the family drama, just as domestic conflicts must always be cast in terms of both old and young, male and female.

All this, in turn, would mean moving toward a theoretical model that integrated the "truths" of radical constructivism with the "truths" of feminist materialism. As an "ecology of ideas" organized by perspectives and metaperspectives (Bogdan, 1984), families are mental entities to which power terms could not apply. As social arrangements made "real" by the very real activities of the larger society, families *are* material structures in which gender inequalities have been, historically, inevitable.

WHICH MEANS WHAT IN PRACTICE?

It means, first, recognizing that every family, as well as every family therapy session, is as much about the politics and meaning of gender as it is about the politics and meaning of growing up. In other words, there is no such clinical entity as a "gender case" any more than there is a unique clinical entity, a "generation case." Even to ask, "What are the gender issues in this family?" misses the point. Just as it is simply not possible to *think* as a family therapist without using a generational or life cycle perspective, it is equally nonsensical to presume anything fundamental has been said about a case until it has been considered through the lens of gender.

Gender and the gendering of power are not secondary mediating variables *affecting* family life; they *construct* family life in the deepest sense. Taking this assertion as a given (which would include the corollary that gender is organized hierarchically with men in the dominant position) should not mean conceding anything to feminists, because it should be, by now, a commonplace truth at the level of "the earth is round." Indeed, by making this our starting point and integrating gender and gender inequality into the formal infrastructure of our theory, we will have, *de facto*, depoliticized these terms by granting them a presumptive status.

This would improve the working climate for all of us because our old arguments are tiresome and repetitive, and there are new possibilities for theory, research, and practice that we could now begin to address. For example, some of the most interesting questions to consider are those that attempt to unconfound the variables of gender and power. Because men and women have been found to operate differently in personal relationships

(Gilligan, 1982; Keller, 1985), it remains to be seen whether those differences are best explained as a function of the power differential between the sexes or as a function of the sex difference itself. In other words, looking at intimate relationships, when do men act more like men, and women more like women, no matter what their social position, and when do those "on top" (those with more access to institutional power) act more like those on top, no matter whether they are male or female?

Researchers who have taken an interest in such questions have typically studied couples who were observed while interacting around task-oriented matters. In these situations, power rather than gender has been found to be the primary determinant of how each party operates (Howard, Blumstein, & Schwartz, 1986). However, one prominent research team (Kollock, Blumstein, & Schwartz, 1985) has suggested that varying the context of the interaction in which couples are studied could produce a different outcome. They speculate, for example, that for couples dealing with "the reciprocal disclosure of very intimate feelings," the conversational division of labor might be very different than for couples restricted, by virtue of the research design, to task-oriented discussions (p. 44).

Needless to say, family therapists have much to contribute to these questions. We do not have to create a laboratory situation to investigate different kinds of conversation. The clinical situation spills over with possibilities. Given our special proximity to the everyday dramas of romantic and domestic life, we are in a unique position to document and analyze the relative contributions of gender and power in the structuring of intimate relationships.

Moreover, insofar as we recognize that power is gendered, the phenomenon of gender inequality will force us to advance our thinking about the relationship between politics, ethics, and the enterprise of psychotherapy. Any light we can shed on this difficult issue will make a contribution that extends beyond the particular concerns of family therapists, because every clinician and every school of therapy must construct a moral philosophy from which to do business. From the easy critiques of behavior therapy to the historic debates among the early psychoanalysts, the problem of politics, morality, and neutrality remains an ordeal for applied psychology.

Taking the problem of feminism and family therapy as a case in point, we might categorize the excesses in our internal debates in terms of "Left Errors" and "Right Errors," the terms Mao Tse-tung used when educating his political cadres. The Right Error here is the argument that feminists are imposing their values by introducing "political" issues into treatment, as if raising moral questions were the same as being moralistic. Collapsing this distinction makes feminists bad therapists by definition.

In fact, the fear of being moralistic has led to another kind of bad therapy, a therapy that silences discussion of the moral dimensions of intimate life: power, privilege, fairness, and exploitation, issues that are of profound psychological importance. Everyone's life and everyone's mind are organized by value-laden concepts because every one of us has a conscience. To sidestep questions of right and wrong because of a crude misunderstanding of what constitutes the proper domain of psychotherapy is to be inauthentic and psychologically distant from people's experience.

The error from the left is equally profound. It involves collapsing another distinction, the distinction between words and deeds, between therapy and politics. This is the argument that relies on the aphorism "therapy is political" as opposed to working with the more precise phrase, "therapy has political aspects." The problem with the familiar slogan is that it reduces therapeutic conversation to politics, and politics to conversation, which trivializes both enterprises. Not every word a therapist speaks or permits should be "politically correct," and no interview should be "scored" according to how many sexist or egalitarian thoughts are voiced. This kind of vulgar reductionism has no place in the clinical milieu, a setting far too dense with possibility and ambiguity. The "meanings" of therapeutic talk radiate to the edges of the imagination. Absolutes bend out there, paradoxes abound.

Given the difficulties and temptations of both these positions, every serious therapist must find a place to work, think, and talk that, however imperfectly, preserves the integrity of the clinical enterprise. This, in turn, requires a philosophically precise definition of what psychotherapy is, and what it is not.

The best contemporary description we have generated is captured by Maturana's phrase "the conversational domain," although I prefer crediting the idea to its earliest source, "Anna O" (a.k.a. Bertha Pappenheim), who coined the phrase "the talking cure" to describe her work with Breuer almost 100 years ago. Pappenheim's poetic and prescient image, anticipating the modern constructivist view of the treatment situation, provides a point of entry into the problem at hand.

Containing psychotherapy within the conceptual boundaries of a conversation clarifies its limits and possibilities. Therapeutic talk is, of course, all about the politics of influence. It is a conversational domain that is a concrete as well as symbolic platform on which players maneuver for position and control of meaning. If, then, we were to take as our subject the politics of heterosexual relationships, and the means by which those politics organize the politics of family therapy, we could then define our clinical task as the search for a way to talk to families about both these politicized spheres. In other words, the question becomes: How can we make the sexual politics of observed and observing systems a subject for therapeutic conversation?

Bringing sexual politics into the dialogic realm would mean discussing the dilemmas of love and power, and discussing the problems of discussing those dilemmas in relation to a therapist of a particular sex and point of view. For example, in a recent case seen at the Ackerman Institute by Gillian Walker and myself, Walker asked a black man who had been "resisting" our line of questioning, "What best explains your not wanting to tell me too much: that I'm white, female, or highly educated?" The man, married to a white woman, answered immediately, "Mostly that you are a woman. I'm used to white people and I don't care that much about education." This exchange freed up the conversation so that sex, race, and class (in that order) were no longer forbidden subjects, but became the subject of the therapy.

Similarly, in another case that Robert Simon and I saw at the Ackerman, a young, decidedly "unfeminist" wife complained, after some prodding, that she was afraid she would forget what she had to say while waiting for her husband to finish speaking. When I, intrigued, asked her what she thought it meant that I'd asked her husband to speak first, she blurted out, "Well, we live in a patriarchal society. I guess you are caught up in it too."(!)

Once it becomes absolutely clear that psychotherapy is nothing more and nothing less than talk, then it is best to conceive of family therapy as a rhetorical strategy that helps elucidate the dilemmas of love and power between men and women living in a patriarchal society. This means capturing in language a double description of the bonds of love, a description that includes both circular reciprocity and hierarchical inequality. Developing questions, metaphors, and stories that make such talk possible has become the central focus of my clinical work.

What Therapy Is Not

Framing the clinical task as "rhetorical" is a way of saying it is not "technical." Thinking in terms of techniques, solutions, or even interventions muddies the waters conceptually and politically. Leaving the conceptual critique for others, I will focus and close on a political note.

Thinking of family therapy in terms of techniques carries the implication that family problems are technical problems and that technical problems are solvable problems; it's just a matter of finding the right technique. This is a simplistic kind of American pragmatism in which moral, political, historical, and existential dilemmas become trivialized into bureaucratic, organizational problems (she's too close; he's too distant).

This sort of instrumentalism has always seemed, from my point of view, to be infected with a willful strain of naivete. This is because, from a feminist perspective, there is always an element of impossibility that adheres to family life, and to romantic love, which simply cannot be fixed, not even by the most canny and humane systems consultant. Not all, or even most, failures in treatment are therapist-generated, nor can someone else's more artful interview necessarily save a marriage. If we are to see our work clearly,

I think we will have to face a truth about men, women, and families. As long as the world is an unfair place, as long as patriarchy prevails, love will be tainted by domination, subordination will be eroticized to make it tolerable, and symptoms will be necessary to keep families from flying apart.

REFERENCES

Bateson, G. (1958). *Naven*. Stanford, CA: Stanford University Press.

Beechy, V. (1978). Women and production: A critical analysis of some sociological theories of women's work. In A. Kuhn, & A. M. Wolpe (Eds.), *Feminism and materialism*. London: Routledge & Kegan Paul.

Belenky, M., Clinchy, B., Goldberger, N., & Tarule, J. (1986). *Women's ways of knowing*. New York: Basic Books.

Bogdan, J. L. (1984). Family organization as an ecology of ideas: An alternative to the reification of family systems. *Family Process, 23*, 375–388.

Braverman, L. (1986). Beyond families: Strategic family therapy and the female client. *Family Therapy, 8*, 143–152.

Collier, J., Rosaldo, M., & Yanagisako, S. (1982). Is there a family? New anthropological views. In B. Thorne (Ed.), *Rethinking the family*. New York: Longman.

Dimen-Schein, M. (1977). *The anthropological imagination*. New York: McGraw-Hill.

Fox, R. (1967). *Kinship and marriage*. London: Penguin Books.

Gilligan, C. (1982). *In a different voice*. Cambridge: Harvard University Press.

Goldner, V. (1985a). Feminism and family therapy. *Family Process, 24*, 31–47.

Goldner, V. (1985b). Warning: Family therapy may be hazardous to your health. *Family Therapy Networker, 9*(6), 18–23.

Goldner, V. (1987). Instrumentalism, feminism and the limits of family therapy. *Journal of Family Psychology, 1*, 109–116.

Haley, J. (1973). *Uncommon therapy: The psychiatric techniques of Milton H. Erickson, M.D.* New York: Norton.

Haley, J. (1976). *Problem-solving therapy*. San Francisco: Jossey-Bass.

Howard J., Blumstein, P., & Schwartz, P. (1986). Sex, power, and influence tactics in intimate relationships. *Journal of Personality and Social Psychology, 51*, 102–109.

Keller, E. F. (1985). *Reflections on gender and science*. New Haven: Yale University Press.

Kollock, P., Blumstein, P., & Schwartz, P. (1985). Sex, power, and interaction: Conversational privileges and duties. *American Sociological Review, 50*, 34–46.

Lasch, C. (1977). *Haven in a heartless world: The family besieged*. New York: Basic Books.

Lévi-Strauss, C. (1969). *The elementary structures of kinship*. Boston: Beacon Press.

Malinowski, B. (1913). *The family among the Australian aborigines*. London: University of London Press.

Minuchin, S. (1984). *Family kaleidoscope*. Cambridge: Harvard University Press.

Minuchin, S., & Fishman, H. C. (1981). *Family Therapy techniques*. Cambridge: Harvard University Press.

Parsons, T. (1954). *Essays in sociological theory*. New York: Free Press.

Parsons, T. (1964). Age and sex in the social structure. In R. L. Coser (Ed.), *The family: Its structure and functions*. New York: St. Martin's Press.

Rosaldo, M. Z. (1980). The use and abuse of anthropology: Reflections on feminism and cross-cultural understanding. *Signs, 5*, 389–417.

Rubin, G. (1978). The traffic in women: Notes on the political economy of sex. In R. Reiter (Ed.), *Toward an anthropology of women*. New York: Monthly Review Press.

Ruddick, S. (1982). Maternal thinking. In B. Thorne (Ed.), *Rethinking the family*. New York: Longman.

Sluzki, C. E., & Ransom, D. C. (Eds.), (1976). *Double bind: The foundation of the communicational approach to the family*. New York: Grune & Stratton.

4

The Problem of Gender in Family Therapy Theory

RACHEL T. HARE-MUSTIN

FAMILY THERAPY THEORISTS have given little attention to gender issues and feminist critiques, viewing such critiques as micro theory, peripheral to the development of macro theory. It is not surprising that this view is isomorphic to the problem feminist theory addresses, that is, the subordinate status of women in the family and society. Such an isomorphism demonstrates how characteristic modes of thought and perception about gender influence us on a number of levels. Rather than gender being a peripheral issue, gender is the basic category on which the world is organized. The fact that family therapy has had little impact on other disciplines and theories may well be due to its inability to deal with the basic issue of gender.

What feminist theory offers those who are trying to develop family therapy theory is an alternative construction of reality provided by a different lens. Feminism is futurist in calling for social change and changes in both men and women. Feminists have been concerned about the family because the family is the primary beneficiary and focus of women's labor as well as the source of women's most fundamental identity, that of mother. The family meets society's needs by shaping people for the roles in society. Feminists view the socially constructed role differences between the sexes as the basis of female oppression (Eisenstein, 1983).

Revised from *Family Process*, 1987, *26*, pp. 15-33.

A CONSTRUCTED REALITY

Our reality is a constructed reality. As Hume observed, what we learn from our experience is that the future will resemble the past. The way the therapist thinks about the world is the most powerful factor in family therapy. Despite a therapist's presumed neutrality, family therapy is not value-free, whether it involves a psychodynamic stance or a systems approach. Even neutrality itself represents a value. The idea of therapeutic neutrality denies the fact that all therapists hold normative concepts of good and poor functioning, growth and stagnation, male and female. These are so embedded in the therapeutic system and, in fact, in Western thinking as to rarely receive comment.

Family therapy has now developed into a successful, even an international, enterprise. Family therapy once felt its way along a lonely road. Now, we are like a driver on those long straight highways in the Midwest who has put the car on automatic cruise setting and gotten into the lotus position, legs folded on the driver's seat and so forth. Here is family therapy, roaring along into the future and unable to get out of the lotus position.

As Lao Tzu, the Chinese sage said, "Trying to make things easy results in great difficulties." One of the difficulties has become the inability of the family therapy field to respond to new ideas. We must ask ourselves, what functions do our theories serve? Perhaps they merely conserve the past. I will review some aspects of the family which influence our traditional ways of construing the family and lead to gender bias in family therapy. Then I will raise some questions about the gender role dichotomy.

THE CONSTRUCTION OF THE FAMILY

The meanings and symbols associated with the family frame the past and organize the future. Today the family has become a hot political issue, perhaps because less than 10% of American households still consist of the traditional family with a working father, a mother at home, and two school-aged children (Wattenberg & Reinhardt, 1981).

The modern family is a recent social invention, dating from the early 19th century, when work and home became separated in the Industrial Revolution. Workers could be better controlled in factories, and technology moved beyond the little workshops that were homes. For poor women in the early 19th century, the saying was not "A woman's place is in the home," but "A woman's place is in the mill," since the vast majority of mill workers prior to unionization were women and children. We view the past we never knew with nostalgia, for we have forgotten the idiocy and harshness of daily life and the repression of the young and lively associated with the stable family.

The idealization of the home as a haven by social critics like Lasch (1977) is a patriarchal view. As men became the primary wage earners, the home became organized as a place of rest and leisure for them. In those days, women had others to share domestic chores. Today, the American mother has the least help for childcare and housework of any mother in the world (Minturn & Lambert, 1974).

Housewives have been described as remaining at a preindustrial stage, doing work in the private sphere of the family which has no exchange value in the marketplace. Women's depression is often associated with the mindless and unappreciated routines of housework (Sobel & Russo, 1981).

Continuity and Change

In the 1950s, when family therapy began, a particular kind of family existed which was unlike the family of previous or subsequent eras; people married younger and had larger families. Today's one- and two-child families are more consistent with the long-term declining birth rate in the United States (Cherlin, 1979). Abortion is not a recent phenomenon; in fact, abortion was widespread in past centuries, terminating about the same proportion of pregnancies as today, the great majority sought by married women (Degler, 1980). At present, one-fifth of all children live with a single parent, perhaps in part because 25% of all births are now to unwed mothers. However, the most prevalent type of family currently is the two wage earner, two parent family.

The most dramatic change in the family in this century is not broken families, for desertion and early death were widespread in the past, but the entry of women into the world of paid work. Fifty-six percent of American wives work outside the home, albeit the majority isolated in sex-segregated and low-paying jobs (Packwood, 1982; Scanzoni, 1979). The lack of widespread childcare means American women are not about to be freed from domestic responsibilities just because they hold other jobs. Asymmetrical boundaries between work and family are so widely accepted as to be unquestioned by families or therapists (Hare-Mustin, 1988). For women intrusion of family responsibilities into work leads to negative evaluations of women as workers, but for men boundary permeability in the other direction means they can take work home or use family time to recuperate from occupational stress (Hare-Mustin, 1980).

The privacy of the family has led to isolation and made the domination of women less accessible to public scrutiny. We do not permit among strangers the violence permitted in the family. Attacks by husbands on wives result in more injuries requiring medical treatment than rapes, muggings, and automobile accidents combined. One-third of all women slain are killed by their husbands or boyfriends (*New York Times*, 1984). Yet some family therapists within the framework of their theories claim there are no victims. Will feminism free men first? Weitzman's (1985) recent research found that the breakdown of the family has provided freedom for men but poverty for women and children. Divorced women and their children are a new underclass, suffering a decline of 73% in living standard at the same time divorced men are experiencing an increase of 42%.

Rather than the private domain of the family being a refuge from the pressures of public life, public life today may be more attractive to family members. Public life may provide anonymity and a place where family members can live beyond assigned identities, as well as escape from the intensity, intimacy, and responsibility which characterize family life (Sennett, 1981).

The End of Childhood

Given smaller families, many children are growing up in neighborhoods without other children. Instead of having children nowadays, lots of couples are having lifestyles. Children may suffer from being too differentiated (Combrinck-Graham, 1985). Learning about gender differences starts early, and it is fathers more than mothers who teach gender stereotypes to both boys and girls (Hoffman, 1977; Lamb & Lamb, 1976).

Children have learned to expect their fathers to be absent, so they rarely complain about that, but they freely express their anger for mothers being away. Pleck (1977) has noted that, although maternal employment has long and incorrectly been thought to harm children psychologically, it is rarely asked whether paternal employment might harm children.

The Myth of Motherhood

Fathering and mothering are different: to father is to beget; to mother is to raise and care for. The emphasis on mothering in American society results from our peculiarly American view of the child as an innocent and vulnerable creature and of early influences as immutable and a cause for great potential harm. The tenacity of this view has hardly given way to recent research like that of Kagan (1984), which suggests that most children are remarkably robust, and that early influences do not have predominance over later influences in the individual's development.

Women's major identity is that of mother, yet women today spend but a small part of their lives in mothering. The idealization and blaming of the mother are two sides of the belief in the all powerful mother (Braverman, Chapter 12; Chodorow & Contratto, 1982). The formulation of dominant-mother/ineffectual-father as the cause of every serious psychological difficulty is typically made without regard for the responsibilities assigned to women in the family. Society is beginning to espouse equality for women, but not yet for mothers (Hare-Mustin, Bennett, & Broderick, 1983; Hare-Mustin & Broderick, 1979). Despite the idealization of women's mothering role, there is consistent evidence that children have a negative effect on the mental health of women, a fact many family therapists seem oblivious to. Paradoxically, with the birth of each child, the mother's power in the family diminishes relative to that of her husband (Hess-Biber & Williamson, 1984).

Chodorow (1978) and Dinnerstein (1976) have suggested that fear of women may result from childhood helplessness. But that overlooks the fear small children have of men. Fathers are not just romantic strangers, but often fearsome strangers because of their remoteness, unpredictability, and, for the child, large size and loud voices. Fathers can be rivals as well as strangers for both boys and girls. Some therapists have held that everyone fears mothers (Pittman, 1985). It has been suggested that those who fear mothers may become family therapists so they can control mothers.

The Marital State

Marriage remains the preferred state in America, although many women in the baby boom cohort are not finding husbands (Norton & Glick, 1979). Marital problems are the most common problems people bring to therapy, but as Gurman and Klein (1980) observe, we have very little knowledge of what actually goes on inside marriage. Current emphasis on self-fulfillment has meant less tolerance for unhappy marriages. It is of interest that in Freud's day, psychoanalysis lasted a year and marriage lasted a lifetime. Now it's just the opposite.

Marriage is structured to assure the status differences between men and women. That is why in marriage the man is typically taller, older, more educated, hairier, hoarser, and from a higher social class (Bernard, 1973). Marriages where this is not the case we regard as strange. Therapists cannot overlook the fact that the standard of living and social status women have are derived primarily from their relationships with men, first their fathers, then their husbands. Women who have no men, like old women, single women, and divorced mothers, have low status and are the most likely to live in poverty.

Marriage has been found to have a protective effect for men but a detrimental effect for women in terms of both mental and physical health (Sobel & Russo, 1981). Miller (1976) has described women in marriage as de-selfing themselves so as not to threaten men. Although individual males complain that they do not feel powerful, it is rare to find a male who seeks to give up masculine prerogatives. No dominant group has ever relinquished power voluntarily.

BIAS IN FAMILY THERAPY

Traditional constructions of the family on which our therapeutic approaches are based reflect society's male norm and female complementation. The therapeutic models which we have developed for working with families reveal widespread gender bias. Such bias can take two forms. One form of bias exaggerates differences between groups of people. This I call alpha bias. The other form of bias ignores differences when they do exist. This I call beta bias. This is the bias of systems theories.

The alpha-beta schema is in some ways analogous to that in hypothesis testing in research. In hypothesis testing, alpha or type 1 error involves reporting a significant difference when one does not exist; beta or type 2 error involves overlooking a significant difference when one does exist. I use the term "bias" to refer not to the probability of error but rather to a systematic inclination to emphasize certain aspects of experience and overlook other aspects. Here the alpha-beta schema is used to examine ideas about gender but it can also be used to understand ideas about race, class, age, and the like.

Psychoanalysis Deconstructed

There have been a number of critiques of psychoanalysis and how it has disadvantaged women; these do not need to be repeated in detail here (Albee, 1981; Brodsky, 1980; Hare-Mustin, 1983). Freud's pejorative attitude to the feminine, his misogyny, his treating masculinity as the human norm, his viewing female development against the standard of male anatomy are critical components of his theory, not incidental ones. Yet, it is sobering that in a recent survey of family therapists, Freud was ranked second of the 10 most influential theorists in family therapy (Sprenkle, Keeney, & Sutton, 1982).

Why has psychodynamic theory continued to be so influential among family therapists? Psychoanalysis originally was concerned primarily with women as patients, and it is questionable if psychotherapy could have survived without women's pervasive unhappiness. John Dewey's observation in 1922 remains true today:

> The treatment of sex by psychoanalysts is most instructive, for it flagrantly exhibits both the consequences of artificial simplification and the transformation of social results into psychic causes. Writers, usually male, hold forth on the

psychology of women as if they were dealing with a Platonic universal entity, although they habitually treat men as individuals, varying with structure and environment. (Cited in Shields, 1975, p. 752)

Alpha bias is apparent in the way psychodynamic theories have mystified women's psychology by ignoring their subordination. Developmental theories like Erikson's (1968) focus on intrapsychic explanations and are based on male development. Even in object relations versions of psychoanalytic theory the woman is an "object." Object relations theory shifted emphasis to the mother as a noxious influence in human development. Mothers were experienced solely as people who did or did not live up to their children's expectations.

Freud's famous case of Dora is a drama of betrayal involving two unhappy families. It vividly illustrates the psychoanalytic view of women, including the belief that the seduced girl is the seducer. Dora provides an important example of a woman who refuses to behave in accord with sex-role stereotypes (Hare-Mustin, 1983). Freud described her as a young woman of very independent judgment who occupied herself with attending lectures for women and more or less serious studies. It is her resistance to Mr. K's seduction and Freud's purposes when she quits therapy that leads to her being labeled as "disagreeable and vengeful" (Jones, 1955, p. 256). Dora has confronted the K family with Mr. K's sexual advances and her father's affair with Mrs. K, all of which the adults involved deny.

The appeal of psychodynamic theory to therapists may be its reversal of the Western primacy of conscious over unconscious, of logic over feelings. Psychodynamic theory attacks the authority of rationality and parental precepts. This is evident in its lack of interest in the patient's experience compared with its preoccupation with the search for the secret event, a search leading to an infinite regression.

What Dora needs most is confirmation of the truthfulness of her perceptions, and thus confirmation of herself, but Freud and his followers have developed the theory that patients are made ill by their fantasies, not by what happens to them. Object relations theorists would also minimize Dora's situation and attribute her problems to her early relationship with her mother. Freud never meets Dora's mother, but he diagnoses her as having a "housewife's psychosis" (Freud, 1959, pp. 27–28). (This is a diagnosis not found in *DSM-III*.) The frequent blaming of the mother for family problems (Caplan & Hall-McCorquodale, 1985) continues in family therapy. It is notable that the women in this family case — Dora, her mother, the maid, Mrs. K — are seen as the source of problems, not Dora's father or Mr. K.

Psychodynamic theories are marked by deconstruction, for what appears as reality is fiction, what appears literal is metaphorical, and every metaphor involves a distortion. The originating event that is sought is regarded as a fiction, something which never happened. Alpha bias is evident in the widely held belief that women cannot be believed.

Systems Theories

Family systems therapy, including structural and strategic approaches, is characterized by beta bias, ignoring differences when they do exist. Systemic models focus on recursive sequences and circular causality (Sluzki, 1983) and have been accused of rendering the family an abstract and mechanistic structure. From a presumed neutral position the therapist reframes the problem, that is, teaches the family the therapist's construction of reality.

From a wider vantage point, the "metaperspective" may be little more than a view over the moat to the opposite wall. Out of sight beyond the wall are the rules, boundaries, and hierarchies of the society. These are what the metaperspective fails to see. When we alter the internal functioning of families without concern for the social, economic, and political context, we are in complicity with the society to keep the family unchanged (James & McIntyre, 1983; Taggart, 1985). Thus, at the societal level, family therapy is "more of the same."

Systems approaches reflect Western conceptions of an objective, active, ahistoric way of dealing with the world. They are actually reductionistic, for they hold that one can learn about the family by looking only at the microscopic interactions of family members. Family dysfunction is viewed as an internal event, an intrafamily problem, independent of context.

In a recent survey, family therapists considered differentiation and negotiation to be the most important goals of therapy (Sprenkle & Fisher, 1980). These represent stereotyped male values of individuality and rationality. Differentiation and clarification of the self are utopian tasks for women until the structure of the family and society changes. It is notable that the lowest-ranked goal was caretaking, typically the mother's major responsibility.

Beta bias is evident in therapists who set up a quid pro quo bargaining exchange on the assumption that family members are equal. Margolin and her colleagues (1983) have pointed out that the changes women want may be less easily accomplished than those desired by men. When men feel there has been sufficient change, women may be dissatisfied, not only because women have more concerns about relationships, but also because women's requests for affection and understanding may be less easily achieved than the behavioral goals men desire and therapists more readily perceive.

There are four primary axes along which inequalities of power are organized: class, race, gender, and age. Two of these pertain to inequalities within every family: gender and age. Hierarchy is central to systems theorists like Haley (1976) and Minuchin (1974), but their categorizing marker for a position in the hierarchy is solely the person's age (generation). By exclusive use of this category they ignore the fact that males and females of the same generation do not necessarily have comparable positions in the family hierarchy.

Age and gender interact in complex ways. Indeed, since the woman typically has lower status than the man in the family and is in fact regarded by the society as less than a mature adult (child-like), her alliance with a child rather than with the father may not be such a violation of the hierarchy as these theories hold. The therapist who focuses only on generational differences is trying to unbalance a hierarchy which is already unbalanced. Gender, a crucial marker of hierarchy, is disregarded.

Systems approaches, by viewing family members as equal interacting parts in recursive complementarities, tend to ignore differences in power, resources, needs, and interests among family members. Such theories regard the nondifferential treatment of family members as equal treatment, assuming that men and women in the normal family are at the same hierarchical level. Thus, we have beta bias: By ignoring gender differences, the therapist supports them.

THE CONSTRUCTION OF GENDER OPPOSITES

Constructivism points out we do not discover facts; we interact with the world to invent them (Dell, 1985; Watzlawick, 1984). As Einstein noted, our theories determine what we can observe.

We construct oppositions to use for understanding the world. We easily slip into dualities which represent an everyday Manicheanism. Thus, we create two-sided perceptions which alternately cancel each other out (Riedl, 1984). Although we recognize the futility of oppositional models in our methods of treatment as generating "more of the same," in our theories of men and women we accept opposition as if it is reality (Watzlawick, Weakland, & Fisch, 1974).

To see both sides of a problem is the surest way to prevent its solution, because there are always more than two sides. If we assume that one way is right, the other wrong, we are led to what is called the fallacy of opposites.

The symmetrical pseudomutuality of male and female can be challenged. Not-*a* is not necessarily the opposite of *a*. What do we observe in opposition to man? Man or mouse? Man or beast? Man or superman? Man or child? Man or mountain? Man or machine? Man or woman? Which is the opposite?

I believe gendered thinking leads to false dichotomies. Let me point out how we succumb to the fallacy of opposites with regard to gender roles.

Gender Roles: A False Dichotomy

The nature of the world is to be complex, but we assume we can understand better by simplifying. Sex-role stereotypes are such simplifications. Masculinity and femininity are often considered opposites, but the differences in the ways we *perceive* men and women have been found to be much greater than their actual differences (Deaux, 1984).

Within our positivistic culture, claims about cognitive differences are assumed to be free of value judgments (Broughton, 1983). Characteristics associated with men, like rationality and independence, are regarded as ideal and a sign of mental health. Although qualities associated with women may appear complementary, in fact they are not equally valued, an asymmetry which reveals that the norm for behavior is maleness rather than femaleness.

Over 30 years ago, Parsons and Bales (1955) observed that men were instrumental and women expressive. For Parsons, this was a functional explanation of how gender roles are linked to power. The emphasis on distinct sex roles then led to these roles being used as the criterion for distinguishing normal and pathogenic families (Peal, 1975). Although most Americans have applauded the apparent decline in class, geneology, and tradition as determinants of social position, we have still clung to gender classifications as the last remaining insurance against social disorder (Rosenberg, 1982). The debate about gender roles currently going on in other disciplines raises questions for family therapists.

What is Masculinity?

In Western society, Judeo-Christian tradition has fostered the ideal of individualism and autonomy, but without making the ideal possible for all. Aspects of the traditional male role not permitted to females include assertion, intellectuality, and overt sexuality. Accompanying the ideal of individualism is the expectation that every person's conduct will be that person's own responsibility. The focus on individual responsibility ignores social forces and leads to individuals being polarized and categorized on a continuum of success and failure (Ho, 1985). A competitive society is the result.

Masculinity is defined by agonistic activity, by ritualistic combat. Masculinity is only achieved by continually engaging in such activity. From Homer's time until today, the first requirement of heroism is the exclusion of women as participants.

Overconformity is one consequence of gender roles. Men conform more than women because the violation of gender role requirements has more negative consequences for men. Traditionally, a man's greatest fear is to be thought to be like a woman. Aspects of the traditional female role avoided by "real men" include concentration on the home, living through others, and stress on adornment. That is why a man who dresses like a woman is called a "weirdo" but a woman who dresses like a man is called "dressed for success." Calling some men "wimps" is the way to pressure men back into the macho style. But there are no more genuinely nice, sensitive men around than in the past; there is no decline in rape or wife-battering, and no documented increase in men's doing housework. It is hard to go counter to the dominant themes of our cultural moment, which have been described as the politics of macho swagger, social meanness, and possessive individualism.

Feminine Relatedness

As for femininity, the preoccupation with defining the female sensibility has led in some cases to dangerously erroneous generalizations about women. As the theories of Dinnerstein (1976) and Chodorow (1978) were popularized, differences between men and women became viewed as part of their *essential* nature rather than due to gender arrangements in society. In stressing the heretofore undervalued quality of relatedness, some feminists from a psychoanalytic perspective have focused on the development of a gendered personality in the crucible of the early mother-child relationship (Hare-Mustin & Marecek, 1986). These theories of male-female differences rest on yet untested assumptions and ignore subsequent social learning (Kagan, 1984; Lott, 1985).

Gilligan (1982) has harked back to Parson's duality, describing women as relational and men as principled when faced with moral dilemmas. In point of fact, men and women alike may be both principled and relational. We can account better for which aspect is expressed by focusing on who has the power in an interaction rather than on gender. Thus, women's concern with relationships can be understood as the need to please others when one lacks of power. Zuk (1972) has pointed out that the powerful advocate rules and rationality, while the weak espouse relatedness. Thus, in husband-wife conflicts, husbands use logic, wives call on caring. But in parent-child conflicts, parents, including mothers, emphasize rules; it is children who appeal for understanding. Society rewards rationality, not emotions, but which is used is associated with who has the power, not primarily with being male or female.

The gender role ideals of both autonomy and affiliation, when closely examined, can be seen as simplifications and caricatures. Even seemingly self-reliant men are dependent on wives to run their households and raise their children and on female staff at work. Autonomy can be criticized as encouraging "lifeboat ethics," narcissism, and selfishness (Wallach & Wallach, 1983). Paradoxically, the uniform striving for individualism leads to widespread conformity. Relatedness and affiliation are not always positive and fulfilling, either. Family therapists have observed how being helpful can render others helpless. A lifetime of putting others first may not benefit women, and the recipients of their concern may not welcome such caring.

Opposition and Hierarchy

What should be apparent is that men and women are opposites in no real sense at all. In fact, the concept of woman's role has no direct counterpart; men are defined by what they do, not by their sex. Because of the dominance of male institutions, women actually receive dual socialization. They are socialized in the dominant male culture, despite being largely excluded from it, as well as in the female subculture.

Like other dominants, men tend to assume their greater accomplishments are the result of inborn superiority (Goode, 1982). What men do affects women, who are subordinates, more than the converse. Thus, men do not observe carefully many aspects of women's behavior. In order to survive, women as subordinates attend to many seemingly insignificant aspects of behavior, which we call "women's intuition."

Dual socialization tempts women to try assimilation into the masculine culture, but also gives women insight into the artificiality of the value dichotomization. To men, socialized only in the masculine culture, women appear unpredictable and so need to be controlled, in the institution of marriage, or as witches, midwives, or nurses. One cannot help but be reminded of the witchcraft craze of past centuries. As Keller (1985) points out, witchcraft was associated with women's insatiable lust. Male knowledge was regarded as chaste. Historians estimate over 500,000 innocent women were put to death in a few centuries, a dramatic illustration of social control.

What needs to be challenged is the idea that a particular sexual division of labor is inevitable and mutually exclusive. Feminists have pointed out that the very language of sex roles conveys the sense of roles being fixed and dichotomous as well as separate but equal (Boss & Thorne; Chapter 5; Thorne, 1982). Uncritical use of terms like "sex roles" implies a harmonious balance and obscures not only differences in power between men and women but also the presence of conflict.

The concept of gender roles exaggerates other differences between men and women. Conflating autonomy with masculinity and relatedness with femininity leads to their being construed as mutually exclusive. By dividing men's and women's roles, the sexual division of labor also makes it appear that one cannot be a complete person without the other. Thus, each sex's dependence on the other is exaggerated, whether the relationship is characterized, in Bateson's terms, as symmetrical or complementary.

Gender has come to be used to symbolize the relationship between reason and its opposites. Because women have been restricted to the private sphere, it is assumed that they do not *know* things discoverable in the larger realm.

The pronouncements of social scientists like Parsons, Erikson, and Gilligan, regarded as science and popularized in the media, have encouraged the ideology of sex roles. Parson's emphasis on sex-role dichotomy has confused what we see with what should be. Gilligan's research has been criticized as flawed and her claims of universal gender differences have not been corroborated (Benton et al., 1983; Broughton, 1983; Viewpoint, 1986). Why have people rushed to embrace the claims that women do not, cannot, and should not think like men? Why has Gilligan's idea that women who nurture have a moral duty to continue to do so been so widely hailed? Why have unsubstantiated ideas of the essential nature of male-female differences found such ready acceptance? I suggest it is because these ideas preserve the status quo and do not demand that either society or individuals change.

For every problem there is a solution which is simple, elegant, and wrong. Separate but equal is such a solution when the male way involves reason and power while the female way involves relationships.

Equality is difficult to achieve with polar opposites, but our competitive society emphasizes differences, not similarities. Dichotomies imply a zero sum game where if one wins, the other loses. Dichotomized thinking leads to hierarchical thinking where one polar opposite becomes more valued than the other. The hierarchical aspect of gender roles suggests another reason why they are so resistant to change. Gender roles serve to maintain a social system based on power. Note that men's presumed inability to be expressive is linked with power, with "stonewalling," with "toughing it out," with winning. The very definition of power is of instrumentality and control of resources. It may be that the very expressiveness encouraged in women detracts from their perceived competence (Gibbs, 1985).

On the other hand, a hierarchy based on presumed female virtues and morality may not be better. To idealize relatedness and claim an innate female superiority is as counter to the egalitarian spirit of feminism as is the claim of innate masculine rationality (Eisenstein, 1983).

It is our construction of gender that emphasizes difference, polarity, and hierarchy rather than similarity, equality, and commonality of experience in human thought and action.

Conclusion

What can we conclude? Change is the purpose of family therapy. But theories about what should be changed depend on those developing the theories.

Alpha bias exaggerates differences between men and women; beta bias ignores differences. What does it mean to call one aspect of human experience male and the other female? Men's lives are apersonal because women are personal? Women's lives are expressive because men are rational? Construing masculinity and femininity as opposites leads to hierarchy, one considered superior to the other. Construing them as equal ignores current inequities. Because gender inequities are embedded in the larger social system, they are assumed to be part of the natural order. What results is the implicit and often unintended support of sexism. Women have constituted an underclass, and as family therapists we are linked to the failure in society to accord equality to women.

Despite our interest in theory and innovative practice, family therapy has had virtually no impact on our culture and time. I suggest this is so because we have not provided a truly new vision of the family or a truly new way of thinking about changes in the family and society. Theories that once seemed innovative now appear conservative. Instead of looking for solutions to the basic problems of gender, we have looked for problems which correspond to the solutions we have available. Since we do not have a solution to the problem of the disadvantaged status of women, we have ignored the problem and defined it as a non-problem. Libow (1985) has aptly pointed out that we treat gender role issues like a family secret.

Gender is the basic category by which our species, the family, and all societies are organized. True, gender is not the only issue, but the avoidance of this most basic issue in family therapy makes it extraordinary. Until we deal with the question of gender we are unlikely to transcend it. As long as family therapy theory treats gender as but a micro issue, our theory cannot make the epistemological shift that I believe the field requires.

As Maturana has observed, every system functions to keep itself intact (Dell, 1985). Thus it is with the gender role system. Those who have sought to develop macro theory in family therapy have failed to recognize how their thinking is limited by traditional gender-biased ways of construing the family. The discontinuous change in thinking which a macro theory would require seems beyond our capacities. Our present constructions, limited by gender role simplifications, do not admit the complexity of human experience. Our views are impoverished and therefore dehumanizing.

The field of family therapy has been unable to apply its models of change to its own theory and practice. Family therapy is now a continuous process, like a car streaming ahead with the driver comfortably in the lotus position. All we can expect is "more of the same." The solution has become the problem.

REFERENCES

Albee, G. (1981). The prevention of sexism. *Professional Psychology, 12*, 20–28.

Benton, C., Hernandez, A., Schmidt, A., Schmitz, M., Stone, A., & Weiner, B. (1983). Is hostility linked with affiliation among males and achievement among females? A critique of Pollak and Gilligan. *Journal of Personality and Social Psychology, 45*, 1167–1171.

Bernard, J. (1973). *The future of marriage.* New York: Bantam.

Brodsky, A. M. (1980). A decade of feminist influence on psychotherapy. *Psychology of Women Quarterly, 4*, 331 344.

Broughton, J. M. (1983). Women's rationality and men's virtues: A critique of gender dualism in Gilligan's theory of moral development. *Social Research, 50*, 597–642.

Caplan, P. J., & Hall-McCorquodale, I. (1985). Mother-blaming in major clinical journals. *American Journal of Orthopsychiatry, 55*, 345–353.

Cherlin, L. (1979). Work life and marital dissolution. In G. Levinger & O. C. Moles (Eds.), *Divorce and separation.* New York: Basic Books.

Chodorow, N. (1978). *The reproduction of mothering.* Berkeley: University of California Press.

Chodorow, N., & Contratto, S. (1982). The fantasy of the perfect mother. In B. Thorne & M. Yalom (Eds.), *Rethinking the family: Some feminist questions.* New York: Longman.

Combrinck-Graham, L. (1985, May-June). Treating small children. *Family Therapy Networker*, p. 21.

Deaux, K. (1984). From individual differences to social categories: Analysis of a decade's research on gender. *American Psychologist, 39*, 105–116.

Degler, C. (1980). *At odds: Women and the family in America from the revolution to the present.* New York: Oxford University Press.

Dell, P. F. (1985). Understanding Bateson and Maturana: Toward a biological foundation for the social sciences. *Journal of Marital and Family Therapy, 11*, 1–20.

Dinnerstein, D. (1976). *The mermaid and the minotaur: Sexual arrangements and the human malaise.* New York: Harper & Row.

Eisenstein, H. (1983). *Contemporary feminist thought.* Boston: G. K. Hall.

Erikson, E. H. (1968). *Identity, youth, and crisis.* New York: Norton.

Freud, S. (1959). *Collected papers* (Vol. 3). New York: Basic.

Gibbs, M. S. (1985). The instrumental-expressive dimension revisited. *Academic Psychology Bulletin, 7*, 145–155.

Gilligan, C. (1982). *In a different voice.* Cambridge: Harvard University Press.

Goode, W. J. (1982). Why men resist. In B. Throne & M. Yalom (Eds.), *Rethinking the family: Some feminist questions* (pp. 131–150). New York: Longman.

Gurman, A. S., & Klein, M. H. (1980). Marital and family conflicts. In A. M. Brodsky & R. T. Hare-Mustin (Eds.), *Women and psychotherapy: An assessment of research and practice* (pp. 159–188). New York: Guilford.

Haley, J. (1976). *Problem-solving therapy.* San Francisco: Jossey-Bass.

Hare-Mustin, R. T. (1980). Family therapy may be dangerous for your health. *Professional Psychology, 11*, 935–938.

Hare-Mustin, R. T. (1983). An appraisal of the relationship between women and psychotherapy: 80 years after the case of Dora. *American Psychologist, 38*, 594–601.

Hare-Mustin, R. T. (1988). Family change and gender differences: Implications for theory and practice. *Family Relations, 37*, 36–41.

Hare-Mustin, R. T., Bennett, S. K., & Broderick, P. C. (1983). Attitude toward motherhood: Gender, generational and religious comparisons. *Sex Roles, 9*, 643–661.

Hare-Mustin, R. T., & Broderick, P. (1979). The myth of motherhood: A study of attitudes toward motherhood. *Psychology of Women Quarterly, 4*, 114–128.

Hare-Mustin, R. T. & Marecek, J. (1986). Autonomy and gender: Some questions for therapists. *Psychotherapy, 23*, 205–212.

Hess-Biber, S., & Williamson, J. (1984). Resource theory and power in families: Life cycle considerations. *Family Process, 23*, 261–278.

Ho, D. Y. (1985). Cultural values and professional issues in clinical psychology. *American Psychologist, 40*, 1212–1218.

Hoffman, L. W. (1977). Changes in family roles, socialization, and sex differences. *American Psychologist, 32*, 644–657.

James, K., & McIntyre, D. (1983). The reproduction of families: The social role of family therapy? *Journal of Marital and Family Therapy, 9*, 119–129.

Jones, E. (1955). *The life and work of Sigmund Freud* (Vol. 2). New York: Basic Books.

Kagan, J. (1984). *The nature of the child*. New York: Basic Books.

Keller, E. F. (1985). *Reflections on gender and science*. New Haven: Yale University Press.

Lamb, M. E., & Lamb, J. E. (1976). The nature and importance of the father-infant relationship. *Family Coordinator, 2*, 379–385.

Lasch, C. (1977). *Haven in a heartless world*. New York: Basic Books.

Libow, J. A. (1985). Gender and sex role issues as family secrets. *Journal of Strategic and Systemic Therapies, 4*(2), 32–41.

Lott, B. (1985). The potential enrichment of social/personality psychology through feminist research and vice versa. *American Psychologist, 40*, 155–164.

Margolin, G., Talovic, S., Fernandez, V., & Onorato, R. (1983). Sex role considerations and behavioral marital therapy: Equal does not mean identical. *Journal of Marital and Family Therapy, 9*, 131–145.

Miller, J. B. (1976). *Toward a new psychology of women*. Boston: Beacon Press.

Minturn, L., & Lambert, W. W. (1974). *Mothers of six cultures: Antecedents of child rearing*. New York: Wiley.

Minuchin, S. (1974). *Families and family therapy*. Cambridge, MA: Harvard University Press.

New York Times (1984). Violent death rate cited as U. S. Health Concern. 28 November, A-14.

Norton, A. J., & Glick, P. C. (1979). Marital instability in America: Past, present, and future. In G. Levinger & O. C. Moles (Eds.), *Divorce and separation* (pp. 6–19). New York: Basic Books.

Packwood, R. (1982, July 1). The equal rights amendment. *Congressional Record*.

Parsons, T., & Bales, R. F. (1955). *Family, socialization, and interaction process*. Glencoe, IL: Free Press.

Peal, E. (1975). "Normal" sex roles: An historical analysis. *Family Process, 14*, 389–409.

Pittman, F. III. (1985). Feminism and family therapy: Are they compatible? Paper presented at the Family Therapy Network Symposium, Washington, D.C.

Pleck, J. H. (1977). The work-family role system. *Social Problems, 24*, 417–444.

Riedl, R. (1984). The consequences of causal thinking. In P. Watzlawick (Ed.), *The invented reality: Contributions to constructivism* (pp. 69–94). New York: Norton.

Rosenberg, R. (1982). *Beyond separate spheres: Intellectual roots of modern feminism*. New Haven: Yale University Press.

Scanzoni, J. (1979). A historical perspective on husband-wife bargaining power and marital dissolution. In G. Levinger & O. C. Moles (Eds.), *Divorce and separation* (pp. 20–36). New York: Basic Books.

Sennett, R. (1981). A community of difference. Lecture presented at the Graduate School of Design, Harvard University, Cambridge, MA.

Shields, S. A. (1975). Functionalism, Darwinism, and the psychology of women. *American Psychologist, 30*, 739–754.

Sluzki, C. E. (1983). Process, structure and world views: Toward an integrated view of systemic models in family therapy. *Family Process, 22*, 469–476.

Sobel, S. B., & Russo, N. F. (1981). Sex roles, equality, and mental health. *Professional Psychology, 12*, 1–5.

Sprenkle, D. H., & Fisher, B. L. (1980). An empirical assessment of the goals of family therapy. *Journal of Marital and Family Therapy, 6*, 131–139.

Sprenkle, D. H., Keeney, B. P., & Sutton, P. M. (1982). Theorists who influence clinical members of AAMFT. *Journal of Marital and Family Therapy, 8*, 367–369.

Taggart, M. (1985). The feminist critique in epistemological perspective: Questions of context in family therapy. *Journal of Marital and Family Therapy, 11*, 113–126.

Thorne, B. (1982). Feminist rethinking of the family: An overview. In B. Thorne & M. Yalom (Eds.), *Rethinking the family: Some feminist questions*. New York: Longman.

Viewpoint. On "In a Different Voice": An interdisciplinary forum. (1986). *Signs, 11*, 304–333.

Wallach, M. A., & Wallach, L. (1983). *Psychology's sanction of selfishness*. San Francisco: Freeman.

Wattenberg, E., & Reinhardt, H. (1981). Female-headed families. In E. Howell & M. Bayes (Eds.), *Women and mental health* (pp. 357–372). New York: Basic.

Watzlawick, P. (Ed.). (1984). *The invented reality: Contributions to constructivism*. New York: Norton.

Watzlawick, P., Weakland, J. H., & Fisch, R. (1974). *Change: Principles of problem formation and problem resolution*. New York: Norton.

Weitzman, L. J. (1985). *The divorce revolution: The unexpected social and economic consequences for women and children in America*. New York: Free Press.

Zuk, G. R. (1972). Family therapy: Clinical hodgepodge or clinical science? *Journal of Marriage and Family Counseling, 2*, 229–304.

5
Family Sociology and Family Therapy: A Feminist Linkage

PAULINE BOSS   BARRIE THORNE

IN DEVELOPING CONCEPTIONS about the composition, boundaries, and inner workings of families, family therapists have drawn upon frameworks from sociology. In the 1950s, functionalist theories came to prevail, assuming the inevitability of the nuclear family and a traditional sexual division of labor, and emphasizing equilibrium and order. Over the last two decades, the women's movement has challenged these assumptions. Feminists have articulated women's submerged experiences, emphasized alternative family forms, traced lines of gender and generation as sources of power and conflict within families, and developed a more complex understanding of the relationship of families to other institutions. In this chapter, we will review functionalist assumptions and feminist challenges in the linked traditions of family sociology and family therapy. Moving between theory and practice, we will trace the connection between sociological conceptual frameworks and therapeutic strategies, using specific cases as illustrations.

TRADITIONAL THEMES IN FAMILY SOCIOLOGY

Talcott Parsons, a major theorist in the functionalist tradition,* developed a framework that became dominant in U.S. family sociology in the 1950s and 1960s. Parsons likened society to an organism whose parts—the family, the economy, the state—contribute to the maintenance and smooth functioning of the whole. With the emergence of industrialization, Parsons argued, the family lost its productive functions (like farming or candlemaking) and came to specialize in two central activities: (1) socializing the young by inducting them into the values of society, and (2) maintaining the emotional health of its members, especially of men who bridge from the family to competitive work institutions. In meeting these "functional imperatives," the family would help sustain the equilibrium of "the social system" as a whole.

This emphasis on stability and equilibrium masked the presence of conflict in human systems and made the status quo seem inevitable. Parsons' image of the family came, in fact, from the context in which he lived and wrote. In the post-war 1950s, middle-class families migrated to the suburbs, men became more intensely defined by their occupations, and women by domesticity and a set of beliefs that Betty Friedan (1963) called "the feminine mystique." Sociologists Parsons and Bales (1955) took one type of family—more statistically prevalent in the 1950s than today, but by no means the only form even then—and theorized it as *The Family*, defined it as a particular set of people (a married couple and their children) filling two central functions (socialization of children and emotional support) with a fixed division of labor (a stay-at-home nurturing mother and a breadwinning father). This then became known as "the normal family."

Unlike other sociological theorists, such as Emile Durkheim and Max Weber, Talcott Parsons paid systematic attention to gender, at least in his analysis of the family. Parsons translated gender divisions into dichotomous "roles": the (male) "instrumental role" and the (female) "expressive role." He and his collaborator, Robert Bales, believed that it was functional for all small groups to have two "role leaders," one attending to the instrumentality of getting tasks done, the other focusing on the group's social and expressive needs.** Since the family is a small group, they found it significant, and

*Other influential theorists in the functionalist tradition of family sociology include Bronislaw Malinowski (1944) and George Murdock (1949), who both argued that the family (characterized by shared residence, economic sharing, socially approved sexual relationships, and childrearing) is a universal institution that functions to meet the human and social need for nurturing and socializing the young. For a succinct critique of their cross-cultural assertions, see Collier, Rosaldo, and Yanagisako (1982).

**Parsons and Bales based these conclusions on research conducted during World War II with bomber crews who had certain tasks to perform. From this small group research, then, they generalized to families (see Parsons & Bales, 1955). *Note:* Phillip Slater was a collaborator on this work but later broke away and wrote a scathing critique of this work in "Parental Role Differentiation," in Rose Laub (Ed.), *The Family* (2nd ed.), pp. 259–275 (New York: St. Martin's Press).

largely inevitable, that the adult male would play an instrumental role, earning a living outside the family, and that the adult female would play an expressive, nurturing role, located inside the family. They defined these two roles, and hence the positions of men and women, as separate, complementary, and relatively equal.

Parsons believed it was "dysfunctional" for wives to seek paid employment; others in the functionalist tradition coined related terms like "role strain" to encompass situations which didn't fit the model of a strict gender division of labor allocating women to families and men to outside employment. This language suggests the presence of tension, but quickly returns to an image of equilibrium. The family adapts to whatever the larger society needs. During the 1940s, women were in fact applauded for working in defense factories, but during the 1950s, when the men returned to fill these jobs, women were expected to stay home.

Functionalists assume that social change comes from *outside* the family; the family is a relatively bounded and *passive* institution, acted upon by external processes of economic change, such as the move to industrialization or the country's involvement in war. By its very nature this *conserving macro-functionalism* supports the status quo in family structure, giving priority to larger societal needs. If society needs workers, then the family must provide workers unencumbered with demands from babies, children, or frail, elderly parents.

Even at the micro level of the individual family rather than larger society, the status quo is assumed to be functional, governed by values of homeostasis and equilibrium. Therapists follow a *conserving micro-functionalism* when they counsel a wife not to make demands on her husband because he has an important job. She should passively adapt to his schedule and make it easy for him to be gone by being fully responsible for the children and "the expressive role."

FEMINIST RETHINKING OF FAMILY SOCIOLOGY

In the late 1960s, other frameworks gained strength in U.S. sociology and loosened the hold of functionalism. Conflict perspectives, drawn from the traditions of Marx, Weber, and the more radical strands of Freud, challenged the functionalist emphasis on equilibrium and order (see Table 1). Contemporary feminists have drawn upon and reworked these critical traditions, opening fresh perspectives on families and on underlying structures of gender.

Functionalist theory begins with abstract postulates about *the social system*. Feminist theory begins with and validates *women's experiences*, leading to deepened understanding of gender and social life (Smith, 1979; Stacey &

TABLE 1 Two Perspectives for Assessing Families

PERSPECTIVE	VALUE	ASSUMPTIONS	QUESTIONS THAT GUIDE THE FAMILY SOCIOLOGIST AND FAMILY THERAPIST
Structure — functionalist theorists	—Stability —Status quo —Homeostasis —Equilibrium —Balance	—Complementarity between genders —Females expressive/males instrumental —Equal power between genders exist —Conflict is dysfunctional	How does the family benefit larger society? (e.g., an unencumbered worker is beneficial for industrialization so the family supplies that worker)
Conflict theorists (not all are feminists, but all feminists are conflict theorists)	—Change —Equal power between genders and among people —People with less power should benefit as much as people with more power	—Conflict is functional —Conflict-ridden interaction is important in larger society (e.g., the women's movement, the civil rights movement)	Who benefits? (e.g., children, frail elderly, minorities, women?) Can we equalize the power so all people and family members can benefit?

Thorne, 1985). This approach opened a wave of new writings about women's experiences, for example, about intimacy, sexuality, childbearing, mothering, nurture, housework, divorce, wife-beating, and incest — experiences that had been submerged and distorted in dominant modes of thought. For example, the functionalist emphasis on woman's socializing and expressive role glossed over the fact that, although industrialization removed some forms of production, households are still arenas of considerable labor and production, albeit inequitably distributed and economically unrecognized.

Studies of housework and childcare (Berk, 1985; Hartmann, 1981) have shown that, on the average, husbands of full-time employed women do little more domestic labor than do husbands of full-time homemakers. There is, feminists have argued, a politics of time and fatigue. Women's double burden should not just be taken for granted, as if it is in the nature of things that a wife must do most of the housework and childcare even when she is employed full-time. A therapist should do more than counsel adjustment to the status quo when married women are angry about their husbands' minimal contributions to domestic labor or when working parents experience stress because they cannot find affordable, quality daycare. Indeed, therapists focus primarily on the psychodynamics of family life, but these psychodynamics take shape within a larger field of politics and social policies as well as structures of privilege and inequality. Feminists have helped articulate this broader context for families; they have also shown that anger may be a constructive emotion and conflict a constructive behavior in families when used to illuminate sources of injustice and directed towards making social change.

Extending the metaphor of "work," feminists have articulated other, relatively invisible and unsung forms of domestic or private labor that are disproportionately the work of women: care for frail elderly and other dependents (Abel, 1986); the work of feeding and provisioning a family (DeVault, 1988); the "kinwork" of writing letters, visiting, and maintaining other contact across households (DiLeonardo, 1987); "interaction work" in conversations (Fishman, 1983); and "emotion work," or the management of feelings (Hochschild, 1983). New writing on the varieties and complexities of women's experiences of mothering (Chodorow, 1978; Rich, 1976) reveal the extent to which earlier literature on mothers was written *from the standpoint of sons*. By starting with *women's experiences*, feminists cut across conventional divisions of knowledge, inquiring into complex connections between women's paid employment, their activities in politics and communities, and their more domestic lives, with attention to variations by social class, race, and ethnicity.

This rich literature bursts the narrow and tight seams of the functionalist notion of woman's "expressive role" within the family. Activities of both women and men clearly blend the expressive and the instrumental, and historically women's activities have never been confined solely to the family. By putting women's experiences at the center of knowledge, feminists have also revealed the tacitly male standpoint of traditional theories of and research on the family. Parsons claimed that his theory had universal applicability, but in fact it was deeply shaped by his historical context and by the gender beliefs of his time. He took for granted men's control of the economy and politics; he defined women in terms of family and nurturing and thereby suggested that many women (those not married, those employed outside the home) were "dysfunctional" or "deviant." Based on functionalist theory, if a woman was employed outside the home, the family had a "deficit structure." There was, according to functionalist sociologists (and therapists), only one way to be a "normal family."

Although traditional family sociologists often relied on interviews with wives (leading some to ask if the field should be redubbed "a wives' family sociology" [Safilios-Rothschild, 1970]), it was male sociologists—many of them clearly invested in patriarchal assumptions—who in fact usually designed the studies and set the questions. Early on, Jesse Bernard (1973) and Constantina Safilios-Rothschild (1970) pointed to male biases in the field of family sociology, especially in measures of marital satisfaction and conceptions of marital power. But their criticisms fell on deaf ears until a decade of feminist scholarship strengthened their arguments. Not coincidentally, that decade of feminist scholarship followed, and moved forward, the establishment of women's studies at universities and affirmative action in the hiring of faculty.

Feminist scholars have argued that by enshrining the nuclear family as the centerpiece of his theory, Talcott Parsons perpetuated an ideology of the monolithic family that obscured the variety of family/intimacy/household forms (Thorne with Yalom, 1982; Barrett & McIntosh, 1983). The women's movement has worked to make visible and to legitimize a *range* of family structures, including situations of single women and men, single-parent families, extended families, lesbian and gay households, child-free heterosexual couples, elderly unmarried couples, and elderly communities. Feminist scholars have helped make speakable the experiences of domination, conflict, and violence that are silenced by romanticized views of "the normal family." And they have resurrected the issue of power in families, this time to be researched from the perspective of female as well as male researchers and therapists.

One of the most important contributions of the contemporary women's movement has been to make visible the prevalence of incest, rape, and wifebeating, experiences that, along with the prevalence of physical abuse of children, challenge the functionalist emphasis on *family harmony* and *bal-*

ance of power. Terms like *"family* violence" and *"domestic* violence" obscure the fact that sexual and physical abuse within families runs along the contours of gender and generation. Adult men are the major perpetrators of sexual violence against women and children; husbands beat and batter wives with much greater frequency and severity than vice versa; and fathers and mothers are about equally likely to physically abuse their children (Breines & Gordon, 1983; Gelles & Cornell, 1985). As Dair Gillespie (1971) argued in an early feminist critique of the literature on marital power, men's greater power within families has deep structural roots extending into other institutions. The average husband is several years older and has more education, higher earnings, and a more prestigious occupation than his wife. These resources translate into men's having more power and privilege than women within families.

How Old Themes and Assumptions About Families Affect Family Therapy

Positing the post-World War II definition of the "traditional" nuclear family as the normal family — assuming rather than questioning the status quo and emphasizing values of harmony and equilibrium — the assumptions and imagery of functionalist theories perpetuate gender stereotypes and inequality. These assumptions have infused the theory and practice of many family therapists. Over the past decade, critics of mental health institutions and practices have argued that counseling and therapy outcomes for women have been jeopardized by the gender stereotypes of their therapists, stereotypes that mirror the sexist orientation of their society (Brown & Hellinger, 1975; Fabrikant, 1974; Feinblatt & Gold, 1976; Gurman & Klein, 1981a, 1981b; Hare-Mustin, 1978; Weiner & Boss, 1985). In 1975, the American Psychological Association Task Force on Sex Bias and Sex Role Stereotyping was established (APA, 1975), confirming the presence and power of gender stereotyping in the mental health professions.

Take "mother-blaming," for example. A mother of a disabled child is preoccupied and worried about her child. She organizes her life around the child's needs. A functionalist would say this is her prescribed role. Because the child will never develop or walk normally, she must spend more than the usual time tending this child. As she does so, her husband spends more and more time at work and taking long business trips. She is increasingly alone with her task of tending this difficult child. The marriage bonds weaken and soon the couple is in trouble.

A therapist who believes in the Parsonian assumption of "the normal family" may begin with the male: "Well, how does it feel to be married to a woman who is married to the children?" The husband feels understood, but the wife feels blamed. She is, in fact, blamed for neglecting her husband while she is performing the role prescribed for her. (This is a no-win situation for her.) Her husband is never challenged for his absence. Rather than blaming the wife, would it not be better to compliment her on her devotion to a difficult child, one who wears out most other people and irritates the father? (That is not, by the way, meant as a paradox; it is a true statement.) Therapists too often blame mothers for overfunctioning and pay less attention to fathers who are absent. Women who take care of difficult children and sick family members, old or young, must be viewed in a larger context. They are being adaptive, not sick. Mother-blaming will not stop until we, as scientists and therapists, reevaluate the possibility of our distrust, if not abhorrence, of close nurturance and our overgeneralization about the negative impact of caretaking and nurturing in families. Even when a woman's nurturance is conditional—"I can take care of this difficult child (or your sick mother) as long as you back me up"—her expectations of her husband may be reasonable and not manipulation, as labeled by some clinicians.

Women have long been asked to "stand by their man" when he has a demanding job to do in the work world; while needing her to do this, he is not labeled pejoratively as "overfunctioning" but positively as doing his job well. He is labeled as a "success" while she is labeled as "hovering," "smothering," and "overfunctioning." She can't win. As therapists, we must avoid reinforcing such a conflicting message for women by changing *our* perception of the woman's nurturant behavior. If she has the demanding challenge of taking care of a difficult family member, regardless of age or situation, she deserves our respect for her steady and capable functioning in the face of incredible demands.

Another example of gender stereotyping based on functionalist theory in family therapy centers around women as overly emotional. The normative Parsonian prescription for women in families is to be "the emotional smoother of waters." If, however, a woman or girl shows much emotion, it is considered a flaw, even by therapists. This again is the no-win situation for women in families. We see women and girls in families who are highly emotional and may even fit the diagnosis of hysteria, but often they are responding to situations of violence, incest, or other situations of learned helplessness and victimization. Rather than treating such emotional overreaction, it may be more fruitful to investigate *why* a woman or girl is acting that way. Once she realizes she has choices and options for changing her situation, she may be calmed. This is a slow process, but her empowerment and her knowledge of choices can be as calming as a Valium—and with fewer harmful side effects. The women's movement has helped therapists understand that an overly emotional woman may be a signal that something is wrong in her context. Rather than "blaming the victim," an attempt must be made to examine and change the context. Legal and political issues meld here with psychological issues. They are not separate where women and minorities are concerned.

In addition to perpetuating sexist stereotypes, family therapists whose work is based in functionalist theory assume family *balance* and role *complementarity* when there is health, and equal fault and bilateral collusion between spouses when there is trouble. Often therapists who think in this balanced way say, "He drinks because she nags; he batters because she provokes; he doesn't show up for dinner because she is a bad cook; he has an affair because she is sexually cool." When therapists think this way, at the base of their thinking lie several functionalist assumptions: that families are relatively bounded units untouched by the larger context; that families are predicated on equilibrium; that all family interactions are bilateral; that husbands and wives play complementary roles; and that they have equal power.

Even among those therapists who are more enlightened about economic inequality between men and women, we still see a conservation of the idea of balance in families. For example, the "quid pro quo" is continued by saying that, although men have economic power, women have emotional control. From a feminist perspective, we propose another interpretation. Rather than focusing on a bilateral balance, it is more productive to focus on the *overt* versus *covert* use of power (or control). That is, a wife may indeed withhold sex as a *covert* expression of power (and control) when there is *overt* inequity in the couple's decision-making power. The therapist should not read this pseudo-balance as proof of equal power in the marital pair. What it demonstrates is that there is "guerrilla warfare" going on in this marriage, a tactic used historically and even today in conflicts where one side has less power and fewer resources than the other. A woman may turn into a "guerrilla fighter" when she is feeling trapped and overpowered by her husband. In this case, her withholding sex would be a manifestation of *imbalance,* not of balance. It is her attempt to resist domination. To foster change with such couples, family therapy strategies should focus on *empowering* the wife rather than on saying there is equal collusion in the family feud. Indeed, she may be playing a part in keeping a destructive marital dance going, but initially she was adapting to being overpowered. Until her experience is recognized and empathically heard by the therapist, she will resist change — or will come to believe that therapy is just another oppression of women.

To complicate matters, the feeling of being intimidated by a husband (or therapist) may be perceived or real; the real event of oppression may have happened years earlier in the woman's family of origin, or it may stem from victimizing experiences in the workplace. The husband is not always the oppressor; her experience of victimization may precede him, but echoes of previous experience can affect the interaction between a wife and husband now. Carl Whitaker (personal communication) tells of the woman who, in childhood, was beaten by her father. He would take off his leather belt and beat her. Although she married a man who was not physically violent, she had a psychotic break the first time she saw her husband take off his leather belt. It bears repeating: Before change in the couple's interaction can begin, the therapist may have to focus on the wife's empowerment regardless of the source of her helplessness.

In order for a victimized woman's self-destructive adaptation to stop, the therapist has to first recognize an imbalance of power between men and women both *inside* and *outside* the family. Not only access to income but societal laws, religious beliefs, and community mores all affect male and female interaction. Until gender inequities are recognized and addressed by the therapist, a woman's self-destructive adaptation cannot fully change. When a woman doesn't change, therapists may call her resistant, but it may be instead the therapist who is resistant—resistant to acknowledging that something could be political as well as psychological.

There are other political issues besides gender. Doing family therapy with an Asian immigrant family is different from doing family therapy with an American southern Baptist family. Doing family therapy with a rural Minnesota family of Scandinavian Lutheran descent is different from doing family therapy with a Jewish family from New York City. Doing family therapy with a black family from the Woodlawn District in south Chicago is different from doing family therapy with a middle-class black family descended from generations of academics. Nevertheless, there are common strategies for working with all families; these systemic strategies should be honed by our attention to larger social, economic, historical, developmental, and cultural contexts and by concern for women as equal partners in family and intimate relations.

Therapeutic practices that focus on the goal of maintaining homeostasis within families will maintain, if not amplify, trouble in a family system where, for example, one parent is locked into a pattern of alcoholic self-destruction and the other into martyrdom. Such a family is full of tension and anger, yet nothing is allowed to erupt. For example:

The Jones family looked like the ideal, picture-book family—a mom and dad, a son and daughter. Dad earned the living as a broker; mom was a full-time homemaker who was usually there for her children when they came home from school and for her husband when he came home from work. There was, however, a problem. Dad spent more and more time away from home even after work. He drank with his colleagues, often missing dinner at home and sometimes staying out all night. Mom became increasingly upset but, having been socialized to be the "smoother of waters" in the family, she held her tongue and adapted to her husband's philandering. She talked with a therapist about her worry and anger; he told her to be patient, to continue to be nice to her husband, to entice him to come home earlier. This she tried to do. Even when the children began showing anger about their father's absence (and her apparent complacency about that), she scolded them and told them everything was all right. When the father didn't show up again for dinner one night and she gave her usual sigh of martyrdom, her junior high son responded, "Mom, for God's sake, don't you know by now that dad's not coming home. He's an alcoholic. Don't you know that by now?" She grounded her son for a week for saying that. No eruptions would be allowed in her family. She was the emotional smoother of waters.

Functionalists, whether micro or macro, view conflict in the family as negative since it threatens homeostasis. There are examples of counselors telling battered women to "stick it out," of therapists telling women sexually harassed in the workplace that they should "forget about it" so as not to cause trouble. Such therapists and counselors believe in peace at all costs. We have learned that, without conflict to bring about change in human systems, patterns of interaction remain rigid and imbalanced; pathology continues and grows to dangerous levels. Feminists have joined others in questioning the status quo and in pointing to the *realities* and, in fact, the *value* of processes of conflict and change.

Feminist Questioning of "The Normal Family"

Parsons and other functionalists posited the nuclear family, with a traditional division of labor between men and women, boys and girls, as the normal and hence ideal family. Feminists have joined others in questioning the search for "the normal family." They have helped make visible the wide range of family and household arrangements and the fact that, in contemporary society, relatively few fit the family as imaged by Parsons. And feminists have rejected the assumption that going against conventional norms means pathology. It is not, for example, pathological for women or men to raise children outside of marriage, or for fathers to nurture, or for mothers to be employed. Indeed, rebellion and deviation from the norm may sometimes be healthy.

In a country with so diverse a population as the U.S., the search for "the normal family" is, we believe, a useless exercise. One set of norms cannot be used to describe health or pathology for *all* American families; we reject the traditional assumption that family normalcy lies only in the isolated nuclear family with strict role delineations of male as instrumental and female as expressive. We reject the traditional assumption of family conflict as evidence of family pathology. Feminist perspectives and values lead us to posit the following assumptions:

1. Family structures can differ; single parent, extended, and remarried families are frequent variations found in both urban and rural areas of the United States. Single people — lesbian, gay, or straight — and lesbian and gay couples also construct families. And as all of us pass through our life cycles, we will live in and pass through varied family structures. This is as it should be. Change is more normative than is status quo.

2. Both instrumental and expressive *tasks* — not roles — have to be accomplished in a family system. Both males and females should learn how to handle *all* family tasks so there will be more flexibility in the system over the life cycle. Women and men, girls and boys need to know about earning money, making hard decisions, and working with machines; men and women, boys and girls need to learn about cooking, mending, laundering, housekeeping, and childcare. The focus is on *tasks*, not on roles. Issues of equitability regarding these tasks must be taken into account; the double burden carried by many employed women, who do the bulk of domestic work as well as holding full time jobs, must be shared by men.

3. Simply put, females and males are of equal human value. In our work as family therapists and researchers, we must wrestle with our own socialization regarding gender equity. If, even after doing this, our ideal remains a patriarchy or matriarchy, we must make this value *explicit* to our clients (or readers). This is a matter of ethics.

IMPLICATIONS FOR FAMILY THERAPISTS

So how do we, as therapists, use sociological theory? The traditional functionalist assumption that the father's role is to be the breadwinner and the mother's role is to care for children has led therapists to speak of "overfunctioning mothers" and absent or peripheral fathers. When centrally defined in terms of family, women are more often blamed for family troubles. And when men are too rigidly defined in terms of occupation and breadwinning, they are reinforced to "underfunction" inside the family. Therapists may then excuse fathers/husbands from involvement in therapy because of work schedules and demands deemed important, whereas mothers are expected — and expect themselves — to take responsibility for therapeutic change. If a family therapist uses functionalist theory as a basis for diagnosing child and family troubles, mothers end up in a no-win situation.

In contrast with this mode of analysis, feminists start with a belief in the equal value of women and men; therapy proceeds from acknowledging the following realities:

1. Women make up the majority of people who seek therapy, for themselves as well as for families. They are the ones who most often take the initiative to call for the appointment. If we as therapists excuse the father or tread more lightly with him, we invalidate the woman's desire for change with our own "emotional smoothing of waters" and our own fear of conflict.

2. Women develop differently than do men, report their experiences differently, and indeed *have* different experiences. Biological factors interact with sociocultural factors to produce significant differences in the female and male experience. This means the experience of marriage and family is indeed different for husbands and wives. Research has consistently documented the marriage experience as being more negative for wives than for husbands (Bernard, 1973). We need to listen to this consistent finding and do something to rectify women's more negative experience with marriage if we really want to improve family life for all concerned.

3. The power of socialization cannot be overlooked when assessing gender issues generically and women's experiences specifically. Complex patterns of difference and similarity characterize the socialization of girls and boys (Block, 1979; Maccoby & Jacklin, 1974). This is good news. With learned behavior, change is possible, although it may take concerted and collective action. For our children's options to be different, we need to press for change in a variety of institutions — schools, childcare centers, places of work — as well as the interior of families.

4. Families as well as the individuals within them differ over the life cycle. Getting older matters; older women and men have different economics, different medical issues, different physiology, and a different view of the world than do younger women and men. Family therapists must take these realities into account.

5. Human experience takes place within a larger context — economic, developmental, political, and above all, cultural (Boss, 1987, 1988; Carter & McGoldrick, 1980). A woman's experience cannot be assessed apart from the context in which she has lived. Exploring how the role of women was defined at other times and places in a person's history, as well as now, is critical if we are to understand the present behavior of individuals, couples, and families. For example, although passivity has more often been the family rule for women than men, finding it otherwise or discovering that passivity did not serve ancestral women

well is useful information when one is contemplating change. Exploring the context of development recognizes the interaction between the individual, family, and larger society over time.

Based on these realities, we present new assumptions for family therapists to consider in their support of women as well as men in therapy.

NEW ASSUMPTIONS*

Women as Able to Refuse Nurturance

It is healthy for a woman to refuse to be nurturant at times. There is no reason why a woman should be solely responsible for the emotional well-being of husband, children, and aging parents, hers as well as his. There is no reason why men and boys cannot perform nurturant, caregiving tasks as well as women and girls. Since nurturance is primarily learned behavior, this behavior may disappear, especially in males, if it is not socially reinforced early and through life. It should not always fall on women and girls to do the nurturing tasks (Boss, 1986b).

Rather than rigid gender differentiation in marriages and families, what is needed is a new flexibility in the attitudes of both men and women about setting limits on nurturant behavior and the healthy use of boundaries in relationships. Women have traditionally not been as good as men in setting limits around their nurturant role. They take care of others before they take care of themselves; even today, some eat only when everyone else has been fed; many bake brownies for the PTA even if it means they have to get to work late or get up at dawn. Therapists need to give women permission to set limits, to establish boundaries, to say "No" at times and to be entitled to care for themselves as well as others.

According to the Parsonian paradigm of a healthy family, women and girls were supposed to be the "emotional fixers" for the family; they were not to refuse men and boys when they were emotionally needy. A wife could not refuse to tend to her husband's needs after a hard day at work, regardless of the difficulty of her own day; a sister could be told to wait on her brother, but not vice versa; and, carrying it to an extreme, a young daughter could not refuse her father if he came into her bed when her mother was indisposed. Women and girls from such intrusive families may even today have trouble saying "No" to demands for nurturance, even when they are extreme. Their compliance is not an innate seductiveness; it is simply a result of rigid

*These assumptions are based on Boss and Weiner, 1988.

socialization for women to be passive, nurturant, and selfless *at all times*. It leads often to a *learned* helplessness in family interaction (Boss, 1987, 1988).

Resulting from Parsonian beliefs, then, women more than men will have difficulty setting boundaries around caregiving tasks. They can become overwhelmed by tasks of caring for husband, children, parents, and in-laws. When women are exclusively prescribed the job of tending to human and social connections, they may see any breach or friction as their fault — or at least as something they should be able to fix if they are really a "good wife," a "good mother," a "good daughter," a "good daughter-in-law," or a "good sister." They may, for example, tend an elderly parent to the point of exhaustion without asking a brother or husband to share the burden. A single-parent mother may overcompensate by focusing on her child's well-being to the exclusion of her own health and well-being. Another example is found in the research on older families. Although adult male children help frail elderly parents with financial support, the female relatives, wives or daughters, are still left with the physical care of frail elderly (Abel, 1986). Even in older families, then, the no-win situation for women is replicated. Men earn money and women take care of people. But in fact, the majority of women caregivers also earn money, so they have an even heavier burden than Parsons and Bales intended.

Women as Equal: Periodic Dependence is not Solely a Female Condition

While it is true that women are usually smaller, less muscled, and shorter than men, technology and other such equalizers have now made differences in physical power much less relevant for married couples in terms of problem-solving, earning income, caring for children, and doing the mundane tasks of family living. Individual differences across gender and subculture and during certain life cycle events must be recognized. Indeed, women's endurance in childbearing and other rigorous activities may more than equalize male strength in the long view. And although negative attitudes about women's reproductive functions have always been used to justify the limits imposed on women in the arenas of intellect and achievement and to reinforce notions of female inferiority, in fact, mortality and morbidity statistics favor females overall from the fetal stage to old age and death.

Rather than viewing women as the "weaker sex," therefore, we assume that *both* males and females in families, old and young, will need help at times and should be able to ask for it and accept it from the other sex without negative sanction, shame, ridicule, or conditions. We all need help at times; periodic dependence is not solely a female condition.

Women as Sexual Beings

A woman's healthy sexual development is based on the assumption that both biology and environment matter. From our perspective, the latter (environment) gets more weight over the long run and the former (biology) receives more weight situationally (especially during pregnancy, lactation, and menopause). We assume females as well as males are interested in sex, but recognize that socialization and reinforcement can influence interest positively or negatively for *both* genders. For women, however, especially from middle-class American culture, social reinforcement has been guilt-laden and inhibiting. Today, the AIDS epidemic will also influence women's sexual development.

A woman's level of education or social class may alter her earlier socialization, so marital and family therapists must begin with an exploration of the client's assumptions about sex. The therapist must also be aware of his or her own feelings about female sexuality. It is sometimes a shock to find that limiting assumptions are woven deeply into our professional assessments of a client's behavior. At some level, we may all too easily agree with a client that a woman has indeed failed if she has not met her partner's sexual needs. And if she has deviated from society's double standard by having an extramarital affair, we, as therapists, may have to work at avoiding a punitive and shaming response.

Motherhood Defined Beyond Nurturance

The idealization of motherhood, pervasive pronatalism, and the assumption that mother is all-responsible for the child's well-being can cripple women in families.

A child's personality development is deeply influenced by what both parents do; rigid gender divisions can therefore lead to negative developmental outcomes. A family having a rigid gender division of labor—where the mother is defined by expressiveness and nurturance while the father is more instrumental—is a fragile system since it depends upon two parents *always* being present. If either one is absent (because of illness, work demands, death, or divorce), we then have, according to Parsons and Bales, a "deficit family structure" or a "broken family." These old assumptions normalized father absence (because it was for the instrumental reason of employment) and blamed mothers for being absent for the same reasons. Today, we assume that families can function well as long as it is clear to all members "who is in and who is out of the family." This more basic systems criterion has better predicted whether a family, regardless of its structure, can function in providing for the care and health of its members (Boss, 1977, 1980, 1986a, 1986b, 1987).

A woman's development of independence and self-sufficiency will therefore improve rather than threaten family functioning. Her interest in being nurturant must be complemented by her development of self-sufficiency in order to foster more flexibility in the family across the life span. Mothers have a chance to get out of the historical no-win situation this way. They will less likely be accused of overfunctioning, hovering, or clinging if they are also connected to the world outside of home and children. But before our clients can become more open to these ideas, we as therapists must wrestle with our own socialization concerning men, women, and family structure.

CONCLUSION

We have discussed four central sociological themes: (a) the issue of perspective and viewpoint (by starting with women's experiences, feminists have revealed male biases in traditional family sociology); (b) the issue of family form (functionalist reification and celebration of the "traditional" nuclear family versus feminist attention to the range of family forms); (c) the functionalist emphasis on equilibrium and balance versus feminist emphasis on structures of power and on processes of conflict and change; and (d) the functionalist view of the family as a relatively bounded and reactive unit versus feminist attention to context and the active relation of families to other institutions.

It is too simple to say that what is wrong for women in families is due to patriarchy. That is linear thinking. The problem is more complex and more contextual. Neither patriarchy nor matriarchy exclusively causes or solves problems in families. Rather, healthy families result from a continually renewing flexibility of structure and function that is based on equity between the genders and within each generation. Some sociologists fear absence of prescription will lead to anomie, rolelessness, and therefore chaos in society. On the contrary, feminist sociologists believe emphasis on equity and flexibility rather than on prescribed roles will lead to healthier family functioning and a greater enjoyment of marriage by women. The emotional smoothing of waters at all costs should no longer be the exclusive role of women in families; rather every family member, male and female, old and young, must take his or her share of responsibility for peacemaking and for honest confrontation when necessary. This is interactive systems theory at work. Traditional structure functional theory would not allow for such feedback and correction.

Sociologists have historically prided themselves on seeing the bigger picture. While the psychologist focuses on the micro perspective of traits and personalities, the sociologist focuses on social context. This broader perspective has made a major contribution to understanding how families work, but unfortunately it brought with it a focus on roles, prescriptions, proscriptions, and sanctions, defining narrowly what men and women were supposed to do (or not do). It is on this issue of prescribed roles (and thereby normalcy) that feminist sociologists and feminist family therapists have joined and differentiated themselves from traditional sociologists and family therapists. Here there is strong linkage between feminist sociology and feminist family therapy because there is agreement on the value of change and conflict; there is challenge to the singular value of status quo and peace at all cost; above all, there is agreement on the equal worth of women and men and girls and boys.

REFERENCES

Abel, E. (1986). Adult daughters and care for the elderly. *Feminist Studies, 12,* 479–497.

American Psychological Association. (1975). Report of the task force on sex bias and sex role stereotyping in psychotherapeutic practice. *American Psychologist, 30,* 1169–1175.

Barrett, M., & McIntosh, M. (1983). *The anti-social family.* London: Verso.

Berk, S. F. (1985). *The gender factory: The apportionment of work in American households.* New York: Plenum.

Bernard, J. (1973). *The future of marriage.* New York: Bantam.

Block, J. H. (1979). Another look at sex differentiation in the socialization behaviors of mothers and fathers. In J. Sherman & F. Denmark (Eds.), *The psychology of women: Future directions in research.* New York: Psychological Dimensions.

Boss, P. (1977, February). A clarification of the concept of psychological father presence in families experiencing ambiguity of boundary. *Journal of Marriage and the Family, 39*(1), 141–151.

Boss, P. (1980). Normative family stress: Family boundary changes across the lifespan. *Family Relations, 29*(4), 445–450.

Boss, P. (1986a). The process of gatekeeping in scientific publications. In M. Sussman (Ed.), The Charybdis complex [special issue] *Marriage and Family Review, 10*(1), 33–39.

Boss, P. (1986b). Psychological absence in intact families: A systems approach to a study on fathering. In M. Sussman (Ed.), The Charybdis complex [special issue] *Marriage and Family Review, 10*(1), 11–32.

Boss, P. (1987). Family Stress: Perception and context. In M. Sussman & S. Steinmetz (Eds.), *Handbook on marriage and the family* (pp. 695–723). New York: Plenum.

Boss, P. (1988). *Family stress management.* Newbury Park, CA: Sage.

Boss, P., & Weiner, J. P. (1988). Rethinking assumptions about women's development and family therapy. In C. J. Falicov (Ed.), *Family interactions: Continuity and change over the life cycle* (pp. 235–252). New York: Guilford Press.

Breines, W. & Gordon, L. (1983). Review essay: The new scholarship on family violence. *Signs, 8*(3), 490–531.

Brown, D., & Hellinger, M. (1975). Therapists' attitudes toward women. *Social Work, 20,* 266–270.

Carter, B., & McGoldrick, M. (1980). *The family life cycle: A framework for family therapy.* New York: Gardner Press.

Chodorow, N. (1978). *The reproduction of mothering, psychoanalysis, and the sociology of gender.* Berkeley: University of California Press.

Collier, J., Rosaldo, M., & Yanagisako, S. (1982). Is there a family? New anthropological views. In B. Thorne with M. Yalom (Eds.), *Rethinking the family: Some feminist questions* (pp. 25–39). New York: Longman.

DeVault, M. (1988). Doing housework: Feeding and family life. In N. Gerstel & H. E. Gross

(Eds.), *Families and work: Toward reconceptualization*. Philadelphia: Temple University Press.

DiLeonardo, M. (1987). The female world of cards and holidays: Women, families, and the work of kinship. *Signs, 12*(3), 440–453.

Fabrikant, B. (1974). The psychotherapist and the female patient: Perceptions, misperceptions, and change. In V. Franks & V. Burtle (Eds.), *Women and therapy*. New York: Brunner/Mazel.

Feinblatt, J., & Gold, A. (1976). Sex roles and the psychiatric referral process. *Sex Roles: A Journal of Research, 2*(2), 109–122.

Fishman P. (1983). Interaction: The work women do. In B. Thorne, C. Kramarae, & N. Henley (Eds.), *Language, gender and society* (pp. 89–101). Rowley, MA: Newbury House.

Friedan, B. (1963). *The feminine mystique*. New York: Norton.

Gelles, R. & Cornell, C. (1985). *Intimate violence in families*. Beverly Hills, CA: Sage Publications.

Gillespie, D. (1971). Who has the power? The marital struggle. *Journal of Marriage and the Family, 33*, 445–458.

Gurman, A., & Klein, M. (1981a). Marital and family conflicts. In H. Brodsky & R. Hare-Mustin (Eds.), *Women and psychotherapy*. New York: Guilford Press.

Gurman, A., & Klein, M. (1981b). Women and behavioral marriage and family therapy: An unconscious male bias? In E. Blechman (Ed.), *Contemporary issues in behavior modification with women*. New York: Guilford Press.

Hare-Mustin, R. (1978). A feminist approach to family therapy. *Family Process, 17*(4), 181–194.

Hartmann, H. (1981). The family as the locus of gender, class, and political struggle: The example of housework. *Signs, 6*(3), 366–394.

Hochschild, A. R. (1983). *The managed heart*. Berkeley: The University of California Press.

Maccoby, E., & Jacklin, C. (1974). *The psychology of sex differences*. Stanford, CA: Stanford University Press.

Malinowski, B. (1944). *A scientific theory of culture*. Chapel Hill: University of North Carolina Press.

Murdock, G. (1949). *Social structure*. New York: Macmillan.

Parsons, T., & Bales, R. F. (1955). *Family, socialization and interaction process*. Glencoe, IL: The Free Press.

Rich, A. (1976). *Of woman born*. New York: Norton.

Safilios-Rothschild, C. (1970). The study of family power structure: A review of 1960–1969. *Journal of Marriage and the Family, 32*, 539–552.

Smith, D. (1979). A sociology for women. In J. A. Sherman & E. T. Beck (Eds.), *The prism of sex* (pp. 135–187). Madison: University of Wisconsin Press.

Stacey, J., & Thorne, B. (1985). The missing feminist revolution in sociology. *Social Problems, 32*, 301–316.

Thorne, B. with Yalom, M. (Eds.) (1982). *Rethinking the family: Some feminist questions*. New York: Longman.

Weiner, J. P., & Boss, P. (1985). Exploring gender bias against women: Ethics for marriage and family therapy. *Counseling and Values, 30*(1), 9–23.

6
Epistemological Equality as the Fulfillment of Family Therapy

MORRIS TAGGART

SEVERAL YEARS AGO, at a time when my interest in feminism was barely begun, I heard a tribute to the poet, Muriel Rukeyser, on a National Public Radio newscast. Her name and work were quite unfamiliar to me, but I found my attention suddenly riveted by the reading of one of her poems:

Waiting for Icarus

He said he would be back and we'd drink wine together
He said that everything would be better than before
He said we were on the edge of a new relation
He said that he would never again cringe before his father
He said that he was going to invent full-time
He said he loved me that going into me
He said was going into the world and the sky
He said that all the buckles were very firm
He said the wax was the best wax
He said Wait for me here on the beach
He said Just don't cry.

I remember the gulls and the waves
I remember the islands going dark on the sea

I remember the girls laughing
I remember they said he only wanted to get away from me
I remember mother saying: Inventors are like poets, a trashy lot
I remember she told me that those who try out inventions are worse
I remember she added: Women who love such are the worst of all.

I have been waiting all day, or perhaps longer
I would have liked to try those wings myself.
It would have been better than this.

—Muriel Rukeyser (1978, p. 495)

What I experienced at that moment is hard to express. I remember a feeling of intoxication and release, a sense of something important happening, and an odd sensation that I was seeing something for the first time. I was of course familiar with the story of Daedalus and his son Icarus: how they had escaped the Minotaur's Labyrinth on wings of leather and wax, and how Icarus, unheeding of his father's warning, had flown too close to the sun. Like most people, I suppose, I understood the story as a cautionary tale of what happens to sons who disobey their fathers. Now, Rukeyser's extraordinary poetic vision had turned everything upside down. No longer was the event cast as something exclusively between men and their monsters. The sheer audacity of introducing a WOMAN as observer, commentator, and fellow-yearner after freedom was enough to call everything in the standard version into question.

In the weeks that followed, I noticed that the standard version of the Icarus tale demanded, *sotto voce*, allegiance to a particular cosmology designed to keep (some) men in their places and women absent altogether. Laws of Nature ("the way things *really* are," etc.) always loom large when the "haves" need to keep the "have-nots" in line. By contrast, Rukeyser's female witness seems much more interested in pragmatic details, such as the firmness of buckles and the quality of wax, when accounting for Icarus's death. Rather than saying "Amen" to a cosmic lesson well learned, she insists on personalizing everything—the loss of a lover, the loss of a dream. Yet, in a strange way that poets and women know about, the dream is not always lost by acknowledging its loss on this or that occasion. On the contrary, the dream of a place in the story lives on in the very realization that its time is not yet.

It is this audacity of women to insert themselves into the story, as well as the consequences for the story itself, that pull me into an interest in feminism. If for Rukeyser's nameless watcher the time was not fully yet, women family therapists have decided that the time for them "to insert themselves into the story" is *now*. What happens to family therapy's ancient cosmologies now that women define the field from their vantage points? What happens to *me*?

Being intrigued by feminism does not of course exempt me from its challenge, nor from the personal and professional disorientation that the challenge brings. The story into which women have now rightly and radically inserted themselves used to be, in a manner of speaking, *my* story. Is my place in it now contingent on my resisting these intruders and defending to the death the old truths? As a man, can I make common cause with women in the matter of their oppression at the hands of patriarchy? Do *I* have a place in the new story emerging as women reconstruct family therapy theory and practice along feminist lines? How do I deal with the anxiety that comes from feeling like a guest in (what I had assumed was) my own house? These, and the questions they beg, are complex issues and not, at least for me, amenable to facile solutions.

Despite welcoming the feminist critique, then, I am both witness to and target for it. In consequence, and at the most immediate level of writing this chapter, I bump up against a paradox. As a man, what can I say about epistemological equality in the context of a book largely written by women? Despite the fact that what I have to say may have all the appeal of a discussion on barnyard security to a chicken by the fox, I am obviously prepared to take the risk. I do so for several reasons. The first is that these particular "chickens" are not nearly as vulnerable as the patronizing metaphor above suggests. A decade-long awareness of the feminist critique of family therapy has enabled women to take very good care of themselves. Secondly and selfishly, I find I come alive intellectually and professionally when thinking about the feminist reconstruction of family therapy, and not the least part of this comes in the form of feedback from women who respond to what I write. Thirdly, I want to explore the paradox I find myself in, including whether men have anything to offer in support of women's cause. Fourthly, I write the chapter because I was invited by the editors to do so. Their invitation, typical of the support I have received from feminist colleagues, tells me they are willing to enter into the paradox with me. I trust that readers, particularly women readers, will be willing to do the same.

INTRODUCTION

Women have had stolen from us 'the power of naming', the power to put 'words' (i.e., interpretations and meanings) to the experiences we have and the images we see . . . As women have lost the power of naming, the intellectual landscape has lost the power of women. (Sheila Ruth, 1981, p. 45)

The rarefied realms of epistemology—that aspect of philosophy dealing with the origins, nature and limits of knowledge—may seem far removed from the down-to-earth practicalities of a family therapy that takes women's place seriously. Theory, especially in as abstract a form as a theory of knowledge, seems altogether too *male* a phenomenon to be of much use to women. Theorizing, the argument goes, is something that *men* do, and as often as not they do it *to* women.

Yet, the struggle by women to define *themselves* in this or any context raises profound theoretical and epistemological questions (cf. Taggart, 1985). Women's realization that *they* are the ones to define their nature and place in human affairs points to a radical break with past definitions of both theory and knowledge. When women criticize how the standard theories routinely construct them (as therapists *and* clients), they call those theories and their basic assumptions radically into question.

To reconstruct family therapy, then, feminists begin at the beginning. Knowledge as constituted in patriarchal tradition is defined so as to exclude women's participation as subjects in its production or as critics of its products. To the knowledge industry, women are designated consumers only. As Sheila Ruth (1981, p. 45) describes it: "Male voices, perspectives, interests, ideas, and modes dominate all thinking. For all intents and purposes, 'official' intellection and male intellection have become coextensive."

But who, it may be asked, argues for male hegemony with respect to thinking in family therapy? Have any family therapists—male or female—suggested that women are unable to think, or are otherwise incompetent to contribute to the ongoing development of family therapy? Are feminists implying that the journals and publishing houses are closed to them, or that they are not free to circulate their ideas at conferences and workshops? Have there not been in recent years many articles by feminists in the professional journals, even some books published, as well as a minor avalanche of feminist-oriented presentations at professional meetings?

Feminists, however, take little comfort from such recognition of their activities, especially if its major purpose is to present family therapy as bias-free. Despite its liberal pretentions, family therapy has failed to take feminists' activities seriously. Indeed, there is little evidence that, apart from other feminists and a few sympathizers, the field's writers are even aware of what feminists have written. Again, men simply do not attend feminist-oriented presentations at professional meetings. One feminist trainer (Bograd, 1987) has admitted that she has been toying with instituting a "Sadie Hawkins Rule" at her workshops—every woman who attends must have a man in tow in order to be admitted!

The ignoring by family therapy of its feminist theorists is all the more appalling in light of the field's insistence that *systems* theory provides its basic rationale. Whatever else the "systems" in "systems theory" refers to, it presumably conveys a sensitivity to what are punctuated as events within a particular system. If the family therapy literature systematically fails to take notice of, never mind grapple with, what feminist family therapists are saying, feminists will be excused if they view the implications as ominous. One implication is that the feminist critique is considered trivial, redundant, extraneous or otherwise unworthy of attention by the majority of the field's writers. But the ordinary standards of scholarship governing judgments of this kind require that they be made and substantiated *publicly*. Only then can the membership-at-large of a professional discipline be afforded the courtesy of participation in the discussion. What starts off as an insult to feminist theorists ends up as an affront to all family therapists. Further, the feminist critique, like the present volume, is concerned with remedying the invisibility of *women clients* in our formulations of the family. It is women in general, then, who bear the ultimate outrage.

From an explicitly systemic point of view, an equally sinister implication emerges. Could it be that feminist family therapists themselves are considered *outside* the family therapy system? Is "feminist" so alien and powerful a qualifier that it disqualifies the substantive "family therapist" altogether (cf. Taggart, 1987)? Putting feminists, and their potentially disruptive commentaries, outside the pale allows the orderly production of traditional family therapy to proceed with the minimum of interference. This way of defending the "established order" of closed systems is as well known to establishment theorists as it is to establishment politicians. In speaking of those who have a vested interest in things remaining as they are, Wilden (1980, p. 348) has observed. "Deviations, disturbances, contradictions, conflicts are therefore necessarily and consequently the work of OUTSIDE AGITATORS."

There are, of course, considerable advantages, to the proponents of mainline theories of keeping such agitators out. The exclusion of feminist criticisms of family therapy lends an air of unity to the field and helps substantiate its claims to the kind of seasoned maturity that presumably impresses public and private funding sources. Anyone raising questions as to how these considerations influence the theory and practice of family therapy (cf. Taggart, 1985) is clearly asking too much.

If feminist family therapists have indeed written and spoken of their vision for family therapy, and do so again in this volume, it is plainly not lack of opportunity that has robbed other authors of taking them seriously. That they have largely failed to do so is no simple sin of omission, but a continuation of patriarchy's historical attitude toward the aspirations of women. By continuing to produce "family therapy" as if the feminist critique did not exist, family therapy theorists intensify the patriarchal project of presenting as comprehensive and normative that which is partial and atypical.

It is this last comment that provides the central theme of the chapter. The question is whether or not family therapy can relinquish gender partiality as a defining feature of its evolution and move toward the equal acknowledgment of women's place in the family and women's place in family therapy. As we shall see, the issues implicit in the question have to do with whether family therapy is committed to equality at the deepest levels of its thinking and practice or whether, indeed, it can continue to be a safe place for women (and men) to be found.

EPISTEMOLOGICAL INEQUALITY AT THE CORE OF FAMILY THERAPY

Since the early 1970s, research has documented the ways in which such intellectual disciplines as history and psychology, literature and the fine arts, sociology and biology are biased according to sex. This work has revealed that on at least three counts the disciplines fall short of the ideal of epistemological equality for women: they exclude women from their subject matter, distort the female according to the male image of her, and deny value to characteristics the society considers feminine. (Jane Martin, 1985, p. 3)

Equality is such an instrinsically attractive notion that it is difficult to imagine serious opposition to it. This is particularly the case among family therapists. The field's radical beginnings almost ensured that those who made the break with traditional ways of doing psychotherapy were of a relatively liberal style and temperament. In its early days, family therapy had all the respectability of a floating crap game, and family therapists relished their maverick role. In such a context, it would have been unthinkable to suggest that the field's treatment of women was in any way traditional or biased. If anything, women were more active in creating the new field of family therapy than had ever been the case with more orthodox models. True, male leaders were still very much in the majority and, apart from Virginia Satir, few women achieved the status of such fathers-in-the-faith as Nathan Ackerman, Murray Bowen, Jay Haley, Don Jackson, Carl Whitaker, and Lyman Wynne.

It might be thought, then, that the first, critical test of family therapy's attitudes toward women came in the mid-1970s, when the feminist critique finally overtook the field. But, as Broderick and Schrader (1981) remind us, pioneers such as Mary Richmond (1908, 1917, 1928), Charlotte Towle (1948), Emily H. Mudd (1951), and many others were blazing the family therapy trail before most of our "founding forefathers" were out of grade school! As happened in so many fields, the *founding foremothers* of family therapy have been largely ignored and consequently have fallen into oblivion. The feminist challenge of the 1970s and 1980s (cf. Ault-Riche, 1986; Avis, 1985; Bograd, 1984; Carter, Papp, Silverstein, & Walters, 1983, 1984; Goldner, 1985a, 1985b, 1987a, 1987b, Chapter 3; Goodrich, Rampage, Ellman, & Halstead, 1988; Hare-Mustin, 1978, 1980, 1987, Chapter 4; Hare-Mustin & Marecek, 1986; James & McIntyre, 1983; Libow, Raskin, & Caust, 1982; Margolin, Talovic, Fernandez, & Onorato, 1983; Wheeler, 1985) has thus fallen upon a field that was instinctively patriarchal in its values. The liberal self-image of family therapists only served to make their rejection of feminist contributions all the more piously acrimonious, that is, when they deigned to note them at all.

Additionally, the feminist critique of family therapy appeared on the scene at a time when the field was preoccupied with its own theoretical and professional consolidation. Winning the battle for recognition with governmental and professional bodies (becoming "one of the boys"?) was judged to be more important than paying attention to what a "few women" were saying. Whatever benefits that consolidation has resulted in — accreditation structures, licensing, NIMH grants, successful lobbying, peer status with the "big boys" among other professional associations, etc. — we do well to remember that in effect they have been bought at the price of ignoring women's claims to be taken seriously.

What in all of this is hardest to understand is that the pattern of ignoring the feminist critique extends to that aspect of family therapy which has had least excuse for doing so. I refer to those working to renew the field's epistemological assumptions. Here, one would have assumed, feminist formulations might have made some inroads, if only because of their obvious relevance to any theory of how knowledge in family therapy is constructed or comes about. "Thinking about thinking" presumes an interest in *thinkers and what might operate to shape their thinking*. Feminists insist that knowledge is socially constructed, i.e., it is invented by human beings who have "limited access to explanations and limited claims to infallibility" (Spender, 1981, p. 1). It would seem, then, that an analysis of the gendered power relations inherent in the production and codification of knowledge is an indispensable ingredient of epistemological work. Feminist theorists (cf. Belenky, Clinchy, Goldberger, & Tarule, 1986; Harding, 1986; Keller, 1985) have already proposed theories of knowledge that address these issues directly. For all the notice taken by epistemological pundits within family therapy, one might never know that they had done anything of the sort.

The issue here is not just a general one. Specifically, issues have been raised about how *context* is handled in family therapy (cf. Goldner, 1987a; James & McIntyre, 1983; Taggart, 1985), which go to the heart of the field's understanding of itself as *systemic*. This work has noted the ways in which established theory fails to take account of how social context defines both theory construction and clinical practice in family therapy. When "the family" is viewed as a-thing-in-itself, cut off from the social and political contexts that constitute it and its problems, women's issues tend to be ignored, reframed as something else, or recast as women's fault. When the "theorist-and-his-theorizing" is likewise viewed as a-thing-in-itself, cut off from the social and political contexts that constitute *it*, the ignoring of feminist theory follows without difficulty.

To take just one typical example, it is one thing to write: "One of the most central among our own epistemological presuppositions, is that reality—for human beings, at least—is always necessarily contextual" (O'Hanlon & Wilk, 1987, p. 183). But it is clearly something else to find, among the nearly 300 pages this quotation represents, any acknowledgment that feminists have written about these topics or, indeed, that feminists and their writings are a part of the context of any "reality" of interest to these writers.

But the invisibility of women in family therapy is not just a matter of being left off the canvas. It happens equally at the finest brush-level of a sentence fragment: "A cybernetic system, whether it involves man and canoe or a husband and wife, can be defined as follows . . . " (Keeney & Ross, 1985, p. 51). Since, as every schoolboy knows, *man/husband* is the measure of things, *he* survives the cybernetic metaphor. *Wife*, as if we didn't already know, disappears into a thing.

It could be argued, I suppose, that these volumes deal with *clinical* epistemology and therefore cannot be expected to deal with the kinds of fundamental assumptions that the term "epistemology" typifies. But this defense only lends substance to Bogdan's (1987) criticism that "epistemology" is a misnomer here, and that the term should be dropped in favor of, say, a more fruitful consideration of the domain of social psychology. Bogdan's arguments have merit, though I would contend that the misuse of "epistemology" in much that goes by the name of "clinical epistemology" has at least the value of drawing attention to the unfinished epistemological tasks. Consequently, I am reluctant to assign questions about the system/context relations of family therapy to the vague hope that family therapists will begin to pay attention to social psychology. Questions of context are basic to family therapy's claim to be systemically based (cf. Taggart, 1985), and as such are quite properly designated as epistemological.

The ignoring of feminist colleagues, as well as the exclusion of their substantive contributions, is an *epistemological* crisis and throws serious doubt on the validity and adequacy of knowledge-making in family therapy. As long as androcentric theory continues to represent its partial and defective account of family therapy as somehow full and complete, to that extent family therapy—theory, practice, politics—is unfulfilled. It is for this reason that I refer to epistemological equality — the attempt to achieve theories that take women and their aspirations fully into account — as the *fulfilling* of family therapy. The search for epistemological equality has to do with whether or not the field of family therapy can become a safe place for women as therapists *and* clients. It is hard not to see this as a question of the field's survival.

EPISTEMOLOGICAL EQUALITY AS THE FULFILLING OF FAMILY THERAPY

The phrase "epistemological equality" does not mean equal participation in male rationality; it means equal acknowledgement for male and female minds, lives, and histories. (Elisabeth Young-Bruehl, 1987, p. 211)

The position taken in this chapter so far has been that, compared with the status granted males, family therapy lacks equal acknowledgment of female minds, lives, and histories. In consequence, its account of how its knowledge base is constructed, justified, and translated into practice is *necessarily* incomplete and incompetent. An important question is: Can there be alternative modes of knowledge-seeking which are not structured by family therapy's androcentric biases? Is a specifically feminist epistemology of family therapy possible? If possible, would a feminist epistemology be of relevance only to women, or would it be designed to replace the existing epistemology for both women and men?

The Forms and Functions of Feminist Epistemology

While the term "epistemology" has not figured much in feminist family therapy literature, it is clear that an epistemological intent underlies most of what feminists have had to say. As Jean Baker Miller (1976, p. 136) foresaw in 1976, when women take the responsibility of seeking their self-determined goals, "it advances and fosters both attempts at knowledge and a personal conviction about the content and methods of getting knowledge. It creates a new sense of connection between knowledge, work, and personal life." As women explore what Carol Gilligan (1982, p. 173) calls "the tie between relationship and responsibility, and the origins of aggression in the failure of connectivity," they prepare the ground for an approach to knowledge and knowledge-making that does not demand the disowning of large parts of their experience. The quest for self and voice — through the positions of *received, procedural*, and *subjective* knowledge to a position of *constructing* one's own frames for knowing — not only calls the dominant epistemology radically into question, but also enables women to integrate their knowledge-*making* with the caring, cooperative, and committed dimensions of their everyday lives (Belenky et al., 1986).

While the epistemological significance of the feminist viewpoint for psychology and family therapy is becoming more and more explicit, it is to the longer-established debate within social science generally that we turn to get a sense of where this concern with knowledge and knowledge-making might be taking us. The issues surrounding the emergence of feminist epistemologies in both the natural and social sciences have been taken up most directly perhaps by Sandra Harding (1986, 1987a, 1987b). In discussing the significance of these issues for family therapy, I can do no better than follow her argument closely, applying it to the case of family therapy along the way.

AMBIVALENCES. Harding (1986, pp. 137–141) notes several ambivalences among feminists themselves regarding the construction of distinctively feminist epistemologies. One is the appeal to the argument (p. 137): "Men see the world in one way, women in another; on what possible grounds other than gender loyalties can we decide between these conflicting accounts?" If family therapy *is* a social product—i.e., its claims to knowledge *always* reflect the social location (including gender) of its theorists and practitioners—does this mean that a feminist account of family therapy has no more (or less) validity than an androcentric one?

In response, Harding would undoubtedly wonder if such extreme subjectivism fails too much to challenge the split between facts and values claimed by traditional science. With Keller (1982, 1985), Harding (1986, p. 138) insists that "the leap to relativism misgrasps feminist projects." The main interest of feminist theories, she argues, is not to supplant "man-centered" with "woman-centered" formulations, but rather to develop theories that are free from gender loyalties. Given where things are, this means that feminists first of all have to devise a woman-centered formulation just to understand what a gender-free one would look like. The ultimate goal, however, is "to achieve theories that accurately represent women's activities as fully social, and social relationships between the genders as a real—and explanatorily important—component in human history" (1986, p. 138). She goes on to emphasize that there is nothing relativistic or "subjective" about such a project. It is rather traditional thought that subjectively distorts its projects through its androcentric bias.

Yet another ambivalence is raised by Harding (1986, p. 138) in relation to the work of Elizabeth Fee (1981). Fee argues that, in the absence of a feminist society, it is simply not possible to imagine what a feminist science would look like. What is feasible currently is a feminist critique of existing science, and all talk of a feminist epistemology is premature. We should look instead for an alternative science by paying attention to the methods and modes of *practice* that feminist scientists use.

Fee's argument will undoubtedly appeal to some feminist family therapists. The search for a feminist epistemology of family therapy at this stage, they argue, smacks too much of (male) grandiosity, and feminists are better employed in developing a distinctively feminist *practice*. But, as Goldner (1987a) has suggested, when theory is too much the handmaiden of clinical practice, the moral, political, historical, and economic dilemmas of family life are ignored. This is the "black hole" aspect of practice that tends to capture all wider concerns and renders them invisible. "Theory" becomes clinical theory and ends up a mere justification for what therapists want to do in any case. "Epistemology" becomes "clinical epistemology" and finds its major function in the refinement of a clinical technology which itself is immune to criticism.

FEMINIST EMPIRICISM. For feminists working in areas where traditional empiricism still dominates (e.g., the natural sciences and the "harder" social sciences such as psychology and sociology), feminist empiricism has emerged as an epistemological alternative (cf. Harding, 1987b, pp. 182–184). Feminist empiricists argue that it is possible to eliminate the gender biases of traditional research by paying closer attention to the existing procedural norms of scientific inquiry. It is thus the incomplete way that empiricism has been practiced — its failure to adhere to its own rules — that feminist empiricism challenges. The social values and political agendas of feminist perspectives, it is argued, work to enlarge the scope of topics chosen for study, as well as generating greater care against sexist bias in the conduct of research.

It is clear that feminist empiricism is an important alternative for those who work where traditional empiricism still holds sway, and can be a powerful tool in challenging established procedures along lines that the establishment presumably respects. Thus, feminist empiricists play a similar role to that of feminist family therapists who accuse their colleagues of failing to live up to their systemic heritage. It may, nevertheless, have little to offer feminists in family therapy, simply because of the (unfortunate?) fact that empirical research plays such a small role in the field. This is not to say, however, that women doing empirical research in family therapy do not deserve all the support they can get from feminist colleagues. For one thing, their work and witness are an important aspect of the overall pattern of feminist activity in the field and, in any case, they have the right to justify their feminist strategies in *their* particular way. For another, the paucity of empirical research in family therapy paradoxically inflates the importance of what does get done. Such work tends to be overvalued by nonresearchers, especially in the Congress and other important arenas. Feminists need their feminist empiricist colleagues to support the case for equality where only their research talents will gain a hearing.

FEMINIST STANDPOINT EPISTEMOLOGIES. Of potentially greater interest to feminist family therapists are what have come to be known as feminist standpoint epistemologies. A standpoint is defined as "an interested ('interested' in the sense of 'engaged,' not 'biased') social location the conditions for which bestow upon its occupants scientific and epistemic advantage" (Harding, 1986, p. 148). At the core of standpoint arguments (cf. Hartsock, 1984, 1987; Rose, 1983, 1984) lies the insistence that feminist claims to knowledge are *more complete* and *less distorting* than are men's because they arise out of a more complete and less distorting kind of social experience. In both the epistemology and the society constructed by men, the real and material relationships between human beings, as well as those between humans and the natural world, are obscured. Committed as they are to severing culture from nature, knowledge from politics, biology from history, the self from the body, and family therapy from a fully human way of life, men avoid material (corporeal, sensuous, practical, relational) reality and structure their social relations (and their understanding of social relations) in abstract and idealized terms. Though women have the potential to experience their lives differently, men's conceptual schemes are the ruling ones. Women are thus alienated from their own experience, and this is the essence of their oppression.

The significance of the feminist movement is that it helps women to envision a world very different from that doled out to them by the patriarchy. As the scales fall away from their eyes, new knowledge emerges for the oppressed through the intellectual and political struggles they wage with their oppressors. The pursuit of justice and the quest for truth become one, in that women's experience can be made to yield up a truer (or less false) image of social reality than that available to men of the ruling classes and races.

There are several factors which, I believe, make standpoint theories attractive to feminist family therapists. It seems obvious, first of all, that feminist family therapists are already engaged in, and *understand themselves to be engaged in*, formulating "a truer image" of both family relations and family therapy than any developed by traditional theories. Despite the patriarchy's claim that such feminist theories represent the political interests of only a segment of family therapy, there is an important sense in which feminist theories are *more inclusive* than the standard ones. The latter maintain their hegemony by ignoring the misery generated by their exclusion of women from knowledge-making. Feminist theories, on the other hand, necessarily include the standard theories *and* their oppressive aftermath.

Another advantage of standpoint theories is their clarifying function with respect to a more unified relation between feminist theory and feminist practice. A feminist standpoint is not an attitudinal perspective to be claimed, but a political and intellectual *struggle for liberation* in which to be engaged. Since theory can now be seen as having an emancipatory aspect, no longer need it be a self-contained activity in opposition to practice. A common purpose, i.e., the struggle against oppression, now unites the three modes of feminist knowledge-making — theory, political activity, and clinical practice — into a fully recursive alliance. No longer will the family be considered a convenient void on which theorists may map the attributes of abstract and ideal systems. The struggle for justice and equality assures that family therapy will address, and be informed by, the real and material relations of family life.

TRANSITIONAL EPISTEMOLOGIES FOR TRANSITIONAL CULTURES. Whatever the tensions at play among feminist attempts to reformulate epistemology, and there are many (cf. Grimshaw, 1986), these are signs of vitality rather than implications of failure. Feminists are well aware that they live in a transitional culture in which the formerly solid understandings of family therapy are coming apart at the seams (cf. Harding, 1987b, pp. 186–187). There is no reason to expect that the epistemologies born out of such changes will be any less transitional. In any case, feminism arose out of a commitment to take women's experiences and formulations seriously. Implicit in this is a pledge by feminists to treat their differences with other feminists as what Bateson (1972, p. 454) called "news of a difference" — the *only* source of information about who, where, and what we are. In this way, hopefully, feminism can avoid the internecine warfare that plagues male discourse.

Perhaps, then, there will be a major difference between how tensions and contradictions are handled among feminist epistemologists as compared with their male counterparts. Young-Bruehl (1987), whose quotation opened this section, has stated that philosophizing among women need *not* take the usual patriarchal forms. Men, she says, set up in the knowledge business as solitary entrepreneurs, each in cut-throat competition with the other. Women, given their ability to live in relational reality, are more likely to be aware of their supporters — those who have encouraged them to do what the dominant culture says they cannot or should not do: *think*. As often as not, the stimulus to think comes courtesy of those with whom we differ.

EPISTEMOLOGICAL EQUALITY: BY WHOM FOR WHOM?

Men must learn to be silent. This is probably very painful for them. (Marguerite Duras, 1981)

If a critical need in family therapy is the securing of epistemological equality, on whose shoulders does the task mainly fall? At one level, this asks who will actually create models of knowledge-making in family therapy that measure up to the ideals of epistemological equality. Given the argument thus far, it seems clear that the task belongs primarily, even exclusively, to feminist family therapists themselves. On epistemological grounds, only women can *know* the reality of their exclusion from knowledge-making, and only women can *know* what would constitute equality for them.

It is difficult to imagine what a man could say on the matter that would not be, as it were, hearsay (i.e., derivative of what women have already said). Whether men have *any* role here is an enormously complicated question, and some mention is made of it later in the chapter. But, further, on empirical grounds, nonfeminists in family therapy have had a decade or more to acknowledge feminist claims to knowledge-making, with little to show for their opportunity. To look to such for initiatives along these lines, or even support, seems unproductive. In any case, the situation is analogous to all movements for liberation. Freedom cannot be granted. In a manner of speaking, it must be taken. For the women in family therapy to take their epistemological destiny into their own hands seems altogether congruent with a struggle for liberation.

Some may be troubled by the apparent conflation of "feminist" with "women" in the preceding paragraphs. There may be situations where it is not useful to treat "feminist" and "women" as if they were identical (cf. Gordon, 1986), but the epistemological discussion is hardly one of them. There is, I suppose in theory at least, the possibility of a nonfeminist, womanly epistemology which, if realizable, would be competent to raise its own issues as far as epistemological equality is concerned. More likely, other oppressed groups within family therapy (blacks, Hispanics, male homosexuals, lesbians, etc.) may at some point experience their oppression at the epistemological level and construct models of knowledge-making more consonant with their concerns. Even so, only feminists are competent to unravel the questions that only they can raise.

It seems clear that family therapy has need of (some) women to take up directly the task of creating epistemologies that more equitably reflect women as knowledge-makers. For some to make this their major sphere of teaching and research would guarantee that the fundamental issues which epistemology treats would gain a more explicit presence among us. Another advantage of this development would be a readier access to the contributions of feminist epistemologists in other fields.

But there is another level at which the question—on whose shoulders does the task of creating epistemological equality fall?—must be asked. This refers not to the relatively few feminist epistemologists actually constructing the new models, but to the much larger, but equally indispensable, community of their readers. Epistemologies, after all, do not originate with those who formulate them. They arise instead in response to the new ventures in knowledge-making which cannot be contained by the old epistemological structures. Feminist epistemology in particular is not constructed by a few "masters" who then must market their product to "consumers." Authorship and readership are in a much more explicitly interactional and nonhierarchical relationship in which one influences (is influenced by) and nurtures (is nurtured by) the other. Thus, there is a need for informed readers who can enter into a mutually instructive and supportive relationship with authors.

Within the family therapy field itself, this mutual interaction between feminist writers and their readership appears to operate freely. The feminist commitment to women's solidarity, as well as the relatively small size of the family therapy community, makes for easy access between feminist theorists and their readers. Networking has become a way of life for feminists generally, and feminists at all levels in family therapy make contact with each other routinely at workshops, conferences, and other settings. In addition, the fact that the authors themselves work primarily as therapists, as well as trainers of therapists, helps guarantee a community of interests with their readers and a common language for dialogue.

It is at the point of introducing the epistemological contributions of feminists in other fields that a mutually supportive relationship between writers and readers will be most vital. On the one hand, readers will be challenged to grapple with the relatively unfamiliar vocabularies and forms of argument found in such areas as the feminist critique of science (cf. Harding, 1986, 1987a, 1987b; Keller, 1982, 1985, 1986; Rose, 1983, 1984), feminist philosophy (cf. Grimshaw, 1986; Ruth, 1981; Young-Bruehl, 1987), feminist political and legal studies (cf. Hartsock, 1984, 1987; MacKinnon, 1987), and feminist literary criticism (cf. Jehlen, 1982; Miller, 1986; Modleski, 1986). On the other hand, authors will surely be encouraged to render such treasures in terms their family therapist readers can appreciate. Only as feminist authors and feminist readers continue to influence and nourish each other can the full riches of feminist scholarship meld with the rich experience of feminist family therapists.

Do Men have a Place?

If, as I have so far suggested, the task of securing epistemological equality is one that belongs to the women in family therapy, do men have any role in this enterprise? To put the question more bluntly — why should anything in this chapter be taken seriously by women since it is in fact written by a man? Feminist consciousness, after all, arose from women's realization that they stand outside the system of male reference. A core part of that consciousness emerges out of the discovery that women's direct experience of their lives has the power to transform women's vision. What credibility can be attached to a man's view of women's oppression?

Spender (1985) insists that such questions have profound practical as well as theoretical implications. On the practical side, she wonders (p. 110) what will happen to *women's authority as feminists* if and when men are allowed validity in the feminist frame of reference:

> Do we welcome men as feminists, in the knowledge that men are disproportionately promoted even in women's fields, and that there is the possibility that men will become the authorities on feminism and define it in their own terms? Or do we claim that this is the unique area of women's authority and that, while men can give support, can be pro-feminist, they are not the real thing — and this in the knowledge that we are defining men as suspect?

Nor are the theoretical issues (p. 109) less thorny:

> If feminism is women's claim for full humanity in a society where full humanity is a male birthright, what does it mean when a man claims to be a feminist? Is it a mark of merit when a man identifies with women's cause? . . . Knowing that it will carry more weight, among women and men, should feminists seek to have men espouse their cause? Is it the *same* cause?

For Stanley and Wise (1983, p. 18), the answer is hardly equivocal:

> We reject the idea that men can be feminists because we argue that what is essential to "being feminist" is the possession of "feminist consciousness." And we see feminist consciousness as rooted in the concrete, practical and everyday experiences of being, and being treated as, *a woman*. . . . No men know what it is to be treated as a woman; and even fewer interpret such treatment in the ways we shall define as central to "feminist consciousness."

Spender (1985) takes a slightly different view. On the crucial issue of whether or not it is necessary to have *direct* experience of a state or event in order to have an authentic view of it, she recalls that *direct experience*, in general, constitutes only a fraction of what we know. She argues that, as human beings, we have the means of transcending our own immediate realm and are able to learn from the direct experience of others. What is required, however, is a *willingness to learn*, and herein lies the stumbling block (p. 110):

> . . . it has been necessary for women to learn about men in the interest of their survival. There has been no such compulsion upon men to learn from women.

And in a society predicated upon male authority there has been no *need* for men to learn from women.

When neither force nor necessity requires men to seek knowledge from women, it would be an unusual if not inexplicable act for a man to take a woman as his teacher.

In trying to locate myself among these questions, I am inclined at this point in my journey to follow Stanley and Wise (1983) in concluding that a man cannot be a feminist. Men who say they are feminists claim too much and too easily. The fallacy, I believe, arises from the typical liberal conceit that "feminist" refers to a personal trait connoting the opposite of "biased." Such a definition totally ignores feminism's historical philosophical, and political character, and supports the notion that the feminist critique of family therapy can be met by changing an unfortunate attitude or two. Further, it assumes that family therapy as traditionally formulated is preserved while such minor adjustments are made.

At the same time, I recognize the force of Spender's (1985) suggestion that a man can be pro-feminist, but only if he takes the "inexplicable" step of taking a woman as his teacher. In family therapy tradition, "taking a teacher" has come to have a very specific meaning. It is more than reading books, attending workshops, or otherwise exposing oneself in a limited way to some teacher's store of knowledge. "Taking a teacher" in our context means above all *getting into supervision with a woman* (say, a feminist family therapist), opening up one's work to the supervisor's scrutiny, and dealing directly with the implications of her input for one's thinking and doing. This will never make a man a feminist, but may help to raise his pro-feminist consciousness beyond the more usual liberal reflex of claiming identification with women's cause.

But these clarifications still do not imply that a "pro-feminist man" carries any more *authority* within the feminist frame of reference than any other man. Perhaps, and it will be up to women to decide, what a pro-feminist man has to say about women's causes may be experienced by feminists as interesting, infuriating, informative, insensitive or whatever, but it can never be taken as authoritative. Whatever colleagueship can exist between feminists and pro-feminist men, there are important senses in which the latter can only be marginal to the feminist project.

Having declared himself pro-feminist, the pro-feminist man in effect also establishes his marginality with respect to men in general, and it may, paradoxically, be here that his major, though modest, contribution to the discourse on women's cause appears. The pro-feminist male family therapist represents a position of "thirdness" (triangularity) with respect to what traditional (androcentric) family therapy might otherwise consider to be a purely either/or struggle between its own views and those of feminist family therapy. A pro-feminist male presence in the discourse serves to undermine the patriarchy's disposition to treat the feminist message of *difference* as an *unmediated opposition* (cf. Wilden, 1980, p. 220) between "us" (men) and "them" (women).

Whether or not an authentic pro-feminist position will actually emerge to play a role in these matters depends on the capacity of pro-feminists to develop a point of view which is more than an echo of the feminist position (cf. Kaufman, 1987). The question is surely not whether pro-feminists are being nice to feminists or, alternatively, trying to steal the revolution. The matter is more one of whether feminists and pro-feminists can be collaborators without either group usurping the other's unique authority. Even here it is worth remembering that, as Spender (1985, pp. 109–110) puts it, " . . . such a coexistence presumes an end of male authority — a lynchpin in male supremacy, and one which feminists are determined to remove."

CONCLUSION

When my paper, "The Feminist Critique in Epistemological Perspective: Questions of Context in Family Therapy," was accepted for publication, I sent out 50 preprints to friends and colleagues across the United States and abroad. It so happened that 25 copies went to women, and 25 to men. Within three weeks, I had heard in writing from all the women except two. Of these two remaining, one wrote after several months, and the other I never heard from. In the year and more between the paper's acceptance and its appearance in print, I heard from two of the 25 men. One is a family therapist with whom I had enjoyed a couple of conversations on things philosophical, while the other is a neuropsychological psychologist who comes at epistemology from his interest in perception.

Apart from the pattern of responses, I was intrigued with the comments that the women made and the questions they raised. They *were* interested in the "baby" and commented at length on the paper's content. But they were also interested in the "pregnancy," and wondered about *me* and the process by which the paper had come about.

In closing, it is thus with some confidence that I put into practice for myself one of the ideals held up for others in the chapter. This is to invite the kind of collaborative feedback-loop between readers and myself that will lead to a mutually supportive, nurturing, and instructive relationship for all of us.

REFERENCES

Ault-Riche, M. (1986). *Women and family therapy*. Rockville, MD: Aspen.
Avis, J. M. (1985). The politics of functional family therapy: A feminist critique. *Journal of Marital and Family Therapy, 11*, 127–138.

Bateson, G. (1972). *Steps to an ecology of mind*. New York: Ballantine.
Belenky, M. F., Clinchy, B. M., Goldberger, N. R., & Tarule, J. M. (1986). *Women's ways of knowing: The development of self, voice, and mind*. New York: Basic Books.
Bogdan, J. (1987). "Epistemology" as a semantic pollutant. *Journal of Marital and Family Therapy, 13*, 27–35.
Bograd, M. (1984). Family systems approaches to wife battering: A feminist critique. *American Journal of Orthopsychiatry, 54*, 558–568.
Bograd, M. (1987). Private Communication.
Broderick, C. B., & Schrader, S. S. (1981). The history of professional marriage and family therapy. In A. S. Gurman & D. P. Kniskern (Eds.). *Handbook of family therapy* (pp. 5–35). New York: Brunner/Mazel.
Carter, B. A., Papp, P., Silverstein, O., & Walters, M. (1983). *Mothers and daughters*. Monograph Series, 1(1). Washington: The Women's Project in Family Therapy.
Carter, B. A., Papp, P., Silverstein, O., & Walters, M. (1984). *Mother and sons, father and daughters*. Monograph Series, 2(1). Washington: The Women's Project in Family Therapy.
Duras, M. (1981). Interview in S. Horer & J. Socquet. *La création étouffée*. Paris: Horay. Excerpted in E. Marks & I. Courtivron (Eds.). *New french feminisms* (pp. 111–113). New York: Schocken Books.
Fee, E. (1981). Women's nature and scientific objectivity. In M. Lowe & R. Hubbard (Eds.). *Woman's nature: Rationalizations of inequality*. New York; Pergamon Press
Gilligan, C. (1982). *In a different voice: Psychological theory and women's development*. Cambridge: Harvard University Press.
Goldner, V. (1985a). Feminism and family therapy. *Family Process, 24*, 31–47.
Goldner, V. (1985b). Warning: Family therapy may be dangerous to your health. *Family Therapy Networker, 9*, 19–23.
Goldner, V. (1987a). Instrumentalism, feminism, and the limits of family therapy. *Journal of Family Psychology, 1*, 109–116.
Goldner, V. (1987b). Generation and gender: Normative and covert hierarchies. *Family Process, 27*, 17–31.
Goodrich, T. J., Rampage, C., Ellman, B., & Halstead, K. (1988). *Feminist family therapy: A casebook*. New York: Norton.
Gordon, L. (1986). What's new in women's history? In T. de Lauretis (Ed.). *Feminist studies/Critical studies* (pp. 20–30). Bloomington, IN: Indiana University Press.
Grimshaw, J. (1986). *Philosophy and feminist thinking*. Minneapolis: University of Minnesota Press.
Harding, S. (1986). *The science question in feminism*. Ithaca, NY: Cornell University Press.
Harding, S. (1987a). Introduction: Is there a feminist method? In S. Harding (Ed.). *Feminism and methodology* (pp. 1–14). Bloomington, IN: Indiana University Press.
Harding, S. (1987b). Conclusion: Epistemological questions. In S. Harding (Ed.). *Feminism and methodology* (pp. 181–190). Bloomington, IN: Indiana University Press.
Hare-Mustin, R. T. (1978). A feminist approach to family therapy. *Family Process, 17*, 181–194.
Hare-Mustin, R. T. (1980). Family therapy may be dangerous for your health. *Professional Psychology, 11*, 935–938.
Hare-Mustin, R. T. (1987). The problem of gender in family therapy theory. *Family Process, 26*, 15–27.
Hare-Mustin, R. T., & Marecek, J. (1986). Autonomy and gender: Some questions for therapists. *Psychotherapy, 23*, 203–212.
Hartsock, N. (1984). *Money, sex and power*. Boston: Northeastern University Press.
Hartsock, N. (1987). The feminist standpoint: Developing the ground for a specifically feminist historical materialism. In S. Harding (Ed.). *Feminism and methodology* (pp. 157–180). Bloomington, IN: Indiana University Press.
James, K., & McIntyre, D. (1983). The reproduction of families: The social role of family therapy? *Journal of Marital and Family Therapy, 9*, 119–129.
Jehlen, M. (1982). Archimedes and the paradox of feminist criticism. In N. O. Keohane, M. Z. Rosaldo, & B. C. Gelpi (Eds.). *Feminist theory: A critique of ideology* (pp. 189–215). Chicago: University of Chicago Press.
Kaufman, M. (Ed.). (1987). *Beyond patriarchy: Essays by men on pleasure, power, and change*. New York: Oxford University Press.

Keeney, B. P., & Ross, J. M. (1985). *Mind in therapy: Constructing systemic family therapies.* New York: Basic Books.

Keller, E. F. (1982). Feminism and science. In N. O. Keohane, M. Z. Rosaldo, & B. C. Gelpi (Eds.). *Feminist theory: A critique of ideology* (pp. 113–126). Chicago: University of Chicago Press.

Keller, E. F. (1985). *Reflections on gender and science.* New Haven: Yale University Press.

Keller, E. F. (1986). Making gender visible in the pursuit of nature's secrets. In T. de Lauretis (Ed.). *Feminist studies/critical studies* (pp. 67–77). Bloomington, IN: Indiana University Press.

Libow, J. A., Raskin, P. A., & Caust, B. L. (1982). Feminist and family therapy systems: Are they irreconcilable? *American Journal of Family Therapy, 10,* 3–12.

MacKinnon, C. (1987). Feminism, Marxism, method, and the state. In S. Harding (Ed.). *Feminism and methodology* (pp. 135–156). Bloomington, IN: Indiana University Press.

Margolin, G., Talovic, S., Fernandez, V., & Onorato, R. (1983). Sex role considerations and behavioral marital therapy: Equal does not mean identical. *Journal of Marital and Family Therapy, 9,* 131–145.

Martin, J. R. (1985) *Reclaiming a conversation: The ideal of the educated woman.* New Haven: Yale University Press.

Miller, J. B. (1986). *Toward a new psychology of women* (2nd ed.). Boston: Beacon Press.

Miller, N. K. (1986). Changing the subject: Authorship, writing, and the reader. In T. de Lauretis (Ed.). *Feminist studies/critical studies* (pp. 102–120). Bloomington, IN: Indiana University Press.

Modleski, T. (1986). Feminism and the power of interpretation: Some critical readings. In T. de Lauretis (Ed.). *Feminist studies/critical studies* (pp. 121–138). Bloomington, IN: Indiana University Press.

Mudd, E. (1951). *The practice of marriage counseling.* New York: Association Press.

O'Hanlon, B., & Wilk, J. (1987). *Shifting contexts: The generation of effective psychotherapy.* New York: Guilford Press.

Richmond, M. E. (1908). *A real story of a real family.* Publisher unknown.

Richmond, M. E. (1917). *Social diagnosis.* New York: Russell Sage.

Richmond, M. E. (1928). Concern of the community with marriage. In M. E. Rich (Ed.). *Family life today: Papers presented at the fiftieth anniversary of family social casework in America.* Boston: Houghton Mifflin.

Rose, H. (1983). Hand, brain and heart: A feminist epistemology for the natural sciences. *Signs, 9,* 73–90.

Rose, H. (1984). Is a feminist science possible? Paper presented to MIT Women's Studies Program, April.

Rukeyser, M. (1978). Waiting for Icarus. In M. Rukeyser. *The collected poems of Muriel Rukeyser.* New York: McGraw-Hill.

Ruth, S. (1981). Methodocracy, misogyny and bad faith: The response of philosophy. In D. Spender (Ed.). *Men's studies modified: The impact of feminism on the academic disciplines* (pp. 43–53). Oxford: Pergamon Press.

Spender, D. (1981). Introduction. In D. Spender (Ed.). *Men's studies modified: The impact of feminism on the academic disciplines* (pp. 1–9). Oxford: Pergamon Press.

Spender, D. (1985). *For the record: The meaning and making of feminist knowledge.* London: The Women's Press.

Stanley, L., & Wise, S. (1983). *Breaking out: Feminist consciousness and feminist research.* London: Routledge & Kegan Paul.

Taggart, M. (1985). The feminist critique in epistemological perspective: Questions of context in family therapy. *Journal of Marital and Family Therapy, 11,* 113–126.

Taggart, M. (1987). Clinical pragmatism's relation to systemic complexity: Vital tension or network "noise." *Journal of Family Psychology, 1,* 117–119.

Towle, C. (1948). Treatment of behavior and personality problems in children. The 1930 Symposium: The social worker. *Orthopsychiatry 1927–1948.* New York: American Orthopsychiatric Association.

Wheeler, D. (1985). Fear of feminism in family therapy. *Family Therapy Networker, 9,* 53–55.

Wilden, A. (1980). *System and structure: Essays in communication and exchange,* (2nd ed.). London: Tavistock Publications.

Young-Bruehl, E. (1987). The education of women as philosophers. *Signs, 12*(2), 209–221.

7

An Evolutionary Approach to Revolutionary Change: The Impact of Gender Arrangements on Family Therapy

RONALD TAFFEL   ROSEMARY MASTERS

REGARDLESS OF OUR EXPERIENCE or skill, none of us can be fully aware of the gender biases we bring to the clinical situation. We suggest, however, that family therapy's historical allegiance to the concept of revolutionary, "magical" change makes the application of the feminist perspective even more problematic than it might be. This allegiance often prevents us from understanding the extent to which gender arrangements place serious limitations on the possibilities for dramatic reorganization in families. Our efforts to create revolutionary change may, in fact, contribute to a therapeutic impasse when we fail to take into account socioeconomic forces on women in families and on families in psychotherapy.

The specific case we have chosen reached just such an impasse after several years and several forms of treatment had produced few positive effects. A year and a half ago, we began to collaborate about the family. This chapter reviews the ways the study of gender changed our thinking and how we applied these changes clinically.

The authors would like to thank Betty Carter and Virginia Goldner for their contributions to the development of these ideas.

CLINICAL DESCRIPTION

The Fisher household consisted of Lenny, a handsome, somber man in his late forties, his wife Doris, plump, friendly, also in her late forties, "Nannie," Doris's 70-year-old mother, and Nicole, 19, the identified patient. Nicole, even at 5'4" and 84 pounds, was a charming, strikingly beautiful, auburn-haired girl. She had been anorectic for two and a half years, her weight dropping slowly over this time from 115 pounds.

Mother, father, and grandmother worked in the family-owned store, and all lived in their small apartment. Within this tight living arrangement, Doris and Nicole were particularly "enmeshed." Each was the other's "best friend," believing that she knew what the other was thinking before it was said. They often (correctly) finished each other's sentences. They spent hours a day together, Nicole demanding comfort, Doris unable and unwilling to turn her away. The degree of their enmeshment was apparent when during one session Doris turned to Nicole and said, "I'm warm in here. Nicole, why don't you take your gloves off." Nicole objected, but removed her gloves.

In a house of women, Lenny was both "peripheral" and sporadically intrusive. Occasionally he would enter, blustering and criticizing. Sometimes he was superficially listened to; other times he was shouted down by different combinations of the women. His experience was of being left out and impotent. And, in fact, the three women had a language of their own, as well as quite a few ongoing secrets that they fiercely nurtured. Outside the household, Lenny's difficulties steadily mounted. He was in constant trouble with creditors and his business was failing. Lenny's attitude was "things will take care of themselves." This drove Doris, Nicole, and Nannie crazy and seemed to be his one source of reliable power—a kind of dynamic passivity that ended up in disconnected phones, shut off gas and electric, and so on.

Except for occasional flareups of adolescent whining, Nicole was indeed a "good girl." Being "parentified," she worried about everyone. She worried about Lenny's business problems, pushing him to take care of things, acting as a pseudo-career counselor. She worried about the fate of her grandmother, although her main concern was that her mother had trouble saying "no" to Nannie. She especially worried about Doris—her hypertension, her overeating, her disagreements with Lenny. Despite her illness, Nicole saw herself as the "mature" one in the family, being surrounded by a mother she thought was too much of a "wimp," a grandmother who was "selfish and nagging," and a father who was usually "too dense" to understand things properly.

In the middle of everything was Doris, the "centralized" mother. She felt responsible for Nicole's illness and her aging mother's growing neediness.

She helped Lenny with business problems, paid creditors, got the phone turned back on, etc. No disciplinary action was taken in the house without her approval; no information escaped her examination. Doris's sense of herself was of the martyr—a description she used with no sign of self-pity. And indeed, after all the fights about "who should be doing what" were over, Doris would take on the task anyway.

We began our work with the Fishers after several therapists and almost three years of therapy had failed. During the first two and a half years of this period individual treatment had produced no visible effects. A course of structural family therapy was then initiated. The goals were the reorganization of hierarchy and boundaries so that Doris and Lenny could work as a team and set effective limits. Several months later considerable structural reorganization was apparent: (1) The parents arranged to have Nannie move into her own apartment in a senior citizens complex; (2) Doris and Lenny began to make demands of Nicole around issues of work (she had been at home neither studying nor working for over a year); (3) Nicole began to work, first in the family store and then for an office temporary agency as a receptionist.

After another few months went by, however, it became clear that Nicole's gains were more apparent than real. Her anorexia and social isolation were worsening. Her weight was near 80 pounds, dipping at one point to 79 pounds. She could not hold a job. She had no friends. Nicole's chronic physical debilitation began to be worrisome and hospitalization became a real possibility.

In this growing crisis atmosphere, the case was reviewed and the authors decided to take on the therapy and reorganize it from a feminist perspective.

In approaching the Fishers (or any other family), we need to keep in mind Hare-Mustin's key point in Chapter 4: "Systems approaches, by viewing family members as equal interacting parts in recursive complementarities, tend to ignore differences in power, resources, needs and interest among family members." The idea that power differences are illusory and that family relationships are complementary ignores hierarchical differences between women and men.

As in many families, the web of day-to-day responsibility in the Fisher family was much more tightly drawn around Doris than Lenny—she was caretaker to three generations, a central actor in the family business, and mediator of intergenerational disputes. One can view this in traditional family therapy terms as powerful centralization (which in some ways it is); however, several factors make this an incomplete and romanticized view:

1. Doris's sense that she had no choice about whether to be the caretaker or not;
2. the degree of family criticism aimed at Doris about how well she handled her jobs;
3. the insidious cultural blame directed at the mother of a "sick" child such as Nicole;
4. Doris's chronic stress-related physical symptoms;
5. lastly, one operational fact — *Doris had absolutely no economic power within the marital system:*
   (a) Doris worked full-time in the family store as the co-manager. She received no salary or recognition of her role. Her participation was labeled as "helping Lenny out."
   (b) Family income was banked in an account under the name of the family business. Only Lenny could draw checks on that account.
   (c) Lenny handled the family's investments and taxes; thus, at any given time, only he had a clear picture of how much money was available for what purposes.
   (d) Savings accounts were in Lenny's name, as was ownership of the family apartment, their single largest asset.
   (e) Given her age, work history and education (a high school diploma), Doris had no way of earning an income remotely equal to Lenny's.

The idea that power differences are illusory and that family relationships are complementary indirectly supports *traditional family therapy's view that "revolution" can be created in all families.* Whether it is called, on a theoretical level, "discontinuous" change, "schismogenesis," or "leap theory," or, on a clinical level, a "one-session turnaround" or a "magical" intervention, the widespread belief in the possibility of "revolutionary" change cannot be minimized; it is central to family therapy lore.

"Revolutionary" family therapy techniques, e.g., structural, strategic and paradoxical approaches, drew many people into our field. Our history is filled with images of dramatic sessions in which surgically applied interventions brought about seemingly immediate and magical "cures." Revolutionary interventions block old behaviors, create intense confusion and anxiety, and "explode" systems into discontinuous "leaps" of family reorganization. From such "sweat box" therapy a "transformation occurs in which a set of completely different . . . options and possibilities emerge" (Hoffman, 1980, p. 56).

But what happens when the "options and possibilities" are limited by cultural-political forces to such an extent that one member of the system has less *actual* freedom to change? The chance for dramatic structural reorganization within the couple is less probable. In such cases, the idea of systemic revolution may be inconsistent with the family's context. A more "evolutionary" approach is then indicated.

Evolutionary techniques, in contrast to revolutionary ones, cool a system down and reduce anxiety, with the hope of gradually changing family members' approach to their situation. These techniques do not make great theater; consequently, they have not been as much a part of family therapy's historical tradition. Yet, recently, evolutionary models have been receiving greater attention. Carol Anderson's psychoeducational work with schizophrenics and their families and Murray Bowen's transgenerational therapy are examples of evolutionary approaches in which change is cumulative and piecemeal.

In terms of the Fishers, we decided to evaluate and apply a combination of revolutionary and evolutionary techniques that we felt could be supported by their context. To do this in any family, one must be clear about the factors that significantly affect a person's freedom to change his or her life situation.

THINKING ABOUT THE THERAPY

My husband is the head of the house. He takes care of all the big items — politics, war and peace, the atomic bomb. . . . I take care of everything else. (popular folk story)

While family theoreticians have been involved with the "big items" regarding systemic change — homeostasis, resistance, ecosystemic epistemology, and so on — feminists have been "discovering" that some of the most significant variables affecting a woman's freedom to change her life are everyday conditions that we often take for granted. Five variables seem particularly important:

1. number of children in the family;
2. age of the children;
3. economic viability — whether a woman would be able to support herself if she had to;
4. a woman's career plans — whether she has an ongoing career or is in school or job training;
5. perceived empathic support — whether a woman can turn to her partner, her friends, or her extended family for empathic support.

To see whether family therapy outcome could be related to these variables, we informally reviewed 77 working- and middle-class families and couples that the first author had seen over the previous five years. We divided the families into a "successful" group (symptom improvement for at least one year), a "mixed" group (general symptom improvement, with fluctuating periods of improvement lasting several months at a time), and an "unsuccessful" group (initial improvement often occurred, but symptoms always returned — usually within three to six months).

We were surprised by the degree of concordance between our findings and the feminists' assertions: The average number of children in the successful cases (40) was .6; the average number in the unsuccessful cases (17), was 1.6; the median age of children in the successful cases was 14, in the unsuccessful cases it was 4; comparing the successful and unsuccessful groups, four times as many women in the successful group were economically viable when they began treatment and five times as many had been preparing for future work; lastly, in the successful cases twice as many women felt they had empathic support.

In clinical terms, the most "resistant" families usually contained a wife or mother who had the least economic leverage, the most caretaking responsibility, the fewest career options, and the least empathic support from her partner, friends, and family.

This review helped us understand why with the Fishers traditional family therapy interventions had not worked and the treatment had become stalled.

1. "Revolutionary" change seemed temporarily out of the question. Doris's freedom in real economic terms, in her lifelong self-concept as a caretaker, and in her web of actual responsibilities was too limited to support disruptive reorganization.
2. Because of Lenny and Doris's own hierarchical inequalities, they could not have equal power in setting limits. Consequently, we decided not to emphasize the kind of hierarchy one thinks of as "limit-setting."
3. Removing Doris from her central role, a common revolutionary strategy, would take her away from her only power base.

When we put aside expectations for revolutionary change and a major emphasis on effective hierarchy and appropriate boundaries, our family therapy cupboard appeared a little bare. It was disheartening how feminist ideas had seemingly narrowed our options with the Fishers.

Psychodynamic theory and family systems theories describe the core problem in anorexia as a failure to separate and individuate and gain a sense of autonomy. (Steiner-Adair, 1986, p. 96)

The biggest obstacle in coming up with an alternative treatment plan in which we did not try to "decentralize mother and bring in father" was the belief that Nicole and Doris needed to separate from each other. For decades personality theory has assumed that healthy development proceeds from a starting point in which an infant cannot tell the difference between her/himself and mother (Mahler, 1968). Pathology, then, is almost always seen in terms of incomplete separation from mother.

The notion of early fusion between mother and infant deeply affects us clinically. It is unusual to find a case example in the literature where the enmeshment, the fusion, the cross-generational coalition, the too richly joined subsystem that is challenged is *not* that between mother and child. Given this state of affairs, we were having difficulty coming up with an alternative model of healthy differentiation that did not, in one way or another, depend on figuring out how to separate Nicole and her mother. Daniel Stern's infancy research began to help us with this dilemma.

According to Stern, infants do not have to separate from "an undifferentiated ego mass" with mother. They are born into the world differentiated: "Our observations show that connectedness is a success of psychic functioning, rather than a . . . failure of differentiation" (Stern, 1985, p. 241). A major part of their struggle in development is to actively search out and regulate a balance of connectedness and differentiation with significant others. Central to this struggle is the development of empathic relatedness between parent and child. Ideally, a sense of shared understanding begins early—at approximately six to nine months; eventually, it becomes an important part of what people need in order to differentiate throughout the course of life.

Unfortunately, the power arrangements in many marriages profoundly erode empathic relatedness between women and men, parents and children. Gender imbalance creates, as it were, a *politics of empathy*, in which those who have the least socioeconomic power (most often women and children) are the ones whose reality is least often understood or considered. In unbalanced arrangements, the distribution of empathic support often mirrors the economic-political context. Along with other services, women are expected to provide empathy without being recompensed in kind. Jean Baker Miller observes: "[women] have developed the sense that their lives should be guided by the constant need to attune themselves to the wishes, desires and needs of others" (1976, pp. 60–61).

Reversing this equation is problematic. Empathic support is almost always necessary to help someone challenge gender definitions. Yet a woman in an unbalanced gender arrangement often lives in an environment that directs the flow of empathy away from her own needs and experience. It is at the point of wanting or needing change that many women, feeling stuck, misunderstood, and unentitled at home, present their families to us for help.

If empathic support is in short supply for many disempowered women, what is family therapy's view on the matter?

Traditional family therapy has been consistently ambivalent regarding the importance of empathy. On the one hand, it has been family therapy's unique contribution to view the child's symptomatology as an empathic effort to protect his/her parents from a "worse fate." In approaching a problem, we are always searching for the empathic connections among family members, trying to unearth the shared meanings of symptomatology. Yet traditional family therapy has had little to say about the importance of empathy in normal family development. Empathy, it seems, is almost always one step away from pathology. Family therapists spend considerable time dealing with the empathic underbelly of family life, focusing on such matters as "covert alliances," "parentified" children, "enmeshed" parents, "pathological" coalitions, "dirty games," and, of course, "overinvolved" mothers.

At first glance Doris and Nicole were just such an overinvolved mother and daughter. However, if we look at them through the lens of Stern's hypotheses, they were anything but *close*. Their capacity to understand one another and respond in a way that furthered the process of differentiation had become seriously impaired. Their view of each other was as imbalanced as the gender arrangements with which they both grew up. Doris and Nicole were locked in a struggle in which each could fully empathize with the other's weaknesses while consistently underestimating the other's strengths. As a result, mother and daughter's "closeness" was in part organized around a shared sense of ineffectiveness and an awareness of each other's resentments and angers. While this kind of empathic connection offered significant support, it was only half the picture.

In the 77 families we reviewed, the less freedom the wife or mother had, the more likely it was that she had accepted the cultural belief that women are the providers and not the receivers of empathy. Almost without fail, a wife or mother would then be involved in just such an "enmeshment of ineffectiveness" with one of her children, her own mother, a sibling, and so on. A central paradox of this situation is the *aloneness* that can exist within enmeshment — regardless of the fact that there may be a crowd of demanding people all around. Since there are economic, social, and family-of-origin sanctions against leaving such a system, family members remain "fused." And, since enmeshment is often accompanied by the experiences of disconnection and ineffectiveness, family members keep trying to establish greater attachment and competence, even as they try to break away. Our review helped us understand this central paradox for the Fishers, as well as several other paradoxes that needed to be clinically addressed:

1. In order to promote differentiation, we initially had to facilitate more empathic connectedness and attachment.
2. Because of Lenny's economic control and control over the direction of their lives, the women in the family had adapted to his views about how to negotiate life problems. In order for them to differentiate, this fact and its everyday implications needed to be addressed.
3. In order for Doris to become less enmeshed, she had to become more effective and central.
4. In order for the parentified child, Nicole, to differentiate, her sensitivities and worries about her mother and father needed to be taken seriously.
5. In order to promote family "revolution," we had to work in an evolutionary manner.

The Feminist Approach

We recognized that the Fishers had created a gender imbalance that was highly impervious to change. Rather than futilely attacking the existing arrangement, we chose to facilitate more effective functioning in just those areas one would label as stereotypical gender definitions. Our belief was that family members, as they developed more self-esteem in their assigned gender roles, would become freer to explore a less rigid arrangement. In the process of doing this, we hoped to gradually address patriarchal beliefs about family living that had contributed to the dysfunctional organization of their family. The treatment was conducted by a female therapist who met with Nicole once a week and with different combinations of family members every couple of weeks.

Initial Phase of Treatment

HELPING THE "ENMESHED" MOTHER AND DAUGHTER BECOME MORE CONNECTED. An earlier history of individual and family therapy had attempted to pull Doris away from Nicole, suggesting that others—a therapist, Lenny, or a hospital—would be less harmful to Nicole than her mother was. We did not think that Doris's relationship to Nicole would improve or that her self-esteem would be strengthened if we "brought Lenny in" to succeed where she had "failed." In addition, Doris's economic dependence and years of deprecation by the whole family ensured that she would not be able to abandon her maternal role, no matter how powerful our intervention.

With this in mind, our first intervention was aimed at helping Doris develop a greater sense of competence in her maternal functioning and helping Doris and Nicole become more attached without feeling it was shameful. Given the presenting problem of anorexia, Doris and Nicole were asked to eat a meal together every day while Lenny was at work.

A minimum weight was established for Nicole to stay out of the hospital. Any weight gain was labeled secondary to the fact that Nicole and Doris needed to develop their *own approach to eating*. The therapist told them that developing even the smallest bit of self-confidence in this area would help them gain the self-confidence to go on in life and tackle other things. Since doctors and hospitals were always telling them what they were doing wrong, the therapist assured them that she would stay out of their way. She also said to Lenny that she would help him control his need to get progress reports from Doris. "Some things," she told Lenny, "are best left to mothers and daughters to work out themselves."

Doris immediately liked the idea. She said confidently that she was sure she had the patience to do it right. Lenny insisted at first that the *therapist*, rather than Doris, feed Nicole. He finally agreed to go along with the plan. Nicole quietly (and diplomatically) agreed to give it a try.

HELPING NICOLE BECOME A MORE EFFECTIVE "CARETAKER." According to Janet Surrey (1984), "reciprocal caretaking" is a normal developmental experience between parent and child, especially mother and daughter. Using this perspective, we believed that the problem was not in daughter's parentification, but rather in her inability to take care of her mother and father effectively. Nicole's self-esteem and self-confidence had been impaired enough by this "failure" to prevent her turning her attention elsewhere. Rather than interpreting Nicole's considerable worries about her family as Nicole's "sacrificing" herself or as her being part of an "inverted family hierarchy," we tried to help her become more effective in her role. Concretely, this meant using Nicole's sensitivities as a barometer to help establish therapeutic direction. We thought that Nicole would let us know soon enough whether her meals with Doris were a good idea for the family.

As one would expect, the first at-home eating sessions did not go smoothly. Doris reported that she had sat with Nicole for over an hour on several nights and after great effort could only persuade Nicole to eat a small portion of tuna salad. Two weeks later the following exchange took place:

DORIS   You won't believe this. Last night she had a biscuit and a potato. This morning she had an omelette, two slices of bread, cream cheese, and jelly. I can't believe it. I sat with her. It was hard.

THERAPIST   Tell me how you did it.

DORIS   Just by talking calmly. I said, "I understand how you feel, but it's medicine. You have to take it even though you don't like it. I take Robitussin when I have a cold. I hate it, but I still take it." I just love to sit with her and talk and watch her eat. I light up inside like an electric lightbulb.

Nicole said little about the task, but her weight had begun to edge up slightly. We were anxious to see what dynamics would be triggered.

HELPING THE "PERIPHERAL" FATHER BECOME LESS CONTROLLING. Within weeks the family was fiercely squabbling. The issue seemed to be Lenny's insistence that Nicole was already well enough to get a full-time job. Despite the women's initial disregard of his opinion, when father would voice his disapproval at the rate of progress, a pall would eventually settle over the family. No matter how obstinate they seemed, neither Doris nor Nicole could hold onto her own beliefs in the face of Lenny's opinions.

Socioeconomic imbalance makes the differentiation of values and beliefs problematic for dependent family members. Peripheral as he often seemed, Lenny's attitudes about solving problems had been taken on by the women around him and had developed into a kind of family ethic. In some families such an adaptation may work, but for the Fishers it did not. This was because Lenny brought to his marriage a number of attitudes and characteristics that hampered effective problem-solving. Some examples of his approach to problems were the following:

- *Wishing makes it so.* Lenny informed us that he had stopped paying medical and hospital insurance for his 80-pound daughter. He explained his thinking as follows: "If we don't pay insurance, that means she won't get sick." No one in the family thought anything was unusual about this notion.
- *Progress often leads to disappointment.* Each time a small step was taken, for example, Nicole working part-time or gaining a pound, Lenny became anxious and critical. In his cognitive framework, progress (because it indicated how much more needed to be done and how much had not been done in the past) was closely associated with disappointment. The rest of the family was easily disappointed as well, believing that "good things only happen to other people."
- *Things should be free.* Lenny's chronic sense of disappointment was organized around the issue of money. He believed that many services in life were owed to him. As a consequence, the family also felt cheated when they were not given preferential treatment in jobs, stores, social situations, etc.

For Doris and Nicole to differentiate their own beliefs from Lenny's, the impact of his ideas had to be made explicit and directly *tied to the presenting problem*. The therapist said:

> I know you feel that you don't have real influence in this family, Lenny. But, in fact, your wife and daughter are exquisitely sensitive to your attitudes. When, for example, you become overly disappointed about Nicole's progress, they feel like failures. Whether or not they give you the satisfaction of saying "you're right," they are deeply influenced by the way you approach life's problems. Because of this, Nicole's anorexia will be helped if you can teach her by example. By that I mean she will learn from watching you strengthen how you deal with your own problems.

How did Lenny react? At first he vacillated between polite lip-service to the therapist and criticisms of the women in the family. We did not, however, let his reaction move us from the position that Nicole's anorexia and Lenny's behavior and attitudes were connected. We were prepared to lose the case rather than let them continue believing that Nicole's condition and its treatment were the mother's responsibility alone.

The most effective way of helping Lenny focus on his own issues was through family-of-origin work. This cognitive approach was particularly useful for such a man, who considered therapy to be "women's work." Each of Lenny's approaches to problem-solving ("wishing makes it so," "things should be free," etc.) was traced through his family of origin. It quickly became apparent how fearful Lenny was that he would suffer his father's fate—his father had become disabled and never worked after the age of 50. The more Lenny talked about his family, the less doomed he felt and the less he was an "armchair quarterback" to Doris and Nicole. Within six weeks Lenny decided to deal with his business's impending failure. He made plans to sell the store.

Empathy

As Lenny's empathy for himself and his family of origin increased, we were somewhat surprised by how much less critical he was of Doris and Nicole, and how much less fearful they were of him. Our surprise was a measure of how far we had been inducted into the patriarchal framework of this family. Specifically, Lenny had lived his entire life "trivializing" the importance of such "maternal" functions as the provision of empathy (Goldner, 1987). Because of their dependent positions, Doris and Nicole had gradually adopted the male view that empathy is a luxury (even an indulgence) or something women provide as a "given." As the therapy progressed, we began to appreciate more fully that consistent empathy had reparative psychological effects, even if it was not connected to a powerful intervention.

At first glance, this may seem obvious. But, as we suggested earlier, family therapy's views about the therapeutic value of empathy are rather complex. There are few direct references to it in the clinical literature. When reference is made, impersonal terminology is invariably used — we "join," we "socialize," we "stroke." Empathy is almost always considered a vehicle in the service of establishing something else — toward creating a different therapeutic reality, as a way to "sell" an idea or task, as a necessary "stroke" to prepare for a well placed "kick." Family therapists value action above all else. Our teaching methods are a reflection of this. The one-way mirror, the one-session consultation, the one-shot demonstration (all manifestations of revolutionary expectations) — reinforce the need to make something happen quickly. This overemphasis on speed and action underestimates the gradual reparative effect of empathy in and of itself.

Recognizing the relationship between the patriarchal devaluation of empathy in the Fisher family and in the family therapy field in general, we decided to focus on the issue directly in treatment. We told the Fishers that labeling empathy as self-indulgence or women's work was a family belief that made problem-solving much more difficult. Given the almost phobic reaction of many people, especially men, to the idea of empathic connection, we approached this matter in several ways:

1. The need for empathy in family living was presented in an educational, cognitive way.
2. The capacity for empathic relatedness was traced, as any other issue would be, through both families of origin: Who listened to whom? Who was afraid to listen? Who was uninterested? Who was a good listener? Who was not?
3. Lenny was coached during the family sessions to listen without lecturing or criticizing.
4. Doris and Nicole were coached to stop protecting Lenny by trying to "read his mind" or by letting him go on and on when they were not listening.

Whether their communication improved dramatically or not was secondary to our challenging the patriarchal myth that people should be able to function well in an empathy-starved system.

At this point, approximately three months into our approach, the therapy appeared to be on solid ground. The principles we were following seemed to have been translated into clinical practice:

1. Nicole and Doris were trying to create a more connected relationship with each other.

2. Lenny's sporadic entrances into the world of the women via criticism had diminished.
3. Nicole trusted that her concerns about her mother and father were being taken seriously by the therapist and her parents.
4. Lenny was trying to change his own ideas about handling life problems and had taken concrete actions to sell the business.
5. The myth that people can function well without receiving empathy was being challenged.

A few weeks later Doris suffered a mild heart attack and was briefly hospitalized. With hindsight we realized this had been predictable. She had been chronically overweight and hypertensive for many years. Her overeating and smoking had remained unchecked. Despite these symptoms, we failed to attend closely enough to the impact of the family's changes on Doris. We had been inducted into taking Doris's position as nurturer for granted and once again had accepted the myth that Lenny was somehow peripheral in the family.

Concretely, what we had failed to appreciate was the increase in responsibility that Doris faced as a result of Lenny's decision to sell the business. This change meant that Doris was working in the store seven days a week to help him liquidate; she also took on the responsibility of selling the family apartment and looking for a new one. These extra duties were added to the usual ones of running a household and taking care of her aging mother and a difficult child. Lastly, though she claimed to feel great pleasure and pride in eating with Nicole, it was still one extra chore to accomplish each day.

The hospitalization was brief and Doris suffered no permanent damage. Even so, the Fishers resumed their usual functioning, *as if nothing had happened*! Their unrealistic expectation that Doris could nurture others without limit was astonishingly powerful: Doris's mother was calling her several times a day for advice and comfort. Lenny began to pressure her to get a job to help him out, even though she had just come out of the hospital (he believed that Doris's fatigue was "mostly in her head"). Nicole, however, was extremely preoccupied with her mother's health. She reported that Doris was sharing her fear that she would start smoking again and that she was eating all the wrong kinds of food. However, despite Doris's illness and the family turmoil, Nicole had not lost a single pound. Since Doris had begun eating with her, Nicole had experienced less and less difficulty over food. This marked the beginning of the second phase of treatment.

The Second Phase

At the start of therapy it would have been futile to challenge directly the family's gender expectations in general and Doris's maternal functioning in particular. Whereas it was still too early to ask Doris to take care of herself for her own sake, we thought she might be able to take better care of herself for Nicole's sake.

THERAPIST   Despite everything, Nicole has managed to keep her weight up. You've done well, Doris. Now it's time to move on to something else. Doris, the better you take care of yourself . . .

NICOLE   . . . the better I feel!

DORIS   We're like a matching set, Nicole and I. The better she takes care of herself, the better I take care of myself.

LENNY   That's right. We feel better or worse, depending on how she's doing.

THERAPIST   You've both got it backwards. Nicole seems to stop eating when she's worried about you. To help her now, Doris, means taking care of your own health. Nicole's weight is like a barometer that tells you if you're protecting yourself.

Whether Doris could be immediately successful in protecting herself was again secondary to challenging another patriarchal myth—that Doris could nurture without limit (being a wife, mother, and daughter) and not eventually harm herself. To challenge this belief, we began sharing the considerable data that the feminist literature has gathered about family living. For example, we mentioned that if Doris continued doing all the household, business, and intergenerational work without setting priorities, medical research almost guaranteed that she would become physically ill again.

Doris seemed quite perplexed by the idea that she needed to become more self-nurturing for Nicole to get better. But, after a couple of months of our endlessly repeating these themes, Doris had not resumed smoking and was eating a little more realistically. She became increasingly disturbed about certain matters around the house. Using "nicotine withdrawal" as the reason for her testiness, she put a stop to a number of things that had gone unchecked for many years. For example, as mentioned earlier, Lenny had been pressuring Doris to get a job. Without coaching, Doris announced to Lenny that she absolutely would not work outside the home until the family apartment was sold and their relocation was complete. As soon as Doris stood firm, Lenny got moving and started looking for a new job. With the therapist's help and with numerous reminders that Nicole would learn by his example, Lenny went about the job search in a step-by-step fashion. In time he found an extremely good position. His realistic approach was not wasted on Nicole and Doris, as they initiated a similar process on their own.

While Lenny methodically explored job opportunities, Doris began assisting Nicole in her efforts to get work, helping her put together a model's portfolio and actually going with her for interviews. Quietly Doris siphoned off $400 from her "allowance" to pay for the resume and portfolio. We were beginning to worry that Nicole and Doris's bonding had gone too far and that we might be promoting an interminable enmeshment between them. However, since Nicole was willing and since Doris's health seemed much improved, we endorsed the project.

A few weeks later, Nicole, whose weight was up to 92 (the most it had been in several years), landed a job doing temporary modeling. Of equal significance, she was referring to her anorexia in the past tense. Doris and Nicole came in for a session together. The following passage illustrates how for the first time it was emphasized that Doris could help herself and Nicole by placing limits on Nicole's demands:

NICOLE (yelling) I don't have any clothes to wear! I won't wear anything from last year. I don't know how in God's name I ever bought those clothes. I was even skinnier then. I must have looked like hell. I will not humiliate myself anymore. I won't have people look at me anymore and say, "Yuch, she's so anorectic!"

THERAPIST I think it's terrific that she thinks she's skinny.

DORIS I do too. I'm thrilled . . . but it's frustrating. I want to help her, but I don't know how.

THERAPIST Nicole, you'd like your mother and father to buy you a new coat, right?

NICOLE But they won't!

DORIS I can understand how she feels, because I want to go get myself a coat, too. But, if I buy Nicole a coat, then I can't get myself those things I need. Do you know what I'm trying to say, Nicole?

THERAPIST Nicole, your mother is not being mean to you. Growing up is finding ways to get yourself what you need.

NICOLE But I want to grow up!

THERAPIST Doris, I'd like to suggest that you listen to Nicole's feelings about growing up for about 10 minutes every day. Stop after 10 minutes, because you don't have endless time for that. You can say to Nicole something like, "I know this is hard, but I have other things to do now and we can talk about this again tomorrow."

This limit-setting move, often the *first type of intervention in "revolutionary" family therapy*, had finally become appropriate. There was no immediate transformation. Doris did not go out and get herself a coat. She was able, however, to begin listening to Nicole for briefer periods without tiring herself needlessly or trying to answer every demand Nicole made.

By a few weeks later Nicole had gained a couple more pounds. The family was involved in another major transition. The business had been liquidated,

Lenny had a new job, and they were selling the apartment. Once again, the changes initiated by Lenny were anything but "peripheral" to the family. Nicole reported that Doris was feeling overwhelmed. And despite Doris's obvious fatigue, Lenny was again pressing her to get a job.

Having learned that Nicole was an accurate observer of Doris's health, we decided to intervene quickly. Believing that no one in the family (including Doris) was cognizant of the pressures that such a move would put on a wife and mother, we drew up a list of everything she would be responsible for during and after the move. The list was long and filled with endless details. It clarified for Doris how absurd it was to get a job outside the home at this time. Instead, she took the bold new step of asking the family for help with the move!

Third Phase of Treatment

At the time Doris drew these limits with the family, she and Nicole seemed on more autonomous, yet parallel tracks. Nicole weighed 100 pounds. She soon got her first steady full-time job. After the family resettled, Doris kept her word and found a job. Nicole weighed 105 pounds and had begun to date. The next month Nicole was up to 110 pounds. Doris decided to quit her first job, for which she was overqualified, and got a better position. By the next month, one year after we had begun working from a feminist perspective, Nicole menstruated for the first time in five years. She weighed 115 pounds.

At this point the Fishers decided that things had improved enough to take a temporary break from therapy. Six months later Doris and Lenny returned alone. Nicole had maintained the same weight and was continuing her improvement on all fronts. Putting her concerns about Nicole aside, Doris wanted to focus on the one thing she had always been afraid to address seriously: Lenny's total control over the family finances. And for the first time Lenny was willing to discuss the matter. After a great deal of evolutionary change this was an important revolutionary step. Doris had progressed from being able to nurture only others, especially Nicole, to pressing for changes in the way of managing money because she wanted them for herself. Lenny also went through an evolutionary process, one we have found typical of men in therapy. As he became interested in his family of origin and more effective at controlling his socioeconomic context, he became less interested in trying to control the family members around him.

Doris and Lenny took different paths. But, as the feminist perspective suggests, women and men are not interchangeable parts in a complementary balance. Sometimes the differences in power, resources, and language become so great that all family members end up sharing are the myths of how families are supposed to be.

The therapy we did had less to do with the dramatic impact or the success of any one intervention than with our various attempts to challenge beliefs about women and men in families. For the Fishers this meant understanding the loneliness of "enmeshment," the control of the "peripheral" father, the dilemma of the child whose "parental" concerns are not taken seriously, and finally, the healing capabilities of the "overinvolved" mother.

REFERENCES

Goldner, V. (1987). Instrumentalism, feminism and the limits of family therapy. *Journal of Family Psychology, 11*, 109–116.

Hoffman, L. (1980). The family life cycle and discontinuous change. In B. Carter & M. McGoldrick (Eds.), *The changing family life cycle*, New York: Gardner Press.

Mahler, M. S. (1968). *On human symbiosis and the vicissitudes of individuation*. New York: International Universities Press.

Miller, J. Baker (1976). *Toward a new psychology of women*. Boston: Beacon Press.

Steiner-Adair, C. (1986). The body politic: Normal female adolescent development and the development of eating disorders. *Journal of The American Academy of Psychoanalysis, 14*(1), 95–114.

Stern, D. (1985). *The interpersonal world of the infant*. New York: Basic Books.

Surrey, J. (1984). Self-in-relation: A theory of women's development, Paper, No. 13, Stone Center for Developmental Services and Studies, p. 1–16.

8
Rethinking Family Therapy Training and Supervision: A Feminist Model

DOROTHY WHEELER   JUDITH MYERS AVIS

LORIE A. MILLER   SITA CHANEY

ALTHOUGH FEMINIST FAMILY THERAPY has been discussed in the literature since 1976 (Hare-Mustin, 1978, 1979; Seidler-Feller, 1976), there has been no clearly defined framework for identifying the specific skills characteristic of such therapy or for the training of therapists. This chapter addresses this gap by presenting a model of feminist family therapy which includes appropriate skills and training methodologies.

Feminism is not a set of techniques or conclusions, but rather a lens through which one views and understands realities. Feminism is "a process that begins with the recognition of the inferior status of women, proceeds to an analysis of the specific forms and causes of that inequality, makes recommendations for strategies of change, and eventually leads to a recognition and validation of women's realities, women's interpretations, and women's contributions" (Wheeler, 1983, p. 1). As a method of analysis, feminism implies an active process as opposed to a static set of conclusions. Hartsock (1975) defines feminism as a "method of approaching life and politics, a way of asking questions and searching for answers" (p. 68).

Author's names are listed in random order and reflect equal contribution to this collaborative paper.
Revised from *Journal of Psychotherapy and the Family*, 1985, *1*, 53–71.

FEMINIST CRITIQUES OF FAMILY THERAPY

Systems theory, the foundation upon which much of family therapy is built, has been criticized by feminists for its abstract, ahistorical, and apolitical assumptions. With its emphasis on circular causality, systems theory has virtually ignored gender inequality within the family. Family dysfunctions are typically assumed to be a result of interpersonal dynamics, rather than a reflection of larger social influences which encourage inequality on the basis of sex. By ignoring social forces, family therapists inadvertently participate in maintaining their negative consequences (James & McIntyre, 1983).

Many family systems theorists deemphasize the origins of family problems, contending that current and ongoing interaction is more important (Hoffman, 1981). Feminists, however, adopt an expanded systems model, one which views women's inferior position as having historical origins, which continue to be reinforced in the family (Thorne with Yalom, 1982). When one ignores history, it is easy to assume mistakenly that women and men have equal impact on their surroundings.

Because family systems theory does not incorporate the history of gender inequality, many family therapists consider women to be as powerful as men and equally as responsible in maintaining dysfunctional family patterns, including those where women are abused or victimized. However, because men and women do not occupy equal positions of power in society, they cannot affect systems equally, as the notion of circular causality seems to imply (Miller, 1983). To adhere to systems theory's circular view of causality is, at least in part, to blame the victim—in this case, women.

In addition to systems theory, other aspects of family therapy have been criticized. Jacobson (1983) argues that family therapists are not sensitive to power differences within the family which favor men. If treatment proceeds with the expectation that each partner will change equally, then pretreatment inequities remain intact. Jacobson suggests that, because families rarely define their concerns in terms of power imbalances caused by socialization, the therapist has an ethical responsibility, regardless of presenting problem, to attempt to redistribute power.

Gurman and Klein (1984) suggest that much of family therapy operates within a system laden with gender bias which disadvantages women. The problem results because family therapists assert an "objective and databased neutrality" (p. 185) and do not adopt a more critical examination of the values which they are implementing. Behavioral marital therapy (BMT), they argue, has a tendency to label behavior as "positive" or "negative." A "good" relationship, one that is positively valued within the BMT frame, is one in which accommodation, personal sacrifice, and lack of conflict are the norms. When a wife who was formerly passive and unassertive begins to demonstrate autonomy, there is often an increase in marital conflict. This behavior cannot be seen as healthy from a traditional marital therapy model because it is viewed systemically and labeled as negative. The value of this behavior to the individual is lost in a normative family framework insensitive to individual needs.

Avis (1985), Gurman and Klein (1984), Hare-Mustin (1978), and others have criticized family therapy for emphasizing the importance of changing performance within roles rather than changing the roles themselves. Avis (1985), for example, challenges functional family therapy for its unequivocal support and legitimization of existing family functions (i.e., the tendency of different family members to seek interpersonal closeness or distance). She suggests that these functions are not, in fact, idiosyncratic or personally chosen by family members. Rather, they are correlated with traditionally prescribed gender-role behavior, with closeness or merging functions (e.g., involvement with children) fulfilled primarily by women and distancing functions (e.g., time away from the family) by men. Functional family therapy, Avis argues, actually perpetuates and encourages such sex-role behavior.

The use of hierarchy in family therapy has also been criticized. Hare-Mustin (1978), in describing a feminist approach to family therapy, pays special attention to the structure of the relationship between the family and the therapist. She proposes the use of a therapist-family contract to minimize the therapeutic hierarchy, to set limits on the therapist's authority, and to provide the opportunity for all family members, but especially women, to negotiate individual and system needs. While Hare-Mustin's suggestions are important first steps in remedying sexism in family therapy, there appears to be a compelling need to develop a family therapy model with specific procedures sensitive to feminist issues.

FEMINIST FAMILY THERAPY: AN ALTERNATIVE

A feminist approach to family therapy incorporates many aspects of family systems thinking: (a) an emphasis on social context as a prime determinant of behavior; (b) the use of reframing and relabeling to shift the conceptual or emotional perspective on a situation; (c) modeling; and (d) an emphasis on action and behavioral change (Libow, Raskin, & Caust, 1982). A feminist approach is also similar to a nonsexist approach to family therapy in its commitment to facilitating equality in personal power between women and men and in its support of clients' rights to design their lives outside of culturally prescribed sex roles (Rice & Rice, 1977).

What sets a feminist approach to family therapy apart from both traditional and nonsexist approaches, however, is its commitment to recognizing the *unique* problems women face as a result of their socialization, as well as to making changes that will benefit women (Gilbert, 1980). Additionally, most feminist perspectives on therapy emphasize the sharing of power in the therapeutic relationship rather than the usual therapist-client hierarchy. Feminist family therapy also demands a more political, institutional, and gender-sensitive viewpoint, which confronts familial and societal barriers, so that women can exercise their individual choices and participate as equals with men. Perhaps as importantly, a feminist approach to family therapy must support and validate women's work both within and outside the family (Rowbotham, 1973). Feminist family therapy is distinguished from other forms of feminist therapy by its particular focus on changing family structure and its involvement of the family system in this process.

While men have also been victims of a sexist culture and its rigid patterns of socialization, men still hold the balance of power and receive a disproportionate share of social rewards and privileges. A feminist approach is concerned with correcting this imbalance as it occurs within the family. The overall goal of integrating feminist ideas into family therapy is, therefore, to change the institution of the family so that women and men who choose to participate in family life can do so cooperatively as equal and intimate partners. This formidable goal requires distinct ways of intervening, as well as a redefinition of healthy family functioning.

AN ALTERNATIVE VIEW OF HEALTHY FAMILY FUNCTIONING

The Family Life Cycle

The family life cycle is usually discussed in terms of stereotypic roles for men and women. An integration of feminist ideas can broaden our thinking about family health and desirable therapeutic outcome to include and validate such options as (a) remaining single and establishing intimacy from within a network of friendships; (b) choosing a marriage without children; (c) choosing to be a single parent; (d) choosing divorce as a mature and responsible decision; (e) choosing homosexual or heterosexual cohabitation with a partner, with or without children; and (f) generally questioning traditional ideas regarding gender-appropriate behaviors from within the family. Healthy outcome, in other words, can be broadened to include one's ability to withstand pressures to conform to stereotypic ideas about how families should be.

Equalization of Resources and Responsibility

In the traditional family, the wife has been expected to subordinate her interests to those of her family, while the husband has been expected to maximize his individuality and autonomy (Kolbenschlag, 1980). A feminist alternative would support each family member's maximizing his/her individuality and autonomy, while at the same time sharing more or less equally in an accommodation or subordination of individual needs.

Roles

It is important to examine both the relationship between roles and gender and the processes by which roles are allocated. From a feminist perspective, a healthy family is one in which males and females have a wide range of roles available to them and the allocation of roles solely by gender is minimal. In addition, the roles are decided on the basis of personal choice and interpersonal negotiation rather than resulting from sex-role prescriptions (Klein, 1976).

Hierarchy and Health

Feminist theory suggests that hierarchical structures both within and outside the family often restrict women (Thorne with Yalom, 1982). Haley (1976) argues that organization and hierarchy are one and the same and that symptoms result when the hierarchy is confused or unclear.

Appropriate differences, separation, and generational boundaries can (and should) exist between individuals and subsystems within the family. However, Haley's emphasis on the inevitability of working out primary and secondary status positions determines a view of behavior and relationships as adversarial, competitive, and unstable. A healthy system, from a feminist perspective, would minimize same-generation hierarchical arrangements (particularly those based on gender), as well as the power struggles that result from such arrangements.

Separating the Personal, Interpersonal, and Social

A healthy family, from a feminist perspective, is one in which the members understand the political and social influences on their personal or interpersonal lives. This often results in a reinterpretation of behaviors; those initially defined as personal inadequacies come to be seen as socially prescribed. Women and girls need to be helped to examine what it is they have been taught about being female in comparison to their actual competencies, interests, and needs. Men and boys need to examine what they have been taught about women. Additionally, both sexes can reexamine their socialized learnings regarding commitment, caretaking, and intimacy.

Individual vs. System Well-Being

Individual well-being and family well-being are equally important in feminist family therapy. Consequently, when individual and family needs conflict, the family should not necessarily be supported at the expense of the individual. For example, if a woman returns to school or work, this may threaten family stability. The feminist family therapist would support such a shift in structure and distribution of functions.

A MODEL OF FEMINIST FAMILY THERAPY

Tomm and Wright (1979) have developed a useful framework for delineating perceptual, conceptual, and executive family therapy skills. This framework will be used to present a model of skills for feminist family therapy. Tomm and Wright refer to *perceptual/conceptual skills* as those "taking place in the mind of the therapist" (p. 228), with perception referring to "the therapist's ability to make pertinent and accurate observations" and conceptualization being "the process of attributing meaning to observations or of applying previous learning to the specific therapeutic situation" (p. 229). Taken together, these comprise the therapist's thinking skills; in practice they are so integrally interrelated that they are difficult to separate. *Executive skills*, on the other hand, refer to the action or response of the therapist, including both the therapist's internal emotional reactions and overt therapeutic actions. Because of the close relationship between thinking and acting, executive skills are dependent on an appropriate perceptual/conceptual base. Thus, although perceptual/conceptual and executive skills can be identified and discussed separately, in practice they form an integral whole, with the former providing a necessary foundation for the latter.

The present model of feminist family therapy presupposes that therapists either have, or are acquiring, basic family therapy competencies and therefore does not detail all the skills in thinking and intervening necessary for effective work with families. Rather, this feminist model is intended to complement existing models of therapy and to elaborate those skills which are particularly feminist in their intent and focus. Since this is a first attempt to articulate such a feminist model, it is not intended to be exhaustive or definitive, but rather to identify a variety of ways in which feminist ideology and goals can be integrated into family therapy practice. This model was developed from the authors' integration of feminist principles into their teaching, supervision, and therapy with families.

Perceptual/Conceptual Skills

A feminist conceptualization of the family provides the therapist with an expanded lens through which to observe and understand family relationships. The change in perception which results from such a conceptualization is analogous to that which occurs when a therapist shifts from a linear to a system/interactional paradigm. Such a shift changes the focus of therapeutic attention, the meaning the therapist attaches to observed behavior, the conceptualization of change, and the intervention strategies selected. In using a systemic lens, for example, the therapist views the behaviors of a nagging wife and withdrawing husband not as isolated personality traits, but as events that must be seen in the context of their relationship system. If the therapist then adds a feminist lens, she/he will shift from the purely interpersonal to the political; "nagging" will be seen as a behavior of powerlessness and "withdrawing" as an exercise of power (Feldman, 1982). This view will influence the therapeutic goals sought and the interventions selected.

Interventions thus grow out of the way in which the therapist thinks about the family. As a result, feminist-informed skills cannot be taught simply through supervision, modeling, or microskill practice (Ivey, 1971). They can be taught only in conjunction with thorough rethinking and reconceptualization of the relations between men and women both in society and in the family. This shift in thinking provides the foundation in knowledge, theory, attitude, and awareness that is an essential prerequisite for learning feminist executive skills.

Executive Skills

Cleghorn and Levin (1973) define executive skills as the ability to "influence the family to demonstrate the way it functions," and to "influence the family's sequences of transactions so as to alter the way it functions" (p. 441). Tomm and Wright (1979) emphasize that executive skills are best understood as consisting of two components. The first is the actual overt intervention a therapist makes, and the second is the ability of the therapist to use her or his "own emotional reactions constructively by channeling them into specific therapeutic activity" (p. 229).

In a feminist approach to family therapy it is extremely important that the therapist be active, directive, and competent. At the same time, however, these skills should be used to influence all members of the family to enter into a collaborative relationship with the therapist, thus minimizing hierarchy.

In a feminist-informed family therapy, as previously noted, it is also vitally important for both the therapist and the family to be able to analyze and place their situation within a larger social frame. Such a view sensitizes family members to the impact of the uneven distribution of power and privilege on men and women and the kinds of relationships they form. In this regard, executive skills are consistently directed at reallocating power.

Tomm and Wright's inclusion of the affective component of executive skills is of particular importance to a feminist approach. Family therapy, in

particular structural and strategic approaches, has emphasized highly instrumental problem-solving while minimizing the importance of affect in
facilitating change. In an attempt to reintegrate and reevaluate emotion and
its usefulness in the change process, we include among feminist executive
skills the ability to both elicit and share emotional responses. It is the affect
aroused by a feminist rethinking of the roles, relationships, and decision-
making patterns within the family that motivates much of the action in the
therapy process.

Intervention Model

The following model of feminist family therapy is outlined in terms of
specific perceptual/conceptual and executive skills. Although many of the
skills are actually used throughout therapy, in the interests of clarity they
have been divided according to the phase in which they are most important
and most useful. The three phases, found in Tables 1, 2 and 3, are each
presented with their relevant perceptual/conceptual and executive skills: (1)
developing and maintaining a working alliance between family and therapist; (2) defining the problem; and (3) facilitating change.

TRAINING AND SUPERVISION IN A FEMINIST MODEL

Content and Teaching Methods

Training in a feminist model is similar to traditional family therapy training
in that many of the same teaching methods may be used. What distinguishes
feminist-informed training is its specific feminist content and its use of
training processes that are isomorphic to feminist-informed therapy. The
isomorphic relationship between training and therapy has been previously
elaborated though earlier authors were discussing a traditional family therapy model (Haley, 1976, 1980; Liddle, 1982; Liddle & Saba, 1982; Minuchin
& Fishman, 1981). The way in which therapy is taught is particularly important in feminist training, where more positive and less oppressive attitudes
toward women, as well as an understanding of power and gender roles, must
be taught both by example and didactically.

The goal of a feminist-informed training program is the acquisition of the
perceptual/conceptual and executive skills presented in Tables 1, 2, and 3.
Because sexist thinking is so pervasive in our society, feminist-based percep-
tual/conceptual skills cannot be taught adequately simply as a part of the
supervisory process. An important first step in learning feminist-informed
therapy is a critical study of women's position in society and in the family.
This can best be accomplished through an academic course dealing with

TABLE 1   Skills for Developing and Maintaining a Working Alliance Between Family and Therapist

---

(a) Perceptual/Conceptual Skills
•Appreciate the heavy load of responsibility which women carry for family well-being and recognize feelings of guilt and responsibility that women in particular feel when family problems develop.
•Realize that both men and women are victims of gender-role socialization and develop a nonblaming attitude towards the socialized behavior of both genders.
•Recognize the importance of joining strongly with men to ensure their participation in a therapy which asks them to give up their privileged position in exchange for unfamiliar benefits.
•Appreciate the value of egalitarian (nonhierarchical) relationships both in the marital relationship and between therapist and family.
•Appreciate the need for an explicit contract which details the expectations and goals of therapy as well as the mutual roles and responsibilities of therapist and family, in the interest of demystifying therapy and reducing hierarchy between the therapist and family.
•Recognize the value of therapist self-disclosure for normalizing gender-role difficulties and for reducing hierarchy in the therapist's relationship with the family.
•Recognize that therapeutic competence can be established by self-assuredness without the need to "take charge" in an authoritarian manner.

(b) Executive Skills
•Define the therapeutic alliance as one in which the therapist and the family members have equal status in terms of their responsibility and capability for problem resolution.
•Avoid defining or reacting to the family as "resistant," as this defines the therapist as "expert" and gives an adversarial and competitive tone to the working alliance.
•Negotiate with the family, as equal partners, for what the goals of therapy will be, how long therapy will last, and what particular strategies or interventions are permissible.
•Selectively use self-disclosure and self-reference in order to emphasize the commonality of sex-role problems and to deemphasize the therapist as a neutral or final authority.
•Overtly influence all members of the family toward a more equitable distribution of costs and benefits of family membership.
•Communicate that an important aspect of therapy is to help the family recognize the negative effects of sex-role socialization where they exist, and to explore behavioral alternatives.

TABLE 2 Skills for Defining the Problem

(a) Perceptual/Conceptual Skills
- Recognize power inequities between husbands and wives as a major dynamic in family problems, and analyze marital relationships in terms of unequal access to influence, control, choice, resources, opportunity, and status.
- Understand the reciprocal relationship between power inequities in marriage and in society, i.e., that the devaluation of women in educational, religious, political, and economic institutions is reflected in and reinforced by their secondary status in marriage.
- Know the theory and research which detail the pervasive negative effects of traditional gender roles on women, men, children, family structure, and interpersonal behavior and relationships.
- Evaluate women positively, including recognizing their strengths and competencies and valuing the important work women do in families.
- Recognize how traditional gender roles reinforce inequities between men and women and thus contribute to family problems. This recognition should include an understanding of how gender-role behavior is taught and maintained in the family.
- Recognize that traditional childrearing arrangements frequently contribute to dysfunctional family structures.
- Appreciate the importance of individual as well as family well-being and recognize that family well-being is oppressive to women when it is accomplished at the expense of their own self-development.
- In assigning meaning to family behaviors, recognize how they contribute to a maintenance of the power structure and to the continuation of women's traditional role as chief nurturer and caretaker of the family.
- Define family problems in terms of power differentials and stereotyped expectations and behaviors.

(b) Executive Skills
- Observe family dynamics for those ideas, behaviors, and interactional sequences which support and maintain power inequities or stereotypic gender roles.
- Assist the family to assess costs and benefits to each individual family member and to the system as a whole of the allocation of roles and responsibilities.
- Determine whether roles result from genuine negotiation and represent the most equitable way to maintain individual and system needs, or reflect instead an unexamined response to social expectations.
- Encourage each family member to share his/her unique view of the problem, while validating and supporting the *affective* as well as rational components of each member's presentation.
- Make explicit statements or ask questions regarding the impact of context, tradition, or socialization on the problem(s) as defined by the family. (e.g., "What is it about the way women are raised that encourages Mom to feel guilty and unsure about her ability to be a good mother?").
- Reframe or challenge, where appropriate, the family's definition of problems to include the impact of sexism, patriarchal structures, or gender bias.
- Resist overt and covert pressure from the family to assume an "expert" role or to take the major responsibility for change during therapy.

TABLE 3   Skills for Facilitating Change

(a) Perceptual/Conceptual Skills
- Identify stereotypical role behavior as it occurs in the session.
- Recognize the political dimension of therapy and the potential for family therapy to inadvertently reinforce traditional gender roles (Jacobson, 1983).
- Recognize the validity of women's world views and perceptions of reality. These perceptions, growing out of their unique life experience as women, are frequently different from men's.
- Value both expressive and instrumental behaviors. Recognize the importance of competence in both modes for both men and women.
- Recognize that a renegotiation of roles and responsibilities is essential for real family change.
- Appreciate the value of insight, awareness, and social analysis in the process of change (i.e., cognitive change is an important tool for effecting behavioral change).
- Recognize the vital importance of working towards individual development and well-being within the context of developing and maintaining family relationships.
- Realize the importance of empowering women within the family, since women usually bear much more than their share of responsibility but much less than their share of power.
- Realize that empowering women often involves helping them to be less accommodating and less responsible for family well-being, while simultaneously helping men to be more so.
- Recognize the importance of the therapist's modeling nonstereotyped behavior in influencing the family's perceptions and beliefs regarding "appropriate" gender behavior.

(b) Executive Skills
- Educate the family, when necessary, regarding those particular roles, structures, or behavioral sequences which support women in one-down dependent positions.
- Direct the family to behave in ways which both challenge stereotypic gender patterns and provide alternatives for their consideration.
- Direct the family to behave in ways that redistribute childrearing responsibilities so that it is shared more evenly by both spouses, enabling children to have the benefits of close involvement with two parents.
- Support competence in women in both their traditional and nontraditional roles.
- Counteract the tendency of women to invalidate or apologize for themselves or to present themselves as helpless and inadequate.
- Model an androgynous style that combines so-called "masculine" (instrumental, problem-solving) and "femine" (affective, nurturing) behaviors.
- Talk to women respectfully and take them seriously in front of their mates and children.
- Minimize hierarchy in the family by (1) consistently questioning male dominance and female subordination when they occur; (2) valuing women's work in the family; and (3) challenging rules or patterns which seem to be gender specific.

(continued)

TABLE 3   *(continued)*

•Explicitly discuss and analyze individual and system behavior in terms of its politics (Jacobson, 1983). This serves to sensitize family members to the influence of such things as economics, sexism, and racism on their interpersonal life.
•Balance pretreatment inequities by (1) temporarily lending power to women; (2) teaching women negotiating skills; (3) validating the expression of feelings of both men and women; and (4) requesting changes which alter roles and not just the quality of role performance.

feminist theory and issues. Ideally, such a course would be oriented to family therapists and taught by a feminist family systems therapist who could help trainees integrate feminist thinking with family systems thinking. However, in the absence of such a specialized course, an introductory course in women's studies or feminist theory could provide a similar foundation. It is important for trainees to be exposed to feminist theory from a wide range of disciplines, so that they may challenge their own culturally prescribed notions of normality, health, appropriate gender roles, and desirable therapeutic outcomes.

The following content areas are specifically recommended for study: the historical and religious roots of gender inequity; feminist analyses of the masculine assumptions underlying philosophical and scientific theories; feminist analyses of the family and of the institutions of marriage and motherhood; the process and effects of gender-role socialization; the psychology of women; economic issues such as paid and unpaid work, pensions for women, the gross overrepresentation of women in poverty statistics and on welfare rolls, the effect of capitalism and competitive economics on the family; issues related to violence against women such as rape, incest, wife abuse, and pornography; women's health issues such as menopause, aging, abortion, overmedication with psychotropic drugs, and unnecessary surgery; an examination of alternative lifestyles for women such as lesbianism, singleness, single parenting, and childlessness; critiques of traditional psychotherapy as oppressive to women; the principles of feminist therapy, and the small but growing literature which deals specifically with feminist issues in family therapy.

This type of course usually results in trainees' heightened awareness of their own socialization, gender biases, and experiences of oppression. Such awareness may be further encouraged through small group discussions and through requesting that trainees keep a personal journal for the duration of the course.

Class discussions present a special challenge to the instructor in this type of course, since the material tends to be emotionally evocative. Discussions must be well monitored so that they do not degenerate into blaming sessions and so that a positive, action-oriented atmosphere is maintained. As women first become aware of the facts of their oppression, it is not unusual for them to become intensely angry (Josofowitz, 1980). It is essential for an instructor to validate female trainees' anger when it occurs and to help them use it as a mobilizing force toward assertive action in their lives and in the therapy they provide, rather than assuming an angry victim role. As male trainees first become aware of their privileged position in society and of their complicity in the oppression of women, they often react with defensiveness followed by guilt (Josofowitz, 1980). Validation of these feelings is imperative in helping male trainees move beyond defensiveness to a new evaluation of women and an acceptance of partnership in fighting oppression.

When a class or supervisory group is composed of both male and female trainees, instances of the usual male-female power differential may occur spontaneously within the group itself. For example, even when males comprise a very small contingent, they often dominate discussions, while women often lack confidence and hesitate to communicate their ideas. Men frequently interrupt, while women politely defer to them. So insidious is this process that, unless instructors are alert, even they may find themselves giving greater attention to male input than to female. The instructor has a unique opportunity to identify such processes as they occur and to use them to demonstrate feminist concepts. As trainees express feelings about their interactions, they experience a highly meaningful and immediate lesson about the power of gender-role socialization.

Once trainees have achieved awareness of women's oppression, they have a cognitive foundation upon which to base executive skills. Training in feminist executive skills may proceed simultaneously with that in perceptual/conceptual skills. The supervisor may use typical family therapy training methods, such as roleplaying, analyzing videotaped sessions, live supervision, pre- and post-session discussions, and feedback. Examining videotaped therapy sessions through an interactional lens and then through a feminist lens enables therapists to see the differences and similarities between the two and to plan interventions that integrate both. Reviewing videotapes also provides an opportunity for the instructor/supervisor to challenge trainees' stereotypical thinking and behavior and to present alternatives.

Live supervision is particularly useful for teaching feminist perspectives and skills. The supervisor may direct the therapist's attention to underlying power and gender issues, as well as coach the therapist to challenge the family's stereotypic expectations and behaviors. When there is a team present, the "Greek Chorus" (Papp, 1980) may be used to elevate and empower women by validating their perspective and feelings, providing support in taking firm positions, encouraging self-development, and applauding efforts to take less responsibility for the family. Such live supervision should be feminist in nature, in that peer observers work as an egalitarian team. Rather than developing all interventions, the supervisor stimulates discussion of the immediate case by asking the team members' opinions, generating an atmosphere open to creative ideas and suggestions, and helping each team member to become an active part of the supervisory process. This involvement includes sharing responsibility for phoning in interventions which have been discussed and agreed upon by the team.

The Supervisory Relationship

The relationship between supervisor and trainee is a crucial element in the training program, one which should embody the feminist values and behavior the therapist is learning. The major characteristics of this relationship are the minimization of hierarchy and the use of social analysis.

MINIMIZING HIERARCHY. Hierarchy may be minimized in the following ways:

(a) *Contracting*. In a feminist training approach, the purpose of contracting is somewhat different from that in traditional family therapy training. Here contracting is used to minimize the hierarchy between supervisor and therapist by stipulating shared responsibility for change and learning. The contract becomes a vehicle for negotiating the roles of both supervisor and trainee. At the beginning of training, the supervisor works with each therapist to specify goals, objectives, areas of improvement, and ways in which the supervisor can be most useful. The responsibility for the therapist's learning is shared equally by supervisor and therapist, with the supervisor as active as the therapist, but not more so. The contract is used to underscore this cooperative attitude.

(b) *Evaluation*. Hierarchy is also minimized via shared responsibility for evaluation. The learning goals and objectives outlined in the contract become criteria by which progress can be measured. During and following training, therapists will discuss their own progress and receive and offer feedback from other trainees regarding each one's achievement. As an equal partner in this process, the supervisor is also evaluated in terms of his/her effectiveness in helping trainees meet their goals.

Feedback is given in an atmosphere where trainees' unique capabilities, individual strengths, and competencies are valued and built upon. One responsibility of the supervisor is to challenge respectfully any stereotypic behavior and to encourage more balanced, androgynous skills. One way to empower a female trainee is to challenge passive, diffident, overly polite behavior. Encouraging her to be active (Caust, Libow, & Raskin, 1981) while also displaying empathy not only validates traditional female behavior but also fosters growth in an instrumental direction. Encouraging expressions of feeling, self-disclosure, warmth, empathy, and intuition in male trainees while still appreciating an active, directive therapeutic posture promotes the widening of behavioral repertoires. It is important, then, for supervisors to push both male and female trainees to explore areas of technique, style, and attitude beyond the traditional, and simultaneously to validate those traditional behaviors which are effective, useful, and positive.

(c) *Use of language.* Therapists' questions are encouraged, respected, and responded to with clear, uncomplicated language and ideas. Such clarity reduces power and status differentials and facilitates learning.

The supervisor, aware of gender bias implicit in our culture, is careful to avoid sexist language and encourages trainees to be equally aware. For example, referring to women clients or therapists as "girls," attending to a woman's appearance rather than her intelligence or competence, and using derogatory labels in regard to female clients demean female clients and trainees alike.

SOCIAL ANALYSIS. Social analysis by the trainee and supervisor clarifies and politicizes a therapeutic issue. For example, a supervisor might say, "You're being too polite with these clients. As women we've been taught to be passive, polite, and not to challenge other's ideas or values. But this often isn't useful to us either as women or therapists. Direct your couple to talk to one another rather than asking them so politely to do so. This models an active and competent woman." Building a cognitive bridge between therapist behavior and traditional socialization empowers therapists while teaching them to make broader political connections for themselves and their clients. Such social analysis is all the more powerful when accompanied by appropriate self-disclosure by the supervisor regarding the effect of his/her socialization on his/her therapeutic style.

Social analysis also should take into consideration the gender issues implicit between supervisor and therapist. As Okun (1983) has stated, "Gender issues are inevitable in processes of family systems therapy and supervision, and these require primary consideration in establishing and implementing the training curriculum" (p. 45). A major gender issue is the possibility of the supervisor-trainee relationship falling into destructive traditional patterns, indicated by the following behaviors: submissive or seductive behavior in women; a patronizing or seductive attitude in men; male trainees not taking female supervisors seriously; male therapists' ideas, behaviors, and progress valued above those of women (Okun, 1983). Social analysis may be used to make connections between these incidents and traditional attitudes and behaviors supported in society.

CONCLUSION

We have presented a model of feminist family therapy and supervision designed to promote a more gender-sensitive approach to working with families. This approach provides family therapists with an expanded lens through which to view families and encourages greater role flexibility, equality, and choices for all family members. The supervisor who employs this model is responding to recent feminist critiques of family therapy by pointing not only his/her trainees but also the field in a new direction — one which will require both courage and commitment.

REFERENCES

Avis, J. M. (1985). The politics of functional family therapy: A feminist critique. *Journal of Marital and Family Therapy, 11*(2), 127–38.

Caust, B. L., Libow, J. A., & Raskin, P. A. (1981). Challenges and promises of training women as family systems therapists. *Family Process, 22*, 439–447.

Cleghorn, J. M., & Levine, S. (1973). Training family therapists by setting learning objectives. *American Journal of Orthopsychiatry, 43*(3), 439–446.

Feldman, L. (1982). Sex roles and family dynamics. In F. Walsh (Ed.). *Normal family processes.* New York: Guilford Press.

Gilbert, L. A. (1980). Feminist therapy. In A. M. Brodsky & R. Hare-Mustin (Eds.). *Women and psychotherapy: An assessment of research and practice.* New York: Guilford Press.

Gurman, A. S., & Klein, M. H. (1984). The family: An unconscious male bias in behavioral treatment? In E. Blechman (Ed.). *Behavior modification with women.* New York: Guilford Press.

Haley, J. (1976). *Problem-solving therapy.* San Francisco, CA: Jossey-Bass.

Haley, J. (1980). *Leaving home: The therapy of disturbed young people.* New York: McGraw-Hill.

Hare-Mustin, R. T. (1978). A feminist approach to family therapy. *Family Process, 17*, 181–194.

Hare-Mustin, R. T. (1979). Family therapy and sex role stereotypes. *The Counseling Psychologist, 8*(1), 31–32.

Hartsock, N. (1975). Fundamental feminism: Process and perspective. *Quest: A Feminist Quarterly, 2*(2), 32–43.

Hoffman, L. (1981). *Foundations of family therapy.* New York: Basic Books.

Ivey, A. E. (1971). *Microcounseling: Innovations in interviewing training.* Springfield: Thomas.

Jacobson, N. S. (1983). Beyond empiricism: The politics of marital therapy. *The American Journal of Family Therapy, 11*(2), 11–24.

James, K., & McIntyre, D. (1983). The reproduction of families: The social role of family therapy. *Journal of Marital and Family Therapy, 9*(2), 119-129.

Josofowitz, N. (1980). *Paths to power*. Reading, MA: Addison-Wesley.

Klein, M. H. (1976). Feminist concepts of therapy outcome. *Psychotherapy, Theory, Research, and Practice, 13*, 89-95.

Kolbenschlag, M. (1979). *Kiss sleeping beauty good-bye*. New York: Bantam.

Libow, J. A., Raskin, P. A., & Caust, B. (1982). Feminist and family systems therapy: Are they irreconcilable? *The American Journal of Family Therapy, 10*(3), 3-12.

Liddle, H. (1982). Family therapy training: Current issues, future themes. *International Journal of Family Therapy, 4*, 31-97.

Liddle, H. A., & Saba, G. W. (1982). On teaching family therapy at the introductory level: A conceptual model emphasizing a pattern which connects training and therapy. *Journal of Marital and Family Therapy, 8*(1), 63-72.

Miller, L. A. (1983). Feminism, families and family therapy. Presentation at American Association for Marriage and Family Therapy, Washington, D.C.

Minuchin, S., & Fishman, C. (1981). *Techniques of family therapy*. Cambridge, MA: Harvard University Press.

Okun, B. F. (1983). Gender issues of family systems therapists. In B. Okun & S. T. Gladdings (Eds.), *Issues in training marriage and family therapists*. Ann Arbor, MI:ERIC/CAPS.

Papp, P. (1980). The Greek chorus and other techniques of family therapy. *Family Process, 199*(1), 45-57.

Rice, D. G., & Rice, J. K. (1977). Non-sexist "marital" therapy. *Journal of Marriage and Family Counseling, 3*, 3-10.

Rowbotham, S. (1973). *Woman's consciousness, man's world*. Middlesex: Penguin.

Seidler-Feller, D. (1976). Process and power in couples psychotherapy: A feminist view. *Voices*, Fall, 67-71.

Thorne, B. with Yalom, M. (Eds.) (1982). *Rethinking the family. Some feminist questions*. New York: Longman.

Tomm, K. M., & Wright, L. M. (1979). Training in family therapy: Perceptual, conceptual and executive skills. *Family Process, 18*, 227-230.

Wheeler, D. (1983). Feminism's treatment of women in the family: Implications for family therapy. (Unpublished manuscript)

9

Women as Therapists, Trainees, and Supervisors

JANET WARBURTON

ALICE NEWBERRY   JAMES ALEXANDER

THE DIFFERENTIAL EFFECT and therapeutic implications of gender are rarely specifically addressed in family therapy theory, research, and practice. Specifically, while the literature describing family therapy practice and training reflects the complexity of such theoretical and practical aspects as joining (e.g., Minuchin, 1974), the social phase (e.g., Haley, 1963), and the need to establish credibility (e.g., Alexander, Barton, Waldron, & Mas, 1983), the impact of therapist gender has not been well conceptualized or articulated, although it is a critical aspect of the therapeutic process. While female family therapy trainees had a number of female role models, in the early development of the field such as Virginia Satir, Kitty LaPerriere, Peggy Papp, and Lynn Hoffman, how their behaviors and methods differ from those of male therapists has rarely been discussed. Though many of us know better, the "classic" family therapy training literature implies that male and female therapists can enter and manage family therapy process in the same way.

This is clearly not true. Male and female therapists have different experiences in therapy sessions resulting from differences in societal expectations of appropriate sex-role behavior, as well as the assumptions and behaviors of family members and therapists themselves. In a series of studies of functional family therapy, we examined the effects of therapist and client gender on the therapy process. In the following pages we briefly review these findings, concentrating on the female therapist's experience, highlighting potential problem areas, and providing a conceptual framework to understand them. In addition, we will suggest ways women can deal with these problems successfully, as well as ways male trainees and supervisors can be sensitized to their own issues of power and status which arise in the context of therapy. Although our studies are primarily of inexperienced therapists employing a specific family model, the themes are likely to apply in other situations as well.

THE THERAPEUTIC PROCESS: A DIFFICULT CONTEXT FOR WOMEN

In our studies of initial therapy sessions of two-parent families with an adolescent identified patient, therapist trainees and clients were rated on a number of process measures. These included the ratio of supportive to defensive communications; the amount of talk time for parents, therapist trainees, and adolescents; and the proportional use of structuring techniques by male and female trainees. Alexander, 1973; Warburton, Alexander, & Barton, 1980; Newberry, Alexander, & Turner, 1987; Mas, Alexander, & Barton, 1985). In general, we found that both male and female trainees can expect pulls for affiliation with the same-sex parent and defensiveness from the opposite-sex parent. Female therapists, however, tend to encounter more defensiveness from family members and other unique problems that male therapists are spared.

Rates of defensive and supportive communications in families of delinquents differed significantly, with the gender of the therapist (Warburton, Alexander, & Barton, 1980). Mothers made more supportive comments to female therapists, while fathers were more supportive to male therapists. Fathers were more defensive toward female therapists than toward males; however, mothers were not more defensive toward male therapists than females. Early in therapy, each parent placed strong affiliative demands on the therapist of the same sex; there were significantly fewer affiliative communications from the opposite-sex parent. The magnitude of the differences between the affiliative behaviors of the parents suggests that parents initiate interactions in an effort to form or avoid a coalition with the therapist. Therapists, meanwhile, are trained to equalize system interaction, or at least to serially join with each parent (Alexander & Parsons, 1982; Ficher & Linsenberg, 1976; Haley, 1963; Minuchin, 1974; Zuk, 1971). The data suggest that a female therapist must work harder to attain this therapeutic goal, since fathers are more defensive with her, while mothers are not more defensive with a male therapist. She must find a way to connect with and win over a defensive father without alienating and losing the support of the mother. This, of course, is no easy task, since parents are often in conflict.

Further analysis shows that the behavior of family members isn't the only factor that differs on the basis of gender. Unfortunately, female trainees themselves respond more defensively than their male colleagues to these already defensive fathers. Thus, there is a risk of escalating reciprocal negative messages between these female therapists and fathers, resulting in a therapeutic context in which producing positive change will be difficult, if not impossible (Warburton & Alexander, 1985.)

Women therapists have another disadvantage in beginning family therapy with this group: getting adolescents to talk. While this is generally a problem in family therapy, it is exaggerated with female therapists. In a separate investigation of the same therapy sessions, Mas, Alexander, and Barton (1985) found that adolescents talked approximately one-half as much as their parents in first sessions with male therapists, but only one-quarter as much as their parents with female therapists. Since these adolescents were the identified patients, their general reluctance to talk was not surprising. It is likely that they had been coerced to attend therapy and felt on the spot. However, equality of talk time among family members by the end of therapy is predictive of positive outcome, while lack of equality predicts poor outcome (Parsons & Alexander, 1973). Consequently, in the interest of producing positive change, this issue must be addressed. Once again, we see a more difficult therapy context for female therapists. They must do more than their male colleagues to actively involve adolescents.

The difficult nature of the therapeutic context may be further complicated by the fact that female therapists, even those with some experience, tend to underestimate their influence on families (Woodward et al., 1981). In judging therapy outcome, female therapists rated their families as having changed less in treatment and as having a poorer prognosis than did male therapists, despite the fact that female and male therapists actually produced similar outcomes on more objective measures of recidivism and goal attainment. This result is consistent with other research demonstrating that males tend to overestimate their performance (West & Zimmerman, 1983). Thus, while we can assume female therapists begin therapy with a more difficult set of therapeutic tasks than male therapists, there is no evidence (at least in Woodward's study) that they produce poorer outcomes. Female trainees may benefit from supervision which focuses on helping them value their own skills and strengths and develop confidence in their ability to create positive treatment outcome. Certainly, the point could be made that their skills are at least as good as those of their male colleagues, since they start out at a disadvantage and end up in the same place.

To further understand gender differences in therapist behavior, Newberry, Alexander, and Turner (1987) examined the use and effect of two therapeutic techniques: supportive techniques, which include conveying caring and warmth and encouraging the family to express feelings and to see behaviors in a more positive light; and structuring techniques, which include establishing the rules of interchange, asking process questions, or directing the flow of the therapy session. This study revealed that female therapists were significantly more likely than male therapists to use structuring behaviors in response to supportive behaviors of clients.

It is surprising that female therapists used more structuring techniques, since they would seem to be inconsistent with stereotypically "feminine" behavior. One might even assume that female therapists would receive strong messages from families that they prefer supportive therapeutic behaviors — and, in fact, this seems to be true. Parents were more likely to respond supportively to a female therapist when she engaged in supportive behaviors. In other words, they rewarded her for giving support or behaving in a more traditionally feminine way. They were less likely to respond supportively to supportive behavior from male therapists. Perhaps the female trainees in this study were conscious of the need to gain authority and credibility, thus accounting for their unexpectedly high rates of structuring behaviors. It would be interesting to know if these rates change with increased experience.

THE ISSUE OF GENDER DIFFERENCES: SOCIALIZATION AS "CULPRIT"

The interpretation of psychological data on gender differences has undergone a number of shifts over the past 25 years. Initially, psychological studies did not look at gender differences at all, frequently using only male research subjects. When critiques of these early studies pointed out the lack of knowledge about the female experience, there was a proliferation of research on female behavior, perhaps as a way of correcting decades of inattention to this issue in the psychological literature and of attempting to eliminate the myth of male behavior as the normative standard for psychological health.

In 1974, Maccoby and Jacklin summarized the literature on gender differences in their influential work, *The Psychology of Gender Differences*. Their review emphasized that there are few real differences in male and female abilities and behaviors. This led some to conclude erroneously that gender differences could be minimized and laid the groundwork for the next series of gender studies, which focused predominantly on gender similarities. At the same time, however, Maccoby and Jacklin's conclusions turned attention to the discrepancies between the *experiences* of men and women. It became clear that, although male and female abilities and behaviors appeared to be similar, their social realities were quite different. The increased awareness of this discrepancy led to a reacknowledgment of sex differences (Chodorow, 1974; Gilligan, 1982).

SOCIALIZATION—THE PROBLEM

We have described some different responses of families to female therapists that result from their differing expectations for males and females based on patterns of socialization in families and larger social systems. Male and female children are typically raised differently, girls to be caregivers with an emphasis on interpersonal skills and the importance of intimacy, and boys to be doers with an orientation toward mastery of tasks (Chodorow, 1974; Gilligan, 1982; Hare-Mustin & Marecek, 1986; Westkott, 1986). The social construction of appropriate gender roles affects both the ways men and women behave and the ways others perceive them. Clients may not expect the female therapist to be "in charge" of therapy sessions and thus may have more difficulty accepting her authority or seeing her behavior as appropriate when it is authoritative. Therefore, she may have to work harder and differently to be seen as an authority during sessions.

Differences in socialization also affect the expectations clients and therapists have of themselves. The "feminine" socialization of female therapists may conflict with role expectations that a therapist be assertive and powerful, while males may find the parts of their roles which require warm and empathic behavior to be more problematic. For instance, if the male client's socialization history includes messages such as "hold back," "be strong," "don't feel emotion," "take care of her," or any of a multitude of other culturally approved gender-linked messages, it will take him longer to interact effectively with a female therapist than the male who comes in with past experiences which have led him to believe that female authorities can be helpful. If, in addition, this skeptical male meets a female therapist whose internal socialization has taught her to be subordinate to males, i.e., "be silent, let him have the upper hand, let him have his way," therapy will be further impeded, unless the therapist has learned specific techniques for coping with these underlying issues and themes. These issues will, of course, become easier to handle as therapists and trainees have opportunities to try, and succeed at, new behaviors.

THE THEORETICAL CONTEXT

Power issues in therapy tend to activate gender stereotypes for both therapists and clients. How they behave and respond to one another is affected by their feelings and beliefs about the gender stereotypes that our society has set forth as normal.

The roles of therapist and client are usually seen as complementary, with the therapist being viewed as more powerful. In fact, some therapists, such as Haley (1963), have made this definition of power distribution central to their therapeutic model. However, in the case of a female therapist and a male client, a second status hierarchy can be superimposed on the complementarity of the therapist-client relationship, that of the male-female hierarchy. Males are expected to have more status than females in our society. If the female therapist is also a trainee, the hierarchy is further complicated by a third variable, level of experience. Finally, in family therapy, if the male client is also a father and husband, a fourth hierarchy develops, since he is likely to be viewed as having the additional power of being "in charge of" other family members. Thus, the female therapist who attempts to move into a power relationship under these circumstances is likely to encounter some strong challenges. She had better be prepared.

The defensiveness that often pervades the relationship between male client and female therapist may result from the tension created by the male's desire to hold power in a context in which the female therapist is likely to see that as her prerogative. Since our culture continues to grant males superior status (Janeway, 1980) and since females continue to expect to have less authority and less status (Eagly & Steffen, 1984; Eagly & Wood, 1982), stereotypes continue to downgrade female competence and authority. Competent women tend to be seen as sex-role incongruent (Nieva, 1981), and since competence is not generally expected of a woman, other traits associated with effectiveness and competence (e.g., assertiveness and competitiveness) are seen as inappropriate for women. A woman who behaves in a competent manner disconfirms sex role expectations and usually suffers one of two possible outcomes: She is disliked or excluded from a group (Hagen & Kahn, 1975), or her performance is discounted (Deaux and Emswiller, 1974, Nieva, 1981). Obviously, the implications for therapy are significant. In these situations, the female therapist must engage the male client and the entire system before attempting to use power effectively. If she moves too soon, or if she becomes defensive, she may risk creating more resistance or undermine her power by seeming insecure.

While there is no direct test of this theoretical stance, there is literature to indicate that the conflicting influence of sex status and expert status variables in the confusing and complex status hierarchy of the female therapist trainee–male client dyad results in an unclear sense of who is in charge. The role of therapist gives the female authority, but her gender and lack of experience undermine her power—both in her own view and in the view of family members. This ambiguity could result in a futile and unproductive struggle for control within the therapy. Studies are needed to examine these status variables and their effects on the process and outcome of therapy. This is not to suggest that male trainees do not experience feelings of anxiety and insecurity around their own levels of inexperience. However, they may

not have to cope with as many challenges to their competence from the
family.

A FRAMEWORK FOR TRAINING

Male and female experience has been described as the difference between
vision and voice (Belenky, Clinchy, Goldberger, & Tarule, 1986; Gilligan,
1982), with male authority illustrated by visual metaphor (e.g., "seeing the
truth of the matter") and female authority by the presence or absence of
voice (e.g., "speaking up, being heard"). Women in general have more difficulty being heard; some even come to expect to be discounted and ignored.
The training of the female therapist must counteract these expectations,
developing the formation and expression of voice. A female trainee may
have problems succeeding as a therapist because the role, by its very nature,
demands that she reach a new developmental stage in her use of authority. If
she experiences difficulty being an authority and using power effectively, she
may remain unable to claim an identity as an expert therapist, that is, she
may be unable to speak up or insist on being heard.

Women are frequently socialized to subdue or restrict their authority,
while males are socialized to demonstrate authority in a very direct, task-
oriented manner. If a father conveys, however indirectly to a female therapist in the first few minutes of therapy, the message: "You can't help me or
my family because you are a woman," the female therapist must be prepared
to deal with his challenge to her abilities. If she has been able to express
herself in a way that has been useful to many other families, she is likely to
see his statement as an expression of his resistance to being in therapy or his
discomfort around female authority figures, rather than as a personal challenge. She may have the expertise to engage in a dialogue within the context
of ambiguous power and status. A less experienced female therapist, however, is likely to have a more restricted ability to use herself. She may view the
male client's challenges to her competence as a personal assault and become
intimidated or engage in win-lose debates about her ability to help.

Thus, the model of growth for female therapists should be both cognitive
and behavioral. In order to overcome the inhibitions of traditional gender-
linked socialization, she must be helped to think her way out of nonproduc-
tive habit patterns (which tend to die hard) and helped to develop specific
techniques for managing sessions and meeting the specific challenges to her
competence which she will encounter. Supervisors must be aware of these
issues and explicitly assist their female trainees to develop skills in claiming
authority. The issues around when to respond to direct confrontation and
when to take a one-down position are basic to helping all family therapy

trainees become competent therapists; it's just that they are more crucial for women.

THE REMEDY

Patterns of socialization in our society establish and reinforce the different therapy contexts male and female therapists experience. Since the socialization of client, therapist, and supervisor will not change overnight, certain training issues become critical. Such data as our results demonstrating that male and female therapists face different therapeutic challenges should become common knowledge to trainees and supervisors alike.

We must expand our research efforts in this area to learn more about the problems male and female therapists encounter and how they can develop the skills they need to work successfully with families. We also need to learn about the ways that stereotypic gender roles influence the process of supervision and then make sure that this awareness becomes integrated into family therapy training programs. Since males are socialized to behave in an autonomous manner which lends itself to hierarchical ordering, and females are socialized to behave in a relational, connected manner which is more collaborative, the learning context is likely to be experienced very differently by male and female trainees.

Male trainees supervised by male supervisors find themselves in an apprentice position, one where they learn directly from their male teacher behaviors they will later perform. The one-down male trainee experiences his separateness and watches the modeling of a one-up male supervisor, who imparts learning in male-male supervision.

A female trainee with a female supervisor is likely to experience something different. Rather than a one-up, one-down hierarchical model of learning, the process of female-female supervision tends to be more relational, with the transfer of information occurring within the context of a more collaborative equal relationship. The behaviors modeled are less likely to be power-oriented, but the female supervisor, because she has experienced the problems related to being a female "in charge of" families, is likely to be able to share the techniques she has developed for managing such situations. Because she, too, has had to come to grips with the use of female power in an ambiguous context, the supervision can focus on specific techniques for establishing professional authority while maintaining very positive and useful empathy and relational skills.

More serious problems can be expected when either male or female supervisors supervise a different-sex trainee. Since males have not experienced the particular reactions and challenges their female trainees are likely to encounter, and because they may operate from a conceptual framework which emphasizes separateness and hierarchy, they may not recognize the female trainee's dilemmas. However, being aware of the documented gender differences in therapy and interpreting their own male-female process issues as part of the supervisory relationship may help. Female supervisors, especially those who tend to make a suggestion or offer an alternative when they really mean to give more definite feedback, may need to learn to be assertive with their male trainees. They also may need to deal with the reactions of male trainees to their power and authority.

CLINICAL ISSUES

The female therapists in our studies tended to spend the first few minutes of the initial session establishing their competence and credibility with the father in the family. They initially appeared more likely to talk to the father than to either the adolescent or the mother. Male therapists were significantly less likely to concentrate on the father in this way. The early exchanges between the father and the female therapist can be explained, in part, by the status ambiguity issues already described. Faced with a female therapist, a father may feel more reluctant to give up control. Should he remain "in charge" of his family or should he turn his family over to the expert, who in this case looks to him to be a young and inexperienced female? In such situations, it may seem to the female trainee that her task is to convince the father that she is competent and can help the family. This may be difficult in light of the evidence that females have more difficulty than males in considering themselves to be authorities (West & Zimmerman, 1983), more difficulty in gaining respect from others and being listened to (Aries, 1976), and more difficulty in utilizing their capabilities and training (Gallese, 1985).

Our earlier research (Alexander, Barton, Schiavo, & Parsons, 1976) indicated that it was crucial for beginning therapists to be active to establish their credibility. Nevertheless, beginning female trainees sometimes started the initial session on a hesitant or even apologetic note, communicating their discomfort or inexperience. At times they sought approval or asked permission of family members, i.e., "Is that acceptable to you?" even when there was no alternative if the family did not agree. All of this introduces unnecessary uncertainty when ideally the family should be moving in the direction of feeling comfortable and assuming that the therapist is credible, confident, and capable of helping them. Some female therapists qualify their statements by adding "Ok?" after taking what would be a definitive stand. This tendency to ask for affirmation and add qualifying words or phrases, such as "maybe," "I'm not sure," or "I may be wrong," may undermine the therapist's authority. The more stereotypical male style of making forceful statements of fact (even when there was ambiguity) often seemed to lead to a more positive initial response from the families.

Our female therapists also occasionally became embroiled in a struggle over the father's participation in therapy, either deferring to the father's position that more important work demands precluded his attention or else seeking outside authority to reinforce the position that he should attend. An alternative to getting caught in a struggle about whether the father will come to therapy is to explore the father's reasons for not participating, empathize with them, but eventually give the message that everyone will work together to find the best way for him to be involved (see Anderson & Stewart, 1983, for other strategies).

Female therapists can more readily establish credibility and authority if they are neither apologetic nor uncertain and avoid relying on outside authority to exert their power in the session. A direct, active, but nonblaming style is effective as feelings are clarified and relabeled and topic changes initiated. An alternative response to a father's challenge of her authority might be to change focus. With this technique, the therapist gains or regains authority, modifying the presumed intent of a father's challenging statement by reinterpreting his verbal behavior in a positive way. For instance, to avoid a direct power struggle, the therapist might attempt to identify and label some of a father's underlying feelings, i.e., she might respond, "It sounds to me like you've tried so hard that you just can't think of trying again." This communicates to the father that she is on his side and is not blaming him. On a process level, the therapist maintains her control of the therapy by picking up on the emotional component of father's verbal behavior, thereby suggesting another way that behaviors can be interpreted without directly confronting him. The therapist establishes that the father is free to express his feelings, including his feelings of frustration and despair. The struggle for control is sidestepped; the therapist does not simply accept the father's terms but expands those terms to include her own expert view. A new context is established for the father's behavior, e.g., one expanded to include love and caring for his child. Female therapists may have an advantage over male therapists in these relational strategies because of their socialization.

In a case in which the father is openly defensive, as sometimes occurs, particularly in the beginning phases of therapy and particularly with a female therapist, it is important to remember that defensiveness begets defensiveness. The wise therapist avoids a direct confrontation. In our view, during the first phases of therapy overtly defensive statements should not stimulate the therapist to engage in an overt struggle for control (Alexander et al., 1983). Typically an active therapist can use structuring and relabeling techniques to avoid direct confrontation.

It is useful to understand the sources of fathers' behaviors that directly challenge the authority of the female therapist. Traditionally, such challenges are explained as reflecting anxiety and insecurity about an unfamiliar setting and an unknown therapist; such questioning probably also is the result of fathers' stereotypes about appropriate roles for men and women (Bloom, Weigel, & Trautt, 1977; Eagly & Steffen, 1984). In the beginning of therapy, the female therapist must both establish her credibility as an expert who is in charge *and* remain sufficiently sex-role congruent to engage traditional families and male clients. Some attributes that are typified as feminine can be strengths for a female therapist, while others undermine her effectiveness. A relationship focus, warmth, and empathy work to the female therapist's advantage in establishing relationships and credibility (Alexander et al., 1983). What the female therapist must avoid in working with certain families is confirming the typically stereotypic view of women as passive; instead she must strive to take an active stance. The trainees we studied were clearly working to do so.

In our particular model, there are a number of ways female therapists can work to establish their authority. They can do it directly by creating "interaction rules" in the beginning phase. For example, a therapist who "takes the heat" off each individual by interrupting blaming sequences of interaction is establishing a relationship focus as a rule in therapy. By using active strategies of intervention and overtly prescribing desirable behaviors, she communicates an ability to take charge and to give instructions. The female therapist can also take charge by using *her* own behavior assertively. For example, when she redirects the flow of therapy by changing the subject or turning to another person and asking for a comment, the therapist is establishing her control over the therapy process.

Another way in which all therapists, but particularly female therapists, establish rules is by reframing behaviors. For example, if a father says, "All the little brat does is run away," the therapist might respond, "It sounds as if it's very frustrating for you when your son runs away." With this statement the therapist not only demonstrates empathy for the father's pain but also links the father and son in an explanation of the problem. This potentially adds to each member's understanding and demonstrates the therapist's ability to define the meaning of behaviors interactionally in the context in which they occur.

It is useful for the therapist to state explicitly what the family can expect of her and what her expectations are of family members. Such activities establish "interaction rules" and support the credibility of the therapist as an "expert"—someone with the knowledge and techniques to solve the family's problems. The therapist can thus "direct the flow" of therapy, creating the context in which behavior occurs. The therapist can also actively shape the therapy process by structuring therapeutic interventions, overtly stating therapy rules, directly teaching skills, and so forth (Newberry & Alexander, 1987; Patterson, 1985). Establishing therapist credibility is a crucial initial goal of therapy (Alexander & Parsons, 1982; Warburton & Alexander, 1985).

RECOMMENDATIONS

We suggest several solutions to the difficulties female therapists, most notably less experienced female therapists, face in family therapy, especially when sessions include husbands/fathers:

1. Trainers have a responsibility to promote an awareness of the contextual differences produced by the gender of both the therapist and the client. However, in generating solutions to problems, such as rebalancing differential treatment of male and female clients, we risk reinforcing stereotypes (McCauley, Stitt, & Segal, 1980). In telling beginning male therapists to expect less support from mothers and beginning female therapists to expect less support from fathers, we may set up negative expectations about opposite-sex clients that then perpetuate negative interactions. However, unless attention is given to these issues, we perpetuate the naive belief that no differences exist and thus no special skills are required. Therapists will fail and not know why.
2. Two stereotypic female characteristics, empathy and a relational focus, work for the female therapist, while a third, passivity, works against positive therapeutic outcome. Female therapists are advised to take an active role and to develop a style that helps them to deal with power effectively.
3. Female therapists have an ambiguous power position with male clients unless they clearly establish control of sessions and the process of therapy. We have suggested they do this directly by establishing the interaction rules in the beginning phase.
4. It is important for female therapists to be able to change the meaning level or focus of a discussion, thereby shifting to a therapeutic metalevel and "creating knowledge" through alternative explanations and expanded possibilities for family members.
5. We may need to remind our female trainees not to overuse qualifiers such as "maybe" or "I'm not sure" and our male trainees to insert such qualifiers and not always be so sure.
6. Finally, the differentiated gender experience for males and females in the supervisor/trainee relationship must be addressed in family therapy training.

REFERENCES

Alexander, J. F. (1973). Defensive and supportive communication in normal and deviant families. *Journal of Consulting and Clinical Psychology, 40*, 223–231.

Alexander, J. F., Barton, C., Schiavo, R. S., & Parsons, B. V. (1976). Systems-behavioral intervention with families of delinquents: Therapist characteristics, family behavior, and outcome. *Journal of Consulting and Clinical Psychology, 44*, 656–664.

Alexander, J. F., Barton, C., Waldron, H., & Mas, C. H. (1983). Beyond the technology of family therapy: The anatomy of intervention model. In K. D. Craig & R. J. McMahon (Eds.), *Advances in clinical behavior therapy*. New York: Brunner/Mazel.

Alexander, J. F., Mas, C. H., & Waldron, H. (1987). Behavioral and systems family therapies — or Auld Lang Syne: Shall old perspectives be forgot? In R. Dev. Peters & R. S. McMahon (Eds.), *Marriages and families: Behavioral systems treatments and process*. New York: Brunner/Mazel.

Alexander, J. F., & Parsons, B. V. (1982). *Functional family therapy*. Monterey: Brooks/Cole.

Anderson, C. M., & Stewart, S. (1983). *Mastering resistance: A practice guide to family therapy*. New York: Guilford.

Aries, E. (1976). Interaction patterns and themes of male, female, and mixed groups. *Small Group Behavior, 7*, 7–14.

Belenky, M. F., Clinchy, B. M., Goldberger, N. R., & Tarule, J. M. (1986). *Women's ways of knowing: The development of self, voice, and mind*. New York: Basic Books.

Bloom, L. J., Weigel, R. G., & Trautt, G. M. (1977). "Therapeugenic" factors in psychotherapy: Effects of office decor and subject-therapist sex pairings on the perception of credibility. *Journal of Consulting and Clinical Psychology, 45*, 867–873.

Chodorow, N. (1974). Family structure and feminine personality. In M. Z. Rosald & L. Lamphere, (Eds.), *Woman, culture and society*. Stanford: Stanford University Press.

Deaux, K., & Emswiller, T. (1974). Explanations for successful performance on sex-linked tasks: What is skill for the male is luck for the female. *Journal of Personality and Social Psychology, 29*, 80–85.

Deaux, K., & Major, B. (1987). Putting gender into context: An interactive model of gender-related behavior. *Psychological Review, 94*(3), 369–389.

Eagly, A., & Steffen, V. J. (1984). Gender stereotypes stem from the distribution of women and men into social roles. *Journal of Personality and Social Psychology, 46*, 735–754.

Eagly, A. H., & Wood, W. (1982). Inferred sex differences in status as a determinant of gender stereotypes about social influence. *Journal of Personality and Social Psychology, 43*, 915–928.

Ficher, I. V., & Linsenberg, M. (1976). Problems confronting the female therapist doing couple therapy. *Journal of Marriage and Family Counseling, 2*(4), 331–339.

Gallese, L. R. (1985). *Women like us*. New York: William Morrow.

Gilligan, C. (1982). *In a different voice*. Cambridge, MA: Harvard University Press.

Hagen, R. L., & Kahn, A. (1975). Discrimination against competent women. *Journal of Applied Social Psychology, 5*(4), 362–376.

Haley, J. (1963). *Strategies of psychotherapy*. New York: Grune & Stratton.

Hare-Mustin, R. T., & Marecek, J. (1986). Autonomy and gender: Some questions for therapists. *Psychotherapy, 23*, 205–213.

Janeway, E. (1980). *Powers of the weak*. New York: Alfred Knopf.

Maccoby, E., & Jacklin, D. (1974). *The psychology of sex differences*. Stanford, CA: Stanford University Press.

Mas, C. H., Alexander, J. F., & Barton, C. (1985). Modes of expression in family therapy: A process study of roles and gender. *Journal of Marital and Family Therapy, 11*(4), 411–415.

McCauley, D., Sitt, C. L., & Segal, M. (1980). Stereotyping: From prejudice to prediction. *Psychological Bulletin, 87*(1), 195–200.

Minuchin, S. (1974). *Families and family therapy*. Cambridge, MA: Harvard University Press.

Newberry, A. M., & Alexander, J. F. (1987). *Therapy coding manual*. Unpublished manuscript, University of Utah, Salt Lake City, Utah.

Newberry, A. M., Alexander, J. F., & Turner, C. W. (1987, November). *First session family therapy process*. Paper presented at the 21st convention of the Association for Advancement of Behavior Therapy, Boston, MA.

Nieva, V. (1981). *The perception of and reactions to female competence*. Paper presented at the meeting of the American Psychological Association, Los Angeles, California.

Parsons, B. V., & Alexander, J. F. (1973). Short-term family intervention: A therapy outcome study. *Journal of Consulting and Clinical Psychology, 41*, 195–201.

Patterson, G. R. (1985). Beyond technology: The next stage in developing an empirical base for parent training. In L. L'Abate (Ed.), *The handbook of family psychology and therapy* (Vol. 2). Illinois: Dorsey Press.

Warburton, J. R., & Alexander, J. F. (1985). The family therapist: What does one do? In L. L'Abate (Ed.), *The handbook of family psychology and therapy*. Homewood, IL: The Dorsey Press.

Warburton, J. R., Alexander, J. F., & Barton, C. (1980, August). *Sex of client and sex of therapist: Variables in family therapy process study*. Paper presented at the Annual Convention of the American Psychological Association, Montreal, Canada.

West, C., & Zimmerman, D. H. (1983). Small insults: A study of interruptions in cross-sex conversations between unacquainted persons. In B. Thorne, C. Kramarac, & N. Henley, (Eds.), *Language, gender, and society* (pp. 103–118). Rowley, MA: Newbury House.

Westkott, M. (1986). Historical and developmental roots of female dependency. *Psychotherapy, 23*, 213–221.

Woodward, C. A., Santa-Barbara, J., Streiner, D. L., Goodman, J. T., Levin, S., & Epstein, N. B. (1981). Client, treatment, and therapist variables related to outcome in brief, systems oriented family therapy. *Family Process, 20*, 189–197.

Zuk, G. (1971). *Family therapy: A triadic based approach*. New York: Behavioral Publications.

SECTION II

Women and Families in Context

10

Ethnicity and Women

MONICA McGOLDRICK   NYDIA GARCIA-PRETO
PAULETTE MOORE HINES   EVELYN LEE

When a newborn baby comes into the world, if it is a boy as strong as a wolf, his parents are still afraid that he might be too weak; whereas if it's a girl as sweet and gentle as a mouse, her parents still fear she might be too strong. (Han Shu, Confucian Text, cited in Kristeva, 1986)

A young man is bothered till he's married; after that he's bothered entirely. (Irish Proverb)

I most sincerely doubt if any other race of women could have brought its fineness up through so devilish a fire. (W. E. B. DuBois, Cited in Giddings, 1985)

DISCUSSING GENDER in the context of culture is a very thorny task; at the same time, however, it may offer us an important perspective on both subjects. It may also help us see the problems of all women more clearly, while highlighting some aspects of cultural differences which are otherwise hidden. Since volumes can and have been written on the role of women and culture (see, for example, Duley & Edwards, 1986; Rosaldo & Lamphere, 1974; Tonnensen & Van Horne, 1986), we will attempt in this chapter to highlight a few key differences to show the importance of this topic for our clinical understanding. One of the most problematic aspects is how to intervene clinically in a way that respects culture and at the same time challenges cultural inequities in gender arrangements.

There are wide differences among cultures in the definition of acceptable behaviors. We are keenly aware of the potential negative effects of cultural stereotyping. We hope the reader will accept the generalizations presented here as attempts to highlight some questions we need to keep in mind in our clinical work (McGoldrick, 1982a; McGoldrick, Garcia-Preto, Hines, & Lee, in press; McGoldrick, Pearce, & Giordano, 1982). We urge the reader to consider the characterizations made here not as statements of absolute fact that apply to all men and women in a given culture, but as suggestions of patterns to increase our cultural awareness.

The attitudes toward women in the dominant culture affect women of specific backgrounds differently. Women from ethnic groups that are particularly stigmatized within the larger culture are under extreme pressure to adapt to the dominant society's conventions. Often cultural stereotyping focuses on the physical characteristics of a group; this is much more problematic for women than men, since women's value is determined above all by their looks. For example, compared to Jewish men, Jewish women are much more likely to have been ridiculed for their appearance and to have had surgery to change the shape of their noses. Black women have spent fortunes straightening their hair, and the pressure on them to approach the dominant norm in looks is much more intense than it is on black men. Women from different cultures have tried to look like the youthful ideal of the dominant group, so those from fair-skinned backgrounds try to become suntanned and those whose skin is dark try to appear lighter.

Rules for female behavior vary considerably from one culture to another. Groups differ, for example, in the distance women are allowed to go beyond the confines of the family, what work is considered acceptable, and how roles are distributed within the home. In traditional Japanese culture wives were expected to walk two steps behind their husbands. Once their sons reached 13, mothers were expected to be under their power as well (Morsbach, 1978). In most groups women are still expected to love, honor and obey their husbands. However, the rules have varied. Women in black culture have consistently been expected to work outside the home to support the family (Staples, 1978). Among blacks there tended to be greater role flexibility between the sexes than in many other groups. Scandinavian women have enjoyed greater freedom and have participated in the labor force to a greater extent than most other European women (Woehrer, 1982). Italian and French women, by contrast, have never been expected to work outside the home, but they have played a pivotal role within the family and the home was considered sacred by the culture. Italian women were supposed to turn a blind eye to their husbands' affairs while remaining faithful themselves. They did have a considerable degree of power inside the home and were allowed to be expressive and passionate, as long as they did not challenge the overall rules of the system (Rotunno & McGoldrick, 1982). And Greek mothers traditionally have not been allowed even to attend the christenings or funerals of their children.

Cultures vary considerably in the roles assigned to women. Results of a study we conducted of the ethnic patterns of family therapists' own families suggested that some of the traditional stereotypes regarding cultural differences still prevail even among sophisticated therapists several generations removed from immigration (McGoldrick & Rohrbaugh, 1987). Italians, Hispanics, and Asians described men and women as having separate and defined roles—men to protect, women to nurture. Greeks said women were expected to stay in their place, Hispanics that women had to put up with what men did to them, and Asians that men were expected to handle the outside world. Italians and Greeks defined men as dominant, while Jews, WASPS, and blacks described male–female roles as more egalitarian and democratic. The latter cultures expect both men and women to be strong and able to make it alone, and blacks reported that both men and women expected to be nurturing and supportive of each other.

In American society the acculturation of men and women from different backgrounds has varied greatly. Women are generally raised to be adaptive to others, which is a particular strength in the experience of migration. Men, on the other hand, are generally brought up with much less sensitivity to their context, and therefore are often at a disadvantage in the migration experience, becoming more rigid in the face of uncontrollable changes. Yet it is men who are generally expected to deal with the outside world, while women's sphere has been primarily the interior of the family. For some this has meant that the immigrant wife has not learned the new language and has grown old in her "old country" domestic sphere. Her husband and children, who have engaged with foreigners in the new land, have learned the new language and customs.

In recent years, however, because of our increasing technological society, immigrant men from traditionally patriarchal cultures (for example, Hispanic, Greek, Italian, and Chinese) have been at an increasing disadvantage. Their wives and children often have more flexibility in adapting to the new culture. The balance between the spouses shifts as the wife gains power—she more easily learns the language, she more easily finds a job, and she learns, particularly through her children, about the ways of the new culture. This may lead to a severe sex-role imbalance for the couple (Wolfe & Witke, 1975).

The men in these cultures have diminished control over their environment, particularly when they cannot find employment. In response they often attempt to intensify their control in the one place it remains—within the family. Given the rapidly changing role of women in the United States, women from rigidly structured cultures soon learn about the increased options in this society and are less likely than before to put up with a subservient role. This cultural clash between the spouses, often played out in alcoholism or violence on the part of the husband, is one of the most common presenting problems for many recent immigrant groups. The wife comes to embody the wish for change, and the husband takes a stand for the traditional culture. She may feel she has much to gain in the changing situation. He feels he has everything to lose. The children more often side with the wife, since they too are usually more adaptive.

There is no easy solution to these complex problems. It is essential, however, that our interventions take into account the complex context of the couple. We must help the spouses evolve new patterns out of the old cultural arrangements; otherwise they will both be hurt, as the complex web of their traditional cultural structure, with its multigenerational richness, is torn apart. Therapists looking for the "quick fix" in such situations are ignoring the deeply rooted problems with which the family is struggling. To minimize the seriousness of their struggle is to leave these immigrant couples isolated. In fact, they need all the cultural supports that can be mustered to help them evolve toward new ways of relating.

Because of the vastness of the topic of ethnicity and women, we have decided to focus on five groups: Irish, Jewish, Chinese, black, and Hispanic women. For each group we will discuss very briefly the following issues: (1) women's characteristics and roles in general; (2) male–female relationships; (3) women's roles within the family as mothers, daughters, and sisters, and in particular, their responsibilities regarding religious and traditional rituals, caretaking, illness, and death; (4) the role of women alone, including especially that of older women; and (5) women and work.

We realize that any one of these questions applied even to a single group involves enormous complexity. Many factors intersect with ethnicity: religion, class, geography, length of time since migration, and the particular family's unique experiences (McGoldrick, Pearce, & Giordano, 1982). We trust that the few suggestions offered here will be taken not as stereotypes but as highlights to help steer us in the direction of increased awareness of our culture, which is always evolving in our diverse and rapidly changing multi-ethnic country.

IRISH WOMEN

In legend, literature, and life, Irish women are seen as formidable and tenacious. Throughout Irish history they have been celebrated in legends as powerful rulers and in families they frequently played the dominant role

(Diner, 1983; MacCurtain & O'Corrain, 1978, McGoldrick, 1982b; Power, 1976; Reynolds, 1983). Even the earliest Irish legendary hero, Cuchulainn, had to go to a female warrior for his final lessons in arms. The real heroine of the legend is Queen Maeve, a masterful, boastful, willful, power-loving and uninhibited woman, who is depicted as the equal of any man. Maeve's husband tries to devalue her and reduce her to the status of a weak woman in need of a man's protection. He says, "Today thou art better than the day I married thee." And she responds: "I was good before ever I had to do with thee" (Reynolds, 1983, p. 13). In war it is Maeve who stands out and who gives the orders. Her husband recedes into the background. Irish men are often viewed as shadowy figures or even buffoons to be treated as children. As one Irish woman said, when the therapist asked about whether she felt there should be different rules for men and women:

> I do. Women are much, much stronger than men, and men are just big babies in a good many ways, and you have to treat them as such. When I got married my husband told me to shine his shoes and I said, "Do it yourself." I didn't want to be a mother to him. I had never been raised to be a mother to any man. I was raised to take care of children because they can't take care of themselves, but he seemed to feel I should do the same for him. I do think that men never grow up. I see women in this country waiting on men hand and foot. Every woman seems to be gloating over a man and pouring tea for him and feeding him, like he was an imbecile or something and couldn't help himself.

Women in Irish families generally raise their daughters to follow in their footsteps — to take responsibility. In fact, they tend to raise their daughters more like sisters, not allowing them to be children (Byrne & McCarthy, 1986). Some lip service is given to the role of the man as the titular head of the family, but not much. Women do not particularly expect to be able to rely on men for support or leadership. And men often take the attitude that women are beyond their control: "One word from me and she does what she likes" (Byrne & McCarthy, 1986). Irish men have a complex and deeply ambivalent attitude toward Irish women. From a distance they admire their fire, strength, and martyrdom, but up close they are often tense, scornful, and hostile and underneath deeply frightened of their power (Byrne & McCarthy, 1986; McGoldrick, 1982b; Murphy, 1975). Murphy (1975) has suggested that the secrecy, obfuscation, and distrust felt by Irish men break down only in the presence of alcohol and in the absence of women (that is, in the pub).

The Irish tend to maintain a social environment of gender segregation and an ethic of intense gender animosity (Diner, 1983). Because of the common pattern of separating when they become uncomfortable in personal relationships, the forced separations of family members brought on by the Irish famine of the 1840s and resulting immigration did not lead to disorganization of the Irish family. It may even have strengthened it, because those who left ceased to be a drain on family resources.

In traditional Irish culture husbands and wives often lived fairly separate lives. They rarely attended church together and would even come and leave other social functions separately, often not interacting with one another (Diner, 1983). Husbands and wives spent very little leisure time together, with men particularly seeking out the company of other men. In public spouses never referred to each other by their Christian names, instead referring to "himself" and "herself." They rarely sat or even ate together. Not only did Irish men and women, particularly of marriageable ages, function in separate worlds, but they became enmeshed in an ethos of gender hostility, where each sex had an elaborate rationale to explain the faults of the other (Diner, 1983). They placed little value on romance or lyrical love. Women's hopes were articulated much less often in romantic terms than in economic aspirations, and a surprisingly large number who had immigrated as servants were ambivalent about the prospects of giving up their freedom and economic independence for marriage.

A wife's apparent subservience often appeared as a symbolic soothing of the male ego. In fact, the wife ruled in many areas of life and might even be physically assertive. Women typically controlled the family's earnings. Husbands and children turned over their earnings to the wife. Children tended to speak of "my mother's house," dismissing the father's role altogether. Wives tended to maintain more autonomy from the family they married into than women of other groups and many continued to use their maiden names. Irish women never expected that men would take care of them. They had no tradition of chaperonage, and they had the sense that it was possible to live without men. They hadn't come from a context in which marriage was their only option or defined their status (Diner, 1983, 1986).

Sons in traditional Irish families tended to be pampered and protected longer than daughters. Daughters appeared to emerge less overwhelmed by their mother's intensity. Their mothers dominated and manipulated them less. Traditionally, infant sons were believed to be greatly desired by the fairies and envied by the neighbors, whereas female infants were seen as having little fascination by either. Mothers were warned never to leave their sons alone prior to baptism, for fear of losing them. Girl babies received no such attention. In fact, the greatest protection against harm to an infant son was to trick the fairies into believing that he was a girl (Scheper-Hughes, 1979). Boys were seen as constitutionally more delicate and in need of pampering. As Scheper-Hughes describes:

Mothers unselfconsciously defend their preferential treatment of sons (i.e., allowing them more sweets, punishing them less harshly, demanding less cooperation
and fewer chores), saying that little boys need more attention and comfort than
little girls, that they are hurt more easily and are more prone to illness. (p. 170)

Whereas girls were often perceived as "catty, sharp, and underhanded,"
little boys were often described as "helpless, innocent, and guileless"
(Scheper-Hughes, 1979). Girls were given serious chores much earlier than
their brothers. Sons were thus often overprotected, while daughters were
underprotected (Scheper-Hughes, 1979). Interestingly, in adult life, Irish
daughters have a very low rate of psychiatric hospitalization compared to
their brothers (Diner, 1983).

Relationships among siblings, especially siblings of the same gender, constituted the most positive and least problematic relationships in Irish society
(Diner, 1983), although males often bonded most closely with male peers
outside the family, especially their "drinking buddies" (Fallows, 1979). Unlike parents and children, adult siblings functioned on a plane of general
equality, without duty or obligation obscuring feelings. Traditionally, brothers and sisters did not shoulder obligations to their unmarried siblings after
marriage, nor did brothers have any particular social responsibility to protect their sisters' honor, as did brothers in Italy. Yet, brother–sister relationships constituted the only cross-gender relationships sanctioned by the society, and sibling bonds often provided an additional obstacle to marriage.
Sibling solidarity affected migration patterns as well, since a brother or
sister might postpone marriage to save money so that a sibling could follow
him or her to the new country (Diner, 1983).

Woehrer (1982) found that the Irish are one of the few groups to visit their
siblings as often as their parents and, in fact, to feel a sense of guilt when
they are not friends with their siblings. The ideal relationship for them is
based on congeniality and common interests. They tend to evaluate all kin in
terms of their capacity to act as friends. The strongest bond is same sex,
same generation, especially sisters.

Irish daughters left Ireland more willingly than sons, and their leaving
involved very little emotional pining by the family (Diner, 1983). In fact, the
Irish are the only group in which the rate of emigration of women far
surpassed that of men. Of the total Irish immigrant population, 53% were
women, compared to 21% of the southern Italians, and 4% of the Greeks.
The only group that came near the Irish in percentage of women were Jews,
who migrated in almost equal numbers, but 28% of the Jewish immigrants
were children, indicating that a large proportion of this group was families.
Among the Irish only 5% were children. Irish immigrants were primarily

single men and women. As time went on, an increasing percentage of the Irish immigrants was women, which meant depopulating rural Ireland of its women. Sisters and other female kin played strikingly important roles in bringing over other sisters (Diner, 1983). Studies of newspaper listings indicate over and over the strong bonds of sisters and of siblings in general.

The Irish have had the latest age, the highest rate of celibacy, and lowest rate of marriage of any country in the world (Kennedy, 1978). In the United States Irish women continued to be reluctant about marrying. They enjoyed a comparatively open range of economic options in domestic work, nursing, and school teaching. This, along with the high rate of desertion of Irish men from their families, augmented female family authority. The intense animosity in Irish male–female relationships, the deemphasis on romance, and the generalized lack of interest traditionally displayed by Irish men for women have continued to some extent in the United States, although obviously modified over time.

Those who have written about Irish family life repeatedly remarked on the high level of tension within Irish families produced by the confluence of female assertiveness within the framework of a culture that supposes male dominance, a high level of mutual disdain across gender lines, and the lack of an arena for male-female social interaction, not to mention the impact of extremely high rates of alcoholism and the burden of so many children in a family (Diner, 1983; Greeley, 1972; McGoldrick, 1982b; McKenna, 1979). Irish women in play and poem have carried the burden for the economic well-being of the family, hoarding the money their husbands would otherwise squander. As late as 1920 one study indicated that Irish men were much less successful than Irish women when immigrant groups were compared (Diner, 1983).

The "martyrdom" of Irish mothers seems to be a response to their being given an increased burden of responsibility without a corresponding degree of status—a state of affairs destined to create dissatisfaction (Humphreys, 1966)—along with deeply held fatalistic, religious beliefs about sin and suffering as the human condition. The dissatisfaction, which relates primarily to the lack of support a woman receives from her husband, may be taken out on her children. McKenna (1979) found that the more support the Irish mother got from her husband, the less controlling she was with her children. She found that Irish mothers were "controlling" but pointed out that this behavior, understood in context, did not have the same pejorative meaning as it would in an American situation. Irish mothers generally favor discipline, strictness, and control in childrearing, and have less democratic attitudes toward children than many other groups (McKenna, 1979). Education made a difference here, in that more educated mothers were less controlling.

Irish mothers often do not recognize their own strength or their ability to intimidate their children, especially their sons. One Irish mother in therapy described her son's arrest for a drunken episode with his friends:

> The policeman expected when I came down to the station to pick Joey up that he'd see a witch of a woman coming through the door, because Joey had said to him, "Just promise me one thing, just protect me from my mother." But I didn't do anything. When I went down there, I just gave him a smack across the face, because I didn't need that nonsense!

As so often happens, this Irish mother had no idea of her power, which is often all the more intimidating because, unlike Portnoy, who could complain about his mother, just as she could complain about him, this Irish son could not complain about his "sainted" mother.

The Irish may do better with a female therapist than some other groups (such as Greeks or Hispanics), because they are accustomed to women with authority. However, the tension that Irish sons (especially those labeled "black sheep" or "weak" by the family) often feel toward their mothers is likely to be played out in subtle resistance to a female therapist, even as they seem to comply. It is important for the therapist to counter the different expectations Irish families have for their male and female members, while at the same time conveying a nonjudgmental attitude toward the family, since family members are all too likely to blame themselves for whatever goes wrong (McGoldrick, 1982b). It helps for the therapist to be delicate in questioning about gender roles, with some gentle humor and reframing and a good deal of understanding for the family's current patterns of behavior. The Irish tendency to use denial, mystification, exaggeration, confabulation, and numerous other techniques to avoid facing painful emotions is extreme. A therapist who is blunt and logical and favors "laying all the cards on the table" may only heighten the family's already rigid denial and avoidance. Stories, metaphors, dreams and parables may all be useful in helping an Irish family modify its beliefs about sex roles, while allowing for avoidance of many issues too painful for explicit exploration. This will often be crucial to a successful therapy.

HISPANIC WOMEN

In most Hispanic countries women learn early how to be female in a man's world. They are raised to be virgins until marriage, while men are to be "machos." Women, taught to repress or sublimate their sexual drives, usually regard sex as an obligation. From infancy they are trained to be extremely modest, which often leads to shame about their bodies. However, since their main goal in life is to be good mothers, they must also be sexually attractive and seductive in a passive and virginal way in order to attract a good husband. Men, on the contrary, are encouraged to know about sex, to be seductive and experienced. Machismo, according to Sluzki (1982), dictates to a man that he must signal that he is always ready for sex. In most situations, seductive behavior is expected of him when interacting with women who are not members of his family system. The paradox is that, since virginity is so important, men are also expected to be responsible for protecting the honor of the women in their families.

Traditionally, Hispanic women have been expected to be responsible for taking care of the home and the children and for keeping the family together. They often feel obligated to sacrifice themselves in order to accomplish this goal, relying on other women within the extended family for support and strength. This sacrificial role is reinforced by the admiration that women who do this well receive from society. A good mother is glorified when she puts her children's welfare above everything else and protects them to the end. Although her role as wife is also important, it is not as romanticized as that of mother. As a wife she must be respectful of her husband and his family. This expectation was eloquently defined by a Puerto Rican client who said to his wife, "Respect between husband and wife means that as a wife you must be loving, considerate, and never have negative thoughts about me."

Women are expected to be submissive and passive in comparison to men. However, while overtly supporting their husband's authority, wives usually assume power behind the scenes. Because they are responsible for keeping the family together, they tend to develop very strong relationships with their children and other family members. Often alliances are built between mothers and children against the father, who is perceived as authoritarian and lacking in understanding of emotional issues. Relationships between sons and mothers in particular are close and dependent, and it is not uncommon to see a son protecting his mother against an abusive husband. Mothers and daughters, in turn, have close relationships, but these are more reciprocal in nature. Mothers teach their daughters how to be good women who deserve the respect of others, especially males, and who will make good wives and mothers.

There is a feeling of sisterhood stemming from the strong ties that exist among the females in Hispanic families. Women in the extended family feel an obligation to help each other out with household chores and childcare. For most Hispanics babysitting is a new concept when they come to the United States, as well as a cause for discomfort, since in their cultures there was usually a female relative who took care of the children. The support that women provide for each other enables the culture to maintain certain gender roles, such as not expecting husbands to perform household tasks or help with childrearing. Without the extended family to offer this support, a woman is likely to experience her situation as unbearable and begin to demand her husband's help. He may resent it and become distant and argumentative, in some cases turning to drinking, gambling, or affairs. Without relatives or friends to intervene in the arguments and to advise the spouses to respect each other, serious difficulties may develop.

Although women are raised to be dependent on males for protection, they are also expected to be strong and to take care of themselves emotionally as well as to take care of men's emotional needs. Among Hispanic groups women have always been influential at home, as well as a strong force in politics and academia. For instance, in Argentina it was the movement led by mothers and other female relatives of those who had disappeared that created a change in government. Additionally, many Hispanic women have always worked outside the home to help support the household. In Puerto Rico, where in 1920 women constituted 25% of the work force (Fernandez & Quintero, 1974), a large percentage of women has always worked to supplement the family's income. For men this can present problems, since it challenges their basic role as provider and protector of the family. They seem to have less difficulty with women working when they themselves are employed and their authority at home is not challenged. At a deeper level, however, they may fear that women who work outside the home run a greater risk of being seduced and of having affairs, an act that would threaten the innermost core of any Hispanic "macho." The potential for conflict is certainly less when couples are well educated and when the man is employed and earning more than the woman.

In the United States, Hispanic women are often forced to work in order to survive. Most are not well educated and tend to occupy the lowest paid, unskilled blue collar and service occupations (Romero, 1986), a fact which is also true for Hispanic males in this country. To obtain legal status, many of them work as domestics, leaving their children in their countries of origin until they can establish themselves here and can afford to send for them. Because women perform menial jobs and tend to adapt faster than men to this culture, it is often easier for them to find employment. Although in most cases they continue to respect their husbands' authority as the head of the household, wives who work may feel more independent and self-confident, and in cases where the husbands are not working they may challenge their "machismo."

If the husband is unable to regain his dominant position through employment, he may experience panic, confusion, and a sense of emasculation. The wife in turn may develop contempt for her spouse when he no longer fulfills his "macho" role (Mizio, 1974). Some women may also experience emotional pain and feelings of helplessness in such a situation. Marital discord and separations commonly result. In these cases women are more likely to seek help from friends, family, and sometimes the church or spiritual healers. If by chance they come to therapy, they find it difficult to complain about their husbands and are highly ambivalent about accusing them. On the one hand, they feel disloyal, and on the other, they feel betrayed. They try to justify their husband's behavior by saying that he is basically a good human being and that his behavior is caused by the alcohol, the lack of job opportunities, the friends, or in general, the way of life in this country.

Unfortunately, because of the adaptations that Hispanics have to make to live in this country, the extended family does not function in the idealized manner that most of these cultures dictate. The expectation is that family members will take care of each other, especially in old age. Both sons and daughters are expected to provide support and protection for their elderly parents, but their roles are different. Men are more likely to contribute financially, and women to do the caretaking. It is usually daughters who take care of their elderly parents and who take their mothers into their homes when they are widowed. In turn, older women will help out at home, making it easier for their daughters to go to school or to work. It is not uncommon for at least one of the females in the family to remain single and to assume the role of caretaker for older relatives. Interestingly, although this woman may have the respect of others in the family, she may also be the source of gossip and concern. Ultimately, a woman without a man to protect her is not safe. Her honor, and therefore the family's honor, is at risk. A woman alone does not have the same rights as a man, especially when it has to do with sexual behavior. Affairs are not tolerated for women, while they are almost expected of men.

Women are more likely than men to attend church and to follow religious rituals. They are very active in planning weddings, christenings, and other events that tend to bring the family together. When they marry they have the responsibility of bringing the two families together and of avoiding conflicts with in-laws. They are also expected to take care of the ill and at times to devote themselves full-time to these duties. These expectations sometimes lead women to assume a martyr role and to express their resentment through somatic complaints and depression. They have much less freedom than men to confront their spouses or to express dissatisfaction with their role. In some cases the pressure that women feel is expressed through emotional outbursts. This behavior is accepted in women, but leads others to perceive them as weak and out of control.

Expressing emotion and losing control are certainly more acceptable among women than men in Hispanic cultures. During funerals this difference is obvious. Women have greater permission to cry and in some groups, such as Puerto Ricans, they may react by having hysterical seizures called "ataques." Women and children are viewed as fragile and after a death are protected, mostly by females less affected by the death. Men are expected to be strong, but are allowed a greater degree of emotional expression than in many other cultural groups. The message that both males and females receive is that they must be strong and continue with life (McGoldrick, Hines, Lee, & Garcia-Preto, 1986). While men who lose their wives are likely to remarry, especially if there are children, women in a similar situation tend to have more difficulty finding a new husband. For a man such a marriage implies taking on a financial burden — and after all, the woman is no longer a virgin. These women may instead end up living with relatives and working to support their children. Leaving this support system to live alone may be very difficult to do, even when women can afford it financially.

Leaving the family system is extremely risky for both men and women, because it implies loss of control, support, and protection. For couples experiencing difficulties adjusting to the American culture, the loss of that system can be disastrous. Helping them make connections with relatives, friends, or community supports may be the therapist's most crucial task. In situations where the woman adapts more readily than the man, the risks are greater. It is important to encourage the man to move forward by finding programs where other Hispanic men are learning English and seeking job training. Asking the spouses to visualize a future together may help them see the present as a transition in their lives. Engaging them in discussions that force them to reflect on cultural contrasts and on what they see as positive and negative about each culture may lead them to ways of relating that take from the old and the new. The idea that to make it in this country both men and women need to struggle together is generally accepted by Hispanics and can be used to join the couple in a more egalitarian relationship. After all, they chose to come to this country because they wanted to improve their situation.

CHINESE WOMEN

Throughout history Chinese women have been victims of oppression, persecution, subjugation, and aggression. In the last few generations, however, their roles have undergone a dramatic transformation from bound-feet concubines to today's assertive, professional career women. In our understanding of Chinese women, we have to take into account the diverse historical, educational, and economic backgrounds of women of different age groups (Sidel, 1982; Wolf & Witke, 1975).

Traditionally, Chinese women were destined to occupy a subordinate position to men and were victimized throughout their individual and family life cycles. Because of the patrilineal and patriarchal principles governing Chinese agricultural society, the birth of a son who carried on the family name was far preferable to the birth of a daughter. Many young girls were "sold" or married off in times of family hardship or subjected to various forms of physical and emotional abuse. During childhood and adolescent years, Chinese girls seldom enjoyed the advantages of a formal education, which was usually reserved for the sons. A girl's "lack of talent" was considered a virtue. Women were taught to follow the Confucian precept of the "Three Obediences"—to obey father at home, husband after marriage, and sons when widowed—and the "Four Virtues"—chastity, reticence, pleasing manner, and domestic skills. From the 10th century to the 19th century, countless girls suffered from the practice of "foot binding," in which their feet were bound so tightly that the arches were broken and the toes permanently bent under. Such a cruel tradition, besides identifying women as being "of genteel birth," served to foster women's dependence, helplessness, and immobility.

Roles for Chinese women were also rigidly assigned according to birth order. The oldest girl in the family was expected to assist her mother with the household chores and to attend to the younger siblings. She usually had much less power than her brothers, especially the oldest son. Historically, women had no choice in the selection of their husbands. Betrothed at a young age through a matchmaker, most were not allowed to meet their spouse until the wedding night (Yung, 1986). Marriage was arranged to ensure the family's prosperity and continue the man's family line. For many women (especially from peasant families), marriage symbolized a lifetime of hardship and drudgery. As wives, their value was judged by their ability to produce male heirs and to serve their in-laws and other extended family members. Infertility usually led to abandonment or the dissolution of the marriage.

Traditionally, men were permitted freely to commit adultery, divorce, remarry, and keep as many concubines and mistresses as they could afford, whereas women were severely punished for adulterous behavior. Once widowed, women were expected not to remarry; further, they had no legal right to ask for divorce or to own property (Yung, 1986). When women faced life crises, very few were able to seek comfort from their own parents or childhood friends. Marriage often symbolized the death of their relationship with their own natal family. They were allowed to visit them only rarely on festival days. In arguments between the wife and the husband's parents, the husband was expected to ally himself with his parents. For some women, the only way to cope with conflicts was to commit suicide, in the hope of returning as a spirit to haunt their oppressive husband and in-laws. For many, it was not until old age that they could look forward to rest, and then only when their in-laws and husbands had passed away (Yung, 1959). Because of the respect for the elderly in Chinese culture, women did in general gain a certain power and respect with age. Unfortunately, elderly women born into a traditional society were raised to expect respect for the aged, but they now live in a youth-oriented culture, where economic control is highly valued. They have lost out both in youth and in old age.

The inequitable social norms prevalent in traditional China did not diminish with migration of Chinese to America in the later half of the 19th century. Anti-Chinese sentiments and discriminatory laws prevented the establishment of Chinese families in America. For instance, the Chinese Exclusion Act of 1881 prohibited the entry of Chinese women. Consequently, many wives in China had virtually no husbands and were compelled to endure a "mutilated marriage" (Sung, 1967).

Because of the highly disproportionate number of Chinese men to Chinese women in the United States, and the racist law which barred interracial marriages, there was really no possibility for continuing the Chinese family structure here. Many Chinese women were forced into prostitution to satisfy the sexual needs of single or married Chinese men in America. Many were lured to the United States by false promises of marriage or even sold into slavery. In 1860 an estimated 85% of the Chinese women in San Francisco were prostitutes (Hirata, 1979). When immigration laws were relaxed, many Chinese women were able to join their husbands after many years or decades of separation. Some came as "picture brides," arranged by relatives or matchmakers. These women often had their expectations of good life in the "Gold Mountain" shattered by the cruel reality of poverty, hard work, social isolation, and racial discrimination. As the victims of sexism, racism, and classism, many Chinese women turned their anger and unhappiness inward toward the self, as reflected in high suicide rates. Sung (1967) reported that the suicide rate for Chinese Americans in San Francisco was four times greater than the rate for the city as a whole, and that Chinese American women rather than men tend to commit suicide. Hanging was reported to be the most frequent mode of suicide.

The roles of Chinese women in America have changed dramatically in the past three decades. The civil rights and women's movements, an expanding technological economy, and a new social consciousness in many Chinese communities have led to improved conditions for Chinese American women. A large number of them are well educated and have achieved economic success and high social status. Nevertheless, many of the acculturated Chinese professionals still face immense problems and barriers. They are still subjected to the stereotypes of Asian women projected by the media—sexy, submissive, shy, unassertive, quiet, and gentle. In striving for success and positions of leadership, they must overcome the "nice Chinese girl" image. At the same time, they have to deal with the internal pain caused by cultural conflicts and identity crises. To be effective and assertive is contrary to the Chinese values of passivity and modesty. Although encouraged to be better educated than their predecessors, they are still handicapped by traditional notions of female inferiority at home and the lack of positive role models outside (Yung, 1986).

Although some educated and acculturated Chinese women have entered the American mainstream, many newly arrived immigrant women are still struggling with economic hardships and discrimination. More than half of the population of Chinese American women today are immigrant women from Hong Kong, Taiwan, China, Vietnam, and other parts of the world. Some are English-speaking, educated professionals, but many are survivors of China's Cultural Revolution and the Vietnam War. The "boat people," many of whom were Chinese women, were traumatized by rape and torture. Having arrived at a time of economic recession and anti-Asian racial backlash, many of them are having a difficult time coping with economic survival and adjusting to a new way of life. Because of cultural and language differences, they are often victims of stereotyping and discrimination at work.

Within their families, women must still sometimes confront traditional sexist attitudes that descredit their ability to achieve economic and social independence. Generally speaking, immigrant Chinese women are more flexible and successful in their initial adjustment than their husbands. Many men deal with frustration and oppression at work by demanding more control within the family. At the same time, many wives, having experienced the rewards of economic independence and a greater degree of freedom, are reluctant to accept their traditional submissive roles. This conflict then becomes a source of family discord, which has at times resulted in domestic violence and divorce.

Chinese women have come a long way. In spite of the many barriers still to be overcome, the overall condition of Chinese women has improved. Strengthened by the long years of struggle and new accomplishments and social advancement, Chinese American women today are more aware of their civil rights and are better prepared to deal with conflicts and challenges of contemporary American life.

WOMEN IN BLACK CULTURE

No other racial, ethnic or religious group of females in the United States has undergone as much degradation, stereotyping and actual punishment as Black women. (Joyce Ladner, 1973, p. 3)

Black women have been portrayed in literature and the media as masculinized females, overweight mammies, sexually promiscuous and domineering seductresses, and tireless superwomen. They have been held responsible for the so-called demise of the black family, the emasculation of black men, and every other ill in the black community. These stereotypes and myths have grown in part out of the reality that black women have never played passive roles in their families and communities. While independence and the ability to survive harsh circumstances have been recognized as strengths among some groups of women, such as pioneer women, black women have been denigrated and attacked not only for surviving, but also for achieving.

In order to understand contemporary black womanhood, it is critical to consider these women's African heritage, strong religious beliefs, the caring roles they have been placed in through socioeconomic circumstances, and the need for mutual aid to survive a hostile environment (McCray, 1980; Rodgers-Rose, 1980). While most pre-slavery African societies were male dominated, women played an important role in the economic and political organization of various tribal societies. They had major military, governmental, and family responsibilities as part of a polygamous and patriarchal system. Procreation was viewed as their sacred duty.

Initially almost all the slaves imported from Africa were men brought as fieldhands to southern plantations. As the slave masters became more aware that their wealth was tied to their human slavestock, black women were also forced into slave ships and brought to plantations, where they too worked long hours as fieldhands. Some were granted the "privilege" of working in the masters' households, where they did housekeeping. They cared for and loved not only the masters' children and their own children (sometimes the product of the masters' rape), but also the children of other slaves who worked in the fields, had died, or had been sold away from the plantation. This role as child caretaker did not end with slavery but continues to be common today (McCray, 1980).

Black women were defeminized by being forced to wear men's clothing and do the same work as men. "As cruel and as dehumanizing as slavery was, it ironically equalized the black man and black woman in ways hardly dreamed of in traditional Africa" (Martin & Martin, 1986, p. 192). Sojourner Truth, a famous slave woman, eloquently commented:

> . . . Nobody every helped me into carriages or over a puddle, or gives me best place. . . . I have plowed and planted and gathered into barns, and no man could head me and ain't I a woman? I could work as much and eat as much as a man (when I could get it), and bear de lash as well and ain't I a woman? . . . And when I cried out with a mother's grief, none but Jesus heard. (Loewenberg & Bogin, 1976, p. 235)

The rape of black women allowed white males to act out a double standard of sexual freedom for themselves, while white women were kept chaste and pure and put on a pedestal. House slaves were most subject to exploitation by plantation owners, their friends and field masters; the laws of the land protected this brutal oppression. Black men attempted to protect black women, but their efforts often cost them their lives or at the very least resulted in punishment and failure, which repeatedly reinforced their sense of powerlessness, just as the whites intended.

In the post-slavery period, skilled black workers were denied the chance to practice their crafts and farmhands entered a new form of enslavement called sharecropping. Women were not allowed to own land and many continued to work in white households, often undergoing continued sexual exploitation in order to protect their lives and their families, as well as to keep much needed jobs. Black men were perceived as a threat to the power of white men and to the chastity of white women. Consequently, the economic survival of black families became dependent on black women, who were able to find employment as domestics.

Even today black daughters are reared with the expectation that they will work outside their homes and generally do so even if they do not have to. However, the majority of black women, even when their husbands are employed and when they are of middle- or upper-income status, work not by choice but by necessity. Black women have always had to work long hours for low pay, often with no benefits or chances of advancement. The median income earned by black women in 1980 was $4,674; this represents 87%, 36%, and 60% of the median income of white females, white males, and black males, respectively (U.S. Dept. of Commerce, 1983). Even professional black women do not escape the effects of racism and sexism; they encounter frequent clinical dilemmas because they do not meet the image their clients expect, namely a white male. They tend to be restricted to the lower rungs of the occupational ladder and frequently feel that they must perform like superwomen in order to be rewarded for their skills and effort.

In 1980 there were 14 million black women and only 12.5 million black men in the United States (U.S. Department of Commerce, 1986). In some geographic areas the ratio of women to men is as high as 7 to 1. The number of men who are available is further limited because of military enlistment, unemployment, and the ills of urbanization (e.g., drug abuse). Staples (1981), noting that eligible black men are as rare as "hen's teeth," wrote that, "Many a Black male's shortcomings must be tolerated for the sake of affection and companionship. In a sense, many Black women have to take love on male terms" (p. 32). Black men more often marry up, even though they often cannot fulfill the male requirements that society dictates and then blocks. Many black women are unable to find mates of equal education and social class. Black women of nonworking, working and middle-income status are slow to consider legal marriage when it cannot guarantee them stability or security. An increasing number of black women at all income levels are choosing to have children outside of marriage rather than missing out on motherhood altogether. Black women who do marry tend to be younger, have larger families, and have less of a gap between marriage and the birth of their first child than their white counterparts (Spanier, Roos, & Shockley, 1985). Education influences, but does not wipe out, these racial differences. Black women expect to be the glue that holds their families together:

> The Black woman has made her home a sanctuary in which she has taken some of the sting out of many of the painful realities of the Black experience. She has ministered to the needs of her man, her children, other women's children, and the community. It is to "my woman" and "my momma" that men and children turn to have mended the wounds inflicted by this society. (Hale, 1980, pp. 82–83)

It is hard to generalize about the quality of blacks' marital relationships. While there are class differences, relationships do not escape the pervasive effects of the many forces mitigating against intimacy and satisfaction. Too little money, little or no recreational time, conflicting work schedules, assaults on the self-esteem of men, displacement of anger and frustration onto one another take their toll. There are no rules inhibiting men and women from socializing together, as exist, for example, in Irish culture. There is an openness about sexuality; black men do not tend to practice a double standard where sex is concerned. While premarital sex is frowned upon by the church and discouraged by parents, a woman is not ostracized for having premarital sexual relations or for becoming pregnant outside of marriage. Men and women do not tend to be openly affectionate, although they may use terms of endearment with each other. Men are allowed greater freedom to socialize away from the home, to drink, and particularly among the poor and working classes, to have extramarital relationships. The expectation is that these practices will drop off by midlife.

While there are couples, particularly among lower-income blacks, whose roles and decision-making are staunchly traditional, with the power balance skewed in the direction of the male, black men and women tend to have egalitarian relationships relative to other ethnic groups (Bell, 1971; Rutledge, 1980). Staples (1981) suggests that the myth of black matriarchy adds insult to injury for black women, since it contradicts the empirical reality of their status and history. It suggests dominance, power, control, and a high position in society. Moynihan's (1965) thesis was that the black family is crumbling in part because of the black matriarchy. He and others have suggested that black men have been exploited by black women. Staples (1981) argues that it is insensitive to deny the crucial roles black women have played as survivors, achievers, and agents of social change in the black community. The myth of the matriarchy promotes racism by pitting the sexes against each other and blaming black women for most of the problems evident among the black population. The suggestion that the "overachievement" of black women, rather than the forced underachievement of black men, has been responsible for increasing family breakups and creates guilt and ambivalence for black women (Giddings, 1985).

Certainly, black women have played major, central roles in their families and, because of the advantage they have been afforded in the labor market, they have, in fact, tended to be more active in family decision-making. Clearly, black women have not been passive or unassertive as a group; their strength, creativity, and ability to rise to whatever the occasion requires have been essential to the survival of their families. This is not to deny that some do underfunction and that there are some black women who are accurately characterized as controlling in personality and behavior. Even among these women, however, it is questionable how much control they assume by choice versus necessity.

For most blacks, major decisions are made by both marital partners or by the wife with her husband's agreement. Men are respected privately and publicly as "head of household." Even when the woman assumes control of the household and contributes to or at times supports the family, this is not synonymous with her dominating her spouse or children.

The most obvious and ominous indicator of stress on black couples and families lies in the rising number of single-parent households (largely headed by women and living below the poverty line). One-third of black women heading families have never been married. Even though more than half (53%) of all black families were still maintained by couples in 1983, the divorce and separation rates among blacks were higher than for any other racial group (U.S. Department of Commerce, 1986). Black women also stay single longer after a divorce. Staples (1985) suggests that this does not represent a devaluation of marriage, but rather is a function of limited numbers of desirable husbands in a restricted pool of potential partners.

This does not necessarily mean that these women or their children have no relationships with their children's fathers. Many maintain connections, and even when they do not, the paternal kin system, particularly the father's sisters and mother, traditionally maintain contact and provide emotional support and resources not only to the children but to the mother as well.

Motherhood tends to be more highly valued than the marital role for black women. The birth of a child marks the transition to womanhood for young women and the fulfillment of one's basic function in life for more mature women. The teenage pregnancy rate among blacks is extremely high. Often these young women are not prepared for the emotional or concrete demands of the mothering role and so their own mothers may assume the bulk of the responsibility for childrearing. In these instances the young mother usually functions more like an older sister and her child is likely to develop stronger ties with the grandmother than with the mother, who experiences conflict about reclaiming the child when she matures or when circumstances (e.g., illness of the grandmother) demand that she do so.

While there are class variations in childrearing, black mothers tend to be firm disciplinarians. They are usually responsible for ongoing supervision, while fathers get involved primarily when major disciplinary action is required. Middle- and upper-income couples share childrearing functions more equally. Physical punishment is a common disciplinary technique, but used more by lower-class mothers. While they have definite aspirations for their children and tend to openly communicate any negative sentiments, black mothers do not withdraw love when their children fail to meet their expectations; they are all too aware that a child's lack of accomplishment may relate to factors beyond his or her effort. Because open emotional expressiveness is so highly valued, when conflicted relationships do exist, negative feelings tend to be communicated in a direct fashion.

Black mothers attempt to instill a sense of self-acceptance that is strong enough to counteract the negative messages of the larger society. This may account for the fact that relationships between mothers and their children tend to be very positive. Children are raised to be assertive, emotionally expressive, and independent. Poor and working-class mothers emphasize being moral, honest, hardworking, and keeping a good name. Middle-income mothers tend to put more emphasis on school achievement and inhibiting sexual and aggressive impulses. Although mothers do not seem to prefer their sons, they do fear more for their safety; too much temper or ambition might mean their lives. Sons are perceived as much more vulnerable to getting into trouble than daughters, who tend to spend more time sharing household responsibilities with their mothers. Regardless of social class, black mothers generally do not allow their children to "talk back" or question parental authority. The struggle, strength, and unselfish love of black mothers do not go unheeded by their children, who are generally loyal and attached.

As sisters, friends, mothers and daughters, black women tend to look to one another for support. Bonded by their sense of common struggle, they provide one another with a cushion that includes help with childcare, financial assistance, advice, and emotional support. Young black women often try to emulate the strength and output of their mothers and grandmothers and then feel guilty when they perceive themselves to be failing in this regard, even when the support systems available to them are much less extensive, as is the case when women are separated from their extended families by geography.

The cultural value of extending help to others in their kin system has promoted survival but at times may be a heavy burden on black women. Elderly black women, though likely to be poor, are often still involved in giving resources to their kin. They seldom experience an empty nest and are looked to for advice, to transmit religious and cultural values, and to encourage family unity. They are generally important figures in the lives of their grandchildren and provide stability for children when the circumstances of the parents do not permit it. The extended caretaker role is not necessarily assumed because this is their preference, but because children's needs are presumed to be more important than their own. They are much more likely to take relatives into their own households than to move in with others. When these women do have financial assets, they may be in the form of farmland in the south that they own with relatives. Even when they need the money to live, many refuse to sell this property because of the value they put on having a place to call their own.

For the most part, black women have not participated in the women's liberation movement (Stone, 1979). Racism is viewed as a greater oppressive force than sexism; most regard the elevation of black males to be equally important to that of black women. Black women are aware and concerned about their status as women; however, most perceive the goals of the women's movement as being narrow and irrelevant to their lives and history. As Terrelonge (1979) points out,

> Racism is so engrained in American culture and so entrenched among many White women, that Black females have been reluctant to admit that anything affecting the White female could also affect them. (p. 583)

Black women have never led sheltered lives and are sensitive to having been oppressed by white women as well as by white men over the years. In addition, black women tend to spend more time than men in the church, where religious doctrine encourages them to play a supportive role. Thus, the bottom line for black women has been to sympathize with their men for the devastating oppression the larger culture has caused them, and often to tolerate and try to be the mainstay for them when they are overcome by a sense of powerlessness. Conflicts over this may at times make black women tolerate poor treatment or even abuse from their husbands, which is hard for others to understand, because others cannot know the torments that generations of racism have caused for both black men and black women.

Thus, failure to immerse themselves in the women's movement does not mean that black women have been passive as change agents. To the contrary, since the emancipation era, black women have been major players in the development of black communities, where they have founded daycare facilities, schools, libraries, recreational facilities, etc. Black women participated in the women's suffrage movement, but were not always accepted by their white peers; they were active in the civil rights movement and have positively influenced black life through their service and political activities in women's organizations. Not surprisingly, black women with more income tend to be much more active in such organizations than those who are poor, the hub of whose social activity outside the home is likely to be the church.

In general, black families are not likely to be inhibited by the gender of the therapist. While the politics of the therapy context (the client being in a "one-down position") is a major deterrent to the participation of black men in therapy, because of their need to feel in control of their lives in whatever ways possible, role overload is a common deterrent for black women. That is, they typically have so much to do that, unless they really understand what therapy can do for them and how long it will take, it is hard to commit themselves to the effort. It helps for the therapist to highlight a black woman's sense of being a survivor, her strength, and her ability to find her own solutions. Black women may be more responsive to the therapist's referring to a fair distribution of responsibilities and to each mate deserving greater life satisfaction than to the importance of women's rights, particularly where it puts them in competition with the men in their lives.

It is also not unusual for black women to underrate the complexities of their lives, because they have received the repeated messages that, by comparison, their role models (their mothers, aunts, and grandmothers) had to survive far more difficult situations. It is important for therapists to help them to validate their experiences, even if black women in earlier times experienced the strains of racism, family disruption, and poverty in more dramatic ways. Poetry, movies, music, and books, because of the immediacy of the emotional response they engender, can be used to amplify therapeutic messages regarding the dilemmas and choices in their lives.

JEWISH WOMEN

Traditional Jewish culture was male-oriented. Women ignored their own needs to play the role of helpmate: patient, submissive to God and to their husbands, and devoted to their children (Baum, Hyman, & Michael, 1975; Herz & Rosen, 1982). In fact, in traditional Jewish culture men began the day with a daily prayer thanking God for not having been born a woman (Hertz, 1960; Herz & Rosen, 1982). Orthodox Jewish women traditionally shaved their heads after marriage, in order not to be attractive and thus seduced into relationships with other men. During menstruation women were considered unclean and had to attend the mikva and receive a ritual cleansing before again having sexual relations with their husbands. In Orthodox practice women are still kept apart in the synagogue and not allowed any central role in religious services. For centuries boys have celebrated the transition to manhood in the bar mitzvah, but the bas mitzvah for girls is a very recent cultural addition.

The other side of this very constricting role for women in traditional Jewish families, and evidence of their strength, is the great success Jewish women have shown in all areas of professional and educational achievement in the United States. Jewish women have also been in the forefront of the fight for women's rights, and they are very much overrepresented in the movement for women's advancement and equality (Schneider, 1984).

Among the greatest conflicts for Jewish women today are the competing demands of family and career (Goldenberg, 1973; Herz & Rosen, 1982; Koltun, 1976). Traditionally, because women's participation in religious services was strictly limited, their domain became the home. The mother was the center of family life. She was the primary educator of children and was held responsible for their success. But, as Herz and Rosen have described it:

> Since she is merely the instrument of their success, her enjoyment must be vicarious. She values intelligence and achievement, but her mission is to work only for the development of others within the family. She is not expected to use her intelligence and drive for personal accomplishments outside of the home, and thus she finds herself deeply invested in the accomplishments of her children. Since the mother instills the educational and achievement values of the culture, she internalizes these values and thus thinks less of her homemaking. This creates a dilemma for the modern Jewish woman. Historical circumstances have given women greater opportunities for personal development and Jewish women have become very successful (Luria, 1974). However, the problem is that the ambivalence of her role often remains unresolved. The competing values of success and caretaking create a conundrum. (pp. 278–279)

Although Jewish couples tend to have more democratic relationships than couples from many other groups, Jewish women often think of themselves more as mothers than as wives (Herz & Rosen, 1982). They seem to have a greater feeling of personal responsibility for the emotional, intellectual, cultural, and physical well-being of their children than do women from other groups, such as Irish, WASP, or Italian mothers.

As portrayed in the media the stereotypic Jewish woman is verbally and emotionally overpowering to her less articulate husband; in the worst versions of the stereotype she is intrusive and domineering to her children

(Bienstock, 1979), while inducing guilt through her endless self-sacrifice. The stereotype of the Jewish daughter reflects the opposite side of this coin: self-centered, demanding, aggressive, and materialistic (Schneider, 1984). These caricatures ignore the important survival value in Jewish culture of a mother's self-sacrificing concern for her children, as well as the value of having a daughter well taken care of as a symbol of the newly successful Jewish man (Schneider, 1984). These stereotypes reflect, probably, fears Jewish men have of Jewish women, fears which men in other cultures have of women as well. They also seem to reflect a pattern common in groups that have experienced the most prejudice and racism from the wider culture: a turning against each other when they cannot deal with the hatred in any other way.

Alongside the limited role Jewish women appeared to play in traditional society existed a tradition of women in business, which provided a model for the enormous success of so many Jewish women in education, business, and the professions. In the Jewish shtetl male piety and religious scholarship were so highly honored that women sometimes undertook to support the family by running small businesses, which left the husband free to study the holy books (Zborowski & Herzog, 1952). In the United States there was little room for men to play this role, so these first-generation Jewish men lost their status, had no skills for the labor market, and were discriminated against in the new culture. Their wives, long trained in the practical arts of making ends meet while maintaining a humble acceptance of male prerogatives and prestige, became the emotional and economic backbone of the family, dedicated totally to self-denial while meeting the needs of others and to performing miracles with the family budget and menu (Bienstock, 1979). Since parental (primarily motherly) sacrifice for the benefit of the children had always been a pivotal Jewish value, mothers at times played a mediating role between their husbands, who were having difficulty adapting to the new culture, and their children, who were trying to succeed in the new world, tacitly choosing the children's path (adapting to the new situation).

It has been suggested that when the children grew up, they became resentful of the powerfully central role their mothers played in their lives, while their fathers seemed almost not to exist. Mothers had indeed focused their expectations on their sons. Their husbands could not fulfill their dreams, and the husbands, experiencing so many obstacles to their own success, often withdrew from their wives, feeling themselves to be failures. As their wives turned to their sons, the mother-son relationship became an intense one in Jewish families. In time the negative stereotyping came to include not only the mother's materialism but also the eroticism of her intense attachment to her son. Further, because mothers had the role obligation to ensure the transmission of Jewish values and traditions to the children, they tended to be blamed for whatever ambivalence members of the next generation felt about their cultural identity (Baum, Hyman, & Michael, 1975).

Unfortunately, because of the widespread denial of anti-semitism in this country, Jews themselves often focused their anger and shame on the interior of the family, particularly on mothers, who had the dual and conflicting tasks of transmitting traditional Jewish culture and promoting their children's success in the gentile world. The Jewish mother was pathologized and blamed by psychologists starting with Freud and continuing in the popular press, where she has become the caricature of anti-semitic portrayals. By the 1960s books like Dan Greenberg's *How to Be a Jewish Mother* made fun of her upward mobility, intensity regarding materialistic security/success, and involvement with her children's lives. Other works, such as Philip Roth's *Portnoy's Complaint* (1967), drew a picture of the "nice Jewish boy" who is self-doubting and self-obsessed, trying to cope with a domineering, enticing, meddling mother, who refuses her son a life of his own (Bienstock, 1979).

Compared to other immigrant groups, Jewish immigrants moved with remarkable speed into the American mainstream (Schneider, 1984), probably helped immensely by the adaptability and intensity of the mother's determination to achieve success for the family and to inculcate in her children the traditional values of education and achievement. As Bienstock has put it:

> Seeking success in American terms, these children learned to shrug off a whole network of traditions, beliefs, and relationships. Yet an inheritance of this size cannot be cast away without guilt, and it may be guilt we see surfacing in much of the literature written by American Jews. Toward the mother the child feels most grateful and consequently most guilty. Recalling the ruthless way in which he left her behind to pursue the American dream he defends himself by converting her into a monster of motherhood. The modern Jewish writer perpetuates the Jewish Mother image in response to several complementary urges. In portraying her, he can draw upon his emotional ambivalence while intellectually exploring a current social phenomenon. Moreover, he can appeal both to those readers (Jews and non-Jews alike) whose guilt feelings mirror his own and to those who find in the Jewish Mother an unambiguous source of fun. (Bienstock, 1979, p. 190)

The relationship between Jewish mothers and daughters was different from that between mothers and sons. There was, until recently, a concentration on the daughter's finding a successful husband, with her own accomplishments being secondary. In part this was for practical reasons and in part it probably reflected the importance of carrying on Jewish culture. Anything that threatened the continuity of Jewish culture, which was carried on primarily through the mother's efforts in the family and the father's efforts in the synagogue, was feared as potentially producing catastrophic results for the survival of the entire Jewish people. And the long history of anti-semitism, pogroms, and the recent memory of the holocaust supported these concerns. The responsibility for carrying on the culture may present Jewish women with serious conflicts, since they have also internalized the values of education and success and now have, for the first time in history, a chance and a need to achieve for themselves (Koltun, 1976).

An important strength of Jewish women is the intimate relationship that generally exists among women. Mother and daughter are often more like sisters, sharing even the details of their relationships with men. Furthermore, the closeness with the extended family and community within Jewish culture means that Jewish women are very good at working together and working with others to improve things for the group. The major difficulty may be a conflict between older Jewish women and their daughters who have made different life choices. The older women may feel unappreciated, since the dominant culture so often undervalues their efforts in cooking, homemaking and attending to the details of their children's development. And women of the younger generation, who are trying to break out of the old ways, may indeed have difficulty sympathizing with their mother's life decisions. Luckily, both generations tend to value discussion of different beliefs and conflictual issues, which means there is a fair likelihood that mothers and daughters will improve their mutual understanding over time (Myerhoff, 1978).

CLINICAL INTERVENTION

Since gender arrangements are transmitted through the culture, challenging the sexism of a family involves challenging its culture in a way that could be experienced as extremely threatening. It may also happen that, as women become conscious of the sexual inequality of most cultural patterns, they will reject their entire culture and its richness in an effort to break the bonds of sexism. Such a revolutionary stance may be temporarily necessary, but in the long run women benefit from a positive cultural identification. We urge women to seek out the hidden strengths of women in their particular culture, to learn about the "herstory" of their people—their mothers, their aunts, their grandmothers, their ancestors, and the successful women in their group's history, women in the arts, women whose creative talents also expressed the culture in a positive form, since culture never reflects a single perspective or set of values (see also Laird, Chapter 21).

Case Study

Elizabeth Kosary, a 50-year-old Hungarian woman, sought therapy out of concern about her relationship with her two grown daughters, from whom she had become estranged. She had been cut off from her community by her divorce, which she had sought fearing her alternatives were suicide or insanity because she could no longer tolerate her husband's domineering behavior.

As we explored her feelings of pain over the loss of her daughters and depression about her own delayed "launching," it became apparent that she had been forced to sacrifice a great deal in order to develop her authentic self and to obtain economic security. Now she felt she was still paying the price. As she said, "I have no family, so what do I have to show for all my years of sacrifice?" When the therapist asked her about her "Hungarian connections," she became very upset, saying that the patriarchal values of Hungarian culture had given her nothing but pain in her life and she wanted no "Hungarian connections." She had very infrequent contact with her mother in Hungary, who lived alone since the death of her father many years before. Elizabeth said her mother had disapproved of her divorce, blaming her for her "selfishness," and that her mother too was "locked into the view that women should take whatever a man does to them in life."

Challenging her one-sided view of the culture, the therapist said she feared she might be throwing out the baby with the bathwater, since Hungarian culture had also produced her and her daughters (whom Elizabeth admired, though she did not feel close to them). The therapist suggested that there must have been positive aspects of Hungarian culture carried on through women's artistic or musical values, strengths that helped them survive, and that there had to be a "herstory" to Hungarian culture, just as there was for every culture. Even if it was not dominant, it must exist and she was urged to seek it. The therapist talked with Elizabeth about her mother's struggles in Hungary after her father died, about her mother's ambition to go to medical school (which Elizabeth had mentioned in passing), and about many other hopes, dreams, and experiences of women in her family.

With a minimal amount of coaching, Elizabeth began to search for the writings of Hungarian women authors and to ask her mother about her life in her developing correspondence with her. In her attempt to reestablish former friendships, she found a Hungarian friend with whom she shared her efforts to learn about Hungarian culture. When her daughters returned on college vacation she was able to approach them with much less defensiveness about her "inadequacies" as a mother. She was also able to hear them say that they appreciated her struggles as a woman, even though they loved their father and had felt his pain when she left. They both said that they now realized that the divorce was probably necessary, and that they had been angry earlier mostly because they felt hurt that the family could not stay together.

Therapists need to be as inventive as possible in helping female clients reframe their traditional culture in ways that work for them and enable them to take along into the future what they will need from the past. There are no simple answers here, and we do not believe that most people will be able to make revolutionary changes overnight (see Taffel & Masters, Chapter 7). There is much to be gained for women in exploring the multigenerational struggles of their mothers, sisters, and grandmothers, as well as taking on for themselves identification with the strengths of their fathers, brothers, and grandfathers.

REFERENCES

Baum, C., Hyman, P., & Michael, S. (1975). *The Jewish woman in America*. New York: Dial Press.

Bell, R. (1971). The relative importance of mother and wife roles among Negro lower class women. In R. Staples (Ed.), *The black family: Essays and studies*. Belmont, CA: Wadsworth.

Bienstock, B. G. (1979). The changing image of the American Jewish mother. In V. Tufte & B. Myerhoff (Eds.), *Changing images of the family*. New Haven: Yale University Press.

Byrne, N., & McCarthy, I. (1986). Irish Women. Conference at U.M.D.N.J., Robert Wood Johnson Medical School, September 15.

Diner, H. R. (1983). *Erin's daughters in America*. Baltimore: Johns Hopkins University Press.

Diner, H. R. (1986). Irish women. Conference at U.M.D.N.J., Robert Wood Johnson Medical School, September 15.

Duley, M. I., & Edwards, M. I., (Eds.), (1986). *The cross-cultural study of women*. New York: The Feminist Press.

Fallows, M. A. (1979). Irish Americans: Identity and assimilation. Englewood Cliffs, NJ: Prentice-Hall.

Fernandez, C. C., & Quintero, R. M. (1974). Bases de la sociedad sexista en Puerto Rico. *Revista/Review Inter Americana, 4*(2), 130–135.

Giddings, P. (1985). *When and where I enter: The impact of black women on race and sex in America*. New York: Bantam Books.

Goldenberg, J. O. (1973). The Jewish feminist: Conflict in identities. *Response, 7*, 11–18.

Greeley, A. M. (1972). *That most distressful nation*. Chicago: Quandrangle.

Greenberg, D. (1964). *How to be a Jewish mother*. Los Angeles: Price/Stern/Sloan.

Hale, J. (1980). *The black woman and child rearing*. In L. Rodgers-Rose (Ed.), *The black woman*. Beverly Hills, CA: Sage Publications.

Hertz, J. H. (1960). *The authorized daily prayer book*. New York: Bloch.

Herz, F., & Rosen, E. (1982). Jewish families. In M. McGoldrick, J. K. Parce, & J. Giordano (Eds.), *Ethnicity and family therapy*. New York: Guilford.

Hirata, L. C. (1979). *Free, indentured, enslaved: Chinese prostitutes in nineteenth century America*. Boston: Houghton-Mifflin.

Humphreys, A. (1966). *The new Dubliners*. New York: Fordham University Press.

Kennedy, R. E. (1978). *The Irish: Marriage, immigration and fertility*. Berkeley: University of California Press.

Koltun, E. (Ed.). (1976). *The Jewish woman*. New York: Schocken Books.

Krista, J. (1986). *About Chinese women*. New York: Marion Boyars.

Ladner, J. (1973). Foreword. In Staples, R. (Ed.) *The black woman in America*. Chicago: Nelson Hall.

Loewenberg, B., & Bogin, R. (Eds.). (1976). *Black women in nineteenth-century American Life: Their words, their thoughts, their feelings*. University Park, PA: Pennsylvania State University Press.

Luria, Z. (1974). Recent Women college graduates: A study of rising expectations. *American Journal of Orthopsychiatry, 44*, 109–120.

MacCurtain, M., & O'Corrain, D. (Eds.). (1978). *Women in Irish society: The historical dimension*. Dublin: Arlen House.

Martin, E. P., & Martin, J. M. (1986). The black woman: Perspectives on her role in the family. In W. A. Van Horne & T. V. Tonnenson (Eds.), *Ethnicity and women (Vol. 5)* (pp. 184–205). Milwaukee: University of Wisconsin System American Ethnic Studies Coordinating Committee/Urban Corridor Consortium.

McCray, R. (1980). One-child families and atypical sex ratios in an elite black community. In R. Staples (Ed.), *The black family: Essays and studies* (pp. 177–181). San Francisco: University of California Press.

McGoldrick, M., Garcia-Preto, N., Hines, P. M., Lee, E. (In press). Families and ethnicity. In A. Gurman (Ed.), *The handbook of family therapy*. (2nd ed.). New York: Guilford Press.

McGoldrick, M. (1982a). Overview. In M. McGoldrick, J. K. Pearce, & J. Giordano (Eds.), *Ethnicity and family therapy*. New York: Guilford.

McGoldrick, M. (1982b). Irish Americans. In M. McGoldrick, J. K. Pearce, and J. Giordano (Eds.), *Ethnicity and family therapy*. New York: Guilford.

McGoldrick, M., Hines, P., Lee, E., & Garcia-Preto, N. (1986). Mourning rituals: How culture shapes the experience of loss. *Family Therapy Networker, 10*(6), 28–36.

McGoldrick, M., Pearce, J. K., & Giordano, J. (Eds.). (1982). *Ethnicity and family therapy*. New York: Guilford.

McGoldrick, M., & Rohrbaugh, M. (1987). Researching ethnic family stereotypes. *Family Process, 26*(1), 89–99.

McKenna, A. (1979). Attitudes of Irish mothers to child rearing. *Journal of Comparative Family Studies, 10*(2), 227–251.

Mizio, E. (1974). Impact of external systems on the Puerto Rican family. *Social Casework, 55*(1), 76–83.

Morsbach, H. (1978). Aspects of Japanese marriage. In M. Corbin, (Ed.), *The couple*. New York: Penguin.

Moynihan, D. (1965). *The negro family: The case of national action*. Washington, DC: U.S. Department of Labor.

Murphy, H. B. M. (1975). Alcoholism and schizophrenia in the Irish: A review. *Transcultural Psychiatric Research, 12*, 116–139.

Myerhoff, B. (1978). *Number our days*. New York: Simon & Schuster.

Power, P. (1976). *Sex and marriage in ancient Ireland*. Dublin: Mercier.

Reynolds, L. (1983). Irish women in legend, literature and life. In S. F. Gallagher (Ed.). *Women in Irish legend, life and literature*. Totowa, NJ: Barnes & Noble Books.

Rodgers-Rose, L. (Ed.). (1980). *The black woman*. New York: Sage.

Romero, M. (1986). Twice protected? Assessing the impact of affirmative action on Mexican-American women. In W. A. Van Horne & T. V. Tonnensen, (Eds.), *Ethnicity and women*. Madison, WI: University of Wisconsin System American Ethnic Studies Coordinating Committee/Urban Corridor Consortium.

Rosaldo, M. Z., & Lamphere, L. (Ed.). (1974). *Women, culture and society*. Stanford, CA: Stanford University Press.

Roth, P. (1967). *Portnoy's complaint*. New York: Fawcett.

Rotunno, M., & McGoldrick, M. (1982). Italian Americans. In M. McGoldrick, J. K. Pearce, & J. Giordano (Eds.), *Ethnicity and family therapy*. New York: Guilford.

Rutledge, E. (1980). Marital interaction goals of black women: Strengths and effects. In L. Rose (Ed.), *The black woman*. Beverly Hills, CA: Sage Publications.

Scheper-Hughes, N. (1979). *Saints, scholars and schizophrenics*. Berkeley, CA: University of California Press.

Schneider, S. W. (1984). *Jewish and female*. New York: Simon & Schuster.

Sidel, R. (1982). *Women and child care in China*. New York: Penguin Books.

Sluzki, C. (1982). The Latin Lover revisited. In M. McGoldrick, J. K. Pearce, & J. Giordano, (Eds.), *Ethnicity and Family Therapy*, New York: Guilford.

Spanier, G., Roos, P., & Shockey, J. (1985). Marital trajectories of American women: Variations in the life course. *Journal of Marriage and the Family, 47*(7), 993–1003.

Staples, R. (1978). The black family: Essays and studies, (2nd ed.). Belmont, CA: Wadsworth Publishing Company.

Staples, R. (1981). The myth of the black matriarchy. *The Black Scholar*, Nov/Dec, 26–34.

Staples, R. (1985). Changes in black family structures: The conflict between family ideology and structural conditions. *Journal of Marriage and the Family, 47*(7), 1005–1013.

Stone, P. T. (1979). Feminist consciousness and black women. In J. Freeman (Ed.). *Women: A feminist perspective*. Palo Alto, CA: Mayfield Publishing Company.

Sung, B. L. (1967). *Mountain of gold*. New York: Macmillan.

Terrelonge, P. (1979). Feminist consciousness and black women. In Freeman, J. (Ed.), *Women: A feminist perspective*. Palo Alto, CA: Mayfield Publishing Company.

Tonnensen, T. V., & Van Horne, W. A. (Eds.). (1986). *Ethnicity and women*. Milwaukee: University of Wisconsin System American Ethnic Studies Coordinating Committee/Urban Corridor Consortium.

U.S. Department of Commerce, Census of Population. (1983). General, social and economic characteristics, Volume 1.

U.S. Department of Commerce, Bureau of the Census. (1986). *We the black Americans*. Washington, DC: Government Printing Office.

Woehrer, C. E. (1982). The influence of ethnic families on intergenerational relationships and later life transitions. *Annals of the American Academy of Political and Social Science, 464*, November, 65–78.

Wolf, M., & Witke, R. (1975). *Women in Chinese society*. Stanford, CA: Stanford University Press.

Yung, C. K. (1959) *A Chinese family in the Communist revolution*. Boston, MA: M.I.T. Press.

Yung, J. (1986). *Chinese women of America: A pictorial history*. Seattle: University of Washington Press.

Zborowski, M., & Herzog, E. (1952). *Life is with people*. New York: Schocken Books.

11

Women Through the Family Life Cycle

MONICA McGOLDRICK

WOMEN HAVE ALWAYS played a central role in families, but the idea that they have a life cycle apart from their roles as wife and mother is relatively recent, and still not widely accepted in our culture. The expectation has been that women would take care of the needs of others, first men, then children, then the elderly. Until very recently "human development" referred to male development, while women's development was defined by the men in their lives. They went from being daughter, to wife, to mother, their status defined by the male in the relationship and their role by their position in the family's life cycle. Rarely has it been accepted that women have a right to a life for themselves (see Hicks and Anderson, Chapter 16).

Women's roles throughout the life cycle in their families and at work have changed dramatically in recent years. Since 1980 childbearing has fallen below replacement levels, as many women are electing not to have children or to postpone childbearing in order to pursue career aspirations. Many more women are concentrating on jobs and education. In fact, for the first time more women than men are now enrolled in college (Bianchi & Spain, 1986). The differential role of men and women in the larger context is illustrated by the fact that in the American workplace women still make an average 64 cents on the dollar a man makes for the same job.

As difficult as traditional patterns may be for many women, changing the status quo may be even more painful. Even as women are rebelling against having responsibility for making family relationships, holidays, and celebrations happen, they typically feel guilty for not continuing to do what they have grown up expecting they will do. When no one else moves in to fill the gap, they feel that the family is breaking down and that it is their fault. A fascinating and little publicized finding suggesting the contrary is that high achievement of mothers is even more predictive of high achievement of both their sons and their daughters than is the high achievement of fathers (Hoffman, 1972, 1974; Losoff, 1974; Padan, 1965).

Women are exposed to higher rates of change and instability in their lives than men (Dohrenwend, 1973) and, because of their greater emotional involvement in the lives of those around them, are more vulnerable to life cycle stresses. Compared to men, they are more responsive to and feel responsible for a wider network of people. Their role overload is exacerbated when unpredictable stresses, such as illness, divorce, or unemployment, occur. This means they are doubly stressed—both exposed to more network stresses and more emotionally responsive to them (Gove, 1972). Kessler and McLeod (1984) found women to be much more emotionally affected than men by the death of a loved one and other network events. Men respond less to events at the edge of their caring networks; they actually hear less about stress in their networks. The help-seeking literature indicates that people in need of emotional support more often seek out women as confidants; thus women experience more demands for nurturance. At times their networks are so demanding that a degree of cutting off may be necessary for their mental health (Cohler & Lieberman, 1980). As Avis (1985) summarizes, "Many writers have concluded that adherence to traditional family roles not only oppresses women, but can have a pernicious effect on all family members, on marriage relationships, and on family functioning" (p. 131).

In recent years women have been marrying later and less often and having fewer children. They are divorcing more—current estimates are that 50% of marriages will end in divorce (Weitzman, 1985; Glick, 1984)—and those with the most education and income are the most likely to divorce and the least likely to remarry. By contrast, the wealthier men are and the more educated they are, the more likely they are to stay married or to remarry quickly. Women are likely to move down to the poverty level after divorce, experiencing an average 73% decline in their standard of living. In contrast, their former husbands experience a 42% average rise in their standard of living (Weitzman, 1985). Presently, 75% of the poor are women and children, most living in one-parent households. After divorce, men have an ever larger pool of marriageable women to choose from, because they prefer and can attract younger women. For first marriages, the wife is on the average three years younger than her husband; for second marriages the wife is on the average six years younger than her husband.

Traditionally, women have been held responsible for the maintenance of family relationships and for all family caretaking—for their husbands, their children, their parents, their husbands' parents, and any other sick or dependent family members. Even now, almost one-fifth of women aged 55 to 59 are providing in-home care for an elderly relative. Usually one daughter or a daughter-in-law has the primary care of elderly women. Clearly caregiving to the very old (who are mostly women) is primarily a woman's issue. Increasingly, younger women are in the labor force and thus unavailable for caretaking without extreme difficulty. Presently more than half of all women between the ages of 45 and 64 are in the labor force, most of them working full-time. Increasingly, with more and more four-generation families, the caregivers themselves are elderly and struggling with declining functioning. Thus, today's middle-aged women are caught in a "dependency squeeze" between their parents and their children (Baruch & Barnett, 1983; Belle, 1982; Brody, 1981; Lang & Brody, 1983).

The laws which regulate social services to support families are determined primarily by men and do not support the women who bear the burden of family responsibilities but do not wield power. Contrary to the claim that government services sap the strength of family supports, the failure to provide public services to families will most likely exacerbate intergenerational conflicts, turning family members against each other (Hess, 1985). The overwhelming majority of lawmakers in our society is male. Their record on legislation in support of family caretaking is very poor. This is a critical issue for divorced women, mothers of small children, minority women, the elderly (who are mostly women), and other groups who do not have the power to make the laws and thus get doubly burdened—with the responsibility and without the resources to take care of their families.

MALE AND FEMALE DEVELOPMENT

There has always been a "his" and "hers" version of human development, although until recently only the former was described in the literature. Female development was seen only from an androcentric perspective and involved learning to become an adaptive helpmate to foster male development. Most male theoreticians, such as Freud, Kohlberg, and Piaget tended to ignore female development. Only very recently has female development been described in the literature at all (Dinnerstein, 1976; Gilligan, 1982; Miller, 1976). While separation, differentiation and autonomy have been considered the primary values for male development, caring and attachment, interdependence, relationship, and attention to context have been primary in female development. At the same time these latter values have been devalued by male theoreticians (such as Erikson, Piaget, Levinson, Valliant, and others).

Women have tended to define themselves in the context of human relationships and to judge themselves in terms of their ability to care. As Gilligan has described woman's place in man's life cycle, it has been that of "nurturer, caretaker, and helpmate, the weaver of those networks of relationships on which she in turn relies. But while women have thus taken care of men, men have, in their theories of psychological development, as in their economic arrangements, tended to assume or devalue that care" (Gilligan, 1982, p. 17). The major theories of human development have generally equated maturity with autonomy. Concern about relationships has been seen as a weakness of women (and men) rather than a human strength. The studies of Broverman and her colleagues on sex-role stereotypes (1970, 1972) have made eminently clear the biases in our cultural attitudes which equate "healthy adulthood" with "maleness." As these studies have shown, we have equated maturity with the capacity for autonomous thinking, rationality, clear decision-making, and responsible action, and have devalued as undesirable the qualities our culture has defined as necessary for feminine identity, such as warmth, expressiveness, and caring for others.

Male theories have failed to describe the progression of relationships toward a maturity of interdependence. Though most developmental texts recognize the importance of individuation, the reality of continuing connection is lost or relegated to the background. Perhaps this is why there is almost no discussion in developmental literature of the important role children play in redefining one's adult identity (Daniels & Weingarten, 1982).

Erikson's (1963) eight stages of development suggest that human connectedness is part of the first stage, trust vs. mistrust, which covers the first year of life. This aspect does not appear again until stage six, intimacy vs. isolation. All of Erikson's other stages leading to adulthood involve individual rather than relational issues: autonomy vs. shame and doubt; initiative vs. guilt; industry vs. inferiority; identity vs. role confusion. Identity is defined as having a sense of self *apart from* one's family. In addition, from age one to twenty those characteristics that refer to interpersonal issues: doubt, shame, guilt, inferiority, and role confusion (all of which are associated with female characteristics) signify failure. It is unfortunate that doubt, guilt, a sense of inferiority, and awareness of role confusion are thus defined out of a healthy identity. Do we not need these qualities to deal with others realistically, just as we need other qualities? Given this idealization of healthy development, it is not surprising that many men have an impaired capacity for intimacy and experience difficulty in acknowledging their vulnerability, doubt, and imperfection.

The amazing development of the ability to talk or communicate, which occurs between the ages of one and three and is the primary differential characteristic between us and other animals, is not even mentioned in this schema. In fact, girls demonstrate greater and earlier verbal ability than boys (Romer, 1981). And remarkably, Erikson's phase of generativity occurs *after* the time of greatest human generativity, producing children, which does not even enter into his schema. The last stage of adulthood — ego integrity vs. despair — again appears to relate to individual rather than interpersonal aspects of development. Thus, Erikson's ideal characteristics of a healthy adult — autonomy, initiative, industry, and a clear identity apart from one's family — create a seriously imbalanced human being. In our view all stages of the life cycle have both individual and interpersonal aspects. The failure to appreciate this has led to seriously skewed conceptions of human development.

In Levinson's (1978) account the most significant relationships for men in early adult life are the mentor and the special woman or helpmate who encourages the hero to shape and live out his dream. Thus, the significant relationships of early adulthood have been construed as "transitional figures" that are the means to an end of individual achievement (Gilligan, 1982, p. 152). George Valliant's (1977) study of male development among high achieving Harvard graduates, interestingly called *Adaptation to Life*, rather than *male* adaptation, also focuses on work and minimizes the importance of attachment to others.

Even the language which has evolved to describe human development uses peculiarly impersonal terms such as "object relations" to refer to human relationships. The sexist bias of our language appears also in the use of the terms "maternal deprivation," on the one hand, but "father absence," a much less derogatory term, on the other, although what is usually meant is a father who was completely unavailable and a mother who was present but did not give all that was expected of the ideal maternal figure, defined in object-relations theory as the "good enough mother."

Developmentally women have been expected from the point of early adulthood to "stand behind their men," to support and nurture their children, and paradoxically, to be able to live without affirmation and support themselves. Adaptability has probably been the major skill required of women. They were expected to accept being uprooted every time their husbands moved for a better job, to accept their husbands' lack of communication and unavailability, and to handle all human relationships themselves. It is ironic that women, who are seen as "dependent" and less competent than men, have had to function without emotional support in their marriages, to be, indeed, almost totally emotionally self-sufficient. Women have typically had to bolster their husbands' sense of self-esteem, but have been seen as "nags" when they sought emotional support for themselves. In clinical practice, men's marital complaints typically center on their wives' nagging and emotional demands, while wives' complaints center on their husbands' lack of emotional responsiveness and their own sense of abandonment (Weiss, 1985).

Miller (1976) has called for a new psychology that recognizes the different pattern of women's development, based on a context of attachment and affiliation with others. As she describes it, women's sense of self has been very much organized around being able to make and maintain relationships. The threat of disruption of a relationship is often perceived not just as "object loss," but as something closer to a loss of one's identity, and thus requiring a transformation of self and of the system. Basic to this systemic perspective is the sense that human identity is inextricably bound up in one's relationships with others and that complete autonomy is a fiction. Human beings cannot exist in isolation; the most important aspects of human experience are relational. Gilligan's studies suggest that women's moral development has centered on the elaboration of the knowledge of human attachment. In Gilligan's (1982) view,

> Attachment and separation anchor the cycle of human life, describing the biology of human reproduction and the psychology of human development. The conceptions of attachment and separation that depict the nature and sequence of infant development appear in adolescence as identity and intimacy and then in adulthood as love and work. (p. 151)

WORK

While for men, work and family function as mutually supportive and complementary, for women, work and family have posed conflicting demands. As a culture we claim that "love and work" are equally important. But we act as if work is what matters for a man—it is the standard by which we judge him, while we continue to judge a woman solely as wife and mother. Furthermore, we demean the importance of her work, whether within or outside of the home, and value her only for her ability to "love"—that is, to respond to the needs of others. Women have been in a painful bind regarding family and work. Although labor force participation has been found to be a primary determinant of women's psychological well-being (Kessler & McRae, 1984) in the dominant culture the value persists that women belong in the home. We know that women who work show fewer symptoms of psychological distress (Bernard, 1982), and yet there are many pressures preventing women from feeling good about working. The family is seen as supporting and nurturing the male worker for his performance on the job. Women, on the other hand, are seen as depriving their families by working. There is little support for the management of conflicting demands and no sense of the family as a "refuge" for women as it has been for men.

Even though the majority of today's women work, the sharing of family responsibilities to balance the workload is not occurring. While husbands and children participate slightly in housework, the vast majority of household tasks is done by wives—between 74% and 92% of the major tasks according to one study (Berheide, 1984).

Friedan (1985) has warned that,

> If the women's movement didn't move into a second stage and take on the problems of restructuring work and home, a new generation would be vulnerable to backlash. But the movement has not moved into that needed second stage, so the women struggling with these new problems view them as purely personal not political, and no longer look to the movement for solutions. (p. 84)

Friedan is now urging us again to bring the issue to the forefront,

> To free a new generation of women from its new double burden of guilt and isolation. The guilts of less-than-perfect motherhood and less-than-perfect professional career performance are real because it's not possible to "have it all" when jobs are still structured for men whose wives take care of the details of life, and homes are still structured for women whose only responsibility is running their families. (p. 84)

Friedan is urging us once again to tackle the hard political tasks of restructuring home and work so that women who are married and have children can also earn and have their own voice in the decision-making mainstream of society. (For a more extensive discussion of women and work, see Apter, 1985; Baruch & Barnett, 1983; Baruch, Barnett, & Rivers, 1983; Holder, Chapter 17; McGoldrick, 1987.)

Economic independence for women, which has profound implications for traditional family structures, appears crucial for women's protection in the face of abuse (Aguirre, 1985; Strube & Barbour, 1984), divorce (Weitzman, 1985), and old age (Hess, 1985). The increasing feminization of poverty means that by the year 2000 the poor will be primarily women and children. In order to counteract this trend, massive power changes are required in our culture. The importance of work for women's self-esteem seems clear. One group of researchers studying women's attitudes found that:

> Contrary to the traditional notion that marriage is the most important pillar of a woman's happiness, our study is finding that, for employed women, a high-prestige job, rather than a husband is the best prediction of well-being. (Baruch & Barnett, 1980, p. 199)

A recent study indicates that in the past decade women have become more aware of the external constraints on their ability to meet their goals in the labor force. As a result they are seeing themselves as having less control over events than they did in the past. This fits with reports that women are experiencing high rates of sex discrimination in the workplace (Doherty & Baldwin, 1985).

HOUSEHOLDS

The traditional household is fast becoming a relic of the past. Very few families fit into the traditional ideal of working father, stay-at-home mother, and children (Friedan, 1985). Currently only 29% of households consist of couples with children under 18, compared to 44% in 1960. At least half of those mothers work. The total number of families still living in a "traditional family" appears to be no more than 6% (Hewlett, 1985). The number of married-couple and couple-with-children households has decreased steadily since 1970, while the number of single-parent households (mostly headed by women) has more than doubled (Rawlings, 1983). An increasing number of teenagers are giving birth to children who are then cared for by their mothers, aunts, and sisters. Teen fathers are rarely included as part of the picture, and other male family members frequently have no primary role in the family's development.

Finally, the majority of people who live alone are women (11 million women vs. 6.8 million men). They tend to be widowed or divorced elderly (Current Population Reports, 1981).

BETWEEN FAMILIES: YOUNG ADULTHOOD

Young adulthood has, until very recently, been a phase for men only. Women passed from their families of origin to their families of procreation, with no space in between to be independent. For men this phase has tended to emphasize their development of a career, while for a woman career has almost always taken second place to the search for a husband. Women are frequently confronted with a clash between the two roles, family and social pressure conflicting with career demands. The more she focuses on career, the less viable are her marital options. In contrast to the situation for men, where education increases the likelihood of marriage at any age, for women with a college education the chances of marrying after age 30 diminish rapidly.

In our experience, daughters who make full use of young adulthood for personal development tend to distance themselves from their families of origin more often than do sons, probably because there is less family acceptance of women's individual development. It is perhaps for this reason that the next phase, the young couple, represents different patterns for men and women in relation to their families of origin. For women it brings a turning back to their parents for more connection, while for men there is an increasing separation from their families of origin, seeing the marital relationship as replacing the family of origin (Goleman, 1986). As Ben Franklin said: "My son is my son 'til he takes a wife, but my daughter's my daughter all the days of my life." In fact, a daughter is also a daughter-in-law for the rest of her life, since through marriage she typically gains responsibility for the connectedness with her husband's family as well.

While women are tending to stay with their educational and career possibilities longer than in the past, they still tend to drop out of college and employment at higher rates than do men. (Men, of course, have fewer options to drop out of the career or work ladder.)

The pressure on women not to take full advantage of independent living may be intense. They may lower their sights because of educational, social, internalized or family attitudes. Women worry that their families may disapprove of their high aspirations, fearing it will mean the loss of marital possibilities.

Horner's studies (1972) showed that women feel anxiety about competitive achievement.

(Such fear) exists because for most women the anticipation of success in competitive achievement activity, especially against men, produces anticipation of certain negative consequences, for example, threat of social rejection and loss of femininity. (1968, p. 125)

Sassen (1980) pointed out that Horner found success anxiety present only in women whose success was at the expense of another's failure. Thus, once again, women are shown to be sensitive to the interpersonal context.

Working with families at this phase of the life cycle is particularly rewarding because of the options that become available when young adults are able to move toward new life patterns. Interventions directed at connecting young women with the strengths of women in past generations of their families may be especially important in assisting them at this crucial formative phase. Helping them reconstruct their family narrative highlights feminine resources they may learn to appreciate and draw on (see Laird, Chapter 21). It is important to outline all the unrecognized work that their mothers and grandmothers did to raise their families and keep a household going in order to emphasize their courage, abilities, hard work, and strengths as role models for positive identification, since women are typically hidden from history (herstory!).

THE JOINING OF FAMILIES IN MARRIAGE: THE YOUNG COUPLE

In recent years women are marrying later or choosing not to marry at all (12% compared to 3% of their parents' generation), they are having fewer children and having them later, and many (about 25%) are opting not to have children at all.

Marriage and divorce have profoundly different implications for men and women. As Jessie Bernard (1975, 1981, 1982) has described it, "his marriage is very different from and a great deal more satisfying than 'her' marriage." "Generally, the woman has given up more to be married than the man has (her occupation, friends, residence, family, name). She adjusts to his life" (Goodrich, Rampage, Ellman, & Halstead, 1988, p. 16). Although men remain ambivalent about getting married, fearing "ensnarement," women become more symptomatic and prone to stress in the married state on virtually every indicator (Avis, 1985; Baruch, Barnett, & Rivers, 1983; Bernard, 1982; Brodsky & Hare-Mustin, 1980; Kessler & MacRae, 1984; Walsh, Chapter 14). Married women experience more depression and more marital dissatisfaction than married men; in addition, women in traditional marital relationships have poorer physical health, lower self-esteem, less autonomy, and poorer marital adjustment than women in more equal relationships (Avis, 1985).

Several recent researchers have found a continuing difference in the values of men and women about their marriages (Blumstein & Schwartz, 1983; Goleman, 1986; Huston, 1983; Sternberg, 1984; White, 1986). Although during courtship men are willing to spend intimate time with women, after marriage they tend to spend less and less time talking to their wives, often considering doing chores around the house to be an adequate demonstration of caring and intimacy and feeling mystified about what women want when they seek more contact in the marital relationship (Goleman, 1986; Sternberg, 1984; White, 1986). Generally women do want intimacy and are frustrated by the limited degree of relating their husbands' offer.

Women are more willing than men to admit to problems and are much more likely than their husbands to evaluate their relationships as problematic. Men value their wives' looks more, while women consider their husbands' earning potential a major attraction in marriage. Men say that what is important in marriage is their wives' sexual responsiveness and shared interests, while their wives say that the husband's ability to get along with her family and friends is more important. Men generally rate their marital communication, relationships with parents, and sexual relationships as good, while women rate all of these as problematic. Furthermore, it seems that the double standard continues to operate, with women considering their husband's fidelity more important than men do, and men more likely to expect fidelity from their wives than from themselves (Goleman, 1986; Huston, 1983; Sternberg, 1984).

Between 1970 and 1982, the proportion of women in their late twenties who had never married rose from 10.5% to 23.4% (Saluter, 1983). For those in their early thirties the proportion rose from 6.2% to 11.6%. It appears that about 25% of women are still marrying before age 20, but the other 75% are delaying marriage for ever longer periods of time.

For every age bracket, the higher the income of the woman, the lower the rate of marriage, a situation that is just the reverse for men (Bernard, 1982). While this probably reflects the greater freedom that financial security gives a woman about whether to marry, it also reflects her limited options. Since women have always been expected to marry men who were taller, older, smarter and wealthier than they were, they have been at a serious disadvantage in finding a mate. Women whose choices did not reflect these differentials have always been stigmatized, as have men who chose women who were older, smarter, taller or wealthier. Such men might these days be labeled as "wimps," unable to find a more desirable woman. The only category where women were allowed to be "more and better" was in physical attractiveness.

For every ten women between 40 and 50 with a college education, there are only three single men who are older and better educated (Richardson, 1986). As one writer has put it:

> This demographic tendency makes marital equality a joke. A husband may be fairness itself/wash his share of the dishes, encourage his wife in her work, value her opinions, respect her individuality and all the rest of it. But every eye wanders from time to time and the moment comes when he is comparing his wife with other women, while she is comparing him to solitude. (Pollit, 1986)

Couples looking to change the traditional pattern of sex roles can begin by altering traditional rituals around marriage (McGoldrick, 1988). For example, both spouses can be encouraged to develop a ritual which allows them to represent the movement from their parents (not just the woman from her father) to the marital bond. Since marriage requires that both partners redefine themselves in relation to their extended family, such a ritual offers them the opportunity to redefine traditional family relationships in a way that may make their future marital accommodation more equitable (for more about family rituals and gender, see Imber-Black, Chapter 22).

The phase of transition to marriage is an important time for helping young women (and men) look beyond sex-role stereotypes. Patterns that become fixed at this point in the life cycle may have great importance later. Many young women resist looking closely at their romantic myths about marriage, and they often do not appear for therapy until after the marriage when the "honeymoon" ends. Fortunately, in the early years of marriage, it is a lot easier to change patterns than later when they have become entrenched.

Families with Young Children

With the transition to parenthood, the family becomes a threesome, which makes it a permanent system for the first time. If a childless spouse leaves, there is no system left, but if one person leaves the new triad of couple and child, the system itself survives. Thus, symbolically and in reality this transition is a key one in the family life cycle.

The traditional family has often not only encouraged but even required dysfunctional patterns, such as the overresponsibility of mothers for their children and the complementary underresponsibility or disengagement of fathers (Avis, 1985). We suggest a very different way of thinking about parenthood. As Daniels and Weingarten (1983) have described

> Parenthood is a powerful generator of development. It gives us an opportunity to refine and express who we are, to learn what we can be, to become someone different. (p. 3)

One of the mothers in their study put it as follows:

> Children battle you into being more than you thought you were, into giving more than you thought you had it in you to give. Those middle of the nights, you learn something about yourself. (p. 1)

The developmental literature, strongly influenced by the male dominated psychoanalytic tradition, has focused almost exclusively on mothers, giving extraordinary importance to the mother/child relationship in the earliest years of life, to the exclusion of other relationships in the family or to later developmental phases (Lewis, Feiring, & Kotsonis, 1984). As Kagan (1984) has pointed out, an entire mythology has evolved around our assumptions about the importance of infancy and early childhood in determining the rest of human life. The psychoanalytical model also stressed the view of human development as a primarily painful process in which mother and child were viewed as adversaries. Such assumptions about development in the early years led to a psychological determinism that held mothering responsible for whatever happened. The fantasy that mothers were all powerful has led to a tendency to blame mothers for whatever goes wrong and to expect they should be perfect, all giving and all knowing (Chodorow & Contratto, 1982).

Much of the feminist literature has continued to focus on mothering, while locating the mother/child dyad within a patriarchal system (Chodorow & Contratto, 1982; Dinnerstein, 1976). And even the family therapy literature has not avoided this mother blaming (Caplan & Hall-McCorquondale, 1985).

We urge quite a different perspective on human development, which views child development in the rich context of multigenerational family relationships, as well as within its social and cultural context. Literature and the media continue to focus on the mother's presence as crucial to healthy child development. Fathers are still depicted as peripheral adjuncts (usually to provide a bit of extra support for the mother), particularly until the child is verbal and out of diapers. And aunts, uncles, grandparents and other relatives are almost never mentioned in the child development literature (Lewis et al., 1984).

It is also curious how nonsystemic the developmental literature has been in ignoring the powerful impact of children on adult development. Thus, the potential for change and growth in parents as they respond to the unfolding of their children's lives is lost, as Daniels and Weingarten (1983) put it:

> Because men have not traditionally occupied themselves with caring for children, parenthood, the core experience of what Erikson calls generativity, is oddly missing from their sense of their own development. (p. 5)

The major research on the transition to parenthood indicates that it is accompanied by a general decrease in marital satisfaction, a reversion to more traditional sex roles even by dual career couples, and a lowering of self-esteem for women (Cowen et al., 1985; Entwistle & Doering, 1981). This tends to be true even for couples with a more equal distribution of roles in the early phases of their relationship and marriage. The transition to parenthood tends to push them back toward more traditional sex roles. Very few couples share household and childcare responsibilities equally.

Recently there has been much talk about husbands and wives sharing in childbirth classes and in the delivery. However, there is still virtually no preparation of men for the much more complicated and longer lasting tasks of childrearing. In our view, this is an important area for intervention when working with families at this life cycle stage. Since fathers rarely have any experience with small children, they need to learn the skills of intimacy with children. This generally requires time alone, since it is often extremely difficult for them to take primary responsibility for a child in the presence of their wives.

Our culture still leaves women with primary responsibility for childrearing and blames them when something goes wrong. Seventy-three percent of mothers with children in the home work, and 60% of working mothers have no guaranteed maternity leave (a basic right in 117 other countries); also, we have been spending 25% less public money on daycare since 1980. Thus, it is clear that mothers are by no means receiving social support for the tasks that are expected of them in parenting. Even when fathers begin to participate more actively in relating to children, it is mothers, including working mothers, who bear the lion's share of responsibility for seeing that children's needs are met. This includes doctors' appointments, school problems, lunch money, afterschool activities, etc.

It is difficult to determine what behavioral differences between males and females are based on biology, since socialization impacts so powerfully and so early. We do know that females are more likely to survive the birth experience, less likely to have birth defects, and less vulnerable to disease throughout life. Apart from this it is hard to tell which gender differences in behavior are biological and which are based on how children are raised. For example, studies of newborns show that parents tend to encourage more physical activity in boys and more dependence in girls (Lewis & Weintraub, 1974; Maccoby & Jacklin, 1974; Romer, 1981). The major gender difference in early childhood is that girls develop language skills earlier and boys tend to be more active. Studies of infants show that parents talk and look more at girls and engage in more rough play with boys. It appears that girls tend already in their childhood play to be more sensitive to relationships and to avoid competition. Already by age three boys are more oriented to males, to peers, and to nonfamily members, while girls are more oriented toward females, toward family members, and toward adults (Lewis et al., 1984). Thus, boys may be directed away from the home as early as preschool, while girls are being socialized toward family relationships. Already rules become important; boys rarely stop their games because of disputes, whereas girls do (Lever, 1976). We wonder how much richer the patterns of both sexes would be if both men and women participated actively in childrearing.

Given the extent of influence of our patriarchal system, it is indeed amazing that more differences between the sexes have not been found. For example, in a study of the ten top children's television programs four had no females at all and the other six were predominantly male, with females most often portrayed as deferential or as witches or magical creatures (Romer, 1981). As another example, a study of children's stories showed that very few main characters were female; girls and women were primarily observers, not central to the action, and almost always shown wearing aprons (even female animals), as if to reinforce their roles as housekeepers (Romer, 1981). Even on the most popular educational TV show for young children, Sesame Street, not a single one of the primary monster characters is a female.

Kagan and Moss (1962) traced achievement-oriented adults back to their relationships with their mothers (they did not look at their relationships with their fathers, interestingly enough!). They found that males had very close, loving relationships with their mothers in infancy, while females had less intense closeness with their mothers than the average. Hoffman (1972) has suggested that a daughter is more likely to become achievement oriented if she does not experience the training in dependence that has been described as typical for girls.

The data on children raised with only one parent are not clear. Sometimes girls raised without a father have more difficulty in establishing relationships with men, while boys may display extremely "masculine" behavior, possibly because their mothers' sensitivity to the lack of a father encourages her to emphasize this behavior (Romer, 1981), but the pattern depends on many factors, including the presence of other male figures in the children's lives and the age at which they lose their fathers.

In treatment with families at this phase of the life cycle it is important to inquire about household responsibilities as well as the handling of finances and the specifics of childrearing and childcare. Clearly, men who do not develop intimate relationships with their children as they grow up will have difficulty changing the pattern later. It is also important to convey an awareness of the importance of what women have been doing in the family, since their role is most often treated as less important than that of their husbands. Typical questions might be:

- Do both parents go to children's school plays and sports events?
- How are your children changing your perspective on the meaning of your life?
- Does the father get to spend time alone with each child? (It is almost impossible to develop intimacy if he does not.) And is the time spent fairly equally divided among the daughters and sons?
- How are domestic responsibilities divided?
- How is money handled and by whom?
- What are each parent's hopes and expectations for each child in adulthood?

An excellent practical book to encourage such discussion is Stella Chess and Jane Whitehead's *Daughters*.

FAMILIES WITH ADOLESCENTS

Erikson (1968) describes the development of adolescent girls as different from that of boys, in that girls hold their identity in abeyance as they prepare to attract the men by whose name they will be known and by whose status they will be defined, the men who, as Gilligan says, will rescue them from emptiness and loneliness by filling the "inner space" (1982, p. 12). Such attitudes toward girls, which define their development in terms of their ability to attract a male, are bound to be detrimental to their mental health, leaving them lacking in self-esteem, fearing to appear smart, tall, assertive or competent, worrying about losing their chances of finding an intimate relationship with a male. It is in keeping with social norms that during the adolescent years girls often confuse identity with intimacy by defining themselves through relationships with others. It is important to raise questions about such norms, since they put the girl into an impossible bind—you are only healthy if you define your identity not through your self but through your mate.

In spite of the changes that are taking place in the role of women, parents still tend to give more mixed messages to their daughters. While girls tend to do well in school, it is too often for the sake of others rather than for themselves (Romer, 1981). Adolescent girls typically concentrate a lot of attention at this phase on boys, and orient their behavior around male approval. Parents may still be giving messages that the most important thing is to get a mate, and in certain ethnic groups in particular parental concern is focused on the adolescent not becoming sexually active (see McGoldrick, Hines, Lee, & Preto, Chapter 10).

For some reason, during certain phases in development including preschool and adolescence, children seem to hold rigidly to sex-role stereotypes—even more than their parents or teachers do. It is important not to encourage this stereotyping, but instead to encourage girls to develop their own opinions, values, aspirations and interests.

Clinically, when working with adolescents and their families it is important to ask questions about the roles each one is asked to play in the family. What are the chores and responsibilities of boys and of girls? Are sons encouraged to develop social skills or are parents focused primarily on their achievement and sports performance? Are daughters encouraged to have high academic aspirations? Are both sexes given equal responsibility and encouragement in dealing with education, athletics, aspirations for the future, extended family relationships, buying gifts, writing, calling, or caring for relatives? Do both sexes buy and clean their own clothes? Are daughters encouraged to learn about money, science, and other traditionally "masculine" subjects? Clinicians can help by asking questions about these patterns.

We also need to help families find more positive ways of defining for their daughters the changes of the menstrual and reproductive cycle, so that they do not see themselves as "unclean" or "impure." For so long, if sex was even discussed in the family, mothers have taught their daughters that menstruation was "the curse," while sons were taught about their bodily changes as positive, powerful and fulfilling aspects of their manhood.

Although conventional gender values are at an all time high during adolescence, it is also during this phase that crucial life-shaping decisions are made. It is extremely important for the therapist to convey facts about adult life in a compelling manner. As Alexander and his colleagues (1985) say about interventions with delinquent adolescent girls:

> Information about the different salaries of a secretary and heavy-machine operator, statistics about women in the work force, and data on the increase of impoverished, single-parent households, increases the probability that the female delinquent will make thoughtful decisions about her future. (p. 141)

During adolescence, daughters are particularly torn between identification with their mothers and with their fathers. A daughter who is close to her mother may feel a sense of betrayal if she moves in her career aspirations toward a life different from her mother's and toward role identification with her father (Hare-Mustin, 1978).

Commonly, the father-daughter relationship may be problematic in adolescence. Fathers often become awkward about relating to their daughters as they approach adolescence, fearing their budding sexuality. Given the frequently limited masculine repertoire for handling closeness, they may sexualize the relationship or they may withdraw, even becoming irritated or angry as a way of maintaining the distance they feel is necessary. They may need encouragement to engage actively with their daughters rather than avoid them. They may interact more easily with sons, where shared activities such as sports allow companionship without too many pressures for intimate relating. The unavailability of fathers for their daughters may lead daughters to develop an image of the male as a romantic stranger, an unrealistic image that cannot be met when they reach adult life (Hare-Mustin, 1976).

On the other hand, especially for men who have only daughters, this phase may mark their conversion to a feminist position, as they want to support their daughters' having the same rights and privileges that men do. This awareness is important to capitalize on therapeutically. Mothers may be feeling a strain as their children pull away, particularly as they realize the limitations of their own options, if they have devoted themselves primarily to childrearing. On the other hand, mothers may feel a special sense of fulfillment in their daughters' going beyond the constrictions that limited the mothers' own lives.

LAUNCHING CHILDREN AND MOVING ON

Because people are living longer and having fewer children, this is typically the longest phase in the family life cycle, often lasting as long as 20 years. Although women are more often postponing marriage and childbearing until they are in their late twenties or thirties, they are still usually finished with childrearing by about age 50. There is a tendency for men and women to be going in opposite directions psychologically as their children move out into their own lives. Men, perhaps realizing that they have missed most of the intimacy of their children's development, may begin to seek a closeness they have missed, while women, after years of focusing on caring for others, begin to feel energized about developing their own lives—careers, friendships outside the family, and other activities.

The self-esteem and confidence that come from work have always been known to men, at least men of the middle classes. In mid-life they often discover intimacy and relationships, which, of course, women have known from the beginning.

The early part of this phase may be particularly difficult for women, since they are in what has been termed "the sandwich generation." The well-being of both their children and their elderly relatives, who are mostly women, may be gained at the expense of the quality of life of this middle generation of women, who are squeezed by overwhelming demands of caretaking for both other generations; they are squeezed and forced to accept work which limits their options for the rest of their lives (Hess & Soldo, 1984).

For some women the period just after launching their children may be a time of special stress, since they often feel very much behind in the skills to deal with the outside world. Just when their children no longer need them and they are beginning to be defined by the male world as too old to be desirable, they must venture outward. The initial steps are usually the hardest. Once they have begun to move in this arena, many women experience a new confidence and pleasure in their independence—no longer having to put everyone else's needs first. Because of the social and management skills they have generally developed in the previous life cycle phases, women are remarkably resourceful in building a social network. Their lifelong skills in adapting to new situations also serve them in good stead. But the world of work still does not recognize their efforts in a way commensurate with their contribution. And women have typically not been socialized to expect or demand the recognition they deserve.

Obviously, the divergence of interests for men and women, as well as the shift in focus of energies required at this phase, often creates marital tensions, perhaps leading to divorce. Men who divorce typically miss the caretaking functions provided by a wife and remarry rather quickly, usually to a younger woman. For women, whose options are much more limited, the likelihood of remarriage after a divorce at this phase is quite slim. In part this is due to the skew in availability of partners, and in part it appears to be due to older women's having less need to be married and thus, perhaps, being less willing to "settle," particularly for a traditional marriage, which will mean a return to extensive caretaking.

Obviously, women who have developed an identity primarily through intimacy and adaptation to men will be particularly vulnerable in divorce during the launching phase, when they may feel that their very self is disintegrating. Gilligan's observation that women's embeddedness in relationships, their orientation to interdependence, their subordination of achievement to care, and their conflicts over competitive success leave them at risk in mid-life seems more a commentary on our society than a problem in women's development. At present 42% of women aged 55–64 are in the labor force, compared to 27% in 1950 (Bianchi & Spain, 1986), but their benefits will not be equal to men's and the primary types of low-paying, sex-segregated jobs available to them have not changed much in the past 40 years.

It is at this time also that women typically experience menopause. This transition has generally been viewed negatively as a time of physical and psychological distress as women move toward old age. On the contrary, for many women it is a turning point which frees them sexually from worries about pregnancy and marks a new stabilization in their energies for pursuit of work and the social arena.

This life cycle phase has often been referred to as the "empty nest" and depicted it as a time of depression for women, especially for those whose whole lives have been devoted to home and family. However, the recently burgeoning literature on this phase suggests that such a phenomenon is much more apparent than real (Block, Davidson, & Grambs, 1981; Neugarten, 1985; Rubin, 1979; Sangiuliano, 1980). Typically, women are grateful and energized by recapturing free time and exploring new options for themselves. They are not nearly as sorry to see the childrearing era end as has been assumed and often passionately interested in developing themselves and their own personal lives. This phase gives them, for the first time, an opportunity to discover who they are and to develop their own creativity. A study of women between the ages of 35 and 55 by Baruch, Barnett, and Rivers (1983) indicates that many women now feel more positive about this new stage of life and about their future. These women indicated a significant increase in self-esteem and a stronger sense of self-worth than they had experienced in their younger years.

OLDER FAMILIES

The final phase of life might be considered "for women only," since they live longer, and, unlike men, are rarely paired with younger partners, making the statistics for this life cycle phase extremely imbalanced (Congressional Caucus for Women's Issues, 1984):

- Six out of ten Americans over 65 and seven out of ten over 85 are women.

- Seventeen percent of American women over 65 have incomes below the poverty line, as opposed to 10% of men.
- Almost half the older women have median incomes of less than $5,000, as opposed to one in five men.
- More than 80% of elderly female householders live alone and one-quarter of them live in poverty.

The increasing proportion of very old women over the next years presages a number of problems. As Hess and Soldo (1984) put it: "The incomes of women, lower throughout worklife than those of men, remain so in old age. In addition, since the great majority of very old women are widows, and widows typically live alone, their poverty rates increase with advancing age. It becomes ever more difficult to obtain and maintain suitable housing, particularly that which is supportive of declining functional capacity" (p. 2). Since women are the primary caretakers of other women, these problems will affect at least two generations of women, who will be increasingly stressed as time goes along.

Those women who need the care and those who give it, are statistically the poorest and have the least legislative power in our society. As mentioned earlier, legislators have given little consideration to services that support family caregivers. Several studies indicate that the immediate cause of nursing home admission is more likely to be the depletion of family resources than a deterioration in the health of the older relative (Hess & Soldo, 1984).

While the increase in remarried families might create a wider kinship network for caregiving, the increasing divorce rate will probably mean that fewer family members will be willing or available to provide care for elderly parents.

Since both those who give care to the elderly and most of those who receive it are women, the subject tends to escape our view. As therapists we can counter this imbalance by redefining the dilemmas of both the elderly and their caretakers as serious, significant issues. An important general aim of therapy now becomes the rebalancing of skewed caretaking patterns between spouses, not only in relation to children, but also in dealing with the third generation.

Divorce, Single-Parent Households, and Remarriage

The special dilemmas of women in our culture are most evident in divorce and remarriage (see also Herz, 1988; McGoldrick & Carter, 1988; and Stern-Peck & Manocherian, 1988). Our society's arrangements regarding divorce are rapidly pushing more and more women and their children below the poverty level. With the recent trend toward joint custody following divorce, many complex issues are raised for women. Until very recently in human history, women never received custody after a divorce. They had no legal rights at all: They belonged to their husbands, as did their children. Gradually we moved toward a system in which custody went to mothers, unless there was strong countervailing reason. Now many people are moving toward some form of joint custody, but a number of feminist groups are opposing this as not in the best interests of women; the argument is that they continue to have ultimate responsibility for their children anyway, while relinquishing some of the little control they had when they had sole custody through their right to support.

In our view joint custody is an extremely important concept for both men *and* women, but even more so for children. The difficulties are that for men, who may have had little practice in childcare during the marriage, it is hard to learn to share real responsibility for the children after the divorce. Men, and their employers, tend to view their work responsibilities as primary and childcare as secondary. Thus, if a child is sick or either parent will be away, it is usually the mother who will have to make special arrangements. And yet, because they are working, mothers now lose the opportunity to be with their children full-time. In the shifting of roles required by joint physical custody following divorce there is a positive value: It allows the mother some time to herself and, particularly where the husband has overnight contacts with his children, involves him in basic childcare responsibilities such as clothing, brushing teeth and delivering children to school. This increases the likelihood of his developing genuine, ongoing intimacy with them, rather than his remaining in a Sunday-father role. Current research clearly documents the importance for children of having ongoing contact with both parents, and the insufficiency, especially for young children, of seeing their fathers only every other weekend (Kelly, 1987).

It is important clinically not to ignore fathers even if they are not active in the household or in the family picture. At the same time one should not invalidate the mother by assuming that the father must be involved in the current situation. Family therapists have all too often disqualified women alone by assuming that children could only be handled if the father were brought in to control and handle the situation. At least 25% of women do not remarry and stabilize their families in a single-parent household constellation. As Herz (1988) recommends, it is advisable to enter a family system of a single-parent household through the mother, and to move only through respect for her responsibility and power toward engagement of her exhusband.

The custodial mother in a remarried family typically has the major responsibility for juggling her children's needs, those of her new husband and those of his children, who visit at times. In addition, it is usually she who will have to manage arrangements for her children's ongoing contact with their own father and his extended family. Meanwhile, the father may be less cooperative now that his ex-wife is remarried. Finally, the custodial mother must find a way to integrate her own personal needs and her own work—a very complex and burdensome set of demands.

Remarried families offer a number of particularly trying situations for women. Most difficult of all family positions is probably the role of stepmother. Given our culture's high expectations of motherhood, the woman who is brought in to replace a "lost" mother enters a situation fraught with high expectations that even a saint could not achieve. One of the major interventions is to remove from the stepmother the burden of guilt for not being able to accomplish the impossible—taking over the parenting for children who are not her own. Our general guidelines involve putting the natural parent in charge of the children, however difficult that may be with a father who works full-time and who feels he has no experience with "mothering." The problem for the stepmother is especially poignant, since she is usually the one most sensitive to the needs of others, and it will be extremely difficult for her to take a back seat while her husband struggles awkwardly with an uncomfortable situation. The fact is that she has no alternative. Women's tendency to take responsibility for family relationships, to believe that what goes wrong is their fault and that, if they just try hard enough, things will work out, are the major problems for them in remarried families, since the situation carries with it built-in structural ambiguities, loyalty conflicts, guilt, and membership problems.

WOMEN AND THEIR FRIENDSHIP NETWORKS

Friendship is an extremely important resource for women throughout the life cycle. Women tend to have more close friends than men, but the relationships they have are often not validated by the larger society. Men may have acquaintances with whom they spend time, but no close friends in whom they confide. Schydlowsky (1983) shows that the importance of women's close female friendships diminishes from adolescence to early adulthood, as they focus on finding a mate and establishing a marriage, and then increases throughout the rest of the life cycle. Close female friendships were reported as more important than close male friendships throughout the life cycle and were second only to good health in importance for life satisfaction.

We urge family members to respect both sexes' need to nurture friendship systems outside the family and to move away from the traditional pattern of the wife's organizing the couple's social schedule around the husband's business associates. In such situations women were expected to make friends not on the basis of personal interests but because their husbands want to cultivate certain contacts. In such traditional arrangements women were expected to replace friends whenever they moved for their husbands' jobs. Such arrangements do not respect the importance of friendship as a basic support throughout the life cycle and mistake career networking for friendship.

LESBIANS

Lesbians tend to be perceived as unlaunched adolescents, regardless of their age (Krestan & Bepko, 1980; Roth, Chapter 15). An important clinical issue involves helping them deal with their families of origin in relation to their lesbian lifestyle, so that the family comes to respect their subsystem boundaries without their feeling the need to distance reactively from the family. Negotiating a way to maintain a sense of connectedness along with a sense of individuality is probably the most serious challenge for lesbian couples (Roth, Chapter 15). In the face of the family's or society's lack of recognition, the lesbian couple's boundaries may rigidify, pushing them into a fusion and creating an increasingly closed system (Krestan & Bepko, 1980). Several specific problems create difficulty for lesbian couples, in particular their not having "marker events," such as weddings or the birth of children, to define their change in status (Roth, Chapter 15). Other life cycle transitions also tend to be problematic, such as retirement, serious illness, or death. The disqualification of the couple by the larger society may lead each woman to disguise her feelings and the relationship, intensifying the problems rather than promoting a sense of continuity and connectedness through the course of life.

In addition, the lesbian couple's relationship to the community is most likely to be influenced by the extent to which they have "come out." They may be very isolated from their work and social community if they are not open, and they may be pressured in various ways within a lesbian community if they are. Dealing with the issue of "coming out" is an important individual and interpersonal aspect of development for lesbian couples (Roth, Chapter 15). They must deal with the added loss of status for their sexual orientation if they are open, and with the multiple cutoffs if they maintain secrecy about their most important relationship. Because of the negative cultural attitude toward homosexuality, the lifestyle of such couples becomes much more than a matter of choice of love or sexual partner. Necessary secrecy from employers about their relationships, for example, can force them into a closed, rigid context.

CONCLUSION

The patriarchal system that has characterized our culture has impoverished both women and men, and we look forward to a changing life cycle in which both men and women will be free to develop themselves equally inside and outside of the family.

We hope that family therapy can become a force that fosters adaptive changes in human development to allow more latitude for both men and women in their ways of relating to their mates and peers, in their intergenerational connectedness, and in their stance toward work and community. So far the family therapy field has failed to address the gender differences for male and female therapists of different life cycle stages in working with different family members. The little evidence we do have so far suggests that there are significant differences in how women therapists, especially young women therapists, are related to in therapy by men and women in families (Warburton, Alexander, & Mayberry, Chapter 9) and in the way they perceive themselves and their work (Woodward et al., 1981). We hope that more research will be done in this area.

We do not believe that the relational and emotionally expressive aspect of development is intrinsic to women. We see the romanticization of "feminine" values as inaccurate and unhelpful to families (Hare-Mustin, 1983). It is also not enough for women to adopt the "male" values of the dominant culture and to devalue what have been traditionally "female" values.

We aim toward a theory of family and individual development where both instrumental and relational aspects of each individual will be fostered. The "feminine" perspective has been so devalued that it needs to be highlighted, as Miller (1976), Gilligan (1982), Friedan (1985), Belenky et al. (1986), and others have been doing. It is hoped that both men and women will be able to develop their potential without regard for the constraints of gender stereotyping that have been so constricting on human experience until now.

It is clear that traditional marriage and family patterns are no longer working for women, and the statistics reveal their dissatisfaction. In our view it will only be when we have worked out a new equilibrium not based on the patriarchal family hierarchy that these patterns will change.

The dichotomy between the "emotional expressiveness" and "instrumental" spheres and the devaluation and relegation of the former to women have been very costly to all family members, men and women alike. We believe that it is the socialization of women that makes them "intuitive" and that men could be raised to be equally sensitive if our patterns of education were changed to include this as a desirable value. Our world needs to appreciate both perspectives and to move towards a society in which men *and* women have both abilities: to function autonomously and to be intimate. Basic to this change is the notion that nurturing would not be the province only of women and that work and money would not be primarily a male controlled sphere.

REFERENCES

Aguirre, B. E. (1985). Why do they return? Abused wives in shelters. *Social Work, 30*(3), 350–354.

Alexander, J., Warburton, J., Waldron, H., & Mas, C. H. (1985). The misuse of functional family therapy: A non-sexist rejoinder. *Journal of Marital and Family Therapy, 11*(2), 139–144.

Apter, T. (1985). *Why women don't have wives: Professional success and motherhood*. New York: Schocken Books.

Avis, J. (1985). The politics of functional family therapy: A feminist critique. *Journal of Marital and Family Therapy, 11*(2), 127–138.

Baruch, G., & Barnett, R. (1980). A new start for women at midlife. *New York Times Magazine*, December 7, p. 65.

Baruch, G., Barnett, R., & Rivers, C. (1983). *Lifeprints: New patterns of love and work for today's women*. New York: New American Library.

Baruch, G., & Barnett, R. C. (1983). Adult daughters' relationships with their mothers. *Journal of Marriage and the Family*, August, 601–606.

Belenky, M. F., Clinchy, B. M., Goldberger, N. R., & Tarule, J. M. (1986). *Women's ways of knowing*. New York: Basic Books.

Belle, D. (1982). The stress of caring: Women as providers of social support. In L. Goldberger & S. Breznitz (Eds.), *Handbook of stress* (pp. 496–505). New York: Free Press.

Berheide, C. W. (1984). Women's work in the home: Seems like old times. *Marriage and Family Review, 7*(3), 37–50.

Bernard, J. (1975). *Women, wives and mothers: Values and options*. New York: Aldine.

Bernard, J. (1982). *The future of marriage*. New Haven, CT: Yale University Press.

Bernard, J. (1981). *The female world*. New York: Free Press.

Bianchi, S. M., & Spain, D. (1986). *American women in transition*. New York: Russell Sage.

Block, M. R., Davidson, J. L., & Grambs, J. D. (1981). *Women over forty: Visions and realities*. New York: Springer.

Blumstein, P., & Schwartz, P. (1983). *American couples: Money, work, sex*. New York: William Morrow.

Brodsky, A. M., & Hare-Mustin, R. T. (Eds.). (1980). *Women and psychotherapy*. New York: Guilford Press.

Brody, E. M. (1981). Women in the middle and family help to older people. *The Gerontologist, 21*, 471–80.

Broverman, I. K., Broverman, D. M., Clarkson, F. E., Rosenkrantz, P., & Vogel, S. R. (1970). Sex-role stereotypes and clinical judgments of mental health. *Journal of Consulting Psychology, 43*, 1–7.

Broverman, I. K., Vogel, S. R., Broverman, D. M., Clarkson, F. E., & Rosenkrantz, P. S. (1972). Sex-role stereotypes: A current appraisal. *Journal of Social Issues, 28*(2), 59–78.

Caplan, P. J., & Hall-McCorquondale, I. (1985). Mother-blaming in major clinical journals. *American Journal of Orthopsychiatry, 55*(3), 345–353.

Chess, S., & Whitehead, J. (1978). *Daughters: From infancy to independence*. Garden City, NY: Doubleday.

Chodorow, N., & Contratto, S. (1982). The fantasy of the perfect mother. In B. Throne (Ed.). *Rethinking the family: Some feminist questions*. New York: Longman.

Congressional Caucus for Women's Issues (1984). *New York Times*, September 23, p. 38.

Cohler, B., & Lieberman, M. (1980). Social relations and mental health among three European ethnic groups. *Research on Aging, 2*, 445–469.

Cowen, C. P. et al. (1985). Transitions to parenthood: His, hers, and theirs. *Journal of Family Issues, 6*(4), 451–481.

Current Population Reports, October 1981, 20, 365.

Daniels, P., & Weingarten, K. (1983). *Sooner or later: The timing of parenthood in adult lives*. New York: Norton.

Dinnerstein, D. (1976). *The mermaid and the minotaur*. New York: Harper & Row.

Doherty, W. J., & Baldwin, C. (1985). Shifts and stability in locus of control during the 1970's: Divergence of the sexes. *Journal of Personality and Social Psychology, 48*(4), 1048–1053.

Dohrenwend, B. S. (1973). Social status and stressful life events. *Journal of Personal and Social Psychiatry, 28*, 225–235.

Entwistle, S. G., & Doering, D. R. (1981). *The first birth: A family turning point*. Baltimore: Johns Hopkins University Press.

Erikson, E. (1968). *Identity: Youth and crisis*. New York: Norton.

Erikson, E. (1963). *Childhood and society*. (2nd ed.). New York: Norton.

Friedan, B. (1985). How to get the women's movement moving again. *New York Times Magazine*, 3 November, 57-61.

Gilligan, C. (1982). *In a different voice*. Cambridge, MA: Harvard University Press.

Glick, P. (1984). How American marriages are changing. *American Demographics*. January, 4-9.

Goleman, D. (1986). Two views of marriage explored: His and hers. *New York Times*, April 1, C1, 3.

Goodrich, T. J., Rampage, C., Ellman, B., & Halstead, K. (1988). *Feminist family therapy: A casebook*. New York: Norton.

Gove, W. R. (1972). The relationship between sex roles, marital status and mental illness. *Social Forces, 51*, 34-44.

Hare-Mustin, R. T. (1978). A feminist approach to family therapy. *Family Process, 17*, 181-194.

Hare-Mustin, R. T. (1983). Psychology: A feminist perspective on family therapy. In E. Haber (Ed.), *The Women's Annual: 1982-83* (pp. 177-204). Boston: G. K. Hall.

Herz, F. B. (1988). The postdivorce family. In B. Carter & M. McGoldrick (Eds.), *The changing family life cycle*. New York: Gardner Press.

Hess, B. B. (1985). Aging policies and old women: The hidden agenda. In A. S. Rossi (Ed.), *Gender and the life course*. New York: Aldine.

Hess, B. B., & Soldo, B. J. (1984). The old and the very old: A new frontier of age and family policy. Presentation at Annual Meeting of the American Sociological Society, San Antonio, August.

Hewlett, S. A. (1985). *A lesser life*. New York: William Morrow.

Hoffman, L. W. (1972). Early childhood experiences and women's achievement motives. *Journal of Social Issues, 28*(2), 129-55.

Hoffman, L. W. (1974). Effects of maternal employment on the child: A review of the research. *Developmental Psychology, 10*(2), 204-228.

Horner, M. S. (1968). Sex differences in achievement motivation and performance in competitive and non-competitive situations. Unpublished doctoral dissertation, University of Michigan.

Horner, M. S. (1972). Toward an understanding of achievement-related conflicts in women. *Journal of Social Issues, 28*, 157-175.

Huston, T. (1983). Developing close relationships: Changing patterns of interaction between pair members and social networks. *Journal of Personality and Social Psychology, 44*(5), 964-976.

Kagan, J. (1984). *The nature of the child*. New York: Basic Books.

Kagan, J., & Moss, H. A. (1962). *Birth to maturity*. New York: John Wiley.

Kelly, J. C. (1988). Longer term adjustment in children of divorce: Converging findings and implications for practice. *Journal of Family Psychology, 1*(2), 135-42.

Kessler, R. C., & McLeod, J. D. (1984). Sex differences in vulnerability to undesirable life events. *American Sociological Review, 49*, 620-631.

Kessler, R. C., & McRae, J. A. (1984). A note on the relationships of sex and marital status with psychological distress. In J. Greenley (Ed.), *Community and mental health. Vol. III*. Greenwich, CT: JAI.

Krestan, J., & Bepko, C. (1980). The problem of fusion in the lesbian relationship. *Family Process, 19*, 277-290.

Lang, A. M., & Brody, E. M. (1983). Characteristics of middle-aged daughters and help to their elderly mothers. *Journal of Marriage and the Family, 45*, 193-202.

Lever, J. (1976). Sex differences in the games children play. *Social Problems, 23*, 478-487.

Levinson, D. (1976). *The seasons of a man's life*. New York: Knopf.

Lewis, M., Feiring, C., & Kotsonis, M. (1984). The social network of the young child. In M. Lewis (Ed.), *Beyond the dyad: The genesis of behavior series* (Vol. 4). New York: Plenum.

Lewis, M., & Weintraub, M. (1974). Sex of parent × sex of child: Socioemotional development. In R. D. Friedman, R. M. Richart, & R. C. Vandewiele, (Eds.), *Sex differences in behavior*. New York: Wiley.

Losoff, M. M. (1974). Fathers and autonomy in women. In R. B. Kundsin, (Ed.), *Women and success: The anatomy of achievement*. New York: William Morrow.

226 *Women in Families*

Maccoby, E. E., & Jacklin, C. N. (1974). *The psychology of sex differences*. Stanford, CA: Stanford University Press.
McGoldrick, M. (1987). On reaching mid-career without a wife. *The Family Therapy Networker, 11*(3), 32–39.
McGoldrick, M., & Carter, B. (1988). Forming a remarried family. In B. Carter & M. McGoldrick (Eds.), *The Changing Family Life Cycle*. New York: Gardner Press.
McGoldrick. M. (1988). The young couple: The joining of families in marriage. *The changing family life cycle*. New York: Gardner Press.
Miller, J. B. (1976). *Toward a new psychology of women*. Boston: Beacon.
Neugarten, B. (1985). Interpretive social science and research on aging. In A. S. Rossi (Ed.), *Gender and the life course*. New York: Aldine.
Padan, D. (1965). Intergenerational mobility of women: A two-step process of status mobility in a context of a value conflict. Tel Aviv, Israel: Publication of Tel Aviv University.
Pollit, K. (1986). Middle age nears, and rules differ for men and women. *New York Times*, 16 January, C2.
Rawlings, S. W. (1983). Household and family characteristics: March 1982. *Current Population Reports*, Series P 20 (381). Washington, DC: U.S. Bureau of the Census.
Richardson, L. (1986). *The new other woman*. New York: The Free Press.
Romer, N. (1981). *The sex-role cycle: Socialization from infancy to old age*. New York: McGraw-Hill.
Rubin, L. B. (1979). *Women of a certain age: The midlife search for self*. New York: Harper & Row.
Sangiuliano, I. (1978). *In her time*. New York: William Morrow.
Saluter, A. F. (1983). Marital status and living arrangements: March 1982. *Current Population Reports*. Series P-20 (380). Washington, DC: Bureau of the Census.
Sassen, G. (1980). Success anxiety in women: A constructivist interpretation of its sources and its significance. *Harvard Educational Review, 50*, 13–25.
Schydlowsky, B. M. (1983). Friendships among women in midlife. Unpublished doctoral dissertation. University of Michigan. Microfilm.
Stern Peck, & Manocherian, J. (1988). Divorce in the changing family life cycle. In B. Carter & M. McGoldrick (Eds.), *The changing family life cycle*. New York: Gardner Press.
Sternberg, R. (1984). The nature of love. *Journal of Personality and Social Psychology, 47*(2), 312–329.
Strube, M. J., Barbour, L. S. (1984). Factors related to the decision to leave an abusive relationship. *Journal of Marriage and the Family, 46*(4), 837–844.
Valliant, G. E. (1977). *Adaptation to life*. Boston: Little, Brown.
White, K. M. (1986). Intimacy: Maturity correlates in young married couples. *Journal of Personality and Social Psychology*, entire issue.
Weiss, R. S. (1985). Men and the family. *Family Process, 24*(1), 49–58.
Weitzman, L. (1985). *The divorce revolution*. New York: The Free Press.
Woodward, C. A., Santa-Barbara, J., Streiner, D. L., Goodman, J. T., Levin, S., & Epstein, N. B. (1981). Client, treatment, and therapist variables related to outcome in brief, systems-oriented family therapy. *Family Process, 20*, 189–197.

12

Beyond the Myth of Motherhood

LOIS BRAVERMAN

WHEN I WAS 18 years old I aggressively told my mother that I would never marry or have children. As I saw it marriage and childrearing were oppressive to women and sapped their creative energies. My mother lovingly responded that, for her, having me was like no other experience in her life and that she would not have given it up for anything. She hoped that I would follow suit and not miss out. Twenty years later, I found myself consumed with the passionate need to have a second child. My first was already seven years old and my husband and I were beginning again to have weekend afternoons free from childcare as our son ran off with his friends to play. Would I want another child once he or she was here? Who would get up in the middle of the night? Did I even have the energy to get up in the middle of the night? Did my husband? Despite the myriad of questions I had, the power of this desire was so intense that I acceded to it, became pregnant, and joyfully birthed a second son. My mother was again able to say, "I told you so." So what was I fighting about with my mother 20 years earlier? Was I simply young and misinformed? Or was there some truth to my protest? I believe I was trying to get out from under the myth of motherhood. I wanted some of the other options that were embraced and accepted by the culture; the only options the myth seemed to permit then were marriage and motherhood.

With the increasing presence of women in the work force and the expanded career options for women, it is all too easy to argue that women today

have lots of options, motherhood simply being one of them. But the myth
of motherhood is deeply embedded in our conscious and unconscious processes. The core elements of the myth dictate that motherhood is instinctual,
that having a child fulfills a woman in ways that no other experience can,
and that the mother is the best care provider for the child. The myth is
reflected in our belief systems, our patterns of family interaction, what we
think is best for our children, how they should be raised, who should raise
them, and who should be held accountable for their mental health. The
myth is reflected in my mother's message to me 20 years ago and in my own
seemingly irresistible impulse to have a second child last year. As much as we
might wish it were otherwise, it cannot accurately be said that the myth is
full of lies and devoid of truth. Giving birth was like no other experience I
have had. Giving to an infant has pushed me beyond whatever I imagined
my capacity for giving was, and seeing my children grow and develop is
uniquely satisfying. But the power of the myth can be toxic in that it limits
other options and possibilities outside the reality created by the myth. Certainly, women who opt to be childless or who bear children outside the
patriarchal sanctity of marriage are not embraced or idealized by the myth
(Hare-Mustin & Broderick, 1979; Rich, 1976).

Such experiences and observations lead me to question the nature of the
myth's power and its implications for clinical practice. The focus of this
chapter will be on unmasking the myth of motherhood by examining historical, anthropological, sociological, and psychological data. Through case
examples the status and influence of the myth in contemporary clinical
practice will be explored. The assumption here is that how one thinks about
mothers and motherhood will influence how the family therapist proceeds
with formulating the problem, and thus the solution.

THE MYTH IN HISTORICAL AND ANTHROPOLOGICAL PERSPECTIVE

A review of the anthropological and historical data on the myth of motherhood reveals that mothering is a culturally determined role, that the objectives of mothering differ from generation to generation, and that social and
economic realities significantly influence the expectations of motherhood.
Furthermore, not until the Industrial Revolution, when the spheres of work
and home were separated, did motherhood evolve with its current trappings.
As Goldner (1985) observes " . . . the overinvolved mother and the peripheral father of today's archetypal 'family case' emerge as the products of an
historical process two hundred years in the making" (p. 35). But before we
look at these data debunking the universality of the myth, let us clarify its
central themes.

The idea that mothering is a natural and instinctive phenomenon is the most prevalent and pervasive element of the myth of motherhood and is often used to justify the ordering of our family life. As feminist philosopher Elizabeth Badinter states,

> Mother love has been discussed as a kind of instinct for so long that a "maternal instinct" has come to seem rooted in women's very nature, regardless of the time or place in which she has lived. In the common view, every woman fulfills her destiny once she becomes a mother, finding within herself all the required responses, as if they were automatic and inevitable, held in reserve to await the right moment. (1981, p. xx)

Since the woman is biologically equipped to give birth, it must follow that she has maternal instincts which make her a natural parent. The father, on the other hand, is not considered to be bonded naturally to the child. The fact of his biological connection to the child is not seen as a predisposing factor for good parenting. As Badinter (1981) observes, "Because reproduction is a natural function, surely—or so it has been assumed—the biological and physiological fact of pregnancy must carry with it a corresponding battery of predetermined maternal attitudes and patterns of behavior" (p. xx).

In *Mother Love*, Badinter examines mothering practices in urban France from the 17th through 20th centuries and finds patterns of maternal care and attitudes toward children which challenge this idea of mothering as instinctual. In Paris during the late 18th century, the use of wet nurses had spread to all segments of urban society, not simply the upper and middle classes. In 1780, of the 21,000 babies who were born in Paris, 19,000 of these infants were sent to wet nurses outside of Paris, sometimes as far as 125 miles away. It was common practice for the children to remain there for three to five years before returning home. These children often came home sickly, crippled or dying. If motherhood is instinctual, how can we understand the seeming indifference and tendency toward abandonment that were the norm in 18th century urban France? Badinter argues that economic factors cannot satisfactorily explain this practice. Women of all economic classes followed the custom. Most women did not *have* to send their children away. The society simply placed infant welfare subordinate to other objectives. Women of that day were encouraged to organize their lives primarily around their husbands and not their children. Nursing was thought to interfere with a woman's beauty, with modesty, and with fulfilling her husband sexually. (It was believed at that time that sperm spoiled the nursing mother's milk!) The prevailing view was that women had better things to do than take care of children. Thus, Badinter concludes that the notion of innate maternal instinct is absurd. Mothers behave as the culture dictates.

Eighteenth century France was not the only time and place where mothers were not seen as the primary and exclusive caretakers of their children. The practices of colonial America provide us with another example challenging the notion that mothers throughout history have been exclusive or even primary childcare providers. Ruth Block's (1978) analysis of motherhood during this period documents that " . . . motherhood was singularly un-idealized, usually disregarded as a subject, and at times actually denigrated" (p. 101). A distinctive maternal role was incompatible with the realities of life during colonial times. Childrearing was not a separate task, but one that took place within the daily tasks of the home, which included all kinds of subsistence activities. As anthropologist Maxine Margolis (1984) describes it,

> The agrarian economy of the seventeenth and eighteenth centuries presented no clear-cut separation between the home and the world of work; the boundary between the preindustrial family and society was permeable. Male and female spheres were contiguous and often overlapped, and the demands of the domestic economy insured that neither sex was excluded from product labor. Fathers, moreover, took an active role in child rearing because they worked near the household. (pp. 18–19)

Mothers were not held exclusively responsible for the rearing and development of the children. Fathers were specifically held accountable for the religious instruction and moral development of the child, and children themselves were hardly recognized as separate entities with their own needs and capacities. Furthermore, during these times childhood rarely lasted beyond 10 years of age.

Ethnographic evidence further demonstrates the varieties of childcare arrangements and the "ideologies that justify them" (Margolis, 1984, p. 15). A study of 186 different societies around the world found that in only 46% of them are mothers the primary or exclusive caretakers. After infancy, mothers provide the primary care in less than 20% of these societies. In another 40%, siblings provide the primary care. The study concludes, "Mothers are not the principal caretakers or companions to young children" (Weisner & Gallimore, 1977, p. 170). Jessie Bernard, in her review of the ethnographic literature, supports this conclusion and adds that a wide variety of people in the kinship system is responsible for the primary care of children. She further notes, "In most of human history and in most parts of the world even today, adult able-bodied women have been, and still are too valuable in their productive capacity to be spared for the exclusive care of children" (1974, p. 7).

So we see that the American belief in the central role of the mother in childcare—an arrangement that seemed natural and normal and went unchallenged until recently—is not substantiated by the cross-cultural data. What is noteworthy about the cross-cultural differences is that, whatever the childcare arrangement, the people in that culture see their arrangement as natural, normal, and the right thing to do (Berger & Luckmann, 1966; Lambert, Hamers, & Frasure-Smith, 1979).

In the 19th century, with the advent of the Industrial Revolution, we see the mother assume her "natural" role as portrayed by the myth. But economics, not biology, are responsible for this change. Margolis (1984) explains that changes in ideas about motherhood and the degree of maternal responsibility in America and Western industrial nations are related primarily to birth rate and the nature and location of women's work. For example, the emphasis on motherhood in the 19th century increased as the birth rate decreased. This was an attempt to improve the "quality of children" through long-term intensive mother care during an industrial age which needed skilled labor. As production was now centered outside the home, childcare remained as the primary function left inside the home. She argues that, "What we have come to think of as inevitable and biologically necessary is in great measure a consequence of our society's particular social and economic system" (1984, p. 16). The 19th century's idealized vision of the mother and her children split women off from the world of work inhabited by men and placed mothers at the center of their children's development. Every aspect of the child's life—social, moral, physical and psychological—was now the responsibility of the mother.

The turn of the 20th century saw the burgeoning influence of social scientists as specialists in human behavior and development. Childcare experts emerged, primarily men, who told mothers what was best for their children and how they should raise them. Motherhood was now "transformed into a profession for middle-class women" to be instructed by child study experts (Margolis, 1984, p. 40). Women were encouraged to make "careful notes on their children's development and behavior, to provide the raw data for the experts who then devised the rules that mothers were to follow" (Margolis, 1984, p. 40). The prevailing view was that the mothers needed expert advice to carry out their great task. Psychologists, medical doctors, and educators now assumed the central role in determining what was considered good mothering, how childcare should be actually conducted, and finally how mothers judged themselves. Women were to take care of children and were to do so under the guidance of male experts—the perfect patriarchal solution to childrearing!

The best known of these "experts" was the psychologist John B. Watson. His book, *Psychological Care of the Infant and Child*, published in 1928, was the major influence on childcare until Dr. Benjamin Spock's *Baby and Child Care* appeared in 1946. It is useful to review some of Watson's major recommendations in order to see the standards against which mothers were measured. He recommended a scientific childrearing approach that included strict scheduling of the infant in all areas—eating, sleeping and toilet training. Toilet training, for example was to be completed by six months to one year of age. A strong position was also taken against feeding on demand. Separate bedrooms were strongly recommended for each child so that their behavioral conditioning could be more precise.

Watson was most adamant in his condemnation of maternal affection. He warned that too much coddling and affection produced dependent children who would not be able to compete adequately in the world of capitalism. Mothers were told that if they must be affectionate, they were only to "kiss them once on the forehead at night, but shake hands with them in the morning" (1928, pp. 81–82). While mothers were viewed as necessary, they were simultaneously seen as the very people who could emotionally cripple children. Historian Sheila Rothman (1978) notes that the mother during this period was "reduced . . . to the point where she almost seemed a criminal figure, stunting and warping her child's development" (p. 212). This exceedingly negative view of mothers might be traced to the strong influence of the principles of scientific management. In effect, the principles which functioned well for ordering the life of workers in the factory were also seen as good for the raising of children. Mothers should be like factory managers—objective, structured, disciplined, fair, but surely not affectionate.

The childrearing philosophy of the post-war era shifted drastically, reflecting the country's increased productivity and affluence. The experts—most notably Dr. Benjamin Spock—now advocated warmth and affection as the very core of good mothering. Showing affection and following her own instincts were recommended to the mother as central to the goal of encouraging the child's spontaneity and self-expression. Furthermore, the mother should make her childcaring tasks fun and enjoyable. It seems that American society's focus on the "mother as the child rearer par excellence, the insistence that no one else could take her place, and the assumption that women's most important task in life was the rearing of healthy, well-adjusted, offspring" (Margolis, 1984, p. 61) prevailed no matter what the specific recommendations of the childrearing experts. Thus, the myth of motherhood which took root in the 19th century was nourished by the childcare experts through the first half of the 20th century and beyond.

THE MYTH OF MOTHERHOOD IN A NEW GUISE: THE CURRENT DILEMMA

What is the status of the myth in the 1980s? Its validity has been disproved by the historical and anthropological research reviewed in the last section. Yet the authority of the myth appears to persist, though it now exercises its power in ways made more subtle and difficult to detect by changed social and economic realities.

Gerson, Alpert, and Richardson (1984, p. 446) note that "the number of mothers entering the labor force increases every year, and this increase is most striking for mothers with preschool children." The traditional nuclear family with a breadwinning father, a homemaking mother, and children in school is evident in only 7% of American families. The motherhood myth continues to influence how we view mothers in view of their employment outside the home. As psychologist Nancy Russo says, the myth promotes the idea that "a 'good' mother must be physically present to serve her infant's every need. As the child enters school, a mother may pursue other activities — but only those permitting her to be instantly available should her child 'need' her" (1979, p. 8). These versions of the myth persist despite compelling data marshalled by social scientists which suggest that constant availability is not necessary: Children are not harmed by maternal employment. Neither their intelligence, their independence, their self-esteem, their school functioning, their sex-role concept, nor their ability to make relationships with others are impaired as a result of their mothers' work. This has been demonstrated with infants (Hock, 1980), preschoolers (MacKinnon, Brody, & Stoneman, 1982; Schachter, 1981), elementary school children (Baruch, 1976; Gold & Andres, 1978, 1980; Rosenthal & Hansen, 1981), and adolescents (Dellas, Gaier, & Emihovich, 1979; Joy & Wise, 1983; Rosenthal & Hansen, 1981).

Equally well researched is the relationship between maternal separation anxiety and maternal employment. These studies reveal that a *mother's own attitude* toward her employment is closely tied to her own anxiety level and ultimately to how well her child adapts (Alvarez, 1985; Farel, 1980; Lamb, 1982). That is, if the mother believes in the importance of exclusive maternal care for her infant, she is more likely to experience maternal separation anxiety and her child will have more problems adapting to her absence. On the other hand, if she believes that mother-child separation contributes to the child's interpersonal skill, and that flexibility in responding to new people and new situations increases independence and fosters a sense of self-esteem, then she will experience less separation anxiety and her child will accept her working as a normal and natural part of life. The most recent studies confirm that *a women's preference* to be at home or employed is the most critical factor "in determining her feelings about being separated from her infant" (DeMeis, Hock, & McBride, 1986, p. 627). What is notable here is that it is the mother's *attitude* which affects her own well-being and that of her child, not the fact of whether she is at home or not, and of course, a woman's attitudes about mothering are very much a function of the authority exercised over her by the myth.

Thus, it appears from the data on maternal employment, maternal separation anxiety, and the increasing presence in mothers working outside the home that the power of the myth is on the wane. Yet it is significant that the research does not examine the effects of father employment on children. Nor does it investigate fathers' separation anxiety (or lack of it). The very fact that social scientists investigate the effects on the child of absent mothers and not of absent fathers shows that the myth still has the power to "create reality" and direct our concern. In effect, the research questions imply that the father's absence makes no difference.

Anne Fausto-Sterling, in her book *Myths of Gender*, demonstrates that the very questions we research are reflections of a patriarchal world view. For example, she reveals that the research on menopause and menstruation reflects a decidedly male bias in the construction of the scientific goals, methods, and explanations. This research is guided by the premise that the male reproductive life cycle is the norm against which the female reproductive life cycle is to be compared. In such a context, female processes like menopause are viewed as diseases in need of medical attention and hormone therapy. Similarly, the research on maternal employment and separation anxiety reflects a continual concern with how the mother's behavior and choices impact on the child, with a decided lack of attention to the father's behavior and its impact.

The power of the myth continues. The very question of how to "balance work and family" for women is a graphic example of how the myth perpetuates itself. The question is asked primarily by women and reflects a continual struggle with "How can I be a good mother to my children and work at the same time?" There is an inherent assumption that women are hurting their children at some level by working. This is not an assumption most men make about themselves. This is not to say that the question of balancing work and family is not important; the problem is that it is viewed only as the mother's question. Additionally, we should note that concern with this issue is limited to White middle-class women. Historically, poor Black women have always worked outside the home as a matter of survival and necessity.

The irrepressible myth surfaces in another subtle form in discussions within the women's community about whether it is better to stay home with the children or to work and put the children in someone else's care. Reasoned discussion of the issue is rare, as each camp justifies itself and condemns the stance of the other side. The myth is so powerful that it does not allow the diversity of options to lie side by side within a nonjudgmental, conversational frame. The emotional intensity with which this question is discussed exemplifies the continuing power of the myth to affect new realities — in this case the discourse among women as they try to cope with new decisions. The myth persists as an authoritative story guiding women in how they think about, talk about, and live out their lives. Social scientific data alone cannot create a new story or entirely undo the old.

THE PSYCHOLOGICAL PERSPECTIVE:
THE PERPETUATION OF THE MYTH

From Fromm-Reichmann's coining of the term "schizophrenogenic mother" to Bowlby's descriptions of "maternal deprivation," mothers have been held accountable for the mental health of their children. As motherhood was idealized in the 19th century, so motherhood in the 20th century has become inexorably "psychologized." The child's psychological flaws became the exclusive responsibility of the mother. The cause for all psychopathology, "from simple behavior problems to juvenile delinquency to schizophrenia, itself, was laid at the doorstep of the mother" (Chess & Thomas, 1982, pp. 213–214). Caplan and Hall-McCorquodale's (1985) study of mother blaming in the psychological literature is striking. Their investigation of the clinical literature (nine major journals, including *Family Process*) finds that mothers are blamed for at least 72 kinds of pathology. They summarize the situation thus:

> Although fewer mothers are at home all day now than formerly, child rearing is still primarily considered the mother's responsibility.   Mothers are there. They are there for professionals who assess and treat their children: they are there to be identified, studied, and questioned by these professionals; and they are there for the general public to see, raising their children. Thus, they, more than absent fathers, are easy targets for blame. (p. 351)

But blaming mothers is not simply a function of the structural arrangement that makes mothers available and central in childcare. The cornerstone of Freudian theory, the Oedipus complex, perpetuates the myth by putting the mother at the center of the lifelong struggle of males. Adrienne Rich (1976, p. 194) writes,

> No one aspect of his (Freud's) theory has been more influential than the so-called Oedipus complex. Women who have never read Freud are raising their sons in the belief that to show them physical affection is to be "seductive," that to influence their sons against forms of masculine behavior they as women abhor, is to "castrate" them or become "the devouring, dominating creature that their sons will have to reject in order to grow up mentally healthy."

Only by rejecting her can the male child free himself from the dependent relationship with his pathology-producing mother. Rejecting his mother is not enough; he must then identify with his father in order to have a relationship that is empowering. "Through the resolution of the Oedipus complex, the boy makes his way into the male world, the world of patriarchal law and order" (Rich, p. 196).

The problem of how a mother, particularly a feminist mother, should proceed with her son is particularly confusing. Rich's analysis poignantly articulates the confusion:

> The fear of alienating a male child from "his" culture goes so deep, even among women who reject that culture for themselves every day of their lives. What do we fear? That our sons will accuse us of making them into misfits and outsiders? That they will suffer as we have suffered from patriarchal reprisals? Do we fear they will somehow lose their male-status and privilege, even as we are seeking to abolish that inequality? (p. 204)

> Yet the fear that our strength, or our influence, will "make our sons into homosexuals" still haunts even women who do not condemn homosexuality as such, perhaps because the power of the patriarchal ideology still makes it seem a better fate for the boy to grow into a "real man." (p. 210)

And what of the daughter in the psychodynamic scene? Here the classic view was that the girl child, at the recognition that she lacks a penis, suffers a "castration" reaction, and that to resolve this loss, she must "substitute pregnancy and a baby for the missing male organ" (Rich, p. 196). Of course, in order to do that the daughter must reject her mother and transfer her affections to a man. The mother is in the paradoxical position of encouraging her daughter to become a wife and a mother, at the cost of severing the bonds of female attachment.

In the past decade there have been powerful critiques from feminist voices in the psychoanalytic community (Chernin, 1984, 1986; Chodorow, 1978; Chodorow & Contratto, 1982; Dinnerstein, 1976). Yet, despite increasing attention to the role of patriarchy in shaping the lives of women, the mother-child dyad remains the focus of analysis (Lerner, 1988). With brutal realism, Lerner's critique exposes the subtle perpetuation of mother-blaming in the feminist psychoanalytic literature in general and in the work of Chernin (1984, 1986) and Jordan and Surrey (1986) in particular. Chernin (1986), for example, argues that eating disorders and obsession with food "reflect problems of identity that are rooted in a mother-daughter separation struggle" (Lerner, p. 265). Although Chernin cautions against mother-blaming by citing the historical and political limitation of our mother's own lives, she rests her analysis solely on the mother-daughter dyad and argues that only by acknowledging and understanding our rage at our mothers can we move on. Lerner criticizes Chernin's analysis for never extending beyond the mother-daughter dyad, that she depicts as singularly pathogenic in nature. Who the daughter is and what she becomes — from the establishment of "basic trust" to the exertion of her will and the belief in her own initiative — rests on how the mother responds and how she does or does not meet her daughter's earliest needs. (p. 265)

Although Jordan and Surrey's (1986) self-in-relation theory positively redefines the mother-daughter bond as the place where sameness of sex facilitates empathy and relatedness and leads to the daughter's "heightened relational capacities," their theoretical contribution, according to Lerner, idealizes the mother-daughter bond and "implicitly holds mothers responsible (even if intended otherwise) . . . " (p. 276). Lerner notes that, when compared to Chernin's deficiency model, Jordan and Surrey's idealization of the mother-daughter bond is found to be the opposite side of the same coin. Both analyses isolate the mother-daughter dyad from the nuclear and multigenerational family process and, despite attempts not to mother-blame, do so by assuming "what happens to a child is largely the product of who the mother is and what she does and does not do" (Lerner, 1988, p. 258).

Does the systemic framework of family therapy correct such limitations? Here we can argue that the drama is no longer limited to the mother-daughter dyad. We understand symptoms in the context in which they occur — family transactions, circular sequences, and multigenerational processes. Our assessment includes the identification of rigid triads, interlocking triangles, family projection process, and hierarchical incongruities. No more of this narrowly focused intrapsychic mother-child dyad stuff for us. But as Goldner (Chapter 3) has pointed out, our entire framework for understanding and assessing families is based on a theory that has ignored gender and elevated generation as the primary variable around which we assess and argue for change. We have assumed that mothers and fathers participate in the family arena with equal power and rights, as if the world of the family is *inexorably* divorced from the workplace and the social and political order. Concurrently, given the very gendered ordering of family life, we are dependent on mothers to bring their families to therapy, to understand and put into action the recommendations we make, and to bring the family back again. The feminist critique of family therapy points out how handicapped the theory is by viewing context as limited to the family and not acknowledging the larger social, economic, and patriarchal context (Avis, 1985; Goldner, 1985; James & McIntyre, 1983; Lerner, 1988; Taggart, 1985). The literature of family therapy, despite its expanded context from the psychodynamic dyad, in the final analysis continues the tradition of mother-blaming, although in much subtler or obfuscated forms (Caplan & Hall-McCorquodale, 1985a; Goldner, 1985). Avis (1988) argues that subtle assumptions of women's primary responsibility for childrearing underlie much of family therapy practice, resulting in a tendency to view children's problems as primarily caused by their mothers. Although emphasis is placed on involving fathers in family therapy, it is often with a view to helping mothers out, giving her a holiday or teaching them more effective parenting skills. (p. 7)

With this in mind, we will look at the clinical implications of the myth of motherhood.

CLINICAL IMPLICATIONS

Awareness of the myth and denial of its factual truth do not constitute clinical solutions. It is not enough to say to a mother of a newborn struggling with her sense of guilt for working outside the home that the pressure to be home has resulted from a complex set of variables involving low birth rate and the separation of work and home spheres or that a mother's guilt is culturally determined. To think that all you have to do with myths clinically is dispel them by presenting a gestalt of the historical and anthropological data is a simplistic solution that only folds in on itself.

What makes myths myths is, of course, their power to create reality. Saying that they aren't true is not enough to make them disappear. Both therapists and clients are aware of the near impossibility of moving against the myth. Myths do not allow for an honest consideration of differences. The myth of motherhood organizes the individual woman, her family, and the society in which she lives. The myth pervades every phase of the mother's life cycle — pregnancy, childbirth and the postpartum period, childrearing and maternal employment, and late parenting with adult children. Perhaps what keeps women tied to the myth is the satisfaction they receive from fulfilling the myth — satisfaction that they do not get by struggling against it. Following the myth satisfies a certain dramatic working out of a situation. Proceeding without a myth is like being without an authoritative script. In my own case, having my newborn fall asleep on my breast as we dozed in the early afternoon together brought me an incredible sense of joy. I reveled in how the entire scene fit into my images of what moments between mothers and infants should be. In my mind's eye, we appeared like a Mary Cassatt painting. When the sacred eight weeks of staying home were up and I returned back to work, there were no images to guide me. I was left with no paintings, no poems, to guide my journey. When the myth can not be fulfilled, what is to direct the mother?

The primary manifestation of the myth of motherhood in its unfulfilled state is guilt. The myth has the power to induce guilt — by saying that if you do not fulfill the role of good mother as defined by the myth, then your life is wrong. If your children have significant problems, then somehow it must be your fault. If you don't love your children or want to give your all to them (even when you can afford to), you are a bad mother. If you don't want children at all, then something must be wrong with you. Motherhood is so idealized that guilt is inescapable. "That guilt is one of the most powerful forms of social control of women; none of us can be entirely immune to it" (Rich, 1976, p. 205).

Guilt is the predominant theme in my work with mothers. No matter what the structural or strategic solution offered for symptom relief, the mother is often left wondering, "What did I do wrong?" Some even articulate this concern and, despite reassurances from family therapists, remain unconvinced.

The following two brief vignettes represent clinical examples of mothers struggling with guilt—one for not protecting a child and the other for not wanting to help. There are no clear solutions here, only some ways to glimpse a bit more of the light at the end of the tunnel.

"He's Not the Mother!"

Jeanne is a 42-year-old lawyer, married to a 42-year-old healthcare adminis trator. They have two daughters ages 16 and 12. Jeanne's distress began three years ago when the older daughter began to get increasingly depressed and ran away. The family went to therapy and was treated by a family therapist using basically a structural and strategic approach. Things improved. The parents got more structured, set more consistent rules, and dealt with some of their differences regarding parenting. The daughter's depressive symp toms were alleviated. The father became more involved with his daughter. The couple's relationship became stronger. Yet, despite the gains resulting from family therapy, the mother was plagued with guilt. She held herself responsible for the depression of her daughter. Three years later, she still blamed herself and believed she had to understand this relationship better in order to keep it from happening again either to this daughter or to the next one. She vacillated between feeling totally inadequate as a mother and thinking "I am a damn good mother but no one has ever told me so." When I asked her if her husband felt any guilt, she looked at me in amazement and asked, "Why should he? How could he? He's not the mother!"

In Jeanne's case, multigenerational work revealed that for three genera-tions the family tended to idealize fathers and depreciate mothers. Jeanne carried on this legacy by idealizing her deceased father—"He was a saint"— and feeling distant from and critical of her own mother. Although the issues were more complicated, one could say that all that went well with children was attributed to fathers in this family and all that went wrong was attributed to mothers. Jeanne's struggle with her guilt was a reflection of this process continuing through one more generation. Jeanne was encouraged to talk with her mother about her notions of mothering. By understanding her own mother's struggles with mothering in the multigenerational schema of idealized men and depreciated women, she was able to be less reactive with her mother and simultaneously less blaming of herself.

"Maybe, I am a Bad Mother."

Mary and Tom were both 46 years old and had been married for 23 years. They had three adult children ranging in age from 19 to 22 years old. Mary came to therapy because she felt she was a bad mother for not wanting to continually support their oldest daughter. This daughter, age 22, had two children, was married to a drug addict, and continually came to her parents for financial help. She refused to "go on welfare." Mary felt that the time in her life had come to be able to do other things. She worked full-time and now wanted there to be enough money to take some trips or go back to school. She wanted there to be some options. But the financial problems of this adult daughter took up to $500 a month of their income. She felt she couldn't say no. Whenever she even thought of refusing to support this life style, her husband became angry and argued that she was "selfish" and a "bad mother." "How can you let your daughter and grandchildren go without housing or food?" he protested. Mary wondered if indeed she could ever stop supporting her daughter. Her guilt was exacerbated by the fact that at times she felt she did not love this daughter. She had always had a difficult time relating to her, even when she was a child. "I feel so guilty—maybe he is right, maybe I am a bad mother."

In Mary's family of origin men were seen as irresponsible and mothers as reliable. Mary, in an effort not to repeat the pattern, married a terribly responsible man, a man who has taken responsibility for his children "to a high art," as she later joked. Her investigation of her family of origin helped her conclude that she was indeed quite different from the immigrant women before her. They were driven by different imperatives. What she came to feel she must do was to help her daughter only in the way that made sense to her, that did not leave her feeling exploited or angry—despite the protests of not only her husband, but also his mother and sisters and her own parents and brothers. In the long run, she decided that she was willing to provide money for daycare for her grandchildren, so that her daughter would be free to work. She would not provide rent or food money. Her husband was initially appalled, but she remained firm. Other family members called and argued with her that the children should not be separated from their mother and be placed in daycare "with strangers." The power of the myth of motherhood operated in full force. Initially, Mary was shunned by all family members. Eventually, they softened. She had to separate her funds from the joint checking account she had with her husband—an unprecedented act for a wife in either her family of origin or her spouse's. Her daughter, after a few months of working, confessed to her mother that being home with the children all day had been awful for her, that she was not good with them and had worried that she might abuse them but had never felt safe enough to tell anyone. Coming to terms with the kind of help she was willing to give without rage or guilt became possible for Mary only after she sorted through the history of mothering and fathering in her own family of origin. She began to trust her own judgment and felt confirmed in her belief that a mother does not have to have perfect love for her children.

Both these women came to therapy to alleviate the legacy of guilt inherent in the myth of motherhood. Both were encouraged to go beyond the history of their own families to study the institution of mothering. This provided a way for both clients to place their mothering attitudes and actions in a historical context and thus lessen the transgenerational force of myth-induced guilt. The therapist in such cases must work hard to help the woman confront the constricting aspects of the myth and simultaneously acknowledge how painful and powerful the feelings of being an inadequate mother are. Moving too quickly to reassure the women that "your guilt is absurd—you are a fine mother" or "it is not your fault" can therapeutically explode in the therapist's face. The woman needs to be made aware of the internalized myth of motherhood gently, carefully, and firmly. Most importantly, the therapist must prepare her client for the likely response of family members as she begins to think and move differently.

Guilt induced by the myth of motherhood can take many forms, as our two cases illustrate—one for not protecting a child from depression and the other for not wanting to help a child or feeling as much love for that child as the culture expects. Multigenerational work offers a way a mother can trace the attitudinal and behavioral history of mothering in her own family of origin. Such data allow a woman to see how she is different from or similar to others who came before her and help her open up greater possibilities for legitimizing her own attitudes toward mothering. This sense of self is deepened by putting her own family's myths in the context of the deeply ingrained sociocultural myth of motherhood. By examining the history of motherhood, in the same way she has examined her own family history, a woman is better able to manage her guilt and thus make more thoughtful and self-defining choices about how to live her life. Exploring historical contradictions of the myth by no means destroys the myth's power, but it begins to lessen its force and makes it more manageable in other ways.

The myth of motherhood that so influences family life and women's sense of self has heretofore been neglected in the family therapy literature. Fathers, not just mothers, must begin to take responsibility for childcare in more than token ways. Until responsibility for parenting is taken seriously by men and not just women, we shall continue to perpetuate, in one form or another, the myth of motherhood. As family therapists, we need to ask ourselves: How does the myth of motherhood explicitly and implicitly implant itself on the very systemic solutions we construct for the families we see?

REFERENCES

Alvarez, W. F. (1985). The meaning of maternal employment for mothers and their perceptions of their three-year-old children. *Child Development, 56,* 350–60.

Avis, J. M. (1985). The politics of functional family therapy: A feminist critique. *Journal of Marital and Family Therapy, 11,* 127–38.

Avis, J. M. (1988). Deepening awareness: A private study guide to feminism and family therapy. In L. Braverman (Ed.), *Women, feminism, and family therapy.* New York: Haworth Press.

Badinter, E. (1981). *Mother love: Myth & reality.* New York: Macmillan.

Baruch, G. K. (1976). Girls who perceive themselves as competent: Some antecedents and correlates. *Psychology of Women Quarterly, 1,* 38–39.

Berger, P. L., & Luckmann, T. (1966). *The social construction of reality.* Garden City, NY: Doubleday.

Bernard, J. (1974). *The future of motherhood.* New York: Penguin Books.

Block, R. H. (1978). American feminine ideals in transition: The rise of the moral mother. *Feminist Studies, 4,* 101–26.

Bowlby, J. (1951). *Maternal care and mental health.* Geneva: World Health Organization.

Caplan, P., & Hall-McCorquodale, I. (1985). Mother-blaming in major clinical journals. *American Journal of Orthopsychiatry, 55,* 345–53.

Chernin, K. (1984). *In my mother's house: A daughter's story.* New York: Harper & Row.

Chernin, K. (1986). *The hungry self: Women, eating and identity.* New York: Perennial Library.

Chess, S., & Thomas, A. (1982). Infancy bonding: Mystique and reality. *American Journal of Orthopsychiatry, 52,* 213–22.

Chodorow, N. (1978). *The reproduction of mothering: Psychoanalysis and the sociology of gender.* Berkeley, CA: University of California Press.

Chodorow, N., & Contratto, S. (1982). The fantasy of the perfect mother. In B. Thorne & M. Yalom (Eds.), *Rethinking the family: Some feminist questions.* New York: Longman.

Dellas, M., Gaier, E. L., & Emihovich, C. A. (1979). Maternal employment and selected behaviors and attitudes of preadolescents and adolescents. *Adolescence, 14,* 579–89.

DeMeis, D., Hock, E., & McBride, S. (1986). The balance of employment and motherhood: Longitudinal study of mothers' feelings about separation from their first-born infants. *Developmental Psychology, 22,* 627–32.

Dinnerstein, D. (1976). *The mermaid and the minotaur: Sexual arrangements and human malaise.* New York: Harper & Row.

Farel, A. M. (1980). Effects of preferred maternal roles, maternal employment, and sociodemographic status on school adjustment and competence. *Child Development, 51,* 1179–1196.

Fausto-Sterling, A. (1986). *Myths of gender: Biological theories about women and men.* New York: Basic Books.

Fromm-Reichmann, F. (1948). Notes on the development of treatment of schizophrenics by psychoanalytic psychotherapy. *Psychiatry, 11,* 263–74.

Gerson, M. J., Alpert, J. L., & Richardson, M. S. (1984). Mothering: The view from psychological research. *Signs: Journal of Women in Culture and Society, 9,* 434–53.

Gold, D., & Andres, D. (1978). Developmental comparisons between 10-year-old children with employed and nonemployed mothers. *Child Development, 49*, 75–84.

Gold, D., & Andres, D. (1980). Maternal employment and the development of ten-year-old Francophone children. *Canadian Journal of Behavioral Science, 12*, 233–40.

Goldner, V. (1985). Feminism and family therapy. *Family Process, 24*, 31–47.

Hare-Mustin, R. T., & Broderick, P. C. (1979). The myth of motherhood: A study of attitudes toward motherhood. *Psychology of Women Quarterly, 4*, 114–28.

Hock, E. (1980). Working and nonworking mothers and their infants: A comparative study of maternal caregiving characteristics and infant social behavior. *Merrill-Palmer Quarterly, 26*, 79–01.

James, K., & McIntyre, D. (1983). The reproduction of families: The social role of family therapy? *Journal of Marital and Family Therapy, 9*, 119–29.

Jordan, J. V., & Surrey, J. L. (1986). The self-in-relation: Empathy and the mother-daughter relationship. In Bernay, T., & Cantor, D. W. (Eds.). *The psychology of today's woman: New psychoanalytic visions*. Hillsdale, NJ: The Analytic Press.

Joy, S. S., & Wise, P. S. (1983). Maternal employment, anxiety, and sex differences in college students' self-descriptions. *Sex Roles, 9*, 519–25.

Lamb, M. (1982). Maternal employment and child development: A review. In M. E. Lamb (Ed.), *Nontraditional families: Parenting and child development* (pp. 45–69). Hillsdale, NJ: Erlbaum.

Lambert, W. E., Hamers, J. F., & Frasure-Smith, N. (1979). *Child-rearing values: A cross national study*. New York: Praeger.

Lerner, H. G. (1988). Is family systems theory really systemic? A feminist communication. In L. Braverman (Ed.), *Women, feminism, and family therapy*. New York: Haworth Press.

Lerner, H. G. (1988). *Women in therapy*. New York: Jason Aronson.

MacKinnon, C. E., Brody, G. H., & Stoneman, Z. (1982). The effects of divorce and maternal employment on the home environments of preschool children. *Child Development, 53*, 1392–1399.

Margolis, M. (1984). *Mothers and such: Views of American women and why they changed*. Berkeley. University of California Press.

Rich, A. (1976). *Of woman born: Motherhood as experience and institution*. New York: Norton.

Rosenthal, D., & Hansen, J. (1981). The impact of maternal employment on children's perceptions of parents and personal development. *Sex Roles, 7*, 593–98.

Rothman, S. M. (1978). *Women's proper place: A history of changing ideals and practices, 1870 to the present*. New York: Basic Books.

Russo, N. F. (1979). Overview: Sex roles, fertility and the motherhood mandate. *Psychology of Women Quarterly, 4*, 7–15.

Schachter, F. F. (1981). Toddlers with employed mothers. *Child Development, 52*, 958–64.

Spock, B. (1946). *Baby and child care*. New York: Pocket Books.

Taggart, M. (1985). The feminist critique in epistemological perspective: Questions of context in family therapy. *Journal of Marital and Family Therapy, 11*, 113–26.

Watson, J. B. (1928). *Psychological care of the infant and child*. New York: Norton.

Weisner, T., & Gallimore, R. (1977). My brother's keeper: Child and sibling caretaking. *Current Anthropology, 18*, 169–90.

13

Sisters

MONICA McGOLDRICK

You know full as well as I do the value of sisters' affections to each other; there is nothing like it in this world. — Charlotte Brontë

Reengagement with the actual sister of our early years is only the beginning; it leads to an exploration of the ongoing meaning of that relationship throughout our lives, toward an understanding of how it reappears, transformed, in many of our friendships and love affairs, and to a deeply challenging revisioning of our innermost self. . . . It is the interactions among sisters that instigate the heroine's journey toward self, toward psyche . . . our sisterly relationships challenge and nurture us, even as we sometimes disappoint and betray one another. — Christine Downing, 1988, pp. 3–4

THERE ARE PROBABLY many reasons for the complexity of sister relationships: the familial bonds, the length of these relationships, the caretaking responsibilities sisters share, and their competitiveness for male attention and approval. Sisters often have a particular problem defining their separate identities and trying to make up for not having the special status given to brothers, probably because women are raised to define themselves more in relation to men and to their families than in relation to each other. This is probably also influenced by the fact that women have not been raised to have an individual identity; their identity has been seen more as a receptacle for the needs of others. This perhaps influences the special fusion and at times even identity confusion that may exist in the relationship of sisters. As McNaron (1985, p. 6) has described it; "A sister is both ourselves and very much not ourselves — a special kind of double." The desire for and experience of fusion lie at the heart of the difficulty many sisters have in seeing themselves as distinct from each other.

> Likeness and difference, intimacy and otherness — neither can be overcome. That paradox, that tension, lies at the very heart of the relationship. For a woman the sister is the other most like ourselves. She is of the same gender and generation, of the same biological and social heritage. We have the same parents; we grew up in the same family, were exposed to the same values, assumptions, patterns of interaction. . . . The sibling relationship is among the most enduring of all human ties, beginning with birth and ending only with the death of one of the siblings. Although our culture seems to allow us the freedom to leave sibling relationships behind, to walk away from them, we tend to return to them in moments of celebration — marriages and births — as well as at times of crisis — divorces and deaths. At such moments we often discover to our surprise how quickly the patterns of childhood interaction and the intensity of childhood resentment and appreciation reappear. There are many times along the way when the pull to reconnect, to understand, becomes imperative. Yet no matter how well or how poorly these earlier reencounters go, the sister bond will have to be reviewed again in this last life phase — even if we have decisively given it up as hopeless, even if it seems long ago successfully resolved. (Downing, 1988, pp. 10–11)

There is a special complexity, intricacy and intimacy in sister relationships (Holden, 1986). It is almost as if we see in our sisters a reflection of aspects of ourselves. Our responses to and experiences with men are usually from the perspective of greater distance, often very great distance. We are led by that distance and by the patriarchal power structure to romanticize and idealize men. On the other hand, our response to women, and to our sisters in particular, is influenced by their closeness to us and by sharing our culture's devaluation of female characteristics.

Elizabeth Fishel writes in *Sisters* (1979):

> My dearest friend and bitterest rival, my mirror and opposite, my confidante and betrayer, my student and teacher, my reference point and counterpoint, my support and dependent, my daughter and mother, my subordinate, my superior and scariest still, my equal. My sister is someone who lives out another part of myself, freeing me or limiting me to my role, which is by definition "not her." (p. 16)

Much of our literature has denied the sharing of sister relationships. As Bernikow (1980) has pointed out, if we think of the most famous sisters in literature — Rachel and Leah in the Old Testament, Cordelia and her sisters in *King Lear*, Cinderella and her "wicked" stepsisters, or Chekhov's *Three Sisters* — a man always stands between the sisters, who are not supportive of each other. And mothers are hardly mentioned at all, unless divisively, as in *Cinderella*. Bernikow reminds us how, in spite of the myth of devotion among sisters, as portrayed in *Little Women*, most of our intellectual inheritance shows sisters deep in antagonism, and almost always the specific conflict is over a man. What he thinks or does determines what happens between them. Rachel and Leah in the Bible are married to the same man and competing to have his child. In *Cinderella*, the prince, who is virtually an off-stage presence, motivates the women at home to compete for his love. In Chekhov's *Three Sisters*, the sisters are competing to get hold of a man's property. In *King Lear* the father asks all his daughters to pay obeisance to him, his law, his will, his language, his property. When Cordelia, the youngest, refuses, her sisters do not support her. Older sisters in literature are usually depicted as evil, while the youngest is "Daddy's Girl," the infantilized baby and favorite, receiving Daddy's love and wealth in return for her loyalty and willingness to be his "love object." The price she pays of conflict with her mother and sisters and loss of their affection is overlooked. As Bernikow says:

> They do each other no good, these female siblings, if the stories are to be believed. One would be better off without them. In this masculine vision, all women would be better off without other women, for the woman alone, motherless, sisterless, friendless — can fix her eyes solely on father, brother, lover, and therefore peace will reign in the universe. (p. 77)

This is the kind of annihilation of the role of sister that we need to counter in our clinical work by validating and encouraging the sister bond.

The relationships in life that last the longest are those between sisters. Our parents usually die a generation before we do, and our children live on for a generation after us. Our spouses rarely know us for our first 20 or 30 years, and it is rare for friendships to last from earliest childhood until the very end of our lives. Thus our siblings share more of our lives genetically and contextually than anyone else, and sisters even more, since sisters live longer than brothers. In fact, we can divorce a spouse much more finally than a sibling (Downing, 1988). The permanence makes this the safest relationship in which to express hostility and aggression — safer than with parents, because we are never quite so dependent on our siblings — and thus the bond between same-sex siblings is likely the most stressful, volatile, and ambivalent one many of us will ever know (Downing, 1988).

Nevertheless, siblings generally seem to have a commitment to maintaining their relationships throughout life, and it is rare for them to break off their relationship or lose touch completely with each other (Cicirelli, 1985). Sister pairs tend to have the closest relationships of all (Adams, 1968). Sisters seem to provide a basic feeling of emotional security in life. The more sisters a woman has, the more concern she tends to have with keeping up social relationships and helping others (Cicirelli, 1985). Sisters can provide role models for successful aging, widowhood, bereavement, and retirement. They act as caretakers and exert pressures on each other to maintain values.

Yet there is little attention given in our culture to this most important relationship. Surprisingly little literature exists on this subject, and it seems a topic of almost no interest for most therapists, who focus primarily on marital or parent-child relationships. Unbelievably, even a 1987 book (Hoopes and Harper) on sibling patterns in individual and family therapy makes no mention of the difference between brothers and sisters and doesn't even list "sister," "brother," or "gender" in the index. Indeed, the excellent classic book on sibling relationships in the family therapy literature, *The Sibling Bond*, also does not mention sister in the index, and makes only one incidental reference to gender differences.

Women tend to be the caretakers and bearers of the emotional responsibility for relationships in families. They are the ones who maintain the networks, who make Thanksgiving, Christmas and Passover happen, the ones who care for the sick, and who carry on the primary mourning when family members die. They are central in family process, more often taking responsibility for maintaining family relationships than their brothers. Sisters not only do more caretaking, but also tend to share more intimacy and to have more intense relationships, as well as more family responsibility, although they typically get less glory than brothers. From childhood on, most sibling caretaking is delegated to older sisters, with brothers freed for play or other tasks (Cicirelli, 1985). In the classic story of childhood, *Peter Pan*, the only sister, Wendy, is immediately inducted into the role of mother, not only for her own brothers but for Peter Pan and for all the "lost boys."

Parents tend to see themselves as having achieved the ultimate when they have a son. While we have come a long way from the infanticide other cultures practiced when they had daughters instead of sons, the remnants of those attitudes still exist. (In Greek culture a typical response to the question "How many children do you have?" is: "Two and, excuse me, also three daughters." The word for child refers only to male children.) Even though this is a diminishing trend (Entwhistle & Doering, 1981), in our culture families are still more likely to keep trying for a son if they only have daughters, than to keep trying for a daughter if they only have sons (Broverman, Vogel, & Broverman, 1972). They are also more likely to divorce if they only have daughters, and if they do divorce, fathers are more likely to lose contact with the children if they are daughters.

Sisters, like all women, are generally taught by the culture to compete for the attention of men, usually beginning with their father. The deep, if turbulent, bonds they often have with each other are not validated or supported by our culture. Sister relationships, like those of women friends, are often disqualified more than peer relationships involving men, brothers, male peers, or men and women.

A woman who wants to avoid a move made necessary by her husbands' job in order to remain near her sister is considered strange indeed. She will probably be labeled "enmeshed" or "undifferentiated." And yet, it is the sister who was there at the beginning, before the husband, and who will most likely be there at the end, after he is gone. In fact, a strong sense of sisterhood seems to strengthen a woman's sense of self (Cicirelli, 1982, 1985; Noberini, Brady, & Mosatche, in preparation).

Sister Roles

The roles in the Brontë family are interesting examples of the limitation of roles allowed to women. Their mother died very early, leaving the children reliant on one another. Charlotte, at age 10, became the functional oldest when her two older sisters died. Next came the family "genius and prodigy," Branwell, who was scheduled for glory. The two younger sisters, Emily and Anne, although a year apart in age, grew up almost like twins. As children, the Brontës collaborated on writing together, with Branwell originating the idea and Charlotte becoming an equal partner. In adult life Branwell could not live up to the expectations for male achievement his father had for him. He became addicted to drugs and alcohol and was involved in various scandals. It was not until he had begun his final deterioration that Charlotte "came upon" Emily's poetry and decided to publish under male pseudonyms the poetry that all three sisters had been writing. Emily, the middle sister, was the most isolationist. When Charlotte and Anne finally went to tell their publisher that they were women, Emily refused to go along. They never told their brother that they had become famous authors and they informed their father only after the fact. But the sisters became each other's primary support. If they had not had each other in this way, the world might not have had the remarkable literature this sisterhood created.

The roles the Brontë sisters played are common sister roles: Charlotte — the director and social organizer; Emily — the isolationist, the stubborn, independent one; and Anne — the darling, the sweet one.

Bossard and Boll (1955) have described eight roles that children often assume:

1. The responsible one (typically the oldest daughter, a mother substitute).
2. The studious one.
3. The popular, well-liked one.
4. The socially ambitious one; the "social butterfly."
5. The self-centered, isolated one, who often withdraws from the family.
6. The physically or emotionally weak one, who is perceived as ill.
7. The irresponsible one, who withdraws from family responsibilities.
8. The "spoiled" one, typically a youngest, whose needs and desires are met by others in the family.

Other common sister roles in a family typically refer to family relationships: "Daddy's girl," "Mother's confidante" (a sister substitute role); Mother's helper or replacement, and finally "Grandmother," who is prissy and serious or who tells mother what to do.

To this list we might add the "tomboy"—the one who rejects or defies conventions for female behavior, and "the princess"—who may be either the dainty "virgin" beauty or the "dangerous siren." Both of these roles derive specifically from the stereotypic roles allowed to women. The tomboy rejects the image and the princess accepts the focus on "feminine" appearance and the subservient role.

Historically, the weak or ill role may have been a type of rebellion against the constraints of a woman's prescribed role. Emily Brontë and Elizabeth Barrett Browning, for example, seem to have used their illness in a way to avoid the social behavior that was otherwise forced on a woman in their era. Both had brothers for whom the father had extremely strong expectations, and both lost sisters and their mothers at an early age, which probably increased their role conflict as strong women who temperamentally could not well fit into the stereotypic role prescribed for women. On the other hand women who took on "masculine" roles as achievers often did not marry as in the extraordinary Blackwell family, which produced five daughters, none of whom married: Elizabeth was the first woman physician in the United States; Emily followed her sister into medicine; Anne became a distinguished poet and translator; Ellen became a successful artist, and the fifth, Marion, took on the opposite role: that of invalid (Horn, 1983).

The roles outlined by Bossard and Boll are, in fact, primarily responses to the prescribed gender characteristics of our culture. The "masculine" roles include "the studious one" and "the self-centered one"; the "feminine" roles include the "well-liked one," "the socially ambitious one," the "emotionally weak one," and the "spoiled one." Our stereotypes for sex-role behavior give a different meaning to the terms "responsibility" and "irresponsibility" for a sister or a brother. Responsibility for sons usually refers to financial and work responsibility, while for daughters it refers to caretaking responsibility. The "irresponsible" brother is probably educationally or professionally irresponsible, while the "irresponsible" sister is probably sexually free, impulsive, and "self-centered." As for the label "spoiled," it is rarely applied to men at all, perhaps because spoiling men is taken for granted to such an extent by their wives and sisters.

PROBLEMATIC SISTER RELATIONSHIPS

Especially in two-sister families we may see a polarization between the "good" sister and the "bad" sister, the sweet, compliant sister and the rebel or tomboy. Of course, the closer two sisters are in age, the more likely they are to get caught up in either close "twin" relationships or complementary relationships of opposites. A major feature of such complementary relationships is the way they reflect triangles with parents. Sometimes parental conflicts will be detoured through the children, with one sibling siding with each parent. Often a parent who cannot deal with his or her spouse can more easily react against the same characteristics when reflected in a child. A polarization may get set up with another child, especially a sibling of the same sex, who develops the opposite characteristics.

Sometimes two sisters will play out opposite sides of their mother—one the adventurous, risk-taking, assertive extrovert, and the other the compliant, conventional, gentle, quiet, giving sweetheart. If the mother has given up her dreams of the more nonconforming role herself, she may then subtly encourage those behaviors in one of her daughters, while overtly reacting against this daughter for living out a side of her self she dared not express. In such instances both daughters may end up feeling rejected—the nonconformist as the object of her mother's direct criticism and the conformist for her subtle feeling that her mother finds her uninteresting and deep down prefers her sister's expressiveness, even though the conformist sister may have dedicated her life to obeying her mother's prescription to assume a "feminine" role. Often the older sister is more serious, conservative and achievement oriented, and the younger sister plays the complementary more popular, creative, flexible, empathic, and less dogmatic role (Holden, 1986).

It is crucial to remember, when hearing stories about sibling rivalries or siblings who are "total opposites," that their assessment of their relationship is most likely a reflection of family tensions passed down the family tree. Such problems are very rarely a matter simply of "totally different temperaments" or of having "nothing in common."

The naming patterns in the family often give a hint of the program each daughter was meant to play out. In one family, for example, the oldest daughter was named Emily Josephine and the second Katherine. It turned out that this reflected a struggle over naming which had actually taken place between their maternal grandparents over the naming of their daughter. The grandmother wanted her to have her own name, Katherine. The "flamboyant, hard drinking, ne'er-do-well" grandfather, who was the one to handle the official naming, gave her the name "Emily" for an actress he greatly admired, and "Josephine" for himself, Joseph. However, the daughter was called Katherine and never even knew about her christened name until she applied for working papers and had to get her birth certificate. She then named her first daughter Emily Josephine and her second Katherine! Could it be a surprise that the oldest daughter became the rebel and the iconoclast, while Katherine III became the compliant, conformist "saint," like her mother and her grandmother.

In understanding problematic sister relationships it is also useful to ask about the family rules for sister relationships. In one family we saw there had been a total cutoff between two sisters for three generations. In other families the sisterhood is the strongest bond generation after generation, with males having trouble finding a place in the family.

The most common sister problem mentioned is probably a reflection of caretaker conflicts: Who did more? Who got more love and attention? Who was treated as special and got out of doing the dishes, because she was going to become a pianist or because she was "sickly"? Who always got into trouble and required mother's intervention? And who was always "the good girl" and demanded so little care, but was always doing for others?

Often, when one sister has been treated as fragile or vulnerable in childhood and has required special parental attention because of an illness or disability, the other has played the role of "good" sister for the special attention she received. This more vulnerable sister, in turn, has resented her sister's health, abilities, independence, and freedom. Each has come to see the other as "having it all." Coaching such sisters to change their relationship is often gratifying, because, once either one can decide to move past the resentment, they are both aware of the hurt they have experienced in not having a relationship (something not always true of brothers, probably because women are raised to attend to and feel responsible for emotional relationships).

Given the pivotal caretaking role that sisters typically have in a family, it is remarkable that there has been so little research on siblings from a systems point of view. There is hardly any research looking at family interactions or even involving siblings — often sibling research involves only the mothers' impressions of sibling adjustment (Vadasy, Fewell, Meyer, & Schell, 1984) or interviews of just one sibling (Cicirelli, 1985). And there is even less research on longitudinal aspects of sibling relationships.

Among the few findings that we have, we do know that siblings of the handicapped, especially the sisters, are more vulnerable to emotional problems and to increased emotional demands from their families (Cleveland & Miller, 1977; McCullough, 1981; McKeever, 1983; Skrtic, Summers, Brotherson & Turnbull, 1983; Vadasy, et al., 1984). Involving siblings in planning and treatment obviously benefits the whole family, and yet very few programs for the disabled include work with siblings (whether children or adults) as a focus of their intervention. Small families tend to experience more pressure when there is a handicapped child, because there are fewer siblings to share the responsibility. The pressure seems increased when the handicapped sibling is a brother, probably because of parental reactions, especially a father's injury to his pride in having a disabled son. Sisters seem more readily able to accept the role of caretaker for a brother and to have more sibling rivalry or competition with a handicapped sister.

In a study of siblings of retarded children, older sisters were found to be more impaired than older brothers, undoubtedly because they got the lion's share of the caretaking responsibility for the retarded child (Cleveland & Miller, 1977). They experienced the greatest demands and their career and family decisions were the most influenced by the retarded child. Sisters tended to be closer to the impaired child than brothers and had the most responsibilities. Sisters had less time for peer involvement, were more informed about the handicapped sibling and tended to adopt the parents' point of view on the handicap more than brothers. These older sisters were found to enter the helping professions more often than other siblings.

We need to plan therapeutically for the lifelong implications that having a handicapped sibling has for the caretaking responsibilities and adjustment of the other children in the family. Oldest sisters are at greatest risk because of increased parental demands. These very parental expectations need to be questioned, as we help parents to modify demands so that brothers can be included in caretaking and sisters not unnecessarily overburdened.

An extremely problematic sister relationship sometimes develops when an older sister has served a parental function for younger sisters, or when inadequate parental attention has resulted in the oldest's becoming a parental figure, later causing the younger sister to feel resentment towards her for her caretaking and "bossiness." There are indications that the older sister is in a less felicitous role, even more so if the younger sibling is a brother (Holden, 1986). The older sister experiences herself as unappreciated for all the sacrifices she has shown the younger sibling. In adulthood the younger sibling may completely cut off the older one emotionally. At times the younger sister is quite intractable and unavailable to the older sister, no matter what efforts she makes. The older sister experiences a great sense of emptiness, isolation, and frustration with the lack of closeness. The cutoff between the sisters seems to reflect a triangle with the parents, especially with the mother. In adulthood the younger sister does not feel the same need for a caring bond with her sister that she might for one with her mother, which could mobilize her to overcome a similar cutoff from her mother. All efforts by the older sister to develop an intimate relationship with the younger sister are perceived by the younger as intrusions or as new attempts at dominance and bossiness, and no degree of distance seems adequate to bring the younger sister closer, as the following case illustrates.

Mary Petrie sought therapy because of marital conflicts, but exploration of her genogram indicated that she was looking to her husband to make up to her for the many hurts she experienced in her family of origin. She was the oldest of five children, the two youngest of whom were sons. Her mother, a Czech immigrant from a deprived background, suffered from depression on and off throughout her childhood. Her father, a midwestern WASP of very stoical stock, was a farmer who struggled to keep the family going and to keep up appearances.

It appeared that Mary and her mother had at first been extremely close, but when the children followed quickly one after the other, the mother became over-burdened and depressed and Mary was left to tend to her sisters and brothers. As an adult Mary had civil but distant relationships with her two youngest brothers. She guessed she would never see them if she stopped taking the initiative, but as it was she called and wrote them, and whenever she went home they acted friendly to her. However, she was totally out of contact with her two sisters, in spite of numerous efforts to develop a rapport with them. In both instances the cutoffs had developed over "minor" incidents in which the sisters interpreted Mary's behavior as "bossy." Mary was three years older than the next daughter, Jane, and four years older than the third, Sandy, for whom she had played a special protective role throughout childhood. Now Sandy lived 2000 miles away and, while she made rare contact with others in the family, she never responded to Mary's phone calls or letters. Over a period of several years of work, Mary was able to establish a limited rapprochement with Jane, but no response came from Sandy.

By contrast, it is my experience that younger sisters generally have very good luck when they attempt to repair relationships with their older sisters. However much a younger sister may have been unable to win the attention of her older sister in childhood, in adulthood older sisters, perhaps because of their tendency toward overresponsibility in relationships, tend to be responsive to efforts by younger siblings to approach them.

Katherine Bailey, the middle of seven siblings, sought help because she felt totally overwhelmed when her only daughter stopped talking to her. Her isolation had developed many years before when she left an abusive husband (she told no one about the abuse) and returned with her infant daughter to her parents' home. She had then gone to work to support herself and her parents. She took care of the parents as they deteriorated and finally died. Her sisters apparently saw her as taking advantage of her parents' hospitality, while she felt abandoned in dealing with her father's alcoholism and her mother's serious physical disabilities. Over the years she had also become the primary caretaker for one schizophrenic brother and another who was severely alcoholic.

When, after a few individual sessions, it was suggested that Katherine invite one of her sisters in for a session, she had no difficulty deciding that the oldest sister, Martha, would be the easiest to approach. During the joint session Martha readily responded to her younger sister, and for the first time they discussed many issues about Katherine's painful life and her caretaking for her parents and brothers. The sisterhood, which had been quite hidden for many years, surfaced, and Katherine proceeded to work on her relationships with her other siblings to modify her overburdened and isolated role.

SISTERS AND THE LIFE CYCLE

In early childhood sisters are often caretakers of one another and of their brothers, as well as rivals and competitors for parental attention. Although all cultures have gender stereotyped roles, there are some variations. Certain cultures, such as Italian and Hispanic, teach daughters from an early age to wait on brothers. Irish and Black mothers are extremely overprotective of sons, and equally underprotective of their daughters, holding very high expectations of their daughters' ability to handle responsibilities. Other groups, such as WASPs, pay at least lip-service to expecting equal chores from both brothers and sisters (see McGoldrick, Hines, Lee, & Garcia Preto, Chapter 9). But, in general, we know that there are gross differences in how parents tend to behave toward their daughters and sons from birth onward (see McGoldrick, Chapter 10).

By the time adolescence begins, sisters provide important models and alter-egos. As Downing (1988) has put it:

> I am who she is not. The inner sister—my ideal self and shadow self as strangely one—figures so significantly in the process of individuation that she is there whether I have a literal sister or not. Yet like all archetypes she demands actualization and particularization, demands to be brought into the outer world of distinct images. When there is no actual sister, there seem always to be imaginary sisters or surrogate sisters. Even when there is an actual sister, there are often fantasy figures or substitutes, as if the real sister were not quite adequate fully to carry the archetype. (p. 13)

As sisters individuate during adolescence, one often begins to live out a life path for the other, so that they become alternate selves. But they also often share secrets, clothes, and sensitivities about their parents and especially their parents' problems.

As they reach young adulthood sisters often grow further apart, each one focusing on her own friends, work, and relationships, developing her own family. The marriage of one sister may put a distance between her and her siblings, as she redefines "family" with her husband and no longer with her sisters, brothers, or parents. Holidays may be shared at the parental home, but the focus now may be primarily on the relationship of each to the parents or spouses rather than on the siblings' relationships with each other. Competition may be strongest at this point: Who went to the better school? Whose husband and children are more successful? Whose life is happier? The images each develops of the other are often colored less by their personal interchanges than by the rivalries carried over from childhood or by the parental images that get transmitted as they each hear from parents about the other's life. It is during this phase that sisters may move into different social classes as they marry and move, according to the culture's expectations, to adapt to their husband's socioeconomic context. They themselves are not expected or able to define this context. It is usually defined by the husband's education, work, and financial status. Although some cultures, such as Black and Irish, emphasize friendship between siblings more than other groups, such as Scandinavian or Jewish culture (Woehrer, 1982), the sister bond is generally continued through a mutual sense of shared understanding and responsibility for the family, rather than through common interests, especially where class differences between the sisters have developed.

Often it is not until mid-life that sisters reconnect with each other, through the shared experiences of caring for a failing or dying parent, a divorce in the family, or perhaps a personal health problem. Such events inspire them to clarify their priorities and to redefine the relationships in life that really matter to them. Downing (1988) even suggests that the true working out of the meaning of sisterhood is associated with death and with getting one's priorities in order. In any case, there are indications that sisters grow closer in adulthood than they had felt while growing up (Adams, 1968).

Sometimes it is at this point that relationships which have been maintained at a superficial level break under the strain of caretaking or under the pain of the distance that has grown between them. On the other hand, sisters may be brought closer to each other by sharing the life transitions. Their relationships may solidify through the realization that their parents will not always be there and that they themselves must begin to put the effort into maintaining their own relationship.

Sisters are generally the caretakers of parents and other unattached older relatives or at least the arrangers of such caretaking. In other cultures, such as Japanese, this role goes to the wife of the oldest son, but in our culture, if sisters do not do the primary caretaking, they often feel guilty about it, because the cultural message to do so is so strong and others hold them responsible for it.

It is at the point of the death of the last parent that sibling relationships for the first time in life become voluntary. While parents are alive, siblings may have contact with and hear news about each other primarily as a function of each of their relationships with their parents. If there are unresolved problematic issues in a family, they are likely to surface at this time in conflicts over the final caretaking, the funeral, or the will. Once the parents die, siblings must for the first time decide for themselves whether to maintain contact with each other.

Because women tend to be so central in maintaining the emotional relationships in a family, sisters may focus their disappointments on each other or on their sisters-in-law, more than on their brothers, who are often treated as superior and not expected to give emotional or physical support when caretaking is required. Brothers may give financial support, but their need to earn a living often provides an excuse for little emotional involvement, while for sisters neither family commitments nor even professional commitments prevent a sense of responsibility for the needs of others.

Older women are especially likely to rely on their sisters, as well as their daughters and even their nieces for support (Anderson, 1984; Lopata, 1979; Shanas & Streib, 1965; Townsend, 1957). Often they even live together. Anderson (1984) found that sisters were the ones most often turned to by older widows, more often than children, even though they were not more available geographically. She speculated that the reasons might include their history of shared experiences and life transitions. She concludes that siblings, especially sisters, take on added significance for women as confidantes after they have been widowed.

Because siblings share a unique history, reminiscing about earlier times together is an activity they engage in at many points in the life cycle. Such reminiscing tends to become even more important later in life. It helps all siblings to validate and clarify events and relationships that took place in earlier years and to place them in mature perspective; in addition, it can become an important source of pride and comfort (Cicirelli, 1985). This seems especially meaningful for sisters who tend anyway to define themselves in terms of context and to place a high value on the quality of human relationships. Cicirelli (1982) found that having a relationship with a sister stimulates elderly women to remain socially engaged with others as well. Although the relationships of sisters, like all female relationships, tend to be invisible in the value structure of the culture at large, sisters tend to sustain one another in time of need throughout life. In old age they become indispensable. As Margaret Mead described it:

> Sisters draw closer together and often, in old age, they become each other's chosen and most happy companions. In addition to their shared memories of childhood and their relationships to each other's children, they share memories of the same house, the same homemaking style, and the same small prejudices about housekeeping. (1972, p. 70)

Mead's comment is interesting in its focus on the details of life. Especially as we grow older, it is the details — of our memories, or our housekeeping, or of our relationships with each other and with each other's families, that may hold us together.

Jungians have suggested several stages in the development of sister relationships through the life cycle: an initial rivalrous stage, related primarily to triangles with the mother, a competitive stage, more focused on adolescence, when triangles with the father are perhaps more apparent, a third stage in young adulthood, when each is developing her self and the sisters grow apart as each develops primary relationships with a partner or with work or other interests, and finally, at midlife a more spiritual coming together, whether through an appreciation of one's sister as opposite or as mirror, in which the sister deepens the other's sense of self (Freudenberg, 1982). While the specifics may not characterize all sister relationships, the characteristics of rivalry, competition, mirroring, sensing the other as a shadow figure or opposite, and the spiritual bonding are all part of sister relationships at various points in the life cycle. As Kahn and Bank (1981) have suggested, perhaps the rivalry of siblings and the downplaying of their "sibling solidarity" have been so influential in psychology because of the influence of psychoanalytic concepts which focused so on competition for parental favor and studied sibling relationships in the early years of the life cycle, not in later adulthood.

SIBLING CONSTELLATION

The role of sisters in a family is always influenced by their birth position, the distance between the siblings in age, and whether they are from all-sister families, as well as their temperament and other personal characteristics, the family program for them, and the timing of their birth in the family history (Emst & Angst, 1983; Toman, 1976). It is important to remember, however, that as the sibling group gets older, the birth order becomes less central in determining the nature of their current relationship, since other issues in their lives — dealing with aging parents, having families of their own, becoming aunt or uncle to each other's children — will play an increasing role in defining their relationships (Kahn & Bank, 1981). Obviously a great many variables influence the personality of each child. Therefore, the following descriptions of sister patterns are meant to be suggestive, rather than "true" for all siblings.

The oldest sister tends to be the prima donna, the leader, single-minded, self-centered, the mother replacement, as well as the most responsible one. In fact, she cannot avoid taking responsibility for organizing the siblings and directing their activities. Fishel (1979) describes her as dispensing her worldly wit and wisdom, even if it falls on deaf ears. Oldest sisters are under considerable pressure to succeed and are often singled out for blame: "You're the oldest, you should know better." The oldest child is more often the recipient of parental pressures, anxieties and hopes, which later children are more likely to escape. Parents are generally overattentive and overambitious with the oldest, eager to validate themselves as parents and fearful that the child may depart from some ideal standard.

As indicated above, an oldest brother generally receives constant encouragement and adulation along with the responsibilities of being the oldest, while an oldest sister more often experiences the pressures, responsibilities and high expectations, but without the glory meted out to the oldest son.

The oldest sister can hardly avoid becoming the surrogate mother to her younger siblings. Margaret Mead, for example, who was followed by a brother and then by three sisters, describes having been enlisted by her grandmother (who lived with them) to take notes on her younger sisters' behavior.

> I learned to make these notes with love, carrying on what Mother had begun. I knew that she had filled thirteen notebooks on me and only four on Richard; now I was taking over for the younger children. In many ways I thought of the babies as my children, whom I could observe and teach and cultivate. I also wanted to give them everything I missed. (1972, p. 64)

But, unlike oldest sons, who typically have a clear feeling of entitlement, oldest daughters often have feelings of ambivalence and guilt about the responsibilities of their role. Whatever they do, they feel it is not quite enough, and they can never let up in their efforts to caretake and to make the family work right.

It is interesting that in the Hennig study (Hennig & Jardim, 1977) of highly successful women in business, all 25 of them were oldests or only children, and not a single one had a brother. The profiles of these remarkable women suggest strongly that, if the parents had had sons, the emotional energy that went toward these women would have been redirected toward their brothers. It was only because there were no brothers that they were allowed to follow the path of achievement and success.

The middle sister is under less pressure to take responsibility, but she needs to try harder to make her mark in general, because she has no special role. She remembers running to catch up with the older sister from childhood, and running frantically from the younger one, who seemed to be gaining on her every minute (Fishel, 1979). The position of middle stimulates competitive feelings and leaves her vulnerable to maladjustment, if she cannot find a place to stand. She is the compromiser, the go-between, and tends to be gregarious and a good negotiator if she can define a middle path, a compromise between extremes. Kate Millet, the feminist author, is the middle of three sisters, with five years between each of them. She defines herself as the go-between, splicing together the differences between her younger and older sisters, between different generations, different temperaments, different professional and creative milieus, with a tochold in each world, while solidly standing on her own turf:

> I've always felt that I was the medium between the two. Since my older sister's a lawyer and in politics, and my younger sister is in the theatrical and art world, and I, being sort of in politics and much longer and more retiring an artist — I'm as reasonable as the elder and as sort of detached from the world as the younger. (Fishel, 1979, p. 73)

A younger sister tends to be protected, showered with affection, and handed a blueprint for life. She may either be spoiled (more so if there are older brothers) and have special privileges or, if she is from a large family, frustrated by always having to wait her turn. Her parents may have just run out of energy with her. She may feel resentful of being bossed around and never taken quite seriously. If she is the only girl, the youngest may be more like the princess, and yet the servant to elders, becoming, perhaps, the confidante to her brothers in adult life and the one to replace the parents in holding the family together.

Sisters of sisters tend to have very different sibling patterns than sisters of brothers, because of our society's strong preference for sons. If the brother is older, he is often idolized and catered to. If the brother is younger, he may be envied and deeply resented by the sister, who is more likely to have perspective on the family's gender bias, since she can remember an era before he was born. To cite one example:

> My brother was the personification of the Holy Grail. He became the end-all and be-all. When he appeared, I disappeared. Up until that time, I was visible as a thorn in my sister's side, but now nothing. He could do no wrong and I hated him

for it. As a child, I wished him dead many times. However, I instinctively protected him and cherished him. I think this was to get our parents' love. If I treated him as they did and saw in him all they did, they would love me. My sister was still indifferent to me and had the privilege because of her age of taking care of my brother. I now envied the time and energy spent on him. I don't think I ever envied any one person more than him. (Fishel, 1979, p. 78)

Gloria Steinem summed up the issue by saying that, "A boy and a girl can come out of the exact same household with two very different cultures" (Fishel, 1979, p. 81). While there has not been a great deal of research done on the subject, there are a few interesting findings on the differences between brothers and sisters: It appears that sisters of brothers are more likely to adopt opposite-sex characteristics than are their brothers, probably because male attributes seem more prestigious in our society. By contrast, brothers of sisters may, if anything, have intensified male characteristics, probably out of a desire not to be identified with the sisters (Forer, 1976).

Both brothers and sisters report feeling more positive about sisters and closer to them (Cicirelli, 1982; Troll & Smith, 1976). Cicirelli (1983) found that the more sisters a man has, the happier he is and the less worried about family, job, or money matters. And it appears that younger siblings are more willing to accept direction from an older sister than from an older brother (Cicirelli, 1985). There appears to be more rivalry, competitiveness, ambivalence, and jealousy in the relationship of brother to brother, while sister relationships are characterized by more support and caretaking (Adams, 1968; Cicirelli, 1985). Overall sister-sister relationships seem generally more intensely intimate than sister-brother or brother-brother relationships.

SISTERS-IN-LAW

Sister-in-law relationships would seem to offer some of the positives of sister relationships without the tensions, but things rarely work out this way. Sisters-in-law share a future, but not a biological or childhood history. As Bernikow (1980) has put it:

At the border of family and friends stands my sister-in-law Marlene. We do not share a mother, do not worry about the pull of likeness and the need for separation. Much of the conflict and tension between sisters is missing for us. Still, as sister-in-law, it is possible that she might be my sister in spirit. The things that arise between us are things that arise between other women, touched by our family affiliation. (p. 105)

Bernikow continues with a description of an evening spent with her brother and sister-in-law:

It (his job options) was the subject of the evening—him, his choices, his problems—and he did not tyrannize us into giving him our total attention, we gave it automatically. The fortunes of his family appeared to rest upon the outcome of his choice. It was a very important matter.

At the same time, Marlene had a critical problem, which she mentioned only once. Her work life depends on childcare. The baby-sitter had resigned that day. It was as severe a crisis to Marlene as my brother's problem was to him, yet we, all three, gave it little attention. I did not notice until afterward. . . .

I managed to tell my brother that I shared his anxiety, but was also envious. He smiled at what I said—we have understood, at last, our rivalry, acknowledged it, and maneuvered around it. But Marlene said she too was jealous.

It was the first time she and I made contact all evening long. The look that passed between us was one of rueful understanding, sympathy and identification. Each of us, of course, knew exactly what the other meant, but my brother did not. He was surprised and, I think, hurt. Whatever happened to him happened to her. She was as much a part of the good fortune as he.

"But," she said, "I'd like to have done it myself."

She is struggling to be Wife, Mother and Marlene, to balance work of her own, her home, her family, to be all of the women she can be, to grow, to participate in life, to not be slave to the sandbox. And her baby-sitter had resigned. I understood. She understood that I understood. In this mutual resentment and struggle we touched and the touching passed. . . . Phantom sister, I thought. (pp. 107–108)

Bernikow has captured very well the potential for sisterhood and the subtle ways that this bond is undercut by the larger processes in a family.

Sisters-in-law who marry into families with only brothers probably have the greatest likelihood of developing positive connections to the new family. And the wife of a youngest brother of older sisters is probably in the most difficult position, since this brother was probably treated most like a prince. He may be resented, though protected by his sisters, whom he probably tried to avoid for their "bossiness." When he finds a wife, his choice is likely to reflect in part his need for some protection against other powerful females, and she then becomes the villain, keeping him from having a closer relationship with his sisters. The structure of the family tends to determine relationships with in-laws, even though family members may be sure they are reacting to "personality characteristics."

Mary Miller was four years older than her only brother, "Prince" George. Mary and her parents had doted on George, a star athlete though a mediocre student, who became a career officer in the air force. George married Linda, a friend of Mary's from college. Sparks began to fly between the sisters-in-law almost from the moment of the wedding. Mary decided that Linda had very materialistic values and was influencing George to distance from the family. George began "making excuses" for not coming on holidays, because he had to go to Linda's family. Mary increasingly avoided dealing with Linda and went around her in attempts to "get back the old closeness with George." She often called him at his office to invite him over. He would say he had to ask Linda about it. Linda would then call to turn down the invitation and Mary silently blamed her for blocking her closeness to her brother.

Finally, as part of therapy for depression, Mary was coached to reconnect with George by first developing a personal relationship with Linda. She now began to go through Linda in initiating contacts with George. She confided to Linda how much she wished for more closeness with George and how much he seemed to pull away from her.

Linda responded that George was often distant from her too and she did not know how to handle it. She began bringing George around to visit. Mary realized that she and Linda had a great deal in common and a new era was initiated in which Mary began to develop personal relationships with both Linda and George.

About a year later, reminiscing about their childhood, George admitted to Mary how intimidated he always was by her. He said he had always felt she was telling him what to do and she was so smart that she was usually right. He said he had often used the excuse of Linda's family so he wouldn't have to deal with Mary directly. Now that she seemed less "strident and demanding" he said, he felt he could tell her this.

This case illustrates how the sister-in-law's function in a family was to handle the brother's problematic family relationships. It is typically fruitless to try to go around this in-law in dealing with family relationship problems.

TWINS

Twins have been a source of fascination, awe, and sometimes even fear for many centuries (Lindblad-Goldberg, 1986). Since a primary factor in the childrearing of girls is to make them more responsive to human relationships, the level of fusion of twin sisters is much greater than that of twin brothers. A kind of mind-reading and emotional connection, which is expected of women in any relationship, is taken to the extreme in a relationship of identical twin sisters. It appears that identical twin brothers are more competitive, more threatened by having a "double," and have more identity problems than identical twin sisters (Fier, 1988). Levine et al. (1979) found that identical twin sisters were more satisfied than twin brothers with their total self-concept, their families, their behavior, and their moral/ethical values. It would seem that women, being raised to think of life relationally, are more comfortable with the idea of a twin who shares their thoughts and feelings. As Lindblad-Goldberg (1986) describe it:

Being an identical twin means never knowing absolute alienation, disapproval, or rejection, because one's twin is always there. Somewhere in the universe the mirror-self radiates this shared acceptance of joy and sorrow . . . between (my twin) and me there is one part that is both of us. We're totally separate beings, yet it does exist, this oneness. (p. 47)

Of course, twins also have at times the experience that they are not as fused as others expect them to be, or even as they may expect themselves to be (Ainslie, 1985; Cohen, 1988). Nevertheless, the remarkable aspect of "telepathic bonding" is a special and undeniable feature of twin relationships.

It is surprising how often the powerful experience of twins can be overlooked clinically by therapists, who have not usually been trained to attend to sibling patterns, even where, as in this case, they are primary in a person's identity.

Mildred Brown sought help for her marital problems. She was an identical twin who had been inseparable from her sister, Martha, until their senior year of college, when Martha met and became engaged to a classmate within two months. Mildred felt abandoned and devastated. After graduating in accounting, Mildred took a job and soon began dating Sam, one of the company salesmen. Mildred was not really in love with Sam but he cared about her and she was lonely. They were married in a double wedding with Martha three months later. The marriage was not very satisfying from the beginning. Sam's complaint was that Mildred never communicated her expectations directly and was then resentful when he didn't meet them. She, on the other hand, thought that if Sam really loved her he would know her feelings without her having to explain everything.

During the early years of marriage Mildred and her twin sister became more and more distant. Martha became a social worker and her husband a professor. Sam was convinced that they looked down on him and felt uncomfortable with them. Mildred also felt awkward. The twins' father died suddenly when they were 26 and they became momentarily closer, but this did not last longer than the week of the funeral, during which Sam felt slighted by Martha and her husband. Mildred, feeling caught between her sister and her husband, thought she had little choice but to side with her husband and stop seeing her sister. Over the years the twins each raised a son and daughter. Mildred concentrated her energy on her children, giving up work during their childhood but returning when they were in high school.

When the younger child went off to college, Mildred became more aware of the lack of understanding that existed in her relationship with Sam. She complained more; he tried, but never seemed able to get it right. The more he tried, the more she thought there was no point trying to explain ideas to someone whose every move indicated a basic lack of sensitivity to her. The frustration now that the children were gone had gotten to the point where they were both thinking it might be better to separate.

Therapy focused on helping them both put the marriage back into some perspective. For Mildred, this meant exploring the many ways in which the special twin relationship she had had with Martha while growing up had led to frustrations when Sam was not able to "read her mind." The marriage came into better perspective for her when she decided it was time to reconnect with her sister and quit letting "class" or "personality differences" between their spouses form the basis for their relationship. She decided to approach Martha individually, not as a couple as she always had before. Martha was immediately responsive to Mildred's frank overtures. Mildred said that by the end of their first meeting it was as if the intervening 25 years had never occurred. Their mental synchrony was such that they were laughing about being able to finish each other's sentences, just as in childhood.

The reconnection of this relationship eased the pressure on the marriage for Mildred, who found that she was no longer so easily irritated by Sam's need to verbalize everything or the lack of total intuitive understanding in their relationship.

CONCLUSION

In our era families are getting smaller. Children are spending more time outside the family from an early age in daycare or with baby-sitters. At home television is so often the focus of attention that siblings spend less time interacting than they did before. Sibling patterns are changing rapidly. With fewer siblings available, there may be more pressure on those there are to fulfill whatever legacies a family may have for the next generation. It is important for us as therapists to encourage families to balance the expectations they have of their children, so that no sibling is shortchanged by the self-fulfilling prophesy of limited parental expectations or the burden of unattainable ones. And with the high rate of divorce, which so often disrupts parent-child relationships, we need to validate and strengthen other family bonds, including especially those primary bonds between siblings.

We urge therapists to challenge traditional assumptions about the sister's responsibility for caretaking and maintaining relationships. We should also help one sister to question the negative focus she may have on another sister for letting her down, rather than appreciating the unreasonable expectations she or the family may have for the sister, which match the overly demanding expectations she has for herself to be sensitive to everyone else. We must validate the sisters' experience of the burden of family responsibilities and encourage them to use each other for support rather than viewing each other as competitors.

Most therapists rarely even ask about siblings, let alone bring them in for sessions or validate their importance to a client's resolution of a problem. It is often helpful to invite adult sisters into therapy sessions and validate through clinical attention to these relationships the bonds that join sisters and brothers in a family. In such meetings, as Kahn and Bank (1981) have shown: "The distorted images, or 'frozen misunderstandings' of their earlier relationships can now be challenged and corrected" (p. 86). Bank and Kahn (1975, 1982) have discussed the value of meeting with sibling groups, using siblings as consultants, holding "sibling rehearsals" and "sibling rallies" to mobilize a client to shift her/his role in the family.

One situation where it is particularly useful to involve siblings is when an adult child is struggling with an aging parent. It is useful to contact not only the adult child's siblings, but also the siblings of the aging parent, thus encouraging the adult child to validate and reinforce the importance of the parent's sibling relationships as well. We routinely inquire about family wills that may set siblings against each other and encourage siblings to deal with these inequities before their parents die. And we urge the sharing of caretaking responsibilities among *all* siblings. It is important not to accept the status quo: "My brother gives money, but never helps because he doesn't have time."

When clients view themselves as competing for the special attention of men, we work to reframe this perspective, expanding each sister's view of the other and emphasizing their shared experiences and bonds.

Finally, we encourage families to rebalance demands and expectations for sons and daughters. It is important to challenge parents who are making daughters into "little mothers" to their siblings, while making their sons into princes. An excellent resource in helping parents change their perspectives in this area is the popular book by Stella Chess and Jane Whitehead (1978), *Daughters*, which suggests many of the areas in which parents reflect their stereotypic sex role expectations in childrearing. We try through our questioning about family rules and roles to challenge any other patterns which reveal different expectations for sons than daughters.

REFERENCES

Adams, B. N. (1968). *Kinship in an urban setting.* Chicago: Markham Publishing.

Ainslie, R. C. (1985). *The psychology of twinship.* Lincoln, Nebraska: University of Nebraska Press.

Anderson, T. (1984). Widowhood as a life transition: Its impact on kinship ties. *Journal of Marriage and the Family, 46*(1), 105–14.

Bank, S. P., & Kahn, M. D. (1982). *The sibling bond.* New York: Basic Books.

Bank, S. P., & Kahn, M. D. (1975). Sisterhood-brotherhood is powerful: Sibling sub-systems and family therapy. *Family Process, 14*(3), 311–39.

Bernikow, L. (1980). *Among women.* New York: Harper & Row.

Bossard, J., & Boll, E. S. (1955). Personality roles in the large family. *Child Development, 26,* 71–78.

Broverman, I. K., Vogel, S. R., & Broverman, D. M. (1982). Sex-role stereotypes: A current appraisal. *Journal of Social Issues, 28*(2), 59–78.

Chess, S., & Whitbread, J. (1978). *Daughters: From infancy to independence.* New York: Doubleday.

Cicirelli, V. G. (1985). Sibling relationships throughout the life cycle. In L. L'Abate (Ed.), *The handbook of family psychology and therapy*. Homewood, IL: The Dorsey Press.

Cicirelli, V. G. (1982). Sibling influence throughout the life span. In M. E. Lamb & B. Sutton-Smith (Eds.), *Sibling relationships: Their nature and significance across the lifespan*. Hillsdale, NJ: Lawrence Erlbaum.

Cicirelli, V. G. (1983). Adult children's attachment and helping behavior to elderly parents: A path model. *Journal of Marriage and the Family, 45*, 815–25.

Cleveland, D. W., & Miller, N. (1977). Attitudes and life commitments of older siblings of mentally retarded adults: An exploratory study. *Mental Retardation, 15*(3), 38–41.

Cohen, K. (1988). Personal communication.

Downing, C. (1988). *Psyche's sisters: Reimagining the meaning of sisterhood*. San Francisco: Harper & Row.

Entwiste, D. R., & Doering, S. G. (1981). *The first birth*. Baltimore: Johns Hopkins University Press.

Ernst, C., & Angst, J. (1983). *Birth order: Its influence on personality*. New York: Springer.

Fier, R. (1988). Personal communication.

Fishel, E. (1979). *Sisters: Love and rivalry inside the family and beyond*. New York: William Morrow.

Forer, L. (1976). *The birth order factor*. New York: Pocket Books.

Freudenberg, B. E. (1982). The effect of sisters on feminine development. *Dissertation abstracts international*. University of Michigan: DAI, 43(03), Sec A, PO 672.

Hennig, M., & Jardim, A. (1977). *The managerial woman*. Garden City: Anchor/Doubleday.

Holden, C. E. (1986). Being a sister: Constructions of the sibling experience. *Dissertation abstracts international*. University of Michigan (0127), April. DAI V47(10), SECB, PP4301.

Hoopes, M. H., & Harper, J. M. (1987). *Birth order roles and sibling patterns in individual and family therapy*. Rockville, MD: Aspen.

Horn, M. (1983). 'Sisters worthy of respect': Family dynamics and women's roles in the Blackwell family. *Journal of Family History*, Winter, 367–82.

Kahn, M., & Bank, S. (1981). In pursuit of sisterhood: Adult siblings as a resource for combined individual and family therapy. *Family Process, 20*(1), 85–95.

Levine, C. S., Eller, B. F., & Whitmore, H. L. (1979). An analysis of the differences in self concept of male and female monozygotic twins. *Social Behavior and Personality, 7*(1), 93–96.

Lindblad-Goldberg, M. (1986). Gemini. *Family Therapy Networker, 10*(6), 45–47.

Lopata, H. Z. (1979). *Women as widows: Support systems*. New York: Elsevier.

McCullough, M. E. (1981). Parent and sibling definition of situation regarding transgenerational shift in care of a handicapped child. *Dissertation abstracts international*. 42, 161B. (University Microfilm No. 8115012).

McKeever, P. (1983). Siblings of chronically ill children: A literature review with implications for research and practice. *American Journal of Orthopsychiatry, 53*(2), 209–18.

McNaron, T. A. H. (Ed.). (1985). *The sister bond: A feminist view of a timeless connection*. New York: Pergamon Press.

Mead, M. (1972). *Blackberry winter*. New York: Washington Square Press.

Noberini, M. R., Brady, E. M., & Mosatche, H. S. (in preparation). Personality and adult sibling relationships: A preliminary study.

Shanas, E., & Streib, G. F. (1965). Social structure and the family. Englewood Cliffs, NJ: Prentice-Hall.

Skrtic, T. M., Summers, J. A., Brotherson, M. J., & Turnbull, A. P. (1983). Severely handicapped children and their brothers and sisters. In J. Blacher (Ed.), *Severely handicapped young children and their families. Research in review*. New York: Academic Press.

Toman, W. (1976). *Family constellation*. (3rd ed.). New York: Springer.

Townsend, P. (1957). *The family life of older people*. London: Routledge and Kegan Paul.

Troll, L. E., & Smith, J. (1976). Attachment through the life span. Some questions about dyadic bonds among adults. *Human Development, 19*, 156–70.

Vadasy, P. F., Fewell, R. R., Meyer, D. J., & Schell, G. (1984). Siblings of handicapped children: A developmental perspective on family interactions. *Family Relations, 33*(1), 155–67.

Woehrer, C. E. (1982). The influence of ethnic families on intergenerational relationships and later life transitions. *Annals of the American Academy of Political and Social Scientists, 464*, November, 65–78.

14
Reconsidering Gender in the Marital Quid pro Quo

FROMA WALSH

IN THE ATLAS MOUNTAINS of Morocco sheepherding Berber tribes gather annually, as they have for centuries, for the traditional "Bridal Market" where eligible men shop for wives. According to custom, each prospective bride strolls through the marketplace, cheeks brightly painted and wearing a headdress that reveals her marital status: Her scarf is peaked if she is an unmarried virgin or folded over if she is divorced or widowed. Each carries a blanket she has woven. As a man catches the eye of someone who interests him, she displays her blanket. They examine each other indirectly as they engage in a conversation about the merits and flaws in the blanket, and he decides whether he wishes to purchase the blanket as she decides whether or not she wishes to sell it to him. If not in agreement, both move on to other prospects. When interest is mutual, they then barter over the price of the blanket. If the blanket pleases him enough and he meets her price, the couple goes off to the local official who legalizes their intention to marry. Their families become involved in the bartering process, as sheep and other valuables are weighed in to each side of the bargain. By tradition, the new bride moves into her husband's family tent, tribal norms shaping the nature of the relationship they will construct. Should she fail to meet the approval of her husband and her mother-in-law, who heads the household, or if she fails to bear a male child, her husband could end the marriage by announcing, "I divorce you; I divorce you; I divorce you!"

Couples in every culture make some sort of metaphorical bargain at the outset of their relationship, determining not only whether they will marry, but also setting the rules for the relationship. Jackson (1977b) has aptly termed this important and largely covert contract "the marital quid pro quo":

> When two people get together, they immediately exchange clues as to how they are defining the nature of the relationship; this set of behavioral tactics is modified by the other person by the manner in which he responds. The definition which is agreed to (and if the marriage is to work some sort of agreement must be reached), this definition of who each is in relation to the other can best be expressed as a quid pro quo. (p. 25).

Contemporary couples are attempting to work out non-traditional gender arrangements in their marital contracts. Jackson, ahead of his times, argued against the presumption of proper sex-linked marital roles in favor of a mutually agreed upon relationship bargain worked out by each couple. Nevertheless, shared belief systems contribute to the formation and maintenance of all interactional patterns and culturally based gender beliefs exert a powerful, and often unintended, influence in every marital quid pro quo. This paper examines the construction of the marital quid pro quo in terms of the operation of gendered rules in the organizational patterns and communication processes of contemporary couples, considering them from a family life cycle perspective and in social context. The gender-linked dilemmas confronting a typical couple combining dual career and childrearing commitments are explored in a clinical case illustration, with recommendations for helping couples to construct a more gender sensitive quid pro quo to fit personal preferences and life cycle challenges.

CULTURE, GENDER AND THE MARITAL QUID PRO QUO

Quid pro quo — literally "something for something" — is an expression of the legal nature of a contract, in which each party receives something for what he or she gives, consequently defining the individuals' respective rights and duties. Jackson likened marriage to a bargain "which defines the different rights and duties of the spouses, each of which can be said to do X if and because the other does Y" (1977b, p. 25).

Jackson challenged the Parsonian model of the "normal" family whereby the rights and duties of spouses were prescribed and limited in adherence to biologically determined gender roles (see Walsh & Scheinkman, Chapter 2 in this volume). In Parson's view, conformity to the "proper" gender-linked role was presumed to be essential, "not only to sexual compatibility, but to the mental health of the spouses and their children and the performance of the marriage" (Jackson, 1977a, p. 18). Jackson opposed the "theoretical and cultural" preconceptions about "proper" sex roles, such that men are supposed to work, be strong, and not openly emotional, defend the home, etc., while women are to keep house, stay inside it, be soft, loving, maternal. Such stereotypical role expectations do not consider the relationship which underlies this arrangement or the possibility of a variety of ways of working out relationship rules.

Instead, Jackson emphasized the active process of working out relationship tasks and challenges through agreement in the marital quid pro quo. He attributed the stresses and successes of marriage to the functioning of rules for collaboration that must be constructed by each couple, with consideration of inevitable similarities and differences of partners. In an ongoing marital relationship, two individuals are confronted with the challenge of collaboration on a wide variety of tasks — moneymaking, housekeeping, social life, love-making, parenting — over a presumably long period of time. The way couples handle this crucial relationship problem is by contracting a marital quid pro quo.

While progressive in his aims, Jackson erred in three ways that contributed significantly to a gender blindness in the field of family therapy (see Walsh & Scheinkman, Chapter 2). First, he mistakenly regarded roles as "individual" constructs and dismissed any attention to roles as inappropriate to an interactional view. He saw the definition of the self, the relationship, and the other as an indivisible whole, comprised of the individual-in-this-relationship-with-this-other. However, roles are actually interpersonally and contextually constructed, and can be thought of as a set of rules defining the position of an individual *in relation to* another position. The role of "wife" exists only in relation to that of husband.

Second, Jackson erred by assuming that any *descriptive* use of the concept of roles implies the *prescription* of roles. The same caution might be warranted for use of the construct of rules, which could, presumably, lead to a prescription of rules. While we would agree that stereotyped preconceptions of proper sex roles *should* not predetermine the relational possibilities in a couple's relationship, nonetheless biologically based gender differences and societal beliefs *do* need to be recognized.

Third, family relationship rules were viewed by Jackson as norms unique to each family unit, with "broader social or cultural considerations remaining secondary, even though we assume that a given set of norms or relationship rules is more common in one culture than another" (1977a, p. 12). Values were considered only as one kind of homeostatic mechanism, serving a function in affirming or reinforcing desired relationship rules. Values were seen as representing coalitions with religion, society, or culture, invoked by a partner as interpersonal tactics to exert leverage on a relationship. What is insufficiently taken into account in this formulation are the macrosystemic rules in societal values and practices that frame, supraordinately, all rules that any couple constructs.

Thus, the construction of relationship rules and roles is a circular process, each influencing the other over time. No couple initiates a relationship as a blank slate; each individual enters with a set of beliefs and expectations for marriage that are shaped by experiences in one's family of origin (McGoldrick, 1988) and previous couple/marital relationships (Walsh, in press), all embedded in one's community and the larger culture. Such values are not merely used by individuals to serve a homeostatic function. They permeate our ways of thinking about marriage and behaving as husband and wife.

The notion of family paradigms, developed by Reiss (1981), is useful in conceptualizing values and beliefs from a systems perspective. Couples, like families, develop a shared construction of reality: basic premises each partner brings to a relationship and that are mutually shaped, reinforced, or modified over time through the partners' experiences together. These include values, assumptions, myths, and expectations for the future—both their highest hopes and their catastrophic fears. This shared belief system is the life blood of a relationship. It guides ongoing interaction and planning for the future. At each major transition, the paradigm undergoes transformation to meet the requisites for reorganization of the system. A couple's belief system might be considered the foundation of the marital quid pro quo.

Jackson was ahead of his time in opposing the prevailing belief that biology-is-destiny in determining how men and women inevitably will—and ought to—function in a marital relationship. Contemporary couples are attempting to construct a variety of nontraditional relationship paradigms that can be functional. However, we can't dismiss gender as an influence in the marital quid pro quo. As couples experiment with new relationship bargains, gender issues continue to come into play, largely out of awareness. Family-of-origin and cultural belief systems concerning the proper roles, rights, and responsibilities of husband and wife and of mother and father influence the bargains that are made and the interactional patterns that evolve over the course of the couple's life cycle.

In fact, men and women receive quite different myths about marriage from our culture, from contemporary media representations to classic literature and folk tales. For example, little girls today are still as taken as in past generations with the stories of Cinderella, Sleeping Beauty, and Snow White, in which the prince rescues the fairest maiden and carries her off to his castle, where they live happily ever after. (For feminist revisions of such fairy tales, see Zipes, *Don't Bet on the Prince*, 1986). Although we know such fantasies and happy endings aren't realistic, they become parables that serve as models of the ideal relationship women are seeking.

For men, the metaphors have been less romantic and more concerned with the balance of power in the marital relationship. Two options are juxtaposed: The husband is either "king of his castle" or imprisoned there. Courtship is feared as entrapment; a man with a promising career is regarded as a "good catch." A man is pursued; when he is caught, the prison door slams shut and he is locked in, constrained by a "ball and chain." Shakespeare's *Taming of the Shrew* has served as a timeless parable: For a happy marriage, a man must establish himself as the boss and subdue the independent and rebellious aspects in his bride's nature, so that he will not be controlled or manipulated by her. Yet, despite widespread beliefs that marriage should be dreaded by men, research reveals that married men are mentally and physically healthier and achieve greater job success than single men, while the opposite is true for women (McGoldrick, 1988).

Our society idealized and labeled as "normal" a particular family form that actually represented only a cross-section of life in post-World-War-II middle-class suburban America. Men and women were given clear messages about what they should do to be regarded as successful in life: Men were to be the financial providers and instrumental leaders in the larger world, while women were to carry the responsibilities for household maintenance, childrearing, and physical and socioemotional caretaking of husband, children, and both extended families. Individual identity was inexorably linked to the performance of gender-linked roles. To the extent that this model worked in earlier times, it did so largely because it was supported by a high value on homelife and mothering and by the close proximity of a vital kin and friendship community, all of whom shared similar values and life styles and were available in times of need. Men tended to maintain their strongest relational ties in the male sphere outside the home, while women did so with other women within the large family and neighborhood circle (Bernard, 1982). However, with increasing job pressures, men became peripheral to family life and unavailable to their wives at the same time that women in the suburbs experienced more isolation from their extended family and community. Yet, more expectations were loaded onto marriage, in the mythology that the couple's relationship should provide all socioemotional needs for partners, in a utopian quest for intimacy (Wynne, 1986).

Over the past two decades, marriage practices have been changing dramatically. In the early phase of the women's movement, questioning of the rigid gendered roles and rules bound up with the institution of marriage led increasing numbers of women to invest in career pursuits, along male paths to fulfillment and greater financial independence. Over 60% of married women — and over 55% of mothers — are currently in the workforce, with numbers increasing to 80% in the coming decade. Many young adults have elected to postpone or forego marriage and childrearing and unprecedented numbers of women have left traditional marriages. Now a second phase of change is occurring, focused on rethinking assumptions and possibilities for marriage and family (Friedan, 1981). As our actual life patterns have shifted dramatically, our paradigms for a healthy, satisfying marriage have lagged behind and are a poor fit with the complexities of life for most couples.

The construction of a marital quid pro quo is more challenging for contemporary couples because the rapid social change over the last two decades has called into question the merits and relevance of traditional marriage bargains, of the standards that operated for their parents and grandparents. Their lives have changed so dramatically that couples are uncertain how to construct a viable marriage. There are as many myths about the normal or ideal marriage as there are about the normal family (Walsh, 1983). Numerous books and programs promoting marital enrichment continue to assume, if not prescribe, traditional gender roles. Increasingly, couples are experimenting with new forms and contracts, lacking models to guide them, and turning to marital therapy or divorce in their distress. Yet, despite a current divorce rate at nearly 50% and the complexities of remarriage (see McGoldrick, Chapter 11), individuals are choosing to marry and remarry more than ever, expressing the deep need for a satisfying and lasting couple relationship. The marital quid pro quo they construct will be crucial in the success or failure of their endeavors. In particular, the covert gender-linked rules that guide a couple's patterns of organization and communication must be more carefully examined and renegotiated where dysfunctional for the marriage or for either partner.

GENDER AND ORGANIZATIONAL PATTERNS

Family and Work Systems

When considering the structural arrangement and tasks involved in the functioning of a marital couple, the interaction of family and work systems must be taken into account (Blumstein & Schwartz, 1983; Walsh & Scheinkman, Chapter 2). In a discussion of implicit and explicit marriage contracts, Weitzman (1981) defined the traditional marriage contract in terms of the division of responsibilities and areas of concern. The woman's domain, primarily in the home, carries responsibility for household management and childcare, while the man's domain, primarily in the workplace, holds responsibility for the family's financial support.

The dual-career (or two wage-earner) marriage has become the dominant family form. In *principle*, this contract is characterized by more nearly symmetrical roles of wives and husbands. The underlying assumption in this relationship bargain is that the job investment of wife and husband will be of equal importance to the couple and, as a matter of equity, each will share responsibility for childcare and home management chores (Weiss, 1985).

Although most wives are now active participants in the workforce, the vast majority of marriage contracts are still based on a traditional belief system. The marital quid pro quo has lagged behind actual social changes, such that women have added on employment outside the home while retaining their traditional charge in the home. Despite increasing interest expressed by many men for greater involvement in parenting, research reveals that most men in dual-career marriages actually carry little more *responsibility* at home than do men who are sole wage earners in traditional marriages. Working wives, on average, continue to carry 80% of household and childcare tasks, including the overall coordinating responsibility (Baruch, Biener, & Barnett, 1987; Piotrkowski & Repetti, 1984; Pleck, 1985). Such findings document a serious structural imbalance in contemporary marriages.

The result is often a breakdown in the contract of equitable, shared leadership in the family, a disparity between the initial bargain and the actual day-to-day patterns of living. In effect, a double standard operates in the marital quid pro quo. For couples who entered marriage with a traditional quid pro quo, the woman typically adds job responsibilities on top of family obligations. For couples who initially contracted a dual career relationship, difficulties commonly arise when the couple enters the phase of childrearing. In the reorganization required by this transition, the wife typically assumes additional responsibilities at home, in most cases compromising or sacrificing her own career aims while her husband continues in full pursuit of his work goals. When she does continue to work outside the home, childcare arrangements are largely her responsibility and viewed as a "women's issue" by the culture.

In a study of occupationally successful men, Weiss (1985) found that all had maintained traditional marriages. While the men valued work and family above all else, work priorities removed them from ongoing active participation in family life. Although most wives worked at least part-time, a wife's job was viewed as chiefly for her own benefit, whereas the husband's employment was regarded as more important, since it was considered his responsibility to provide financially for the family. Husbands believed themselves to be demonstrating concern for their families when they worked hard. Absence from family involvement on evenings and weekends, as well as minimal responsibility for household and childcare tasks, tended to be justified by the shared belief in the primary importance of their role as financial provider. They stated a desire to be involved in decisions at home, but since their jobs consumed most of their energies, they found the activities necessitated by decision-making and the day-to-day implementation to be too burdensome to carry out. Moreover, because they viewed children as in their wives' domain, they felt ineffective in opposing their wives' practices and believed that their wives had the power to decide what really happened.

Power and Egality

The balance of power between husband and wife is a fundamental issue in the organization of marital systems (Goldner, Chapter 3). Achieving that balance is critical to couple functioning and to the well-being of both partners, and yet power has been the most neglected issue in the theory and practice of family therapy (Walsh & Scheinkman, Chapter 2). Beavers (1986) found that couples in successful marriages were able to work out both complementarity in task performance *and*, at the same time, a sense of equitability and shared leadership. In contrast, dysfunctional families were characterized by a power imbalance in the marital unit: The greater the skew toward one partner's maintaining an authoritarian and dominant stance over the other, the more dysfunctional and unsatisfying was the marriage.

The distribution of power is an issue distinct from whether a couple's organizational arrangement is more complementary or symmetrical. Couples in more asymmetric relationships, with dissimilar roles and functions, can negotiate an agreement that feels equitable in terms of their respective contributions, but they are prone to power imbalance if one domain (e.g., household) is less valued (Scheinkman, 1988). In more symmetrical relationships, where both are committed to job and parenting roles, equitability does not mean that husbands and wives must do the same tasks, in identical fashion and amounts (Margolin, Fernandez, Talovic, & Onorato, 1983). Partners may be symmetrical at a macrolevel of role-sharing and still work out complementary allocation of tasks within that domain. While symmetry can generate competition, it can also facilitate greater collaboration, as, for example, both partners share parenting responsibilities.

What is required in any structural arrangement is a mutual sense of long-term *reciprocity*, such that partners believe that each is carrying a fair share of responsibilities and that their contributions are valued and balance out over time. A persistent skew or power imbalance in the relationship can lead to marital dissatisfaction and to symptoms such as fatigue, decreased sexual desire, and depression, more likely in the wife who is carrying a disproportionate share of family responsibilities. While marital partners are becoming more symmetrical in the job domain, with women increasingly doing "men's work," they continue to confront discrimination and lag behind in salary and advancement. At the same time, reciprocal changes by husbands in the home, doing what has been traditional defined as "women's work," have yet to be realized, largely because that domain has been culturally devalued.

Ironically, although men hold higher status than women by all objective measures, most men tend not to experience themselves as powerful in the work domain or larger society, and typically view their wives as in control of family life, which has been defined as the wife's domain. Subjective feelings and beliefs about power and control and their expression in the marital quid pro quo need to be more fully explored in marital therapy.

Adaptability

A chief requisite for well-functioning marital and family systems is adaptability, which involves a balance between maintaining a stable structure and allowing for flexibility in response to life challenges (Olson, in press). The stresses confronted by dual-career couples strain the relationship on this dimension. With commitments to two jobs and to raising a family, the constant conflicting demands in work and family spheres demand both firm structure and high flexibility.

Such couples need to set clear rules that, yet, must often be broken and renegotiated. Given the complexity of demands in everyday living, clarity and consistency are essential for order, predictability, and accomplishment of the myriad of family and work tasks. At the same time, the unexpected variations in routine, crises, and added responsibilities require flexibility and tolerance for occasional chaos.

Cohesion

Another crucial aspect of family organization involves cohesion (Olson, in press). Well-functioning couples tend to work out a balance between connectedness and a respect for separateness and individual differences. In the marital quid pro quo, there is a shared commitment to the relationship and its continuity, with boundaries set to protect the couple's relationship from intrusion or disruption by children, extended family, or extrafamilial involvements. The impact of work system pressures on marital cohesion requires more attention. It is difficult to maintain connectedness and specialness in a couple's relationship when job commitments limit investment in the relationship and are regarded in our society as more important than family commitments. When work priorities take precedence with regularity, a spouse tends to feel alienated and devalued. In traditional marriages wives are expected to defer to their husbands' career demands, to sacrifice or postpone fulfillment of their own individual or relationship needs. To the extent that cohesion is maintained, it is achieved largely through the wife's "adjustment" to fit with her husband's priorities. Respect for separate, individual needs is skewed toward the husband's pursuits, with his work-related needs taking precedence and her needs considered less legitimate. This pattern of deference persists in most dual-career marriages, where the husband is still thought of as the "provider," since he is more likely to hold a full-time job and to have higher earnings and job status than his wife.

Typically, women, carrying the burden of making family relationships work, coordinating the household, and primary caretaking of family members, have found little time for themselves. Men, on the treadmill of job demands, have also lacked personal time, although by comparison women's combined responsibilities leave even less energy for themselves. Especially in dual-career couples, separate time is consumed by job and family demands, the relationship strained by the lack of both shared couple time and individual time. Adding childcare demands to heavy work commitments can push partners toward disengaged positions, with little sense of couple connectedness apart from shared burdens. In low-income families, couples may have no choice; one may have to work a daytime shift and the other a night shift just to make ends meet. As one husband lamented, "Our relationship is like two trains on separate tracks, pausing to unload at the station before racing on."

Many young couples entering marriage with expectation of dual careers contract for a relatively separate relationship, each on a different career track. It may work until the arrival of children when there may not be enough cohesiveness to make it work. Lacking sufficient connectedness to collaborate around parenting, they may slide into disengagement.

When such couples seek therapy, it is imperative that clinicians not assume that their distress is necessarily an indication of individual psychopathology or a pathological marriage. They may request individual therapy for the partner believed to be deficient, or they may seek a divorce, hoping to find a better partner. It is crucial for therapists to help them recognize the contextual aspects of their distress and gain perspective on common dilemmas inherent in the kind of lifespace they have constructed. Gathering information about a typical week may reveal that they spend almost no time together, and what little time they have is consumed by responsibilities and maintenance issues that require constant problem-solving. They may lack pleasure or leisure time together and rarely go out in the evening or take vacations.

Couples carrying the traditional model of the mother/wife as perfect homemaker may not have considered, or felt comfortable, hiring a housekeeper. It is useful for couples to consider that, in hiring and delegating chores, they are still in charge. Often, despite a genuine desire for husbands to carry a more equitable share of home responsibilities, it is hard for women to yield control in the domain where their competence and sense of identity are centered, while experiencing less status in extrafamilial arenas. Contributions by husbands need to be reframed from "helping" their wives, which only maintains the skew, to sharing responsibility with their partners and assuming responsibility for their own part.

GENDER AND COMMUNICATION

In formulating the marital quid pro quo, Jackson (1977a) elaborated on Bateson's observation that communication has two distinct functions: a content (report) aspect conveying information, opinions, feelings, and experiences, and more importantly, a relationship (command) level defining the nature of the relationship between participants. With couples, each partner offers definitions of the relationship, seeking to determine its nature. Each, in turn, responds with a definition that may affirm, deny, or modify that of the partner. In an important, ongoing relationship, the give-and-take of relationship definitions must stabilize or else lead to a run-away, endangering the continuity of the relationship. These relationship rules organize interaction into a reasonably stable system. While considered to be agreements, most relationship rules are outside of awareness. Relatively few rules can explain the complex patterning of a range of behaviors, since couples interact in repetitive sequences in various areas of their lives. Rules are considered to be inferences, abstractions, or metaphors to cover observable redundancies. In short, a rule is a formulation for a relationship, such as: "No one shall control anyone else, Father shall overtly run the show but Mother's covert authority shall be respected, Husband shall be the wooer and Wife the helpless female" (Jackson, 1977a, p. 11). The question of who controls the very definition of relationship rules is fundamental to the marital quid pro quo and concerns the balance of power.

Clarity of rules, roles, and messages is necessary to facilitate a healthy couple relationship. With so much complexity and ambiguity in contemporary lives, spouses must continually redefine and make explicit their assumptions and expectations for marriage, for their partner, and for themselves. Balancing the demands of two jobs and family commitments requires a high level of communication, coordination, and monitoring of arrangements simply to manage the ordinary tasks of family life without mishap. A minor miscommunication can result in no one picking up a small child from day-care because each parent assumed the other was attending to that task or other demands intruded. Unless both partners are clear and consistent in follow-through, misunderstandings occur repeatedly, with a pile-up effect of frustration and conflict. Congruence between stated relationship bargains and actual behavior is crucial. When a relationship is explicitly based on equality, yet the wife continually defers to the husband's needs and priorities, she is left feeling cheated and resentful.

Emotional expression is another vital aspect of communication. Each couple has to work out an understanding as to how husband and wife can mutually express their loving, caring feelings. Misunderstandings about this are a common source of marital tension. When couples entering treatment report communication problems, husbands and wives may mean quite different things. Women tend to complain that their husbands don't demonstrate enough affection, whereas husbands are more often distressed about their wives' lack of sexual interest. For wives, the two are more likely to be connected: They would feel more sexual desire if their husbands would express more affection, respect, and appreciation. Typically, husbands from traditional backgrounds believe that they are demonstrating their love by providing financially for their wives and family and feel that their wives do not sufficiently appreciate those efforts. Often, in dual-career marriages, husbands who have genuinely supported their wives' career aspirations nevertheless feel unloved when their wives do not prepare meals for them, because cooking was regarded as a wife's expression of love in their families of origin. Therapists can help couples to work out a quid pro quo for expression of caring that fits their needs for mutual respect, support, and intimacy (Wynne, 1986).

Men and women often differ in what comprises a satisfying relationship and what is problematic and requires change. Typically it is the wife who requests couples therapy for her distress. Often the husband comes reluctantly, his only complaint being that his wife complains too much. She would like him to change by doing more for her and the relationship; he would like her to change by becoming less needy and demanding. Where he is favorably comparing his family involvement to his own more peripheral father, he may not appreciate his wife's overburdened and undervalued position. If he believes the cultural myth that women control relationships, he may have difficulty responding to her needs, viewing accommodation as yielding to her control.

In a common pursuer-distancer pattern, wives are more likely to become the pursuer as husbands are more likely to become distancers. The more she requests, the more he withholds or withdraws. Punctuating the interaction differently, the more he directs his attention to extrafamilial pursuits, the harder she tries to involve him. Also, husband and wife commonly miss each other when she needs comforting words or a hug at the end of a difficult day but he, socialized to be a problem-solver, assumes that to meet her needs he must solve her problem — or offer advice for managing it better next time. A wife, raised not to ask directly for her own needs to be met, may not express clearly—or even know herself—what she would like her husband to do. Expected to be the emotional caretaker for others, she may be uncomfortable asking her husband to give to her. Raised to intuit others' needs and to meet them even before they are articulated, she may expect that he should be able to know what she needs, or feel that, if she has to ask, it won't be the same. Men who have not been so trained may seem impervious to the needs of their wives, despite genuine caring.

The traditional division of labor and separate domains create a marriage with few areas of shared emotional experience (Weiss, 1985). In his study of men and the family, Weiss found that work challenges and constant performance evaluations generated powerful emotions in men, especially those related to self-appraisal of success or failure, as well as fear of demonstrating uncertainty or weakness. Weiss posited that, to function effectively, to advance, and to retain the respect and confidence of others, men have learned to control emotions and to hide insecurity or anxiety. This tends to carry over into the marriage, blocking communication of emotions with partners (see Bepko, Chapter 20).

One exception Weiss found was the expression of anger in response to frustration. Men acknowledged that at times they lost control, exploding in angry outburst. The socialization of men to control all emotional expression but anger has its most serious consequences in cases of wife abuse. Systemic therapies need to understand more fully the societal context that contributes to patterns of abuse (Bograd, 1984). Taking responsibility for one's own expression and control of emotions is crucial. Each partner needs to be assertive and responsible for his and her own feelings. Women have had the burden of being the emotional caretaker for men, expected to protect them from uncomfortable or dangerous feelings and behavior, while men have been out of touch with their own feelings and needs. Helping men to express the full range of emotions enriches relationship possibilities (Feldman, 1982) and enables men to share in socioemotional tasks that have been borne by women, such as the expression of grief and comforting of others in loss and adversity (Walsh & McGoldrick, 1988).

Problem-solving

The operation of gender-based assumptions and differences in problem-solving processes is largely unrecognized by clinicians (Jacobson, 1983). First, accepting the culturally shared belief that men are the "instrumental problem-solvers" fails to appreciate the complex responsibilities of coordination and problem-solving carried out daily by wives in homemaking and family caregiving. The household domain and work therein must be accorded greater legitimacy, and women's competencies in problem-solving need to be recognized.

Covert relationship rules underlie striking gender differences in the process of decision-making. Most marital and family therapists focus on problem-solving without recognizing that husbands and wives participate differently in the process based on gendered relationship rules and models of negotiation. Men and women enter negotiation with different basic premises. Men are socialized to argue their positions as forcefully and convincingly as they can, with the aim of meeting their needs as fully as possible. Since women are raised to put the needs of others before their own, they tend to defer and accommodate. It can be helpful in therapy to frame this dilemma in terms of different rules for negotiation. The male rule for good negotiation is to make the strongest case and push for one's own position. For women, rules for good negotiation start with consideration of the other's position and compromise to take the other's needs into account. As one wife responded to this intervention: "Since I never play by his rules and he never plays by my rules, things always end up his way." This pattern may be stable and unnoticed, since it is complementary in the sense of a reciprocal fit. However, over time the continual deferral and lack of reciprocity skew the balance of power and privilege to the disadvantage of wives and can result in feelings of powerlessness and selflessness (Lerner, 1985).

"A Matter of Deference"

Anna and Bob requested brief couples therapy when she was eight months pregnant with their first child. They were both in the same profession, with the same degrees; he was two years older and slightly ahead on his career path. From the start of their relationship they had shared the expectation and desire of having a dual-career marriage, each actively engaged in their jobs and, with an intention to raise a family together, each planning to take an active role in parenting. During the pregnancy, they started to worry that having a baby would disrupt their pattern of living in ways that might slide into a traditional marriage. Anna, like many women, was not permitted by her employer to cut back from full-time to part-time employment, so she quit her job during the pregnancy, uncertain what job she could find on a part-time basis after the baby came and certain only that she wanted to work part-time while her children were young. Bob commented: "She'll probably take off two years — uh, I mean two *months* — before she goes back to work." He laughed, noting his slip, saying there probably was a part of him that would like Anna, like his mother, to be at home with their child, having dinner ready for him at the end of his workday.

Two years later the couple returned for therapy, Anna still at home with their child. Even though this couple had entered the marriage with a different quid pro quo, the contract had shifted, without either of them recognizing it. She called to request therapy for herself to adjust to a move to another state because of a job opportunity for her husband. They both agreed that she needed individual therapy to help her with her adjustment problem. They were asked to come in together initially. Anna burst into tears: "Somehow I always seem to defer to him. And this decision is too important. I just feel cheated; I want my needs to matter, too."

These bright, capable, and well-meaning individuals were attempting to construct a marriage that was radically different from those of their parents and grandparents. Their marriage was at risk for failure as the gulf between them widened and the lack of fit increased. They had slid, unintentionally, into a pattern that neither had bargained for, and she now saw leaving the marriage as the only alternative to "adjustment." Their dilemma is a familiar one for the current cohort of young married couples who have, as Anna put it, "one foot in the fifties and one in the eighties."

She has made one clear choice: to be home at least part-time while her child is young. Yet she began to resent her husband's advancement while she was taking time out. She was conflicted about her choice, judging herself deficient by both traditional male and female standards, since she was not fully engaged in either domain and had to compromise each for the other. She believed that she was underfunctioning on both counts because she compared herself to her husband, committed (as she had been) to a full-time career, while also comparing herself unfavorably to her mother, who made a full-time commitment to homemaking and parenting. In terms of professional development, she lagged further behind each year and expected to fall even further behind with the plans to have a second child.

It's interesting that he noted that he would never make the choice to stay at home and accept a part-time job because, he acknowledged, he was probably more selfish in pursuing his career. He admitted that, since his identity and worth were measured in terms of job success, he would always feel like a failure if he didn't succeed. Now that he is assuming the traditional role as breadwinner and because the decision has been made for his own career advancement, he feels an increasingly burdensome sense of financial responsibility and pressure for performance and success.

A circular feedback loop operates in such relationships: The biological imperatives in pregnancy and nursing and the significance our culture places on mother-infant bonding lead women to forgo other commitments in order to center on childcare. Then, because she is home more than her spouse, it follows that she assumes more of the homemaking and family coordination responsibilities, as the husband assumes the larger proportion of financial responsibilities and the demands of a full job schedule. The more time she spends at home, the more natural it seems to both that she be the one to pick up all chores. As he advances professionally, her career development is put on hold; as his financial contribution lends more primacy and legitimacy to his job demands, the less he is expected to contribute to daily family functioning. The more central she becomes for family functioning through taking care of others' needs, the less energy and focus she has for her own career. When he says he is more selfish, it is true that he, typical of men in our culture, has been raised to be self-centered and to define and pursue his own interests and ambitions. Since our culture doesn't accord the same value to family life as to job performance and personal achievement, her relationship needs and preferences are subordinated to his work-based priorities (Gilligan, 1982).

In most contemporary marriages, the couple never makes an explicit bargain that she is expected to defer to him (the traditional marriage vow of "love, honor, and obey" has been altered), but many out-of-awareness relationship rules contribute to that pattern.

It is useful to examine the decision-making process in arriving at the decision to move. The husband stated: "I told Anna, 'I just got a terrific job offer in California. What do you think about it?'" Yet she also participated in the process, deferring to him and only afterwards feeling depressed, resentful, and "cheated." I met with her individually and encouraged her to consider the possibility of not moving, legitimizing her feelings and needs. It was important to shift her position from passive, powerless victim to a woman with a voice to contribute and priorities to be weighed in major decisions. Instead of feeling that it was his decision imposed on her, she had to participate actively in the decision-making process and share power in determining the outcome.

The issue of legitimacy requires a fundamental rebalancing of priorities between family and work systems. If both partners are to participate actively in marriage and childrearing, family and personal needs must be valued as much as job requisites, so that family and work are regarded as equally legitimate domains.

A CO-EVOLUTIONARY, LIFE CYCLE PERSPECTIVE

Couples in therapy should be encouraged to examine their marital quid pro quo and to consider how gendered beliefs and premises both shape and constrain their patterns of interaction, largely out of their awareness. The therapeutic goal is to recontract new relationship rules for a more functional balance in the partners' lives.

To achieve this, we need a co-evolutionary life cycle view of marriage in order to recast the static mold of marriage from castle or prison to a flexible form that can be shaped and reshaped by both partners over time to fit changing needs, priorities, and constraints. Each successive phase in the relationship poses normative (i.e., expectable, typical) challenges and tasks (Carter & McGoldrick, 1988; McGoldrick, Chapter 11). At each transition the marital quid pro quo needs to be reconsidered and renegotiated. In courtship, couples need to be more forward-looking when planning marriage. Few couples seek premarital counseling, reluctant in the phase of romantic togetherness to broach the troublesome issues that are likely to arise in the future course of their relationship (McGoldrick, 1988). Marital therapy may not be sought until problems have become chronic and severe, or when one partner is already on the verge of divorce. At any phase in the couple's life cycle, clinicians can help spouses to become more forward-looking, thinking and planning ahead and clarifying expectations for self and partner in the relationship.

The expectation that marriage vows will be kept "till death do us part" is much harder to achieve simply by virtue of the fact that we live much longer than people in the past. It has been said that adults today need at least three marriages: for youth, one based on romance and passion; for childrearing, one based on shared responsibility; and later in life, one strong in companionship and mutual caretaking. Rather than requiring new partners, couples need to construct different relationship bargains to fit changing life cycle needs, since the qualities valued for a satisfying relationship are likely to vary over the course of adulthood.

The life cycle perspective is also useful to punctuate current dilemmas in terms of transitional stresses and to view the transition as an opportunity for change. Often couples therapy can get bogged down in a backward review of cumulative dissatisfactions over the years; this leaves couples—and therapists—pessimistic about change. It can be helpful to frame the problem in terms of a dysfunctional relationship bargain that needs to be renegotiated. It may be that a bargain made in earlier phases of a relationship fit the partners' needs or expectations at that time but is no longer workable. Their quid pro quo needs to be updated to reflect changing needs and circumstances.

Rituals (Imber-Black, 1988 and Chapter 22) are important in marking transitions in a couple's relationship. Our culture lacks such rituals for entry into new phases in the couple's life cycle. The anniversary, our sole celebration, is backward-looking, filled with reminiscence of the wedding, with celebrants marking the time the marriage has lasted. Clinicians can help couples to construct new rituals, meaningful to them, that symbolize the recontracting of each new marital quid pro quo.

Cultural stereotypes regarding proper roles interfere with constructing new couple paradigms. At the same time, clinicians need to appreciate the diversity in couples' preferences and to be careful not to impose their own beliefs and standards for men and women in marriage. Couples worry a good deal about whether their relationship is "normal"; also, when they consider the marriages of their friends, they don't find many that they would consider desirable. I routinely ask couples their views about "normal" couple relationships—what they think is typical and what they imagine would be ideal for couples in their life circumstances, cultural orientation, and life stage. What are their paradigms? Asking partners what their relationship rules are and how they were decided upon can be useful in making covert assumptions and agreements explicit and in generating dialogue about other possibilities.

In exploring how patterns developed over time and have been mutually shaped and reinforced by the couple, it may be useful to track the evolution of the relationship and the transitions at critical life transitions. How did their view of their parents' model of marriage impact on the contract they envisioned for their own marriage? Couples may decide that they want to do it differently, but lack a blueprint and skills for a new model. Therapy is insufficient if it simply reduces conflict without considering how gender-based relationship rules reinforce dysfunctional interaction patterns. Couples need assistance in constructing guidelines and building new interactional skills. Therapy can normalize and contextualize distress, offer information from research on adaptational challenges and strategies of other couples in similar problem situations and relationship phases, and promote more functional and satisfying relationship options.

Since a new family paradigm emerges out of a major transition, as a family reorganizes in response to life challenges (Reiss, 1981), clinicians can help couples to renegotiate their quid pro quo at each transition to a new phase in the family life cycle and in relation to emerging work, childrearing, and personal priorities. This requires recontracting their relationship according to the preferences, competencies, resources, and constraints of each partner; it may also require building new competencies. I would urge the removal of the labels of "feminine" and "masculine" that have categorized certain aspects of functioning in traditional marriages. To argue that a man should become "more feminine" imposes a label and identification that is prima facie discrepant with his actual gender; it implies that he should be "less masculine," less oneself and more other. It is more useful to work toward disengaging gender from relationship rules and the definition of roles of wife and husband, mother and father. The marital quid pro quo can be constructed—and reshaped—to meet the challenges and tasks that must be accomplished, as marital partners and co-parents, while balancing the individual needs and worth of husband and wife.

REFERENCES

Baruch, G. K., Biener, L., & Barnett, R. C. (1987). Women and gender in research on work and family stress. *American Psychologist, 42*, 130–36.

Bernard, J. (1982). *The future of marriage.* New Haven, CT: Yale University Press.

Beavers, W. R. (1986). *Successful marriage.* New York: Norton.

Blumstein, P., & Schwartz, P. (1983). *American couples: Money, work, sex.* New York: William Morrow.

Bograd, M. (1984). Family systems approaches to wife battering: A feminist critique. *American Journal of Orthopsychiatry, 54*, 558–68.

Carter, B., & McGoldrick, M. (1988). *The changing family life cycle.* 2nd ed. New York: Gardner.

Feldman, L. (1982). Sex roles and family dynamics. In F. Walsh, (Ed.). *Normal family processes.* New York: Guilford Press.

Foster, S. W., & Gurman, A. S. (1984). Social change and couples therapy: A troubled marriage. In C. Nadelson & D. Palonsky (Eds.), *Contemporary marriage.* New York: Guilford Press.

Friedan, B. (1981). *The second stage.* New York: Summit Books.

Gilligan, C. (1982). *In a different voice.* Cambridge, MA: Harvard University Press.

Hafner, J. (1986). *Marriage and mental illness: A sex roles perspective.* New York: Guilford Press.

Imber-Black, E. (1988). Idiosyncratic life cycle transitions and therapeutic rituals. In B. Carter & M. McGoldrick (Eds.). *The changing family life cycle.* 2nd ed., New York: Gardner Press.

Jacobson, N. (1983). Beyond empiricism: The politics of marital therapy. *American Journal of Family Therapy, 11*, 11–24.

Jackson, D. D. (1977a). The study of the family. In P. Watzlawick & J. Weakland (Eds.), *The interactional view.* New York: Norton.

Jackson, D. D. (1977b). Family rules: Marital quid pro quo. In P. Watzlawick & J. Weakland (Eds.), *The interactional view.* New York: Norton.

Lerner, H. (1985). *The dance of anger.* New York: Harper & Row.

McGoldrick, M. (1988). The joining of families through marriage: The new couple. In B. Carter & M. McGoldrick (Eds.). *The changing family life cycle.* New York: Gardner Press.

McGoldrick, M., & Carter, B. (1988). Forming a remarried family. In B. Carter & M. McGoldrick (Eds.). *The changing family life cycle.* New York: Gardner Press.

Margolin, G., Fernandez, R., Talovic, S., & Onorato, R. (1983). Sex role considerations and behavioral marital therapy: Equal does not mean identical. *Journal of Marital and Family Therapy, 9*, 131–45.

Olson, D. H. (in press). The circumplex Model. Special Issue, *Journal of Psychotherapy and the Family, 4.*

Piotrkowski, C. S., & Repetti, R. L. (1984). Dual-earner families. *Marriage and Family Review, 7*, 3–4.

Pleck, J. (1985). *Working husbands/Working wives.* Beverly Hills: Sage.

Reiss, D. (1981). *The family's construction of reality.* Cambridge, MA: Harvard University Press.

Scheinkman, M. (1988). Graduate student marriages: An organizational/interactional view. *Family Process, 27.*

Walsh, F. (1982). Conceptualizations of normal family functioning. In F. Walsh, (Ed.). *Normal family processes.* New York: Guilford Press.

Walsh, F. (1983). Normal family ideologies: Myths and realities. In C. Falicov (Ed.), *Cultural dimensions in family therapy.* Rockville, MD: Aspen Publications.

Walsh, F. (In press). *Treating severely dysfunctional families.* New York: Guilford Press.

Walsh, F., & McGoldrick, M. (1988). Loss and the life cycle. In C. Falicov (Ed.). *Continuity and change.* New York: Guilford Press.

Weiss, R. S. (1985). Men and the family. *Family Process, 24*, 49–58.

Weitzman, L. (1981). *The marriage contract.* New York: The Free Press.

Wynne, L. C. (1986). The quest for intimacy. *Journal of Marital & Family Therapy, 12*, 383–94.

Zipes, J. (1986). *Don't bet on the prince.* New York: Methuen.

15
Psychotherapy with Lesbian Couples: Individual Issues, Female Socialization, and the Social Context

SALLYANN ROTH

THE MOST IMPORTANT characteristics distinguishing lesbian couples as a clinical population arise from these few but significant attributes: (a) both members of a lesbian couple are women; (b) the female couple is not a socially sanctioned family unit; and (c) full commitment by the members to their couple requires the acceptance of a stigmatizable identity. Although these attributes may seem obvious, they often are neglected, and they have profound implications for the couple and for the therapy. This chapter addresses these issues in the belief that effective clinical intervention with troubled lesbian couples requires full attention to the individual psychology of each partner, the cultural patterning of female development, and the tenuous social position of the committed female pair.*

The author wishes to acknowledge that discussion with four colleagues—Richard Chasin, M.D., Ann Fleck Henderson, M.S.W., Jo-Ann Krestan, M.A., C.A.C., and Bianca Cody Murphy, Ed.D.—was particularly helpful in the formulation of many of the ideas presented in this chapter.

An earlier version of this material was presented at the Mental Health Service, University Health Services, Harvard University, on December 17, 1981. This chapter is a revision of an article by the same title that was published in the *Journal of Marital and Family Therapy*, 1985, *11*, 3, 273–286.

*These points have, of course, counterparts of similarity and difference in therapy of male couples, but consideration of these issues as they apply to such couples is outside the scope of this discussion.

The six major issues most often presented by lesbian couples at the beginning of treatment are: (a) problems of distance regulation and boundary maintenance; (b) problems of sexual expression; (c) problems related to unequal access to resources; (d) problems arising from stage differences in coming out and in the development and management of each partner's lesbian identity; (e) problems related to choosing to have children and/or co-parenting them; and (f) problems about ending the relationship, even when one or both have decided to do so. Of these issues, all but the fourth are also often presented in early work with heterosexual couples. Although the rest are common to all sorts of couples, the way in which they are manifest in lesbian couples has a systematic regularity which seems related to the exclusively female composition of these couples.

The clinical experience reflected in this chapter — work with over 65 lesbian couples and families during the last eight years — is limited by the nature of my clinical setting, a private practice with a family institute base, in a university dominated area with large and organized women's and lesbian communities. Highly educated white lesbians, lesbian couples rearing children, and women too young to have known what it was like to come out before the women's movement and gay liberation are probably overrepresented, compared to their numbers in the national population. Therefore, it is difficult to say to what degree my specific conclusions are generalizable. My aim has been less to provide specific conclusions than to offer a model for looking at coupling issues through a lens that takes in multiple embedded contexts and their reverberating interrelationships.

DISTANCE REGULATION AND BOUNDARY MAINTENANCE

One of the most common problems for couples is difficulty achieving a range of behaviors that allows enough closeness as well as enough distance to satisfy the needs of each individual to feel both connected and separate (Feldman, 1979; Karpel, 1976). The anxiety and behavior activated by the experience of too much closeness and their counterparts, the anxiety and behavior activated by the experience of too much distance, form the presenting complaint of most lesbian couples requesting treatment (Krestan & Bepko, 1980).

Although developmental psychology historically has attended principally to male development, recent writers have addressed gender differences in development and psychological style (Chodorow, 1978; Gilligan, 1982; Henderson, 1984; Miller, 1976), elaborating a previously unacknowledged, uniquely female voice and vision. The female world view described in these newer studies includes an orientation to achievement and relationship from which one could predict that the negotiation of contact and separateness would be problematic in female couples. In our society, in which men and women are groomed for gender-specific social roles, women have learned (a) to define themselves in relation to others (Chodorow, 1978); (b) to define morality in terms of responsibility and care (Gilligan, 1982); (c) to develop exceptional sensitivity in noticing the needs of others and to demonstrate empathy even by experiencing the needs of others as their own (Chodorow, 1978); and (d) to suppress aggressive and competitive desires in order to avoid hurting others and to prevent the feared result of such self-expression, social isolation (Miller, 1976).

With this legacy of learning about how to be in relationships, it is not surprising that lesbian couples in treatment report experiences of extraordinary closeness, described alternately as exhilarating and terrifying, as containing the possibility of such intimacy that the experience of self as separate is momentarily inconceivable, so that the possibility of never again being separate seems a realistic fear. Nor is it surprising that many lesbian couples in a clinical population report long periods of extreme and unbreachable distance, in part a response to a fear of loss of self, or fusion (Krestan & Bepko, 1980).

One member of a lesbian couple in treatment presented her version of the couple's problem this way: "We go from Velcro—which is wonderful—to no contact at all, and then it seems like too much to go back. There is no middle place. We don't know how to do that." This difficulty in moving with ease—indeed, in moving at all—from deep connectedness to solid separateness and back again is a difficulty affected in its magnitude and form by the particular social surround of a given lesbian couple, as well as by the nature of female socialization.

Krestan and Bepko (1980) have detailed the complex interaction between the position of lesbian couples in the heterosexual community and the boundary-regulating behavior within individual couples. These authors note, as does Toder (1979), that when the lesbian couple's attempts to define their bond meet with no response or one that is invalidating, the partners may rigidify their couple boundary to ensure couple integrity, thereby developing an increasingly closed couple system.

Within the confines of any closed couple system, individual boundaries are easily blurred. Typical distancing strategies called into play in response to the experienced dangers of fusion and overcloseness include (a) distancing by one partner or, in alternating sequence, by each; (b) open conflict (sometimes including physical violence); (c) triangling in of a third element (e.g., a child, a romantic involvement with another person or increased involvement with a job); and (d) repeating cycles of fusion and seeming unrelatedness (Feldman, 1979; Karpel, 1976; Krestan & Bepko, 1980). Although any of these four responses to overcloseness, exaggerated in a closed couple system, may precipitate entry into therapy by couples of any composition, it is helpful if the therapist is aware that an even greater exaggeration may occur where the closed couple system is lesbian. Distance regulation problems, inevitable for any couple, are amplified for the female couple by the bond-invalidating activities of the heterosexual world in conjunction with certain aspects of female development: the ability to lose the self in the other, the sense of responsibility for the affective well-being of intimates, and the reluctance to openly declare difference if such difference may create difficulties.

Many lesbian couples in therapy show mutual understanding and concern, each member listening carefully to the other and asking challenging but kind questions. Sometimes it is difficult to recognize that they are fighting until it becomes evident that continuing discussion seldom achieves resolution and neither experiences the other as close. Frequently members of lesbian couples in a clinical population neither openly state differences nor make strong statements about what each partner needs for herself.

Indeed, individual and social forces combine to push members of the couple toward the denial of their separateness. Some therapists (Hall, 1978, 1984; Krestan & Bepko, 1980) report working in direct ways to encourage lesbians in couples therapy to make self-declaring and individuated statements. Krestan and Bepko (1980) emphasize the usefulness of sharing information about concepts such as boundaries, triangling, and fusion. They suggest that these concepts may provide the couple with new ways of thinking about their relationship that can point the way toward greater individual autonomy within the couple. Roth (1984) suggests that reframing caretaking but undifferentiated behavior as a lack of respect each partner has for the other's ability to protect and care for herself alters each partner's vision of her own caretaking behavior; any continuation of caretaking by self-denial becomes seen as diminishing both partners and as a demonstration of lack of care.

The position of the lesbian couple in relation to the lesbian community also affects boundary-maintaining behavior within the couple. Partners who are isolated from the lesbian community frequently have a more difficult time negotiating distance between themselves than those who are well connected with a community of lesbian friends. The provision of recognition, acceptance, and respect for the couple unit by members of the lesbian community may make it less necessary for the couple to "pull in" and form a tight circle of two for mutual protection.

Examining the influence of female development on coupling issues of lesbians in areas of distance regulation and boundary maintenance is not a trivial exercise. In the past it was common for clinicians to see the behaviors associated with these difficulties in lesbian dyads as indicative of serious pathology. Although some members of some lesbian couples may suffer developmental arrest, there is no justification for assuming that coupling difficulties of the sort described here are necessarily indicators of such problems.

Some of the ways in which the boundaries around lesbian couples are affected by the heterosexual surround are unique to each couple; others are events—and sometimes nonevents—that affect all lesbian couples. The lesbian couple has no marker event to define the change in status from dating or cohabiting couple to "married" couple. As much as it recently has been criticized, the heterosexual wedding ritual provides a legitimization of boundaries, declares public expectation of the continuation of the dyadic unit into the future, and assists young adults in separating and differentiating from their families of origin. The addition of children to the marital unit usually furthers the same processes. There is community celebration around such events. Such ceremonies and celebrations contrast markedly with the usual societal invalidation of the lesbian couple. Invalidating activities range from acting as if the relationship did not exist, rendering it invisible, to acting as if it exists but disqualifying it as "not genuine," "a stage," or as evidence of pathological disturbance. The committed lesbian couple may even be invalidated within the lesbian community, where there are some women who see such commitment as imitative of negative aspects of heterosexual culture and who actively promote non-monogamous forms of coupling.

Direct invasion of the lesbian couple boundary by the heterosexual surround takes such forms as not including the partner as a relative at holidays and other major family-of-origin events, giving the partners separate rooms during visits to families of origin, depriving one partner of access to the other and/or of decision-making power in time of serious illness, and depriving the partners of legal protection in mutual ownership of property and in survivorship unless they take special legal actions.

An extreme form of boundary invasion exists in those instances where a couple may be unable to live together or even to see each other in the presence of one member's children because of the threat that exposure of a mother's lesbianism may result in her losing custody of the children or visitation rights.

These bond-invalidating activities, along with the difficulties they compound, complicate, and sometimes create, frequently motivate couples to seek therapy early in the development of their relationship, when they actually need therapy less than they need witness and validation of their coming together. In these situations, the therapist may discover her role to be primarily that of witness and validator, a social role performed by ministers, rabbis, and others in the heterosexual world. At later points in the development of the couple relationship, therapy more often focuses on the couple's complex arrangements for negotiating separateness and closeness as they have evolved between its members within the context of heterosexual society.

Problems of Sexual Expression in Lesbian Couples

Lesbians, being women, "have their share of sexual problems . . . similar to the general [female] population" (Loewenstein, 1980, p. 35), a fact sometimes denied within the lesbian community where the myth exists that lesbians, being women, know how to please each other (Toder, 1978). "Lesbians may have primary or more often secondary dysfunction, when relationship problems are expressed in the sexual realm" (Loewenstein, 1980, p. 35). Some lesbians report fears of being touched, sexual inhibitions (discomfort with particular sexual acts, often oral sex) and rigid lovemaking patterns. In many instances these concerns are not particularly associated with lesbianism. In other instances they may be associated with lingering conflicts about lesbian identity (Loewenstein, 1980). Rigid lovemaking patterns and discomfort with particular sexual acts as tied to a lesbian partner choice are especially prevalent among older lesbians who came out prior to the women's movement, and among women who have been isolated from the emerging women's culture and community and who may have difficulty shifting from early stereotyped ideas of "how a lesbian is supposed to behave." In these groups, some members hold beliefs and expectations tied to "butch" and "femme" role models, stereotypes which, in settings where they are socially outmoded, may still serve a current defensive role.

Many self-help and professionally led lesbian groups have been established, focusing on roles and sexuality, exposure to lesbian literature, and contact with the lesbian community. The goals of such groups include, but are not limited to, expanding role possibilities and addressing the internalized homophobia which may be operating to reduce sexual freedom.

Since numerous other writers address the sexual issues of women in general, and since there are two sexual problems which appear regularly in couples treatment with lesbians in my urban clinical context, this discussion will be limited to those two most commonly named problems: infrequency of genital sexual contact, and heterosexual fantasies and behavior.

Infrequency of Genital Sexual Contact

Although lesbian couples generally report substantial satisfaction with the quality of their sex life (Bell & Weinberg, 1978; Blumstein & Schwartz, 1983; Tanner, 1978; Toder, 1978), they complain about infrequency. Blumstein and Schwartz (1983) report in their comparative study of lesbian couples, gay male couples, heterosexual cohabitors, and heterosexual married couples that lesbians report the lowest frequency of genital sexual contact across all stages of couples' life histories. Their data also indicate that frequency of sexual contact for lesbian couples drops off more markedly after the second year of the relationship than it does with the other three kinds of couples studied. Infrequency of and unequal desire for genital sex are the primary sexual complaints of lesbian couples even in nonclinical populations (Blumstein & Schwartz, 1983; Tanner, 1978; Toder, 1978). Hall (1984) proposes that infrequency of genital sex is a response to distance-regulation problems. She explains the decrease in sexual contact over time by saying that, as the relationship becomes more intimate and the lovers spend more time together, or live together, the increased tightness of the female pair bond requires greater distance. An expanded view of this sexual infrequency, however, addresses additional aspects of female socialization and the influence of the social surround on sexual expression.

Women in our culture learn to inhibit and repress their sexuality; they learn to express it in terms of "other's" needs and wishes, being less attuned than men to the sexual messages of their own bodies (Henderson, 1984; Rubin, 1976), less comfortable with being sexually assertive, and less comfortable in initiating sex (Nichols, 1987). Predictably, when two people are paired who share societal injunctions against sexual self-assertion, sexual self-knowledge, and recognition of their own sexual desire, sexual encounters may be reduced until they discover mutually acceptable redefinitions of self and couple that allow substantial sex-role rule breaking.

Blumstein and Schwartz (1983, p. 303) note that in heterosexual couples where women are "assigned" the sexual initiative and men are sexually "coy, then both frequency and satisfaction suffer." Lesbians, especially those who are younger or who came out after the women's movement, are in a particular bind, since they usually place a high value on equality: neither partner can readily take on the role of the "initiator" or "aggressor" on any regular basis. Additionally, should the couple manage to make an agreement that one would initiate more frequently, this would create yet another problem. In any couple where there is a more frequent initiator, that person is sometimes turned down. Heterosexual men are used to this; they accept as truth that women have less frequent interest in sex than they do and generally perceive a "no" as an indication of this difference between them. Women, on the other hand, are far more likely to understand a negative response to a sexual approach as a rejection of them, not of the sexual act (Blumstein & Schwartz, 1983), and to experience the anxiety associated with an emotional cutoff. This, too, is a factor in the diminishing over time of the number of sexual approaches women make to their partners. In addition, the impact of women's need to be in good emotional contact with their partners before engaging in genital sex must not be minimized (Henderson, 1984; Nichols, 1987; Rubin, 1976). Thus, the sexual relationship of female partners is substantially more vulnerable to the personalization of sexual refusal than is the sexual relationship of heterosexual partners.

For many lesbians, lesbian sexual expression is a learned response, and for some it is hard won. Some lesbians today make their partner choice on the basis of emotional preference and assume that they can develop an interest in lesbian sexuality (Henderson, 1979). Others feel immediately physically attracted and responsive to women, but are so imbued with cultural proscriptions against such contact that they have to work to overcome these barriers. The difficulty of learning to be comfortable with lesbian sexuality in a culture that disapproves of such sexual expression has been partly lessened by the publication of several informed and explicit books that serve to desensitize the subject (Loulan, 1984; Sisley & Harris, 1977). Although these books are very informative about lesbian sexuality, their major contribution is to offer positive models, models largely unavailable in the general culture.

The position of the couple within heterosexual society also affects their sexual expression. There is often great discontinuity between traveling in the outside world where any overt show of sexually tinged affection may put a lesbian couple at serious risk, and arriving home, where all levels of contact are fine. The warming-up process may thus be significantly attenuated or interrupted, just as it may sometimes be enhanced, by the social context, depending on the degree of acceptance or safety the couple experiences.

Given the operation of these psychological and sociological forces, it is not surprising that some lesbian couples go without genital sex for considerable lengths of time. The greater the duration of time, the more mutually avoidant of sex the partners become. Requests for therapeutic help with this issue do not usually arise until an impasse has been reached. Some couples broach the topic by requesting normative information about other lesbian couples.

Occasionally the partners do not experience infrequency of sexual contact as a problem, but are concerned that they *should* be worried about it. More often, the partner defined as more desirous experiences the infrequency as a serious problem, one which has been played out so many times that she has withdrawn all approaches.

Plans for treatment are as numerous as couples in therapy and may be tied to any unsettled issue in a couple relationship. Therapists who are called upon to assist lesbian couples in interrupting recurring sequences of sexual apprehension must take into account not only whatever models they have for addressing such sexual dysfunction; they must also be alert for the ways in which the social surround for the couple influences this private aspect of their lives and the ways in which the partners have learned their societally designated roles so well that they are inhibiting the expression of their sexuality.

Although this section has addressed the problem of infrequent genital sex in lesbian couples, it is important to note that lesbians as a group "prize non-genital physical contact — cuddling, touching, hugging — probably more than other couples do. But more important, they are much more likely to consider these activities as ends in themselves, rather than as foreplay leading to genital sex" (Blumstein & Schwartz, 1983, p. 197). While the need and desire for non-genital lovemaking may well be equal among heterosexual and lesbian women, heterosexual women make an adaptation to male sexuality, accepting the snuggling and touching as foreplay, even when they might prefer only non-genital pleasuring (Blumstein & Schwartz, 1983).

Heterosexual Fantasies and Behaviors

Many lesbians are privately distressed by sexual feelings, fantasies, and dreams about men, and they experience their awareness of these interests as threatening to their lesbian identity and membership in the lesbian subculture. There is no more justification to consider these thoughts and feelings, even when acted upon, as demonstration of the lesbian's "basic heterosexuality" than there is to consider the sometime homosexual fantasy of the heterosexual person evidence of "basic homosexuality." Since the lesbian community largely looks with disfavor upon these heterosexual interests and behaviors and with even greater disfavor upon bisexuality, lesbians in the treatment context are often relieved to be able to speak of these interests at all; and they are doubly relieved, though often uncomfortable at first, to speak of them with their lovers.

Toder (1978, p. 111) notes that there is a taboo within the lesbian community against talking about these experiences and that "many lesbians assume that other lesbians never have them and literally panic when they have a sexual fantasy or a dream that includes men." It may be useful to term this reaction *heterophobia* to point out that it has a parallel in the well-known homophobia of heterosexual life and to indicate that in the lesbian community heterosexuality is often stigmatized.

For the heterosexual therapist, the exploration of these issues is a delicate matter, because lesbian women are ever alert for signs that the therapist disapproves of or does not support their lifestyle and object choice, and may suspect the therapist's reason for raising these issues. It may not be possible, in fact, for some lesbians to discuss these issues in such a context. In some cases, if the heterosexual therapist suggests that the clients discuss these matters with a lesbian therapist, the heterosexual therapist's demonstration of openness may render the consultation unnecessary for the clients. Although the sexual orientation of the therapist may make an important difference in dealing with this topic, the therapist's values and attitudes and communication of them to the clients are usually far more significant.

Intolerance of bisexuality or of inconsistent sexual preference is very great in the lesbian community. Thus, those many women who experience themselves as having the potential for significant relationships with women *and* with men often feel lonely and trapped with their feelings. These feelings are frequently named in therapy in times of deepening commitment within the lesbian couple, when the member experiencing them is addressing her own grief over the loss of social acceptance of her partner choice, of heterosexual privilege, of the possibility of having a child who is biologically related to both parents, and sometimes, of sexual relations with men.

STRESS RELATED TO UNEQUAL ACCESS TO RESOURCES

Lesbians who came out after the women's movement began usually strive for the ideal of individual autonomy within an egalitarian relationship. The strain they experience in their strivings is analogous to that of heterosexual partners who are working to develop relationships of autonomy and equality in a context that has few such models. Female couples may actually have an advantage in this enterprise, as women's culture historically has assumed a model of collaboration among women, and the women's community is consistently supportive of such values and efforts. Nevertheless, the same beliefs that place high value on egalitarian relationships also place enormous strain on those relationships in which women earn widely discrepant amounts of money or have other discrepancies in access to such resources as inheritances or child-support payments.

Lesbians sometimes meet in settings where the commonality is sexual orientation, and they frequently connect with partners whose financial and social status is different from their own. Heterosexual society accepts—and even expects—major differences in partners' incomes. In fact, women are generally reared to believe that they will marry men who will either support them or at least have greater earning power and professional status. In a heterosexual couple, when the woman has more money than the man, the same discrepancy between expectation and reality confronts her as confronts the lesbian who has more money than her lover. Disappointment about unmet dependency expectations is seldom verbalized as a problem in lesbian couples where this discrepancy occurs. The more frequently named difficulty is the violation for both women of the philosophical and political ideal of equality. In fact, Blumstein and Schwartz (1983) report that heterosexual and male couples described differences around allocation of financial resources as power struggles, whereas lesbians consistently described similar differences as the avoidance of dependency and the establishment of equality. The ideal of equality, endorsed by the lesbian community, offers the couple exemption from the trade-off made by traditional heterosexual women of individual autonomy for financial dependence and status sharing.

Lesbian couples often develop extraordinarily creative financial arrangements to avoid power imbalances in decision-making and planning, with the goal of maintaining a sense of interdependence without a loss of independence. It is common for partners to keep money separate for the early years of the relationship and to keep detailed accounts of exactly who has spent how much for what, with attempts made to keep contributions for living expenses substantially equal. Often large "debts" are built up which may never be paid but which allow the illusion or promise of equal contribution.

Sometimes the partner who "owes" feels burdened by the debt. She believes that it is fair to owe it and, in fact, wants and intends to pay it in order to keep things "equal," but the continuing greater financial contribution of the higher-income partner to their lives together becomes increasingly burdensome to the lower-income partner as she falls deeper into "debt." Thus, a lower-income partner may become upset should her higher-income partner purchase something defined as a luxury for them both, such as a vacation, new appliance, or restaurant dinner, while the higher-income earner may resent not having the freedom to use her full earning power to enhance their lives.

Although there are variations, the practice of keeping money separate and contributions evenly balanced, at least on paper, is usually the pattern of the early years. One variation which sometimes occurs as a second phase of arranging finances is that of keeping contributions to joint expenses proportional to the income of each partner. Toder (1978) sees the separation of finances as destructive to lesbian couples and suggests that an earlier mingling of resources might encourage partners to work harder at their relationship during difficult times. Blumstein & Schwartz (1983) report that merging of money takes place gradually and is related to the process of deepening commitment, the belief that the relationship will last and the belief that it can survive the increased potential for conflict once money and property are pooled.

Lesbian couple relationships, like those of other couples, are tentative in their beginning stages. Because no ritual clearly marks the change for lesbian couples from living together or dating to being "married," from experimenting with a possibility to making a commitment, there is no point designated by social tradition at which the mingling of resources begins or is expected to begin. Thus, the financial arrangements can sometimes serve as an indicator of a developmental stage of the relationship. Additionally, in a society in which relationship models of equality are rare and evolving, it may take many interactions of such concrete nature as specific account balancing before the partners can believe themselves sufficiently equal in other respects that their sense of equality does not stand or fall with their financial arrangements.

In the lesbian community, as elsewhere, the subject of money is seldom discussed outside the individual family unit. Consequently, information about arrangements for sharing unequal resources within a relationship of equality is seldom freely exchanged, leaving couples isolated in their attempts to meet this challenge. They may also lack information about ways to manage resources that permit both financial pooling and legal protection. Here, legal and financial consultants are essential, and the therapist cannot take their place (English, Blair, Gertner, & Rivera, 1978).

All of the ramifications of pooling resources are rarely clear at the outset. One woman added her partner's name to the deed to the house they had shared for eight years, without realizing that subsequent mortgage statements would be addressed to both of them. She was unprepared for the anxiety she experienced from the realization that information she considered private and potentially damaging to her was now possessed by bank and postal employees and was no longer under her control. Lesbians must face and somehow resolve the dilemma that combining financial sharing with legal protection involves some loss of control of personal information and some degree of exposure, with all of its attendant risks, in the outside world.

Stage Differences in Coming Out and Development of Individual Lesbian Identity

Many women engage in emotional and sexual relationships with other women, sometimes for long periods of time, without construing their involvements to mean that they are lesbian (Ponse, 1978). Thus, it is possible that a woman who is in a couple relationship with another woman may not have identified herself as a lesbian or may not have embraced fully a lesbian identity with all of its extensive ramifications and profound implications for both members and their couple.

When members of a female couple who have not defined themselves as lesbian are deepening their commitment to one another, identity issues that have been kept at a distance will enter the heart of the relationship. In couples in which the members are moving on different time schedules through the stages of accepting a lesbian identity and coming out, the slower movement of one member may be experienced by the other as threatening to the relationship (Roth & Murphy, 1986). The faster movement of one partner may be experienced by the other as threatening to her own sense of self and her safety from stigma and ostracism. It is common for the behavioral manifestations of these stage differences to be interpreted within the couple as acts of alienation, assault, or abandonment. For these reasons, female couples commonly seek therapy in periods of forward movement, when they are mutually deepening their relationship and identity issues are stirred up, or when one partner's demonstration of greater comfort with her lesbian identity is frightening to the other.

Coming out as a lesbian is not a single event but a process. Lehman (1978) describes five levels of coming out: to self, to another woman through sexual activity, to family and friends, to the larger community, and to society at large through political action. For the therapist's purposes, these "levels" might be more usefully seen as social fields or contexts. Although Lehman's levels are logically ordered, from smaller to larger contexts, the individual lesbian may not come out in all these contexts or in this specific sequence. Additionally, the process may be differently weighted and organized for women whose relationship history includes primary heterosexual relationships, for those women who have children from prior relationships, and for those who come to relationships with women having had little significant emotional contact with male partners.

One woman had left a marriage of 15 years and had lived with another woman in a couple relationship for five years before stating to herself, and then to her partner, that she was a lesbian. This couple began therapy at the point when the last of the children was leaving home. In retrospect, one partner described her slow acceptance of a lesbian identity as related to the meanings it might have to her children, and to her reluctance to cause them greater pain than the divorce had caused them already: "I had advocated for myself enough to be living with the person I wanted to live with, but I couldn't do any more. I didn't think my husband would try to take the children from me. I thought they might just leave." Even though these women had lived together at that point for seven years, issues concerning acceptance of lesbian identity were primary aspects of the therapy.

Asynchrony between the partners in coming out in the more intimate contexts of self, of the dyadic relationship, and of families or origin and/or friends is experienced differently within the couple than asynchrony in coming out in the broader contexts of society and the political realm. Where one woman has been slower to declare herself a lesbian or to let family, friends, and coworkers know about her relationship, her faster-moving partner may personalize this slower schedule as a rejection of herself or as a devaluation of their relationship. Even when the faster-moving partner is sympathetic to extenuating circumstances that explain her partner's reluctance, such as high risk of job loss, family-of-origin estrangement, or loss of children through rejection or court action, the requirement of secrecy is often experienced by her as her lover's lack of commitment to their relationship. If the difference in degrees of comfort with acceptance of lesbian identity and with revealing the nature of the relationship in these intimate contexts continues over time, patterns associated with this difference become part of the ongoing life and myth of the couple relationship, and great upheavals can be expected within the couple system when these patterns shift.

One woman who had objected for years to her lover's reluctance to reveal the nature of their relationship to her parents said, "I had a hard time recognizing her after she came out to them. That had always been the one thing I didn't love about her, and then I didn't have any way to think that she was a crumb. It took months to adjust and find something else I could think she was a crumb about. But the bigger result for me is that I feel more committed to the relationship, safer, and I don't need as much distance anymore." Her lover said, "I was finally saying to my parents, 'My life isn't with you anymore. This relationship is where my life is and will be.' They haven't changed any. They still ignore our relationship. But I feel different inside it . . . and differently about myself."

When asynchrony in coming out is central to the present struggle, the initial therapeutic task often is to challenge this commonly occurring and paralyzing set of constructs: "If she doesn't come out to X, then she's not committed to me," and "If she needs me to come out to X, then she can't really love me."

Exploration with couples experiencing this dilemma generally reveals the previously undeclared contributing fantasy that they can be members of multiple conflicting relationships without experiencing major losses. In actuality, all of the three possible moves for the lesbian involve loss. She can give up her relationship, accept and declare her lesbian identity with all the loss that follows from that action, or she can remain socially closeted, giving up the possibility of being more fully known by important others in her social world. If she decides to stay in the relationship and to identify herself as lesbian in contexts broader than that of her couple, she achieves an identity which is continuous across all of the contexts of her life, and relief from the burden of "passing" and the incessant decisions about where, how, and to whom it is safe to self-reveal. The cost may be high, endangering both wishful fantasies and concrete realities, but the gains may be high as well.

One woman reported losing a valued teaching position as a direct result of allowing her partner choice to be known. Another, when asked why she had not come out to her parents earlier, said, "I believed that if I held on, my mother and I would develop a close enough relationship so that she would want to know me really well. It was only when I got it that no one in our family ever wanted to know anyone that well, and that that would *never* happen, that I was able to actually tell her." Another woman stated that she was the sibling in her family who never caused any trouble. "I didn't know," she said, "if there would be a place for me in my family at all if I made trouble by telling." A fourth woman feared the loss of her inheritance through parental retribution.

Most lesbians report that as they become more open about their relationship, their friendship networks shift. Friends who are uncomfortable with the new information fall away; others become substantially closer with the lessening of barriers to personal sharing.

Since human relations in the broader context generally proceed on the assumption that a woman is heterosexual unless she declares otherwise, the lesbian who comes out changes her relationship to the society in which she lives. Riddle (1978), in describing what a lesbian must give up in coming out, states that coming out " . . . means stepping outside the system of gaining respect and prestige by virtue of the man with whom you are identified, and being willing to be related to on your own merits." Many lesbians — and heterosexual women as well — are willing to be related to on their own merits. However, when a lesbian corrects the societal assumption that she is heterosexual, she trades being seen by society through its sets of assumptions about women for being seen by society through its sets of assumptions about lesbians. Far from being prepared to relate to the lesbian on her own merits, society, if it sees a woman as less of a person than a man, sees a lesbian as less of a woman than a heterosexual woman.

A lesbian who carries another stigmatizable identity may see coming out in larger contexts as placing herself in even greater jeopardy. A lesbian who already is stigmatized in some other way, as, for example, in her identity as a woman of color or as a physically disabled woman, may be unwilling to incur the further loss of status and acceptance that coming out involves. Or, she may feel herself sufficiently outcast by society already that she believes she has more to gain than to lose by coming out to the larger community and by becoming politically active.

When one partner is moving into a more public or political level of being out, the other is in danger of being, as one woman said, "yanked out of the closet," and it is here that the differences between coming out in the more intimate and the broader social contexts become evident. The increased visibility of the more open lesbian may threaten the closeted existence of her partner, whose career, livelihood, and family-of-origin relationships may hang, or appear to hang, in the balance. The more closeted partner's protestations and fears may be perceived as attempts to control and limit the behavior of the other and to hinder her development, while the activities of the more open partner may be perceived as destructive power plays within the relationship. Although these dynamics may be operative, it is also true that the larger context for, and developmental needs of, each partner may be so different that they do not permit a balance that respects the needs of each while the relationship continues. Here the therapist's task is to help the clients to develop a vision of the entire situation that includes the accommodations each has made to society, each one's individual social context and developmental needs, and the couple's larger context, in the hope that this broad picture can reduce the need for blame as the partners move toward whatever resolution they can find for their difficult situation.

The crucial time for self-confrontation about lesbian identity is the time of relationship commitment, a situation easily comprehensible in a culture where women make their fundamental definitions of self through relationship (Chodorow, 1978). One of the therapeutic dilemmas where such identity and commitment issues are raised by a couple is that identity conflicts may be presented in the service of avoiding commitment to the relationship, and relationship problems may be presented in the service of avoiding commitment to a lesbian identity. The therapeutic task is to explore openly and fully both sides of the dilemma with an educated recognition of the costs and benefits to each woman of fully embracing her partner and her lesbian identity.

Self-defined and openly lesbian and gay male therapists may have more investment in seeing the costs of staying closeted, while heterosexual therapists or closeted lesbian and gay male therapists may see more easily the benefits of staying in the closet. Therapists of all persuasions are likely to overcompensate for any position they are not entirely comfortable with, and may also feel stuck with their clients in the chicken-and-egg problem of relationship commitment and acceptance of lesbian identity.

CHOOSING CHILDREN AND CO-MOTHERING

Lesbians have always raised children. Prior to the 1980s however, co-parenting of children by lesbians usually involved rearing children born of prior heterosexual unions, and was often fraught with secrecy based on fear of losing custody and actual punitive court action. Many mothers lost custody of their children; others were able to keep their children by agreeing never to have a lover in the house when the children were present (Pollack & Vaughn, 1987). When therapists were called in, it was often to be expert witnesses in legal proceedings, to help partners deal with the grief of losing children, to assist couples in dealing with the complexities of parenting in a secret relationship, and, occasionally, to deal with the ordinary stress of integrating a new parenting figure or ordinary disruptions of family development. Although the first kinds of difficulties still occur, they are now less often the subject of therapeutic intervention than are other, new phenomena.

CHOOSING CHILDREN

Today lesbian couples sometimes seek therapy in distress around differences in their wanting or not wanting to have children, and around differences over the method of getting a child (adoption, insemination by a known or unknown donor, by intercourse or indirect transfer of semen, by medical or at-home insemination). Although therapy is sometimes indicated, connection with sources of medical and legal information may suffice, just as more general support from "choosing children" conferences and short term "choosing children" groups can serve the need. Certain books and articles are particularly useful for lesbian couples struggling to make these choices (Pies, 1985; Pollack & Vaughn, 1987). When information and community support for choosing to have or not to have children are available, and the couple is still having trouble making decisions, then the therapist must explore the usual arenas that contribute to such an impasse in any couple, with special attention paid to those additional issues specific to lesbian couples. Perhaps the most commonly noticed of these special issues is the increased pressure to come out or to be secret about the relationship.

One woman had been comfortable being closeted to her family until her lover wanted to adopt. Although holding her lesbian identity secret from her family of origin had been acceptable to her during the first ten years of her couple relationship, it was no longer acceptable as her identity as a couple member expanded to include the possibility of parenting. She wanted her parents to be grandparents to the child her partner would adopt and they would parent together. She thus experienced her partner's wish to adopt as an unplanned impetus in her own coming out. Another lesbian couple who had been very active politically in the women's community believed that their desire to protect a child from potential ostracism would dictate that they go back into the closet.

Another less recognized pressure which emerges in some therapy and consultation meetings is that felt by the woman who, not wanting children, embraced a lesbian identity at a time when it was generally accepted that membership in a lesbian relationship precluded having them. She may experience her partner's wish to have a child as a choice between reopening a satisfactorily closed issue or losing her lover. Conversely, her partner may experience pressure to choose between having a child or losing her partner. As the heterosexual world and the lesbian community become more open to child-rearing by lesbians, presentation of this kind of problem should diminish substantially.

CO-MOTHERING

Co-mothering places particular stresses on the lesbian couple that go beyond the co-parenting stresses of a heterosexual couple (Crawford, 1987). For example, the role of co-mother is not recognized by society, yet lesbians who have or plan to have children need to negotiate and develop this role. In only the tiniest handful of instances are co-mothers legally recognized as such (Polikoff, 1987). Who can serve as their reference group? Other lesbians, who may not be parenting? Heterosexual parents who may not know of or accept the lesbian couple's life-style? How will members of the lesbian couple deal with pressures to come out to the children? How will they deal with pressures to not come out to their children? How will they deal with a child's invalidating request that only the legal mother show up at school? How will they deal with the pressures of having a child who wants both mothers to come to school? While I have occasionally addressed these issues in therapy, it is my impression that on-going peer groups of lesbian mothers and major conferences on lesbian parenting have been more useful than therapy to women struggling with these issues.

Often lesbians become coupled with partners who are already raising children. Here, it is important to recognize both the similarities and differences between their situations and that of heterosexual step-families. Sometimes it is helpful to suggest reading material about step-families. It is too easy for lesbians — and their therapists — to assume that difficulties they may be having in establishing a cohesive family group are merely consequences of their unusual societal position.

Sometimes, especially when the children are older and subject to peer pressure, or when they are moving from living in a heterosexual family to living in a lesbian family, there are complex issues of anger, confusion, doubts about what to call this group of people, and even doubts about whether the children want to claim membership in this group. They may not want to call it a family. The children (or each group of children, when both women bring them to the new family unit) and their "first" or biological mother may have trouble incorporating a co-mother role for which there are few societal models and for which there is a great deal of ostracism, a role which may even be invisible within certain families. The co-mother, especially if she is the newcomer to the family, may be conflicted about how much mothering she wants to do. She may be shocked to discover how strong her opinions are about how things should go, or how violated she feels by not being taken into account in decisions that she herself may have opted out of, or that the other family members may not have seen as her prerogative — at the same time that she may not feel entitled to put forth her wishes and ideas. If the partners have not come out to their children, her position in managing the younger persons in the group is especially tenuous.

When these issues are central, it is generally helpful to establish an ongoing conversation about them within the couple, and later, in the larger family. The usual mutual protections in the family group may mitigate against such open discussion; hence a therapist can often play an important role in providing a context safe enough to open this conversation and to keep it going. Questions such as "What do you call this group of people?" and "Does everyone in it call it the same thing?" are especially useful in getting the conversation started. It is best for the therapist to make no assumptions, but to allow system members' self-definitions of the situation to emerge.

BREAKING UP

Lesbians sometimes stay in their relationships long past the point when the relationships seem workable to them (Hall, 1978). Although there are doubtless many reasons for this holding on, one of the most common is that women experience the act of initiating a breakup as a violation of the female ethic of care and as a failure to obey the societal injunction to nurture and work at relationships. Less common but recurring reasons include (a) angry rebellion against the heterosexual world's view that homosexual relationships do not last and fear that the breakup of a relationship is evidence that the dominant society's vision is accurate, and (b) recognition of the difficulty of finding a suitable partner in a limited and largely invisible population. When a lesbian couple has been parenting together, the decision to separate may be complicated by the lack of legal protection of the parenting bond for the non-custodial parent.

If the two who are breaking up have been together for a long time and have pooled their money, made major joint purchases, or shared parenting, the therapist may be called upon to provide a setting and an emotional climate that will facilitate the negotiation of visitation arrangements and/or property distribution as the relationship ends. The partner's legal protection can be only as extensive as the specific contracts they have made with each other or are willing to negotiate at the time of the break-up, and mediation by a neutral outsider may be necessary. The symbolic value of the act of mediation may be as great as its pragmatic value, as it provides witness and ritual to the ending of the partners' lives as a couple.

It is not uncommon in the lesbian community for former partners to become part of each other's continuing friendship network after the immediate pain of the breakup subsides and one or both are reconnected with other partners (Krestan & Bepko, 1980; Roth & Murphy, 1978; Tanner, 1978). Krestan and Bepko (1980) note the opportunities this custom provides for triangulation of former lovers into new relationships. Whereas it may indeed provide an easy avenue for distance regulation in the new relationship, it also may, and frequently does, provide a sense of continuity and connection as former partners become transformed into long term "family friends."

When a lesbian whose relationship is secret loses her partner, she is denied the aid, comfort, and understanding usually available to heterosexuals experiencing loss of a mate. The grief can be greatly compounded and complicated by her isolation from others. She may feel anger toward those who do not recognize or understand her pain, those who did not even know she was in a relationship. Therapy may provide the only, or rare, place where she can bring the full force of these feelings, and the therapist's first task is a simple but very important one, to bear witness to the loss.

CONCLUSION

The patterning of relational themes in lesbian couples has systematic regularities in its variations from the patterning of those themes in heterosexual couples. Every couple, of whatever composition, develops unique patterns of coupling deriving from the members' individual psychology and the nature of their connection with each other as these evolve in the dominant heterosexual society, a culture which has distinctly different models of sex role development for men and women. The dominant culture, however, contextualizes and interacts with the lesbian couple system in a way that differs from the way it contextualizes and interacts with the heterosexual couple system. Additionally, the lesbian couple system's relationship to its heterosexual environment will differ depending on whether the couple system and the macrosystem are in direct contact most of the time or whether the couple system is partly embedded in, and hence buffered by, an intermediate context such as a lesbian subculture that is accepting of the relationship.

Effective therapy with a lesbian couple requires that the therapist be skilled at seeing the interrelationships among the individual, couple, and larger social systems. Attempts to normalize lesbian couples by addressing themes only as unique and personal ignore the complex reverberations of female socialization and societal homophobia. Attempts to relate problems of lesbian coupling merely to the individual's or couple's position within the dominant society ignore the uniqueness of each couple. A vision is required that encompasses all of the relevant systems and comprehends their many complex and often subtle reciprocities.

REFERENCES

Bell, A. P., & Weinberg, M. S. (1978). *Homosexualities: A study of diversity among men and women*. New York: Simon and Schuster.

Blumstein, P., & Schwartz, P. (1983). *American couples*. New York: William Morrow.

Chodorow, N. (1978). *The reproduction of mothering: Psychoanalysis and the sociology of gender*. Berkeley: University of California Press.

Crawford, S. (1987). Lesbian families: Psychosocial stress and the family building process. In Boston Lesbian Psychologies Collective (Eds.). *Lesbian psychologies: Explorations and challenges*. Urbana: University of Illinois Press.

English, K., Blair, S., Gertner, N., & Rivera, R. (1978). Legal planning for loving partnerships. In G. Vida (Ed.). *Our right to love*. Englewood Cliffs, NJ: Prentice Hall.

Feldman, L. T. S. (1979). Marital conflict and marital intimacy: An integrative psychodynamic-behavioral-systemic model. *Family Process, 18*(1), 69–78.

Gilligan, C. (1982). *In a different voice: Psychological theory and women's development*. Cambridge: Harvard University Press.

Hall, M. (1978). Lesbian families: Cultural and clinical issues. *Social Work, 23*, 380–85.

Hall, M. (1984). Lesbians, limerance, and longterm relationships. In J. Loulan, *Lesbian Sex*. San Francisco: Spinsters Ink.

Henderson, A. F. (1979). College age lesbianism as a developmental phenomenon. *Journal of the American College Health Association, 28*, 176–78.

Henderson, A. F. (1984). Homosexuality in the college years: Developmental differences between men and women. *Journal of the American College Health Association, 32*, 216–19.

Karpel, M. (1976). Individuation: From fusion to dialogue. *Family Process, 15*(1), 65–82.

Krestan, J., & Bepko, C. (1980). The problem of fusion in the lesbian relationship. *Family Process, 19*(3), 277–90.

Lehman, J. L. (1978). What it means to love another woman. In G. Vida (Ed.) *Our right to love*. Englewood Cliffs, NJ: Prentice Hall.

Loewenstein, S. (1980). Understanding lesbian women. *Social Casework, 61*, 29–38.

Loulan, J. (1984). *Lesbian sex*. San Francisco: Spinsters Ink.

Miller, J. B. (1976). *Toward a new psychology of women*. Boston: Beacon Press.

Nichols, M. (1987). Doing sex therapy with lesbians: Bending a heterosexual paradigm to fit a gay life-style. In Boston Lesbian Psychologies Collective (Eds.) *Lesbian psychologies: Explorations and challenges* (pp. 242–60). Urbana: University of Illinois Press.

Pies, C. (1985). *Considering parenthood: A workbook for lesbians*. San Francisco: Spinsters/Aunt Lute.

Polikoff, N. (1987). Lesbian mothers, lesbian families: Legal obstacles, legal challenges. In S. Pollack & J. Vaughn (Eds.). *Politics of the heart: A lesbian parenting anthology*. (pp. 325–32). Ithaca, NY: Firebrand Books.

Pollack, S. and Vaughn, J. (Eds.) (1987). *Politics of the heart: A lesbian parenting anthology*. Ithaca, NY: Firebrand Books.

Ponse, B. (1978). *Identities in the lesbian world: The social construction of self*. Westport: Greenwood Press.

Riddle, D. I. (1978). Finding supportive therapy. In G. Vida (Ed.). *Our right to love*. Englewood Cliffs: Prentice Hall.

Roth, S. (1984). Psychotherapy with lesbian couples: The interrelationships of individual issues, female socialization, and the social context. In E. Hetrick & T. Stein (Eds.). *Innovations in psychotherapy with homosexuals*. Washington, DC: American Psychiatric Press.

Roth, S., & Murphy, B. C. (1978). *The importance of "loss" as a clinical issue with lesbian couples*. Presented at the Third Annual New England Feminist Therapy Conference, Boston.

Roth, S., & Murphy, B. C. (1986). Therapeutic work with lesbian clients: A systemic therapy view. In J. C. Hansen & M. Ault-Riché (Eds.). *Women and family therapy*. Rockville, MD: Aspen Press.

Rubin, L. B. (1976). *Worlds of pain: Life in the working class family*. New York: Basic Books.

Sisley, E., & Harris, B. (1977). *The joy of lesbian sex*. New York: Simon and Schuster.

Tanner, D. (1978). *The lesbian couple*. Lexington: Lexington Books.

Toder, N. (1978). Sexual problems of lesbians. In G. Vida (Ed.). *Our right to love: A lesbian resource book*. Englewood Cliffs: Prentice Hall.

Toder, N. (1978). Lesbian couples: Special issues. In B. Berzon & R. Leighton (Eds.). *Positively gay*. Millbrae: Celestial Arts.

16

Women on Their Own

SHARON HICKS   CAROL M. ANDERSON

There are times when I'm lonely, but usually I enjoy being alone. . . . And I've always had the feeling that it would be very hard to have both marriage and my performing. Although I have said I would like to do both things, I never quite figured out how you would do it. Perhaps it takes more flexibility than I've been able to muster. (Baruch, Barnett & Rivers, 1983, p. 270)

ALTHOUGH MOST WOMEN in our society marry (Brock & O'Sullivan, 1985), almost all will spend substantial portions of their lives without a mate. There have been a number of major cultural and sociological changes occurring in the last few decades that have directly influenced these two phenomena. Increases in birth control, divorce, education and career opportunities, extended life spans—all have had an impact on the amount of time women spend alone. Until relatively recently, for instance, most women left the protection and homes of their parents only to enter the protection and homes of their husbands. In fact, marriage was regarded by many as the only acceptable way for women to emancipate. Today, it has begun to become a socially acceptable alternative for a woman to spend at least a limited period between these two households "on her own," although a woman still must be seeking a spouse and be disappointed if she cannot find one. There continues to be considerable social pressure to become a part of a couple, but many women marry later than they did a few decades ago, and three times as many as in the previous generation never marry. Of those who marry, most are likely to find themselves alone again, or at least without a husband, following divorce, separation, or the death of their partner.

This chapter will attempt to review the issues of women alone at various life stages — young, middle-aged, and older women before marriage, after marriage, between marriage. It will also discuss the issues of the never-married woman, a population group on which there has been little focus, and the implications for therapists attempting to help women who are dealing with the issue of being alone. For our purposes, women alone have been defined as women not currently married or cohabiting with a committed sexual partner. The special issues of lesbian women are not addressed, although they too are represented in the categories of never-married, divorced and widowed women; in addition, they must deal with the added complication that their lifestyle is often not validated or sanctioned by society. Some of these women have established "new" support systems resembling extended families; this type of social network is discussed in greater detail later in this chapter. The reader may find a thorough discussion of lesbian women and their special issues in Chapter 15.

MYTHS AND REALITIES

Someday My Prince Will Come

Although many, if not most, women will be alone for decades, if not forever (Johnston & Elkund, 1984), the universal assumption seems to be that women who are alone are in some sort of transitional life stage (Rothblum & Franks, 1986). A woman's being alone is regarded by almost everyone as temporary. As professionals, we assume that women will connect with a partner as soon as they can, at the very latest after a period of mourning and/or adjustment to a previous loss. Women themselves appear to make the same assumption. They want to be married and spend years planning, hoping, waiting. When they divorce, they may take on a negative view of their last marriage, but their negative feelings usually do not generalize. They continue to idealize marriage, to want and hope for a good man and a good union.

Even if this marital connecting and reconnecting were desirable for most women, the reality is that it is not statistically possible. The likelihood is that many women who are unmarried at mid-life, or even earlier, will remain unmarried as a permanent lifestyle, whether they like it or not. In addition, since the divorce rate is so high and men have shorter life spans than women, many women will spend the last 20 to 30 years — up to a third of their lives — "on their own." Unfortunately, a substantial proportion of these women remain "ladies in waiting," thinking that sooner or later a man will come

along to rescue them. Waiting prevents them from adjusting to the reality of
the present and planning for the reality of the future. Minimally, an unmarried state should be regarded as an expected, significant, and prolonged life
cycle phenomenon for women.

The Numbers of Women on Their Own

Although choosing to be unmarried and/or childless is only just beginning
to be marginally acceptable, singles on their own are an ever increasing
group. For instance, while in 1950 they represented only 5.1% of a demo-
graphic sample, by 1976 they represented over 29% (Michael, Fuchs, &
Scott, 1980). The number of single people in America in the 20-to-30-year-
old age group almost doubled between 1969 and 1978 (Haber, 1981); in
1982, one-fifth of all women aged 25 to 29 were single (O'Rand & Henretta,
1982). According to the 1980 census, the number of single people *and* single
households is increasing dramatically. In 1984 it was estimated that nearly
10% of the adult population fell into the never-married category (Johnston
& Elkund, 1984), many choosing to be alone as a way of life. (Of course,
many of the women in these groups are not actually "alone," but rather live
with families of origin, a male partner or another woman, with whom they
may or may not be sexually involved.)

The incidence of divorce has also increased, leaving more and more
women on their own. There were nearly 1.2 million divorces in America
during the 12-month period ending in December 1981 (Goethal et al.,
1983), and 50% of today's married couples can be expected to divorce or to
be involved in a significant separation (Weiss, 1979). Some reports suggest
that an increasing number of well educated and economically viable women
are actively choosing to not marry at all or to dissolve their marriages and
become unmarried heads of families (Tcheng-Larouche & Prince, 1979). In
fact, 90% of custodial single parents are women (O'Rand & Henretta,
1982).

Widowhood also takes its toll and accounts for a considerable number of
women alone, particularly older women. Nearly two-thirds of women over
the age of 65 are widows, and the likelihood of either older widows or
divorced women remarrying is small and decreases with age (National Institute on Aging, 1978). As women age in our society, the number of eligible
men decreases significantly; in addition, many single older men seek out
younger women as their mates. Estimates suggest that in America by the
year 2000 there will be two women for every man over the age of 65 (Brock &
O'Sullivan, 1985). Not only are older women, particularly widows, less
likely to marry, but they are also much more likely to live alone than their
never-married contemporaries. For instance, 48% of never-married women

reported living with someone else as opposed to only 31% of widows (Hoeffer, 1987).

Views of Single Women

Perhaps one of the reasons women are so eager to marry is the predominant image of those who do not. Singles in general are seen as selfish, irresponsible, hedonistic, immature, possible victims of pathological personality development, even "schizoid." Whatever the reasons, singles do not have "good press." While both male and female singles are viewed negatively, single women are perceived in an even more negative light than single men. Since women are "supposed" to be invested in relationships and naturally suited to nurturing others, and since our culture is so dependent on women to maintain and care for families, women who are unable or unwilling to marry are perceived as undesirable or abnormal. In fact, about the only way for a single woman to be completely acceptable is to be a nun, or perhaps a saint. Few would say that Mother Teresa is lonely, unfulfilled, or incapable of love, few also would call her a tragic figure—yet these are viewed as predominant characteristics of most single women.

It is likely that adjusting to the single state is complicated by the pervasiveness of these negative stereotypes of single women. Literature, plays, movies, and popular culture are much less kind about an older, unmarried woman than about an elderly bachelor who goes to his club to eat and socialize and who employs a housekeeper to look after him. It is assumed that a "spinster" or "old maid" must keep cats, be terminally neurotic, and have been rejected by men. The bachelor "swinger," on the other hand, is accepted, even envied. Rarely he is regarded as lonely; rather, he is seen as having chosen to be "footloose and fancy free," to have sports cars, boats, and sequential relationships rather than a marriage and children.

Part of the problem may be that the never-married woman is not viewed as having *chosen* her life. It is assumed that if anyone had asked to marry her, she would have accepted; thus she is a pathetic, tragic figure who clearly cannot be happy without the joys of a husband and children. Even the single career woman is rarely viewed as enjoying what success she may have achieved. In fact, if she were not defective when she started, her climb up the ladder would inevitably have made her too aggressive, too cold or too masculine, maybe even desperate or castrating. No one believes she is fulfilled. The following quote reflects the opinion of one psychoanalyst practicing in the 1960s, but the attitudes would be shared by many today:

> It is useless, not to say cruel, to say that a woman's work or profession should meet her needs. It can and may do a very great deal to help, and some profes-

sions, such as nursing—both sick nursing and nursery work and teaching, certainly offer a fair substitute for one part of a woman's normal instincts, those of motherhood. But a woman is more than a potential mother; she is also, and chronologically first, a potential mate, and both her mating and her maternal instincts have to be taken into account, understood, made use of and controlled, if her personal contacts with her own sex are to do anything of enduring value to alleviate her basic loneliness. . . . (Hutton, 1960, p. 6)

Women who are single following divorce also are often viewed negatively. They, too, are seen as rejected or cast aside, unable to hold onto a man. They are described as bitter, angry, and often to blame for the dissolution of the marriage. If they are not seen as at fault, they are pitied, infantilized, or thought to be wanton. In times past, divorced and widowed women were the only unattached and unprotected women who obviously were not "virgins," so they were also fair game for sexual advances, welcome or not. Widows, in particular, have been regarded as tragic figures, awkward and even threatening additions to social occasions based on "twosomes."

Why do these views persist when there are so many examples of women who do well on their own and when the facts fail to support the view that life for a woman is always enhanced by a man? For instance, unmarried women appear to be less prone to depression or anxiety and to enjoy a higher level of educational and professional success (Johnston & Elkund, 1984). Clearly, failure to marry is not a totally negative outcome. In fact, the belief that a married woman must place her needs and priorities after those of her husband and children creates its own set of problems. Married women living with their husbands at best must divide their energies and commitments, while single women are more free to pursue their own interests or vocations and to develop their independence and creativity.

It's not surprising, therefore, that many women who have left their mark on history have been single when they did their most important work. Women like Helen Keller, Emily Dickinson and Anna Freud, who never married, Eleanor Roosevelt, who was a widow, Golda Meir, Katherine Hepburn and Margaret Mead, who were divorced, and Amelia Erhart, who was separated from her husband for most of their marriage, were all unencumbered by marital relationships when they achieved greatness. Had these women and many others who have enhanced our history and culture been married, would they have had the time or the freedom to have a "brilliant career," to travel, study, write? Had Karen Horney or Georgia O'Keeffe been married during the time they were most creative, would either have been able to manage the demands of a husband and children without causing their careers to suffer? Nevertheless, our basic assumptions make it difficult to even consider that the state of being single could actually be good for women, could actually help them to lead interesting lives or do creative, vibrant work.

Assumptions about the pathological nature of single women are deeply embedded in our unconscious, in our theories of psychological health and illness, in the entire way our social order is organized. Marriage is central to our views of adulthood, and women in particular are defined by their marital status, as is evidenced by the continued widespread use of the titles Miss and Mrs. (Although some have grudgingly accepted Ms., it is not used equally with Mr. but rather is regarded, often with some hostility, as another way of indicating a single state). Almost all theories of human development and models of psychotherapy propose that the state of marriage is a natural and necessary one, especially for women (Johnston & Elkund, 1984). Erikson's theories about the stages of human development (1959, 1964) examined young adults who remain single in only a cursory way. His major focus was on the decision to marry and on young married couples before they had children. The years between emancipation from parents and marriage were discussed primarily as a time when young women and men should explore the world, a world which women should explore with the hidden (or not so hidden) agenda of finding a mate as a primary task. Their identity would be achieved only when they committed themselves to the future father of their children. Erikson stated:

> The stage of life crucial for the emergence of an integrated female identity is the step from youth to maturity, the stage when the young woman, whatever her career, relinquishes the care received from the parental family in order to commit herself to the love of a stranger and to the care to be given to their offspring. (Erikson, 1968, p. 265)

The emphasis on the primacy of marriage continues to the present day (Johnston & Elkund, 1984). For instance, one author suggests that "our emotional needs can be reduced to three dimensions; intimacy, power and meaning" (Foley, 1979). These, he proposes, are to be met through a heterosexual relationship, career or work development, and the act of childrearing. In a very few instances it may be possible to meet these basic emotional needs without marriage and children, but these situations are clearly regarded as unusual (Johnston & Elkund, 1984). This view seems to be well represented in the family therapy literature as well:

> In the second major task of young adulthood, marital choice, the strongest factor at play will again be the degree of solid personal identity achieved in the process of separation from the family of origin. This sense of self, coupled with other family influences, will inform the young adult's conduct of intimate relationships.

> . . . In the conduct of intimate relationships, the spectrum goes from those who maintain a marital relationship with one person for life, to those unable to engage in an intimate relationship at all. In between are those who marry and divorce; those who can maintain an intimate relationship as long as there is no marital commitment; and those unable to maintain an intimate relationship beyond a few years, months or weeks. (Meyer, 1980, p. 74)

While a legitimate case could be made that all humans need and desire this sort of connectedness, it is interesting that women are far more likely to be viewed as lonely and unfulfilled if they do not mate or mother. Perhaps because our assumptions about the essential nature of marriage for women are so basic and pervasive, therapists do not have a great many reference works to use to understand the psychological development of women. Since even the existing literature is not routinely a part of most training programs, most therapists are not particularly attuned to the special issues facing women in general, much less to those facing single women.

BECOMING WOMEN ON THEIR OWN

To understand the problems of women alone, it is important to look at the route women take to becoming "women on their own," since the issues of single women differ depending on how they got that way. The woman who has never married, the woman who is alone post divorce, and the woman alone after her husband's death have some issues in common but also some very different emotional and practical dilemmas and tasks.

Unmarried Having Never Been Married

When young adults are finishing high school or college, they have a sense of unlimited time, choices, and options. For most women the expectation that one can choose one's life path includes the choice to marry and have children. When a woman has put this particular choice "on hold" until she completes school or during her drive for career advancement, she may find the option has been taken away by biological time (infertility increases as women age) or opportunity (the number of appropriate eligible men diminishes).

Because of all the negative views of single women, it is not surprising that women appear to drift into singlehood, rather than to choose it (Rothblum & Franks, 1986). For instance, in recent years a number of women have become so committed to their careers that they discover too late that the time when most of their peers were marrying has passed them by and the remaining choice of available partners is not a stellar one. As one 37-year-old woman said, "I never consciously decided to be single and have no children. I woke up one morning and realized that I was divorced, 35, and in graduate school." It was, she claimed, almost like the comic strip where the woman looks around and says, "Oops, I knew I was forgetting something— I forgot to have children." When a woman comes to such a realization, she is likely to have feelings about it, whatever her priorities. For those single women who genuinely want to marry, but find it impossible to do so, both being alone *and* not feeling in control of their fate may be problematic. Women who feel they have not actively chosen a single lifestyle may have a sense of frustration, failure, or anger. They must cope with lost dreams and lost options. Other single women may have consciously or unconsciously made the choice they really wanted to make, but, for reasons of their own, maintain the fiction that they want to marry. Perhaps admitting their real preference, even to themselves, is too foreign to everything they have been raised to value and thus is seen as potentially increasing their unacceptability to their families and social communities. They may claim to be unhappy about their lives, but the evidence is that many do well both emotionally and financially.

Whether or not single women come to grips with not having a partner, they are likely to have to deal with the issue of not having children. In some subcultures in our society it is possible and even desirable for a single woman to have a baby, but it is not acceptable for a middle-class woman to have a child out of wedlock. It does happen, but such children are more likely to be born either to lower-class teenagers or to movie stars who choose to flaunt their disregard for social norms and have the money and independence to do so. Somewhat more acceptable, but still unusual, is the decision to adopt, although for single women adoption usually means a third world or multiple problem child. Raising a child alone, or even with the help of relatives, is not an easy task. For some, however, it is a better alternative than forgoing the joys of children altogether. It seems to be a matter of which set of problems the single woman would rather live with.

Therapists find that women who have never married are less likely than widowed or divorced women to be coping with new adjustments and "new" problems created by the loss of a long-term relationship. They will have had years to develop the set of coping mechanisms necessary to survive outside the commitment of a permanent union. Nevertheless, since our society does not regard the choice of a single lifestyle for women as a "normal" one, these women will have had other problems dealing with the social stigma of their status.

Behavioral science theorists have suggested that because never-married women do not occupy the important female roles of wife and mother, their self-esteem should be lower than the self-esteem of other women, they should be less happy and less well-adjusted (Baruch et al., 1983). There is no empirical support for these contentions, however, since almost no research has been done on this population. One researcher described never-marrieds as "statistical deviants who have been virtually ignored in social theory and research" (Baruch et al., 1983). One of the few existing studies in this area found that there are two distinct groups of never-married women: those who are thriving, enjoying their lives, and those who are not. Those who do well tend to be those women who enjoy their careers and prefer to be single or who have come to terms with the fact that they have not married. Those who do poorly tend to be those women who do not get pleasure from their jobs and to whom singlehood means that they have been rejected or "not-chosen" (Baruch et al., 1983).

Of comfort to those women who do choose to be on their own, or who are "forced" into this way of living, there is some anecdotal literature which suggests that women alone in their thirties and forties are finding the lifestyle an easier one today than women found it to be 10 or 20 years ago. It may be that society and women themselves are more accepting of the single role, or that the existence of multiple alternative lifestyles makes all unusual choices more acceptable. Certainly the sexuality of single women is somewhat more acceptable, along with the notion that women can obtain sexual satisfaction outside the boundaries of a long-term relationship (Baruch et al., 1983). Of course, the "double standard" remains; there is stigma about a woman being the sexual aggressor or openly stating her sexual needs, but greater latitude in behavior has been allowed in recent years, at least until the recent proliferation of AIDS and other sexually transmitted diseases.

In addition to the issue of sexuality, the issue of the ability to develop close, intimate relationships is an important one for single women. Despite their single status, most single women are not actually alone. Most report extensive contacts with relatives or the existence of a special circle of friends who stay connected over a very long period of time. The social support single women cultivate and receive through these resources may be their way of building a nontraditional family, beyond our usual conceptualizations of what family means. When such "families" work, they may provide even more intimacy, support, and love than conjugal families for women in traditional marriages. In one study of married women, for instance, it was shown that, when they did report having a confidant, they most often reported that this person was not their husband (Baruch et al., 1983).

Overall, data about never-married women do not reveal a negative picture, just a different one. A comparison of the concepts of single and married women after 30 revealed that, compared to married women, single women saw themselves as more assertive and independent and valued achievement, personal growth, and autonomy more highly. Married women placed higher value on interpersonal relationships (Gigy, 1980). It may be either that marriage nurtures affiliative values and skills in women or that highly independent women avoid marriage. As the author suggests:

> Such a sense of independence may easily be seen as incompatible with the role demands inherent in a traditional marriage and thus may well account, in large part, for non-marriage in many women. It also may account for the fact these single women appear to be able to withstand the negative social sanctions they most probably have encountered for their non-conformity. (Gigy, 1980, p. 335)

Professional women appear to do particularly well in coping with the single state. Some have described the typical single female professional as a bright woman from a lower-class background who did well in school and found achievement to be a way to make a place in the world without needing to rely on feminine charm and wiles:

> As an adult, she tends to be very work-oriented, depending on work for both personal satisfaction and economic independence. Often, she sees herself channeling her "feminine" qualities of nurture into the world of work. The single professional often sees marriage as incompatible with her work life, fills her personal life with relationships with friends and co-workers, and sees her life as happy and productive. (Birnbaum, 1975, p. 415)

The positive feelings of the successful professional women in this study are not surprising. Unfortunately, there appear to be no related data available on less successful single women, who do not feel excited and challenged by their work, but one would assume that their perceptions of their lives would be considerably more negative. Nevertheless, the positive feelings of successful professionals would seem to reinforce the notion that marriage and family are not the only route to happiness and fulfillment for women. Perhaps the more important variable is that women feel they have had choices and control over the direction of their lives. This sense of self-determination may be the factor that relates most to ultimate feelings of satisfaction.

Despite professional success, a surprisingly high number of otherwise intelligent women do not manage their finances well. Checkbooks do not balance, investments are not scrutinized, savings are a myth. The never-married woman may tend to have fewer financial problems than those women who are widowed, and fewer still than those who are divorced, but she still has problems. Even when she has a career, she is less likely to have adequate fiscal arrangements for times of adversity. Too often, a never-married single woman has adopted the view that she will someday marry a man who will provide for her financially. Given this assumption, she may work on her career, but she probably will not concentrate on managing her finances in the way her male counterparts do; she is less likely to consider investing her money, signing up for retirement benefits, or buying a home. When the realization dawns that she must permanently depend on herself for support, she may be faced with very real financial problems and little time to come to grips with them.

On the social side, as the years go by, the picture is brighter for never-married women. In fact, they appear better prepared to adapt to late-life singlehood than widowed, divorced, or separated older women (Hoeffer, 1987). They are better educated and in better health. They also appear to be less lonely, more positive, and more socially connected. It has been suggested that these women have dealt with the problem of singlehood and developed the necessary coping mechanisms and attitudes (social support, social networks, career involvement) over a lifetime, while once married women who were naturally more dependent on their husbands often have not learned how to create alternative supports for themselves.

Unmarried After Divorce

In the past, people who married were likely to stay married however unhappy they were. Social pressures forced even the most unhappy couples to make the best of it. Today almost 50% of marriages will end in divorce. These divorces will produce more single women than men, since women are less likely to remarry. In a long-term study of 60 divorced families requesting clinical services, half the women, as opposed to only a third of the men, had not remarried 10 years post divorce (Wallerstein, 1986). The women in this study, however, were more likely than the men to have improved the quality of their lives: Sixty-four percent of the women reported improved psychological functioning, compared to only 16% of the men, and 90% of the women, compared to only 70% of men, reported contentment with the quality of their lives (Wallerstein, 1986). Nevertheless, divorced women are likely to be poorer and to have more dependents than their never-married female counterparts. More divorced women fear remaining alone, and many report having had a very difficult time, particularly during the initial post-divorce period.

One of the main contributing factors to problems for divorced women making it on their own appears to be financial. Divorce is often a financial disaster for women. The immediate transition to being alone is dramatic, since it can be accompanied by a move from an upper-middle-class to a near-poverty-level lifestyle. Even if the change is not so dramatic, in most divorces men improve their financial picture while women lose financial stability. It has been estimated that the post-divorce standard of living of men actually increases by 42%, while the standard of living of women decreases by 73% (Weitzman, 1985). The phenomenon of a lowered standard of living for women is a complicated one, with many different causes. If children are involved, the divorced woman is usually the custodial parent and does not find it easy to work. Even if such women are able to reenter the work force, it is difficult for them to find a job if they have spent a period of time out of the job market. As a result they are less likely to obtain satisfying, desirable, or highly paid work. In addition, they confront the discrepancies between men's and women's salaries, since women continue to earn only 60% of what a man earns for comparable work (Fox, 1986). Even in those few situations in which men become custodial parents, financial inequities exist. One study, for example, demonstrated that male parents on their own earned $347 per month more than female parents (Bloom & Hodges, 1981). In addition, women are likely to receive inadequate child support if they receive any at all, not to mention inadequate or nonexistent alimony.

The financial problems caused by divorce have ramifications beyond the loss of money. For instance, the correlation between financial security and self-esteem and/or status is high; people with money *feel* better and are thought to *be* better. The divorced woman who once enjoyed a status based on her husband's salary and position must learn to cope not only with having less money, but also with friends, relatives, acquaintances, and shopkeepers who regard her as less important.

If divorced women have children, they are also left with a myriad of childcare, household and life management tasks that can be overwhelming for even the most organized. Combining these issues with the fact that they also come to the single life with fewer skills in managing alone than nevermarried women, it is not surprising that divorced women have difficulty adjusting to being "single" (Wallerstein, 1986).

Societal differences in perception of divorced as opposed to widowed women may also contribute to some of the difficulties in post-divorce adjustment. For instance, widows are encouraged to mourn the loss of their marriage, while divorced women are expected to be happy to have gotten out of it (Schwartz & Kaslow, 1985). Therefore, the mourning done by divorced women is often done alone, if it is done at all. When divorced women express feelings of sadness, some perceive it as a bid for pity or as a failure to adjust to the reality of the divorce or to admit their own contribution to the end of the marriage (Schwartz & Kaslow, 1985). These factors can contribute to the social isolation of single women post divorce. Nevertheless, it is important to remember that, despite their financial problems and childrearing responsibilities, divorced women do adjust over time and do report improving the quality of their lives. Many, in fact, report greater freedom and increased self-esteem once they have had time to create a new life for themselves.

Unmarried After the Death of a Spouse

Another large group of single women consists of those women who were married and then widowed. Despite the fact that widows increasingly account for the largest proportion of older women, the experience of being single in late life has been studied infrequently (Hoeffer, 1987). Nevertheless we do know that there are different responses to living alone after the death of a spouse; some women do well, others do poorly. A strong predictor of the psychological well-being of widows appears to be the degree to which these women perceived themselves as dependent on their identity as wives before their husbands died (Brock & O'Sullivan, 1985). In other words, women who had a greater sense of their own separate identity prior to widowhood adjusted better to being widowed.

Whatever the reasons, elderly widowed women are particularly vulnerable to loneliness and its negative effects on quality of life (Kivett, 1978). Many older widows have spent their lives nurturing, playing the roles of wife and mother, only to find themselves at a loss when faced with the new and for them unwelcome role of woman alone. Many widows never had to cope with major decision-making, or did so only with the companionship, guidance or support of their husbands. It is truly a shock for them to assume sole responsibility for themselves, financially, socially, and emotionally.

Widows are in a unique position. Not having chosen to give up the role of wife, many attempt to continue to define themselves in relationship to their husbands. However, the essential functions which reinforce their role as wives are unlikely to be primary, necessary, or even possible after the death of a spouse. For older widows, mothering tasks also will have lost significance. Thus, for many widowed women, role deprivation or negative roles (i.e., not a wife, not a mother) could be a major factor in contributing to their risk of decreased self-esteem and social functioning (Brock & O'Sullivan, 1985).

Most of the clinical focus on widows has been on their reaction to the initial stress of loss, grief, and bereavement, rather than on long-term adjustment or the development of effective coping skills for managing life alone. Since women have longer life spans than men, their ability to make a new life for themselves following the death of a spouse is an extremely important issue. The literature which does address long-term adjust seems to suggest that the variable most highly correlated with life satisfaction after death of a spouse is the development of strong, reciprocal, social supports

(Brock & O'Sullivan, 1985; Goldberg, Kantrow, Kreman, & Lauter, 1986; Gubrium, 1975; Hirsh, 1980; and Rook, 1987).

Clearly, many women not only adjust well to widowhood, but are able to make these years the most productive of their lives. Eleanor Roosevelt, who was highly productive during the many years of her marriage when she had little contact with her husband, became more so after he died. Grandma Moses did not even begin to paint until she was in her late seventies. Indira Gandhi became prime minister of India six years after the death of her husband. Each of these women appears to have found that the loss of the wife/mother role opened other doors. This phenomenon is probably not limited to women who are rich and famous. It is not uncommon to find a woman who discovers her own abilities and begins to blossom only when she is "forced" to do so. Each of us probably knows at least one elderly widow who was able to "start living her own life" or at least to make a satisfying second life after the death of her spouse.

CLINICAL IMPLICATIONS

. . . we are guilty of omission when we (for example) provide empathy and reassurance to female clients who seek therapy because they are unmarried or childless rather than pointing out the difficult aspects of the married-with-children status and its negative mental health implications. (Rothblum & Franks, 1986, p. 366)

Awareness of the issues and problems confronting single women is important for family therapists, since these issues touch the lives of all families in one way or another. Wives and mothers in family treatment may well come to find themselves single as a result of death or divorce, young women in families may "emancipate" and need help in dealing with their families of origin about the "single" issues they face, and most extended families have single members who may need help in connecting with or fitting into the larger family system in a way that allows each to be a resource to the other. Furthermore, most family therapists also treat individuals. As we have come to see the relevance of historical and current contexts in understanding any problem, we are less likely to limit our definition of family therapy to sessions with the entire family in the therapy room.

Our ability to be helpful to women on their own is dependent in part on our ability to accept them as potentially whole and healthy regardless of their marital state. Unfortunately, this ability on our part isn't as common as one might suppose. Most family therapists would be surprised by the suggestion that they might be prejudiced against single women, or that they are insensitive to their special issues or needs. They would claim to approach such women with the best of intentions and/or no preconceived notions about what is right or wrong. Most of us, however, have biases which favor "normal" family patterns and tend to equate single marital status with pathology and failure (Bequaert, 1976). Unfortunately, if we as therapists believe that women cannot be both healthy and alone, this attitude will permeate treatment, subtly influencing goals, methods and outcome. We will underestimate the strengths of single women and their satisfactions with life. We will miss the special issues that these women face and fail to reinforce the legitimacy of their choices.

All work with women on their own must begin with a realistic and unbiased appraisal of the issues and a woman's own feelings about them. To often therapists are convinced they know the "real" issue and unwittingly disempower, infantilize, or fail to validate a woman's own reality. Therefore, to be helpful to a single woman, therapists must first avoid the imposition of unilateral goals and unexamined biases. For example, a 30-year-old, never-married woman interested in discussing her career concerns told us of beginning therapy with a male therapist who repeatedly pressured her to talk about the feelings of failure and jealousy he assumed she must be experiencing since she was not married and her younger sister was. Even if such feelings existed, they were not her *perceived* priority in requesting treatment and she was not aware of any current ambivalence about her life choice. She terminated treatment and found another therapist who was less prone to imposing his own agenda and more willing to help her to explore her career problems.

Both male and female therapists may have other problems dealing with single women attempting to make it on their own. Male therapists may fail to empower women or to help them maximize their strengths. They are more likely, for instance, to step in to play the absent father's role rather than to help a single-parent mother develop her own solutions. They also are more likely to get angry when a single mother is not nurturant to her children and less likely to see how overwhelmed she is. Male therapists may also be more likely to fail to appreciate the contextual issues influencing the psychological and financial survival of women, believing that women have the same options and resources as men. Female therapists, though often more naturally empathic, are likely to err on the side of trying to provide too much support to their single female clients, especially if they themselves have dealt with recent divorce or widowhood. Such support, unless it is very short term, can foster excessive dependence on the therapist. If the therapist is too sympathetic and does not actively help women to face their problems, begin to create a support network, and define their own solutions, the risk of overdependence on the therapist is increased and the likelihood of the woman's maintaining any growth she attained from therapy is lessened. All of these tendencies reflect a therapist's irrational involvement in a woman's "single-hood" and thus are more common in therapists who are inexperienced. Some of these tendencies, however, exist in experienced therapists who have not thought about the issues. These issues are common to many therapists and will often recur throughout our careers; thus they require vigilance and/ or consultation.

Helping Women to Come to Terms with the Single State

Women who have lost a partner and are unlikely to find another, or who have never had a partner, sooner or later may need help in dealing with their awareness of a loss of options. Whether she has decided to put her career or education above a family, has unconsciously opted to forgo family life, or has simply let fate creep up on her, such a woman will have a number of emotional reactions. She may be deeply sorry and regretful that she has not married or had children, or she may be neutral or even relieved. She may be bitter that she "could not have it all" as she was led to believe, or angry and frustrated that the culture makes doing both more difficult than it has to be. She may feel guilty that she is not fulfilling her "duty to produce grandchil-dren" and may be made to feel even more guilty by members of her family of origin who put pressure on her to "settle down and get married." Whatever the pressures and whatever the feelings, a woman must come to terms with the choice she has made. Only then can she begin to address the fact that her choice to be single may be a permanent one. In particular, the therapist must begin to challenge the assumption that single women are simply temporarily "between men," which makes it difficult for these women, and those who care about them, to adjust to reality and thus to really make a life for themselves. Without painting a negative picture, the therapist needs to dis-cuss the unlikelihood of marriage and/or remarriage, especially for older women, to help them begin to mourn the loss of one way of life or at least the dream of that way of life, and then to help them move on to develop another. This does not have to be a depressing process. In part, coming to terms with the single state means helping women reconnect with their strengths and the joys available to them and helping them modify their primary identities to highlight other roles (friend, career woman, aunt, etc.) which can contribute to a viable life and a place in the community. Activities that facilitate the meeting of new people (not just men), activities that promote a sense of belonging to a neighborhood or extended network, activities which allow them to give nurturance and love, activities which give a sense of purpose—all can be encouraged. The single woman may need help in seeing her opportunities to play real and meaningful roles in other people's families and other people's lives. Who would not welcome the zest for life and vitality of an Auntie Mame at family gatherings? The single woman's lack of primary responsibility for childrearing may in fact free her to be more indulgent, more available, and more special.

Dealing with the Loss of a Relationship

Marriages do not end easily, even when they are unhappy ones. Hope for better times dies hard, and fear of having failed, being alone, or having to cope with worse alternatives contributes to the postponement of an actual divorce. Thus, by the time a marriage collapses, there are likely to be many serious emotional ramifications. Often, one of the early tasks in therapy with divorced women is to begin the process of mourning the loss of the marriage.

The newly divorced woman, however, must deal with a number of issues in addition to the loss of a relationship. However unhappy a marriage may be, it is largely a private unhappiness. When a woman divorces, she must come to grips with the public exposure of her unhappiness and a "bad" marriage. She must deal with the stigma of divorce, the personal feelings of failure and disappointment, and the reactions of her family. A recently separated woman with three children said, "When I was part of an unhappy marriage, no one except my very close friends knew that there were problems. My husband and I had drifted apart so he had not been a vital part of my life for some time by the time we separated. Then the whole community became aware of it and I became the object of pity. People who I didn't know very well inquired about how I was doing and that attention made me feel even worse." Therapists can help divorcing women to understand that it is normal and expected to feel anger, regret, shame, and a sense of loss, and to wonder whether or not the divorce was the right step, even if they also feel relief. Discussing these reactions in therapy can be the first step in getting past them.

Although divorce is an increasingly common phenomenon, there continues to be a sense of stigma for those who have been divorced or those who are currently in the process of divorcing. Public stigma can be compounded by a divorced woman's own sense of failure, which may be unwittingly reinforced by her family and friends. Questions about what happened may imply to her that if she had only tried hard enough she could have prevented the divorce. Perhaps because marriage is viewed as more desirable for women than for men, and relationship maintenance is viewed as a woman's responsibility, the dissolution of a marriage is also often viewed as a woman's problem and a woman's failure. Since most women already feel guilty about the failure of the marriage, these reactions from their "support" systems are particularly painful. Even if they don't blame her, some friends avoid newly separated or divorced women because of their own feelings of discomfort about the divorce or the woman's grief, anger and stress.

Recently widowed women also are usually coping with major issues of loss, grief, loneliness, and anger. Again, mourning is in order if it is not already underway. Both widowed and divorced women also find that an identity crisis is not uncommon. Often women who have been widowed or divorced for many years continue to regard themselves as married; some do so, in fact, for the remainder of their lives. Giving up their primary public identity as "Mrs." can be very threatening, both because it is a public acknowledgment of loss, and because it leaves them vulnerable to overtures for a new relationship. In addition, both groups must confront the loss of any instrumental help spouses once provided. For instance, widows and divorced women who have been married for a long time must begin to be responsible for the day-to-day chores of life, many for the first time in years. Paying bills, contacting repairmen, doing the taxes—all may be new tasks. These day-to-day stresses can compound the larger stresses of loss of identity, grief, and loneliness (especially if the woman is childless, her children are very young, or her children have emancipated).

It is not surprising, therefore, that the early years on her own are likely to be difficult ones for the once-married woman. Over time, most women develop coping mechanisms to handle the hurt, blame, and stigma. In the long run, the more common problems are isolation and loneliness for adult relationships, as well as chronic burden when they must manage household and childcare tasks alone. Thus, early on, therapists should concentrate on helping women to manage loss and identity issues. For those who have been single for some time, the emphasis can be on minimizing burden and maximizing social contact.

For both divorced and widowed women, the step following grief work is to help them discover that a woman can be satisfied and fulfilled with her life outside of the parameters of a marital relationship. One way of doing so is to help a woman acknowledge her own strengths and interests and then to actively encourage her to pursue them. Not all elderly widows who like painting can be Grandma Moses, but all can take art classes or get involved in art appreciation groups. Often it helps to encourage women initially to try these new "risky" behaviors with a trusted relative or friend. Later they can be helped to do more on their own.

Managing Children

Issues for newly single parents are even more complicated than those of women totally on their own. In survey studies, single parents appear much less satisfied with their lives than either married parents or childless single people. For instance, one study reported that 41% of married mothers and

26% of childless single women describe themselves as very happy, while only 16% of single mothers described themselves in this way (Weiss, 1979).

The problems of single mothers do vary depending how they became single, as do the feelings of women in relation to motherhood. One study reported that 30% of never-married mothers stated that they would forgo having their children if they had to make that choice again. This compared to 20% of separated mothers, 15% of divorced mothers, and 10% of widowed mothers (Weiss, 1979). Obviously, never-married mothers have the most difficulty in dealing with the varied and complicated issues of childrearing. This is a population that is growing, as more teenage mothers choose to have and keep their children, and such women are less likely to have financial or social resources to cope effectively when their families are unable to help. Single mothers, more than other groups of unmarried women, may need special help in developing a beneficial social support network. Because they have to provide care for their children both financially and emotionally, they have difficulty finding the time or energy to survive, much less to address their own needs or go to therapy to make things better.

Divorced mothers also have their troubles. Other issues, such as adjusting to living alone, becoming a single parent, becoming responsible for taxes and finances, explaining the absence of the children's father, are just as important for them and may be even more overwhelming than dealing with the loss of the partnership. Often it is the single mother who is left to deal with the anger of the children, since they may feel too much anxiety about being overtly angry with the father whom they rarely see. If they express their anger to him, he'll spend even less time with them, or not see them at all. It is much safer to be angry with the mother, because she will continue to be involved. The single mother then is often placed in the position of having to defend the father and accept the children's anger, even if she feels a great deal of anger at her ex-husband herself. Thus, the newly divorced woman may be dealing with stigma, single parenting, work, and the need to connect with a new network all at once.

Mothers tend to put their children first, and single mothers are no exception. A recently divorced mother of three children, all with behavioral problems, reports that she leaves her job at 5:00, drives for 40 minutes to pick up her children and then drives another 40 minutes with her children to a family therapy clinic near her workplace. She willingly makes this commute weekly because it is for her children's benefit. On the other hand, she responds to her clinician's suggestion that she take some time out of her week for herself by saying that she can see no way in which that could be possible in her already overloaded schedule. She is willing to sacrifice for her children, but not for her own needs.

Since children also provide joys and comforts, even with all the problems, the lives of single mothers are often quite satisfying. Nevertheless, therapists working with single mothers must make a special effort to understand the social, economic, and emotional issues these women face, and most especially must help them to avoid defining the very real problems inherent in their situation as evidence of psychological problems or inadequacy on their part. Perhaps the most crucial and difficult task is to understand and support what the single mother must do to survive, and yet help her to avoid sacrificing everything to the needs of her children. Permission along with *repeated* encouragement and practical advice about spending some time meeting her own needs is important.

The Need for Stronger Support Networks

The development of a support network is imperative for women who live outside the boundaries of marriage. Never-married women do not have children or in-laws, and thus their immediate automatic networks tend to be smaller than those of other women. On the other hand, there is evidence that never-married women are more successful at maintaining extrafamilial social support systems than widows. Still, they may need help in forming surrogate families of friends to fill some of their human needs to belong.

For those recently divorced, being involved in a deteriorating marriage has probably meant living with an ongoing lack of meaningful intimate communication and a gradual decrease in social contacts as a couple. A strong support network is crucial in beginning the healing process and continuing it once it has begun. The difficult and ambivalent feelings of the recently separated or divorced woman may be hard to discuss with friends who are also loyal to her ex-husband, friends who may even find it awkward to include her in their gatherings.

With newly single women therapists may need to facilitate the process of developing new friends and acquaintances who can help them establish a new life. These friends may be able to help a woman learn new skills for coping with ordinary tasks, like money management, finding daycare, obtaining good legal advice, etc. For some women, even those who have been single for some time, it may be necessary to address the development of skills in meeting people before they can form an effective network. Some women may need help in seeing that the same friends do not have to serve all needs. For instance, some friends may help them to attend social functions, others may help with chores, others may give emotional support. However it happens, if a woman can become active in her community, join women's groups, develop relationships with those who have similar interests, the new single state can provide a sense of freedom, independence, or autonomy that can be very satisfying and enjoyable.

Nevertheless, as the single woman builds networks of friends from which she can draw support and familial intimacy, she must be helped to understand that her married friends may not give her the same priority that she gives to them. Family comes first for most people. Married friends are not likely to think of her when there is a family issue or problem, and they are unlikely to be available when the needs of their spouses or children conflict with hers. However close and intimate the friendship, limitations are imposed by the mere existence of other people's family relationships. The unmarried woman, then, must be encouraged to develop a diverse support network that includes a number and variety of people, so that the chances of someone's being available to her when she is in need are increased.

It is often particularly difficult for older women to cultivate a new support network. Married women are often not encouraged to nurture a range of close friendships with other women, a tendency exacerbated for those women with an intense family orientation and complicated by the myth that women must be rivals for the attention of men. The result is that some women who have been married for many years have only their families to depend upon. Family and friends who knew a woman primarily as one-half of a now extinct couple may feel uncomfortable hearing about the mixed feelings of relief, anger, and grief that are common following death or divorce. A woman's own feelings of guilt over having such feelings might be reinforced and she might become alienated from her network. While no one can take the place of a lifetime helpmate, widowed women are more likely than divorced women to be able to seek comfort during the acute phase of loss from their children and other family members. Over the long haul, however, these women may lose portions of their natural support networks, and those friends who remain may not be particularly helpful in facilitating adjustment to the new single role. In the years or decades following the loss of a spouse, family-oriented women may need extra help from therapists in learning how to develop extrafamilial contacts and make connections to a new life. In particular, older women must be helped to see that creativity and vibrancy do not have to end with youth or the loss of their partner. Role models can be used to make the point — e.g., such women as Helen Hayes or Martha Graham who have continued to have new experiences and make contributions to others well into their eighties.

Dealing with Sexual Needs

All people are sexual beings. Issues of sexuality for women in our culture are confusing enough, but when they are compounded by being single, they present additional problems. Even today "nice" women are not really supposed to want sex and, if they do, they certainly should not be aggressive in pursuing a sexual relationship. Whether or not women accept this traditional cultural norm, it creates problems for them. If a woman is inhibited, she may need help identifying and admitting her sexual needs; she may even believe that having sexual feelings when she has no partner is abnormal. Even if she is not inhibited, her sexual needs may or may not return before she is willing, interested, or able to negotiate them socially.

If a woman was once married, how she viewed herself as a sexual being during her marriage will color her feelings about her sexuality after the relationship is over. Women who had satisfying sexual relationships within their marriages are likely to want to continue this part of their lives. They may, however, feel guilty for wanting to seek gratification in another relationship; widows particularly may be unable to do so without feeling unfaithful to their dead spouse.

Older women, especially, may find that the very family support network they most need actively attempts to deny or negate their sexuality. Grown children may at times attempt to sabotage any moves their mother makes to date or reenter the sexual arena. Because women may be uncomfortable initially discussing this topic, it is important that therapists explore this area of a single woman's life and help her to address it in a way she finds comfortable, perhaps most easily as part of her larger need for closeness and human contact. In this process, therapists should help women to respect their own needs, to develop ways of meeting them, and to find ways to negotiate their relationships with any extended family members who may disapprove.

Dealing with Family Relationships

Extended family members can be a genuine resource for single women. They can provide psychological support and instrumental help in managing household and daily tasks. Unfortunately, families of unmarried women may, instead of giving support, inadvertently cause problems or stress. In part, this may occur because there is a tendency to regard unmarried women, regardless of their age, as not quite emancipated, like adolescents who are not totally responsible. The single woman is less likely to have had the experience of childbearing and rearing to reconnect her with her family of origin and move her to resolve some of the childhood struggles she experienced with that family. This is not to imply that all unmarried women have unresolved issues with their families of origin that need to be addressed in treatment, but rather to highlight the ongoing invisible ties with them that may be having an effect. A woman may need to help her family to form a new image of her, one that reinforces her self-respect and autonomy. She may need "coaching" to be able to negotiate this process of establishing an adult-to-adult relationship with family members.

In part, a new way of relating may begin to be negotiated by the way a single woman handles the issue of family pressure to marry. For instance, parental pressure for an ambivalent woman to marry may stimulate guilt or anger; the same pressure on a woman who would like to get married but has not been able to find a suitable partner may cause feelings of inadequacy and frustration. Pressure on the woman who wants to remain single may increase friction and frustration. Taking a stand which demonstrates her autonomy without becoming reactive can begin to redefine the parent-child relationship. In any case, unless an effort is made to develop new ways of relating, the result may be alienation between the single woman and her family. If this happens, she becomes even more alone without the vital support they could provide, and they are left without the special experience she could bring into their lives as a single person. In these situations, the clinician may be able to help family members to resolve tense feelings towards one another and begin to reconnect.

Widows and divorced women will also have issues with their families of origin and their families of marriage. Family contacts can at times impede the process of healing, especially if there is friction or unresolved loyalties, or if they do not understand the need for a woman to move on to the next stage of her life. It is not only the single women who must come to grips with these dilemmas. Families, too, may have to work at being able to understand the issues that face their unmarried, widowed or divorced family member, as well as losses of their own that may occur as a result (grandchildren, etc.). Since these issues may not be the presenting complaint, therapists may have to actively inquire about the family issues of their single clients or about "invisible" single family members.

Minority Women Alone

This chapter does not address all the issues facing all single women. Minority women, for instance, must cope with many confounding variables in addition to the basic issues of single life. Black families, for instance, are greatly overrepresented among those below the poverty line; thus, single black women are particularly likely to experience financial problems as a source of stress (Turner & Turner, 1983). For example, the 1985 median income for white male heads of family (any household with or without children headed by a male) was $16,322, as compared to $13,551 for black male heads of household. The median income of white female heads of family for the same year was only $5,561, and was even less for black females, only $3,917 (Wetzel, 1987). An unmarried, black woman faces many challenges, including a relatively high likelihood of single parenthood at an early age. Black women account for 14% of the total adolescent female population, yet they account for about 30% of teenage women who have given birth and almost half of the unwed teenage mothers (Wetzel, 1987). In addition, the divorce and separation rate is higher for blacks than whites, and two-thirds of all black marriages last less than 10 years (Staples, 1978). These data suggest that the likelihood of black women being unmarried at some point in their lives, either with or without children, is far greater than the likelihood for white women. Furthermore, they are more likely to be given a "caretaking" or provider mandate, with little if any support from the men in their lives.

Black mothers tend to have higher expectations for their daughters than for their sons (Turner & Turner, 1983). Black females seem to have responsibility for holding the family together and maintaining family ties, regardless of their marital state. On the positive, side, many black families seem to form viable groupings without the presence of a mate or spouse, since the extended family tends to play a more active and important role. Thus, single black women may in fact have more extended family support and contact than their white counterparts.

To help these and other minority women, clinicians may have to examine their own biases regarding race, gender, and economic status. Few poor minority clients are able to get treatment at all, much less respectful treatment. Many mental health centers that provide for those who cannot afford private care are understaffed, and many employ undertrained, underpaid, overworked therapists. Even the process of asking for help under such circumstances can be dehumanizing. The single minority woman of a lower socioeconomic status may find herself at the bottom of everyone's list of priorities. Therapists must acknowledge the strengths these women must have to be able to survive and even sometimes thrive in a world many other women or men could not negotiate for a day.

CONCLUSIONS

Women who are unmarried may have a variety of issues about their marital state. They may need to be given permission to grieve or feel relief — or both at the same time; they may need to be helped to learn specific skills; they may need to work on their self-esteem; they may need to be helped to be more assertive. Almost always they will need to address financial issues. Whether it be the stress of adjusting to a lower standard of living, the need to develop very specific skills for managing finances, or the need to overcome a socially ingrained fear of handling money, women must be helped to get control of financial matters. Without this control they will never fully experience their own power, self-esteem, pride and autonomy. Whatever therapy we do should reinforce the notion that single women can be happy, productive, and even more free than their married counterparts to realize their creative and career goals. Single women, whether never married, divorced, or widowed, can also be a vital part of family and friendship circles.

There is a need for family clinicians to begin paying attention to the prevalence of unmarried women in the families we know and treat. We must routinely inquire about and perhaps even try to involve the widowed grandmother, the maiden aunt, the recently divorced sister. We must allow our clients to define for us whom they feel their families are, yet not unwittingly exclude important members of their social networks by not asking about people who do not actually live in the home. We must think about resources for single women by considering extended family and friends. We must encourage the development of new pseudo-families for those who are not getting the support and love they need from their biological relatives.

We pay attention to women after the loss of a spouse, whether through death or divorce. We are sensitive to the immediate, acute issues of loss, loneliness, grief. After the crisis has passed, however, the single woman largely becomes invisible in our writings, our thoughts, and our culture. If we think about these women at all, we assume that they have made their peace with a life that works for them. In the family therapy literature we attend to remarriage extensively, and we deal with the parenting aspects of single-parent families. However, we rarely discuss the long-term personal adjustment of women who have been previously widowed or divorced. Never-married women are even more rarely discussed, particularly not in relationship to their long-term adjustment to a single lifestyle. Every indication suggests that clinicians should look at the chronic issues that confront single women, in addition to the acute issues they confront during the initial crisis of how they "got that way." Like any other group of diverse people who make up a segment of our society, these women defy generalization. We know that they are not necessarily totally unfulfilled, but we know little about their daily struggles. We need to know more.

We do know that reality for single women isn't always as bleak as myths would lead us to believe. There are more chances for women who are unencumbered by a family to achieve in the other aspects of their lives. Real life and fictional characters can provide role models to help women see these opportunities. Golda Meir and Indira Gandhi would have had more difficulty running their countries if they had had the demands of a family; Auntie Mame would not have been so free and lively if she had had a spouse and children of her own; Miss Marple might not have solved so many mysteries; Mother Teresa may not have saved so many children's lives. It is hard, perhaps impossible, for women to have it all. When women must juggle their own needs with those of their families, often times their own needs lose out. Clinicians who have an understanding of the issues that might confront unmarried women in our society, who are sensitive to the need to help women clarify their roles in their social and work lives, will be able to focus more productively on the positives and negatives in the lives of single women without assuming that every woman can and/or should marry.

Given the prevalence of single women in our society, and the fact that the single state will occupy such a large portion of nearly every woman's life, the mental health profession has paid insufficient attention to their needs. This chapter has attempted to outline some of the issues of single women and to suggest that unmarried women can be happy, successful, and in close emotional contact with a "family" like network. The task for family therapy may be to increase our understanding of how to help our clients build these networks in a successful and emotionally satisfying way.

REFERENCES

Baruch, G., Barnett, R., & Rivers, C. (1983). *Lifeprints*. New York: New American Library.

Bequaert, L. (1976). *Single women: Alone and together*. Boston: Beacon Press.

Bernard, J. (1975). *Women, wives, mothers*. New York: Aldine Publishing Company.

Birnbaum, J. (1974). Life patterns and self-esteem in gifted family-oriented and career committed women. In M. Mednick, S. Tangri, & L. Hoffman (Eds.), *Women and achievement: Social and motivational analysis*. New York: Hemisphere-Halstead Co.

Bloom, B., & Hodges, W. (1981). The predicament of the newly separated. *Community Mental Health Journal, 17*, 277-93.

Brock, A., & O'Sullivan, P. (1985). From wife to widow: Role transition in the elderly. *Journal of Psychosocial Nursing, 23*, 6-12.

Erikson, E. (1959). Identity and the life cycle: Selected papers. *Psychological Issues, 1*, 50-100.

Erikson, E. (1964). (rev.). *Childhood and society*. New York: Norton.

Erikson, E. (1968). *Identity: Youth and crisis*. New York: Norton.

Foley, V. (1979). Family therapy. In R. Corsini (Ed.), *Current psychotherapies*. Itasca, IL: F. E. Peacock Publishers.

Fox, M. (1986). Women in the labor force: Position, plight, prospects. In J. Figueira-McDonough & R. Sarri (Eds.), *The trapped woman*. Newbury Park, CA: Sage Publications.

Gigy, L. (1980). Self-concept of the single woman. *Psychology of Women Quarterly, 5*, 321-40.

Goethal, K., Thiessen, J., Henton, J., Avery, A., & Joanning, H. (1983). Facilitating post-divorce adjustment among women: A one month follow-up. *Family Therapy, 10*(1), 61-68.

Goldberg, G., Kantrow, R., Kreman, E., & Lauter, L. (1986). Spouseless, childless, elderly women and their social supports. *Social Work*, March-April, 104-12.

Gubrium, J. (1975). Being single in old age. *International Journal of Aging and Human Development, 6*(1), 29-41.

Haber, J. (1981). Family therapy with single young adults. *Perspectives in Psychiatric Care, 14*, 174-79.

Hirsch, B. (1980). Natural support systems and coping with major life changes. *American Journal of Community Psychology, 8*(2), 159-72.

Hoeffer, B. (1987). Predictors of life outlook of older single women. *Research in Nursing and Health, 10*, 111-17.

Hutton, L. (1960). *The single woman: Her adjustment to life and love*. New York: Roy Publishers.

Johnston, M., & Elkund, S. (1984). Life adjustment of the never married: A review with implications for counseling. *Journal of Counseling and Development, 63*, 230-36.

Kivett, V. (1978). Loneliness and the rural widow. *The Family Coordinator*, October, 389-94.

Meyer, P. (1980). Between families: The unattached adult. In E. Carter & M. McGoldrick (Eds.), *The family life cycle*. New York: Gardner Press.

Michael, R., Fuchs, V., & Scott, S. (1980). Changes in the propensity to live alone: 1950-1976. *Demography, 17*(1), 39-56.

National Institute on Aging (1978). *The older woman: Continuities and discontinuities*. National Institute of Mental Health Workshop.

O'Rand, A., & Henretta, J. (1982). Women at middle age: Developmental transitions. *The Annals of the American Academy of Political and Social Science, 404*, 57-64.

Rook, K. (1987). Reciprocity of social exchange and social satisfaction among older women. *Journal of Personality and Social Psychology, 52* (1), 145-54.

Rothblum, E., & Franks, V. (1986). Custom fitted straight jackets: Perspectives on women's mental health. In J. Figueira-McDonough & R. Sarri (Eds.), *The trapped woman*. Newbury Park, CA: Sage Publications.

Schwartz, L., & Kaslow, F. (1985). Widows and divorcees: The same or different. *The American Journal of Family Therapy, 13*, 72-76.

Staples, R. (Ed.) (1978). *The black family*. Belmont, CA: Wadsworth.

Tcheng-Laroche, F., & Prince, R. (1979). Middle income, divorced female heads of families: Their lifestyles, health and stress levels. *Canadian Journal of Psychiatry, 24* (1), 35-42.

Turner, C., & Turner, B. (1983). Black families, social evaluations, and future marital relationships. In C. Obudho (Ed.), *Black marriage and family therapy*. Westport, CT: Greenwood Press.

Wallerstein, J. (1986). Women after divorce: Preliminary report from a ten year follow-up. *American Journal of Orthopsychiatry, 56*(1), 65-77.

Weiss, R. (1979). *Going it alone: The family and social situation of the single parent*. New York: Basic Books.

Wetzel, J. (1987). *American youth: A statistical report*. Report commissioned by The William T. Grant Foundation Commission on Work, Family and Citizenship.

Weitzman, L. (1985). *The divorce revolution, the unexpected social and economic consequences for women and children in America*. New York: Free Press.

17

Women's Relationships with Larger Systems

EVAN IMBER-BLACK

Aid to Families with Dependent Children is:

> a supersexist marriage. You trade in "a" man for "the" man. But you can't divorce him if he treats you bad. He can divorce you of course, cut you off anytime he wants. But in that case "he" keeps the kids, not you. "The" man runs everything. In ordinary marriage, sex is supposed to be for your husband. On AFDC you're not supposed to have any sex at all. You give up control over your body. It's a condition of aid. . . . "The" man, the welfare system, controls your money. He tells you what to buy and what not to buy, where to buy it, and how much things cost. If things—rent, for instance—really costs more than he says they do, it's too bad for you. (Tillmon, 1976, p. 356.)

STANDING BETWEEN FAMILIES and the wider sociopolitical context, larger systems, such as welfare, public schools, health care and mental health, serve as the culture's carriers of beliefs regarding women, minorities, social class, and appropriate family organization. The place of women in larger systems, as professional and nonprofessional workers in those systems and as consumers of the services of those systems, has been shaped by beliefs in traditional sex roles and mythical two-parent nuclear families who function autonomously, never needing outside help, and by policies which support continued financial and power disparity between men and women in the workplace.

While many changes have occurred in the last 20 years regarding educational and job opportunities for women, larger human service delivery systems within which women work and receive needed services continue to operate from norms which simultaneously blame women for problems in their families and hold them primarily responsible for problem resolution (Imber-Black, 1986a, 1988d; Webb-Watson, in press).

The current chapter will examine women's positions as workers and consumers in larger systems in order to enable the practicing family therapist to appreciate and intervene effectively in the complex relationships of women, families, and larger systems.

LARGER SYSTEMS AS MIRRORS OF WOMEN'S ISSUES

Many issues regarding women's positions in the culture at large and within families can be examined by looking at the norms, values, attitudes, and practices of larger systems. Historically, women have been "one down" in such systems, barred from key decision-making roles as workers and frequently infantilized and patronized as consumers. Brief looks at the health care and welfare systems will serve as examples.

Health Care

The establishment of medicine as a profession requiring university training began in the Middle Ages. Since most universities were closed to women, only men were trained as doctors. The male-run institutions of law, medicine, and religion then came together to attack and outlaw female witches who were the competing health care system of the time (Hole, 1957). Cultural assumptions regarding men and women's capabilities and proper roles, as defined by men in power, were immediately ingrained in the developing health care institutions.

During the 17th and 18th centuries in Europe, the attack on women as medical providers shifted to midwives and was mounted this time by "barber surgeons" who were allowed by law to use forceps, a surgical instrument barred from women's hands. In the 19th century, midwives were outlawed in the United States, relegating women to the far less autonomous position of nurse in the health care system (Kobrin, 1966). Simultaneously, pregnancy became a "disease" requiring a doctor (Ehrenreich & English, 1973a). Nursing began and remained as "women's work," an extension of the mothering role. Even today, male nurses are the subject of sexist jokes, as nursing remains a "feminine" occupation, whose positions are largely filled by overworked and underpaid women.

During the 19th and most of the 20th century, medicine became a male-dominated larger system. Women were banned from most medical schools. Those women who did perservere and gain entry to medical training were often harassed by the male majority, refused access to anatomy classes, unable to attain internships, and barred from membership in the growing medical societies that were shaping the profession. Paternalistic arguments were mounted against women as doctors, including the beliefs that women were simply too delicate for the work and that women could not be allowed to travel alone at night to emergencies. Making the streets safe for women to travel at night was certainly not considered. Sexism and racism converged in the developing medical profession, as philanthropic contributions supported white, male medical schools, resulting in the closing of six out of eight black schools and the so-called "irregular" schools where women trained (Ehrenreich & English, 1973a).

As the health care system developed in the 19th and early 20th centuries with men as the doctors and women as the nurses, affluent women who were not allowed to work outside the home were encouraged to become the patient population in a growing cult of invalidism. The myth of female frailty operated to disqualify women as doctors while making them imminently qualified as patients (Ehrenreich & English, 1973b).

During this same period, women's sexuality was viewed by the developing male medical profession as inherently pathological and facilitative of disease. Uterine and ovarian "disorders" were postulated to be the cause of nearly all of women's medical complaints. The surgical removal of ovaries for non-ovarian complaints was practiced routinely for such conditions as "troublesomeness, eating like a ploughman, masturbation, attempted suicide, erotic tendencies, persecution mania, simple 'cussedness,' . . . dysmenorrhea . . . and a strong current of sexual appetitiveness on the part of women" (Barker-Benfield, 1972, p. 1). Clitorectomies were also performed as recently as 1948. While all of this attention was placed on women's sexual organs as explanatory for all manner of disease, no attention was given to developing contraception.

Other treatments developed only for women and aimed at altering so-called female behavior of "restlessness" included isolation from family and friends, with visits only by a nurse, uninterrupted rest, and prescribed passivity. Women were warned to guard against "all sources of mental excitement" (Ehrenreich & English, 1973b, p. 11). A woman writer, Charlotte Perkins Gilman, was so advised by her physician and later wrote, "So I take phosphates . . . and am absolutely forbidden to 'work' until I am well again. Personally, I disagree with their ideas. Personally, I believe that congenial work, with excitement and change, would do me good. But what is one to do? I did write for a while—in spite of them; but it does exhaust me a good deal—having to be so sly about it . . . or else meet with heavy opposition" (Ehrenreich & English, 1973b, p. 34). Thus, qualities of action, personal power, and work were seen to make women ill, while qualities of passivity and inactivity were seen to make women well! Social and cultural beliefs regarding women underpinned the practices of the health care system and, in turn, these practices perpetuated the beliefs.

In the latter part of the 19th century, a new women's "disease" was discovered and labeled "hysteria" (of the womb). This mysterious disease afflicted upper-middle-class and upper-class women. Ehrenreich and English (1973b) note that hysteria became the only acceptable expression of women's rage. At the same time, it affirmed male doctors' and men's belief that women were irrational. So-called medical approaches to hysteria included suffocating women until their fits ceased, beating them with wet towels, ridiculing and embarrassing them (Smith-Rosenberg, 1972). The powerful act of labeling by the medical profession may be seen in the example of hysteria, as independent actions by women came to be called "hysterical." Like other uniquely women's symptoms and their relationship to the larger medical system, hysteria functioned paradoxically as rebellion against women's narrow choices and as that which maintained those narrow choices.

During this same period, women suffered from the very real health danger of tuberculosis, from which young women died at twice the rate as young men. Rather than examine the health care practices that resulted in such a disparity, women's vulnerability to tuberculosis was utilized as proof of their defectiveness, and for a time the disease was considered to result from "hypersexuality." Prevention strategies involved warning women not to masturbate. The double messages to women from the culture and the health care system may be seen in the ideal of female beauty of the period—the woman with tuberculosis who was thin, had bright eyes, translucent skin and red lips (Ehrenreich & English, 1973b). One can draw similarities to anorexia today, as one sees young women choosing life-threatening thinness in an attempt to meet the standards of beauty prescribed by the culture.

While affluent women became patients for the developing medical profession, poor women suffered many health problems, including contagious diseases made worse from overcrowded living conditions and industrial accidents from dangerous working conditions. They lacked access to adequate health care and were certainly not prescribed rest or time off from work. For poor women, missing work for illness or pregnancy usually meant losing one's job. The delicacy and frailty ascribed to middle- and upper-class women, which functioned to keep them at home as ready patients, was distinctly missing from any views regarding poor women and their health care needs. Rather, the need for cheap and replaceable labor, underpinned by classist beliefs, superseded beliefs regarding women's proper roles.

In response to poor women's health problems, many affluent women became volunteers in the public health and birth control movements in the early 20th century. While such reform movements involved important health concerns for women, including birth control and immunizations, they also reified class and racial splits between women who were "reformers" and women "to be reformed." Here, the patriarchal and hierarchical structure of the health care system, in which men are doctors and women are nurses, and men are doctors and women are patients, was replicated *among* women along class lines.

In the health care system today, women are 70% of the workforce, while men remain the overwhelming majority of the leaders (Ehrenreich & English, 1973a). Despite all of the changes in opportunities for women, in 1985, only 15% of all physicians were women. More women enter the lower-paying medical specialties (Klass, 1988). Klass notes that women's strengths of empathy, compassion, and creating equal power relationships with patients are not valued in medical training, which remains under the influence of male norms. In medical research, investigation of particular side or long-term deleterious effects of medications on women lags behind similar research for men (Townsend, 1988).

Women remain the overwhelming majority in the lowest paying and least protected positions in the health care hierarchy. For instance, poor women constitute nearly 100% of home health aides, receiving minimum wage and no benefits in one of the most difficult health care jobs. These women, many of them undocumented or recent immigrants, are given little training for positions involving their care of very sick or disabled poor patients in their homes. When conflicts arise between home health aides and their patients, as they frequently do, the analysis made is individually oriented and the aide is removed or fired. Gender and class issues, played out in the requirement that poor and ill-trained women, who will remain so, are the main care providers for poor patients, remain hidden.

Thus, while many advances in women's issues as both workers and consumers have been made in the health care system, it remains a larger system whose historical context is rooted in sexist assumptions and whose present values reflect the classist and sexist divisions of the wider culture.

Welfare

The welfare system in the United States reflects male-developed policies affecting largely female clients and their children. Such policies have historically supported the traditional nuclear family and punished deviations from that form. The ideology underpinning welfare programs has promoted women's primary role as wife and mother, enforcing women's economic dependence on men and regulating their labor force participation (Abramovitz, 1988).

Early welfare policy of the 19th century divided women into "deserving" and "undeserving" of aid. White widows and deserted wives were considered "deserving," while other single mothers were considered "undeserving." Mother's pensions, whose intention was to keep women at home with their children, were established for those considered "deserving" (Abramovitz, 1988). The women who received such aid were supervised by probation officers, establishing a larger system in which the women clients were "one down." Mental hospitals became a place to send the "undeserving" women (Rothman, 1971). At the same time, larger systems to "save children" emerged, beginning a process of taking children away from single mothers (Abramovitz, 1988).

The supervision of women receiving welfare continued through the various 20th century revisions of welfare policy and systems, including Aid to Dependent Children and the more recent Aid to Families with Dependent Children. Until 1968, when court decisions altered the practices of the welfare system, poor women were subjected to rules that interfered with their privacy, including surprise raids to search for any evidence of a man in the home (Komisar, 1974). Aid could be denied to women who had even brief and casual relationships with men, on the assumption that these men should be supporting the family.

In the 1960s, social services were added to welfare assistance on the assumption that such services could strengthen family life. Such services included help in single-parenting, making friends, developing self-esteem, housekeeping, budgeting, and job training (Abramovitz, 1988). While perhaps well-intended, most of these services ignored the natural support systems of poor women, including their extended families. The jobs for which women were to train were often nonexistent. No childcare system was created for those women who did secure employment. Finally, services directed to raising poor women's "self-esteem" ignored the connection between self-esteem, poverty, and women's position in the culture.

In 1967, federal welfare laws established the Work Incentive Program, requiring all welfare mothers to register for work, accept referrals for training, and take any job offered or else lose welfare. This coincided with an increased demand for cheap female labor in the wider economy. Eligibility for welfare became increasingly defined by the mother's behavior, as funds were frozen to families with out-of-wedlock births, and the ability to remove children from the home due to "illegitimacy" was strengthened (Abramovitz, 1988). Such policies were supported by wider cultural attitudes of this period, reflected in surveys which indicated that most people believed that poverty was the fault of the poor (Patterson, 1981).

In the 1980s, under Reagan, there have been major cutbacks in all social programs. While this has been presented as a money-saving venture, policy and law have also been used to champion and attempt to reestablish the traditional patriarchal family form. Many states have implemented mandatory "workfare" programs, requiring women to work off their welfare grants at unpaid jobs. Current federal welfare reform efforts all involve mandatory work at extremely low-paying jobs. These programs imply that poor women need to be forced to work (Abramovitz, 1988). The present popular language of welfare reform is that welfare is a "contract" of mutual obligations between the government and the mostly female recipients. The "contract" concept is a mystification of the relationship between poor women, the welfare system, and the government, obscuring that the parties to the contract are far from equal and that the women have not participated in developing the terms of the contract.

Like the health care system, the welfare system has historically supported patriarchy and traditional family form. Both systems developed within a wider sexist, racist, and classist context. Similar to the health care system, the welfare system has supported sharp splits between poor women and middle-class women, as poor women form the client population and middle-class women hold the great majority of case worker jobs, in a system where men remain the main policymakers. Women who live and work in these and other larger systems as consumers or employees must deal with the sexist practices and policies that inform these institutions. In these larger systems, women's issues have remained invisible, preventing separate groups of women from seeing their common struggle.

Women, Families and Larger Systems

The relationship of families and larger systems has been discussed in a growing family therapy literature whose focus has been on discernible patterns and interventions at the macrosystemic level (Imber-Black, 1988; Schwartzman, 1985). Similar to other family therapy literature, most of this literature has omitted gender. Larger human service systems, such as hospitals, probation, schools, residential treatment, mental health clinics, have been examined from a perspective that looks for patterns which replicate family patterns (Bell & Zucker, 1968, Bokos & Schwartzman, 1985; Harrell, 1980; Imber Coppersmith, 1985; Schwartzman & Restivo, 1985); however, the contribution of gender to such patterns is missing in these analyses, which look at families and larger systems without reference to the wider social and historical context shaping both.

An analysis of the problems of families and larger systems *within* a sociohistorical context is offered by MacKinnon and Marlett (1984) in their

examination of families with handicapped members, the larger systems
which offer services, and the wider context of prejudice and discrimination
against those with disabilities. Their attention to the interaction of an identified group, the families of this group, larger systems, and the wider social
context provides a model for looking at women, families, larger systems,
and the culture.

This perspective on families and larger systems within a wider context
which shapes the beliefs, attitudes, norms and behavior of each is described
by Imber-Black (1986a, 1988) in reference to women, families, and larger
systems. Issues raised include the following: Many families, larger systems,
and the culture share a belief that problems in families are either the fault of
the mother or her responsibility to solve or both. This results in larger
system practices in which treatment and interventions are oriented primarily
in regard to the mother, whether the identified problem specifically involves
her or not. The tendency to see family problems as "belonging" to the
woman creates unplanned alliances between larger systems and family members who share this view, allowing men to be relieved of the responsibility of
sharing in the solution to family problems.

The unique concerns and experiences of woman are frequently disqualified by larger systems. Pejorative terms such as "overinvolved mother" are
used in ways that criticize and blame women for their children's problems,
while ignoring the historical and social imperatives in the wider culture
which have placed women at home with their children.

Women's close relationships with other women relatives and friends are
often not examined as a source of strength, but designated as "pathological"
or "symbiotic." The importance of such female ties is often overlooked by
larger systems working with poor minority women, as for instance when a
school or health clinic interacts with a young single mother and omits the
crucial role that grandmother plays with both mother and child. Rather than
examining the strengths inherent in such a family, personnel often make
referrals because the family "lacks a male role model."

Women are often the recipients of mixed messages from larger systems,
reflecting similar messages from the wider culture. Poor women who live in
unsafe neighborhoods with their children may find that they are designated
as "hypervigilant" when they keep a close watch on their children, but are
considered "neglectful" if they do not. Women are expected to be their
family's emotional "bank" but are criticized for being "overly emotional."
Both families and larger systems count on mothers to handle the stresses of
family members, but helpers frequently label such women as "enmeshed."
Women are encouraged by multiple helpers to become the family's conduit
to the larger systems. Women who do so may find they are told that they are
"overly central" or "too dependent on helpers." Women who choose not to

cooperate with such referrals may be told they are "resistant" and that they need to be doing more on their children's behalf.

Women clients may find that they are members of triangles with two or more larger systems. Here helpers often assume "parental" roles, positioning the woman client in the place of a "child" whose parents are arguing over "who knows best." Such triangles often function in ways that contribute to the woman's confusion and lack of confidence, frequently resulting in further referrals or increased involvement of the multiple helpers, thus maintaining the woman in a "one-down" position.

Triangles may also develop among traditional larger systems, new feminist informed larger systems, such as shelters or sexual abuse programs, and women clients who are involved with both.

The specific problems of single-parent women have been discussed by Imber-Black (1986a, 1988), Morawetz and Walker (1984), and Webb-Watson (in press). Both Imber-Black and Webb-Watson highlight the ways in which larger systems, particularly schools, let single mothers know that their families are "not complete" without a man. Imber-Black (1988) describes the ways in which larger systems and single parents may join in a belief that the family is incomplete or broken, ignoring the strengths in the family and supporting a practice in which the helper tries to become the missing parent. Morawetz and Walker discuss the problems facing single-parent mothers as they interact with school systems. Single mothers and school professionals interact in ways that support the erroneous notion that the helpers can make the children behave properly, while the mothers cannot. Children, single mothers and helpers form problematic triangles, since to improve with helpers who disqualify the mother is to be disloyal to her, while to remain troubled and symptomatic supports the outside systems in their criticism of the single mother. The lack of adequate daycare, afterschool programs, job training and adequate support is also examined by Morawetz and Walker from a perspective that appreciates how these factors feed back on the difficult relationship between the school and the single mother, highlighting how schools both contribute to the problem through lack of adequate programming and policies and blame single mothers for problems of the wider culture.

Women's roles as workers in larger systems have been described by Imber-Black (1988). Larger systems directed by men often have predominantly female subsystems, such as nurses within the health care system and elementary school teachers within the educational system. The support staff subsystems (e.g., secretaries, clerical workers) within larger systems are almost exclusively female and are often organizationally cut off or excluded from the other women workers within the system. Here larger systems replicate both male-female roles and class splits within the wider culture. Problems related to gender within larger systems include ignoring or disqualifying the complaints of female subsystems, the invisibility of gender as an issue, and criticism of emerging of female leaders within previously male-led systems. As new leaders in larger systems, women may find that they are in binds similar to those of women clients, criticized for whatever behavior they manifest. Thus, women leaders who behave with authority may be called "bitches," while women leaders who behave collaboratively are thought to be "soft."

CLINICAL WORK WITH WOMEN,
FAMILIES AND LARGER SYSTEMS

Several principles emerge from reported clinical work with women, families, and larger systems. Such principles arise from an examination of the macro-system formed by larger system and families within a framework informed by women's issues.

(1) *Examine the implicit sexist, classist, and racist assumptions that are communicated from a referring larger system. Accept referrals in ways that begin to alter those assumptions.*

Webb-Watson (in press) describes a referral for family therapy from a school system whose implicit assumptions about single-parent, female-headed families and Afro-American families were negative and blameful. Rather than simply accept the referral and begin to work exclusively with the family in ways that would fix the locus of blame within the family and on the mother in particular, the therapist conceptualized the problem as belonging to the school *and* the family, developed interventions that worked with strengths in the family and the family's culture, reframed the child's problems as the problems of all concerned in making transitions from one culture to another, utilized the mother as a key resource for her child and enabled the school to see this single-parent mother, the child and Afro-American culture from a new perspective. School personnel and the single-parent mother were designated as necessary to solve the child's problem, a problem now framed in ways that challenged old assumptions of the larger system. This work was done in a manner that accepted the school's desire to help the child, but offered the larger system a new way to do so that obviated prior criticism of single-parent women and minorities.

Webb-Watson's work illustrates a way to accept referrals from larger systems in ways that neither join the family therapist with oppressive attitudes and behavior nor create untenable triangles for clients between warring systems. Such work requires careful analysis of the beliefs underpinning the practices of the larger system and an adept use of systems concepts within a progressive sociopolitical framework.

(2) *Examine the macrosystem formed by larger systems and the family for patterns of escalating complementarity and triangulation that function to disempower women. Develop interventions that introduce symmetry among the participants and detriangulate women clients from inherently childlike positions between larger systems who are arguing over "who knows best for her."*

In a case exemplifying these issues, Imber-Black (1986a) describes a single-parent, female-headed family in which several male helpers representing different larger systems entered the family sphere because an adolescent son refused to go to school. During a consultation, the mother explained how she felt pressured to accept the advice of the different men regarding her son, but that the advice conflicted and she felt "caught in the middle," increasingly unable to cope. Each helper saw his appropriate role as directing the family towards the "right" solution, and none approached the mother as a person who was capable of making good decisions for her children. Messages regarding the boy's need for a "male role model" abounded in the macrosystem, while no one examined the mother's natural support system, which included an available uncle. A major triangle, consisting of two male helpers arguing over what was "best" for the mother to do, functioned to reduce her effectiveness. As the mother appeared more confused with the panoply of conflicting advice, the helpers gave her more advice in a pattern typical of escalating complementarity. In a poignant moment in the interview, the son remarked that if the help stopped his mother would be hurting less because the help "made her feel helpless."

The major intervention in this case offered the mother a decision-making task regarding her son and the issue of the nature of future help, explicitly delineating her as the head of her family and as the person who knew best what manner of help might be helpful. Utilizing an "odd days/even days" format, she was asked to consider future options regarding help for her son and her family. Rather than being the one-down recipient of conflicting advice, the mother was now in a symmetrical position with the helpers. The mother responded with a decision that normalized her son, interdicting a direction set by the helpers, who pathologized him.

(3) *Examine the macrosystem for beliefs that engender doubt in women regarding their own decisions and actions and that disempower women.* Included in such beliefs are (a) women are at fault for whatever happens to their children; (b) women should be dependent on helpers; (c) women are "overly close" to female relatives and should be more "independent"; (d) single-parent, female-headed families or lesbian parents are deficient and require helpers as "male role models." Examine and question the labels placed on women by larger systems that communicate these beliefs, such

as "overinvolved mother." Look for strengths in adult female relationships, such as mothers and daughters, and seek ways to utilize these, rather
than to intervene in them with strategies for separation. Examine and use
the network of extended family and friends of single parents, rather than
assuming that temporary helpers should become "role models." Develop interventions that challenge these beliefs, both in the family and in the larger
systems.

A single-parent mother with three teenage girls was referred for family
therapy by her welfare worker, who stated that the "household was chaotic"
and strongly implied that all of the problems were the fault of a deficient
mother. In examining the macrosystem, the clinician uncovered a pattern
involving multiple referrals for family therapy. Each try at therapy had
ended by the therapist's deciding that the mother had grown "too dependent
on therapy." The mother was not involved in these decisions; instead she
found herself to be the recipient of yet another referral within a short time.
The welfare worker stated that the family "had no hierarchy" and that the
mother did not "know how to be a mother." A thick file, consisting of reports
by various therapists, pointed to the mother's faults in organizing her family.
Each new therapy existed in the context of these beliefs. The mother, in turn,
found herself to be the recipient of a mixed message from the macrosystem:
"Go to therapy and be dependent on helpers, but if you become dependent on
helpers, we must stop therapy." In a discussion regarding prior therapy, the
mother said she felt the past therapists simply didn't understand how her
family worked. She also expressed confusion regarding the continued referrals
and endings, all of which felt out of her control.

The new therapist wanted to work in a way that would not replicate prior
treatment failures. He began by asking the mother what she meant about
prior therapists not understanding how the family worked. The mother
explained that she saw her family as four women living together, and that
this had been their way to be since the girls became teenagers. She said that
this worked most of the time, except when there was a dispute. At those
times, she would attempt to be the final authority, but the daughters would
refuse to listen. The mother would tell her welfare worker about the incident
and a referral for therapy would ensue. The mother, who was fairly isolated,
found therapy sessions to be enjoyable. In each therapy, however, the therapist would attempt to impose on the family a more hierarchical arrangement, which did not suit their needs.

After discerning the family's experiences with help and larger systems, the
therapist began by asking the mother and daughters to look closely at what
was working in their current arrangements and what was not. To this one
daughter said that no other therapist had asked them what was working

well! They agreed that things worked well for them most of the time with their arrangement of four women living together, but that problems arose when there were disagreements. The daughters said they believed their mother should have the final word during disputes, but that at other times they wanted their more collaborative style to prevail. Therapy ensued and several disputes between mother and daughters were negotiated successfully.

After four months, during which the family members developed what they called their "two ways to be together" the therapist felt it was time to end; however he did not want to replicate previous endings, which had excluded the mother in decision-making. In a session he raised the question of stopping therapy and asked the mother's opinion. She stated that she felt therapy was the reason things were going so well and expressed reluctance to stop. She compared therapy to a cookie jar of which the therapist held the lid. When he took the lid off the jar, it was safe for the family to talk together. Here, the therapist realized that a further step in therapy was required for the mother to "own the cookie jar." Rather than stipulate that she had become "too dependent" on therapy, he asked the four women to go shopping and to decide together on "just the right cookie jar." His instructions for the shopping trip affirmed the family's collaborative style. He then asked them to have a meeting at home when they would ordinarily come to therapy. The mother was to begin the meeting as the one who held the cookie jar lid and to pass the lid to the daughters when they wished to speak, thus incorporating both parental hierarchy and collaboration. He set an appointment for two weeks later and asked that the mother bring the cookie jar to the session. At this session, the mother began before the therapist. She reported that they had had a successful session at home and then she passed the lid to him. At the end of the meeting, the therapist again inquired about therapy, and the mother replied that she wanted to have three weeks of meetings at home and to then return. This time arrangement was repeated once more at the mother's request. At the final session, the mother brought the therapist a second cookie jar to keep for other families.

This therapy proceeded in ways that challenged the beliefs of the various larger systems about the mother. Initially delineating her as the expert on what had occurred in the prior therapies and on her family's organization, the therapist joined her in a more collaborative style. Within that collaborative framework, elements of workable hierarchy were negotiated rather than imposed. The mother's multiple experiences with helpers had functioned to make her feel incapable. The ritual intervention involving the cookie jar communicated the therapist's belief in her capabilities and enabled her to enact an empowered position vis-à-vis both her family and larger systems (Imber-Black, 1988).

(4) *Utilize effective advocacy when larger systems have created the problem (Webb-Watson, in press) and when the larger system seems unlikely to alter its position and a woman's rights are being violated (Imber-Black, 1988).* Interventions arising from an advocacy stance are enhanced by familiarity with a systemic paradigm, enabling the therapist to work in ways that de-escalate conflict and blame. Such advocacy also involves coaching the woman to advocate for herself and her family rather than simply doing it for her. Advocacy requires familiarity with the laws and policies affecting clients' lives.

A case involving such advocacy work involves a single mother and her mentally handicapped daughter, age 12. The mother received no support from the father, who left the family shortly after the child's birth. The school referred the family for therapy, stating that the child was unmanageable in her special education class and blaming the mother. Rather than simply accept the referral, the therapist decided to find out more about the larger system and arranged to visit the school. The child was in a special education class, which the school had placed in a far corner of the building, away from other classes. The handicapped children were not allowed to eat lunch in the cafeteria; rather, they remained in their room. The school officials said they believed this was for the handicapped children's own good, in order to protect them from other children who would make fun of them. The school took no responsibility for changing the attitudes of the children. Officials also complained that this particular mother had tried to get them to integrate the child for lunch and physical education, and that she clearly did not have her child's best interests at heart in making this request.

Following the school visit, the therapist met with the mother. Rather than focus initially on problems with the child, which would have joined the therapist with the school system, the therapist inquired about the mother's experiences with larger systems regarding her daughter. The mother described many difficulties with larger systems who disregarded her advice and ideas about her daughter. She stated that she felt the principal and counselor at her daughter's school treated her as if she were "retarded." She was unsure what her rights were regarding her daughter. She said she felt criticized by teachers and other helpers and had found over the years that getting services for her child was extremely difficult. She wondered aloud how the school might treat her if she had a husband with her at the many meetings.

Rather than begin therapy, which would fix the locus of blame on the mother and relieve the school of responsibility, the therapist chose a very different process. She began by teaching the mother some principles for interacting with larger systems and coaching her to get information regarding her legal rights as the parent of a handicapped child. The therapist advised keeping distant from the school during this research phase, in order to obviate the conflictual interactions that usually left the mother feeling hopeless. The mother quickly discovered that the school was, in fact, violating the law regarding educating handicapped children in the least restrictive environment. Instead of confronting the school alone, as she had done in the past, the mother was encouraged by the therapist to call a meeting of other parents of handicapped children in the school. The mother responded that she had always wanted to do such a thing, but had felt so beaten down by her interactions with the school that she had not had the energy. Now she felt ready and organized the meeting. Eventually the resulting parents' self-help group developed and planned strategies to require the school to comply with the law.

This work involved coaching and advocacy at the family-larger system interface. The therapist formed a partnership with the mother initially and developed methods that enabled the mother to effectively advocate for her daughter with the larger system. An activist stance regarding both women and the handicapped informed the therapist's work.

CONSULTATION TO LARGER SYSTEMS—MAKING GENDER VISIBLE

Recently, the role of the family therapist has expanded to include the application of systemic assessment and intervention skills to the problems of larger systems (Wynne, McDaniel, & Weber, 1986). The family therapist may be invited as a consultant to a larger system struggling with intrasystem issues pertaining to its relationships and operations, or to two or more larger systems confronting intersystem problems. Such consultations may focus on cases, in-service education, program development, or staff relationship problems (Imber-Black, 1986b).

While women increasingly comprise the workforce in larger systems, few if any consulting requests begin with a recognition of gender and women's positions in larger systems as a salient issue for examination and change efforts. More often, gender is such a hidden dimension in the larger system that the consultant must pay careful attention to such issues as women's positions in the larger system, the criteria by which women are evaluated and promoted, what larger system agendas are women expected to carry, how relationships are structured between men and women and between women and women, and how women are rewarded.

Upon entry, the consultant should ascertain the history of the larger system regarding women employees. Is the system one involving traditionally female subsystems within a larger, male-dominated institution? Examples include the health care system, in which nurses are the predominantly female and subordinate subsystem, the public education system, in which women fill most of the teaching jobs while men fill upper-level administrative and policymaking positions, the university system, where women fill the librarian positions while the majority of professors and administrators are men, and all larger systems that utilize support and clerical staff, the overwhelming majority of whom are women. Traditional male-female roles in the culture are frequently replicated by the relationship configurations in these systems. Just as men often disqualify or otherwise ignore the complaints of women in families, the consultant may find that the issues raised by predominantly female subsystems have been dismissed or not taken seriously.

As an example, in one consultation to a university, it was found that the all-male administrative staff waited a year before taking an escalating problem in the library seriously because they believed it was simply "a bunch of women complaining." Distinctly missing from anyone's analysis prior to the consultation was the place of this female subsystem within the larger, male-led institution.

As female leadership emerges in previously male-led systems, the women may discover that they are in the untenable position of being criticized for "acting like men" (e.g., authoritatively and hierarchically), while also being expected to do so. Conversely, they may find that they are expected by others to be "feminine" and criticized for being so. Women leaders who behave in collaborative ways with an emphasis on relationships may find that they are punished for doing so or that they are not taken seriously by the male hierarchy.

A public high school sought consultation regarding problems in its guidance office. The guidance staff was comprised of six women counselors and three women secretaries. The central administration seeking the consultation was all male. A new director of guidance, Ms. Kraus, had been hired a year earlier, replacing Ms. Appel, who had stepped down due to family concerns, but who continued to work in the guidance department. Ms. Appel had valued collaborative leadership, believing that this suited her style and the values she wished to further with both staff and students. The administration secretly criticized her and sought what they referred to as a "stronger, tougher" leader. When Ms. Kraus joined the system, the administrators instructed her to be "tough." Hearing their criticisms of Ms. Appel, she declined Ms. Appel's offers to introduce her to the system. In a short time, other staff began to ally strongly with their prior director. Ms. Kraus responded by becoming "tougher." Complaints regarding morale began to filter to the administration, but these were ignored until the situation reached a crisis level. No one considered gender to be a salient issue in an institution where several women were fighting with each other within a larger male-run system. By the time of the consultation, Ms. Kraus found herself blamed by her staff for her interpersonal style *and* by the administrators for doing precisely what they had requested. At the beginning of the consultation, Ms. Kraus told the consultant that she felt uncomfortable with the leadership style she had been asked to assume, but believed that the job required it. She said she felt criticized whichever way she moved.

The consultant raised gender issues with the guidance staff and the administration. Initially, gender was dismissed by all concerned. Ms. Kraus, who was under the most stress, and soon likely to quit or be fired, became curious about the consultant's conceptualization and began to examine her leadership style. She initiated meetings with her staff to seek input, and the crisis began to de-escalate. While this was occurring, the consultant had several meetings with the administrators, challenging them regarding their earlier dismissal of the complaints. In meetings with all personnel, the consultant raised questions regarding the different treatment of men and women within the school system, while highlighting that such differential treatment was common in larger systems due to unexamined assumptions from the wider culture. No individuals were blamed. This framing enabled the participants to consider gender issues. The consultation led finally to the implementation of school-wide workshops on sexism, including students, their families, and staff (Imber-Black, 1988).

Larger systems may be organized in ways that promote what is considered to be traditionally female and male behavior. For instance, in a large human service system, a crisis unit served adolescents and their families. A striking characteristic of this unit was that it was composed of seven female social workers and one male psychologist. The women were expected to be on-call seven days a week, 24 hours a day, and to go to clients' homes during crises. The male psychologist worked regular hours and joined the women on home visits "in order to make the families pay attention" to what was being said. Thus, the larger system was organized in a way that perpetuated male and female stereotypes. The women were expected to be available at all times, just as mothers would be expected to be with small children. The man's role was to enter briefly as the one whom the families needed to take seriously, as in "wait 'til your father gets home." In many ways, the client families were regarded as "naughty, out-of-control children," whose family organization fit the ubiquitous "overinvolved mothers" and "peripheral fathers." During the consultation, one woman remarked, "we're expected to be all things to all people." Like many mothers in families, these women felt alternately pleased with their position and on the verge of burnout.

Prior to the consultation, no one in the agency had questioned this arrangement or examined the sexist assumptions that underpinned it. No one had looked at how the organization both mirrored the culture at large and helped to reinforce it through interactions with clients. During the consultation, the participants were able to begin to examine the sexist messages from the wider culture within which the larger system was embedded and which had invisibly informed both their organization and their process of service delivery to families. It is important to note that the consultation had not been sought for problems involving gender issues; rather, the consultant raised these issues as a crucial element both for the larger system per se and for the families it served.

CONCLUSIONS

Larger systems carry the culture's assumptions and values regarding men and women, mothers' and fathers' roles, helping relationships, and appropriate family and workplace organization. As such, they are the silent and powerful transmitters of beliefs regarding women's positions in family and work systems. Family therapists who choose to work at the family-larger system interface, either as therapists who conceptualize their tasks from a macrosystemic perspective or as consultants to larger systems, must examine and utilize gender as a central organizing principle for their work in order to avoid perpetuating sexism and patriarchy in the family and the larger system. The work involves sensitivity to the actual power differentials between men and women in families and larger systems, as well as carefully planned interventions to challenge and address these discrepancies. Such work eschews simplistic hypotheses linking symptoms only to individuals and families in favor of a more encompassing perspective that includes larger systems and their embeddedness in a historical, social, political and economic context that has functioned to constrain women's options and opportunities. Examining families and larger systems from such a perspective entails developing working methods informed by the social policies and cultural history within which particular larger systems took shape. Therapeutic and consultative work with families and larger systems that locates gender at the forefront of assessment and intervention seeks to develop interdependent relationship options and to facilitate women's empowerment across class and racial divisions at all levels of the macrosystem.

REFERENCES

Abramovitz, M. (1988). *Regulating the lives of women: Social welfare policy from colonial times to the present*. Boston: South End Press.
Barker-Benfield, B. (1972). The spermatic economy: A nineteenth century view of sexuality. *Feminist Studies, 1*, 1.
Bell, N., & Zucker, R. (1968). Family-hospital relationships in a state hospital setting: A

structural-functional analysis of the hospitalization process. *The International Journal of Social Psychiatry, XV,* 73–80.

Bokos, P. J., & Schwartzman, J. (1985). Family therapy and methadone treatment of opiate addiction. In J. Schwartzman (Ed.), *Families and other systems: The macrosystemic context of family therapy.* New York: Guilford Press.

Ehrenreich, B., & English, D. (1973a). *Witches, midwives, and nurses: A history of women healers.* New York: The Feminist Press.

Ehrenreich, B., & English, D. (1973b). *Complaints and disorders: The sexual politics of sickness.* New York: The Feminist Press.

Harrell, F. (1980). Family dependency as a transgenerational process: An ecological analysis of families in crises. Unpublished dissertation, University of Massachusetts, Amherst.

Hole, C. (1957). *A mirror of witchcraft.* London: Chatto & Windus.

Imber-Black, E. (1988). *Families and larger systems: A therapist's guide through the labyrinthe.* New York: Guilford Press.

Imber-Black, E. (1986a). Women, families and larger systems. In M. Ault-Riche (Ed.), *Women and family therapy.* Rockville, MD: Aspen.

Imber-Black, E. (1986b). The systemic consultant and human service provider systems. In L. C. Wynne, S. H. McDaniel, & T. T. Weber (Eds.), *Systems consultation: A new perspective for family therapy.* New York: Guilford Press.

Imber Coppersmith, E. (1985). Families and multiple helpers: A systemic perspective. In D. Campbell & R. Draper (Eds.), *Applications of systemic family therapy.* New York: Grune & Stratton.

Klass, P. (1988). Are women better doctors? *New York Times Magazine,* April 10, 32–35; 96–97.

Kobrin, F. E. (1966). The American midwife controversy: A crisis of professionalization. *Bulletin of the History of Medicine,* July–August, 350.

Komisar, L. (1974). *Down and out in the U. S. A.* New York: New Viewpoints.

MacKinnon, L., & Marlett, N. (1984). A social action perspective: The disabled and their families in context. In E. Imber Coppersmith (Ed.), *Families with handicapped members.* Rockville, MD: Aspen.

Morawetz, A., & Walker, G. (1984). *Brief therapy with single parent families.* New York: Brunner/Mazel.

Patterson, J. T. (1981). *America's struggle against poverty 1900–1980.* Cambridge: Harvard University Press.

Rothman, D. (1971). *The discovery of asylum: Social order and disorder in the new republic.* Boston: Little Brown.

Schwartzman, J. (1985). *Families and other systems: The macrosystemic context of family therapy.* New York: Guilford Press.

Schwartzman, J., & Restivo, R. J. (1985). Acting out and staying in: Juvenile probation and the family. In J. Schwartzman (Ed.), *Families and other systems: The macrosystemic context of family therapy.* New York: Guilford Press.

Smith-Rosenberg, C. (1972). The hysterical woman: Sex roles in 19th century America. *Social Research, 39*(4), 652–78.

Tillmon, J. (1976). Welfare is a women's issue. In R. Baxandall, L. Gordon, & S. Reverby (Eds.), *America's working women: A documentary history—1600 to the present.* New York: Vintage Books.

Townsend, J. (1988). Personal communication.

Webb-Watson, L. (in press). Women, family therapy and larger systems. *Journal of Psychotherapy and the Family.*

Wynne, L. C., McDaniel, S. H., & Weber, T. T. (1986). *Systems consultation: A new perspective for family therapy.* New York: Guilford Press.

SECTION III

Special Issues

18

Women, Work, and the Family

DIANE P. HOLDER   CAROL M. ANDERSON

OVER THE PAST TWO DECADES we have witnessed a groundbreaking era for
women in terms of the number of roles and choices available in their lives.
Motherhood is not passé—in fact, more American women have at least one
child than at any other time in history (Hewlett, 1986)—but an unprecedented number of women are also working outside the home, even while their
children are very young. Managing these multiple roles is presenting families, and particularly women, with a new set of challenges and dilemmas.
Interestingly, considerable concern about the potential deleterious effects
for women who exercise these options, taking on multiple roles, is being
replaced with growing evidence that employment benefits women in many
ways—ways that contribute to their physical and psychological survival
(Barnett, Biener, & Baruch, 1987). Nevertheless, strong cultural, social and
political traditions continue not only to make it extremely difficult for wom-
en to balance work and home responsibilities, but also to make it almost
impossible for them to gain parity with men in the workplace. This chapter
will examine the movement of women into the labor force, explore the
opportunities and barriers they experience in the marketplace, and discuss
the reciprocal impact of work and family roles.

WOMEN IN THE WORKFORCE

Women have entered the paid workforce in unprecedented numbers in the
past 30 years. The number of women in the labor force increased 173%
between 1947 and 1980 (Gerson, 1985); moreover, women will account for

the lion's share of new workers until 1995, when an estimated 85% of all women who are in prime childbearing and childrearing years will be in the labor force (BNA, 1986). In 1985 there were over 47 million employed women, making up an unprecedented 44% of the workforce (BNA, 1986). These statistics reflect a major change for families, since much of this growth has occurred in the percentage of mothers of children under 18 who are employed. For example, in 1940, only 8.6% of all mothers who had dependent children were employed, although the rates for Black and immigrant women were much higher (Blau, 1984). But by 1985 almost 60% of married women with children under 18 and nearly 80% of divorced mothers with children under 18 worked outside the home. This means that by the close of the '80s the classic 1950s family with a stay-at-home mother, dependent children, and a breadwinner father will represent less than 10% of American families (BNA, 1986).

Changing Patterns

Changes in work patterns represent an incredible shift for many women. Access to jobs, the ability to earn money, and the option to choose whether or not to conceive mean that women can exercise more control over their worlds than at any time in history. Their life choices are much less predetermined and less exclusively dominated by fertility and childcare tasks, so that there is an increased ability to influence their own destinies. The result has been a tremendous variation in the types and timing of decisions that women make. At age 40 a woman may be a first-time mother with an infant and a career, a traditional homemaker with school-age children, a woman with grown children who is reentering the job market, an unmarried career-oriented professional, a remarried mother with a job and two sets of children, etc. No one family theory or life cycle model adequately captures the issues these women and their families face.

Unlike men, who have been socialized to enter the job market at an early age, to stay there consistently, to achieve, and to define themselves in terms of their work, women have been given mixed messages regarding work and motherhood. Prior to 1940, the average American female worker was young and single (Blau, 1984). Middle-class norms dictated that married women, particularly mothers, seek jobs only when absolutely necessary. Until the last generation, only if a woman "had" to work (which usually translated to "when she was without a competent man") was there social sanction to do so. Today women are trying various employment arrangements, but several factors make working outside of the home difficult: norms regarding the ways that men and women divide their family and work responsibilities; laws and corporate traditions that inequitably shape employment opportunities; and social policies regarding parental work leave and childcare, all of which are lagging significantly behind these sweeping social changes. The result is that most women are now expected to seek employment *and* to have children, without letting either the domestic or the work world impede the other—all this with little support from inside or outside the family.

In addition to the dramatic changes in women's work lives, several other major changes have altered the structure of the American family, including a significant increase in the divorce rate, a decline in the birth rate, an increase in average life expectancy, and an increase in the number of single-parent households (Borman, Quarm, & Gideonse, 1984). These radical changes have many implications for family theories and practice, for, as Goldner (1985) points out, much of the early academic interest in the family and the formative growth of family therapy as a field of specialization took place during the 1950s, the heyday of the traditional family. Our theories and our clinical practice are highly influenced by the assumptions of this era, yet many of them are no longer relevant. Most mothers of the 1950s did not work outside the home, and fewer were forced by divorce or their own career aspirations to become family breadwinners. Fewer women had lifestyles that required them to juggle complex and contradictory tasks and messages, and fewer men had to come to grips with what it means to have a "working wife." As they learn to help families who are confronting contemporary issues regarding home and job responsibilities, family therapists need different templates to place over these problems and the clinical quandaries that result. A first step for therapists is accurate information regarding what is happening.

What Do We Know about the Jobs Women Hold?

Women have always worked for economic gain. How, under what circumstances, at what costs, and for what rewards—these have all varied, but working itself is not a new phenomenon. What *is* new is the shift resulting in the majority of American women being employed outside the home for wages while their children are young, women's expression of strong career goals in addition to or instead of family responsibilities, and their desire to have a more equitable slice of the economic pie.

Unfortunately, jobs in this country continue to be gender stratified. Most women continue to be employed in traditional "female" jobs. One-half of all employed women were in just 17 of the 400 job categories listed by the 1975 Bureau of Census (Blau, 1984). Eighty percent of all women work in female-dominated job categories, and these categories almost always pay lower wages than those that are dominated by men, even when a greater skill level or educational background is needed to do the "female" job. Women have crossed some traditional male boundaries, but unfortunately the economic rewards for doing so have not been great. Only 10% of women employed in 1984 earned over $20,000 per year (Hewlett, 1986). Even the increased stability of women's presence in the workforce during the past 25 years has not bridged the gulf between male and female earnings, a gap which is wider in the United States than in most other advanced industrialized countries. In Britain, Italy, Sweden, Germany, Denmark, and France the earning gap between men's and women's wages closed significantly during the 1970s. Only in the U. S. did the gap remain stubbornly wide, a particularly disheartening fact considering that American women are the best educated in the world (Hewlett, 1986). In 1987, women earned only 68 cents for every dollar men earned (N. Y. *Times* July, 1987).

The growth of female-headed households in the face of this enormous earning gap has resulted in what is commonly referred to as the "feminization of poverty." This translates into the following disturbing statistics: In 1977 two-thirds of poor persons 16 years old and over were women (Goldberg & Kremen, 1987); between 1960 and 1981 the number of poor persons in female-headed households increased 40% while the number of poor people in all other family types decreased 45% (Folbre, 1987); by 1985, 55% of all households below the poverty line were headed by women (Arendell, 1987). Almost 75% of all women who are employed work full-time; however, based on income figures of the Bureau of Labor Statistics, in 1985 the median annual income for women was only $14,404, while for men it was $22,112 (Statistical Abstract, 1987). In general, if you are born female rather than male, the likelihood is twice as great that you will be below the poverty line at some time during your life. If you are born male, you are at greatest risk for being poor during childhood, when you are more likely to be financially dependent upon the earnings of a woman (Shortridge, 1984).

Historical Influences: Separate Spheres

> Something must be wrong in a social organization in which men die a premature death from coronary thrombosis, as a result of overwork and worry, while their wives and widows organize themselves to protest against their own lack of opportunities to work. (Myrdal & Klein, 1956)

These words of protest were voiced in an era that strongly promoted the idea that the world of work and world of the family were two separate spheres—each one independent of the other. Women managed the home and children and were socialized to perform more nurturing activities. Men were schooled to actively compete in the larger community, to influence policy and norms, and to earn money. A man's job status typically determined the status of the entire family; thus, a man's employment was viewed as central to his family's functioning (Asmundsson, 1981). This gender-based division of labor was seen as optimal and various theories evolved to explain and support it (Parsons & Bales, 1955). In recent years, women have challenged the usefulness of this construct (see Boss & Thorne, Chapter 5), and a growing understanding of the reciprocal relationship between work and the family has developed (Mortimer & Sorensen, 1984). Nevertheless, it is partly the legacy of separate gender-determined spheres that continues to keep women's work and men's work so sharply separated and so unequally reimbursed. When we try to figure out why women and men fare so differently in the workplace and why most couples have great difficulties sorting out who should do what, it helps to place the 1980s in historical perspective.

A brief look at the past sheds light on women's choices and opportunities today. There is evidence that, from the time of the hunting and gathering groups through preindustrial society, women actively joined men in work activities: securing, producing, and/or marketing goods and services in addition to performing the work of rearing children (Davis, 1984). During colonial and preindustrial American times, women produced goods and services in the home for sale or exchange and ran households that provided educational, health, and residential services. Since households were workshops, there was no clear separation between work life and family life (Havaran, 1982). American women were particularly adventurous; in fact, during the pioneer era women served a wide range of roles and were even elected to political office in many western townships. In Kansas City, for example, there were 16 women mayors by the year 1900 (Stratton, 1986). Women did not enjoy the legal rights or privileges of their brothers or husbands, but labor shortages and the attending need to use all able hands in a predominantly agricultural society meant that men, women, and children shared the work to keep family farms and businesses alive.

As society became more industrialized, economic and philosophical shifts gradually occurred. One major shift was the emergence of the family "breadwinner" concept. Men increasingly left the home to work in factories or other businesses. The family surrendered much of its previous activity to formal institutions, as hospitals, schools and asylums were built to take over the care and socialization of children and of the mentally and physically ill. No longer did husbands, wives and children share similar tasks within the home workplace, and increasingly men and women worked at different tasks.

As described by Hareven, the changes that evolved in family life varied and depended on class and ethnic origin. There was a major impact on middle-class families, which became more child-focused (although the birth rate was declining), more private, and more idealized as a haven away from the harsh world of work. Motherhood was glorified, while husbands and wives took separate roles and responsibilities. Rae Andre, in tracing the evolution of the modern homemaker, cites economist John Kenneth Galbraith, who suggested that in large part middle-class women's roles changed in post-industrial America due to the need in a modern society for people who would both serve and manage consumption. Women, he suggested, were elected to replace the old servant class and menial labor was redefined as a way to express love. A family structure with separate spheres for men and women became the disguise and the justification for the economic function of women (Andre, 1981).

These changes in middle-class family patterns, which discouraged women from working outside the home, were occurring at the same time that rural and immigrant women and children were being recruited into the New England textile mills in large numbers (Hareven, 1981). Class differences were also apparent in the South, where black women, including one-quarter of all married black women and two-thirds of all widowed black women, were employed outside the home (Blau, 1984). These working-class and minority families continued longer than middle-class families to adhere to the concept of the "family wage," as a much larger percentage of women from lower economic groups continued to work outside the home. In the early 20th century, as immigrant groups became more "Americanized," second- and third-generation families began to adopt middle-class ideology and to view the employment of a wife and mother as representative of her husband's failure and her children's loss. For most families a comprehensive separation between home and work occurred. Mothers were responsible for home and children, the private sphere; men were potent in the public domain. Turn-of-the-century feminists challenged these ideas, but their voices were barely heard. Men's work and women's work became increasingly differentiated, with legal, social, religious, medical, and moral belief systems supporting and enforcing the separation (Gerson, 1985; Goldner, 1985; Rossi, 1986). Severe social sanctions limiting women's activities to "appropriate" choices were erected; we are still feeling the legacy of these sanctions today.

Ushering in the '50s

Events during World War II and the decade immediately following offer an interesting contrast between the roles women can play and highlight the importance of cultural factors in choices that women make. From the early 1900s through World War II American women made gradual educational, economic and civil rights gains, so that by the 1940s they were ahead of their European counterparts in the attainment of advanced degrees and professional status. There had been a slow but steady stream of women into the paid workforce.

During World War II the number of women workers rose sharply and 60% of married women, most with school-age and preschool children, worked in factories and businesses to aid the war effort. The government mobilized to maximize women's participation, state-subsidized daycare was quickly established to encourage women to take jobs, and aggressive advertising proclaimed the availability of "men's jobs for men's pay." Although 95% of the women who took these jobs stated at the outset of the war that they would quit when the war ended, 80% later changed their minds. However, most wartime employees lost their jobs shortly after VJ Day, and many major companies re-instituted their prewar policies against hiring married women. Support for daycare also ceased (Hewlett, 1986). Immediately after the war there was a sharp dip in the number of employed women, but as the '40s waned labor force participation by women crept back, as women slowly returned to the paid labor force. But for middle-class women, the vast majority of women in this country, the 1950s was an era in which they became more housebound than they had been in several decades. A smaller percentage of Ph.D.'s was awarded to women than in the 1920s and 1930s, and the percentage who entered nontraditional fields decreased (Weitzman, 1984). Motherhood, increasingly glorified, became a "profession" in and of itself. For the first time in history, mothering became the middle-class American woman's role to the exclusion of almost everything else.

While the decade of the '50s appears aberrant in the larger context of women's history, it was a formative decade for women who are currently in prime childbearing and rearing life stages. The influential attitudes of this era continue to be reflected in the ways that women view themselves and their roles and to contribute to what others expect from them both inside and outside of the family.

The Post 1950s Era: Legal Challenges

As the 1950s closed, women had regained some of their pre-World-War-II representation in the workforce, but as they tried to pick up jackhammers and scalpels they encountered significant cultural and legal inequities. As the women's movement and civil rights activities again gained strength during the 1960s, American women began to challenge these unfair practices in the courts. As outlined by Opsata (1988), landmark legal decisions since that time have changed the face of the workplace in major ways:

- Prior to 1963 a woman employed in the same job by the same company could legally be paid less money for doing exactly the same work. The Equal Pay Act was passed in 1963.
- Before 1974 a bank could discriminate against a woman who tried to borrow money. This was on the basis that presumably her income was

not predictable because she might become pregnant and lose her job. The Equal Credit Opportunity Act made it illegal to discriminate based on sex or marital status.

- Until 1978, a woman could be fired if she became pregnant. The Pregnancy Discrimination Act of 1978 eliminated this inequity.
- Before 1984 a woman could be paid a smaller pension than her male coworker from the same employer even though she earned the same wage for the same length of time. This practice was defended using the argument that women live longer and therefore would collect the same amount over a longer span of time. The Economic Equity Act of 1984 eliminated this discriminatory option.
- In 1986 and 1987 women obtained legal rights to get their jobs back after pregnancy; to demand company protection from supervisors who were sexually harassing them; to have their applications accepted by all-male business-oriented clubs; and even to be able as civilians to go out to sea on navy submarines (not an irrelevant issue for women scientists and engineers whose work is dependent on this type of access) (Opsata, 1988).

The legal challenges are not over, and additional changes are needed. The next big battle will be fought for women's pay equity in the arena of "comparable worth," a major civil rights issue of the coming decade. As explained by Alice Rossi (1986), "equal pay for equal work" is not the critical variable in correcting the earning gap between men and women; rather, there is a need to employ the doctrine of "comparable worth." This premise suggests that women are commonly routed into job classifications on the basis of sex and are paid less than job classes that are traditionally male-dominated. It is not enough simply to open up male-dominated fields to women; in addition, wage inequities between types of jobs must be rectified. Only then will master's level nurses consistently make more than truck drivers without high school degrees or skilled secretaries more than parking lot attendants (Hewlett, 1986; Rossi, 1986).

The importance of pursuing civil rights activities and corrective legislative and legal action cannot be underestimated if women are ever to obtain economic parity with men. However, legal changes alone will not sufficiently improve the economic condition of women; changes in social policy and the family's division of labor must also take place. If and when legal inequities do not overtly block a woman's chance for advancement, excessive family responsibilities will.

DECIDING ON WORK, MARRIAGE, AND MOTHERHOOD

With increasing options regarding marriage, divorce, birth control, abortion, birth, education, and employment, many women will not, and in many cases cannot, make the same choices that their mothers made regarding family and work activities. In the ways that they structure their lives, women are choosing alternatives to traditional paths; yet each path—marriage with or without children; single whether by choice, death or divorce; work inside or outside the home; parenting alone or with help—has many crossroads and forks. Depending on which set of circumstances a woman chooses or inherits, different benefits and costs accrue.

Which Women are Employed?

A number of factors influence who seeks employment, but the greatest predictor is the availability of adequate income. Those women who are single, separated, or divorced have higher rates of employment than married women (see Table 1). Children also influence who seeks employment. Although percentages are increasing, mothers of young children under age six are still less likely to be employed than mothers with school-age children (see Table 2). The lower rates of employment for women with no children under 18 may reflect the fact that most of the women in this group are older with grown children; coming of age in the 50s, they were less likely to enter the job market than women who came of age in the '70s (Blau, 1984).

Education is also a factor; more highly educated women are more likely to be in the job market. According to the United States Census Bureau, in 1987 two-thirds of college-educated mothers returned to work before their infant's first birthday, compared to one-half of women with less education. For married women, the amount of money that their husband makes is also relevant. All other things being equal, the higher a husband's income, the less likely it is that a wife will be employed and the greater the likelihood that the wife will support the legitimacy of her husband's power in their relationship (Steil, 1984).

Obviously, a woman's earning ability is related to her educational background and past work experience, as is her husband's. Moreover, for both sexes *continuity* of employment is extremely important, since even relatively

TABLE 1   Female Labor Force Participation Rates for Women 16 and Over by Marital Status, 1986

Never Married.	65.3%
Married—Husband Present.	54.6%
Married—Husband Absent.	62.2%
Widowed.	43.1%
Divorced.	76%

(Bureau of Labor Statistics, 1987)

TABLE 2   Labor Force Participation Rates of Women 16 and over by Marital Status and Age of Children

	No Children Under 18	Children 6-17	Children Under 6
Married	48.2%	68.4%	53.8%
Divorced	72%	84.7%	73.8%

(Bureau of Labor Statistics, 1987)

short absences from the marketplace significantly alter income potential. Women are three times more likely than men to have interruptions in their job histories, particularly during the main childbearing years, a time when women's wages begin to fall significantly vis-à-vis their male counterparts (Hewlett, 1986).

In large measure, a woman's choice to seek employment is influenced by what she is giving up financially by not earning a wage. For example, if the earnings she loses by electing to stay at home represent a large fraction of potential household income, there is greater likelihood that she will be employed. If a woman's earnings contribute relatively little, other reasons to seek employment must be sufficiently strong to overcome the burden of the extra tasks associated with employment, particularly if there are young children in the home. Unfortunately, for many women there is a circular phenomenon: When they elect to stay out of the workforce for a period of time, their earning potential diminishes significantly, and the less earning potential they have, the less likely they are to enter the workforce at a decent wage.

INTEGRATING WORK AND FAMILY

In the following pages we look at common work patterns of married women in the current decade — dual-earner couples, dual-career couples, and traditional couples — and briefly address work and family issues for divorced and single women.

Dual-Earner Couples

Most employed women are married and live with husbands and children. This fact has been the cause of much attention and alarm, focusing on the potentially deleterious effects of work on the woman and her family (Barnett et al., 1987). In fact, much of the research on stress and employment has explored the negative consequences for men who are *not* employed and for women who *are* employed (Borman et al., 1984). Barnett et al. (1987), in reviewing the literature on stress and gender, postulates that the search for the negative stress factors for employed women may stem from the assumption that most women already have two primary roles, i.e. wife and mother, which are defined as fully demanding. Since paid employment is also viewed as very demanding, working women would inevitably experience stress. However, there is increasing evidence that women who hold jobs in addition to their roles as wife and mother report greater physical and psychological well-being than their housewife counterparts (Barrett et al., 1987; Baruch, Barnett, & Rivers, 1983; Meri Kangas, Prusoff, Kupfer, & Frank, 1985).

These data would seem to support the expansion hypothesis of human energy, which suggests that people with multiple roles have unique advantages and get different rewards from each of their activities, including financial gain, positive feedback, or self-esteem. These rewards balance the emotional and physical cost of additional activities. Men have traditionally held multiple roles and benefited from them. It appears that women are now beginning to experience some of these same benefits.

There are several additional reasons why employed women may demonstrate better physical and emotional health. Unpaid work has typically been devalued; when wives earn money they gain their husbands' respect and increase the amount of power they have in their marriages (Blumstein & Schwartz, 1983). Even in low level jobs women report benefits, including improved social contacts and an increased sense of accomplishment (Baruch et al , 1983). However, although overall benefits appear to accrue to working wives, most women can plan to have an extended work week by adding paid to unpaid tasks. This results largely from the fact that few couples have achieved anything close to symmetrical roles, even when both husband and wife are employed full-time. The majority of the household tasks continue to fall to women, whether they are employed or not (Blumstein & Schwartz, 1983).

Men have traditionally benefited at home by having jobs that paid money and gave them a way to barter for services. This bartering or role bargaining allows men to avoid some of the worst household/family tasks by offering to compensate in some other way. The average husband/father has been able to offer the money he earns for the extra time his wife might spend on the less desirable tasks related to the children or home maintenance. Because being a "good provider" has traditionally dovetailed with the definition of being a good husband and father, spending more time at work has been seen as positive for the family, and consequently viewed as a way of demonstrating family responsibility. Women who work in dual-earner couples usually earn less than their husbands. Their work is less likely to be regarded as a demonstration of family responsibility; rather, it is seen as optional. The home remains the primary responsibility of women.

Tasks in dual-earner families typically continue to fall along gender lines, with wives having much greater responsibility for the household and childcare. While employed women do less work around the home than their homemaker counterparts, their husbands do not alter their home responsibilities significantly and are unlikely to do more (Mortimer & Sorensen, 1984). Data from one study revealed that full-time housewives average 8.1 hours per day in household jobs, while employed wives average 4.8 hours per day. Husbands, however, averaged 1.6 hours per day whether or not their wives were employed (Portner, 1983). Although there are some data supporting the idea that when a wife's salary approaches her husband's he does more in the home (Model, 1982), gender roles are usually very durable. In fact, even unmarried couples tend to follow traditional patterns in the division of labor (Stafford, Backman, & DiBina, 1977). In sum, when a woman is employed she usually has two jobs. The resultant role strain can be very great, especially for those women employed full-time while their children are young. These women report more physical distress than women with young children who work part-time (Arber, Gilbert, & Dale, 1985).

Since most women maintain primary responsibility for children and home, they often report greater role conflict and worry about balancing activities at home and work than their husbands (Sekaran, 1986). Suckled on the psychological theories of the 1950s, most women of childbearing age have heard over and over again that women must stay out of the workforce or their children will suffer. Even when women reject this theory, there are few who don't experience tightening stomachs as they walk away from the babysitter and hear their child shrieking—even if it's only a ten-second response and the rest of the child's day goes well.

For women the boundary between work and home appears to be more permeable than for men. It is more often the woman who cancels work obligations to stay home with sick children or to handle family obligations that conflict with work schedules. Women report more preoccupation at work with matters at home, and children choose to telephone mothers at work much more often than they choose to interrupt fathers (Sekaran, 1986). Many of these data reflect the fact that, when women add employment responsibilities, there is not a corresponding shift to equal participation by men in the home.

For most working mothers, conflicts and problems related to childcare create the greatest stress. Even such relatively minor problems as snow days, sick children, late babysitters, and summer vacations can create enormously difficult logistical problems. Families with strong networks to help out with crises in daily living have more protection from the impact of these dilemmas (Asmundsson, 1981). Since the United States, unlike most European countries, has no national maternity or paternity leave policies and since most companies do not grant much leave, the childcare problems of parents begin when the baby is only several weeks old and continue throughout infancy and into the school years. Daycare is often expensive or inaccessible — a situation that seems to be getting worse. Federal funds for low cost daycare have decreased significantly since 1982 (Nelson, 1988). The paucity of resources forces many women to choose between giving up their jobs, which they usually cannot afford to do, or leaving their children with inadequate care.

The problems do not evaporate when the child enters school. For the older child with no stay-at-home parent, school days are too short and community-based afterschool and weekend programs too few. In 1986 an estimated five to ten million children fell into the category of "latchkey children," a term that refers to children who stay alone before or after school hours (BNA, 1986). There are insufficient studies to demonstrate the impact of less parental attention on these children, but in clinical settings parents frequently cite the unavailability of adults to provide supervision as a problem. Oftentimes women compromise and take jobs that are less satisfying or lower-paying in order to combine the tasks of home and work more easily.

How well a woman balances job and home tasks depends on numerous factors including: availability of childcare; flexibility in the workplace; attitudes toward employment; and adequate support. As with other life choices, having support to do what you want to do is vital to mental health and marital adjustment. There are some indications that both maternal and child adjustment is related to the congruence between a woman's desires and her actual activities. Mothers who want to be home but cannot afford to be often resent the need to be employed; mothers who prefer to be employed but are home full-time due to internal or external pressure also show dissatisfaction (Demris, Hock, & McBride, 1986). In addition, when a husband disagrees with his wife's work/home choice, tension can run very high.

In general, balancing work and home responsibilities is a challenge for these dual-earner couples. Women frequently are overloaded and ask their husbands for "help" with home tasks; unfortunately, marital conflict is often the result (Blumstein & Schwartz, 1983). Although egalitarian role-sharing may be an ideal for some couples, most women in dual-earner families continue to view themselves as the ones who *should* do most of the home-related tasks, but they often want more "help" than they are getting.

Some researchers have explored how couples resolve conflicts over lack of balance and equality. Rachlin's work (1987) suggests that many couples resolve this difference by striving for "equity," i.e., a sense of fairness rather than equality. In one-half of the "non-egalitarian" relationships that she studied, the individuals viewed themselves as equitably treated even though family roles were not equally divided. Apparently, for many couples a belief that the division of labor is "fair" is more important for marital satisfaction than "equal" division as viewed from an outside perspective. In many cases the husband's providing *any* childcare or doing *any* housework at all is such a net gain from what the partners saw in their families of origin that he is credited with great assistance for minimal support.

Typical clinical issues resulting from work/home imbalances may include:

- No time or energy allotted for the adult couple relationship, including recreational and sexual activities.
- Disagreements over what is equitable in household and childcare tasks.
- Criticism from extended family members, particularly toward mothers of young children who do not stay home full-time.
- Anxiety and guilt stemming from unmet self-expectations: men who think that they should be able to be the sole support of their families, and women who feel that they are bad mothers if they are not home full-time.
- Inappropriate expectations for older children, who may be burdened excessively with childcare responsibilities for younger siblings.
- Inadequate financial resources even with two pay checks to purchase helpful services or products.
- Lack of an adequate network to help with predictable as well as emergency problems.

Clinicians must help these families develop survival skills, since there is relatively little available community or social support. Children need increased training in self-reliance; parents need help reducing their unrealistic expectations that they can do everything well all of the time; couples need help in recognizing that they are not alone in their dilemma and in accessing support networks; women need help adjusting their levels of guilt and self-criticism; and men need help adjusting their attitudes and expectations that they should bear sole financial responsibility for the family and do little at home.

Dual-Career Couples

A dual-career marriage is defined as one in which both heads of a household develop an uninterrupted career (rather than a job) and simultaneously create a family life (Rapoport & Rapoport, 1971). It has been touted as the new form of egalitarian marriage and held up to women as the way to "have it all." The pressures on women in these dual-career arrangements are considerable, perhaps even requiring the "superwomen" described by newspaper columnist Ellen Goodman:

> Super Woman gets up in the morning and wakes her 2.6 children. She then goes downstairs and feeds them a Grade A nutritional breakfast and then goes upstairs and gets dressed in her Anne Klein suit and goes off to her $35,000 a year job doing work which is creative and socially useful. Then she comes home after work and spends a meaningful hour with her children because, after all, it's not the quantity of time—it's the quality of time. Following that, she goes into the kitchen and creates a Julia Child 60-minute gourmet recipe, having a wonderful family discussion about the checks and balances of the U. S. government system. The children go upstairs to bed and she and her husband spend another hour in their own meaningful relationship at which point they go upstairs and she is multi-orgasmic until midnight. (VanGelder, 1979)

Unfortunately, the above scenario is a goal that many women think they should achieve. "If I could only find a way to eliminate the need for sleep, I could probably do all these things," said one woman quite seriously. Many women who are choosing to combine home and family run in high gear most of the time, for there is little evidence to support the notion that most dual-career marriages are egalitarian—even when philosophically both husband and wife say that they want it to be (Gilbert, 1985; Rachlin, 1987).

Only a small percentage, roughly 14%, of dual-earner couples fall in the dual-career category (Portner, 1983), but they have commanded significant interest in the literature. This is due partly to the speculation that this group may increase in number as women continue to advance professionally and partly to the particular challenges that these couples face in trying to integrate home and work priorities. Unlike dual-earner couples, where one person, usually the woman, consistently places home and child needs before work demands, these couples are comprised of two "equal" parents, neither of whom is hypothetically willing automatically to make career compromises. These couples are piloting uncharted territory with few role models. If they are truly trying to share roles not based on traditional gender assignments, then they encounter on a daily basis choice points that often feel unclear, without historical precedent but not without pain. It is not surprising that these are difficult negotiations. The fact that the divorce rate for highly educated women (those with five or more years beyond high school) is higher than for any other group of women except those without high school diplomas suggests that the conflicts of these couples are frequently intense and the marital strains great (Houseknecht & Macke, 1981).

Families with two professional adults have numerous benefits. First of all, financial resources are greater, enabling them to buy help. The couple may develop a sense of collegiality, which can help keep marital satisfaction high. There is evidence that individuals in these marriages are more self-reliant and self-sufficient (Burke & Weir, 1976), and that children of these employed mothers are more independent and highly motivated (Hoffman, 1979).

Still there are difficulties for two partners actively pursuing demanding careers. Corporate America, academic institutions, law firms, and medical facilities are greedy organizations. Becoming a partner, obtaining tenure, or rising up the corporate ladder tends to require long hours, extensive travel, and often relocation. Two professionals equally committed to their careers have to contend with the possibility of incompatible choices and major compromises if they plan to remain married. More often it is the woman who relocates for her husband's career or who turns down offers that require her to relocate (Steil, 1984).

Childless couples have a greater chance than those with children of being able to manage the heavy demands of two careers and yet retain a personal life. It is not always optimal, but each can work a 12-hour day, six days a week, and collapse together in the evening. There is usually money to purchase meals out and household help. The crisis tends to come when there are children or when one must make career sacrifices for the greater good of the other or of the family. The crisis resolution, in combination with subtle discriminatory practices in the structure of the workplace, often leads to women experiencing less professional success (Epstein, 1980). Even when women start with the same education and the same entry level salaries, ten or so years into their professional careers they will have a lower rank and lower salary than their male counterparts (Kaufman, 1984; Morrison, White, & Van Velsor, 1987). Several factors contribute to this from inside and outside the family. Inside the family, women, even in dual-career families, provide more childcare and homemaking services. Women often take time off post childbirth or reduce their work hours to part-time or limit themselves to a 40-hour week. One new mother who asked to return to her Washington law firm half-time after the birth of her baby was told that half-time was possible. But since the average full-time attorney worked 74 hours per week, they would expect her to put in 37 hours. One could say that this is equitable, but one could also say that the world of work makes it unlikely that women who continue to bear children and the brunt of childrearing tasks can compete with men. Many economists suggest that much of the wage gap between men and women can be explained by even brief interruptions in their careers due to childbearing and rearing tasks (Hewlett, 1986).

Outside the family, women face problems in the work environment because they are women. Women at the top of prestigious professions are usually in the lower half of the pay categories of those professions. Women lawyers, physicians, and academics have lower salaries on average and specialize or cluster in subspecialities that are less prestigious (Kundsin, 1974; Kaufman, 1984). Although women are represented in most professions, they are grossly underrepresented in management positions. Several explanations are possible. One is that women are "crowded" into a few traditional female fields and that their lack of appropriate advanced training keeps them out of a broad cross-section of fields. Another is that women continue to be omitted from the upper ranks of almost all types of organizations because women are socialized in families to meet the needs of others, frequently without taking credit. They learn compliance and subordination to others, traits which are not functional in managerial capacities (Dexter, 1985). If this were true, however, simply changing women's behavior could result in their rise into managerial ranks. Unfortunately, the ways in which men perceive women's capacities is highly colored by their history with other women, the majority of whom have not held positions of power. What is seen as assertive in a man can be seen as aggressive or pathologic in a woman. Historically, what have been viewed as normal and desirable traits for a successful manager have been "male" characteristics; when demonstrated by a woman they become suspect. In essence, the very traits that would make a woman an effective leader and a desirable candidate for promotion would make her "odd" in the eyes of men.

Women's progress along the road to the top is also influenced by the availability of mentors, those who inspire, show the shortcuts, and point out the landmines. The lack of appropriate mentors is a problem for women. Too often male mentors of women assume a paternal role or adopt sexualized behaviors which interfere with a woman's goals for achievement. Additionally, the hiring and promotion process is frequently based on personal comfort, which often leads men to choose colleagues of the same sex. Moreover, the informal power network of organizations is often not accessible to women. Traditionally, golf dates, lunches, and private men's clubs have been the arenas in which the real decisions are made, before the meetings begin, leaving women out in the cold.

The fact that most men are used to dealing with women primarily as people to meet their needs for nurturance or sexual gratification may impair their ability to perceive a woman's capabilities accurately. Traditionally, employers have questioned whether a woman is as committed to her job as a male counterpart might be. If she is young, will she become pregnant? If she is pregnant, will she quit? If she is married, will she be able to relocate if need be? "The business of America is business," and people in professional jobs have been expected to put business first, above spouse and children, to engage, in effect, in "corporate bigamy." Professional men have traditionally had wives whose job it is to clean, cook, take care of the children and provide them with emotional support after a tough day. A woman who enters a similar high stress work environment with long hours and unending commitments usually has no spouse, a spouse who is as stressed as she is, or one who does not perceive his role to be one of providing nurturance and support to her and her career. For many women this stress is managed by having fewer or no children and sometimes no spouse. Numerous studies have documented that women executives have a much lower rate of marriage and higher rate of childlessness than their male counterparts or women in nonexecutive positions (Nieva, 1985).

One of the more difficult tasks for clinicians who provide marital therapy to these professional couples (aside from finding a time all three can meet) is to look at their own assumptions regarding the appropriate distribution of tasks and the choices they have made in their own lives. Even then clinicians may have problems helping couples resolve these issues in a way that is equitable for everyone and does not impose biases and assumptions. These topics hit very close to home. Some of the common problems for the dual-career group include:

- Increased power struggles, since roles are less stereotyped and responsibilities must be negotiated.
- Inability to achieve a distribution of tasks that is perceived as fair by both partners.
- Lack of energy available in either partner for mutual nurturance and support.
- Lack of an extended family support network, frequently due to geographic separation from families of origin.
- Problems related to decisions about whether or not to have children.
- Infertility problems which may be less successfully resolved in women who have delayed childbirth decisions in order to establish careers.
- Lack of time for individual or family leisure activities, particularly in households with young children.
- Conflicts regarding one spouse's need for or interest in relocation for career advancement.
- Time conflicts around social activities, some of which may be work related.
- Professional competition between the spouses regarding the rate of career accomplishments.

Traditional Families

By and large the social status of the housewife is determined by her husband's status; however, even when that status is high the role of homemaker is typically devalued. There has been very little economic value placed on the many important tasks these women perform. One study estimated that it takes 60 hours per week to provide physical and emotional support for a family of four (Hewlett, 1986). Most people who have spent time managing a household with children recognize that it takes a fair amount of patience, savvy, and energy to clean, cook, and parent creatively. The fact that the job of homemaker was evaluated by government classifications as requiring the same level of skill as a parking lot attendant would be ludicrous if it weren't so tragic.

Unfortunately, with few exceptions how much a job pays has been the measure of its worth. More than 99% of the over 30 million people in this country who list homemaker as their occupation are women (Andre, 1981). The problems for these women are significant. They earn no wage and have little discretionary income. Lacking financial resources, they are dependent on the will of others, unable to leave even a bad marriage. The change to no-fault divorce laws and the growing societal belief that women have good employment options mean that most women who have spent the bulk of their years at home out of the job market will not receive the support they need if they find themselves alone through divorce or widowhood. They will be left with few skills, no track record of employment, and frequently little self-confidence. Old age for these women may bring poverty. With increases in the divorce rate, a new class of women — "displaced homemakers" — has emerged (Greenwood-Audant, 1984).

There is some evidence that the greater a husband's income, the more likely it is that his wife will believe in her husband's legitimate right to greater power in their relationship, and that White middle-class housewives have less power in marital relationships than any other group of women (Steil, 1984). They have little role-bargaining ability and show higher rates of psychological distress than their employed cohorts (Barnett et al., 1987; Brown & Harris, 1978). Unemployed middle-class women married to professional men frequently have developed a supportive or adjunctive spouse role through which their personal status is derived from their husband's success. It is not uncommon for wives of physicians, ministers, military officers, politicians, academics, corporate executive, etc., to assume a supportive role in which psychological support, household management, clerical or secretarial functions, collegial entertainment, and community liaison roles are an expected and necessary part of her commitment and job, a job that makes his career possible. This "two-person career" (Papanek, 1973) arrangement often translates into institutional expectations for the wife and positive reinforcement (though not independent monetary reinforcement) from the husband and his employer for her helpful behavior. It is noteworthy that there is some evidence that professional men whose wives also pursue careers achieve less professionally (fewer published papers, etc.) than professional men with traditional wives (Hunt & Hunt, 1982). The particular advantages for a man of having an educated wife whose energy is directed toward his career are usually underestimated (Hunt & Hunt, 1977). Professional women usually cannot expect to receive this type of support from their spouses.

For the traditional homemaker, the home is frequently child-centered. Much of daily life and family activity is related to the tasks of childrearing. The impact on children of having full-time care from at least one parent rather than parental substitutes is not completely clear, but so far empirical evidence has failed to uncover negative emotional or cognitive deficits in children of employed versus unemployed mothers (Hoffman, 1979; Lamb, 1984). If, as mentioned earlier, the major factor in children's adjustment is congruence between what the mother wants to do and what she is doing, children of homemaking mothers who choose not to be employed should do well.

Middle age may hit the child-centered woman harder than the employed woman. As children mature, couples often must renegotiate their relationship. In some families, husbands who were supportive of their wives' being homemakers while the children were young may be less supportive of this arrangement once the children reach adolescence. Since this stage of the family life cycle is one in which expenses escalate, a husband might come to prefer a money earning partner. However, a wife at this point may be anxious about her skills or resent pressure to change her lifestyle. There is evidence, however, that when couples disagree, more wives want to be employed than husbands want them to be, and that disagreement over employment correlates with marital unhappiness (Blumstein & Schwartz, 1983). Role disagreements may bring couples into treatment as they attempt to renegotiate their relationship. Spouses who have had some non-child-centered activities as a couple or separate individual interests are less vulnerable to crisis; for many of these women, in fact, mid-life offers new opportunities and options.

With divorce rates hovering near the 50% mark, "until death do us part" can no longer be counted on as a realistic end to marriage. Divorcing homemakers cannot realistically expect full protection under the law. A woman who decides to defer her employment opportunities and care for children while her husband develops his career will find that, if divorce ensues, there is usually no consideration given to the loss of her future earning potential based on their joint decision that she would stay home while he earned the money. Her lack of continuous employment usually means that her reentry salary will be low and her future prospects much less promising than they would have been earlier. Alimony is awarded in only a few cases, and even child support is less than dependable. Only 20% of men are in full compliance with child support orders and only another 15% partially comply (Arendell, 1987).

If divorce occurs, men leave marriage with their status and earning abilities intact. They have pensions and their standard of living typically goes up while a woman's plummets. Studies have found a direct relationship between a woman's economic recovery post divorce and her employment status while married. Four years post divorce, women who worked regularly before the divorce had incomes that were 80% of their average family income while married. Women who were not employed pre divorce were only at the 50% mark (Arendell, 1987). As the statistics discussed earlier confirm, most divorced women with or without young children end up employed. As a group, their salaries are low, and although they need more help and support in surviving job and mothering demands than women with husbands, they can least afford the extra sitters, meals out and household help that many two-paycheck families rely on.

Consequently, women who do elect to remain at home to take care of others can be vulnerable if the marriage breaks up. The problem is that we live in a culture that devalues this role, empowers its members through money, creates laws that give women no financial protection, and permits a fairly high divorce rate. This makes the traditional homemaker role a very risky one!

Clinical concerns in this group include:

- Couples may have disagreements over sex-role expectations – women frequently want more involvement from their husbands regarding home and childcare responsibilities.
- Spouses may disagree regarding whether the wife should be employed.
- Marital power is often unequal and there may be disagreements regarding financial expenditures, personal autonomy and childrearing decisions.
- The emancipation of children may cause role confusion in women who have been predominantly child-focused.
- Displacement of homemaker role through death or divorce can result in financial and/or emotional crisis.
- Overinvolvement in work and corresponding lack of emotional input into family relationships by the husband.
- An increased risk for social isolation of the homemaker.

In summary, a woman's employment status is relevant to her physical and psychological well-being. Access to jobs and the attending ability to achieve in arenas other than mothering and homemaking appear to offer benefits that improve women's lives in financial, psychological, and physical ways. There is no empirical evidence to suggest that children are adversely affected by having two employed parents, although the stress related to lack of social supports, particularly childcare resources, is significant, particularly for single mothers. Increased marital conflict appears to be likely as couples attempt to negotiate these highly ambiguous roles and the competing demands between home and work environments. Therapists will need to recognize the serious problems that most families face as they attempt to negotiate a reasonable home/work, husband/wife balance and must help couples and individuals who are struggling with the confusion that abounds as men and women try on new ways of connecting and achieving in both of these important spheres. In many ways we are living in a time of crisis, bringing with it both threat and opportunity. Men and women have much to gain by helping each other redefine and balance both love and work.

REFERENCES

Aldous, J. (Ed.). (1982). *Two paychecks: Life in dual-earner families*. Beverly Hills, CA: Sage Publications.

Andre, R. (1981). *Homemakers: The forgotten workers*. Chicago, IL: The University of Chicago Press.

Arber, S., Gilbert, G. N., & Dale, A. (1985). Paid employment and women's health: A benefit or a source of role strain? *Sociology of Health and Illness, 7*(3).

Arendell, T. J. (1987). Women and the economics of divorce in the contemporary United States. *Journal of Women in Culture and Society*. The University of Chicago.

Asmundsson, R. (1981). Women at work: Stresses within the family. In C. Getty, & W. Humphreys, (Eds.), *Understanding the Family*. New York: Appleton-Century-Croft.

Bane, M. (1976). *Here to stay: American families in the twentieth century*. New York: Basic Books.

Barnett, R., Biener, L., & Baruch, G. (1987). *Gender and stress*. New York: The Free Press.

Baruch, G., Barnett, R., & Rivers, C. (1983). *Lifeprints: New patterns of love and work for today's women*. New York: New American Library.

Berg, B. J. (1986). *The crisis of the working mother*. New York: Summit Books.

Blau, F. (1984). Women in the labor force: An overview. In J. Freeman (Ed.), *Women: A feminist perspective*. Mayfield Publishing Company.

Blumstein, P., & Schwartz, P. (1983). *American couples: Money, work, sex*. New York: William Morrow.

Borman, K. M., Quarm, D., & Gideonse, S. (Eds.) (1984). *Women in the workplace: Effects on families*. Norwood, NJ: Ablex.

Brown, G. W., & Harris, T. O. (1968). *Social origins of depression: A study of psychiatric disorders in women*. New York: Free Press.

Bureau of Labor Statistics (1987). *Statistical abstract of the United States* (107th Edition). U. S. Department of Commerce.

Bureau of National Affairs, Inc. (BNA) (1986). *Work and family: A changing dynamic*. Books Demand UMI.

Burke, R. J., & Weir, T. (1976). Relationship of wives' employment status to husbands, wife and pair satisfaction. *Journal of Marriage and the Family, 38*, 279–87.

Davis, K. (1984). Wives and work: Consequences of the sex role revolution, population. *Development Review*, September, 397–418.

DeMeis, D. K., Hock, E., & McBride, S. (1986). The balance of employment and motherhood: Longitudinal study of mothers' feelings about separation from their first-born infants. *Developmental Psychology, 22*(5) 627–32.

Dexter, C. R. (1985). Women and the exercise of power in organizations: From ascribed to achieved status. In Larwood et al. (Eds.). *Woman and work*. Beverly Hills, CA: Sage Publications.

Epstein, C. (1980). The new women and the old establishment. *Sociology of Work and Occupations, 7*(3), 310.

Folbre, N. (1987). The pauperization of motherhood: Patriarchy and public policy in the United States. In N. Gerstel & H. E. Gross, *Families and work*. Philadelphia, PA: Temple University Press.

Gerson, K. (1985). *Hard choices*. Berkeley, CA: University of California Press.

Gilbert, L. A. (1985). *Men in dual-career families: Current realities and future prospects*. Hillsdale, NJ: Lawrence Erlbaum.

Goldberg, G. S., & Kremen, E. (1987). The feminization of poverty: Only in America? *Social Policy*, Spring, 279–90.

Goldner, V. (1985). Feminism and family therapy. *Family Process, 24*, 31–47.

Greenwood-Audant, L. M. (1984). The internalization of powerlessness: A case study of the misplaced homemaker. In J. Freeman (Ed.). *Women: A feminist perspective*. Palo Alto, CA: Mayfield.

Hareven, T. K. (1982). American families in transition: Historical perspectives on change. In F. Walsh (Ed.). *Normal family processes*. New York: Guilford.

Hewlett, S. A. (1986). *A lesser life: The myth of women's liberation in America*. New York: Warner Books.

Hoffman, L. W. (1979). Maternal employment: 1979. *American Psychologist, 34*, 859–65.

Hoffnung, M. (1984). Motherhood: Contemporary conflict for women. In J. Freeman (Ed.). *Women: A feminist perspective*. Palo Alto, CA: Mayfield.

Houseknecht, S. K., & Macke, A. S. (1981). Combining marriage and career: The marital adjustment of professional women. *Journal of Marriage and the Family*, August.

Hunt, J. G., & Hunt, L. L. (1982). Dual-career families: Vanguard of the future or residue of the past. In *Two paychecks: Life in dual-earner families*. Beverly Hills, CA: Sage Publications.

Hunt, J. G., & Hunt, L. L. (1977). Dilemmas and contradictions of status: The case of the dual-career family. *Social Problems, 24*, 407–16.

Johnson, C. L., & Johnson, F. A. (1980). Parenthood, marriage, and careers: Situational constraints and role strain. In F. Pepitone & Rockwell (Ed.), *Dual career couples*. Beverly Hills, CA: Sage Publications.

Kaufman, D. R. (1984). Professional women: How real are the recent gains? In J. Freeman (Ed.). *Women: A feminist perspective*. Palo Alto, Ca: Mayfield.

Kundsin, R. B. (1974). *Women and success*. New York: William Morrow.

Lamb, R. B. (1974). Fathers, mothers, and childcare in the 1980s: Family influences on child development. In K. Borman et al. (Eds.). *Women in the workplace: Effects on families*. Ablex Publication.

Merikangas, K. R., Prusoff, B., Kupfer, D., & Frank, E. (1985). Marital adjustment in major depression. *Journal of Affective Disorder, 9*, 5–11.

Model, S. (1982). Housework by husbands: Determinants and implications in two paychecks. In J. Aldous, *Two paychecks: Life in dual-earner families*. Beverly Hills, CA: Sage.

Morrison, A., White, R., & Van Velsor, E., and the Center for Creative Leadership (1987). *Breaking the glass ceiling: Can women reach the top of America's largest corporations*. Reading, MA: Addison-Wesley.

Mortimer, J. T., & Sorenson, G. (1984). Men, women, work and family. In K. Borman et al. *Women in the workplace: Effects on families*. Norwood, NJ: Ablex.

Myrdal, A., & Klein, V. (1986). *Women's two roles: Home and work*. London: Routledge and Kegan Paul.

Nelson, M. (1988). Providing family day care: An analysis of home-based work. *Social Problems, 35*(1), 78–94.

New York Times (1987). 23 February, E6.

Nieva, V. F. (1985). Work and family linkages. In L. Larwood et al. (Eds.). *Women and work*. Beverly Hills, CA: Sage.

Opsata, M. (1988). Legal gains. *Women's Issue: Graduating Engineer*, 41–44.

Papanek, H. (1973). Men, women and work: Reflections on the two-person career. *American Journal of Sociology, 78*, 852–72.

Parsons, T., & Bales, R. F. (1955). *Family socialization and interaction process*. New York: Free Press.

Peplau, L. A. (1984). Power in dating relationships. In J. Freeman (Ed.). *Women: A feminist perspective*. Palo Alto, CA: Mayfield.

Portner, J. (1983). Work and family: Achieving a balance. In H. McCubbin & C. Figley (Eds.). *Stress and the family I: Coping with normative transitions*. New York: Brunner/Mazel.

Rachlin, V. (1987). Fair vs. equal role relations in dual-career and dual-earner families: Implications for family interventions. *Family Relations, 36* 187–92.

Rapoport, R., & Rapoport, R. N. (1971). *Dual career families*. London: Penguin.

Rossi, A. (1971). Sex and gender in the aging society. In A. Pifer & L. Bronte (Eds.). *Out aging society: Paradox and promise* (pp. 111–39). New York: Norton.

Sekaran, U. (1986). *Dual-career families: Contemporary organizational and counseling issues*. San Francisco: Jossey-Bass.

Shortridge, K. (1984). Poverty is a woman's problem. In J. Freeman (Ed.). *Women: A feminist perspective*. Palo Alto, CA: Mayfield.

Stafford, R., Backman, E., & DiBina, P. (1977). The division of labor among cohabiting and married couples. *Journal of Marriage and Family, 39*(1), 45–38.

Statistical Abstract of the United States (1987). 107th Edition. U. S. Department of Commerce, Bureau of Labor Statistics.

Steil, J. M. (1984). Marital relationships and mental health: The psychic costs of inequality. In J. Freeman (Ed.). *Women: A feminist perspective*. Palo Alto, CA: Mayfield.

Stratton, J. (1981). Pioneer women: Voices. In *Kansas Frontier*. New York: Simon & Schuster.

VanGelder, L. (1979). Ellen Goodman: A columnist you can trust. *Ms.*, March.

Weitzman, L. J. (1984). Sex role socialization: A focus on women. In J. Freeman (Ed.). *Women: A feminist perspective*. Palo Alto, CA: Mayfield.

19

Women and Serious Mental Disorders

CAROL M. ANDERSON   DIANE P. HOLDER

> . . . to be born a woman means to inhabit, from early infancy to the last day of
> life, a psychological world which differs from the world of men.
>
> —M. Komarovsky, 1953

WHILE WOMEN MAY inhabit a psychological world different from that of
men, with different behaviors and opportunities, these identified differences
have had surprisingly little influence on the definitions of normality and
pathology that are applied to them. Historically, men have had the power
within the family and within society to define the appropriateness of wom-
en's behavior, as well as the right to control that behavior and to determine
the fate of women both medically and legally. In a recent review of early
mental health treatments for women, Geller reports a story told by Elizabeth
Parson Ware Packard, the wife of a Presbyterian minister in Illinois in 1860,
concerning the events occurring after she expressed religious views which
conflicted with the creed of the church. She recounts:

> Early on the morning of the 18th of June, 1860, as I arose from my bed, prepar-
> ing to take my morning bath, I saw my husband approaching the door with two
> physicians, both members of his church and of our Bible-class, —and a stranger
> gentleman, sheriff Burgess. Fearing exposure I hastily locked my door, and pro-
> ceeded with the greatest dispatch to dress myself. But before I had hardly com-
> menced, my husband forced an entrance into my room through the window with

an ax! And I, for shelter and protection against an exposure in a state of almost entire nudity, sprang into bed, just in time to receive my unexpected guests. The trio approached my bed, and each doctor felt my pulse, and without asking a single question pronounced me insane. . . .

My husband then informed me that the "forms of law" were all complied with, and he therefore requested me to dress my self for a ride to Jacksonville to enter the Insane Asylum as an inmate. I objected, and protested against being imprisoned without any trial. But to no purpose. My husband insisted upon it that I had no protection in the law, but himself, and that he was doing by me just as the laws of the State allowed him to do. . . .

When once in the Asylum I was beyond the reach of all human aid, except what could come through my husband, since the law allows no one to take them out, except the one who put them in, or by his consent; and my husband determined never to take me out. (Packard, 1866, in Geller, 1985)

Examples of men controlling noncompliant but mentally well women in the early days of the mental hygiene movement are not uncommon. Of course, the point could be made that these particular events took place over 100 years ago, when commitment procedures were more subjective and the rights of both sexes more easily abused. However, there are *no* accounts of women inflicting any such blatant injustice upon their husbands.

The power of men at that time was not limited to the physical control, abuse, or coercion of women in the name of mental health treatment; rather, it extended to the right to develop theories about female dysfunction and to define and apply treatments for "mental problems" thus defined. For instance, in the 19th century, when a woman with mental problems was diagnosed as having an "irritable uterus" (hysteralgia), a common treatment was to insert leeches into her uterus (Ashwell, 1845). One of the most popular treatments of women involved removing their ovaries (Morton, 1893); this procedure was recommended for a variety of reasons, including making a woman more "tractable" (Fisher, 1987; Geller, 1985). Despite the fact that men of the day had mental problems as well, there is no record of the development of any theory that located the source of such problems in the male genitalia, and certainly no evidence of leeches being applied to a man's penis or testicles.

During the latter half of the 19th century, the treatment of neurasthenia or "American nervousness" in women included admonitions to avoid straining the brain, to forgo intellectual work, to lead as domestic a life as possible, and to keep the children near at all times (Geller, 1985). One can only imagine the strains caused by prescriptions such as these on depressed women, and only wonder at the elements of social control inherent in defining anything other than domesticity as bad for a woman's mental health.

Certainly, today women cannot be controlled or abused by either their husbands or the mental health system in quite such drastic a way. On the other hand, the use of diagnosis and treatment as a form of social control is still a very real risk. In fact, these early interventions may only seem extreme because they are not based on our current assumptions. Our current practices may be equally problematic for women but may be so much a part of the way things are that we fail to appreciate just how damaging they might be. Nevertheless, we are beginning to be more aware that there are some aspects of our thinking about psychiatric disorders that are damaging to the self-concepts, adjustment, and success of women.

CURRENT VIEWS

Our current standard of psychological health is male. Differences from this standard tend to be regarded as pathological and/or less desirable. The now classic Broverman study (Broverman et al., 1970) documented the influence of sex-role stereotypes on clinicians' judgments of mental health. This project demonstrated that men and women are viewed as having different characteristics, with male characteristics being more highly valued and more closely approximating what is thought to be the mentally healthy adult. Compared to men, a healthy woman was seen as more submissive, more easily influenced, less aggressive, less independent, less adventurous, less competitive, more excitable, more easily hurt, more emotional, more concerned with appearance, less objective. In other words, the definitions of appropriate mentally healthy adult behaviors and appropriate feminine behaviors are at odds, leaving women in the bind of having to choose between two valued but incompatible sets of behavior. If they exhibit the socially valued characteristics of healthy adults, their femininity is questioned; if they behave as women are expected to behave, they are less healthy and attain a "second-class" adult status.

In addition to having their behavior defined as less healthy, women in our culture are more likely to be blamed for their own problems and for those of other family members, a responsibility even women themselves tend to accept. *DSM-III-R* (APA, 1987) includes "masochism" as a diagnosis, one which will lend itself to blaming the female victim of male abuse when she does not leave a destructive relationship, regardless of the fact that she may lack the social, psychological, or fiscal supports for doing so. If a woman's psychological "symptoms" can be explained by the unhealthy or destructive situation in which she lives, then it seems reasonable that we should be less interested in providing either a diagnosis or treatment than in modifying the context of her life.

In addition to theories about how the abused wife might provoke her husband, there also are numerous theories about the role played by the alcoholic's wife in encouraging and maintaining her husband's drinking (Jacob et al., 1978). Mothering has also come to be viewed as the cause of a child's major psychiatric disorder; the concept of "schizophrenogenic mother" (Fromm-Reichmann, 1948) is just one of many examples. For years, and even today, child guidance clinics have emphasized the involvement of mothers—not fathers—in the child's treatment. The implicit message of blame and responsibility is obvious, sometimes even explicit. In fact, mothers with problematic offspring have been described in so many negative ways (cold, intrusive, overinvolved, etc.) that one wonders if any new methods of blaming them are even possible (Chess & Thomas, 1982). Despite the increased popularity of family systems thinking and the use of circular causality to explain interactive behaviors, there has been no decrease in the number of pejorative terms used for mothering and women in the professional literature. In fact, a recent review of several professional journals revealed that mothers were blamed for 72 different kinds of pathology (Caplan & Hall-McCorquodale, 1985).

Oddly enough, men/fathers are rarely held responsible for the mental disorders of their wives and children in anything close to a corresponding way. For instance, in disorders more commonly displayed in women (i.e., depression, anorexia, agoraphobia), there have been no terms coined to describe a potentially destructive role for the woman's husband/father. In fact, some still consider these disorders to be the fault of mothers (Chernin, 1986).

Our predisposition to define women as disordered and to hold them accountable for their own problems and those of others no doubt influences their self-esteem, well-being, and functioning. The treatments provided for these problems may in fact cause additional troubles. For instance, while abuse of alcohol and nonprescription drugs is a serious issue for women, perhaps their most pervasive and neglected drug-related problem is the abuse of sedatives and minor tranquilizers, a problem influenced by gender issues and perpetuated by physicians. Women are more likely to be prescribed minor tranquilizers—some suggest as a way of dismissing their very real complaints. While it is likely that many physicians overprescribe drugs for women for this very reason (Mogul, 1985), it is also possible that "normal" feminine behaviors are viewed as too emotional or even dysfunctional by some male physicians.

On the other hand, there are instances in which the very drugs which might have helped women recover more quickly have been withheld when they were thought to be "good psychotherapy candidates" who should be left depressed or anxious to maintain their motivation for treatment. Which alternative—psychotherapy or drugs—is more effective is a matter for debate; in either case women often are not given sufficient information to make an informed choice about how *they* wish to deal with their symptoms. Unfortunately, even women themselves tend to regard the very real stresses in their lives or the problematic effects of marriage and childrearing as evidence of their personal inadequacy and failure. Thus, they may turn to psychotropic drugs for relief rather than taking action to correct the negative forces acting upon them and their relationships.

These attitudes, as well as other gender-related phenomena such as early sexual abuse, may even influence the development, incidence, or onset of some psychiatric disorders, particularly such disorders as agoraphobia, sexual dysfunction, dysthymia, substance abuse, and borderline states. For instance, there seems to be a correlation between early childhood sexual abuse and later substance abuse in adult women. In a group of walk-ins to a community mental health center, 27% of those women who had been abused had an alcohol problem, compared to 11% who had not been abused; 21% of previously sexually abused women had a drug addiction, compared to 2% of nonvictims (Brown & Finkelhor, 1986). In fact, close to 50% of hospitalized patients report having experienced some type of abuse during childhood. While boys and men are also sexually abused, more than 80% of the victims of family sexual abuse, spouse abuse, and elder abuse are women (Carmen, Rieker, & Mills, 1984; Finkelhor, 1983; Goodwin, 1982; Kosbery, 1982; Pagelow, 1981).

Various anxiety disorders and phobias are particularly problematic for women and affect a disproportionate number (Miller & Kirsh, 1987), severely impeding their lives and curtailing their social and work functioning. In fact, the rates for agoraphobia are typically two or three times higher for females than males (Turns, 1985), and the *DSM-III-R* (APA, 1987) indicates that simple phobias are diagnosed in women far more often than in men. Some feel, however, that since animal phobias were reported nine times more frequently by women than men, the exclusion of this subgroup would leave a less pronounced gender discrepancy (Marks, 1970).

While there is some controversy about research regarding sex differences, we can state unequivocally that women seek treatment for anxiety more often than men (Sturgis & Reda, 1984). One hypothesis frequently cited to explain this finding is that women find it socially acceptable to express feelings of fear, since they are socialized to internalize and express emotion, while men are taught to channel their feelings into physical activity (Barnett & Baruch, 1987) and to cope with them through alcohol. The effects that accompany the diagnosis of women as anxious are usually not discussed, i.e., the imposition of social control, a sense of decreased power and self-efficacy, and the redefinition of possibly legitimate complaints as symptomatology.

There is almost no clinical or empirical literature discussing the etiology or treatment from a woman's viewpoint. Early psychoanalytic thinking about anxiety did not address women separately. Freud and many of his followers felt that anxiety was manifested when the sexual act failed to produce "appropriate psychic satisfaction" (Snaith, 1968). Given the state of understanding and thinking about women's sexuality during that era (women were not supposed to have sexual needs and female enjoyment was not considered essential or even desirable), one might expect that most women would have had anxiety neuroses at least until well into the 1950s and 1960s, which, of course, they didn't.

Does the social context in which women live *cause* serious mental disorders? Probably not. There are developmental differences between men and women which are psychobiological. When impairments occur in these processes by gender, they are likely to manifest themselves behaviorally by gender. Victimization and the politics of labeling can be contributing forces or risk factors for women, since illness, even if totally caused by psychobiological processes, will manifest itself behaviorally in sociocultural context.

Even if the predisposition to major psychiatric disorders, such as schizophrenia and affective disorders, exists independently of social factors, gender-related psychosocial events and relationship issues minimally will influence the presentation, onset, course, outcome, and treatment of these problems. Given this possibility, it is truly surprising that theories, research and treatment programs have failed to differentiate subjects or patients on the basis of gender, and have failed to address the special needs of women with serious dysfunctions. It was not until 1985 that the Public Health Service Task Force on Women's Health Issues published its report urging attention to diseases and conditions of women, resulting in written requests from the NIH that grant applicants and providers *consider* the inclusion of women in study populations for all clinical research efforts and that gender differences be noted and evaluated (Department of Health Services, 1985).

Gender issues are relevant to multiple components of serious dysfunctions, relating to etiology, course and treatment. When a woman becomes dysfunctional, her entire family is disrupted in a variety of ways. When another family member is dysfunctional, women are expected to provide nurturance and caretaking, sometimes in ways that are beyond any normal individual's capacity to cope. When they attempt to perform these impossible tasks, they are criticized for being overinvolved with their offspring.

Because the topic of women and all serious dysfunctions is far too large for this space, this chapter will highlight the gender issues and differences in three major psychiatric problems—eating disorders, schizophrenia, and depression.

EATING DISORDERS

Eating disorders such as anorexia and bulimia are "women's diseases," intricately intertwined with our culture's view of women, how they look and their place in the social order. For the past several decades women have been victims of a standard of beauty that places enormous pressure on them to be thin. Although in our Western world almost all women have enough to eat, we admonish them not to eat too much, and we extol an "ideal" body weight that for most women is impossible to maintain, is physically unhealthy, and may prevent the adequate function of their hormones and biological reproductive systems.

As the pressure to diet and remain thin has mounted and has become a mainstream cultural value, there has been a corresponding increase in the prevalence of anorexia nervosa and bulimia nervosa. Currently an estimated 1% of all teenage girls and women in their twenties suffer from anorexia nervosa and approximately 5% from bulimia nervosa (Crisp, Palmer, & Kalucy, 1976; Hsu & Holder, 1986). The overwhelming majority of anorectic and bulimic patients are women (Garfinkel & Garner, 1982; Root, Fallon, & Friedrich, 1986). These are serious disorders with potentially severe physical and psychological manifestations and consequences; in fact, anorexia has one of the highest mortality rates of any psychiatric illness (Garfinkel & Garner, 1982).

Anorexia nervosa is characterized by the pursuit of a low body weight and an exaggerated fear of fatness, even when a person is in an emaciated state. Over time the drive for thinness becomes excessive and control over food intake is required for the person to feel a sense of mastery over her body and control in her life. Identified by Gull in the 1600s anorexia has typically affected primarily adolescents and young women in their twenties. While the disorder is more prevalent in the upper socioeconomic groups and more common in Caucasian women, there is evidence that it is increasing in older women, Black women, oriental women and across all categories of the socioeconomic spectrum (Garfinkel & Garner, 1982).

Bulimia or "ox appetite" is a syndrome in which people experience a compulsion for excessive food intake or gorging in the context of extreme fear of weight gain. Constant preoccupation with food and self-depreciating thoughts and depressed mood are frequently present. These women are highly critical of their bodies and in perpetual pursuit of a lower body weight. This pursuit means that following episodes of binge eating some type of purging occurs, usually through vomiting or laxative abuse.

There is a question of whether or not anorexia and bulimia are manifestations of the same underlying disorder. Although defined separately, they appear to overlap and to be related; for example, 50% of anorectics develop bulimia and a significant percentage of affected women tend to alternate between the two disorders (Fairburn & Garner, 1986). There are numerous theories regarding the etiology of anorexia and bulimia, including biological, psychological, and cultural explanations. Some have concluded that these disorders represent a final common pathway and that a biopsychosocial perspective with a broad lens is required to understand these self-destructive patterns (Johnson & Maddi, 1985).

There are many intriguing questions related to eating disorders. Why has the prevalence of eating disorders increased in recent years? Why do they tend to develop mostly in women? And why have they been more common in Caucasians and middle- and upper-middle-class women? All cultures have aesthetic ideals and most have strong opinions about women's bodies. Throughout history there have been standards of beauty which required procedures that were actually physically harmful. In pre-revolutionary China, for example, the feet of young well-to-do Chinese girls were bound. This created for them a beautiful "lily" foot and required that they be waited upon and carried about as a sign of their high social status. Unfortunately, their crippled feet did not allow them to walk.

What is considered beautiful varies according to the culture and the era. The plump female body has been considered beautiful in societies in which food is scarce and full-bodied women represent strength, wealth, and fecundity. The paintings of Rubens and Botticelli idealize the female body as curved and rounded; in fact, in some times and cultures plumpness was admired as a secondary sexual characteristic (Garfinkel & Garner, 1982). However, the standards in Western society have shifted dramatically, until now bony, prepubescent figures are considered more attractive and desirable.

The entire culture has become increasingly preoccupied with weight. Most American women do not like their bodies or are critical of some part of them. As a result a large percentage attempt to shape themselves into more acceptable packages. By the late 1970s over 300,000 women annually were having their breasts enlarged and another 20,000 were having them reduced (Chernin, 1981). Millions of dollars are spent annually on diet books, clubs and supplies; fat farms have come a major industry; Miss America contestants have on average become steadily thinner over the past 20 years and each winner has been thinner yet; and *Playboy* magazine's centerfolds have significantly dropped in average weight over the same period (Garfinkel & Garner, 1982). Madison Avenue bombards women on a daily basis—it is difficult to pick up a magazine or turn on a television show without women hearing that their hair isn't shiny enough, their eyelashes aren't long enough, and their bodies aren't thin enough. It is big business in the Western world to help women believe that they must alter themselves in major ways in order to be beautiful, and beauty continues to be a major measure of female worth.

Within this cultural context most female high school and college students begin to diet at some point (Root et al., 1986), and a percentage of these women are ripe to develop an eating disorder. Girls and women who are particularly vulnerable appear to be those who have a premorbid sense of helplessness and powerlessness about their lives. Their family histories are often positive for depression or alcoholism, and their sense of self-efficacy is impaired. Although women with anorexia and bulimia represent a range of severity, most of these women identify problems with appropriate identification of internal feeling states, perfectionistic attitudes, trouble with expression of direct and appropriate anger, difficulty with assertiveness and decision-making, and trouble with appropriate separation and autonomy from the family of origin (Garner & Bemis, 1985; Minuchin, Rosman, & Baker, 1978).

With some of these women their painful condition is obvious. Others, particularly normal-weight bulimic women, may present a competent external picture and function moderately well in a structured work or school environment but deteriorate emotionally when alone or within the context of their relationships with parents or spouse.

Clinical Examples

Molly, a 28-year-old advertising executive, decided to open her own business. After two years, she was able to establish herself financially and turn a profit. She ran a three-person shop, managed the books, handled the public relations and produced a viable product. She had been bulimic for eight years. Her evenings were full of repeated binge eating and purging, self-denigration, and anxiety. She reported that her husband was supportive and tried to be understanding. Each morning, thoroughly upset with herself and unable to make decisions, she would line up five dresses on the bed and ask him to choose what she should wear. She would then go off to run her business.

Carol, a 29-year-old homemaker, began her eating disorder history as an anorectic at age 15; for years she would starve her 5'10" body down to 95 pounds and then, over a period of several months, repeatedly gorge and gain up to 180 pounds. She saw her only strength as her internal ability to "control" her food intake and become beautiful, which, to her wealthy father and jet-set husband, was desirable and a way to "achieve." During treatment her moods became more obviously volatile, and she became more verbal instead of secretly stuffing herself with food. Her husband reacted by asking, "Can't you just go back to binges? I can't take this." Her response— "No I can't, I don't want to die"—was her first assertive statement.

Deborah, a 24-year-old bulimic woman, described all of her relationships with men as centered around finding ways to please them—with her looks, her demeanor, her acceptance of whatever it took to keep them with her. She had no women friends. She talked of a string of relationships in which each man temporarily became the center of her world. Since she dated each boyfriend exclusively, she was afraid to make a demand or to try to negotiate a conflict for fear that he would leave her. Each one did anyway. During treatment increasing her ability to assert herself, to make demands, or at least to expect a compromise, was stressed. "Now that I don't throw up anymore," she said at the end of therapy, "I bring up what I don't like in the relationship. If he won't deal with it I bring it up again—sort of like the way I used to 'bring up' my food—only this at least is healthy!"

There is a wealth of literature that describes these disorders as variants of affective illness (Pope et al., 1983), as separation-individuation failures (Bruch, 1973), as disorders of self (Goodsitt, 1985), as products of enmeshed families (Minuchin et al., 1978) or products of transgenerationally rigid or chaotic systems (Root et al., 1986). They may be. They are also probably disorders of power, at some level expressing the dilemmas of women who are told to achieve but have only faulty avenues for doing so, who are told they matter but only if they're beautiful. Somewhere along the line they have lost their voices and learned to talk with their bodies. For many the process of therapy requires permission to speak, as well as help in learning how to do so.

SCHIZOPHRENIA

There are major gender differences in the onset, course, symptomatology and treatment outcome of schizophrenia. For women the onset of the disorder is later (Flor-Henry, 1985; Seeman, 1982, 1985b). It was once hypothesized that this difference might reflect the fact that disturbed women are less trouble to their families and thus go underdiagnosed and deprived of early intervention, but recent data suggest that there is no significant gender difference in the amount of time between symptom onset and first hospitalization (Gove & Tudor, 1973; Lewine, 1981). The explanation for later onset for women is likely to be a more complicated one.

Whatever the reasons, it is likely that the benefits of a later first break outweigh any possible disadvantages from delayed treatment exposure, i.e., the chance to obtain more education, the opportunity for the development of at least a brief successful work history, the greater likelihood of developing more social skills and social support networks, and even the increased likelihood of marriage and parenthood. All these factors appear to be associated with a more successful outcome and response to treatment for women (Seeman, 1985a). In fact, their hospital stays are shorter than those of men, they have fewer relapses and fewer suicides, and they have remissions of better quality (Hogarty et al., 1974; Sartorius et al., 1978; Tsuang & Woolson, 1978). They are less likely to drop out or resist treatment, are more likely to take their medication, and respond better to the drugs they take, although this response rate may reflect greater compliance with treatments (Hogarty et al., 1974). Perhaps because they are more likely to live in families, their general health and nutrition are also better, factors which may well affect all the other variables (Seeman, 1985b). In fact, throughout the course of their lives, schizophrenic women have a better quality of life than schizophrenic men. They maintain closer family ties, are more likely to marry or have a social life, and are more likely to succeed in the area of employment (Affleck, Burns, & Forrest, 1976; Farina, Garmezy, & Barry, 1963; Muzekari, 1972; Seeman, 1982).

It is unclear whether these successes are possible because both the culture and families have lower expectations and less fear of disturbed women, and thus put less pressure on them; because there is more tolerance of deviant behavior in women; because most women do not become as dysfunctional as men even when they have a severe mental illness; or because there are different pathophysiologies in schizophrenic men and women, with men having a more neurological base to their disorders. Most women certainly have had the chance to develop more skills, assets, and interpersonal loyalties before dysfunction comes to dominate their lives. Furthermore, being fragile, dependent, low functioning, or highly emotional does not necessarily make women undesirable potential mates, particularly if they are attractive. These qualities still approximate female "norms," and may even appeal to men who need to be "one-up." In other words, the fact that they are dysfunctional may make relationships with them less threatening, at least initially. These improved relationships may help to provide a "safety net" to catch them when they fall, to support them when they are shaky.

Unfortunately, while schizophrenic women marry more often than schizophrenic men, in fact at close to the same rate as nonschizophrenic women, a greater percentage of marriages of all schizophrenic individuals do not last. The strain of living with chronic mental illness appears to cause many spouses to eventually opt for divorce. Perhaps because women in general, even when chronically mentally ill, are more likely to stay connected to their families of origin, the ongoing strain of providing primary care for them during episodes and over the years of chronic dysfunction may be even more of an issue for their families than for the families of young males, who will have more frequent hospitalizations and out-of-the-home placements, giving everyone some respite.

The symptoms of schizophrenia also tend to differ by gender. Women have a greater affective component while men show more disturbances in the areas of cognition, behavior, and motivation (Hogarty, 1985). Furthermore, some preliminary data suggest that psychotic episodes for women are more likely to be precipitated by real or perceived interpersonal loss, while the precipitant of episodes for men is more often some assault on self-esteem and major role functioning (Hogarty, 1985; Salokangas, 1983). If schizophrenic women are particularly vulnerable to negative events and/or losses in their interpersonal contexts, this factor should be addressed in treatment programs.

What might account for these gender differences? Evidence for genetic differences does not exist, but there is some suggestion that hormonal factors could operate in either a triggering or protective fashion (Seeman, 1985a). One view suggests that earlier onset for males can be attributed to the influence of androgens on the thymus gland, which in turn compromises immune functions, a process that begins earlier in men than in women (Seeman, 1985b). Early onset for males may also relate to the fact that "all left hemisphere developmental difficulties affect males over females at a ratio of 5 to 1. Schizophrenia may be just one more left hemisphere developmental problem for men" (Shepherd-Look, 1982). Others suggest that estrogens serve a protective function for women. The hypothesized role of endocrine factors is supported by the observation that hormones may in part account for the frequently noted premenstrual flareups of schizophrenic disorders, postpartum schizophrenic episodes, the relative protection pregnant women appear to have during the first trimester, and the higher incidence of middle-age onset of the illness for women (Seeman, 1981).

Other researchers are attempting to understand gender differences by exploring the neuro-organizational system, citing possible sex-linked morphological differences, with females having far better bilateral hemispheric functioning than males (Goy & McEwen, 1980). One hypothesis suggests that this allows women to compensate with right hemispheric functioning when the left cerebral hemisphere is impaired. Different sensitivities of steroid receptors in relevant brain areas dealing with cognition, affect, sex, and reproduction have been noted. Unfortunately, we must conclude that we do not yet know all the ways schizophrenic men and women differ or the impact of these differences on behavior functioning.

Overt behaviors of schizophrenic patients obviously differ based on gender, with schizophrenic females being less active, less aggressive, more sociable, and more dependent (Lewine, 1981). In terms of surviving within one's family, or even within the larger community, these behaviors could be protective, since they are less socially disturbing, especially since dependence is more socially acceptable in women. Furthermore, schizophrenic males are likely to find it difficult to move to a functional independent male role, since their symptoms are discrepant with male role expectations. In fact, all of these behaviors are consistent with the differences between "healthy" males and females described earlier. It is not surprising that disturbed males are apparently more frightening, since their size and their tendency to be aggressive could easily precipitate a series of negative interactional events between family members, increasing everyone's discomfort and level of stress, which in turn could repeatedly precipitate episodes and exacerbate the negative interpersonal consequences of the disorder.

Considering all of these differences, one might expect programs, policies, and treatment techniques for schizophrenic patients and their families to differ based on gender. The fact is that these problems are almost never even conceptualized in ways that make it possible to understand gender differences, much less taken into consideration when treatment programs are designed. Instead, schizophrenia has tended to be regarded as genderless by theoreticians, researchers, and clinicians.

The special needs of schizophrenic women often have been neglected by both professionals and their families. Birth control, for instance, is a complicated issue for seriously disturbed women. Schizophrenic women, whether by consent or through exploitation, are likely to be sexually active. These women are unlikely to take the pill dependably and may have atypical perceptions of pain and discomfort, making them potentially poor reporters of possible problems with an IUD (Talbott & Linn, 1978); additionally, when they do become pregnant, their ability to take the psychotropic drugs they need for their own well-being is compromised or complicated (Bachrach, 1985).

All of these gender-related factors have implications for the treatment provided by family therapists. The family members of severely disturbed patients are always affected by the dysfunctional member, but how they are affected depends in part on the patient's gender. Because of the different ages of onset, for instance, the family-oriented treatment of females is likely to be with the patient's conjugal family, while treatment of males will be focused primarily on the family of origin. This fact alone presents a different series of challenges for the patient, family, and therapist. Women, should they become too disturbing, may find themselves alone, abandoned by their husbands. However, parents of male patients do not have the option of divorcing the patient. A female patient's ongoing insecurity about the potential loss of her husband, along with his level of commitment to the relationship, must be addressed by the family therapist; on the other hand, the "trapped" feelings of both parent and ill child as they struggle to manage both the illness and their relationship to each other must not be neglected.

Even women who are themselves severely disturbed often retain the responsibilities and pressures of home and childcare, a stress which is often underestimated. When told of patient vulnerability to stress, a common response of husbands and other family members is a bewildered, "All she has to do is take care of the children and keep the house clean." The larger cultural myth that childcare and homemaking are not stressful acts to the disturbed woman's serious disadvantage. Not only are these women, like all others, inculcated with the value of providing for the needs of their family members, but they assume that this task should not be problematic or stressful. When they are ill — even when they are hospitalized — they continue to feel guilty that they are unable to take care of others. Many women press for an early or rapid discharge because they are "needed at home," a request often supported by other family members and too often by the treatment team. Even schizophrenic women themselves do not regard their own needs as particularly relevant in the decision-making process.

Therapists should be sensitive to the female schizophrenic patient's tendencies to be compliant. Excessive compliance has often worked against women and the seriously mentally ill are no exception. While compliance with drug and other treatment programs seems to work for them in some ways, it is important to be aware of the fact that these women may not share their dissatisfactions, their doubts, or their concerns. When the therapist makes a special effort to elicit these reactions, the results may include better understanding of the patient, a stronger treatment alliance, and a positive outcome.

When the schizophrenic patient is unmarried, another women's issue is relevant, whatever the patient's gender. It is usually the mother of the patient who carries the primary burden of caretaking, the mother who lives with the burden and stress 24 hours a day. These women are expected to manage very disturbed patients in their homes, with little emotional, financial or community support. Furthermore, they are frequently criticized for their efforts and blamed for the patient's ongoing problems, if not for the illness itself. The automatic assignment of this caretaking role to a woman, who in turn is held responsible for the creation of the illness, is a particularly disturbing and destructive double message, which family therapists should be sensitive to and avoid.

Several family issues are crucial for treating patients with schizophrenia in a gender-sensitive way. Along with the usual tasks of helping family members to be more aware of signs of stress in the patient and each other and of allowing members to come to grips with the problem in their own way and at their own pace, it is crucial to attend to female patients and family members who automatically do more than their share. Mothers who are ill continue to attempt to manage the household. Mothers of patients often attempt to provide the equivalent of hospital support in the home. Sisters of patients curtail their social lives to help their mothers and the patient. Attention to the development of social support networks beyond the nuclear family is vital in helping women to deal effectively with the illness or the burden of caretaking. In addition, a redistribution of these unequally balanced caretaking burdens can help to maintain each individual's mental health, as well as the stability of the family unit. Since women, particularly mothers, are so committed to caretaking, it is not always easy for them to relinquish even a portion of their duties. Therapists may need to support them in doing so, emphasizing the benefits the patient will receive from a wider circle of contacts, as well as the benefit to both the patient and the rest of the family if the primary caretaker does not "burn out" over time.

DEPRESSION

Major depression, that is, depression accompanied by prolonged, serious changes in biological/vegetative functioning rather than in response to a major life event, is significantly more common in women than in men (Boyd & Weissman, 1981; Weissman & Klerman, 1985). Current theories suggest a biological/hormonal and/or genetic component in the pathogenesis of this disorder (Bertelsen, Harvald, & Hange, 1977; Carroll et al., 1981; Kidd et al., 1984; Post & Ballinger, 1984; Schlesser & Altshuler, 1983; Weissman & Akiskal, 1984; Winokur, Behar, & Van Valkenburg, 1978). As in schizophrenia, however great the biological component may be, it is likely that family and societal issues play a role in the disorder, in its etiology, onset, course, and/or outcome. How else, for instance, could we account for differences in the incidence, characteristics, and/or frequency of the disorder between groups of married and unmarried women, working and nonworking women, childless women and women with young children (Brown & Harris, 1978).

Certainly a woman's social context is relevant in the development of depressed symptoms, and our social context is relevant in determining the way we perceive them. Our increased awareness that age modifies the presentation of symptoms has probably led to an increased awareness and earlier identification of depressive illness in younger patients, even children (Kovacs et al., 1984; Orvaschel, 1983; Puig-Antich et al., 1985). This awareness probably also influences the way the complaints of women are seen by clinicians. Thirty years ago a symptomatic woman was likely to be labeled "hysteric" or "neurasthenic"; now she is more likely to be called depressed. Thus, social factors influence a diagnostic label and the way it is applied.

Years from now, we may look back at the 1980s and conclude that depression was as overdiagnosed as hysteria was a few decades ago.

Those who are unhappy, perhaps for good reasons, may be mislabeled as clinically depressed. Once a "clinical" label is applied, certain activities follow. In the case of depression, those activities will depend at least as much on the clinician's theoretical assumptions and prejudices as on the woman's condition. If the clinician has a biological orientation, the label may mean the administration of antidepressant drugs, whether the woman actually needs them or not. If the clinician has a psychodynamic orientation, her emotional pain may be labeled psychogenic and drugs may be withheld, whether she needs them or not. In either case there is a risk of victimizing a woman based on the politics of labeling.

Marriage and depression appear to be intricately intertwined for women (Merikangas et al., 1985). Depressed women are likely to list marital problems as a primary complaint (Merikangas, Prusoff, Kupfer, & Frank, 1985; Weissman & Paykel, 1974); married women are more likely to be depressed than single women (Gove, 1972); married women who do not work are even more likely to be depressed (Brown & Harris, 1978); and those women with three or more children under the age of 11 at home appear to have increased vulnerability for the development of depressive symptomatology (Brown & Brolchain, 1975). The presence of a confidant, often a spouse, appears to serve a protective function, preventing the development of depression in women following exposure to a negative life event. Only 4% of women with such a confidant became depressed after a negative life event, while 42% of those without a confidant became depressed (Brown & Brolchain, 1975). These associations, of course, cannot be claimed to be causal relationships, since all of these issues are complicated by our inability to know what comes first. It may be, for instance, that women predisposed to depression are less able to form "confidant" type attachments rather than that the depression is in part precipitated by their absence.

Depression in women also has an impact on other family members (Coyne et al., 1987; Weissman, 1972). Regardless of age, children of depressed mothers have more symptoms, accidents and school problems (Brown, Harris, & Copeland, 1972; Beardslee, Bemporad, Keller, & Klerman, 1983). Adolescents seem to have the most overt trouble. They are likely to have intense conflict with their depressed mother, and appear to exploit her helplessness rather than to respond sympathetically (Weissman, 1972). Spouses and children appear to have more visits to their family doctor (Widmer, Cordoret, & North, 1980). It's clear that depressed individuals are more difficult to like and even influence the self-perceived moods of those who interact with them (Coyne, 1976; Hammen & Peters, 1978). Whatever the etiology of depression, living with a depressed person cannot be regarded as easy.

Today one of the most common treatments of depression is administration of psychotropic drugs (Elkin et al., 1986), an intervention which appears to improve depressive symptoms without affecting a woman's psychosocial or marital problems. There is at least some evidence to suggest that marital problems fail to resolve automatically when a woman gets less depressed and that those women with marital problems appear to do less well on drugs (Bothwell & Weissman, 1977; Paykel et al., 1969; Weissman & Klerman, 1972). Although we do not know the pre-illness state of these marriages, it is interesting that at least some depressed women who divorced appeared to do better, only to experience a reappearance or exacerbation of their problems when they remarried (Bothwell & Weissman, 1977). These data certainly raise the question of whether marriage is not "depressogenic" for some women. The role of wife seems to inspire many women to be less assertive, to deny their own needs, or at least to see them as less important than those of their husbands. Perhaps these factors eventually lead a woman to feel less in control of her life and her fate. Perhaps heavy doses of self-denial increase anger, an emotion many women find difficult to tolerate. Some may, in fact, as early psychodynamic views proposed, "turn their anger inward." Whatever the reason, women with severe recurrent depressions do express more anger and have more somatic complaints than men (Frank, Carpenter, & Kupfer, 1988).

It is crucial to address the marital and family issues of depressed women. Particularly relevant for the woman herself are issues of perceived control and power and the development of ways to avoid giving up her own needs — at least some of the time. It may be important for family members to allow the woman more room to be her own person, separate from her family roles, and to learn to avoid the cycle of infantilizing/overprotection which turns to distance and anger when it doesn't make things better. In working with depressed women themselves, therapists need to be sensitive to the tendency to expect the wife/mother in the family to do more than an equal share of the changing.

Clinical Examples

Marion, age 52, and her husband, Robert, age 54, were referred for marital therapy following her third abdominal surgery and advice from a psychiatric consultant who was withdrawing the patient from the pain medication to which she had become addicted. History-taking revealed that she had experienced several previous episodes of major depressive illnesses, beginning in her early thirties. During the course of marital treatment, her husband, a

CEO for a large prestigious company, complained that their last sexual encounter had been three years earlier and that his wife was always too sick to entertain and travel as he expected and as she had in the past. Additionally, he was angry that she complained frequently that she did not have enough money. He felt the "allowance" he gave her was sufficient; when she pointed out that he gave each of their young adult daughters more money each week than he gave to her, he said that her demands were excessive. The sibling rivalry this created between mother and daughters became a treatment issue, as did the power imbalance between spouses.

Mid-life for Mr. and Mrs. R, both in their forties, was a time of severe and chronic marital conflict. Mrs. R announced at the first marital therapy session that she had been treated for depression with medication for one year to no avail and that she probably wanted a divorce. Her husband, distraught, stated that he did not want a divorce but felt that he was not able to provide his wife with what she wanted. She explained that over the past several years it became obvious to her that financially he would never be able to buy her what she wanted: a larger house, a better car, and more vacations. Her goal was to begin to look for a wealthier man while she was young enough to make a switch. In part, the therapy focused on her overwhelming sense that only through a man could she access any of the things that she felt she wanted and her husband's acceptance that he was a failure because they owned one BMW and not two.

Mrs. S, a separated 32-year-old mother of three daughters, two with serious learning disabilities, was hospitalized after she attempted suicide during her fourth episode of depressive illness since the age of 16. A survivor of child sexual abuse, she reported that she experienced chronic sexual dysfunction and believed that this was one reason her husband had left her. Prior to her suicide attempt, she had been evicted from her apartment, her mother had died, and her 10-year-old daughter had threatened to kill herself by holding a butcher knife to her stomach. Mrs. S's only form of treatment prior to her attempt had been Valium, prescribed by her local family physician months earlier.

TREATMENT—WHAT DO WE NEED TO DO DIFFERENTLY?

The presence of a mentally ill person has a profoundly disruptive effect on family life. If that person is the wife/mother in a family, the effect can be even more devastating, since the person usually charged with family maintenance and nurturance is the one whose functioning has become most impaired. On the positive side, women do not particularly resist therapeutic intervention. In fact, women use more mental health services than men and are less likely to deny psychological symptoms. They ask for and accept help more easily for both themselves and their families. In some ways women appear more likely to be committed to wanting things to be different, more likely to be invested in the psychological well-being of family members. Perhaps because men are not assigned, nor do they tend to assume, responsibility for attending to the emotional and relationship issues in families, they are less likely to notice problems or more willing to settle for things as they are.

Family therapists instinctively respond to the greater receptivity of women by asking them to do more of the changing, more of the caring, more than their share of nurturance, more of the adapting, even when they are seriously disturbed (Goldner, 1985). The lower expectations we tend to have of husbands/fathers perpetuate an already unequal balance in the family system and may even operate to keep an already troubled woman stressed and dysfunctional. Thus, it is important to avoid accepting without question or self-examination our assumptions about who should do what in coping with the impact of serious mental illness.

Women in caretaking roles may need help in setting limits on what they can and cannot do. We must give increased attention to the needs these women have for nurturance themselves. Although traditionally regarded as "natural" caretakers, women have considerable needs for nurturance, particularly when they are attempting to manage an impossible situation. A unilateral focus on the needs of fathers, husbands, or children, without a reciprocal emphasis on the needs of women, must be avoided. One way to attend more helpfully to caretakers is to give greater attention to the risk for women of losing themselves through their greater capacity for empathy (Goldner, 1985). Women are less likely to act with enlightened self-interest and selfishness within the family system and more likely to put their own needs on hold while attending to those of others. This is particularly dangerous for women who are caretakers of a family member with a serious mental disorder. Their own tendencies to center their lives around the needs of a family member who is unwell are often reinforced and exacerbated by the family system and the culture. Without support, they may endanger their own health and even their ability to give to others. They may well need help in being more assertive in saying "no" in both therapy and in their family. They must be helped to preserve their own energies and identify priorities to protect their well-being.

This is also true for some women in patient roles. When a woman is depressed or schizophrenic, she is likely to be psychologically unavailable to her children. Of course, it is important to develop alternative methods of meeting the needs of children, especially if they are young. Nevertheless, it is crucial that family therapists not limit their work to the accomplishment of this task. Ways must be found to address a woman's own psychological needs, even when she cannot directly express them or request that they be attended to. Too often, non-nurturing women are rejected rather than helped since their behaviors and attitudes are so culturally unacceptable. In working with women with major psychiatric disorders, therapists must give increased attention to sex-role stereotypes and their impact on the functioning of all family members, especially those individuals whose personality characteristics do not fit dominant cultural expectations. Women who are aggressive or who are not prone to nurture are particularly at risk for being mistreated by therapists.

When assessing the family issues relevant to women in cases involving serious disorders, one must examine the presenting complaints and the nature of the patient's and family's premorbid functioning. Too often, the presenting complaints brought by women are put aside or ignored as the complaints of other family members are addressed and/or the therapist looks for the "real" issue. Too often the real issue is determined unilaterally by the therapist. Following a genuine discussion of everyone's views and opinions about the problems and how they should be resolved, a contract that contains mutual goals can be established. In this process, the therapist must be careful to avoid imposing goals unilaterally, even feminist ones. As therapists, for instance, we may want a woman to be more independent or assertive, but she is the one who must live with the ramifications of such behaviors. She must decide if they are worthwhile. We must help these women look at their chances of getting what they want if they confront their husbands or of surviving alone if they leave. Information about the risks and the options available is often useful. What does she lose if this marriage dissolves? What change is really possible for her and what is its cost? Therapists, however, should avoid polarizing these choices, i.e., accepting too easily what may be a depressed woman's view—that she must accept the status quo or be prepared to see her marriage dissolved. It may come to such a choice, but therapists should first work with couples to promote more flexibility in their relationships, to change expectations and then small behaviors, while simultaneously dealing with each partner's fears of abandonment.

To determine feasible goals, it is important to look at the roles, rules and functioning of the family and its members before the onset of a serious mental disorder. In general, it is usually unrealistic to expect to go far beyond the best previous functioning or to modify basic personality characteristics. If a woman was not inclined to nurture before she became depressed, she is unlikely to nurture when she recovers. If a man was intolerant of intimacy when his wife was well, he is unlikely to develop this tolerance just because she is now symptomatic, or even when she recovers. This is not to say that the therapist should always promote a return to the status quo. At times it may be important to look at what needs can and cannot be met in a given relationship and to help the spouses decide whether the good available to each of them is worth the grief that accompanies it. Sometimes divorce or separation actually helps women to find more contentment and even to function better.

In all family therapy it is important to attempt to empower each family member, emphasizing strengths rather than weaknesses. This point is especially relevant in working with severely dysfunctional women. Too many aspects of their lives are already beyond their control. Given the multiple problems inherent in coping with mental illness, these women may give up many of their goals and hopes. Therapists can help them to find ways to make life seem less overwhelming by developing small tasks and specific skills which build on existing assets. In so doing, however, therapists must be careful to leave as many choices as possible in the hands of women — choices about goals, timing, and acceptable methods. Otherwise, the metalevel message of therapy can be a destructive or infantilizing one.

In ongoing therapy, increased attention to blatant issues of power and control is also indicated. The abuse of power (physical violence, sexual abuse) and the abuse of control (intimidation, excess caretaking, intrusiveness) are particularly relevant, since severely disturbed women are vulnerable both within and outside of their families. Therapists must be careful not to dismiss their complaints simply because these women are dysfunctional. However disturbed they may be, they may still be capable of handling increased autonomy and responsibility. If this is a desirable and attainable goal for a particular woman, the therapist must be sensitive to the feelings of those who have been caring for her needs. The caretakers are likely to be women as well, and they are likely to have taken on these tasks out of genuine concern, commitment and fear. The dysfunctional woman can be helped to become more independent without blaming her family for the fact that she has not become so already.

Attention to the larger context in considering options for each family member and the family as a whole is particularly relevant for families with severe acute or chronic disorders, which are likely to tax a family's resources. A limited focus on the nuclear family not only may cause us to miss crucial stresses but may also decrease the likelihood of developing the necessary supports for handling severe illness and stress. Mothers of patients, for instance, may be coping with the additional stress of caring for an aging parent or even for other family members suffering from chronic illnesses. On the other hand, these same mothers may have close friends or siblings who would be willing to provide emotional, social, or instrumental assistance. Each family member may have friendships that can be cultivated in his/her best interests. Promoting the connections of friendships and support in these larger networks also can decrease the tendencies towards excessive intensity in the marriage or nuclear family.

Finally, it is important to remember that even dysfunctional women have dreams and goals that are not related to their spouses and children. Too often, therapists neglect these aspects of a woman's life in their attempt to find ways to manage the immediate crisis of an illness or an episode. Once the crisis has passed, it can be extremely helpful and affirming to begin to help the dysfunctional woman to reconnect with these parts of herself. Because the ability to earn money is so central to our self-concept and the views others have of us, for many of these women paid employment may be useful in promoting recovery and in providing a special sense of self, separate from the family. We know women tend to do better psychologically and physically when they work (see Holder, Chapter 18); thus, it is particularly relevant to assess the possibility of developing a woman's ability to work. As women begin to work and to make work-related social connections, they begin to be less vulnerable to self-definitions entirely dependent on their roles as wife and mother to their husband and children. Having two spheres of activity can provide a woman with an insurance policy; if life is not going well in one sphere, there is at least a chance that the other can provide some small sense of satisfaction.

REFERENCES

Affleck, J. W., Burns, J., & Forrest, A. D. (1976). Long-term follow-up of schizophrenic patients in Edinburgh. *Acta Psychiatrica Scandinavica, 53*, 227–37.

American Psychiatric Association, *Diagnostic and statistical manual of mental disorders, 3rd Ed.*, Washington, DC: APA, 1987.

Ashwell, S. (1845). *A practical treatise on the diseases peculiar to women*. Philadelphia: Lea and Blanchard.

Bachrach, L. (1985). Chronic mentally ill women: Emergence and legitimation of program issues. *Hospital and Community Psychiatry, 36*(10), 1063–1069.

Barnett, R. C., & Baruch, G. K. (1987). Social roles, gender and psychological distress. In Barnett, R. C., Biener, L., & Baruch, G. D. (Eds.), *Gender and stress*. New York: Free Press.

Beardslee, W. R., Bemporad, J., Keller, M. B., & Klerman, G. L. (1983). Children of parents with major affective disorder: A review. *American Journal of Psychiatry, 140*(7), 825–32.

Bertelsen, A., Harvald, B., & Hange, M. (1977). A Danish study of manic depressive disorders. *British Journal of Psychiatry, 130*, 330–51.

Bothwell, S., & Weissman, M. (1977). Social impairments four years after an acute depressive episode. *American Journal of Orthopsychiatry, 47*, 231–37.

Boyd, J., & Weissman, M. M. (1981). Epidemiology of affective disorders: A re-examination and future directions. *Archives of General Psychiatry, 38*, 1039–1046.

Broverman, I. K., Broverman, D. M., Clarkson, F. E., Rosenkrantz, P. S., & Vogel, S. R. (1970). Sex role stereotypes and clinical judgements of mental health. *Journal of Consulting and Clinical Psychology, 34*(1), 107.

Brown, A., & Finkelhor, D. (1986). Impact of child sexual abuse: A review of the research. *Psychological Bulletin, 99*, 66–77.

Brown, G. W., & Brolchain, M. W. (1975). Social class and psychiatric disturbance among women in an urban population. *Sociology, 9*, 225–54.

Brown, G. W., & Harris, T. O. (1978). *Social origins of depression: A study of psychiatric disorders in women.* New York: Lee Press.

Brown, G. W., Harris, T. O., & Copeland, J. R. (1972). Depression and loss. *British Journal of Psychiatry, 130*, 1–18.

Bruch, H. (Ed.). (1973). *Eating disorders: Obesity, anorexia nervosa and the person within.* New York: Basic Books.

Caplan, P., & Hall-McCorquodale, I. (1985). Mother-blaming in major clinical journals. *American Journal of Orthopsychiatry, 5*, 345–53.

Carmen, E., Rieker, P. P., & Mills, T. (1984). Victims of violence and psychiatric illness. *American Journal of Psychiatry, 141*, 378–83.

Carroll, B. J., Feinberg, M., Greden, J. F., et al. (1981). A specific laboratory test for the diagnosis of melancholia: Standardization, validation and clinical utility. *Archives of General Psychiatry, 38*, 15–22.

Chernin, K. (1986). *The hungry self: Women, eating and identity.* New York: Perennial Library.

Chernin, K. (1981). *The obsession: Reflections on the tyranny of slenderness.* New York: Harper & Row.

Chess, S., & Thomas, A. (1982). Infancy bonding: Mystique and reality. *American Journal of Orthopsychiatry, 52*, 213–22.

Coyne, J. C. (1976). Depression and the response of others. *Journal of Abnormal Psychology, 85*, 186–93.

Coyne, J. C., Kessler, R. C., Tal, M. et al. (1987). Living with a depressed person. *Journal of Consulting and Clinical Psychology, 55*, 347–52.

Crisp, A. H., Palmer, R. L., & Kalucy, R. S. (1976). How common is anorexia nervosa? A prevalence study. *British Journal of Psychiatry, 128*, 549–54.

Department of Health and Human Services (1985). *Women's health: Report of the public health service task force on women's health issues.* Vol. II, U.S. Public Health Service.

Elkin, I., Shea, T., Watkins, J., et al. (1986). NIMH Collaborative Research Program: General effectiveness of treatment. Presented to the Society for Psychotherapy Research, June 1986.

Fairburn, C. G., & Garner, D. M. (1986). The diagnosis of bulimia nervosa. *International Journal of Eating Disorders, 5*(3), 403–19.

Farina, A., Garmezy, N., & Barry, H., III (1963). Relationship of marital status to incidence and prognosis of schizophrenia. *Journal of Abnormal Social Psychology, 67*, 624–30.

Finkelhor, D. (1983). Common features of family abuse. In D. Finkelhor et al., (Ed.). *The dark side of families: Current family violence research.* Beverly Hills, CA: Sage.

Fisher, S. (1987). Good women after all: Cultural definitions and social control. In J. Figueira-McDonough & R. Sarri (Eds.). *The trapped woman: Catch 22 in deviance and control* (pp. 318–47). Beverly Hills: Sage.

Flor-Henry, P. (1985). Schizophrenia: Sex differences. *Canadian Journal of Psychiatry, 30*, 319–21.

Frank, E., Carpenter, L. L., & Kupfer, D. J. (1988). Sex differences in recurrent depression: Are there any that are significant? *American Journal of Psychiatry, 145*(1), 41–45.

Fromm-Reichmann, F. (1948). Notes on the development of treatment of schizophrenics by psychoanalytic psychotherapy. *Psychiatry, II*, 263–74.

Garfinkel, P. E., & Garner, D. M. (Eds.). (1982). *Anorexia nervosa: A multidimensional perspective.* New York: Brunner/Mazel.

Garner, D. M., & Bemis, K. M. (1985). Cognitive therapy for anorexia nervosa. In D. M. Garner & P. E. Garfinkel (Eds.), *Handbook of psychotherapy for anorexia nervosa and bulimia.* New York: Guilford.

Geller, J. L. (1985). Women's accounts of psychiatric illness and institutionalization. *Hospital and Community Psychiatry, 36*(10), 1056–1062.

Goldner, V. (1985). Feminism and family therapy. *Family Process, 24*, 31–47.

Goodsitt, A. (1985). Self Psychology and the treatment of anorexia nervosa. In D. M. Garner & P. E. Garfinkel (Eds.), *Handbook of psychotherapy for anorexia nervosa and bulimia.* New York: Guilford.

Goodwin, J. (1985). Family violence: Principles of intervention and prevention. *Hospital and Community Psychiatry, 36*(10), 1074–1079.

Goodwin, J. (1982). *Sexual abuse: Incest victims and their families.* Littleton, MA: Wright PSG.

Gove, W. R. (1972). The relationship between sex roles, marital status and mental illness. *Social Forces, 51*, 34–44.

Gove, W. R., & Tudor, J. F. (1973). Adult sex roles and mental illness. *American Journal of Sociology, 78*, 812–35.

Goy, R. W., & McEwen, B. S. (1980). *Sexual differentiation of the brain.* Cambridge: MIT Press.

Hammen, C. L., & Peters, S. D. (1978). Interpersonal consequences of depression: Responses to men and women enacting a depressed role. *Journal of Abnormal Psychology, 87*, 322–32.

Hinchcliffe, M., Hooper, D., Roberts, F. J., et al. (1975). A study of the interaction between depressed patients and their spouses. *British Journal of Psychiatry, 126*, 164–72.

Hogarty, G. E. (1985). Expressed emotion and schizophrenic relapse: Implications from the Pittsburgh Study. In M. Alpert (Ed.), *Controversies in schizophrenia.* New York: Guilford.

Hogarty, G. E., Goldberg, S. C., Schooler, N. R., Ulrich, R. F. and the Collaborative Group (1974). Drug and sociotherapy in the aftercare of schizophrenic patients II — Two year relapse rates. *Archives of General Psychiatry, 31*, 603–18.

Hsu, L. K. G., & Holder, D. (1986). Bulimia nervosa: Treatment and short-term outcome. *Psychological Medicine, 16*, 65–70.

Jacob, T., Favorini, A., Meisel, S., & Anderson, C. (1978). The alcoholic's spouse, children and family interactions. *Journal of Studies on Alcohol, 39*(7), 1231–1251.

Johnson, C., & Maddi, K. L. (1985). The etiology of bulimia: A bio-psycho-social perspective. *The Annals of Adolescent Psychiatry, 13*, 253–73.

Kidd, K. K., Egeland, J. A., Molthan, L., et al. (1984). Amish Study, IV: Genetic linkage study of pedigrees of bipolar probands. *American Journal of Psychiatry, 141*, 1042–1048.

Komarovsky, M. (1953). *Women in the modern world.* Boston: Little Brown.

Kosbery, J. (1982). *Abuse and maltreatment of the elderly.* Littleton, MA: Wright PSG.

Kovacs, M., Feinberg, T. L., & Crouse-Novatz, M. A., et al. (1984). Depressive disorders in childhood I: A longitudinal prospective study of characteristics and recovery. *Archives of General Psychiatry, 41*, 219–39.

Lewine, R. R. (1981). Sex differences in schizophrenia: Timing or subtypes? *Psychological Bulletin, 90*, 432–44.

Marks, I. M. (1970). The classification of phobic disorders. *British Journal of Psychiatry, 116*, 377–86.

Merikangas, K. R., Prusoff, B., Kupfer, D., & Frank E. (1985). Marital adjustment in major depression. *Journal of Affective Disorder, 9*, 5–11.

Miller, S. M., & Kirsh, N. (1987). Sex differences in cognitive coping with stress. In R. C. Barnett, L. Biener, & G. K. Baruch (Eds.), *Gender and stress.* New York: Free Press.

Minuchin, S., Rosman, B. L., & Baker, L. (Eds.). (1978). *Psychosomatic families: Anorexia nervosa in context.* Cambridge, MA: Harvard University Press.

Mogul, K. (1985). Psychological considerations in the use of psychotropic drugs with women patients. *Hospital and Community Psychiatry, 36*(10), 1080–1085.

Morton, T. (1893). Removal of the ovaries as a cure for insanity. *American Journal of Insanity, 49*, 397–401.

Muzekari, L. H. (1972). Birth order and social behavior among chronic schizophrenics. *Journal of Clinical Psychology, 28*, 483–85.

Orvaschel, H. (1983). Maternal depression and child dysfunction: Children at risk. In B. Lahey & A. Kazdin (Eds.), *Advances in clinical child psychology*, Vol. 6. New York: Academia Press.

Pagelow, M. (1981). *Woman-battering: Victims and their experiences.* Beverly Hills, CA: Sage.

Paykel, E. S., Myers, J. K., Dienelt, M. N., Klerman, G. L., Lindenthal, J. J., & Pepper, M. P.

(1969). Life events and depression: A controlled study. *Archives of General Psychiatry, 21*, 753–60.

Pope, H. G., Hudson, J. I., Jonas, J. M., & Yurgelon-Todd, D. (1983). Bulimia treated with imipramine: A placebo controlled, double-blind study. *American Journal of Psychiatry, 140*, 554–58.

Post, R. M., & Ballinger (Eds.). (1984). *Neurobiology of mood disorders.* Baltimore: Williams & Wilkins.

Puig-Antich, J., Lukens, E., Davies, M., Goetz, D., Brennan-Quattrock, J., & Todak, G. (1985). Psychosocial functioning in prepubertal major depressive disorders. *Archives of General Psychiatry, 42*, 500–17.

Root, M. P. P., Fallon, P., & Friedrich, W. N. (Eds.) (1986). *Bulimia: A systems approach to treatment.* New York: Norton.

Salokangas, R. K. R. (1983). Prognostic implications of sex of schizophrenic patients. *British Journal of Psychiatry, 142*, 145–51.

Sartorius, N., Jablensky, A., Stromgren, E., & Shapero, R. (1978). Validity of diagnostic concepts across cultures. In L. C. Wynne, R. L. Cromwell, & S. Matthysse (Eds.), *The nature of schizophrenia: New approaches to research and treatment* (pp. 657–69). New York: John Wiley.

Schlesser, M. A., & Altshuler, K. Z. (1983). The genetics of affective disorder: Data theory and clinical applications. *Hospital and Community Psychiatry, 34*, 415–22.

Seeman, M. V. (1982). Gender differences in schizophrenia. *Canadian Journal of Psychiatry, 27*, 107–12.

Seeman, M. V. (1985a). Sex and schizophrenia. *Canadian Journal of Psychiatry, 30*, 313–15.

Seeman, M. V. (1985b). Symposium: Gender and schizophrenia. *Canadian Journal of Psychiatry, 30*, 311–12.

Seeman, M. V. (1981). Gender and the onset of schizophrenia: Neurohumoral influences. *Psychiatric Journal University of Ottawa, 6*, 136–38.

Shepherd-Look, D. L. (1982). Sex differentiation and the development of sex roles. In B. B. Wolman (Ed.), *Handbook of developmental psychology.* Englewood Cliffs, NJ: Prentice Hall.

Snaith, R. P. (1968). A clinical investigation of phobias. *British Journal of Psychiatry, 114*, 673–97.

Sturgis, E. T., & Reda, S. (1984). Simple phobia. In S. M. Turner (Ed.), *Behavioral theories and treatment of anxiety.* New York: Plenum Press.

Talbott, J. H., & Linn, L. (1978). Reactions of schizophrenics to life threatening disease. *Psychiatric Quarterly, 50*, 218–27.

Tsuang, M. T., & Woolson, R. F. (1978). Excess mortality in schizophrenia and affective disorders. *Archives of General Psychiatry, 35*, 1181–1185.

Turns, D. M. (1985). Epidemiology of phobic and obsessive-compulsive disorders among adults. *American Journal of Psychotherapy, 39*(3), 360–70.

Weissman, M. M. (1972). The depressed woman: Recent research. *Social Work, 17*(5), 19–25.

Weissman, M. M., & Akiskal, H. S. (1984). The role of psychotherapy in chronic depression: A proposal. *Comprehensive Psychiatry, 25*, 23–31.

Weissman, M. M., & Klerman, G. L. (1985). Gender and depression. *Trends in Neurosciences, 8*(Sept.), 416–20.

Weissman, M. M., & Klerman, G. L. (1972). Sex differences and the epidemiology of depression. *Archives of General Psychiatry, 34*, 90–111.

Weissman, M. M., & Paykel, E. S. (1974). *The depressed woman: A study of social relationships.* Chicago: University of Chicago Press.

Widmer, R. B., Cadoret, R. J., & North, C. S. (1980). Depression in family practice: Some effects on spouses and children. *Journal of Family Practice, 10*, 45–51.

Winokur, G., Behar, D., & Van Valkenburg, C. (1978). Is a familial definition of depression both feasible and valid? *Journal of Nervous and Mental Disease, 66*, 764–68.

20
Disorders of Power: Women and Addiction in the Family

CLAUDIA BEPKO

I'm just a girl who can't say no.

(Hammerstein, 1943)

IN 1943, when Oscar Hammerstein wrote the lyrics of "Can't Say No" for the musical *Oklahoma*, the world was at war and his heroine was meant to lighten the hearts of a country in chaos. Laura's "terrible fix" was of a fairly innocent nature: a failure to resist the romantic advances of an attractive male lead.

Almost a half century later, the world and women's roles have changed dramatically and with these changes the individual and collective dilemmas of self-assertion, relatedness, and emotional health have become more complex. The "girl who can't say no" becomes a metaphor or mirror for what may be a fatal flaw in our social design, since the inability to say no is both the stuff of all addictive behavior and the heart of a woman's role.

As a cultural and an individual process, addiction makes special statements about issues of power and of dependency. The primary characteristic of an addictive process is that the attempt to have power or control over some aspect of oneself through the use of some external agent ultimately renders a person powerless and dependent. Since this statement could be viewed as a description of the dynamics that occur at many levels in male-

The author wishes to acknowledge the help of Jo-Ann Kresten in editing and revising this chapter.

female interaction within a patriarchal culture, the addictive process offers particular clarity as a lens for viewing some of the gender issues currently of concern to family therapists. This chapter will explore the ways in which power and addiction are related constructs, looking specifically at the patterns that are common to different forms of addiction within the framework of gender.

ADDICTIVE PROCESS AND GENDER: MODELS FOR POWER AND POWERLESSNESS

Our hypothesis is that addiction reflects a disordered power arrangement embedded in gender. Not only do patterns of addiction depend on gender, but addiction also mirrors, on an internal, subjective level, the interactional power imbalances and hierarchical constraints imposed by gender arrangements in our culture. And power is no less paradoxical a process at the interactional level than at the internal level.

Family systems theory currently lacks any integrative concept of addictive behavior. As family therapists we tend to see addiction, or those sets of behaviors that we may informally identify as compulsive and habitual, as symptoms of a larger systemic imbalance. Our set is to treat the system and not the addiction, assuming that compulsivity will be reduced or eliminated with the restoration of a more functional balance in the family—a balance which often presumes the restoration of typical gender hierarchies. But, in fact, addiction represents a complex process that occurs on many levels within the system. It is, at its roots, a subjective process that occurs between the addict and his or her drug or compulsive behavior. A fundamental failure to understand the nature and intensity of this subjective relationship has led us to assume that rebalancing a system will eliminate the need for addictive behavior. However, the addiction takes on a life of its own within the individual that, although affecting and affected by the system, cannot be entirely addressed by shifting the system. The relationship between the addict and the drug needs to be disrupted as well. Systemic change is a necessary, but not sufficient, response to an addiction.

At the core of the addictive process is a particular set of beliefs about the nature of our own experience, beliefs which are colored by gender. Gregory Bateson (1972), in his classic essay, "The Cybernetics of Self," describes the fundamental belief system of Western culture as one in which we assume the capacity to dominate, control, or have power over certain aspects of our experience or self-awareness. We assume, for instance, that if we have a painful feeling, we can get rid of it, that if others threaten us, we can dominate them, and that in any interaction with someone or something outside ourselves, we can compete for dominance and win. Bateson suggests that our cultural belief system, which in turn informs our individual think-ing about ourselves, is one in which we pridefully fail to acknowledge limita-tion and vulnerability. Bateson theorized that this belief system is funda-mentally erroneous and leads to addiction. He viewed addiction as a disordered attempt to get to a more "correct" state of mind, one in which we permit dependency, vulnerability, and mutuality. This paradox is the key to the addictive process: We start with an attmept to take power that ends up rendering us dependent. Bateson suggests that thinking of ourselves as inter-dependent is more correct, but we have no culturally sanctioned, non-addic-tive way to allow ourselves to achieve this complementary state.

Bateson describes an erroneous belief system based on notions about power. He fails, however, to comment on the ways in which patriarchal gender arrangements maintain a male sense of power by assuming a comple-mentary arrangement in which men are one-up and women one-down. Men maintain a sense of dominance in this culture primarily by the overt stance of having power over women. Covertly, however, if one is controlled by that which one tries to control, women may dominate men from their one-down position. What sets the stage for the addictive process is the overriding belief system maintaining that men have power and women are the objects of that power. The assumption that men can or should have power over women is as erroneous as the assumption that people should be able to dominate or control their own feeling states. However, our entire culture is predicated on this belief system and most of our social institutions are set up in ways that perpetuate the illusion of male dominance.

Being socialized in an inherently erroneous belief system sets the stage for addiction, since incongruity may arise between what one believes and how one actually feels. If a male must *show* dominance but actually feels vulner-able, he may employ some addictive agent to either disqualify his vulnerabil-ity or enhance his sense of dominance. If a woman must *show* dependence but actually feels powerful, she may use a substance to either enhance or disqualify the impulse to be powerful. The singular difference between males and females in terms of the functions and effects of addiction arises from their prescribed roles in this complementary social heirarchy. Men assume a dominant status and their sense of self is predicated on feelings of entitlement. Women assume a submissive status and their sense of self is predicated on feelings of being dependent on and valued only in relationship to men. In this complementary arrangement, while the status of each role may be systematically equal, the *effects* of operating in either role are not. Individuals in the dominant role are always more insulated from the effects of their dominance than are those in the one-down position. The woman who is battered, for instance, experiences more damaging consequences than the male who batters.

Since symbols of power in our society are highly prescribed and predominantly gender-linked, female addictions take different forms from male addictions. For males, money, sexuality, size, strength, and competitive work convey power and status. Consequently, gambling, sexual addictions, and workaholism tend to be predominantly male forms of compulsive behavior. Women are socialized to concern themselves with physical and emotional nurturing, so that eating disorders, obsessive shopping or cleaning, and compulsive behavior in relationships are common female forms of addictive behavior. Women also typically abuse prescription drugs such as tranquilizers, reflecting cultural support for the notion that their emotions need to be subdued and controlled.

Some addictions express themselves primarily as aggressive, defiant, other-directed types of control, while some are more directed at a self-effacing form of internal control. Males are more likely to engage in addictive behavior that involves having power over others. Often the initial effect of the addiction is a sense of enhanced power. Even if the shift in experience is internal, such as in abuse of alcohol or drugs, which affect internal mood states, the activity of ingesting the drug may be carried out in a context that involves others. Or the high may enhance the male's sense of power in relationships to others. For instance, the heavy cocaine user may become a dealer and thereby exert control over those to whom he sells the drug, or the alcoholic may drink with others in a bar where a routine part of the drinking event is banter directed at putting down other people. For men, drug or alcohol abuse is frequently associated with physical or sexual abuse of others, primarily women. Addictive behavior may also allow a man to express but disqualify his needs for caring, dependency, and tenderness. The man who is romantic, sentimental, or highly emotional while drinking or during a remorseful "morning after" period can disclaim any unacceptable feelings or behaviors as simply the effect of the drug—not his "real" position.

Female addictions usually have the expressed intent of diminishing a woman's impulses; often their effect is to reinforce powerlessness and to disqualify any tendencies to overpower another or even to express herself in a context where this is considered non-normative. Interestingly, research by Wilsnack shows that drinking is becoming more pronounced among women in less traditionally female jobs (in van Gelder, 1987), perhaps because of conflicts they feel about asserting themselves.

Often "female" addictions, such as eating disorders, have the quality of *covertly* controlling the interactional dynamics of a relationship. Instead of controlling others, a woman often tries to control herself, and this ultimately renders others powerless to help or control her. A woman's attempt at control is often focused on her own body. As Orbach states in her work on anorexia, "If a woman's body is the site of her protest, then equally the body is the ground on which the attempt for control is fought" (Orbach, 1986, p. 19).

Addiction helps a woman to play out the dilemmas of female experience at many different levels. It mediates and obscures the conflicts between dependence and independence internally, interactionally, and at the social level. A woman's inability to say "no" to a drug, food, or other compulsion mirrors her inability to say "no" in a relational context where she is expected to be the object of the needs and experience of others rather than the subject of her own. The feelings both underlying and resulting from this dilemma include a sense of powerlessness, inadequacy, rage and shame. Traditional family structure both maintains and is affected by this cultural imperative that a woman's experience is not subject to her own definition and control.

FAMILY PATTERNS UNDERLYING FEMALE ADDICTION

Much of our thinking about the dynamics surrounding addictive disorders in families is basically structural, founded in Minuchin, Rosman, and Baker's (1978) findings describing the interactional patterns common to anorectic and psychosomatic families. These dynamics include rigidity or violation of boundaries, inability to resolve conflict, detouring of parental conflict through the symptom bearer, enmeshment, and overprotectiveness. Others have developed theories that are more specific to the dynamics or characteristics of substance-abusing families (Berenson, 1976; Davis et al., 1974; Stanton et al., 1982; Steinglass, Davis, & Berenson, 1977). Notably absent in these theories, however, has been a focus on gender or on the differential effects of addictive dynamics for men and women in families. Nor has gender hierarchy been considered as an aspect of the larger social context within which families function.

In the structural family model certain optimal family hierarchies are assumed, primarily that of a two-parent system in which the male holds the dominant power and authority. Addiction has never been viewed as a potential comment on power imbalances in families, because a patriarchal, male-dominated family with the wife in the more submissive, caretaking role has always been assumed. Looked at more closely, however, it becomes clear that one of the potential "adaptive consequences" of an addiction is either to disrupt the "normative" power balance in a disqualifying, face-saving way, or to appear to return a family to a balance that has been disrupted in a covert way.

In our own work on alcoholic families (Bepko & Krestan, 1985), we look closely at family interactional dynamics within the context of gender. Our primary assumption as we work with a family is that alcoholism creates and is maintained by an imbalance concerning who is responsible for what or whom. Issues of functional and emotional responsibility and, by extension, power in a family become skewed. As the alcoholic drinks more, he or she does less and becomes less emotionally available. Other family members assume more responsibility, making it possible for the alcoholic to continue to drink. Imbalances in over- and underresponsible functioning become the basic behavioral and emotional building blocks of addictive dysfunction.

Since our notions of who is responsible for what or whom in families are predominantly gender-linked, however, it is clear that gender-role socialization both shapes and is continually challenged by addictive behavior. Males are socialized to be responsible primarily in areas of occupational functioning. Women are socialized to be caretakers to be, in fact, almost totally responsible for the emotional and physical needs of spouse and children. In alcoholic families these roles become highly rigidified; yet the addiction frequently serves the function of relaxing them at the same time. If a male drinks, one possibility is that he is permitted to express dependency and emotion in a face-saving way, because the drug disqualifies his behavior. Equally, his wife gains power covertly as he becomes more and more dysfunctional and she becomes increasingly responsible. If a female drinks, she is able to disqualify any rebellion from her overresponsible role. The drinking functions to suppress or express in a "false" way feelings of resentment or desires for power or autonomy. Her husband, on the other hand, is able to function in a more protective "female" way with the face-saving vehicle of alcohol to disqualify his more nurturant impulses. In either case, the addiction helps to express or suppress feelings and impulses that run counter to the image of appropriate maleness and femaleness. Since family affect and behavior are distorted in the oscillation from dry to wet states, issues of power, dependency, and autonomy can never be overtly clarified or resolved.

One major distinction should be emphasized: A male may become emotionally as well as functionally overresponsible in the same way that women do depending on sibling position and other family dynamics, but this is more the exception than the rule. And this type of overresponsibility in a male frequently leads to an addictive solution. Women, in general, are more likely to be socialized to be overfunctioning emotional caretakers of men, children, and their own parents. They also may drink to relieve this overresponsibility. The difference is that men operate within a context in which both autonomy *and* entitlement to be taken care of are assumed. Women operate within a context in which both dependency on a man *and* emotional overfunctioning are assumed. The contradictions in these prescriptions create a bind: The male is autonomous and taken care of and the woman is dependent and the caretaker. Addiction has been one response to the pain created by this incongruity in our social design.

Similar conflicts and distortions related to sex-role socialization are aspects of the sociocultural backdrop of eating disorders for women. The work of Root, Fallon, and Friedrich (1986), as well as that of Schwartz, Barrett, and Saba (1985), essentially comments on the dilemma of the eating-disordered female, who typically experiences the pressure to be successful in a female way, that is, dependent, thin, physically attractive, and alluring to a male, as well as successful in more a traditionally male way, that is goal-oriented, concerned with achievement, and assertive. Just as an addiction to alcohol ultimately disqualifies a woman's potential movement towards autonomy and assertiveness and returns her to a dependent, powerless state, the bulimic woman's symptoms make a statement of both mastery and powerlessness at the same time (Root et al., 1986). The bulimic process usually represents her attempt to join with her father in his power and her mother in her powerlessness. Because these are incompatible and conflicting loyalties, self-abuse is the result.

The inequity of power is equally at issue in other types of abusive families. Star, Clark, Goetz, and O'Malia (1981) and Walker (1980) conclude that battered women hold extremely traditional views of sex-role functioning. Most report that their husbands were in the overtly powerful position in almost all areas of the relationship, that their own mothers were abused by their fathers, and that a sense of helplessness, powerlessness, and inability to support themselves economically prevented them from leaving the abusive husband.

Similarly, Barrett and Trepper (1986) state that the rigidity of sex-role stereotyped behavior and the degree to which traditional notions of male-female roles are accepted by a couple are significant factors in determining family vulnerability to sexual abuse of children.

We know from research (Sandmaier, 1980) that greater social stigma is attached to women's addiction than to men's because notions of acceptable "out of control" behavior are more narrowly and rigidly defined for women than for men. Women who are addicted are viewed as "sicker" than men (Curlee, 1970). While an addicted man's out-of-control addictive behavior (for instance, excessive gambling, violence, sexual acting-out) is viewed as "manly" and is excusable even if it becomes excessively emotional, a woman who is out of control in similar ways is viewed as contemptible and "sick."

Women have long been blamed by society and the mental health system for their husbands' and sons' addictions (for instance, Futterman, 1953). Thus, even if the male is the addict in a family, the female often experiences the negative stigma and consequences of the addiction. As a wife, lover, or mother, a woman is often the focus of the violent, abusive, controlling behavior that expresses the male's "out-of-control" responses. At the very least, she becomes what the addiction community has dubbed a "codependent." In the face of the male's increasingly out-of-control behavior, the female tends to become more "in control", overresponsible, rigid, and over-functioning in an attempt to maintain the system. In effect, she further gives up self and the male becomes an even more intense focus of attention.

While women are frequently blamed for causing men's addictions, men with addicted wives are usually looked on with sympathy and even revered for their tolerance. While codependency in wives is viewed as a notable form of pathology and frequently studied and commented on in the literature, codependency in men is rarely a focus of attention. Men are more likely to leave women who drink, while women rarely leave men who drink (Fraser, 1973). Essentially, women are "blamed" even for their responses to male addiction.

This differential status of women in addictive families extends to issues of treatment and recovery. In a recent study of differences between women and men entering alcoholism treatment, Beckman and Amaro (1986) found that women find less support for entering treatment in their social and family environment than do men. While women are supported in their attempts to get help primarily by their children and parents, but not by their husbands, men are supported in getting treatment primarily by their wives. Men often refuse to participate at all in their wives' treatment. On the other hand, women are usually the first to seek help for their husbands' addiction. Lack of financial resources, as well as inadequate childcare, seriously impair women's access to treatment. While men are the primary clients of most alcohol and drug treatment programs, women's addictions are routinely misdiagnosed as psychiatric rather than addictive disorders, and they are sent to psychiatric hospitals (Corrigan, 1985).

The systemic dynamics common to almost all forms of compulsive or abusive behavior in families have two major points in common. First there is a typical interactional process in families with addictive problems character-ized by: oscillations between in-control/out-of-control behavior; cyclical patterns of abuse that occur within the nuclear family or in previous genera-tions; either chaotic or rigid boundaries; highly reactive or highly constrict-ed affect; distortion of roles; denial of the effects of addictive behaviors; and a discrepancy between overt and covert messages in terms of who is dependent and who has power over what or whom. Second, sex-role con-straints are a major concomitant of dysfunction in families with problems of addiction. One can speculate either that normative structures constructed around sex-role hierarchies are inherently dysfunctional and that our forms of social organization are unworkable or that families rigidify their sex-role organization as an adaptation to factors experienced as threatening to fami-ly cohesion and stability. For some families it may simply be easier to adapt to change in the larger social environment by remaining more rigidly the same. Certainly the current economic and feminist pressure to change women's roles has resulted in a reactive return to such traditional staples of patriarchy as fundamentalist religious views of the family, which reinforce the value of female submissiveness, as well as to homophobic oppression, in which any departure from traditional gender-defined behavior is attacked as deviant and immoral.

The High Cost of Not Saying No: A Case Study

Miriam, age 39, and Jeff, age 44, have three children, Aaron, age 12, Anna, age 10, and Sarah, age 6. Miriam is addicted to alcohol and prescription drugs and has a history of anorexia. Jeff is an alcoholic. Both were heavy drinkers prior to their marriage.

Miriam came into treatment for help in coping with Jeff's alcoholism and did not initially acknowledge her own addictions. Her initial concern was Jeff's effect on her three children, especially Aaron, who was beginning to have problems in school. She called for help because of an incident in which Jeff, while drunk, had become physically abusive to her and Aaron.

The first stage of treatment with Miriam was focused on encouraging her to become involved with Al-Anon, because she had defined her concern as Jeff's drinking and denied her own. She brought the children in for some initial educational sessions, but was adamant that she did not want her husband Jeff involved in treatment. I agreed to this contract, primarily because I suspected that drinking was an issue for Miriam also and that her unusually compliant agreement to go to Al-Anon masked her reluctance to admit to her own drinking problem. Since participation in Al-Anon frequently leads drinkers to AA, I knew that, if Miriam could achieve sobriety and begin to make changes in her overresponsible functioning with Jeff and the children, the impact of her change might result in his sobriety as well.

As the therapy proceeded, Miriam slowly revealed a history of severe, often life-threatening addiction to prescription drugs and alcohol that had dominated her life since adolescence, as well as a history of early sexual abuse and intense overinvolvement with her father. Along with the addiction, she recounted her teenage promiscuity, out-of-wedlock pregnancy, extramarital affairs, neglectful behavior towards her children, and general abuse of her own health, including a long period of anorectic behavior. Eventually, perhaps very much bolstered by the support and positive response she had encountered in Al-Anon, she made the decision to stop drinking and became actively involved with AA.

After having accomplished this goal, we shifted the focus of treatment back to Jeff's drinking and the children's problems. Miriam finally agreed to have Jeff come in, but he predictably resisted all attempts to talk about his own alcoholism and tended to minimize Miriam's addiction. He soon left treatment because he was convinced that the therapist was "obsessed" with alcoholism. Miriam continued to recover in AA and Al-Anon.

While therapy was primarily supportive in nature during this early sobriety phase, Miriam began to learn in AA that self-focus is desirable and important. She began to differentiate from Jeff in small but important ways, such as insisting on her right to talk on the phone with AA friends and leave the house in the evening to go to meetings. Eventually Miriam joined a group focused on women's issues in alcohol recovery. As the group stirred her thinking, Miriam developed a stronger sense of herself. Therapy now became more interactionally focused, as we began to explore changes in her relationships with her family of origin, Jeff, and her children. Miriam began to encourage her children to expose themselves to Al-Anon and counseling groups at school for children affected by alcoholism. As Jeff became more depressed and withdrawn, Miriam occasionally thought about drinking again, because she feared that her sobriety would necessitate the end of the marriage.

Miriam's story, briefly outlined here, is particularly cogent in terms of the light it sheds on the different subjective experiences of male and female addicts, as well as the gender-based factors influencing their accessibility and reaction to treatment.

In the marriage, Jeff's and Miriam's addictions tended to maintain and balance one another's until Jeff became physically abusive. Before marriage there were some significant differences in their response to their addictions. Miriam had seen a number of psychiatrists, who routinely prescribed medication and failed to diagnose her alcohol problem, causing her the additional problem of drug addiction. Miriam was defined as "sick"for seeing and attempting to get help for Jeff's problem, as women are often scapegoated for challenging rules regarding male behavior. Her own drinking, drug abuse, and disordered eating were kept secret and went largely unnoticed.

Jeff consulted no one about his alcohol problem. He drank openly within a context in which it was socially acceptable and even part of the definition of "maleness" to drink. Because he continued to function as the breadwinner, neither he nor those around him viewed his drinking as a problem. Even his parents felt that Miriam's concern about it was her problem.

Interactionally, Jeff was raised to expect to be the focus of Miriam's physical and emotional attention. While he failed to notice the self-damaging effects of her addiction (she became desperately thin and was often drugged when he came home), what he did notice was that she was unavailable to him. He escalated his attacks on Miriam for her distance until he eventually became physically abusive. His alcoholic drinking reinforced his image of maleness and eventually gave him license to assert his attempts at controlling his wife and children by physically abusing them. His sense of maleness was predicated on his being in control of and providing for his family and on being sexually gratified by his wife. Jeff was able to deny the seriousness and implications of his own behavior. In the face of his increasing loss of control he felt his violence was justified. By overpowering someone else, he avoided facing his own "unmasculine" feelings of fear, abandonment, and dependency. Miriam, on the other hand, was terrified by the abuse and finally recognized that she needed to get help. Typically, she was motivated more by a desire to help her children than to help herself.

It is also typical that Miriam would translate "I take care of Jeff" to mean "he is there for me." While Jeff made abusive attempts to coerce Miriam to give to him, Miriam made self-abusive attempts to control her own need to be given to. For Miriam, giving to Jeff was not a choice but a compulsion; her entire sense of herself depended on it.

Miriam, like most addicted women, felt intense conflict about her femininity and her sexuality. Her experience had been one of having her "self" defined totally in relationship to the expectations of a man. As a result, she never really felt adequate; she acted out sexually and then used alcohol and drugs to numb the pain and to suppress her anger and guilt.

In her marriage, Jeff's increasing hostility and abuse confirmed her failure. She also knew that her own problems had made her less than adequate as a mother. Finally, as she put it, "I decided I didn't need to eat. It was some kind of punishment. I liked the pain of hunger, I enjoyed it—it felt good to be in pain. It was the only thing I could control—it was the only control I had left." If alcohol and drugs could no longer provide the necessary "correction" to make her feel adequately female, then starving herself to death could serve as punishment for her failure.

Some generalizations about patterns of addictive behavior specific to men and women have begun to emerge in the literature, but little research is available on the differences in family-of-origin patterns for male and female addicts. Such research might identify gender-specific patterns across many generations.

Miriam's abuse of prescription drugs speaks to a major distinguishing characteristic between male and female alcoholics. Women are at higher risk than men for abuse of other drugs (Mulford, 1977). They are twice as likely to abuse tranquilizers and sedatives (Curlee, 1970) and are consequently at greater risk for accidental overdose. It is hypothesized that while men are more likely to abuse illicit drugs women like Miriam suffer more from polydrug use because they are routinely tranquilized and sedated by doctors. Symptoms of addiction in women are frequently misdiagnosed as depression, "hysteria," or, as a local doctor termed one client's problem, "husbanditis."

An English study (Beary, Lacey, & Merry, 1986) found that 35% of alcoholic women previously had a major eating disorder, and that bulimic patients in particular are at high risk for later alcoholism. Miriam's reports of indiscriminate sexual encounters, ability to have sex only while drinking, and post-sobriety sexual dysfunction are common among women alcoholics (Wilsnack, 1984). Many women who are promiscuous while drinking (Galbraith, 1982) are seeking comfort, closeness, or love. Miriam talks about not being aware that she had the right to say no to a man's sexual advances, since she felt such an intense need for male approval.

Guilt about indiscriminate sexual behavior tends to be a major issue for addicted women (Evans & Schaefer, 1980). Also, it is important to be aware of the high correlation between women's alcoholism and rape, incest, or sexual abuse before or during the course of abusive drinking (Covington, 1982).

While there have been inconsistent findings about the relationship between female alcoholism and sexual problems, Wilsnack (1984) believes that there is a "mutually reinforcing system" in which 'sexual dissatisfaction' contributes to heavy drinking, which in turn further enhances sexual dissatisfaction" (p. 210). Some studies indicate that, while alcohol in fact decreases physiological arousal, it tends to increase a woman's subjective *sense* of arousal (Covington, 1982; Sholty, 1979).

Finally, Corrigan (1980) and Gomberg (1978) found that alcoholic women tend to characterize their childhood experiences as full of deprivation and rejection. They report such disruptions as the absence, divorce, death, or alcoholism of a parent more frequently than do men. Alcoholic women are more likely to have husbands who drink than non-alcoholic women, and these husbands typically have a role in maintaining their wives' drinking by drinking with them (Corrigan, 1980; Dahlgren, 1979).

The social oppression of women becomes internalized in female addiction as self-abuse and self-oppression. Miriam's experience mirrors that of many female clients, who come to feel that power over one's own self-destruction is the only power left to them.

Interactionally, Miriam and Jeff represent the yin and yang of addictive process. They are both addicted, both ultimately self-destructive, but their individual addictions arise from their different positions in the world and ultimately have different interactional and intrapsychic effects. The view of reality to which they both ascribe is based on a gender-defined family and social structure that perpetuates the addictive process. For both the critical issues are dependency and control.

Jeff reacts to his feelings of getting inadequate attention from Miriam by stepping up attempts to control her. The alcohol serves the function of suppressing his awareness of feelings of inner emptiness and dependency.

His drinking reinforces his sense of power and control — he drinks to emphasize that he will not be controlled by Miriam's distance and failure to give. He operates from a sense of entitlement and sees only that Miriam fails in her prescribed caretaking functions.

Miriam, on the other hand, reacts by attempting to control herself. Addiction and disordered eating function to help her do this. She tries to obliterate the self who needs.

Jeff experiences rage because he is not given to, but Miriam experiences shame at her failure to give enough. Jeff's addiction is visible but denied, while Miriam's addiction is invisible. Miriam will get help to address her addiction and Jeff's, but Jeff will not get help to address Miriam's or his own. Jeff is dependent on Miriam for nurturing and caretaking that reinforce his sense of self. Miriam is dependent on Jeff for her sense of self. At one point in treatment Miriam questions whether her life is "worth putting much energy into." She would not question the importance of putting energy into Jeff or her children, just as Jeff is not likely to be heard asking whether his own life is worth putting energy into. Jeff assumes a self worthy of being cared for by Miriam. Miriam's experience is that she must work to be "given" a self by Jeff.

These are two radically different addictive experiences, representing two radically different positions with respect to power and control. Male addicts tend to enter treatment with "attitudes" of pomposity, grandiosity, or self-pity that may cover shame or inadequacy. Women, however, almost uniformly enter treatment with overt feelings of shame and inadequacy. They start out from a devalued position and are scapegoated and stigmatized for their self-destructive attempts to respond to that devalued position.

Empowering Women: Special Issues in Treatment

For a woman, recovery from addiction requires being freed from the constricting dictates of the female role — that is, those social and psychological pressures that make it difficult for her to assume appropriate responsibility for herself without the addiction serving to return her to a powerless state. Essentially, recovery can allow women to become the "subjects" of their own experience, to be able to "say no" to the expectations of others without guilt and fear of rejection.

Once clinicians help a woman to overcome the initial constraints to entering treatment, their first task is to understand the level of shame (Fossum & Mason, 1986), guilt, anger (Lerner, 1985), and low self-esteem (Braiker, 1984) she has experienced. While her internal reality of feeling shamed and devalued may make her resistant, she needs to be empowered within the therapeutic situation, as she has not been in her other relationships. The therapist's response to this dilemma becomes critical. Most women expect therapists to define them in the same way that men, parents, and society have defined them. Therapy needs to provide an experience of self-definition, self-confirmation, and self-direction.

By contrast, men expect to continue to define themselves as they always have. In early phases of treatment these rigid views may need to be confronted and challenged. Both men and women must be helped to understand that they are co-creators of their interactional system within the context of a larger system in which men have more power and in which husband and wife are not responded to as equals.

The clinician is often hindered in work with addicted women by pervasive gender-role constraints of the larger culture. Conflicting and ambiguous messages from the family or the larger culture about a woman's permitted level of self-control and responsibility for herself should be acknowledged and validated. Women still pay a high emotional price for autonomy and selfhood, especially if they are economically dependent. Many women have highly ambivalent feelings about assuming greater responsibility for themselves. Ultimately they need to be helped to embrace the possibility of choice and then to choose the level of autonomy comfortable for them individually. While space does not allow a review of family therapy approaches to various addictive behaviors, some general statements may be applicable across a range of treatments.

The first is the necessity for understanding the nature of the addictive process as a multilevel process, requiring multilevel treatment. Since addiction evolves over time and the family system adapts and adjusts in phases, it is critical to conceptualize treatment as both long-term and phase-oriented. In the first phase, therapy deals primarily with the *systemic* relationship between the addict and the drug of choice, as well as all the other systemic responses that maintain that relationship. In phase two, the larger family system becomes more the focus of treatment as the family adjusts to the termination of the addict's relationship with the addictive substance or process. In phase three, the family is helped to achieve and maintain a healthy non-addictive interactional balance which will prevent addiction from emerging in the next generation. This balance is often different from the normative imbalance of power arrangements between the sexes prescribed by our culture.

Given the phase-oriented nature of treatment, as well as the differing belief systems of men and women entering treatment, the question of whom to include in therapy and when to include them poses special challenges to both our standard notions of family therapy and our evolving sense of a feminist approach to therapy. Frequently, in the beginning phases of treatment it may be more effective to work primarily with the woman alone, whether or not she is the addict. This approach appears to be linear and nonfeminist in seeming to reinforce the notion that the women is "at fault" and solely responsible for change in the system. Entering the system through the woman has been soundly criticized by feminists, such as Bograd (1986).

> Family therapists are trained to enter and modify systems through their most responsive or malleable member. . . . When family therapists structure their interventions primarily around the woman's behaviors, they reinforce the cultural concept that the woman should adapt herself to the family context, should initiate changes in her husband's actions, and should take primary responsibility for the tranquility of the domestic environment. (p. 43)

In this argument Bograd makes the assumption that the therapist, by putting the responsibility for change on the woman, is automatically asking her to change in the direction of stabilizing the system, that is, to adapt to the man. This is an unwarranted assumption. Work with women, as illustrated by the therapy in Miriam's case, may indeed put the initial burden of change on the woman,· but the change is in the direction of destablilizing the system, challenging the existing power imbalances, and refuting society's definition of the woman as sick. Her addiction is viewed not as pathology, but as her attempt at health. That is, the addiction is viewed as her expression of defiance against her one-down status or at least her need to tranquilize herself into accepting the unacceptable.

In most family systems, whether the woman is the addict or the codependent, addiction reinforces already damaging complementary views about male-female responsibility. Women tend to view themselves as responsible even for the abuse they have experienced from men. When a woman is an addict, it is typical that her own *internal* overresponsibility, rather than an interactional imbalance, maintains the addiction, particularly if the male spouse is also addicted. In effect, the addiction becomes a release from or sedative for overresponsible behavior, thinking, and feeling. In this case working with the woman alone disrupts her tendency to overfunction and devalue herself, so that her underresponsible solution of addiction no longer keeps the system stable.

It is, however, critical to communicate to the woman that, while she *has* a problem, within the larger systemic frame she is *not* the problem. Ultimately, all family members need to change their assumptions about what is problematic and who is "truly" responsible.

This focus was pertinent for Miriam and Jeff. A system in which both spouses are addicted is the most difficult to unbalance. Miriam's overresponsibility maintained Jeff's addiction as well as her own. The initial move of asking her to go to Al-Anon addressed her overresponsibility in a way that was consonant with her own belief system; it maintained a focus on his addiction in a positive way that eventually resulted in her recognizing her own. As she recovered, work in disrupting her overresponsibility continued, so that Jeff would hopefully hit bottom and confront his own addiction.

The nature of the addiction itself determines who to include in therapy. When a male is the addict he will often either refuse treatment or leave when the therapist or the family begins to confront his denial. It is neither efficient nor effective to try to do therapy with an addicted male who denies his problem. Since addicted women are more likely to engage with a therapist, this relationship can be used as leverage to encourage involvement with a rehabilitation or self-help program to address the specific addiction. A male is more likely to become engaged because of a shift in the behavior of his wife, family, or especially, his employer. Therapists must assess each particular system carefully and determine what the major relational sources of motivation are for the addicted person. Including a male spouse, a father, a mother, or a distant uncle in treatment may be beneficial under certain circumstances. If both husband and wife are addicted, it is critical to get somebody sober, and generally the wife is more accessible. Technically, the point is that family therapists need to treat addictive problems flexibly, without being hindered by rigid assumptions of what constitutes family therapy or feminist therapy. We propose a flexible and expanded approach utilizing many resources, with family therapy being one part of a coordinated treatment plan.

We are in danger of using feminism against women if we deny them a chance to focus on themselves in our effort to avoid defining women as the problem or making them responsible for change. A woman is, after all, responsible for herself. To ask a man to change ignores the reality that "no dominant group has ever relinquished power voluntarily" (Hare-Mustin, 1987). Edith Lisansky-Gomberg (1985) makes the point that it is not helpful to reinforce an alcoholic woman's notion that she is a passive victim.

Beyond issues of technique, therapy with addictive systems needs to address clients' behavior, affect, and belief system within the context of the marital, extended family, and societal systems. At the level of behavior, the first obvious goal is abstinence from the addiction. Self-help groups such as AA and Al-Anon are primary resources for maintaining abstinence from most drug addictions. Inpatient treatment programs for alcohol, polydrug addiction, and eating disorders may be an important part of an overall treatment plan as well.

Therapists need to be aware, however, that AA, Al-Anon and other similar groups such as Narcotics Anonymous or Overeaters Anonymous often communicate messages that reinforce gender stereotypes. They are, in fact, very traditional in terms of gender roles and do not necessarily encourage women to change in ways that may result in greater assertiveness or responsibility for themselves. Feminist therapy, for instance, may seem to contradict Al-Anon or Nar-Anon programs, in which women are not encouraged to take differentiated positions, but are told simply to "detach" from abusive behavior. Addicted women often return to rigidly overresponsible behavior when sober and the program does not discourage this. Male alcoholics may revel in the standard assertion that AA is a "selfish" program and use this as an excuse not to take responsibility for emotional issues in the family.

The primary benefit of self-help programs lies in their ability to provide a different context for thinking about the relationship to the drug or to the addicted person. The mutual interdependence and support that form the basis of such programs are primary requirements for recovery. But a therapist must have a strong working knowledge of these programs both to counteract inappropriate gender messages and to confront the tendency of some clients to use the program to maintain dysfunctional behavior rather than to further change.

Beyond abstinence, an important behavioral goal of therapy in this phase is to reverse dysfunctional patterns of over- and underfunctioning (see Bepko & Krestan, 1985). In addition, changing role behavior specifically within the nuclear and extended family is critical to sustained, long-term maintenance of recovery from addiction (Bowen, 1978; Carter & McGoldrick, 1976).

Later in treatment it is critical to deal with affect both within the individual and within the family. Many family therapy approaches have tended to avoid dealing with affect in the interests of focusing on process, but the subjective experience of shame, guilt, rage, emptiness, inadequacy and fear dominates the emotional environment in an addictive family. Since these underlying feelings both prompt and maintain addictive cycles, it is crucial that they be addressed.

Many addicted women have experienced a lack of response to their feelings and needs in their families of origin. If the therapeutic process ignores this, a woman may experience in treatment a reenactment of the original family drama that maintained or triggered the addiction (Middleton-Moz & Dwinell, 1986; Miller, 1983). It is particularly important for women who have experienced rape, incest, or other forms of physical abuse to integrate their own emotional responses to these traumatic events. It is equally important for men who have been abusive to take responsibility for their abuse or for men who have been abused to experience the full emotional impact of that trauma. Techniques for dealing with affect can vary, as may the timing and involvement of different family members. Group treatment, psychodrama, family sculpting, visual imagery, metaphor, ritual, and hypnotic work are all powerful tools for encouraging an exploration and integration of painful emotional realities underlying and resulting from addiction.

For most women a focus on sexuality is critical at some point in treatment. As noted, sexual dysfunction and conflict about sex are major issues for substance-abusing or eating-disordered women. Choosing one's desired level and form of sexual involvement with others may represent a major expression of autonomy for a woman. Conflicts surrounding sexuality need to be addressed at affective as well as behavioral and cognitive levels.

Finally, the cognitive level of treatment is critical, since a woman's low self-esteem and distorted beliefs about herself usually evolve in response to a long history of devaluing communications from her environment. In the early phases of treatment a major focus of cognitive change is to break through the family's denial of the negative consequences of addictive behavior. Educational approaches have been utilized in some treatment programs, for instance, to give clients information about the physiological effects of mixing drugs and alcohol and the risks to the fetus of alcohol and drug use during pregnancy. Similar approaches are often used in the treatment of eating disorders.

A more significant cognitive/affective task for therapists is to validate and reframe negative and traumatic experiences for women. It is important to confirm that what a woman experienced was violating, invasive, or abusive. Moreover, it is critical to connote positively her position with respect to the violation: that she demonstrated strength and resourcefulness in withstanding the abuse and that, while the experience was negative, she herself is not therefore worthless, shameful, or bad. This validation of an experience of abuse, neglect, or trauma may be equally necessary for men, such as those who are sons of alcoholic or addicted parents.

The intensity of the addicted woman's self-negating belief system can be formidable, becoming an internal defense against further abusive experiences. Underlying beliefs may take such forms as, "I deserve to be abused," "I deserve to be unhappy," "I am worthless," "I can't expect anything from anyone." When a woman changes these self-negating beliefs, her family may step up its accusations that she is "bad, selfish, or crazy." When a man overcomes his addiction, his family may also react negatively, but usually because his wife feels as if she is now the bad or deficient one—believing that the "love of a good woman would have changed him," she sees his successful involvement in AA as a statement of her failure. To a man, his wife's involvement in AA is more of the same, another "koffee klatch"; he is threatened not by the idea that AA may succeed where he has failed but by the possibility that she might meet other men in AA. Many women alcoholics accommodate by attending daytime women's meetings or limiting their involvement with the program, to the detriment of their own recovery. It is at this point that work with the larger family system becomes crucial — individual change must be accompanied by change within the larger system, and the larger system will not change unless a woman's roles are fundamentally redefined.

CONCLUSION

Treatment of addictive systems is long-term, phase-oriented work that requires an integrative use of technique and the flexibility to allow for occasional seemingly nonsystemic interventions. Therapists must be aware that an addiction is a more powerful force than most therapeutic techniques and that many resources (such as self-help groups, educational and rehabilitative programs, same-sex support groups, and many combinations of therapy — marital, individual, sibling, group, and extended family group) may serve the family well at some point in treatment. The goal is to maintain family stability without reappearance of the addiction or other rigid role behavior either in the current family or in the next generation. In this respect, it is less likely that short-term interventions will bring about long-range changes with addictive families and more likely that interventions that focus on the family's long-range future, such as Bowen therapy, will maximize sustained intergenerational change.

Beyond technique, as we struggle with the challenges posed by addiction in this culture, a new epistemology of women will hopefully emerge. Recovery from addiction demands that women redefine and reenvision both their social selves and their fundamental ways of thinking about who they are. Ultimately, new directions in family treatment for addictions will almost certainly make greater use of ritual, mythology, and play (see Laird, Chapter 21; Imber-Black, Chapter 22) as we recognize that the job of renewing our entire social structure may reside in women's capacity to re-mythologize and re-ritualize families in ways that are more creatively in tune with their own inner definitions of themselves.

REFERENCES

Barrett, M. J., & Trepper, T. (1986). Vulnerability to incest: A framework for assessment. *Journal of Psychotherapy and the Family, 2,* 13–25.
Bateson, G. (1972). The cybernetics of self. In *Steps to an ecology of mind.* New York: Chandler Publishing.
Beary, M. D., Lacey, J. H., & Merry, J. (1986). Alcoholism and eating disorders in women of fertile age. *British Journal of Addiction, 81,* 685–89.
Beckman, L., & Amaro, H. (1986). Personal and social difficulties faced by women and men entering alcoholism treatment. *Journal of Studies on Alcohol, 47,* 135–45.
Bepko, C., & Krestan, J. A. (1985), *The responsibility trap: A blueprint for treating the alcoholic family.* New York: Free Press.

Berenson, D. (1976). Alcohol and the family system. In *Family Therapy: Theory and practice.* P. Guerin (Ed.). New York: Gardner Press.

Bograd, M. (1986). A feminist examination of family systems models of violence against women in the family. In *Women and family therapy.* M. Ault Riche (Ed.). Rockville, MD: Aspen Systems.

Bowen, M. (1978). *Family therapy in clinical practice.* New York: Jason Aronson.

Braiker, H. (1984). Therapeutic issues in the treatment of alcoholic women. In S. Wilsnack & L. Beckman (Eds.). *Alcohol problems in women.* New York: Guilford Press.

Carter, E., & M. McGoldrick-Orfanidis. (1976). Family therapy with one person and the family therapist's own family. In P. Guerin, Jr. (Ed.). *Family therapy: Theory and practice.* New York: Gardner Press.

Corrigan, E. (1985). Gender differences in alcohol and other drug use. *Addictive Behavior, 10,* 314–17.

Corrigan, E. (1980). *Alcoholic women in treatment.* New York: Oxford University Press.

Covington, S. S. (1982). Sexual experience, dysfunction and abuse: A comparative study of alcoholic and non-alcoholic women. Doctoral dissertation, Union Graduate School.

Curlee, J. (1970). A comparison of male and female patients in an alcoholism treatment center. *Journal of Psychology, 74,* 239–47.

Dahlgren, L. (1979). *Female alcoholics: A psychiatric and social study.* Stockholm, Sweden: Karolinska Institute.

Davis, D. I., Berenson, D., Steinglass, P., & Davis, S. (1974). The adaptive consequences of drinking. *Psychiatry, 37,* 209–15.

Evans, S., & Schaefer, S. (1980). Why women's sexuality is important to address in chemical dependency treatment programs. *Grassroots, 37,* 37–40.

Fossum, M. & Mason, M. (1986). *Facing shame: Families in recovery.* New York: Norton.

Fraser, J. (1973), The female alcoholic. *Addictions, 20,* 64–80.

Futterman, S. (1953), Personality trends in wives of alcoholics. *Journal of Psychiatric Social Work, 23,* 37.

Galbraith, S. "Summary of critical sexuality issues observed among alcoholic women in the skyward women's alcoholism treatment program," Unpublished Manuscript, Rockland, ME.

Gomberg, E. S., (1978), Risk factors related to alcohol problems among women: Proneness and vulnerability. In *Alcohol and Women: Research Issues.* NIAAA Research Monograph No. 1 Proceedings of NIAAA Workshop Jekyll Island, GA, DHHS Pub. No. (ADM) No. 1 Washington, DC: US Government Printing Office, 80-835.

Hammerstein, O. (1943). "Can't Say No." © Williamson Music, Inc.

Hare-Mustin, R. T. (1987). The problem of gender in family therapy theory. *Family Process, 26,* 15–27.

Lerner, H. G. (1985). *The dance of anger.* New York: Harper & Row.

Lisanky-Gomberg, E. & Schilit, R. (1985). Social isolation and passivity of women alcoholics, *Alcohol and Alcoholism, 20,* 313–14.

Middleton-Moz, J., & Dwinell, L. (1986). *After the tears: Reclaiming the personal losses of childhood.* Pompano Beach, FL: Health Communications.

Miller, A. (1983). *For your own good: Hidden cruelty in childrearing and the roots of violence.* New York: Farrar, Straus, Giroux.

Minuchin, S., Rosman, B. O., & Baker, L. (1978). *Psychosomatic families.* Cambridge, MA: Harvard University Press.

Mulford, H. A. (1970). Women and men problem drinkers: Sex differences in patients served by Iowa's community alcoholism centers. *Journal of Studies on Alcohol, 38,* 1624–1639.

Root, M., Fallon, P. & Friedrich, W. (1986). *Bulimia: A systems approach to treatment.* New York: Norton.

Orbach, S. (1986). *Hunger strike.* New York: Norton.

Sandmaier, M. (1980). *The invisible alcoholics: Women and alcohol abuse in America.* New York: McGraw-Hill.

Schwartz, R., Barrett, M., & Saba, G. (1985). Family therapy for bulimia. In D. Garner & P. Garfinkel (Eds.). *Handbook of psychotherapy for anorexia nervosa and bulimia.* New York: Guilford.

Sholty, M. J. (1979). Female sexual experience and satisfaction as related to alcohol consumption. Unpublished Manuscript, Alcohol and Drug Abuse Program, University of Maryland, Baltimore.

Stanton, D. T. and Associates. (1982). *The family therapy of drug and alcohol abuse*. New York: Guilford Press.

Star, B., Clark, C., Goetz, K., & O'Malia, L. (1981). Psychosocial Aspects of Wife Battering. In *Women and Mental Health*, E. Howell, & M. Bayes (Eds.). New York: Basic Books.

Steinglass, P., Davis, D., & Berenson, D. (1977). Observations of conjointly hospitalized "alcoholic couples" during sobriety and intoxication: Implications for theory and therapy. *Family Process, 16*, 1-16.

Van Gelder, L. (1987). The dependencies of independent women. *Ms., 15*.

Walker, L. E. (1980). Battered women. In *Women and Psychotherapy*. A. Brodsky & R. Hare-Mustin, (Eds.). New York: Guilford Press.

Wilsnack, S. (1984). Drinking, sexuality, and sexual dysfunction in women. In S. C. Wilsnack & L. J. Beckman (Eds.). *Alcohol problems in women: Antecedents, consequences, and intervention* (pp. 189-227). New York: Guilford.

Wilsnack, S. & Beckman, L. (1984). *Alcohol problems in women: Antecedents, consequences, and intervention*. New York: Guilford Press.

21
Women and Stories: Restorying Women's Self-constructions

JOAN LAIRD

What would happen if one woman told the truth about her life? The world would split open. — Muriel Rukeyser

THE FIRST STORY:

There was a great tree from which a hornet's nest blew down in a storm. I had been dancing in the wind when it blew down and, still dancing, plunged my hands into it. I can still remember the wind but not the stings with which I was said to have been covered. — Margaret Mead, *Blackberry Winter,* p. 9.

THE SECOND STORY:

All the other houses were strange—houses that had to be made our own as quickly as possible so that they no longer would be strange. This did not mean that they were frightening, but only that we had to learn about every nook and corner, for otherwise it was hard to play hide-and-go-seek. As soon as we arrived, I ran ahead to find a room for myself as far away as possible from everyone else, preferably at the top of the house where I would always be warned by footsteps that someone was coming. After that . . . I was busy exploring, making my own the new domain. — Margaret Mead, *Blackberry Winter,* p. 8

I would like to acknowledge Catherine Kohler Riessman's generous sharing of ideas and helpful comments concerning the relationship between gender and genre.

IN THE ABOVE STORIES from a self-story, Mead describes her child self as irrepressibly curious, a free spirit who understands that the world holds its dangers but who nevertheless decides that the experiences are more than worth the risks. These stories forecast the curiosity of the future anthropologist who must explore every nook and cranny of the world, someone who is willing to stick her hands into hornets' nests, to risk the pain and inconvenience necessary to know the strange and the unknown. After all, how many young women of 23 in those days might venture alone to Samoa, maintaining a firm sense of self in such an exotic world? Her grandmother played running games with her and her brother—"until one day she put her hand to her heart." Margaret, too, ran—as fast as she could, hoping to catch it all, until she could no longer even walk. She knew she would get stung, but that was not the important part. She remembered the wind but not the stings.

The young Margaret, as remembered by an older Margaret, tells us that her family's frequent moves taught her to quickly master new environments, to make them her own. She even forecasts her special cloister in the upper reaches of the Museum of Natural History, a place where she would have privacy from her very public life and would be warned by footsteps that someone was coming.

But what have we here? Clearly these are stories, reminiscences, part of a larger narrative being constructed, deconstructed, and reconstructed from her own words and writings. But are they also "history"? Are they "true" or "real"? Are they apocryphal? Mythical? Does it matter? I begin with these stories because they serve to introduce the two categories or themes to be woven together throughout this chapter, the first of women and women's issues, the second of story, myth, and narrative.

Until the beginning of the feminist critique, women and women's issues had been largely disregarded in the family therapy literature. And until very recently, at least, with the exception of Ferreira and a few others writing in his tradition, almost no attention had been paid to the genres of narrative, story, or myth. However, while women and their stories were still being trivialized in the family therapy field, women as narrators and narrated about and narrative as a primary source of human knowledge were forming major intellectual steams in the social sciences, arts, and humanities.

This chapter weds the genre of story (and its relationships with history, narrative, and myth) with women. The marriage is an important one for two reasons. Until very recently women's stories were largely private and unknown, not of particular interest to the wider intellectual community. The history of anthropology, for instance, is a history of men. To learn about the cultures of the world is still, for the most part, to learn the stories of men and of male production. Women have always had their private stories, as both male and female anthropologists are discovering, but until recently we did not know how to listen to them.

One goal of this chapter, then, is to call attention to the stories of women — in the world, in families, and in our work. The second aim is to explore the category of "story" itself, in the process suggesting that family therapists have cast too narrow a net around a universal human category of understanding, ignoring the rich potential of story, myth, and narrative for understanding family and individual phenomena. This exploration begins with an examination of the definitions of and relationships among narrative, story, myth, and history, along the way making the argument for a broader, more informed view of these categories in family therapy. This material is followed by a discussion of the functions of story and myth in society, in families, and for the individual. Linkages are then made between women and story, as we examine the restorying of women and their lives that is now part of the national discourse. Finally, implications for clinical practice with women, as individuals and in their families, are drawn and illustrated through case example.

NARRATIVES: STORY, HISTORY, AND MYTH

One contemporary narrative, which might be called the "science story," has emphasized narrowly conceived definitions of scientific thought and method in the social sciences and helping professions. The mission of science has centered on discovering the nature of "reality" and measuring it. In such a world, categories such as narrative, story, ritual, and particularly myth are "survivals" from a less scientific time, and are relegated to a realm of unreality, of mysticism, of art, of primitivism.

Some scholars believe, however, that perhaps we have leaned too long and too extensively on the physical sciences for models and on a mathematical metaphor for understanding human behavior. What is needed, says Geertz (1980), is a blurring of the genres. Perhaps it is time to turn more to storytellers, folklorists, dramatists, travelers, artists, anthropologists, and to others who have explored these essential, creative, and powerful but unmeasurable dimensions of human life. Perhaps our naked myths, muses O'Flaherty, are "our last hope for a non-language that can free us from the cognitive snares, a means of flying so low, so close to the ground of the human heart, that they can scuttle beneath the devastating radar of the physical and social sciences" (1980, p. 121).

Many students have searched for definitional distinctions between narrative, story, myth, folklore, life history, history, and so on, attempting to impose order and structure on these dimensions of human discourse. Not only do traditions overlap, but any one explanation is incomplete. Doty (1986), in an effort to cull and synthesize existing definitions of myth, is left with over 50 such definitions, which he has organized into 10 categories ranging over a wide territory of human experience. Making careful distinctions among modes of narrative language and action is not possible here; the discussion must be kept more pragmatic and descriptive than definitive. Nevertheless, some discussion of how these terms are being used is necessary.

Narrative, in a broad definitional sense, is relevant to every level of human experience and social organization, for every dimension of space and time. In family therapy, we tend in general to be more interested in the particular narratives and stories of individuals and families, rather than the sociocultural narratives that construct the contextual realms of possibility from which individuals and families can select the ingredients and forms for their own narratives. Various models of family therapy make particular selections concerning what dimensions of time and space will be attended to, often without worrying about how figure and ground, past and present, or individual and group narratives are interwoven and mutually determining. Perhaps that is one reason why we have failed to recognize the larger narratives that shape and constrain women's stories in families and in family therapy.

Narrative is the prototypical discourse unit, used across cultures, by all social classes, in the widest possible range of contexts (Linde, in press). The fact that similar narrative forms are found throughout the world and over many historical eras means that their basic forms and genesis may be indigenous to the requisites of human interaction (Gergen & Gergen, 1983). Coherence among events, not the events themselves, generates or reduces dramatic tension in life. To understand or interpret a narrative, one must understand the *event* structure, the *evaluative* structure, and the *explanatory* structure, that is, the facts of the narrative, what meaning the speaker makes of these facts, and the speaker's world view or belief system, his or her personal paradigm for making sense of the world (Linde, in press).

In any therapy, and family therapy is no exception, it is the personal narrative, the life history, which is of central interest, as well as how the individual narrative fits with the family/group narrative. In psychotherapy, says Draeger (1983), a living narrated text evolves, with constant selections from and amendments to the rich variety of detail and expression possible. He calls it the building of a "best text." "As therapy progresses, the patient continues to evaluate this text in terms of the context of the past and finally interprets it as an illumination of the present" (p. 374). The self-narrative is an individual's account of the relationship among self-relevant events across time, a way of connecting coherently the events of one's own life. One's identity, then, is built upon the sense one can make of one's own life story. The individual must construct not only an intelligible self (which is not a stabilized state of mind or a set of attributes), but also a capacity for understanding one's own narrative and being able to communicate this understanding to others (Gergen & Gergen, 1983).

As we communicate our personal narratives, we subject them to social alteration or critique. Whether or not a narrative can be maintained depends on the individual's skill in negotiating with others or convincing others that her or his interpretation of events is correct (Gergen & Gergen, 1983). Individuals, families, and other groups drop, add, and revise stories to maintain coherence between the personal and the social. Problems emerge when there is no accepted or acceptable story about what "really" happened, no foundation of assumptions against which either individuals or groups can construct their stories. Examples in our own time include the Nazi Holocaust, the Vietnam War, the Argentinian "Dirty War." When there is no public discourse, only a residue of shame and guilt, it becomes enormously difficult for participants to construct coherent narratives, a general "story" to explain the meanings of these events and one's own place in them. The absence of discourse in these instances may contribute to the extensive difficulties participants have had in making sense of their lives (Lifton, 1973). Similarly, individual and family events, such as incest, abortion, murder and other situations socially defined as deviant and shameful, or individual experiences which are difficult to tolerate or explain, such as suicide or other painful loss, may not be narrativized. One's personal story, as well as the family story, may then lack continuity and meaning.

An issue largely ignored in the literature on narrative, and one crucial to women's lives and women's stories, might be called the politics of storymaking or mythmaking. Clearly there are both obvious and subtle differences in the power individuals and particular interest groups possess to ensure that particular narratives will prevail in family, group, and national life. Not all stories are equal.

NARRATIVE, HISTORY, AND TRUTH

Another relationship frequently debated in the narrative literature is that between narrative and history (for the moment defined as events as they "really" happened) or narrative and "truth." Croce argued that, where there is no narrative, there is no history (White, 1980), while Riceour (1980) pos a dialectic between historicality and narrativity, in which each needs t understood in the terms of the other. Not only do our historical acc vary, but our versions of time itself are shaped by the stories by w live. In the case of individuals, through our constructions of our own biographies, our (his)stories or (her)stories, we recover our identities, we recollect and re-collect our own existences, our very selfhood dependent on the possibilities of constructing a biography (Whan, 1979). Levi-Strauss (1963) has called this process "bricolage." In his view odds and ends, fragments of life, are offered up by chance and the environment. Almost anything will do. These fragments are integrated into a tale, which then is used to explain self or world. This personal story, says Whan, is a "supreme fiction," a way of relating and presenting the self to others.

Wider cultural and historical narratives (as well as the storytelling context itself) provide the frames of reference within which individual narratives can be either constructed or understood. The culture, or the collectivity, provides exemplary story models from which the individual's story draws shape and expression and within which interpretation is possible, connecting the individual to the culture. Whan argues that the issue is not truth or fiction, since very little of human narrative can ever be verified or falsified in any strict empirical sense. We need to understand the "fictional" genres and the literary tropes through which people create and connect themselves with larger collectivities and their own histories.

Bauman (1986), too, takes the position that the fact/fiction or history/story dichotomies are not useful in understanding personal narrative, suggesting that it may be possible that events are not the raw materials out of which stories are constructed but rather the reverse, that events are abstractions from narrative. "It is the structures of signification in narrative that give coherence to events in our understanding, that enable us to construct in the interdependent process of narration and interpretation a coherent set of interrelationships that we call an event" (p. 5). In his view there is an intentionality to narrative. Thus, while narrative may be a linguistic mechanism for making experience or history comprehensible, it may also be used as an instrument for confusing, questioning, obscuring, or distorting events, for keeping the coherence of the narrated event open to question.

Therapy, then, may be described as an effort to help a client not only to comprehend (her) story, to choose among many possible interpretations, to rewrite it, but perhaps, in the cases of those denied their own stories through upheaval or disruption, also to compose new stories which can become models for future action.

Story and Stories

Up to now the terms narrative and story have been used interchangeably. The term "story" is often used to mean narrative. Although the narrative category is a very broad one, not all narrative forms are considered "stories."

Students of language and linguistic form have emphasized various dimensions. Labov's influential work, for example, attends to the structure of the narrative form, identifying narrative (or story) as "one of the many linguistic devices available to speakers for the recapitulation of past experience" (Labov, 1982).

Gergen and Gergen (1983) write of "nested narratives." The self-narrative, that is, the life history or biography, is in part made up of specific vignettes or micronarratives which account for specific events, feelings, interpretations, and so on, or offer an image of self as a worthwhile or moral person. Stories, then, may be thought of as narratives within narrative. We often recognize a particular story in the midst of a longer account because the speaker herself "nests" the narrative, marking its beginning by a shift in tone or affect or with the use of a "once upon a time" sort of phrase that calls attention to the fact a story is about to begin. These vignettes often carry very important messages, as we will see shortly.

The structure of the story or performance event evolves from the systematic interplay of situational factors, which include the roles and identities of the participants, the expressive means used, and the social interactional rules, norms, and strategies for the performance and the criteria for its interpretation, and finally, the sequence of actions that make up the scenario of the event. Context is crucial. Since no two contexts are ever identical in relation to speaker, audience, time, situation, and so on, no story is ever told in quite the same way twice.

Bruner (1986) argues we must go beyond the text (story) in terms of its structure, historical context, linguistic form, genre, and multiple levels of meaning, to discover the ways in which the reader (observer) is affected by and affects the text. Texts are instantiations of the models we carry in our own minds. As reader (listener), we change the "actual" text to a "virtual" text, something in the actual text having triggered our own interpretation. The actual text is unchanged; the virtual text changes almost moment to moment in the act of reading" (Bruner, p. 7).

There are many other perspectives, in a rich and lively field of scholarship, that can offer family therapists a theory and praxis for understanding and participating in the narratives and narrative forms that they and the families they seek to help bring to the therapeutic context.

THE MYTH

For our purposes here, the myth is defined as a story that is more potent and highly symbolic, a story that seems to stand out. Over time, and particularly in the modern era, the term "myth" came to be identified with the notion of fiction or imagination, as contrasted with truth or reality. Myth is associated with belief, with mysticism, a concept linked to the world of fantasy. Linked with religion and the supernatural, myth is considered irrational and primitive, as contrasted with science, which is considered rational and more civilized.

Recently, a large number of scholars from many disciplines have been questioning these distinctions. Doty (1986), for example, argues that myths may be fictional, but they are not irrational, unreal, or unempirical. Furthermore, they are often foundational, special, and sacred, "big stories" that concern the universal themes that individuals face across time, culture, and context. Since every part of our human experience has a claim to reality, the mythic perception is just as "real" as the scientific (Bidney, 1955). Myths, argues O'Flaherty (1980), stand at the boundary line between event and imagination, providing a "cosmic map of the intersecting territories of reality and fantasy, . . . a place where an apparent barrier to human understanding may be forded or breached" (p. 95). Others have argued that science itself is a social construction with its own mythical qualities, a way of languaging the world which gives it a particular kind of coherence and which establishes false dichotomies between truth and falsehood, event and story, reality and fantasy. The scientific mythmaking process provided a context in which the work on myth in the family therapy field took shape, work which now must be questioned.

Stories and myths are something much more than "survivals," relics of the past with mainly or even primarily homeostatic or defensive functions. They are part of the daily discourse for all of us. They are as much about change as about stasis, as much about function as dysfunction. In fact, they are part of our histories, of the ways we think about, interpret, and explain ourselves and our worlds through written and spoken word. The stories that are told and retold in a family may be seen as part of a creative expression of the family's past, its ancient and mythical legacy. The family folklore is not identical with its history. Like the photographs and heirlooms chosen for preservation, stories and myths are "personalized and often creative distillations of experience, worked and reworked over time" . . . moments that are "carefully selected and elaborated through the years, tailored to the demands of the present" (Zeitlin, Kotkin, & Baker, 1982).

The issue, then, is not one of defining what is truth or reality and what is myth, but of understanding that storytelling and mythmaking are themselves definitional. Only when an event has been languaged can it become endowed with cognitive, moral, or aesthetic meaning. There is no world without words or, to paraphrase something Goolishian said some time ago, namely that we can only know the world through our own bumping into it, we can only know the world through our own storying or mythologizing of it.

THE FUNCTIONS OF STORIES AND MYTHS

People tell stories about everything, particularly about important life transitions such as birth and death, arrivings and leavings, and of the important rituals that mark these and other passages. Many such events become richer in the telling; we forget the bee stings, the lost luggage, the disappointing weather after saving all year for a week in the sun. Through our stories and myths we punctuate or bracket our lives in particular ways, revealing our interpretive systems for explaining ourselves, the world, and ourselves in relation to the world.

Storytelling and mythmaking, then, are central devices in the construction of human self and meaning. Like the ritual, they help us to bear witness, to see ourselves mirrored in a collective identity, at once both subject and object. Stories are used to anchor and explain family beginnings. The migration story, for example, not only makes a statement such as "This was the beginning of our family," but also may contain very important prescriptions for how the family is to be, perhaps through a description of the original pioneer or of the way the family adapts to the new country.

Families may have myths for the origin of particular individuals as well. A woman in a workshop recently recounted this tale:

> My father tells this story about my birth: "Your grandfather and I were out hunting one day. A crow flew by and shit on a rock and there you were." He also tells a story about my sister's birth. "Your grandfather and I were out hunting for mushrooms one day. We looked under a rock, and there she was."

The young woman interpreted these stories in the light of her parents' marriage. She saw herself as an unexpected event, an "accident," since her parents were not married when she was conceived. Her sister, however, arrived later; they were "looking for" her. Interestingly, she did not notice that no women were involved in the birth process; in these stories, as in many of the famous creation myths, it is men who give birth/life.

Stories and myths help us to order the world, to sort out, explain, and integrate events in a striving for continuity and coherence; they are social touchstones, mediating a complex, cybernetic feedback process between the personal and the social, meshing one's inner and outer history (Myerhoff, 1978). Myths, argued Malinowski (1954), have both social and pragmatic functions, in that they promote feelings of unity and harmony among the members of a society, negating death and affirming the unity and continuity of life. The elderly Jews in *Number Our Days*, for example, overcame the devastating ruptures from country, religion, and family through their reconstructions and reminiscences. One way we mourn and perpetuate, in altered form, some of what has been lost, is to restore to life those who have come before by making attributions to current figures and connections to current events. Myerhoff reminds us that the issues are not truth and completeness, but rather the understandings, the working-out through memories of our dreams, wishes, and overarching life questions in a kind of "domestic religion" process.

Stories, like rituals, also order and preserve the past, creating and transmitting tradition, providing continuity of experience and meaning. Because they are central culture-bearing mechanisms, they also have ideological and moral dimensions, revealing the family's charter for belief, its system of meanings, and the set of prescriptions and proscriptions that guide behavior.

Stories play a crucial role in socializing family members. They are models for action, telling family members how to master challenges as well as what should be feared or avoided, as in the following anecdote, told by a successful professional woman.

> My mother told me that she was the only girl in the neighborhood who could climb the tree to the boy's club house, and thus could join the boy's club. One day she fell out of the tree and broke her arm.

Jung saw myths serving as exemplars for living and Eliade, too, describes them as models for human behavior. Bettelheim (1977) believes that stories, myths, fables, legends, and tales offer material from which children form important concepts, their notions of the world's origin and its purpose, of the social ideals after which their own behavior can be patterned. In treatment, such stories offer children possibilities for identification and for problem solution. Family narratives, which may take the forms of heroic legends, tall tales, tragic dramas, cautionary stories, or humorous anecdotes, send potent messages concerning admired behaviors and preferred solutions in times of crisis and during important transitions. They tell family members how to behave, as parents, as children, as women, and as men, in their respective ethnic and cultural worlds. Stories and myths are, then, as Kenneth Burke has said, equipment for living (Myerhoff, 1983).

Stories and myths also serve to explain the unexplainable and rationalize the irrational, mediating family paradoxes by both displaying and screening them at the same time. The following story about a story illustrates this point.

> The therapist noted that Jane, who seemed a caring and loving mother, was physically distant from her two small children, rarely spontaneously hugging or kissing them. At one point Jane remarked that when she was three years old, the age her daughter was now, her mother became ill with tuberculosis. Her mother

"cured" at home, and Jane remembered a long period of time when she was not allowed to touch or kiss her mother but had to stand at the door of her mother's bedroom if she wished to see her or talk to her. Her mother, she reminisced at another time, used to tell her many stories. One she remembered in particular was about a great uncle who suffered from tuberculosis. The man traveled the world in search of a cure and, on return from one of these trips, greeted his niece (Jane's mother's aunt) and her baby daughter with kisses. Within one year both the niece and her infant were dead of the dreaded disease.

This story, in the broadest sense, both explained and was an expression of the physical distance customarily maintained in the family. In the case of Jane, it was her mother's symbolic way of explaining to a young child the need for physical distance. This explanatory, cautionary story, its usefulness outlived, was shaping current behavior.

The story or myth can make paradoxes explicit without forcing a risk of serious confrontation between those elements which are truly in conflict or incapable of resolution. Thus, a genuine inquiry into the meaning of the symbols is fended off, preventing change and warding off dissatisfaction with the current state of things. Also, as in larger social, political, religious and other contexts, the control of those in power may be reinforced and enhanced through family story and myth.

This brief discussion of the functions of stories and myths would be incomplete without some comment about the function of what might be called the "unstory." Some families, some women, seem to lack meaningful stories, or what stories exist are so deeply embedded in the family's discourse as to be unrecognizable as story. Migration, geographic and emotional cutoffs, poverty, despair, conflict, and unhappiness may indeed truncate the family's languaging of its experience, giving family folklore a sterile quality. In other families, there may have been a deeply painful or shameful event which the family cannot bring itself to discuss or does not know how to "story." The secretiveness around the most important story, like a communicative disease, contaminates other stories, in a sense placing a quarantine on the family's ability to language its experience. In still other families, the secret story may play a powerful role in maintaining particular balances of power. Much work remains to be done in understanding both the positive and negative functions of secrecy and the unstoried.

WOMEN AND THEIR STORIES

Women and their lives have been largely unsung, unstoried, unmythologized. Their accomplishments, if noted at all, are recorded in small and private ways. The following account of the Objiwa might have been written of almost any tribe, including our own:

Whenever men fulfill their duties creditably, they are lauded. In company they tell endless stories about their adventures, for their duties are always "adventures"; they hold stag feasts of religious importance after a successful hunt. Even the mythology occupies itself with the pursuits and rewards of men. The important visions, which men have been driven all their youth to pursue, bestow power for the masculine occupations. A successful hunter can parade this fact in ways licensed by his visions — songs that he sings publicly, amulets that are conspicuous and worn in public, charms that he can sell. Women's work "is spoken of neither for good nor for evil" — at least in a gathering of men. Conventionally it is not judged in any way, it is simply not given any thought (Landes, 1971, pp. 9–11).

Women's stories, like women's rituals, have been confined, for the most part to a private rather than a public world, as have women themselves (Laird, 1986; 1988). There are two points to be made here. First, the split itself is falsely dichotomous, a megamyth the destruction of which is at the heart of the feminist movement. In this myth, men have created history, culture, and indeed, life itself. They belong to the public world, the world of culture; women to the private world, the world of nature. In this world of nature, women give birth, lactate, rear their children, and take care of the mundane, everyday parts of life, freeing their men for the public and the extraordinary, for the stuff of myth and story. Ardener (1975) points out that the models of society made by most of anthropology are drawn from male visions and male activities; many ethnographers return having spoken only to men about men. He suggests that "the models of society that women can provide are not the kind acceptable at first sight to men or to ethnographers . . . they lack the metalanguage for its discussion" (p. 3).

A second point is that not only have women's stories been untold, but the accepted genres for storytelling and mythmaking are largely defined and controlled by males. "Mythology," says Weigle (and I would add storytelling), "has usually been defined and studied as a public, collective, male-dominated means of communication which pertains to cyclic time and metaphysical or supernatural reality . . . " (1982, p. 293). Not only are women's (private and mundane) lives unstoried, but women's ways of storying are also private, and they are disparaged. Folklorist Claire Farrer argues, "Women's expressive vehicles are the non-legitimate forms, even though they are as ordered and as rule-governed as the male forms" (1975, p. xiv). Women's talk is described as "gossip" or "old wives tales"; with a few notable exceptions it is dismissed and rarely studied (Harding, 1975).

In our own society, not only have men largely been in charge of mythmaking, at least in the public forums, but men also have at their disposal narrative genres not usually associated with women, for example, the tall tale, the war story, or the heroic myth. Men have had virtual control of the most powerful media and the sociopolitical forums and thus of the public mythmaking process around both males and females. In this process, sym-

bols and language are used which define gender-appropriate roles and behaviors and ward off threats to established social and political hegemonies
and to, symbolically, male secret societies. One genre over which men have
had a virtual monopoly (Lily Tomlin notwithstanding) is public humor,
which often becomes a vehicle for keeping women in their place. Many
stand-up comics have made their fortunes, for example, on wife and mother-
in-law jokes. I cannot think of anyone who has become rich on father-in-law
jokes.

These two points have important implications and raise some difficult
questions for students of women's issues, for those who seek change in the
rules for storytelling and mythmaking, and for family therapists who wish to
know women's stories. Clearly women's stories need to be told and they need
to be told in ways that do not humiliate and demean women, as has frequently been the case with the public degradation of many successful
women.

At the present time, in this society at least, we are experiencing a tremendous surge in the storying of women's lives, as well as a conscious effort on
the part of many women to gain control over women's mythmaking. Many
bookshops are devoted exclusively to women's issues and women's writing,
while others have sections for women's literature and women's biography. A
gallery for the display of women's art has opened in Washington, D.C. and
exhibits of women's paintings have toured the country. Reproductions of
women's paintings, long unknown or unavailable, are finding their way into
posters, calendars, and other forms of art.

A restor(y)ing process with the quality and force of a social movement has
been taking shape. In the process, new public heroines are emerging. Today,
for example, we can read about Beryl Markham, an astonishingly talented
writer and courageous aviatrix whose story was virtually unknown, of newly
discovered Black women heroines, of American pioneer women. It should
be pointed out, however, that heroine-making entails significant risk. On
one level at least, a central gender-connected rule is broken; the public-
private myth is undermined. The costs of heroineship (and thus, in the eyes
of many, neglect of women's primary roles) are heavy, and women heroines
are subsequently vulnerable to public contempt and accusations of neglect,
usually from men but also from women. Markham, for example, like
Margaret Mead, is faulted for being a poor mother, promiscuous, a faithless
wife. Public women like Coretta King or Ethel Kennedy, who devote themselves to the memories of their husbands' achievements, fare better. Currently, public women Nancy Reagan and Elizabeth Dole play powerful counter-
feminist roles in the women's mythmaking process.

Women are hungry for women's stories, but not just for the stories of
public women, of women who live their lives in ways usually reserved for
men. As more and more women tell their own stories and as stories are told

about women in biography, novel, play, and poem, and in music, film, television and radio, women's choices for self-construction are enriched and expanded. Women not only begin to connect themselves with other women and to discover new possibilities for their lives, but also have new opportunities to tell the stories of their oppression and of their poverty. Only recently, for example, has Freud's myth of women's rape fantasies been seriously questioned, as growing numbers of women reveal the stories of their actual rapes, by strangers and by fathers and other male caretakers. Women are now telling of the violence they have experienced, making it the shame of men rather than of themselves.

Other women, as mentioned, have taken active roles in both demythologizing and remythologizing women's lives. For example, Kolbenschlag (1979) has analyzed familiar fairytales, exposing the pervasive misogynous images, roles, and cultural attitudes, while Plaskow (1979) has revitalized the ancient Hebrew myth of Lilith, writing a new ending to the story. Her myth transforms the competition between Eve and Lilith for the attention of Adam into a story of women's cooperation, affection and bonding. Jewish women have made special contributions in telling the stories of their mothers, their grandmothers, and themselves, in the process affirming their rightful places in Jewish religion and culture (Kaye/Kantrowitz & Klepfisz, 1986; Koltun, 1976). These narratives of women's lives testify to women's skills in reaching moral resolution through the telling and interpreting of their stories, factual and imaginative, individually and collectively.

PRACTICE

Having written something of narrative and something of women and their stories, it remains to bring the two together in thinking about practice with women and their families. In recent years there has been growing interest in the application of developments in narrative, literary, and linguistic theories to the clinical world. Some psychoanalysts, for example, "began inquiring whether the object of analysis was not so much archaeologically to reconstruct a life as it was to help the patient construct a more contradiction-free and generative narrative of it" (Bruner, p. 9). Spence, in *Narrative Truth and Historical Truth* (1982), argues that the purpose of therapy should not be to rediscover and work through the traumas of the past, but to reconstruct a self and a life in the form of a narrative of the whole. Schafer, too, has challenged what has come to be called Freud's "archaelogical" approach to analysis. Therapy is, in his view:

> a story that begins in the middle, which is the present: the beginning is the beginning of the analysis. . . . Once the analysis is under way, the autobiographical present is found to be no clear point in time at all . . . more and more it seems

to be both a repetitive, crisis-perpetuating misremembering of the past and a way of living defensively with respect to a future which is, in the most disruptive way, imagined fearfully and irrationally on the model of the past. The life history is, in this world, a second-order history, while the analytic dialogue is a first-order history. In the narration of this moment of dialogue lies the structure of the analytic past, present, and future. . . . . Those traditional developmental accounts, over which analysts have labored so hard, may now be seen in a new light: less as positivistic sets of factual findings about mental development and more as hermeneutically filled-in narrative structures. (1981, p. 49)

For Draeger (1983), therapy is the building of a "best text," a living, evolving narrated text, in which emendations and selections are made in a sorting out process. The patient is "a redactor of those oral traditions contained within the expanding narrative," which contains the symbols, beliefs, myths, and metaphors that have "derived from traditions now without individual identity but fused into the complicated unit of the patient's culture and times" (p. 375). Whan (1979) sees therapy as the reconstruction of a "self," a text of identity. "The narrative form provides a primary linguistic structure for giving and having an account of oneself, and thus having a self that is accountable" (p. 490). One recovers an identity from the complexity of existence.

What is the role of the therapist? For Draeger, the therapist is an interpreter, the patient the subject of the exegesis, although he recognizes the multiple layers of meaning in any narrative and the importance of the patient's own interpretations. Whan believes that both client and therapist are telling stories, another way of framing what has come to be called "co-evolution" in family therapy. He suggests that all of us adopt literary genres, schemas through which we view the human condition, through which our visions of temporality are shaped. Our therapeutic interpretations are driven by the poetic and fictional forms and motifs we favor. In this sense, Bowen is clearly a romantic, full of nostalgia for the past, Minuchin, with his optimistic view of overcoming all through reframing, favors the comic mode, Haley with his appreciation for paradox and surprise is a master of the ironic, and Boszormenyi-Nagy and Paul, for whom time is inexorable and full of nemesis, perhaps our best tragedians.

Family therapists, too, have incorporated linguistic theory into their understanding of therapeutic processes in a number of ways (e.g., Watzlawick, 1978; Bandler & Grinder, 1975; 1976), and many family therapists have appreciated the reciprocal relationships between life and art and the lessons to be learned from literature. Some therapists have been master storytellers. Milton Erickson (Rosen, 1982), for example, was noted for his brilliant use of teaching tales, which served as analogues for the patterns he observed or carried a special and often enigmatic message in the form of a metaphor; his many disciples continue to enrich that tradition. Bowen (1978), too, makes use of apocryphal stories, tales loosely based on or made up about other client families, to send a particular message to a family regarding its own dilemma. Friedman, who creates his own fables, sees them as "microcosms of life—rather than didactic sermons or interpretations—they enable one family to learn what I have learned about life from other families" (1985, p. 31). One person who has used such genres most creatively is Peggy Papp, who points out that "tasks, rituals, metaphors, and stories are devices which protect people from being blinded by the truth. They allow analogous messages to be communicated and absorbed according to the family's own tolerance level" (1984, p. 24). Many others who have long appreciated the value of a good story might be cited. Less available, however, are theories and examples from narrative and linguistic theory which help us in a more disciplined way to listen to the stories we are told.

Other family therapists became intrigued with the family myth. Ferreira's creative 1963 paper provided the polestar around which the course of family mythology was charted. He defined the family myth as a series of well integrated beliefs which preserves a particular homeostasis. Byng-Hall (1973, 1979) continued in this tradition, arguing that "family mythology includes false or edited beliefs about the present which may be coupled with family legends which support these beliefs" (1979, p. 103). Byng-Hall contrasts these homeostasis-preserving consensus images, which include family yarns or tales, fables, lies, legends, and secrets, with "recalled events" or attempts at historical accuracy, which he sees as "the building blocks of a healthy family history" (1979, p. 105). Others who have enriched family therapy's mythology of myth include Stierlin (1973), who argued that family myths serve group defensive functions, warding off disintegration, and Bagarozzi, Perlmutter, and Anderson (1985), who have made applications to therapy from a similar theoretical stance. Selvini Palazzoli and her colleagues (1977) are known for their creative work with intergenerational family myths and the use of a ritualized prescription to challenge such myths.

Family therapists have tended to have colorful visions of the destructiveness of myth in rigid, dysfunctional families, but less appreciation of its central role in all families or for the richness and creativity inherent in family folklore and mythology. In some of the work, in spite of unconvincing acknowledgments that families may need their myths and that accuracy does not necessarily imply health, there is the inescapable notion that family mythology is a homeostasis-preserving, rigid category of false belief. It is implied that a little bit of myth goes a long way, that some myth may be necessary to family life, but too much places the family at risk, as if mythology could be quantified. Our mission as truthtellers often seems one of puncturing the fantasies of storytellers, surfacing the secrets implicit in the legends, exposing the liars, and exorcising the deadly myths. In the process, not only do we then spoil many a good story for the sake of the truth, but we may also be guilty of spoiling the family story-meanings and folklores for the sake of our own coherences, which are, of course, as ethnic, gender, political, and ideologically biased, indeed as mythological, as those of our clients.

While no one, to my knowledge, has developed a model of family therapy based on narrative theory, some family therapists have begun to adopt metaphors from the world of narrative and previously ignored branches of literary and linguistic theory. For example, Keeney speaks of the therapuetic "story," while Hoffman (1985) and Anderson (1987) have begun to describe the therapeutic encounter as "conversation." Viaro and Leonard (1983) draw upon the linguistic theories of Sacks and Schlegoff and the notions of conversation and "talk exchange" to analyze the work of the Milan group, and Tomm has borrowed the notion of "reflexivity" from the work of Pearce and Cronen to describe the "relationships among meanings within the belief systems that guide communicative actions" (1987, p. 169), ideas that are connected not only to Bateson but also to the contributions of the great Prague linguist, Roman Jakobson.

Certainly there are some significant differences in the ways linguistic and narrative metaphors are being applied. In Viaro and Leonardi's analysis of the Milan teams' work, for example, the therapeutic dialogue is conceptualized as a "conversational game" in which the therapist is in charge of the rules which organize the talk. This may be contrasted with Anderson's approach, in which the therapist allows the family to choose what they will talk about and how, while "the team ideally tries to figure out the family's own style of reflecting, their rhythm, speed, and modes of communication" (1987, p. 421).

All of these developments have occurred in the context of the "new epistemology" and of the constructivist movement in family therapy; for the most part they seem to signify a movement away from positivism and from normative notions of family structure and functioning, from the search for "truth" to a search for meaning, and toward new ways of comprehending how families construct their worlds. One of the richest sources of meaning lies, of course, in the narratives through which individuals and families explain themselves, their thinking, and their behavior. Furthermore, these developments imply a different definition and role for the family therapist, variously described as family consultant (Hoffman, 1983), facilitator of self-healing (Tomm, 1987), or reflector (Anderson, 1987).

These developments are occurring in tandem with the feminist critique of family therapy and a concern on the part of many female (and some male) family therapists that women's issues are inadequately addressed and women's voices largely unheard in the profession and in families. MacKinnon and Miller (1987) and Taggart (1985; Chapter 6), for example, speculate that the new and so-called "radical" epistemology and related models of therapy ignore factors of social structure and social construction, failing to recognize that "drawing distinctions is . . . not only an epistemological act, it is a political act" (MacKinnon & Miller, 1987, p. 151). In the process, women's and children's stories are unheard or discounted.

LISTENING TO WOMEN'S STORIES: A CO-INTERPRETIVE EXPERIENCE

The narrative metaphor and the ethnographic stance can open up opportunities to listen in new ways to our clients' narratives-in-construction and to the embedded stories that stand out and call for attention. In this section, specific suggestions for a beginning approach to story co-interpretation are made, using women's stories as example. We need to know how to listen to the stories women tell, to search for and respect the ways in which they tell their stories, to further explore the relationships between gender and genre (Riessman, 1987, in press). Women need to be helped to examine the ways their lives are storied and mythologized, to become aware of who the storytellers and mythmakers are, to interpret their own stories, and to make choices about the ways they wish to story their futures.

Individual and family stories may be gathered in a variety of ways in direct practice with individuals, families, and groups. The "best" stories, in the sense of those least influenced by the clinician, are perhaps those that emerge spontaneously, as part of the client's life narrative or in family dialogue. Such stories or myths are likely to surface during the construction of a family genogram or when the woman or family is reminiscing about individual and family experiences. The clinician may also elicit family stories and myths through direct request. For example, one might ask: What stories do your parents tell about you when you were a child? Some clients, particularly those who come from either families or ethnic groups with rich storytelling traditions, will respond easily and even colorfully to such requests. Others may be unable to respond: those whose ethnic traditions do not encourage storytelling; families that are guarded about their histories, even with their own family members; those who have events in their lives they have been unable to story, or who have rigid communication rules. Their stories will be more deeply embedded in the overall family narrative and require more careful searching. The more the therapist is able to explore and observe family culture ethnographically, that is, unfettered by prejudgments of normative structure and functioning, the more likely stories will be remembered and shared.

Family and group contexts aid and enrich the storytelling process, for there is a contagion effect. In family sessions, as family members joke, reminisce, and challenge various versions of a past event, other family members are usually stimulated to tell their versions or to associate to other stories, providing a sense of the context in which stories are told and the family interactions that take place around them. In group sessions, one member's story will trigger the memories of others, freeing everyone to share stories around a particular theme. Sometimes material that has been shielded, such as a powerful superstition, or a story of a family "hex" (common in many families but rarely shared because they are interpreted as "primitive"), will emerge. An individual or family will usually, over time, tell several stories that can be seen to express a theme, a set of messages, beliefs, and meanings, suggesting the importance of that theme in the family, as in the following example.

Elizabeth, 46, was seen individually in family systems treatment primarily focused on self-definition and differentiation issues in the context of family-of-origin experiences. She was at times depressed and expressed rather undefined dissatisfactions with her marriage. Central to her current dissatisfaction with herself and her work was an issue facing many women of her generation, women who grew up in the 1950s and were pulled between traditional women's roles and the public world of work. An English teacher in a small junior college, married, with two grown children, Elizabeth had dreams of becoming a leader in her field, of moving to a prestigious university, but had not finished her doctorate or published. An ardent but ambivalent feminist, she wished to climb the highest mountains but was acrophobic, a pervasive metaphor for her life. While she took some risks, this talented woman was frustrated by her own fears and felt handicapped by her equally pressing need to keep the silver polished, her nest in perfect shape, to entertain, to be available as always to husband and children.

She described her mother as unhappily married, unexpressive, disappointed with most of her own life choices, and saw her as both highly critical and competitive with her, identifying Elizabeth with her maternal grandmother. Her grandmother, in turn, was described as a dominating but highly phobic woman, a self-sacrificing and controlling woman who sighed and suffered a great deal, the matriarch of the family. Elizabeth's mother also identified her with Elizabeth's father, passionately interested in many things, optimistic and ambitious, but unable to follow through with any one project for any length of time. Elizabeth had a highly conflicted and competitive relationship with her mother, as well as with her two brothers, whom her mother favored. She adored her father as a child and young woman, and had been his favorite, but had become increasingly contemptuous of him over the years.

The following women's stories juxtapose just a few of the many images of and choices for women in Elizabeth's family:

A story told by her grandmother about herself:

> You should have seen me at the party (laughing). I got a little tipsy, and I took a pair of scissors and walked right up to Howard Spencer and cut off his tie.

Another story told by her grandmother:

> Mr. Wilson was so disappointed when I got married and left the firm. He hated to lose me, and he told me I was the best secretary he ever had, and that if I stayed, maybe one day I could become a partner.

A reminiscence by grandmother:

> I admired my father so. I always thought he was so strong. My mother was a weak person, she had to get married, and I never had much use for her.

A story told by Elizabeth's mother:

> I was sitting in the Sugar Bowl after school, in a booth with some friends (junior in high school at the time). It was raining out; all of a sudden I looked up and there was my mother, standing there with my rubbers. I was so humiliated.

A story Elizabeth's mother tells of her:

> That reminds me of the time Elizabeth went to the Y camp when she was eight. She went out with a friend in a rowboat, and jumped in the water in the middle of the lake, where it was real deep. She forgot she had her glasses on, and you can imagine what happened. She couldn't see a thing after that, and I had to rush another pair to her right away. She was always losing things, still is.

A second:

> When Elizabeth was 16 and got her driver's license, I let her drive one night when it was snowing. Do you know what she did? She drove right up on someone's front lawn, couldn't tell the road from the yard! She's a terrible driver.

One of Elizabeth's family stories:

> I was at my grandmother's house one day, when it began to snow very heavily. My grandmother always picked my grandfather up at work, and she began to worry that she wouldn't be able to drive down the street. It was finally decided that my

grandfather would take the bus to the corner of the street, and that she and I would meet him at the bus stop to help him home. I will never forget that image. She was on one side and I had hold of his other arm, while we all three trudged through the snow.

Elizabeth interpreted the stories about herself as "stories of humiliation," ways that her critical mother had of embarrassing and degrading her. She saw her grandmother, whom she admired, as dominating and "castrating" of men, as seeing men as helpless and dependent on women, and herself as following in that tradition. She saw her own mother, who had been pregnant with her before marriage, continuing another family tradition, as passive and weak, just as her grandmother had defined her own mother.

In a gradual, co-interpretive process, a view of women, women's lives and the relationships between women and between women and men as envisioned in the family and handed down in stories by and about women began to emerge. These stories were examined in the contexts of the times, of the possibilities for men and for women, and of women's aspirations and disappointments. Men, who carried the public roles, could not do it without women and could not do it "right." All of the women in this family were self-defining and defined by other family members and each other as "phobic," as afraid of things out there, a way perhaps of justifying and accepting their assignment to hearth and home. Women who did enter the public world lost their glasses and could not find their ways, or might get their feet wet.

Elizabeth began to see an element of caring in some of the "humiliation" stories, and began to speculate that perhaps they communicated the notion that "you need your mother," "the world out there is full of dangers for women," and "I don't want you to leave home; I want you to stay connected with me, for when you leave, I have nothing." Her own anxious and phobic responses to new "public" challenges began to make sense to her, as she became involved in a restorying process. On another level she began to move toward a new interpretation of women's relationships in her family, developing new insight into the contexts in which these family stories defined women's lives, reinforcing social mores and establishing constraints on life choices. Elizabeth also began to restory her resentments toward her husband and marriage, making possible a series of renegotiations around role definitions and gender expectations within the family, especially in terms of public/private workloads.

For readers who wish to explore their own stories or the stories of their clients the following set of questions may help:

The storytelling context: Who usually tells this story? To whom is it told?

When and under what circumstances? How do you react? How do others react?

Development over time: Has this story changed over time? (In what ways?)

Variations on the theme: Are there other versions of the story? In family sessions, how does each person remember it, what does each person think of it, and of others' versions?

Portrait of women (or self): How are you portrayed in this story, or series of stories? As competent? Incompetent? Courageous? Cowardly? Daring? Dignified? Silly? Sickly? Saintly?

Interpretations: What meaning does the story hold for you? What does this story say about what you (or other women in the family) are supposed to be like? Loyal, self-sacrificing, independent? How does that differ from the stories that are told about men? What do the stories say about what men are supposed to be like? How do women get to be heroines in your family? Saintliness? Generosity?

Women in context: How do women's stories in your family connect with what was (is, will be) possible for women? How do you understand this story in the context of the times and in the context of the opportunities and constraints in women's lives?

Present self-definitions: Do you see yourself the way you are portrayed here? How do you think this story affects your choices, your behavior, your relationships with men, with women, your life choices, the ways others perceive you?

Future stories: Would you like to change the stories told about you? In what ways? How could you go about doing that? What story would you like your granddaughter to tell of you?

Summary

Women's stories have been largely untold and unheard, and women are part of a gendered mythmaking process in which they are rarely the authors. In family therapy, we have been inattentive to and disqualifying of women's narratives, in families and in the profession itself. This is one of the things the feminist critique is about: Women's stories must be heard and women must have more say in the construction of their own myths; they must be recognized as storytellers and their storytelling modes respected.

On another level, theories of storytelling and mythmaking now in vogue in family therapy must be examined for their limitations as well as their contributions. Much work of value is emerging from the fields of narrative theory, literary theory, folklore, anthropology, linguisitics, and other sources, offering the potential for other ways of understanding, co-interpreting, and reconstructing the texts/narratives that emerge in work with families. Much work remains to be done in studying the relationships between individual and family narratives, perhaps one way of bridging the unfortunate gap between individual and family theories. In fact, therapy itself can be thought of as narrative-in-construction, the restorying not only of the lives of women and men who come for help but of our own as well.

REFERENCES

Agar, M. (1980). Stories, background knowledge and themes: Problems in the analysis of life history narrative. *American Ethnologist, 7,* 223-39.

Andersen, T. (1987). The reflecting team: Dialogue and meta-dialogue in clinical work. *Family Process, 26*(4), 415-28.

Ardener, E. (1975). Belief and the problem of women. In S. Ardener (Ed.). *Perceiving women* (pp. 1-17). New York: John Wiley.

Bagarozzi, D., Perlmutter, M., & Anderson, S. (1985). Family Myths: Personal and familial odysseys. Presentation at 1985 American Association of Marital and Family Therapy Annual Conference. New York: New York.

Bandler, R., & Grinder, J. (1975; 1976). *The structure of magic.* Vols. I and II. Palo Alto, CA: Science and Behavior Books.

Bauman, R. (1977). *Verbal art as performance.* Prospect Heights, IL: Waveland Press.

Bauman, R. (1986). *Story, performance, and event: Contextual studies of oral narrative.* Cambridge: Cambridge University Press.

Bettelheim, B. (1977). *The uses of enchantment.* New York: Vintage Books.

Bidney, D. (1955). Myth, symbolism, and truth. In T. Sebeok (Ed.), *Myth: A symposium* (pp. 3-24). Bloomington, IN: Indiana University Press.

Bowen, M. (1978). *Family therapy in clinical practice.* New York: Jason Aronson.

Bruner, J. (1986). *Actual minds, possible worlds.* Cambridge, MA: Harvard University Press.

Byng-Hall, J. (1973). Family myths used as defence in conjoint family therapy. *British Journal of Medical Psychology, 46,* 239-50.

Byng-Hall, J. (1979). Re-editing family mythology during family therapy. *Journal of Family Therapy, 1,* 103-16.

Doty, W. (1986). *Mythography: The study of myths and rituals.* University, AL: University of Alabama Press.

Draeger, J. (1983). The problem of truth in psychotherapy: A phenomenological approach to treatment. *Social Science Medicine, 17*(6), 371-78.

Farrer, C. (1975). Introduction. Women and folklore: Images and genres. *Journal of American Folklore, 88,* v-xv.

Ferreira, A. (1963). Family myth and homeostasis. *Archives of General Psychiatry, 9,* 456-63.

Friedman, E. (1984). Friedman's fables. *Family Therapy Networker, 8*(5), 30-35.

Geertz, C. (1980). Blurred genres: The refiguration of social thought. *American Scholar, 49*(2), 165-79.

Gergen, K., & Gergen, M. (1983). Narratives of the self. In T. R. Sarbin and K. E. Scheibe (Eds.), *Studies in social identity* (pp. 254-73). New York: Praeger.

Harding, S. (1975). Women and words in a Spanish village. In R. Reiter (Ed.), *Toward an anthropology of women* (pp. 283-308). New York: Monthly Review Press.

Hoffman, L. (1985). Beyond power and control: Toward a second-order family systems therapy. *Family Systems Medicine, 3,* 381-96.

Kaye/Kantrowitz, M., & Klepfisz, I. (1986). *The tribe of Dina: A Jewish women's anthology.* Montpelier, VT: Sinister Wisdom.

Kolbenschlag, M. (1970). *Kiss sleeping beauty good-bye: Breaking the spell of feminine myths and models.* New York: Doubleday.

Koltun, E. (Ed.). (1976). *The Jewish woman: New perspectives.* New York: Schocken Books.

Labov, W. (1982). Speech actions and reactions in personal narrative. In D. Tanner (Ed.). *Analyzing discourse: Text and talk.* Washington, DC: Georgetown University Press.

Laird, J. (1986). Teaching content on women through family myths and stories. Paper presented at the Annual Program Meeting, Council on Social Work Education, Miami, FL, March.

Laird, J. (1988). Women and stories. In E. Imber-Black, J. Roberts, & R. Whiting (Eds.). *Rituals in families and family therapy*. New York: Norton.

Landes, R. (1971). *The Objiwa woman*. Columbia Contributions to Anthropology. New York: Norton. (First pub. 1938).

Levi-Strauss, C. (1963). *Structural anthropology*. New York: Basic Books.

Lifton, R. (1973). *The broken connection*. New York: Basic Books.

Linde, C. (in press). Private stories in public discourse: narrative analysis in the social sciences. In U. Quasthoff and E. Guelich (Eds.). *Narrative analysis: An interdisciplinary dialogue*.

MacKinnon, L. and Miller, D. (1987). The new epistemology and the Milan approach: Feminist and sociopolitical considerations. *Journal of Marital and Family Therapy, 13*(2) 139–155.

Malinowski, B. (1954). *Magic, science, and religion*. New York: Doubleday.

Mead, M. (1972). *Blackberry winter: My earlier years*. New York: William Morrow.

Myerhoff, B. (1978). *Number our days*. New York: Dutton.

Myerhoff, B. (1983). "Rites of passage." Plenary speech, National Association of Social Workers Clinical Conference, Washington, DC, November.

O'Flaherty, W. (1980). Inside and outside the mouth of god: The boundary between myth and reality. *Daedalus, 109*, 93–125.

Papp, P. (1984). The creative leap. *Family Therapy Networker, 8*(5) 20–29.

Plaskow, J. (1979). The coming of lilith: Toward a feminist theology. In C. Christ & J. Plaskow (Eds.), *Womanspirit rising*. New York: Harper & Row.

Ricoeur, P. (1980). Narrative time. In W. Mitchell (Ed.), *On narrative*. Chicago: University of Chicago Press.

Riessman, C. (1987). When gender is not enough: Women interviewing women. *Gender and Society, 1*, 172–86.

Riessman, C. (in press). *Making sense: Women and men talk about divorce*. New Brunswick, NJ: Rutgers University Press.

Rosen, S. (Ed.). (1982). *My voice will go with you: The teaching tales of Milton H. Erickson*. New York: Norton.

Schafer, R. (1981). *Narrative actions in psychoanalysis*. Worcester, MA: Clark University Press.

Selvini-Palazzoli, M. et al. (1977). Family rituals: A powerful tool in family therapy. *Family Process, 16*, 445–63.

Spence, D. (1982). *Narrative truth and historical truth: Meaning and interpretation in psychoanalysis*. New York: Norton.

Stierlin, H. (1973). Group fantasies and family myths: Some theoretical and practical aspects. *Family Process, 12*, 111–25.

Taggart, M. (1985). The feminist critique in epistemological perspective: Questions of context in family therapy. *Journal of Marital and Family Therapy, 11*, 113–26.

Tomm, K. (1987). Interventive interviewing: Part II. Reflexive questioning as a means to enable self-healing. *Family Process, 26*, 167–84.

Viaro, M., & Leonardi, P. (1983). Getting and giving information: Analysis of a family-interview strategy. *Family Process, 22*, 27–42.

Watzlawick, P. (1978). *The language of change*. New York: Basic Books.

Weigle, M. (1982). *Spiders and spinsters: Women and mythology*. Albuquerque, NM: University of New Mexico Press.

Whan, M. (1979). Accounts, narrative and case history. *British Journal of Social Work, 9*, 489–99.

White, H. (1980). The value of narrativity in the representation of reality. In W. Mitchell (Ed.), *On narrative* (pp. 1–24). Chicago: University of Chicago Press.

Zeitlin, S., Kotkin, A., & Baker, H. (1982). *A celebration of American family folklore*. New York: Pantheon Books.

22

Rituals of Stabilization and Change in Women's Lives

EVAN IMBER-BLACK

The cake cutting at modern weddings is a . . . comic ritual that sustains masculine prerogatives in the very act of supposedly subverting them . . . the groom helps direct the bride's hand—a symbolic demonstration of male control that was unnecessary in the days of more tractable women. She accepts this gesture and, as further proof of submissiveness, performs the second step of the ritual, offering him the first bite of cake, the gustatory equivalent of her body, which he will have the right to "partake of" later. In the third step, the master-servant relationship is temporarily upset, as the bride mischievously pushes the cake into her new husband's face, leaving him with a chin full of icing. Significantly, this act of revolt is performed in a childish fashion, and the groom is able to endure it because it ironically demonstrates his superiority: His bride is an imp needing supervision. That the bride herself accepts this view of things is demonstrated in the ritual's final step, in which she wipes the goo apologetically from his face. This brings the play back to the beginning, as she is once again obedient to his wiser judgment. Thus the entire tableau may be seen as a dramatization of potential marital tensions and a theatrical resolution of those tensions in favor of the dominance of the male. (Tuleja, 1987, pp. 63–64)

RITUALS, THOSE RICHLY condensed dramas, composed of metaphors, symbols and actions occurring in the lives of all people, have fascinated me for over a decade. Over the years my interest in rituals has expanded from an initial focus on therapeutic rituals in family therapy to normative, naturally occurring rituals in the lives of individuals and families, to the need for rituals to facilitate, mark and celebrate idiosyncratic life cycle transitions, and most recently to the links between normative and therapeutic rituals. I am continually drawn in by rituals' contradictory possibilities, by the capacity of rituals both to stabilize what is and to change what is, to proclaim and even reify a social system and to transform a social system, to be the tools of totalitarianism and the facilitators of empowerment, to enable constriction and stereotypy and to enable expansion and surprise.

The multiple functions of rituals have been examined by social and cultural anthropologists (Hallowell, 1941; Radcliffe-Brown, 1952; Scheff, 1979; Turner, 1974). Such functions include the maintenance and alteration of social structure; the resolution of contradictions through the simultaneous incorporation of such opposites as loss and union, childhood and adulthood, sameness and difference, individuation and community, feminine and masculine; the facilitation of change and stability through ritual elements, which operate at different levels of a social system; the linkage of past, present and future; the reduction of anxiety regarding change through the use of the familiar to bring about change; and the creation of a safe and manageable context for the expression of strong emotions. Women's positions in rituals and the impact of rituals in the lives of women may be examined in light of these many functions. Does a given ritual maintain traditional social structure in which women are subservient to men, or does it offer a new social structure marked by equality between men and women? How can ritual effectively express and affirm feminine and masculine qualities in ways that make the best of these available to both sexes? Can traditional women's rituals be reclaimed and revitalized, enabling women to be connected to their past, without embedding these in a sexist social order? How can the daily, annual, and life cycle rituals in the lives of individuals, families, and culture be recast in ways that utilize familiar elements to foster change in women's empowerment and sense of self and in the relationship between women and men?

According to Roberts (1988a), ritual works as both a maintainer and creator of social structure for individuals, families, and social communities, as well as a maintainer and creator of world view. These dual functions in the arenas of both structure and beliefs make ritual a powerful lens with which to examine women's past and present positions in families, work settings, and communities, and a potential therapeutic and broader social intervention with which to alter narrow and oppressive gender assumptions and arrangements in the present and the future.

RITUALS IN FAMILY THERAPY—A BRIEF REVIEW

As a therapeutic intervention in family therapy, ritual has been of interest since the mid 1970s, when the concept was introduced by the Milan team (Selvini Palazzoli, 1974). In several papers (1974, 1977, 1978a) and in their book *Paradox and Counterparadox* (1978b), Selvini Palazzoli, Boscolo, Cecchin and Prata reported on the efficacy of therapeutic rituals, while highlighting what they believed to be the extreme difficulties of designing such interventions. Their definition of ritual was loose and shifted over time (Roberts, 1988a), making design issues more elusive.

In the early to mid 1980s, a number of trends regarding rituals emerged. Several creative efforts with therapeutic rituals were reported in the family therapy literature (Bergman, 1985; Imber Coppersmith, 1985; Kobak & Waters, 1984; Papp, 1984; Seltzer & Seltzer, 1983). During this same period, van der Hart's book *Rituals in Psychotherapy: Transition and Continuity* (1983) was published in English, providing both a link between therapeutic rituals and cultural rituals and an early attempt at demystifying the design of therapeutic rituals. Wolin and Bennett (1984) began to point the way to the importance of examining normative rituals in families through their research examining rituals in families with a history of alcoholism.

This first decade of interest in rituals in family therapy contained no specific reference to women's issues or to gender. The reported clinical work was essentially hierarchical in nature, as the therapist *designed* a given ritual and *instructed* the family regarding its application, usually giving specific directions for participation, time, place, symbols and symbolic actions to be used. This hierarchical aspect was further reinforced by the fact that the design of therapeutic rituals was considered to be very difficult for therapists. As stated by Selvini Palazzoli, "The 'invention' of a family ritual invariably calls for a great creative effort on the part of the therapist and often . . . for flashes of genius . . . " (1974, p. 239). Similarly, in Bergman's work (1985), credit for the ritual is given solely to the therapist, and the reader is warned that "there is always nonverbal information given by the family and used by the therapist in the formulation of rituals which by definition cannot easily be described" (p. 116).

More recent work with therapeutic rituals has begun to question the necessity for mystifying the practitioner and family alike, offering rather a perspective that clearly defines ritual, elaborates the elements needed to design effective rituals, and includes family members as active collaborators in the ritual process (Imber-Black, Roberts, & Whiting, 1988). This shift is in keeping with the collaborative and demystifying values of feminist family therapy.

Roberts' definition of ritual underpins the current chapter:

Rituals are coevolved symbolic acts that include not only the ceremonial aspects of the actual presentation of the ritual, but the process of preparing for it as well. It may or may not include words, but does have both open and closed parts, which are held together by a guiding metaphor. Repetition can be a part of rituals through either the content, the form, or the occasion. There should be enough space in therapeutic rituals for the incorporation of multiple meanings by various family members and clinicians, as well as a variety of levels of participation. (1988a, p. 8)

Whiting's emphasis that the elements of designing rituals should be clear and available, rather than mystifying and magical (1988), also informs the present work.

Building on Wolin and Bennett's work with normative rituals, my own work (Imber-Black, 1988a, 1988b) suggests multiple directions for using normative, naturally occurring rituals to enhance the therapeutic process. This focus on normative rituals leads directly to the place of such rituals in women's lives, women's participation in rituals, and the effect normative and therapeutic rituals may have in maintaining or altering social constructions of gender identity and role.

Laird (1988), in the first article specifically examining women's issues, rituals and family therapy, offers an analysis of the ways in which normative rituals function to maintain male power in the public domain, while circumscribing female influence to the domestic sphere. She offers a cross-cultural and life cycle examination of rituals, and in example after example finds that " . . . male rituals in general, throughout the world, tend to be more public and more central to societal cosmology. Women's rituals are usually less dramatic and colorful, less important in terms of power definitions, and tend to confine her assignment to the domestic domain" (p. xx).

The awareness of and attention to women's issues in the family therapy field in general and the emerging trends among some practitioners toward examining normative rituals in families and toward co-creating, rather than imposing therapeutic rituals, combine to make rituals an excellent tool with which to examine and alter women's positions in families.

NORMATIVE RITUALS

Normative rituals may usefully be divided into four categories: (1) daily rituals; (2) family traditions; (3) family celebrations; and (4) life cycle rituals (Roberts, 1988a; Wolin & Bennett, 1984). Each category provides an arena in which to see ways that rituals have functioned broadly to maintain women's positions and roles, how specific rituals function in the lives of the women we see in therapy, and what changes may be possible in gender arrangements by using a normative ritual perspective in therapy. Laird suggests that therapists listen carefully as clients describe their rituals in order to discover how such rituals shape and define women's roles, men and women's relationships, women's self-image, and the value placed on women's contributions to family life (1988). Each of these categories will be discussed from a perspective that looks for the often hidden gender arrangements contained in the rituals, highlighting ways to bring these to awareness in therapy as well as ways to use normative rituals to alter such patterns.

Daily Rituals

Daily rituals, including meals, parting and reentry of members, children's bedtime, and repeated routines, define membership and express norms and beliefs regarding appropriate roles, allowable topics of conversation, and permissible affect. Occurring every day, and frequently unexamined, such rituals powerfully shape the gender rules and expectations in a family.

The daily dinner is an excellent lens with which to examine the ways in which gender is defined. Like most rituals, the meal includes anticipation and preparation, as well as the actual event. According to a 1987 New York *Times* survey, women remain the primary people who "pay attention to how, when, what and where their families eat" (Burros, 1988, p. A1). Regarding the preparation aspect of family meals, the survey reported that 91% of married women do the shopping, including 90% who work full-time, while 3% report sharing the shopping with someone else in the family; 90% do the cooking and 4% share the cooking with another member.

Gender definitions are also maintained by the symbolic action of father carving the meat. Tuleja (1987) suggests that such action is the 20th century equivalent of the centuries' old split between men and women, in which men did the hunting and women the gathering. Thus, it is women who do nearly all of the shopping and cooking, while men's position as the "fearless" leader of the family is demonstrated in his more visible and dramatic knife wielding abilities. According to Tuleja, "the carving ritual . . . celebrates the male's role as 'hunter,' while obscuring the equally essential contribution of female 'gatherers'" (p. 98).

An exception to women's role as cooks can be seen in the backyard barbeque, where men frequently don funny-looking aprons and hats, announcing to one and all that this is play and should not be considered a serious change in gender relationships. They become, not cooks, but chefs. Here men are guardians of the dangerous fire, demonstrating that they are the "captains of carnivores" (Tuleja, 1987, p. 98). Like the reversals that occur in many rituals, this one serves not to change the social order but to stabilize and affirm it through the extraordinary.

Seating arrangements at the family dinner may also announce gender definitions, as well as positions of superiority and inferiority. While a table usually has two ends, only one is designated as the "head," and it is here that father usually sits (Roberts, 1988b). In workshops with family therapists examining rituals in their own families of origin, story after story repeats the scenario of women sitting closest to the kitchen, women sitting last, women sitting closest to the children, or women simply not sitting down with the family at all. Participants have remarked on not being able to remember seeing their mothers eat, only being able to remember seeing their mothers serve.

Gender positions are also defined at the family meal through the actions of serving and being served. Traditionally, women serve and men are served. When men are served first, they also receive the choicest food (Laird, 1988). As this drama plays out day after day in families, girls and boys learn about the privileges and limitations associated with being male and female respectively. In one workshop, a woman recalled a time when her family had less food than usual. Her mother quietly called her aside and said, "Eat less — your father and younger brothers should take more."

Family meals are also opportunities for conversation. Here gender rules may be defined by who picks the topics for conversation, who starts and stops the discussion, who protects and who gets protected. In our workshops, we often use dinner scenes from popular films to examine dinner rituals. In scene after scene, one can see some variation of mothers' warning children "not to upset father at dinner," with the implications being that father is busy with "more important concerns," and that the domestic sphere belongs to mother.

As a daily ritual, the meal can provide important information to therapist and family regarding gender assumptions and rules and can be an available arena for change. In two-parent families where both parents work outside the home and in single-parent families where the mother works outside the home, changes in the gender arrangements regarding meals are essential. Such changes are also important, however, in households where the mother works in the home, as girls and boys are learning about gender through the daily meal. The therapist can raise these issues to the family's awareness through questions regarding the daily meal. Questions comparing a given family's mealtime to that of their families of origin help families begin to see where their familiar maps come from, what crucial circumstances have changed, and what they may be able to do differently. Experiments carried out at home during the daily dinner can alter rigid gender patterns. Dinner rituals held during a therapy session can bring the issues to life, while the preparations for such a session can begin to challenge stereotyped gender roles, as when men are asked to participate in the shopping.

Brief Example — A Dinner Ritual in Therapy

A family whose 11-year-old daughter had developed an eating disorder came to family therapy. The daughter's eating problem was seen by all as the responsibility of the mother. The mother took her to various professionals, fought with her daily regarding food, and was the recipient of advice from her own mother and criticism from her mother-in-law. The family's dinner ritual was a metaphor for family relationships, in which the mother was involved as preparer and executor, with no real power to make anything different happen, while the father remained distant and uninvolved, sending his daughter the covert message that her eating problem was okay with him. In the second session, a dinner was held. Father was asked to go to the store with his daughter to shop for the meal. Everyone laughed loudly at this very strange suggestion! Father and daughter shopped as requested, while mother prepared the meal. During this meal session, the family's stereotyped gender definitions emerged, as the daughters set the table and the father carved the roast prepared by the mother. Following this meal session, the mother began to voice her complaints for the first time, stating clearly that the father did not back her up regarding the children, expressing that she felt undermined, and challenging the father regarding his lack of participation in family life.

In this example, a seemingly small change regarding who shopped for groceries shifted the family's daily ritual, which had defined the mother as central and powerless and the father as peripheral and powerful, thereby enabling the mother to begin to negotiate for other changes.

Family Traditions

Family traditions are those rituals connected to the family's internal calendar, such as birthdays, anniversaries, vacations, and other idiosyncratic traditions that the family may invent. Women's position as keeper of the domestic sphere is frequently played out in family traditions, as, for instance, when women are expected to remember and acknowledge birthdays for both sides of the family, or when women are responsible for all gift selection. In some upper-middle-class families, the "important and busy" executive or lawyer or doctor may show that gift selection is "woman's work" by having his female secretary shop for gifts for his wife. In a workshop, a woman reported being enthralled by her father-in-law's romantic nature, until she discovered that the monthly flower delivery to her mother-in-law in honor of the day they met was arranged for and sent by his secretary!

Du Plessix Gray describes the gender split regarding family traditions as "woman the rememberer and man the forgetter" (1988, p. 63). This split can be heard in couples therapy when women describe remembering everyone's birthday while their own is forgotten, or being responsible for whatever anniversary celebration occurs. Thus, while women are frequently the guardians of family traditions, the meta message remains that men do not need to be bothered with this responsibility. When this pattern is maintained, women describe feeling caught between recognizing the importance of traditions and wanting to keep them alive, on the one hand, and not feeling valued for doing so, on the other.

Examining family traditions in therapy can both raise the issue of gender inequalities and challenge these patterns. Asking questions regarding responsibilities for family traditions opens an area of family life where gender assumptions abound. Women's implicit responsibility for the maintenance of warmth, intimacy, and memories in relationships can become overt and appreciated, rather than dismissed. Men's discomfort with the intimate implications involved in, for instance, taking time to choose a gift that expresses knowledge of and care for the other can be discussed, linked to family-of-origin and larger cultural patterns, and challenged. Questions such as, "What if she didn't keep the family traditions alive?" can result in both an affirmation of this important function and a redistribution of responsibilities regarding family traditions.

Family Celebrations

Family celebrations are those linked to the external calendar, such as Thanksgiving, Christmas, or other national, ethnic, or religious celebrations. Similar to the daily meal and family traditions discussed above, responsibility for preparation of family celebrations most often falls upon women, while men are expected to appear and fill leadership positions for a ritual in whose preparation and anticipation they have not participated. A seemingly playful editorial in the New York *Times*, entitled "Conquering Christmas," suggested preparing for Christmas in January, in order to be able to enjoy the holiday in December (*New York Times*, 1988, p. A18). All references to these preparations were female, implying that if women simply took this responsibility on earlier they would be less worn out. There is no mention of other family members sharing in the ritual preparations.

Since family celebrations are embedded in a wider cultural context, participants usually come to such celebrations with highly unrealistic expectations regarding how the ritual should be enacted and what a "perfect" celebration would look like. These expectations are generally accepted by women in families, who, as noted by Laird (1988) in her discussion of Christmas, frequently end up exhausted and resentful.

Celebrations can be discussed in therapy to discern gender arrangements and to experiment with changes. The therapist can help a family to examine what aspects of preparation for a celebration are, in fact, burdensome and to highlight ways that these aspects can be shared more equitably among family members. Elements of a ritual that implicitly denote male superiority can be questioned and altered. For example, when I was growing up, only the men and boys left the Passover table to wash their hands in a special ceremony. I always wanted to participate in this ceremony, but was told it was only for the males. In my own family, at this holiday celebrating freedom, we have replaced this with a ceremony symbolizing caretaking and equality, in which each person at the table washes the hands of the person sitting next to him or her.

Life Cycle Rituals

Among the most powerful and meaningful of rituals are the life cycle rituals. Such rituals are capable of both marking a transition and at the same time making a transition (Roberts, 1988a). They are the secular and sacred celebrations of such individual, family, and community transitions as the emergence into adolescence, marriage, birth of children, and death. These life cycle rituals may come to our attention in therapy either when a family is anticipating such a transition or when the transition has somehow gone awry. The therapeutic arena can be a place to assist a family in the planning of a life cycle transition ritual, the reworking of a ritual, or the developing of a completely new ritual for an idiosyncratic life cycle transition (Imber-Black, 1988c). In each of these, issues of gender appear and can be worked with effectively.

The transition from childhood to adolescence is one that is not marked well by rituals for girls or for boys in our culture. Looking cross-culturally, one finds more group celebratory rituals marking boys' transition to manhood than girls' transition to womanhood.

In middle-class families, girls may have a "Sweet 16" party, which Tuleja (1987) suggests is a kind of puberty initiation rite. Laird (1988) points out that both the "Sweet 16" party and the debutante ball are rituals that value traditional feminine characteristics. Tuleja reminds us that "Sweet 16 and never been kissed" implies a deficiency that must be remedied. According to Eichler (1924), debutante parties are connected to an ancient ritual in which young women who had reached puberty had to remain secluded before being allowed to marry. During such seclusion, they were kept in cages, and a feast marked their "coming out." Both the "Sweet 16" and the debutante ball can be seen as rituals that announce young women's value only in relationship to men.

Few cultures celebrate the onset of menstruation. Laird (1988) discusses a wide spectrum of responses to this crucial transition to womanhood, ranging from genuine celebration by the Navajo, to rituals that highlight the danger and "uncleanness" of the menstruating woman, to our own culture's lack of ritual that functions to mark the event as secret and even shameful. Starhawk (1987) describes a moving ritual designed to celebrate a daughter's first menstruation. This ritual included advance preparation by a group of women who embroidered symbols of power on a special robe for the girl who was about to become a woman. On a chosen day, the girl and her mother were tied together with a silver cord and ran together for a time until the cord was ceremonially cut, allowing the young woman to run free. All of the women involved in the ritual gave the young woman a special gift and spent time telling her their own story of becoming a woman. Following this, they joined the men, who had cooked a special feast, enabling her young womanhood to be celebrated by the women and the men in the community.

Similarly, Laird (1988) tells of a therapeutic ritual designed in concert with a family in which a girl's transition to womanhood was enhanced and celebrated, first by a special "women's time" in therapy, during which mother and older sisters imparted their knowledge of being a woman to her and the young woman negotiated more autonomous functioning in the family. Then a final celebratory dinner was prepared by father and grandfather. At this celebration, gifts belonging to the women in the family were passed along to the newest woman, along with a special blessing given by the father.

These rituals described by Starhawk and Laird show how to celebrate the transition from girl to woman in ways that utilize the strengths and mutual support of the women in the family and the community, highlight the importance of separate time for women, and involve the men in the preparation of the final celebration meal. Therapists working with families who are approaching such a transition can co-create such rituals with families, introducing the ideas in ways that speak of the value of womanhood as that which can and should be celebrated in a family context.

For women and men who choose to marry, the wedding ritual is one that is filled with implicit symbols and symbolic actions organizing gender arrangements in a male as superior and female as inferior fashion. The very word "wedding" means "bride price," coming from medieval England, where "wed" referred to the money the groom gave to the bride's father. While few men actually ask for a woman's hand any longer, the tradition arises from a Roman marriage custom, during which a father hands his daughter over to the husband in return for a coin. She was, in effect, sold by one man to another. The vestiges of this tradition can be seen in the father's "giving the bride away" and in wedding invitations, which frequently define the bride as the "daughter of," while the groom is defined as his own person who is not being "offered" by his parents. The "giving away" of the bride is linked to selling the bride, which still occurs in many cultures today (Tuleja, 1987). As recently as one hundred years ago in England, men not only bought their wives, but resold them as well (Knowlson, n.d.). The assumption of the cost of the wedding by the bride's family, a still common custom, is also related to the selling of the bride.

Two rituals occurring prior to the actual wedding are the bridal shower and the stag party, which function to reinforce traditional gender roles. The bridal shower involves the giving of domestic gifts, such as kitchen items or linens, or of lingerie. The stag party highlights supposedly macho activities, such as getting drunk and viewing pornography. When working in therapy with engaged couples, these traditions can be discussed and their implicit underpinnings examined and challenged, allowing the couple to plan pre-wedding rituals that make a different sort of statement. For example, some couples have requested that friends give a shower for both, or that same-sex celebrations be celebrations that offer strength, support and guidance, rather than inducting women into the kitchen and bathroom and men into the bottle.

Several symbols of the traditional wedding highlight the value placed on the bride's virginity, while no similar expectation is related to the groom. These include the white dress, the veil, the separation of the bride before the wedding, the throwing of her bouquet as a symbol of her "deflowering," and the removal of her garter by the groom, symbolizing her sexual fidelity to him (Tuleja, 1987). Brasch (1965) notes that the veil also symbolizes a woman's submission to her husband.

The wedding ring contains many meanings. While the circular shape is often taken to denote unbreakable love and commitment, Seligson (1973) believes that the ring symbolizes the woman's capture by the man, further denoted by placement on the left hand, considered to be the hand of subjection. Thus, the movement to double ring ceremonies adopted by many couples in the present may be seen as a welcome change in the meanings of the ring symbol.

Following many wedding ceremonies, tin cans and shoes may be tied to the new couple's car. Tuleja (1987) relates the symbol of the shoes to an ancient tradition of the Anglo-Saxons in which the bride's father gave the groom one of her shoes to symbolize his new authority over her. This ceremony was completed when the groom hit the bride on the head with the shoe! Finally, many wedding rituals are completed when the groom carries the bride over the threshold, not as a symbol of her weakness, but rather as a symbol of her dangerous strength, which is neutralized by the groom (Tuleja, 1987).

The many symbols and symbolic actions involved in the planning and execution of a wedding lend themselves well to a discussion in therapy, both with couples who are planning to marry and with those who are already married and wish to rework the original ritual. It is increasingly common for couples to design their own wedding rituals. Here the therapist can be effective by raising questions and imparting information regarding the chosen symbols and symbolic actions, such that the spouses can begin their married life with a thorough examination of gender assumptions, designing aspects of the wedding ritual to symbolize equality rather than domination and ownership. With couples who are already married, couples therapy offers a unique opportunity to look at their original wedding, utilize the process of therapy as a metaphor for "new wedding vows," and actually make and mark the transition with a ceremony. This can be a time to carefully review gender definitions that underpinned the old "contract" and to make a new contract redefining male and female spheres of influence.

Brief Example — New Wedding Vows and New Rituals

A man who was separated from his wife came to therapy. At an earlier time she had requested that he join her in couples therapy, but he had refused, stating that the problems in the relationship were her concern. The couple had been married for 14 years and had two children. Their marriage had been quite traditional, with rigid gender arrangements. The husband was an executive and the wife worked in the home and considered herself a "housewife." The husband played with his daughter, fought with his son, and frequently humiliated his wife. The couple and family had no celebrations because the husband had decreed early in their marriage that there would be none because of his own unhappy memories of holidays in his family of origin. The wife felt she had no choice, but longed for the rituals of her own childhood. Here the husband had not simply delegated the family's ritual life to his wife, as happens in most families, but had autocratically banned rituals altogether. This pattern regarding rituals, in which the husband laid down the law and the wife felt intimidated and complied, was metaphorical for most aspects of their relationship until the wife insisted on a separation.

In this case, a therapeutic ritual both announced and facilitated the couple's new relationship. The husband not only affirmed his wife's position regarding celebrations, but demonstrated in action that he valued her ideas by his active participation. The change was not one of his grudging acceptance of her need for rituals, which would have resulted in her assuming full responsibility for yet another aspect of family life, but rather a genuine redistribution of responsibilities in and outside the home and co-participation in family events, as exemplified by the ritual they designed together.

During the husband's therapy, which focused both on his family of origin and on his present life, he began to make many changes. At the same time, his wife went back to school, sold one house and bought another, and began to work outside the home. Gradually, the spouses began to spend time with each other and decided to come into therapy in order to work on a reconciliation. The couples therapy focused on "new wedding vows," making their agreements explicit. These included the husband's participation in household responsibilities and childrearing, which had previously been the wife's sole responsibility, and his agreement to learn from her about the rich meanings available in family celebrations. Their reconciliation was punctuated by a ritual, for which both took responsibility and in which the husband fully participated. The couple chose new wedding rings, replacing a prior arrangement in which only the wife wore a ring. A ring exchanging ceremony was conducted involving their children. The wife chose a restaurant and hotel for the celebration. Previously, choices of where the couple would go were solely up to the husband. The husband bought special gold glasses with each family member's name and the new anniversary date engraved on them, and told me proudly that these were now used at special family dinners and holidays. The children, led by the son, who had never before participated in any kitchen activities, baked a wedding cake for the parents.

It is important to remember that many women do not choose to marry. They may be in committed lesbian relationships for which there is no legal marriage, but for which a ritual marking commitment, the contributions of two women to each other, and the support of the community is crucial. Many lesbian and gay male couples design such rituals, as well as anniversary rituals. A therapist can raise the possibility of such an affirming life cycle ritual for couples in therapy who have not designed such rituals (Imber-Black, 1988b).

Laird (1988) notes that there are no common rituals in our culture to mark two important transitions for women: the transition to motherhood, and the transition to being a woman whose children have grown. The transition to motherhood is usually marked only by rituals that celebrate the baby, rather than by rituals that celebrate the mother as well. Starhawk (1987) suggests the need for birthing rituals that celebrate both woman and infant. Further, many ethnic and religious rituals marking the birth of a baby are far more elaborate and celebratory for boy babies than for girl babies, announcing the greater value of a male to the family and the community. A therapist who is working with a pregnant woman or with a couple about to have a baby can raise these issues to the spouses' awareness and help them to plan rituals to make and mark this transition.

Starhawk (1987) also describes a ritual for celebrating menopause as a time when a woman's life experience and wisdom are at their fullest. This stands in contrast to the usual myths regarding menopause as a time of decline. Such rituals may be co-created in therapy, as evidenced by Laird's (1988) example of a 50th birthday ritual in which a woman both reclaimed cutoff aspects of her past and celebrated her future.

In addition to the commonly known and accepted life cycle transitions and their attendant rituals, many people experience idiosyncratic life cycle transitions for which there are no familiar or widely accepted rituals (Imber-Black, 1988c). These may include divorce, the end of a nonmarried relationship, lesbian and gay relationships, family formation by adoption, and losses that may not be affirmed by family and community, such as pregnancy loss. These transitions should be examined for gender aspects, and any rituals that are designed should include women's and men's positions as elements.

Summary

Daily rituals, family traditions, family celebrations, and life cycle rituals all lend themselves well to an examination in therapy regarding gender. Questions to utilize include:

1. Who is responsible for preparing the ritual?
2. What hidden assumptions and values about men's and women's positions in the family and in the outside world are being expressed through the ritual's symbols and symbolic actions? What symbolic actions in rituals maintain notions of male superiority and female inferiority?
3. Is the family's ritual life solely or primarily the woman's responsibility? Are men's activities in the outside world considered "too important" to be "interrupted' for family ritual preparation?
4. What are children in the family learning about gender through watching and participating in the ritual?
5. What unspoken maps from families of origin and the wider culture shape the family's present ritual life?
6. What areas of the family's life have changed (e.g., mother working outside the home) that require concomitant changes in ritual preparation and action?

As the family and therapist examine these questions together, possibilities for reworking and redesigning rituals capable of expressing both greater equality and appreciation for women's contributions to the family's ritual life emerge.

THERAPEUTIC RITUALS

Therapeutic rituals can effectively be viewed as extensions of normative rituals, as they utilize many of the design elements of more naturally occurring rituals, including symbols, symbolic actions, open aspects where improvisation may occur, closed aspects prescribing either form or content, and special time and place (Whiting, 1988). Unlike tasks in therapy, which target the behavioral level and are expected to be done as prescribed by the therapist, therapeutic rituals work at the behavioral, cognitive, and affective levels and are expected to be co-evolved by therapist and client system (Imber-Black, Roberts, & Whiting, 1988).

Therapeutic rituals involving women's issues have been described by Laird (1988), Roberts (1988b), and myself (Imber-Black, 1986, 1988a, 1988b, 1988c, 1988d). Laird highlights the versatility of a ritual approach through several different cases involving rituals for such diverse aspects of a woman's life as the onset of puberty, a single woman leaving home, connection to religion and spirituality, a lesbian relationship, the onset of menopause, and the previously unmourned loss of a grandmother. Common to all of this work is an approach by which rituals are co created by therapist and client, rather than imposed by the therapist, thus modeling a process of empowerment and a valuing of women's contributions to their own development.

Roberts (1988b), in a moving case called "Use of Ritual in Redocumenting Psychiatric History," demonstrates the empowerment of a woman whose 20-year history as a psychiatric patient had maintained her in a disqualified and one-down position of family and helpers alike. Through a therapy focusing on her resources rather than her deficits, this woman ultimately collects all of her psychiatric records and, in a collaborative effort with her husband and her therapist, issues corrections and prepares a new document, challenging her old identity as a psychiatric patient replete with unchangeable labels and describing her new identity as a strong woman willing to struggle with life's problems. Collaborative and nonhierarchical relationships among the woman, her family members, and various helpers are exemplified in this document ritual. The effects of the ritual included the woman's reemergence as a talented artist and a shift in the marital relationship from escalating complementarity and distance to healthy symmetry and connectedness.

I have described the use of rituals to facilitate the empowerment of single-parent women, both within their own families and vis-à-vis larger helping systems, which have defined them in a one-down position (Imber-Black, 1986, 1988d). These rituals included the use of documents and the "odd days-even days" format as design elements; however, the most important aspect of these rituals involved the place of the single parent woman as the leader and decision-maker within contexts that were defining her as unable to take leadership and make decisions. In these cases utilizing ritual, the single parents were enabled to stop escalating processes through which their sons were becoming "career patients." Their positions with regard to the larger helping systems shifted from one where they were pitied or blamed to one in which they were partners in their children's behalf.

I have also described rituals facilitating women's expression of grief regarding the loss of relationships and losses through death (Imber-Black, 1988a, 1988b, 1988c). These rituals involve a process of engaging the woman as co-creator of the ritual, relying on her to set the pace of the letting-go process and to choose the appropriate symbols and symbolic actions. As therapist, my role in these rituals has been to secure a safe context for the expression of grief and loss, to serve as a witness, and to shift the direction to celebration following healing.

Case Example — The House-Cooling Party

Candice Meyers requested individual therapy following brief, unsuccessful couples therapy, during which her husband left her. He was seeing another woman and wanted an immediate divorce. Candice was devastated by this rapid disintegration of her marriage. She appeared frightened and told me that she felt she had no future. Her sense of loss centered both on her husband and on her relationships with his family and their mutual friends. She said she did not want to be a single woman. When I asked her what this meant, she said she felt that single women were not entitled to the kind of social life she had enjoyed with family and friends, and that now she would be alone. As we talked about this, she began to tell me how much her house meant to her. This house held many of her dreams for the future, including having children, which she now felt were shattered. She also told me that the house had been a center of activity with extended family and friends, which she no longer felt she could have. When she was married, all holidays with family were held in her home. In addition, she had prepared a monthly dinner ritual for both sets of in-laws. In short, she felt she had lost not only her husband but all of her familiar rituals as well. She told me that the house was now "her loneliness and her memories." She also painfully and angrily told me that her ex-husband was already setting up a new house with his girl friend, and that she was sure family and friends would now go there.

Since the house was such a central metaphor in her life, I began to ask her to consider ways that she might enliven the house. We talked about how the house could express her identity as a single woman in positive ways. She responded by getting some new furniture, replacing several pieces that she had not liked but had bought because her husband liked them. She said she liked this part of being on her own, and that she was rediscovering her own tastes. However, she did not invite anyone to see her new items, telling me again that she didn't think people would feel comfortable there. Her rule seemed to be "you need a man in order to entertain people in your home." She also said that she felt that inviting people over would somehow be the final admission that she was divorced. She told me she felt like a "prisoner" in her home, adding that she was not locked in but had, indeed, locked other people out.

I was intrigued by Candice's metaphors and symbols. I asked her if she would be willing to purchase a new lock for her house. She said she would. In keeping with her pace, I suggested that she not install the lock, but that she bring it to the next session. She did so. At that session, we talked about what it would mean to put the new lock on the door, a lock that she would have control of, that she could open or close, a lock that would enable her to allow others access to her in her own time. At the end of the session, I suggested that she continue to ponder these questions for one hour each day. We agreed that she would conduct this hour in a different room of the house each day, both because she felt the entire house was her "prison" and because it would enable us to discover if certain rooms evoked particularly painful memories or, conversely, enabled movement into the future.

The ritual began by facilitating the expression of much sadness and grief. Candice told me that she cried a lot during the first three days, as the thought of putting a new lock brought a flood of memories of all wonderful times she had had in the house with family and friends. Following this sadness, however, she was surprised to find that she felt very angry with her husband for what he had done to her. Prior to this, when we had discussed his leaving, she had been unable to feel any anger. She also told me that she realized that many of their social events, celebrations and rituals had, in fact, been at her initiation and that she had done the major share of the preparation and cleanup. She smiled and said, "I did it then. I think I can do it now!"

She then told me about a wonderful idea that had come to her on the fifth day, which was to have a "house-cooling party" in order to celebrate her new status. As she described this idea, it was evident that her sense of humor was returning. During the sixth day, she made invitations to the "house-cooling party" that read "Please do bring gifts appropriate for the lovely home of a single woman — I need to replace the 'his and her' stuff!" Finally, she put the new lock on the door.

This ritual was embedded in a therapy that respected and affirmed Candice's position as a single woman. During our sessions, I raised many questions about the normative rituals in Candice's life, which led to discovering the importance of her home, as well as her sense of isolation and lack of entitlement. Candice's abandonment of familiar rituals had increased her loneliness. An unfamiliar ritual, utilizing Candice's own symbol of the lock and a safe and manageable daily format, facilitated healing, allowed for the expression of sadness and anger, led to the claiming of her own abilities as a maker of rituals, enabled the emergence of creativity and humor, and affirmed her new identity as a single woman deserving of celebrations and a satisfying social life (Imber-Black, 1988b).

CONCLUSIONS

Working with rituals allows a therapist to enter the gender beliefs and patterns in a family and to raise these to the participants' awareness as a first step in a change process. Normative rituals can be examined and talked about with individuals, couples, and families in ways that highlight the conservative aspects and stabilizing effects of these rituals on men's and women's roles. Exceptions to stereotyped positions that are illustrated in the rituals can be brought forth. Women's contributions to the ritual life of the family should be underscored and appreciated, while simultaneously men are held responsible for participation. Care should be taken not to simply reverse roles in a familiar ritual, since this may reify, rather than change, male and female positions. Collaboratively made changes in normative rituals can set in motion a process of transformation that will affect relationships in non-ritual spheres.

In designing therapeutic rituals with women, the process is as important as the specific ingredients. Care must be taken when designing therapeutic rituals to avoid replicating familiar ritual patterns in which the woman is solely responsible for the preparation and execution of the ritual and the man simply has to appear. The therapist needs to listen closely for the woman's choice of symbols and symbolic actions, adding ideas to these but not imposing direction that implies that the woman is not capable of developing her own. The therapist's own "flashes of genius" (Selvini Palazzoli, 1974, p. 238) are much less important than the capacity to co-create an environment in which the woman's own creativity emerges.

REFERENCES

Bergman, J. (1985). *Fishing for barracuda: Pragmatics of brief systemic therapy*. New York: Norton.

Brasch, R. (1965). *How did it begin?* New York: Longman.

Burros, M. (1988). Women: Out of the house but not out of the kitchen. *New York Times*, 24 February, A1, C10.

DuPlessix Gray, F. (1987). Women's rites. *Utne Reader, 24*, 61–66.

Eichler, L. (1924). *The customs of mankind*. New York: Doubleday.

Hallowell, A. I. (1941). The social function of anxiety in a primitive society. *American Sociological Review, 6*, 869–81. Bobbs-Merrill Reprint Series. A-104.

Imber-Black, E. (1988a). Ritual themes in families and family therapy. In E. Imber-Black, J. Roberts, & R. Whiting (Eds.), *Rituals in families and family therapy*. New York: Norton.

Imber-Black, E. (1988b). Normative and therapeutic rituals in couples therapy. In E. Imber-Black, J. Roberts, & R. Whiting (Eds.), *Rituals in families and family therapy*. New York: Norton.

Imber-Black, E. (1988c). Celebrating the uncelebrated. *Family Therapy Networker, 12*(1), 60–66.

Imber-Black, E. (1988d). *Families and larger systems: A therapist's guide through the labyrinthe*. New York: Guilford Press.

Imber-Black, E. (1986). Women, families and larger systems. In M. Ault-Riche, (Ed.), *Women and family therapy* (pp. 25–33). Rockville, MD: Aspen.

Imber-Black, E., Roberts, J., & Whiting, R. (Eds.), (1988). *Rituals in families and family therapy*. New York: Norton.

Imber Coppersmith, E. (1985). We've got a secret: A non-marital marital therapy. In A. Gurman (Ed.), *Casebook of marital therapy*, New York: Guilford Press.

Knowlson, T. S. (n.d.) *The origins of popular superstitions and customs*. J. Pott.

Kobak, R., & Waters, D. (1984). Family therapy as a rite of passage: Play's the thing. *Family Process, 23*(1), 89–100.

Laird, J. (1988). Women and ritual in family therapy. In E. Imber-Black, J. Roberts, R. Whiting (Eds.), *Rituals in families and family therapy*. New York: Norton.

New York Times. (1988). Conquering Christmas. (Editorial). 5 January, A18.

Papp, P. (1984). The creative leap: The links between clinical and artistic creativity. *The Family Therapy Networker, 8*(5), 20–29.

Radcliffe-Brown, A. R. (1952). *Structure and function in primitive society: Essays and addresses*. Glencoe, IL: Free Press.

Roberts, J. (1988a). Setting the frame: Definition of rituals, functions and typology. In E. Imber-Black, J. Roberts, R. Whiting (Eds.), *Rituals in families and family therapy*. New York: Norton.

Roberts, J. (1988c). Rituals and trainees. In E. Imber-Black, J. Roberts, & R. Whiting (Eds.), *Rituals in families and family therapy*. New York: Norton.

Roberts, J. (1988b). Use of ritual in "redocumenting" psychiatric history. In E. Imber-Black, J. Roberts, & R. Whiting (Eds.), *Rituals in families and family therapy*. New York: Norton.

Scheff, T. J. (1979). *Catharsis in healing, ritual, and drama*. Berkeley and Los Angeles: University of California Press.

Seligson, M. (1973). *The eternal bliss machine*. New York: William Morrow.

Seltzer, W., & Seltzer, M. (1983). Material, myth and magic: A cultural approach to family therapy. *Family Process, 22*(1), 3–14.

Selvini Palazzoli, M. (1974). *Self-starvation: From individual to family therapy in the treatment of anorexia nervosa*. New York: Jason Aronson.

Selvini Palazzoli, M., Boscolo, L., Cecchin, G., & Prata, G. (1974). The treatment of children through brief therapy of their parents. *Family Process, 13*, 429–42.

Selvini Palazzoli, M., Boscolo, L., Cecchin, G., & Prata, G. (1977). Family rituals: A powerful tool in family therapy. *Family Process, 16*(4), 445–54.

Selvini Palazzoli, M., Boscolo, L., Cecchin, G., & Prata, G. (1978a). A ritualized prescription in family therapy: Odd days and even days. *Journal of Family Counseling, 4*(3), 3–9.

Selvini Palazzoli, M., Boscolo, L., Cecchin, G., & Prata, G. (1978b). *Paradox and counter paradox: A new model in the therapy of the family in schizophrenic transaction*. New York: Aronson.

Starhawk (1987). Ritual to build community. *Utne Reader, 24*, 66–71.

Tuleja, T. (1987). *Curious customs: The stories behind 296 popular American rituals*. New York: Harmony Books.

Turner, V. (1974). *Dramas, fields and metaphors: Symbolic action in human society*. Ithaca, NY: Cornell University Press.

van der Hart, O. (1983). *Rituals in psychotherapy: Transition and continuity*. New York: Irvington Publishers.

Whiting, R. (1988). Guidelines to designing therapeutic rituals. In E. Imber-Black, J. Roberts, & R. Whiting (Eds.), *Rituals in families and family therapy*. New York: Norton.

Wolin, S. & Bennett, L. A. (1984). Family rituals. *Family Process, 23*(3), 401–20.

Index